PRACTICING
TEXAS
POLITICS

18e

Lyle C. Brown Baylor University

Joyce A. Langenegger Blinn College

Sonia R. García St. Mary's University

Robert E. Biles Sam Houston State University

Ryan T. Rynbrandt Collin College

Veronica Vega Reyna Austin Community College

Juan Carlos Huerta Texas A&M University—Corpus Christi

 CENGAGE

Australia • Brazil • Canada • Mexico • Singapore • United Kingdom • United States

Practicing Texas Politics, Eighteenth Edition

Lyle C. Brown, Joyce A. Langenegger, Sonia R. García, Robert E. Biles, Ryan T. Rynbrandt, Veronica Vega Reyna, Juan Carlos Huerta

Product Director: Laura Ross

Product Manager: Lauren Gerrish

Product Assistant: Martina Umunna

Senior Marketing Manager: Valerie Hartman

Senior Subject Matter Expert: Emily Hickey

Learning Designer: Erika Hayden

Content Manager: Dan Saabye

IP Analyst: Deanna Ettinger

IP Project Manager: Kumaresan Chandrakumar

Production Service: Straive

Compositor: Straive

Art Director: Sarah Cole

Text and Cover Designer: Sarah Cole

Cover Image: iStockPhoto.com/drmakkoy

For product information and technology assistance, contact us at **Cengage Customer & Sales Support, 1-800-354-9706 or support.cengage.com.**

For permission to use material from this text or product, submit all requests online at **www.cengage.com/permissions.**

Library of Congress Control Number: 2021912569

Student Edition ISBN: 978-0-357-50524-3

Loose-leaf Edition ISBN: 978-0-357-50529-8

Cengage
200 Pier 4 Boulevard
Boston, MA 02210
USA

Cengage is a leading provider of customized learning solutions with employees residing in nearly 40 different countries and sales in more than 125 countries around the world. Find your local representative at **www.cengage.com**.

To learn more about Cengage platforms and services, register or access your online learning solution, or purchase materials for your course, visit **www.cengage.com**.

Printed at CLDPC, USA, 07-21

Brief Contents

Detailed Contents

Chapter 4:
Political Parties   130

Chapter 5:
Voting and Elections   165

Chapter 6:
The Media and Politics   212

Chapter 7:
The Politics of Interest
Groups   261

Chapter 8:
The Legislative Branch 298

Chapter 9:
The Executive Branch 340

Chapter 10:
The Judicial Branch 391

Chapter 11:
Finance and Fiscal
Policy 421

Chapter 12:
Public Policy and
Administration 463

Chapter 13:
The Criminal Justice
System 508

State Learning Outcomes

Practicing Texas Politics helps you meet the State Learning Outcomes for GOVT 2306:

1. Explain the origin and development of the Texas constitution.
2. Demonstrate an understanding of state and local political systems and their relationship with the federal government.
3. Describe separation of powers and checks and balances in both theory and practice in Texas.
4. Demonstrate knowledge of the legislative, executive, and judicial branches of Texas government.
5. Evaluate the role of public opinion, interest groups, and political parties in Texas.
6. Analyze the state and local election process.
7. Describe the rights and responsibilities of citizens.
8. Analyze issues, policies, and political culture of Texas.

Chapter in *Practicing Texas Politics*	GOVT 2306 State Learning Outcomes (SLO) that are specifically addressed in the chapter	
1: The Environment of Texas Politics	SLO 1	Explain the origin and development of the Texas constitution.
	SLO 2	Demonstrate an understanding of state and local political systems and their relationship with the federal government.
	SLO 3	Describe separation of powers and checks and balances in both theory and practice in Texas.
	SLO 4	Demonstrate knowledge of the legislative, executive, and judicial branches of Texas government.
	SLO 7	Describe the rights and responsibilities of citizens.
	SLO 8	Analyze issues, policies, and political culture of Texas.
2: Federalism and the Texas Constitution	SLO 1	Explain the origin and development of the Texas constitution.
	SLO 2	Demonstrate an understanding of state and local political systems and their relationship with the federal government.
	SLO 3	Describe separation of powers and checks and balances in both theory and practice in Texas.
	SLO 4	Demonstrate knowledge of the legislative, executive, and judicial branches of Texas government.

(Continued)

Chapter in *Practicing Texas Politics*	GOVT 2306 State Learning Outcomes (SLO) that are specifically addressed in the chapter	
	SLO 7	Describe the rights and responsibilities of citizens.
3: Local Governments	SLO 2	Demonstrate an understanding of state and local political systems and their relationship with the federal government.
	SLO 5	Evaluate the role of public opinion, interest groups, and political parties in Texas.
	SLO 6	Analyze the state and local election process.
	SLO 7	Describe the rights and responsibilities of citizens.
	SLO 8	Analyze issues, policies, and political culture of Texas.
4: Political Parties	SLO 2	Demonstrate an understanding of state and local political systems and their relationship with the federal government.
	SLO 5	Evaluate the role of public opinion, interest groups, and political parties in Texas.
	SLO 6	Analyze the state and local election process.
	SLO 8	Analyze issues, policies, and political culture of Texas.
5: Voting and Elections	SLO 2	Demonstrate an understanding of state and local political systems and their relationship with the federal government.
	SLO 5	Evaluate the role of public opinion, interest groups, and political parties in Texas.
	SLO 6	Analyze the state and local election process.
	SLO 7	Describe the rights and responsibilities of citizens.
	SLO 8	Analyze issues, policies, and political culture of Texas.
6: The Media and Politics	SLO 5	Evaluate the role of public opinion, interest groups, and political parties in Texas.
	SLO 8	Analyze issues, policies, and political culture of Texas.
7: The Politics of Interest Groups	SLO 5	Evaluate the role of public opinion, interest groups, and political parties in Texas.
	SLO 8	Analyze issues, policies, and political culture of Texas.
8: The Legislative Branch	SLO 3	Describe separation of powers and checks and balances in both theory and practice in Texas.
	SLO 4	Demonstrate knowledge of the legislative, executive, and judicial branches of Texas government.
	SLO 8	Analyze issues, policies, and political culture of Texas.
9: The Executive Branch	SLO 3	Describe separation of powers and checks and balances in both theory and practice in Texas.
	SLO 4	Demonstrate knowledge of the legislative, executive, and judicial branches of Texas government.
	SLO 8	Analyze issues, policies, and political culture of Texas.
10: The Judicial Branch	SLO 3	Describe separation of powers and checks and balances in both theory and practice in Texas.
	SLO 4	Demonstrate knowledge of the legislative, executive, and judicial branches of Texas government.
	SLO 7	Describe the rights and responsibilities of citizens.
	SLO 8	Analyze issues, policies, and political culture of Texas.

Chapter in *Practicing Texas Politics*	GOVT 2306 State Learning Outcomes (SLO) that are specifically addressed in the chapter	
11: Finance and Fiscal Policy	SLO 2	Demonstrate an understanding of state and local political systems and their relationship with the federal government.
	SLO 3	Describe separation of powers and checks and balances in both theory and practice in Texas.
12: Public Policy and Administration	SLO 8	Analyze issues, policies, and political culture of Texas.
13: The Criminal Justice System	SLO 2	Demonstrate an understanding of state and local political systems and their relationship with the federal government.
	SLO 4	Demonstrate knowledge of the legislative, executive, and judicial branches of Texas government.
	SLO 7	Describe the rights and responsibilities of citizens.
	SLO 8	Analyze issues, policies, and political culture of Texas.

A Letter to Instructors

Dear Texas Government Instructor:

Texas politics is a dynamic enterprise. As Texas moves from being a majority-minority state to becoming a majority-Latino state, the changing demographics will alter election outcomes and public policy decisions. An economy that fluctuates with the rise and fall of oil and gas prices results in a surplus of funds in one legislative session and a scarcity in the next session. Reliance on money from the federal government, especially for funding social-welfare programs, regularly brings state officials into conflict with federal authorities and conditions placed on use of those funds. Limited water resources and a decaying infrastructure require innovative government solutions before these problems erode the state's economic success and growth. Uncommon events, like the COVID-19 pandemic and 2021's Winter Storm Uri, bring into sharp relief the importance of government and the fragility of the state's economy and infrastructure. Government officials play an active role in negotiating and resolving policy issues in the context of an ever-changing demographic, economic, and ideological environment. Students in our classrooms will be the ones who select policymakers and policies to deal with a multiplicity of concerns that face the Lone Star State in the 21st century. Understanding their government and appreciating its dynamism is critical to our students' future role as active, informed citizens.

- *Practicing Texas Politics* analyzes **the practices and policies** of the Lone Star State by giving students a realistic introduction to how public policymaking is conducted in Texas. The state's individualistic and traditionalistic political culture, together with the role of Texas's rapidly changing demographics, are referenced throughout to aid students in placing policy decisions in a historical and cultural context. Students are introduced to current policymakers, their decisions, and the impact of the resulting policies. Roles of political parties, special interest groups, voters, and the media in influencing public policy are also explored. Policymaking and process are integrated within each chapter throughout the book with a special emphasis on public education, higher education, social services, and infrastructure needs both from a budgetary perspective in Chapter 11, "Finance and Fiscal Policy," and as policy issues in Chapter 12, "Public Policy and Administration."

- Through **learning outcomes, learning checks, and other pedagogical features**, students are given an organizational structure that helps them learn, understand, and remember the material.

New to This Edition

In this edition, we have continued to focus on aligning our narrative with the **state learning outcomes** for GOVT 2306 and the skills-based **core objectives** required of the discipline, as defined by the Undergraduate Education Advisory Committee (UEAC) of the Texas Higher Education Coordinating Board (THECB).

- This edition has been designed to support students' development of these core objectives, with the expansion of core objective questions that prompt students to engage in critical thinking, develop communication skills, evaluate social responsibility, and reflect on their own sense of personal responsibility.

- **The role of the emerging Latino majority** in reshaping Texas politics is addressed in several areas, including political party dominance, representation in all branches of state government, the media, and public policy.

- Effects of social change, including the death of fellow Texan George Floyd and the Black Lives Matter movement are discussed throughout.

- **"Keeping Current: The Impact on Texas"** analyzes the outcome and effect of both the national and state 2018 and 2020 elections on aspects of Texas politics and the 86th and 87th legislative sessions.

- The text has been updated to include the effects of **recent court decisions** and other changes in laws and procedures.

- Updates highlighting **new laws enacted by the 87th regular session** are included.

- The role of the COVID-19 pandemic on the state's health care system, economy, and relationships with federal and local officials is included.

MindTap

As an instructor, MindTap is here to simplify your workload, organize, and immediately grade your students' assignments, and allow you to customize your course as you see fit. Through deep-seated integration with your Learning Management System, grades are easily exported and analytics are pulled with just the click of a button. MindTap provides you with a platform for easily adding current events, videos, and RSS feeds from national or local news sources.

Our goal, first and foremost, is to help you engage your students in the dynamic process of politics and develop them into active, informed participants in their democracy. We have attempted to present a realistic and up-to-date picture of how Texas politics is practiced in all branches and at both local and state levels of government. We welcome your feedback on any material or feature in this book.

Sincerely,

The *Practicing Texas Politics* Author Team

A Letter to Students

Dear Student:

Welcome to Texas government. Whether you're a native-born Texan or a newly arrived Texan, you can feel the energy of change all around you. You live in a state that no longer has a majority population from any race or ethnic group and in a few short years will have a majority Latino population. You're in a state that continues to respond to a global pandemic, erratic weather, and active social change. Even with the unpredictability of the energy sector and related uncertainty about jobs, the number of new Texans continues to increase. Four of the 11 largest metropolitan areas in the nation are in Texas: Dallas-Ft. Worth, Houston, San Antonio, and Austin. All are projected to experience significant population growth in the coming decades. This same state, however, has the most uninsured children and adults in the nation, one of the greatest gaps in earnings between the wealthy and the poor in the United States, and lower-than-average college graduation rates. A decaying transportation infrastructure and depleted water resources will require multibillion-dollar solutions. And who will solve these problems? You, the future voters and taxpayers of Texas, will have that responsibility. That's why you need to understand your role and how the system works so you can keep Texas the vibrant state we all want it to be. Helping you become an effective participant in that system is why we wrote *Practicing Texas Politics.*

In this book, you'll be introduced to today's important policymakers and learn what we all have a right to expect of them. You'll meet students just like you, who have chosen to get involved and make a difference at their colleges and universities, in their communities, and in this state. You'll learn about ways you can become involved by voting and through political campaigns. You'll see how Texas compares to other states, and you'll be exposed to the diversity and uniqueness of the Lone Star State—a state that responded quickly to the threat of COVID-19 by conducting the first virtual court hearings and trials in the nation and a state that continues to experience exponential population growth in its major cities and boomtown population growth and busts in many of its rural areas. You'll come to understand what this state could be in the future and how you can shape the outcome.

- Updated **"Students in Action"** features in each chapter help you make a personal connection to the content. The features highlight how Texas students like you have participated in the community or provide information on internships and other opportunities for interested students.

- **"Point/Counterpoint"** examines a key controversial issue in Texas politics from both sides of the controversy and asks you to take a stand on each issue.

- **"Learning Checks"** provide a few factual questions at the end of major sections for you to use in checking your knowledge. Answers are provided at the end of the chapter.
- **"How Do We Compare?"** boxes compare Texas with other states.
- A **Marginal Glossary** allows you to access terms as they are needed for easier understanding of the text.
- **End-of-chapter materials** include a conclusion that wraps up the chapter and offers final thoughts for you to consider, a chapter summary organized by learning outcome, Key Terms, and Learning Check answers.
- **Skills-based, core objective** questions with all images ask you to engage in critical thinking, develop communication skills, evaluate social responsibility, and reflect on your personal responsibility by thinking about your political opinion and beliefs on a variety of important issues in this state.
- **Charts, graphs, and maps** are used to give you a visual image for understanding concepts.
- **Keeping Current: The Impact on Texas** provides insight into what recent state and national elections and legislative decisions mean for the Lone Star State.

The Benefits of Using Mindtap as a Student

As a student, the benefits of using MindTap with this book are endless. With automatically graded practice quizzes and activities, an easily navigated learning path, and an interactive eBook, you will be able to test yourself in and outside of the classroom. On your computer, phone, or tablet, MindTap is there when you need it, giving you easy access to flashcards, quizzes, readings, and assignments.

You will guide Texas through the 21st century. It is our hope that when you understand how to get involved in Texas politics, you will choose to do so. And that once you are involved, you will use your vote and influence to create the kind of Texas in which you want to live. It is to you, the students of Texas, that we dedicate this book.

Sincerely,

The *Practicing Texas Politics* Author Team

Resources

Students

Access your *Practicing Texas Politics* resources by visiting **www.cengage.com**.

If you purchased MindTap access with your book, click on "Register a Product" and then enter your access code.

Cengage Mobile App

Complete course work on the go with the *Cengage Mobile App*, which delivers a seamless course experience on a smartphone or tablet. Read or listen to your textbook whether online or offline and study with the help of flashcards, practice quizzes and instant feedback from your instructor. You can receive due date reminders and complete assignments from the convenience of your mobile device!

Cengage Unlimited

Cengage Unlimited saves students money, time and hassle when accessing course materials. One student subscription includes access to every Cengage etextbook, online homework platform, print rental benefits, study tools, and more–in one place, for one price. Cengage Unlimited eTextbooks is an option for courses that use textbooks only. Available for students in bookstores and online.

Details at **www.cengage.com/unlimited**. Available in select markets only.

Instructors

Access your *Practicing Texas Politics* resources via **www.cengage.com/login**.

Log in using your Cengage Learning single sign-on user name and password, or create \ a new instructor account by clicking on **"New Faculty User"** and following the instructions.

MindTap for *Practicing Texas Politics*

MindTap for *Practicing Texas Politics* is an immersive, outcomes-driven online learning experience built upon Cengage content and correlated to a core set of learning outcomes. MindTap is the platform that gives you complete control of your course–to craft unique learning experiences that challenge students, build confidence and elevate performance. The design maximizes how the brain learns new information and minimizes distraction for students, guiding them through their course material. Each Mind-Tap activity is anchored to a single concept, and pairs content and assessment in a visually captivating side-by-side presentation. These activities engage students with a variety of content types–including graphs, infographics, and explanation videos–that extend learning experience beyond the textbook, while also providing students with ample opportunities to check themselves for where they need extra help. The Cengage Mobile app enables greater flexibility for students to fit learning into their day, wherever they are, through bite-sized content and the ability to complete activities on a phone or tablet.

Cengage Infuse

Cengage Infuse for Political Science is the first-of-its-kind digital learning platform solution that uses your Learning Management System (LMS) functionality so that you can enjoy simple course set set-up and intuitive management tools. Offering just the right amount of auto-graded content, you'll be ready to go online at the drop of a hat.

Instructor Companion Website for *Practicing Texas Politics*—for instructors only

ISBN: 9780357505250

This Instructor Companion Website is an all-in-one resource for class preparation, presentation, and testing. Accessible through **www.cengage.com/login** with your faculty account, you will find available for download: book-specific Microsoft® PowerPoint® presentations, a Test Bank compatible with multiple learning management systems (LMSs), an Instructor Manual, and more.

The Test Bank, offered in Blackboard, Moodle, Desire2Learn, and Canvas formats, contains learning objective-specific multiple-choice and essay questions for each chapter. Import the test bank into your LMS to edit and manage questions, and to create tests.

The Instructor's Manual includes information about all of the activities and assessments available for each chapter and their correlation to specific learning objectives, an outline, key terms with definitions, a chapter summary, and several ideas for engaging with students with discussion questions, ice breakers, case studies, and social learning activities that may be conducted in an on-ground, hybrid, or online modality.

The Microsoft® PowerPoint® presentations are closely tied to the Instructor Manual, providing ample opportunities for generating classroom discussion and interaction. They offer ready-to-use, visual outlines of each chapter, which may be easily customized for your lectures.

A guide to teaching online presents technological and pedagogical considerations and suggestions for teaching the Introduction to Texas Politics course. Access the Instructor Companion Website for these resources and more at **www.cengage.com/login**.

Cognero for *Practicing Texas Politics*, 18e—for instructors only

ISBN: 9780357505304

Cengage Learning Testing Powered by Cognero is a flexible, online system that allows you to author, edit, and manage test bank content from multiple Cengage solutions; create multiple test versions in an instant; and deliver tests from your LMS, your classroom, or wherever you want. The test bank for *Practicing Texas Politics*, Enhanced 18e, contains Learning Objective–specific and core competency–specific multiple-choice, critical-thinking short answer, and essay questions for each chapter.

Practicing Texas Politics on Twitter

https://twitter.com/PracTexPol

Follow the *Practicing Texas Politics* author team's Twitter feed @PracTexPol for the latest news and updates that affect politics in the Lone Star State. The feed also regularly posts tips for studying and thriving in college and engaging in active and informed citizenship.

Acknowledgments

We are indebted to many personal friends, government officials and their staffs, political activists, lawyers, and journalists who have stimulated our thinking. Likewise, we owe much to librarians and archivists who located hard-to-obtain facts and photos. We also appreciate the professional assistance rendered by the editorial, production, and marketing staff of Cengage Learning. Without the benefit of their publishing experience, this textbook and its ancillaries would be of much less value to students and instructors.

Of course, expressions of appreciation are due to spouses, family members, and others important to us who helped to produce this new edition of our book and have learned to cope with the irregular working hours of authors struggling to meet deadlines. We are especially grateful to the many students who assisted us in writing *Practicing Texas Politics*, especially those who willingly gave of their time and expertise in the production of the *Students in Action* feature, as well as those who assisted us by providing input to some of our early drafts. We give special thanks for the assistance and support of Anastacia De Gorostiza, Avery Stewart, Patrick Alan Hall, Sirena L. Casper, Julia Ann Cloudt, Jessica Marie Green, Diane Vecchio, and Annaleesah Pina of Austin Community College; and, Citlalli Rivera, a student and political science major at St. Mary's University and a participant in the Texas Civic Ambassadors Program.

We would also like to thank John Osterman, for authoring this edition's Instructor's Manual and PowerPoint, and MPS North America, LLC, for authoring this edition's Test Bank. Our hope is that through the efforts of all, this book will help Texas students better understand the practice of Texas politics and their role as participants.

Reviewers
We would also like to thank the instructors who have contributed their valuable feedback through reviews of this text:

New Reviewers

Reynaldo Flores
Richland College

Dawna Montanelli
Texarkana College

Raymond Sandoval
Richland College

Previous Edition Reviewers

Eric T Lundin
Lone Star College—Kingwood

Neal Tannahilll
Houston Community College

Jamey Crane
Houston Community College

Reisha Beaty
Houston Community College

Jennifer Bachan
Houston Community College

Daniel Allen
Hardin-Simmons University

Alicia Andreatta
Angelina College

Dorris Robinson
Texas Southern University

Vida Davoudi
Lone Star College—Kingwood

Margaret Richardson
San Antonio College

Kevin T. Holton
South Texas College

Olivia Wilson
Angelina College

Dr. Ashley D. Ross
Texas A&M University Galveston Campus

Prof. David E. Birch
Lone Star College—Tomball

Mario Marcel Salas
Northwest Vista College

Brian R. Farmer
Amarillo College

Billy Hathorn
Laredo Community College

Amy S. Glenn
Northeast Lakeview College

Jim Startin
University of Texas at San Antonio

Sandra Creech
Temple College

Patrizio Amezcua
San Jacinto College—North

Debra St. John
Collin College—Preston Ridge Campus

Evelyn Ballard
Houston Community College—Southeast College

Aaron Knight
Houston Community College—Northeast College

About the Authors

Lyle C. Brown is professor emeritus of political science at Baylor University, where he served as departmental director of graduate studies and director of Baylor's Foreign Service Program. His international academic experience includes teaching at Mexico City College (now University of the Americas) and postgraduate study at the Instituto Tecnológico de Monterrey in Mexico. He received his M.A. from the University of Oklahoma and Ph.D. from the University of Texas at Austin. Dr. Brown served as president of the Southwestern Council of Latin American Studies. His writing experience includes coediting *Religion in Latin American Life and Literature* and authoring numerous articles. His political activities include serving as a delegate to county and state party conventions.

Joyce Langenegger teaches government at Blinn College and is the college's Executive Director of Academic Success. She received M.A. and J.D. degrees from Baylor University, and an M.A. and Ph.D. from Fielding Graduate University. Dr. Langenegger has been named to "Who's Who Among America's Teachers" and received a NISOD Award for Teaching Excellence, Teacher of the Year for Blinn College-Bryan, and "Most Valuable Player" award from San Jacinto College for her work as a professor and administrator at that institution. She is a frequent workshop presenter on innovative teaching strategies. Before beginning her teaching career, she practiced law in Houston.

Sonia R. García is a professor of political science, coordinator of the women's studies program, and a pre-law advisor at St. Mary's University in San Antonio. She has also served as chair and graduate director of the political science department. Dr. García received her undergraduate degree in political science from St. Mary's University, master's degree from the University of Arizona, and her Ph.D. in political science from the University of California, Santa Barbara. She has published articles on Latina politics and is a co-author of *Mexican Americans and the Law: El Pueblo Unido Jamás Será Vencido* and lead author of *Políticas: Latina Public Officials in Texas*. Her involvement in politics includes leadership development for various Latino/a-based organizations.

Robert E. Biles, professor emeritus and former chair of political science at Sam Houston State University, has taught college students about Texas politics in Texas, Colombia, and Ecuador. He received his M.A. and Ph.D. from The Johns Hopkins University-School of Advanced International Studies. Dr. Biles is the author of numerous books and articles. His involvement in politics includes serving as a school board member, county party chair, county election supervisor, and staff member of the U.S. Senate Foreign Relations Committee. He has advised state agencies and held leadership positions in statewide lobbying groups and professional organizations. Dr. Biles has received four Fulbright grants, as well as awards for his research, teaching, and administrative service.

Ryan T. Rynbrandt is a professor of political science at Collin College in Plano, Texas, where he teaches American Government and Texas Government. Professor Rynbrandt leads campus initiatives that help students improve academic and life skills, develop mental and emotional resilience, and increase civic engagement. His research and writing examines the role of the pursuit of happiness in American political history, culture, and public policy. He earned his master's degree from the University of Michigan in Ann Arbor. He has been active in politics at the local, state, and national levels.

Veronica Vega Reyna is associate professor of government and assistant dean of Social and Behavioral Sciences for Austin Community College. She has been faculty advisor to a civil rights organization at ACC. Professor Reyna earned her M.A. in Political Science from St. Mary's University in San Antonio, where she taught as adjunct faculty. Her political involvement has included interning for Congressman Ciro Rodriguez, working as a union organizer, and volunteering in various Texas campaigns. She has also taught Texas politics at colleges and universities in San Antonio.

Juan Carlos Huerta is a professor of political science at Texas A&M University—Corpus Christi. He earned his M.A. and Ph.D. in political science from the University of Houston. Dr. Huerta is active in promoting teaching and learning in political science and has served as president of the Political Science Education Organized Section of the American Political Science Association and the Southwestern Political Science Association and was nominated to serve as Vice President of the American Political Science Association. He is the founding president of the Learning Communities Association. His research and writing examines political representation, public opinion, Latino/a politics, political science education, and learning communities. His most recent research (with Beatriz Cuartas), "Red to Purple? Changing Demographics and Party Change in Texas," is published in *Social Science Quarterly*.

Career Opportunities: Political Science

Introduction

It is no secret that college graduates are facing one of the toughest job markets in the past 50 years. Despite this challenge, those with a college degree have done much better than those without since the 2008 recession. One of the most important decisions a student has to make is the choice of a major; many consider future job possibilities when making that call. A political science degree is incredibly useful for a successful career in many different fields, from law to policy advocate, pollster to humanitarian worker. Employer surveys reveal that the skills that most employers value in successful employees—critical thinking, analytical reasoning, and clarity of verbal and written communication—are precisely the tools that political science courses should develop. This brief guide is intended to help spark ideas for what kinds of careers you might pursue with a political science degree and the types of activities you can engage in now to help you secure one of those positions after graduation.

Careers in Political Science

Law and Criminal Justice

Do you find that your favorite parts of your political science classes are those that deal with the Constitution, the legal system, and the courts? Then a career in law and criminal justice might be right for you. Traditional jobs in the field range from attorney or judge to police or parole officer. Since 9/11, there has also been tremendous growth in the area of homeland security, which includes jobs in mission support, immigration, travel security, as well as prevention and response.

Public Administration

The many offices of the federal and state governments combined represent one of the largest employers in the United States. Flip to the chapter on the executive branch of this textbook and consider that each state department and agency you see looks to political science majors for future employees. At the federal level, a partial list of such agencies would include the Department of Education, the Department of Health and Human Services, and the Federal Trade Commission. Texas offers similar opportunities including the Texas Education Agency and the Health and Human Services Commission. There are also thousands of staffers who work for members of Congress or the Congressional Budget Office, and at the state level for legislators and the Legislative Budget Board. Many of these staffers were political science majors in college. This does not even begin to account for the multitude of similar jobs in local governments that you might consider as well.

Campaigns, Elections, and Polling

Are campaigns and elections the most exciting part of political science for you? Then you might consider a career in the growing industry based around political campaigns. From volunteering and interning to consulting, marketing, and fundraising, there are many opportunities for those who enjoy the competitive and high-stakes electoral arena. For those looking for careers that combine political knowledge with statistical skills, there are careers in public opinion polling. Pollsters work for independent national organizations, such as Gallup and YouGov, or as part of news operations and campaigns. For those who are interested in survey methodology, there are also a wide variety of nonpolitical career opportunities in marketing and survey design.

Interest Groups, International and Nongovernmental Organizations

Is there a cause that you are especially passionate about? If so, there is a good chance that there are interest groups out there that are working hard to see some progress made on similar issues. Many of the positions that one might find in for-profit companies also exist in their nonprofit interest group and nongovernmental organization counterparts, including lobbying and high-level strategizing. Do not forget that there are also quite a few major international organizations, such as the United Nations, the World Health Organization, and the International Monetary Fund, where a degree in political science could be put to good use. While competition for those jobs tends to be fierce, your interest and knowledge about politics and policy will give you an advantage.

Foreign Service

Does a career in diplomacy and foreign affairs, complete with the opportunity to live and work abroad, sound exciting to you? Tens of thousands of people work for the U.S. State Department, in Washington D.C. and in consulates and embassies around the world. They represent the diplomatic interests of the United States abroad. Entrance into the Foreign Service follows a very specific process, starting with the Foreign Service Officers Test—an exam given three times a year that includes sections on American government, history, economics, and world affairs. Being a political science major is a significant help in taking the FSOT.

Business

Knowledge and skills gained in a political science major are well suited to pursue a career in business. Understanding governance and how government influences the economy is critical knowledge for a successful business career. In addition, analytical, quantitative, and communication skills provide political science majors with a strong foundation for any profession. Visit with career counselors to select appropriate electives.

Graduate School

While not a career, graduate school may be the appropriate next step for you after completing your undergraduate degree. Following the academic route, being awarded a Ph.D. or Master's degree in political science could open additional doors to a career in academia, as well as many of the professions mentioned earlier. If a career as a researcher in political science interests you, you should speak with your advisors about continuing your education.

Preparing While Still on Campus

Internships

One of the most useful steps you can take while still on campus is to visit your college's career center in regard to an internship in your field of interest. Not only does it give you a chance to experience life in the political science realm, it can lead to job opportunities down the road and add experience to your resume.

Skills

In addition to your political science classes, there are a few skills that will prove useful as a complement to your degree:

Writing: Like anything else, writing improves with practice. Writing is one of those skills that is applicable regardless of where your career might take you. Virtually every occupation relies on an ability to write clearly, concisely, and persuasively.

Public Speaking: An oft-quoted 1977 survey showed that public speaking was the most commonly cited fear among respondents. And yet oral communication is a vital tool in the modern economy. You can practice this skill in a formal class setting or through extracurricular activities that get you in front of a group.

Quantitative Analysis: As the Internet aids in the collection of massive amounts of information, the nation is facing a drastic shortage of people with basic statistical skills to interpret and use these data. A political science degree can go hand-in-hand with courses in introductory statistics.

Foreign Language: One skill that often helps a student or future employee stand out in a crowded job market is the ability to communicate in a language other than English. Solidify or set the foundation for your verbal and written foreign language communication skills while in school.

Student Leadership

One attribute that many employers look for is "leadership potential" which can be quite tricky to indicate on a resume or cover letter. What can help is a demonstrated record of involvement in clubs and organizations, preferably in a leadership role. While many people think immediately of student government, most student clubs allow you the opportunity to demonstrate your leadership skills.

Conclusion

Hopefully, reading this section has sparked some ideas on potential future careers. As a next step, visit your college's career placement office, which is a great place to further explore what you have read here. You might also visit your college's alumni office to connect with graduates who are working in your field of interest. Political science opens the door to a lot of exciting careers. Have fun exploring the possibilities!

1

The Environment of Texas Politics

Learning Objectives

1.1 Describe the relationship between the social history of Texas and the political characteristics of the state's diverse population.

1.2 Analyze how political culture has shaped Texas's politics, government, and public policy.

1.3 Discuss the political implications of Texas's size in both geography and population, along with the geographic distribution of its residents.

1.4 Describe the industries that formed the historic basis for the Texas economy, the diversification of the modern Texas economy, and economic implications for Texas politics.

1.5 Identify four major policy challenges Texas faces in the 21st century.

Image 1.1 Governor Abbott uses social media to announce Executive Orders relating to COVID-19.

> GOVERNORABBOTT
> **Posts** Follow
>
> **governorabbott** ⦿
> Texas State Capitol
>
> ♡ ▢ ◁   ▢
>
> **2,173 likes**
>
> **governorabbott** Today we issued a series of Executive Orders to mitigate spread of the #COVID19 in TX.
>
> It temporarily closes schools, restaurants, and bars while limiting gatherings to less than 10 people.
>
> We are continuing to strengthen TX's ability to safeguard & protect our communities.

Source: Instagram

— Competency Connection —
⚙ **CRITICAL THINKING** ⚙

How can the Texas government most effectively work to continue the state's success and address its challenges?

"Yesterday is not ours to recover,
but tomorrow is ours to win or lose."

—*Lyndon B. Johnson*

Everything Is Changing in Texas

On March 13, 2020, less than a month after Texas officially recorded its first case of COVID-19, Governor Greg Abbott declared a state of disaster for all Texas counties. Six days later, the Texas Department of State Health Services responded to the threat caused by the novel coronavirus by declaring a public health disaster for the first time in almost 100 years.[1] Local governments began issuing a patchwork of "shelter-in-place" orders for individuals and restrictions on organizations of all kinds. Life in Texas had been changing rapidly for decades, but the life-threatening coronavirus transformed life for nearly every resident of the state (and indeed almost every human being on the planet). Beyond damage to life and health, social and governmental responses to the pandemic devastated the economy, exacerbated political divisions, and unleashed social unrest. Individuals, private organizations, and government institutions struggled to adjust to the new reality and clashed over the proper balance of liberty, safety, and equality.

If you live here, these transformations and the way our political system handles them have a significant impact on your life. State governments arguably have more direct effect on your quality of life than does the national government. The varying state responses to the pandemic show how different they can be.

If you don't live here, pay attention anyway. Because of the sheer size of Texas, what happens here also has an impact on the direction of the United States as a whole.[2] In 2020, the U.S. Census Bureau ranked Texas second largest among the 50 states, with a population over 29 million. That placed the Lone Star State between California with 39.5 million residents and Florida with more than 21.5 million.[3]

Our analysis of the politics of Texas's state and local governments will help you understand political action and prepare you for active and informed participation in the political life of the state and its counties, cities, and special districts. As Texas Congresswoman Barbara Jordan once said, "The stakes are too high for government to be a spectator sport." It's time to suit up and play. To help you play effectively, we will introduce you to the playing field (government, political culture, land, and economy of the state), the players (ordinary citizens, activists, politicians, public employees, and opinion leaders), and the rules of the game (state and federal constitutions, laws, and political processes).

Follow *Practicing Texas Politics* on Twitter **@PracTexPol**

◩ Managing Change: Government, Policy, and Politics in Texas

Restrictions on liberties, such as governmental responses to COVID-19, along with expressions of liberties, such as protests sparked by some instances of police brutality, have inspired passionate disagreement about the proper powers and responsibilities of national, state, and local governments. There has never been full agreement in democratic societies about such issues. Views vary widely and are held deeply. Yet aside from a handful of anarchists (who oppose all governments), there *is* agreement that society needs rules, or public policies, by which to live. Making, implementing, and enforcing these policies is the job of **government**. The government of the state of Texas is a representative democracy or "republic" modeled on the government of the United States. As such, it incorporates U.S. political principles, discussed in other chapters, such as popular sovereignty, political equality, separation of powers, due process of law, civil rights, and personal liberties. Our government is thus responsible for representing all citizens of this diverse state as political equals. Power of state government to make policy is divided among legislative, executive, and judicial branches. Each branch has its own powers, and each has some ability to limit or check the power of the other branches. The state government also delegates some policy-making power to local governments, including counties, cities, and special districts. As a result, **public policies** take different forms.

Many policies are laws passed by the legislature, approved by the governor, implemented by an executive department, and interpreted by the courts. Others are constitutional amendments proposed by the legislature and ratified by the voters of Texas. Some policies derive from rules promulgated by state agencies and ordinances passed by local governments. What all of these efforts share in common is that they are attempts to meet a public need or reach a public goal. Government tries to meet public needs by allocating resources. For example, state or local government may formulate, adopt, and implement a public policy, such as raising taxes to pay for more government services or shifting tax revenue from police departments to violence prevention programs. Government tries to meet public goals by using policy to encourage or discourage specific behaviors. The state can encourage some behaviors using incentives—for example, establishing scholarships or student loan programs to encourage getting an education. It can discourage other conduct with punishments, such as imposing civil penalties (fines that must be paid) for price gouging after a disaster. In addition, the government can encourage or discourage behaviors through public relations and information campaigns, such as social media posts and press conferences encouraging social distancing and wearing masks during a pandemic.

government
A public institution with authority to formulate, adopt, implement, and enforce public policies for a society.

public policy
What government does or does not do to and for its citizens

In the political realm, you may think of public policy as the product and government as the factory in which policy is made. If that's the case, then **politics** is the process that produces public policy. In fact, critics have compared government to a sausage factory—even if you like the product it produces, the process isn't pleasant to watch. The politics of policymaking often involves conflict among government officials, political parties, interest groups, media figures, citizens, noncitizen residents, and other groups that seek to influence how policies in Texas are enacted and implemented. Conflict over power and resources can encourage the worst behavior in people, and opportunities for corruption and greed abound. Yet politics also requires cooperation and can inspire noble and courageous action. In sum, politics is the moving force by which government produces public policy, which in turn determines whether and how we use the power of the state to address our challenges and take advantage of our opportunities.

⭐ The People of Texas

LO 1.1 Describe the relationship between the social history of Texas and the political characteristics of the state's diverse population.

Texas is amazingly diverse in racial, ethnic, and cultural terms. Defining groups is not a straightforward exercise, but is important because people often receive differential treatment depending on their perceived race and ethnicity. Genetic research has revealed that human beings are not clearly divisible into what we call "races," or "ethnicities."[4] Such divisions are not scientific facts but **social constructs**. "Race" is a construct based on physical or social characteristics commonly considered distinctive; and "ethnicity" is a construct based upon shared characteristics such as language, ancestry, homeland, cultural heritage, and the like. All this can make proper terminology difficult and confusing.

For example, the racial category of "White" has changed dramatically over time. Prior to the 1940s Americans commonly recognized numerous "White races" with persons of Anglo-Saxon, Germanic, or Nordic ancestry considered superior and those of Irish, Italian, Eastern European, and other ancestries ranked in a hierarchy from less inferior to more inferior. While all "White races" received the right to vote, discrimination against the supposedly inferior Whites in hiring, housing, and lending was common. The country also operated on the "one drop rule" according to which Whites with one drop of African blood were to be considered Black. For a time, those with one Black grandparent were classified by the U.S. Census Bureau as "quadroons" and anyone with one Black great-grandparent was classified as an "octoroon." By contrast, the U.S. Census Bureau now classifies anyone "with origins in any of the original peoples of Europe, the Middle East or North Africa" as "White" and allows those of mixed ancestry to choose multiple races. The terms "Black" and "African American" are now used by the Census Bureau interchangeably to indicate "a person having origins in any of the Black racial groups of Africa." Yet in common usage "African-American" is nation-specific and generally used to indicate Black people born in the United States or whose direct

politics
The process of policymaking that involves conflict and cooperation between political parties and other groups that seek to elect government officials or to influence those officials when they make public policy.

social construct
concept or belief developed and maintained by the collective views of a society rather than existing inherently or naturally.

ancestors were enslaved in the United States. "Black" is a more inclusive term that is more likely to be embraced by people who come from or trace their roots more directly to Latin America (usually the Caribbean region), Europe or Africa.[5]

Further complicating matters, a person categorized by the U.S. Census Bureau as ethnically Hispanic may be of any race. "Hispanic" is used to indicate someone of Spanish-speaking ancestry. It overlaps with, but is distinct from "Latino," which indicates ancestral roots in **Latin America**, where a variety of languages are spoken. While any label for a group is necessarily imperfect, the authors of this book aim to use the most inclusive language possible as consistently as possible. They diverge from this practice only when it is clearly not applicable or when referring to specific U.S. Census Bureau data. In reference to race, they will use the terms White, Black, Native American (which includes American Indians and Indigenous Hawaiians, Pacific Islanders, and Alaskans), and Asian (which includes persons with origins in the original peoples of the Far East, Southeast Asia, and the Indian subcontinent). When referring to ethnicity, they will use the term Latino/a.[6]

According to the U.S. Census Bureau, more than one-half of all Texans are either Black or Latino. The remainder are predominantly non-Hispanic Whites, with a small but rapidly growing Asian population and approximately 320,000 Native Americans. More than one-third of all Texans speak a language other than English at home. More than 145 languages are spoken in the Houston metropolitan area, which replaced New York City in 2012 as the most ethnically diverse city in the country. In 2021, Dallas ranked as the 4th most diverse city in the country. The historical changes that brought about this diversity were not always free of conflict.

Texans Throughout History: From Conflict Toward Cooperation

The politics of democracy is about forging a path for diverse groups with sometimes opposing interests to live together peaceably. Racial and ethnic tensions in recent years have been high; and there are strong disagreements about the nature, extent, and proposed remedies for discrimination. Nevertheless, one of the remarkable facets of Texas is that most members of its diverse population live together peacefully. Historically, peaceful coexistence was difficult. Texans have a reputation for toughness, and that reputation was formed over hundreds of years of surviving an often-unforgiving terrain, made harsher by a social atmosphere that historian and political scientist Cal Jillson calls "breathtakingly violent."[7]

The First Texans Few specifics are known about the people who inhabited what would become the Lone Star State for more than 10,000 years before Spanish explorers planted the first of Texas's six flags here in the 1500s. When Spaniards arrived, the land was inhabited by more than 50 Native American tribes and nations. Population estimates for that time vary widely, ranging from 50,000 to perhaps a million people. In East Texas, the Caddo lived in organized villages with a complex political system. The state's name comes from the word *tejas*, meaning "friendly," which was the tribal name for a group of Indians within the Caddo Confederacy. The Comanche were arguably the most important

Latin America
Countries in the western hemisphere south of the United States where Spanish, Portuguese and French are the official languages.

tribe in shaping Texas history. Excellent horsemen and valiant warriors, these buffalo hunters maintained a successful resistance to the northward expansion of Spaniards and Mexicans, and later to the westward expansion of Whites.[8] Native American tribes were not unified. For example, the Tonkawa of Central Texas often allied with Whites in fights against the Comanches and the Wichitas, another important South Plains tribe.

European Colonization Accurate estimates of the Native American population are not available, but whatever the true size, their numbers declined rapidly after European contact in the 16th century. With Spanish explorers and their African slaves came diseases like smallpox that decimated native communities. Though sometimes peaceful, early contact also included the taking of slaves, torture, and even cannibalism.[9] Spain and France claimed Texas, but neither country actively ruled all of the territory. Their activities involved exploring, surveying, and fighting. Spanish activities also included trading, farming, and livestock herding. Missions and towns were established around present-day Nacogdoches and San Antonio, and in a few places along the Rio Grande like Laredo and El Paso, but the area remained sparsely populated through the Mexican War of Independence (1810–1821). In 1824, three years after Mexico overthrew Spanish rule, the area that is now Texas became part of a federal republic for the first time.

Mexican Texas Around the time of Mexican independence, White American settlers began coming to the Mexican province of *Tejas* in greater numbers. The first non-Spanish-speaking immigrants to Texas were largely of English ancestry, along with some other European nationalities. Arrival of White settlers sped decline of the Native American population, which had already been reduced to between 20,000 and 30,000 people. Violence between the native population and immigrant Whites was constant and pervasive. Despite the Mexican government's authorization of Stephen F. Austin to offer free land to settlers willing to work it, Mexican officials were concerned about these immigrants. Many White newcomers would not learn Spanish and resisted the constitution and laws of Mexico that established Catholicism as the state religion and abolished slavery. (See Chapter 2, "Federalism and the Texas Constitution," for more discussion of the historical context).

When General Antonio López de Santa Anna was elected president of Mexico in 1833, most Texans did not expect him to repudiate the principles of the federal democratic republic he was elected to serve. When he did so, one result was the Texas Revolution with its famous battles at Goliad, the Alamo, and San Jacinto. Much blood was shed to establish the independent Republic of Texas in 1836.[10]

The Republic of Texas The two elected presidents of the Republic, Sam Houston (twice) and Mirabeau B. Lamar, along with members of the Texas Congress, struggled to establish Texas as an independent nation, even as many in the government sought to join the United States. Burdens of establishing and maintaining an army and navy, operating a postal system, printing paper money, administering justice, and providing other governmental services were made difficult by conflicts within and without the Republic's borders.

Warfare between Whites and Native Americans continued because of increased immigration from the United States and because some **Texian** leaders pursued policies of removal and extermination. Fighting was so fierce that two decades after independence, one observer in 1856 estimated the state's Native American population at only 12,000, with most having been killed or driven from the state.[11] While many **Tejanos** (Latino Texans) had fought for Texas's independence, Cal Jillson notes that "some Texas leaders sought to equate Indians and Mexicans and urge the expulsion or extermination of both."[12] From the time of Texas independence until 1890, immigration from Mexico all but ceased. Latinos remained concentrated in settlements such as San Antonio that were founded during the 18th century and within Central and South Texas. Conflicts, in some cases violent, among White Texians, Native Americans, and Tejanos, continued into Texas's statehood, which came about in 1845, less than a decade after its independence.

The Lone Star State In South Texas, Latinos comprised a majority of the population despite the increased number of White arrivals after the Mexican-American War of 1846–1848 (which followed admission of Texas into the Union). White immigration dominated much of the rest of the state. Before the Civil War, more than one-half of the state's White residents had migrated from Alabama, Arkansas, Georgia, Kentucky, Louisiana, Mississippi, Missouri, and Tennessee. Many of these new immigrants were slaveholders, so the Republic of Texas legalized slavery and entered the federal Union as a slave state. By 1847, Blacks accounted for one-fourth of the state's population, and most were slaves.

Yet slavery was not universally accepted in Texas. Some estimates suggest as many as 24,000 German immigrants and descendants settled in the Hill Country of Central Texas by 1860. Most opposed slavery on principle, whereas others simply had no need for slaves. As a result, 14 counties in the region voted 40 percent or greater against secession in 1861. Despite Sam Houston's opposition, the secessionists won and Texas joined the Confederate States of America in February of that year. In the Ordinance of Secession and in an official explanation of the causes of secession issued the following day, Texas leaders repeatedly cited northern attacks on the institution of slavery, along with the alleged failure of the federal government to protect White Texans against Mexican and Indian banditry, and other grievances.[13]

The Civil War and Reconstruction Although Texas experienced less fighting than other southern states in the Civil War, ravages of combat were felt. In addition to battles with Union troops, Central Texas was scarred by what has been called "a civil war within a Civil War," as hundreds of opposing Union and Confederate sympathizers died in armed confrontations. The Confederacy lost the war, and Texas was brought back into the Union through Reconstruction, a period in which the U.S. government sought to protect freed slaves and to remake the political and economic structures of southern states.

Governor Edmund J. Davis's active work to enfranchise freed slaves during Radical Reconstruction temporarily made political participation safe for Black Texans. This change even led to a small wave of freedmen migration from other

Texian
A term referring to early White settlers of Mexican Texas and the Republic of Texas, especially those who supported the Texas Revolution. All residents of Texas today are referred to as Texans.

Tejano
A term referring to early Mexican settlers of Mexican Texas and the Republic of Texas. All residents of Texas today are referred to as Texans.

southern states into Texas. Disenfranchised White citizens who had supported the Confederacy considered Davis's tactics heavy-handed and sought to re-establish White control once Reconstruction ended.

The Great State of Texas Texas was fully readmitted to the United States in 1870, but civil strife continued. Although White migration into the state declined during the Civil War and Reconstruction, it resumed by the 1870s. Westward settlement further displaced Native Americans and converted the prairies into cattle and sheep ranches. A combination of White in-migration and Black out-migration reduced the percentage of Black Texans in the population from 31 percent in 1870 to 13 percent by 1950.

Black Texans who remained in the state faced great difficulty. Slavery was replaced for many by a different form of servitude in the form of sharecropping, in which they farmed land as tenants for a portion of the crops grown. *De jure* segregation, or segregation by law (also known as Jim Crow laws), resulted in denial of adequate education, scarcity of economic opportunities, and incidents of racial violence. Texas saw more than 700 lynchings of Blacks and Latinos between 1882 and 1968.[14]

Early in the 20th century, waves of Mexican immigrants escaping the Mexican Revolution and its aftermath fed the American need for seasonal laborers. Many worked for White farmers and ranchers. The Great Depression and resulting competition for work greatly increased anti-immigrant sentiment and policy in Texas. Violence sometimes erupted as a result.[15]

After World War II, many Mexican immigrants left agriculture and sought manufacturing jobs in cities. Most of them experienced improvements in wages and working conditions as unskilled or semiskilled laborers. Nevertheless, a growing number entered managerial, sales, and clerical professions. Many Texans joined Latino/a and Black civil rights groups in the fight for equality.[16] In the 1960s, the federal government began to enforce the desegregation decisions of the U.S. Supreme Court, and Texan President Lyndon Johnson signed a series of new anti-discrimination civil rights laws. Public schools, workplaces, and some neighborhoods, especially in urban areas, began to integrate.

Integration has reduced, but not eliminated, intergroup tension in Texas. Events within Texas and outside the state have sparked dramatic incidents of racial animosity in the Lone Star State in recent years. Protests of deadly encounters between police and Blacks—along with statistics demonstrating continued discrimination in housing, employment, and criminal justice—have heightened long-simmering tensions in the Lone Star State.

On May 25, 2020, videos were released to the public of Minneapolis police officer Derek Chauvin kneeling on the neck of George Floyd until he died. Floyd, a Black man originally from Texas, had been arrested for allegedly passing a counterfeit bill. Within days, large protests against police violence toward Black people spread through the nation and Texas cities, large and small. While the vast majority of the tens of thousands of protesters remained peaceful, some looting and property damage occurred in several Texas cities and some instigators threw objects at police. Police response to protesters varied from police firing tear gas, pepper spray, rubber bullets, and beanbag rounds (beanbags filled with metal pellets) at protestors in Austin to uniformed bicycle police kneeling with and hugging protesters in Fort Worth. In response to the protests, Governor Greg Abbott activated the Texas National Guard and declared a statewide state of disaster, issuing statements affirming the First Amendment right to protest while condemning violence and destruction.[17] Some local governments imposed curfews and continued to make arrests.

With the **Black Lives Matter** movement at the forefront, Texans of all ages, races, and ethnicities took to the streets. Demands for police reform divided Texans but did result in a few policy changes. Some counties and cities enacted reforms including bans on police using chokeholds or firing at moving vehicles, requiring de-escalation training, limiting no-knock warrants, banning the use of deterrents such as pepper spray and beanbag rounds, and requiring police officers to intervene when another officer uses excessive force. In addition, local governments removed numerous Confederate monuments around the state and renamed schools that had been named for Confederate leaders.[18] Conflicts over police use of force and over monuments celebrating the Confederacy are part of a larger debate in Texas and across the United States about **systemic racism**.

The concept of systemic racism argues that racially and ethnically discriminatory laws and policies have resulted in segregated housing; isolation of many members of historical minority groups into low-income neighborhoods; disparate treatment in the criminal justice system; and fewer life opportunities, such as education, quality health care, and the opportunity to accumulate wealth. Systemic racism is different than individual racism in that it refers to disadvantages inherited by people of color because of multiple racist practices, systems, and institutions that shaped the society we live in today.

Although Texas continues to struggle with individual and systemic racism, historical minority groups have made major strides in education, employment, and political representation in recent decades. In 2020, Texas ranked second on a list of best states for Black entrepreneurship.[19] In increasing numbers, Texans work, live, socialize, date, and marry across racial, ethnic, and religious lines. Evidence shows that young people use more social media than other groups and that persons who use social media have more racially and ethnically diverse social networks. Generation Z, the generational designation for those born between 1997 and 2012, is the most racially and ethnically diverse generation in American history and is poised to become the largest generation in the United States. The U.S. Census Bureau projected racial/ethnic categories in Texas for 2019 at the following percentages:

White, non-Latino/a	41.2
Hispanic/Latino	39.7
Black/African American	12.9
Asian	5.2
American Indian or Alaskan Native	1.0
Native Hawaiian or other Pacific Islander	0.1
Two or more races	2.1

Totals exceed 100 percent because some people report in more than one racial or ethnic category.

Black Lives Matter
A decentralized social movement advocating non-violent protest and civil disobedience in reaction to police brutality and racially motivated violence against Black people.

systemic racism
Systems, structures, procedures, or processes that disadvantage people of color. Also known as "institutional racism" or "structural racism."

Texans Today

Texas ranks among the most racially and ethnically diverse states in the nation. There really is no such thing as a "typical Texan." Five groups comprise the major racial and ethnic groups in the state: Native American, Asian, Black, Latino, and White.

Native Americans Although some counties (Cherokee, Comanche, Nacogdoches), cities and towns (Caddo Mills, Lipan, Waxahachie), and other places have Native American names, by 2019, Texas Native Americans only numbered about 320,000. Most Native Americans live and work in towns and cities, with only a few remaining on three reservations. Approximately one-half of the 1,291 members of the Alabama-Coushatta tribe reside on a 4,351-acre East Texas reservation. On the U.S.–Mexican border near Eagle Pass, a few hundred members of the Kickapoo tribe are allowed by the governments of Mexico and the United States to move freely between Texas and the Mexican state of Coahuila. At the far western boundary of the state, the 1,700-member Tigua tribe inhabits a reservation near El Paso.

As of mid-2021, all three tribes operated casino-like facilities. The Kickapoo have done so continuously since 1996, transforming their 850-member tribe from poverty to a middle-class lifestyle. The Tigua and Alabama-Coushatta tribes gained federal recognition later than the Kickapoo. At that time federal treaties allowed Texas to apply all state laws to Native American tribes, including those regarding gambling. Though both tribes opened successful casino-like facilities, a federal judge ordered them closed in 2002. Since then the Tigua and Alabama-Coushatta have organized politically to gain gaming rights on their reservations, making substantial campaign contributions, using the courts, and engaging in lobbying activity. In 2015, the National Indian Gaming Commission and the U.S. Department of the Interior declared that they would allow certain types of casino-like facility gambling on both the Tigua and Alabama-Coushatta reservations. Despite repeated attempts by Texas Attorney General Ken Paxton to close the facilities, both tribes used some forms of gambling to generate tens of millions of dollars each year. In 2020 the U.S. Fifth Circuit Court of Appeals upheld a 2019 District Court ruling declaring tribal gaming facilities to be in violation of state law and ordering them to halt operations. In that same year, a resolution in the U.S House authored by Brian Babin (R-Woodville) seeking to allow bingo-style gaming and to clarify that tribes fall under the Indian Gaming Regulatory Act failed in the U.S. Senate. U.S. Senator John Cornyn caused the Senate Indian Affairs Committee to postpone hearings regarding the resolution until Texas state government and the tribes reached agreement.[20] In 2021, the U.S. Supreme Court ordered the U.S. Department of Justice to weigh in on the issue of tribal gaming facilities in Texas, allowing gaming to continue during the appeals process.

Asians The Lone Star State is home to one of the largest Asian populations (more than 1.5 million) in the nation. "Asian" is a broad term encompassing those with roots in East Asia, Southeast Asia, and the Indian subcontinent. Texas has long received immigrants from these regions. In recent years, Asian immigration increased, while immigration from Latin American countries declined. Census data indicate that the Asian population of Texas is diverse, with the largest groups claiming ancestry from Vietnam or the Indian subcontinent, but with substantial populations of East Asian (Chinese, Japanese, and Korean) or Filipino heritage. Most Asian Texans live in the state's largest urban centers. Fort Bend County near Houston has the greatest percentage of Asian Americans in the state at almost 21 percent.

More than one-half of Texas's first-generation Asian Americans entered this country with college degrees or completed their degrees after arrival.[21] The intensity with which the state's young Asians focus on education is revealed by enrollment data at major Texas universities. Although Asians account for less than 4 percent of the total population of the state, they comprised 31 percent of the undergraduate enrollment at Rice University and 37 percent of the enrollment at the University of Texas at Dallas in the fall 2020 semester. Asians have the highest median household income of any racial group in Texas, at $111,900. Four Asian representatives served in the 87th Legislature. In 2020 Jacey Jetton was elected to the Texas House of Representatives. Jetton's father is a sixth-generation White Texan and his mother is South Korean, making him the first Korean American elected to the Texas Legislature.

Blacks By 2019, Texas was home to approximately 3.7 million Black residents, approximately 12.9 percent of the state's population. The Black population has continued to grow, but more slowly than other ethnic or racial groups. Today, Texas has the second highest number of Black residents in the nation (after New York) with most residing in southeast, north central, and northeast Texas. More than one-half of the state's Black population lives in and near major urban areas. In recent years, a significant number of people seeking employment and a higher standard of living have immigrated from the African continent to the United States and settled in Texas. Although Black people constitute a majority in some small towns, they do not constitute a majority in any Texas county or large city. According to the 2014–2018 Community Survey, the city of Beaumont had the highest percentage of Black residents among larger Texas cities at more than 48 percent.[22]

For more than 80 years from the end of Reconstruction until 1958 (when Hattie White was elected to the Houston School Board), no Black person held elective office in the state. Over the last 50 years, the political influence of Black Texans has increased in local, state, and national government. In 1972, Barbara Jordan became the first Black politician since Reconstruction to represent Texas in Congress. In 1992, Morris Overstreet became the first Black person to win a statewide office when he was elected to the Texas Court of Criminal Appeals. In 2018, Eddie Bernice Johnson became the first Black Texan to chair a standing committee in the U.S. House. The number of Black voters, candidates, and officeholders in Texas has continued to rise in recent years.

Latinos Although many Texas Latinos trace their ancestry to Central America, South America, and the Caribbean, more than 88 percent are of Mexican origin. By 2020, Texas ranked second in the nation behind California in the number of Latino/a residents with more than 11.4 million and second in the nation behind

New Mexico in percentage of Latino/a residents with approximately 39 percent of the state's population. More than one-half of all newborns in the state are Latinos. Based on current population trends, some demographers suggest that by 2022 Latinos will be the largest population group in the Lone Star State. Though poverty rates are significantly higher for Latinos than Whites, Texas's Spanish-surnamed residents are gaining economic strength, and the number of Latino/a-owned businesses is growing rapidly.[23]

As Latinos continue to be the fastest-growing ethnic group in Texas (in terms of numbers), their political influence is increasing. Between 1846 and 1961, only 19 Latino politicians were elected to the Texas legislature. Since 1961, however, Latinos have won election to many local, state, and national positions. In 1984, Raul Gonzalez became the first Latino in a statewide office when he won election to the Texas Supreme Court. Though group solidarity among Latino/a voters is lower than other groups and they do not always support Latino/a candidates, organizations such as the League of United Latin American Citizens (LULAC) and the Southwest Voter Registration Education Project have worked to increase voter registration and turnout in recent years. By 2019, Texas had almost 2,740 Latino/a elected officials, by far the largest number of any state and approximately 40 percent of all Latino/a elected officials in the country.[24] Henry González was the first Texas Latino elected to the U.S. House in 1963, and in 2012, Ted Cruz became the first elected to the U.S. Senate. Texans reelected him to the Senate in 2018 and sent the state's first two Latinas, Sylvia Garcia and Veronica Escobar, to the U.S. House of Representatives. Of the 29 officials elected on a statewide basis, as of 2021, three were Latino/a.

Whites According to the 2000 census, more than 52 percent of Texas's population was composed of "non-Hispanic Whites," a category including people of European ancestry but also those of Middle Eastern and North African heritage. That percentage dropped to less than 50 percent in 2004, when Texas joined Hawaii, New Mexico, and California as majority-minority states. By 2019, the White population of Texas was almost 12 million, or about 41.2 percent of the state's population. Projections indicate that the percentage of Whites in the state will continue to decrease and the percentage of other racial/ethnic groups will continue to increase. Although White Texans trace their roots to all parts of Europe, North Africa, and the Middle East, White Texans of English ancestry predominate in eastern, central, and northern Texas and those of German ancestry predominate in central and western Texas. Many small towns in Texas remain exclusively, or almost exclusively, White. The Whitest large city in Texas is Spring (near Houston), with over 88 percent of its more than 205,000 residents identifying as non-Hispanic White.[25]

Poverty rates among Texas Whites remain dramatically lower and incomes remain significantly higher than all groups except Asians. The poverty rate for Texas Whites was 8 percent in 2018, compared to 20 percent for Blacks and 21 percent for Latinos.[26] In 2018, Black and Latino/a households had median annual incomes below $49,000 whereas White households averaged $102,000. Despite making up less than half the state's population, more than two-thirds of all businesses in Texas are owned by White people. An advantage in resources

Image 1.2 Protesters march in Austin demanding reforms to end police discrimination and excessive force.

Competency Connection
± PERSONAL RESPONSIBILITY ±

In an increasingly diverse political landscape, how might you contribute to the representation of your community's interests?

also translates into political advantage. White Texans are more likely to vote, to contribute to campaigns and interest groups, and to run for office than any other racial group. As a result, they also continue to hold a disproportionate share of local, state, and national political offices in the Lone Star State.

Implications of Racial and Ethnic Diversity The changing demographics of Texas lead many to speculate that the partisan makeup of Texas will soon change. "Demographics Is Destiny," as the saying goes. Many point to the increasingly small margins by which Republican candidates won elections over the past several election cycles as evidence that Texas will soon become a Democratic state.

Yet the ascendance of Democrats over Republicans in Texas is not a foregone conclusion. While a sizable majority of Texas Latinos identify with the Democratic Party, many are ineligible to vote. Among those who are eligible, voting rates have been increasing but continue to be lower than the voting rates of White voters, a sizeable majority of whom identify with the Republican party. Moreover, Texas Republicans have historically done better among Latino/a voters than Republicans at the national level and are making efforts to continue that trend.

✓ 1.1 Learning Check

1. How has the size and political power of Texas's Latino/a population changed in recent decades?

2. What is systemic racism?

Answers at the end of this chapter.

✪ Texas Political Culture

LO 1.2 Analyze how political culture has shaped Texas's politics, government, and public policy.

Types of Political Culture

In a state as diverse as Texas, people may not all agree on the proper role of government or what makes good public policy. Yet when certain widely shared values, attitudes, traditions, habits, and general behavioral patterns develop over time, they shape the politics and public policy of a particular region. We call this concept **political culture**. According to political scientist Daniel Elazar (1934–1999), "Culture patterns give each state its particular character and help determine the tone of its fundamental relationship, as a state, to the nation."[27] Based on the settlers in the original colonies, Elazar identified three distinct subcultures that exist in the United States: moralistic, individualistic, and traditionalistic. Although elements of each exist in Texas, proponents of the individualistic and traditionalistic subcultures have historically dominated the state and controlled the political system.

Texas Moralism In the moralistic subculture that originated in Puritan New England, citizens view government as a public service. They expect government to improve conditions for the people through economic regulation and to advance the public good in order to create a just society. Citizens see it as their duty to become active in governmental decision-making through participation in politics and government, and they hold the government accountable to their high expectations.

The moralistic subculture in Texas has historically been the domain of those who lack power, yet moralists have helped shape Texas through numerous movements to use government for the betterment of society. Radical Republicans of the post–Civil War era sought to use government to end a White supremacist political system and achieve racial equality. Radical Republican Governor E. J. Davis's aggressive use of state government power in an effort to protect Black political participation made him many enemies among conservative White Democrats who regained control of the government when Reconstruction ended. Reaction to Davis's administration resulted in the decentralized, weak government established by the 1876 Texas Constitution, which is still in operation today.

In the late 19th and early 20th centuries, **progressive** groups like the Farmers' Alliance, the Populist Party, and the Socialist Party surged in popularity in Texas as they challenged government to control the damaging effects of rising corporate capitalism.[28] From the mid-1800s into the early 1900s, a powerful Temperance movement in Texas sought to use government to end the sale and consumption of alcohol. From the earliest days of the civil rights struggle, Blacks and Latinos in Texas engaged in organized political activism to change the traditionalistic political structure of the state.

political culture
Widely shared attitudes, habits, and general behavior patterns that develop over time and affect the political life of a state or region.

progressive
Favoring and working for progress in conditions facing the majority of society or in government.

Texas Individualism The individualistic subculture grew out of the focus on individual opportunity, especially in business, in the mid-Atlantic colonies. Business leaders advanced this subculture, often viewing government as an adversary that used taxes and regulations to limit their economic freedom. Therefore, they saw government as mostly negative and wanted to limit its size and scope. Today, the individualistic subculture is dominant in a majority of the midwestern and western states. Elazar asserted that the political culture of Texas is strongly individualistic, in that those in positions of power have tended to believe that government should maintain a stable society but intervene as little as possible in the lives of people.

An important source of Texas's individualistic subculture is the mostly English-speaking, White settlers who came to Texas in the early 19th century from the United States either individually or because they were recruited by *empresarios*, such as Stephen F. Austin. These settlers, without significant government backing or restraint, established farms and communities while persevering through extreme hardships.[29]

Elements of the individualistic subculture in the Lone Star State are its limited government and excessively restricted powers. Per capita government spending for social services and public education is consistently among the lowest in the nation. Power at the local level is dispersed among more than 5,000 governments—counties, cities, school districts, and other special districts. The public perception of government and elected officials remains negative, although this viewpoint appears more directed to the federal government. Texans consistently report levels of trust in state government that are almost twice as high as their trust in the government in Washington, D.C. In response to the COVID-19 pandemic, the Lone Star State's individualistic political subculture has been displayed by strong resistance to business closures and shelter-in-place orders.[30]

Evidence of individualistic subculture can also be seen in Texas's economic conservatism and deference to the power of wealthy businessmen and corporations. Texas remains one of the few states without a personal or corporate income tax, and it has adopted **right-to-work laws** that hinder the formation and operation of labor unions. The state and its municipalities offer public funding and tax abatements to encourage private corporations and businesses in other states to relocate to Texas. A traditionalistic-individualistic political culture is reflected in the important role powerful individuals and families continue to play in local and state politics, and in their influence on public policies.

Texas Traditionalism The traditionalistic subculture grew out of the Old South. It is rooted in feudal-like notions of society and government that developed in the context of the slave states, where property and income were unequally dispersed. Governmental policymaking fell to a few powerful families or influential social groups that designed policies to preserve their dominant role in the social order. Poor Whites and minorities were often disenfranchised. In traditionalistic subculture, government is a vehicle for maintaining the status

right-to-work laws
Laws that limit the power of workers to bargain collectively and form and operate unions, increasing the power of employers relative to their employees.

quo and its hierarchy. This subculture has often developed one-party systems that tend to strengthen people who are already powerful. Today, traditionalistic subculture still remains dominant throughout the South.

The traditionalistic subculture in Texas can be traced to the early 19th century and the immigration of Southern cotton plantation owners. Before Texas joined the Confederacy, much of its wealth was concentrated in a few plantation-owning families. Although slave owners represented only a quarter of the state's population and one-third of its farmers, these slave owners held 60 to 70 percent of the wealth and controlled state politics.[31] After the Civil War (1861–1865) and Reconstruction, **Jim Crow laws** limited Black Texans' access to public services, such as education, and to both public and private facilities, like restrooms. In the late 19th and early 20th centuries, poll taxes and all-White primaries further restricted voting rights.

Today, many Texans are the descendants of migrants from traditionalistic states of the Old South, where conservatism, elitism (upper-class rule), and one-party politics were entrenched. In addition, the traditionalistic influence of Mexico, as evidenced by the *patrón* (political boss) system that dominated some areas of South Texas, has also affected political attitudes of some Texans of Mexican ancestry.

For most of its history, Texas has been a one-party-dominant state (first Democrat and later Republican), which is one of the key identifiers of a traditionalistic political subculture. Although urbanization and industrialization, together with an influx of people from other states and countries, are changing Texas, the traditionalistic influence of the Old South lingers. With few exceptions, participation in politics and voter turnout are consistently low, averaging less than 50 percent for presidential elections and below 30 percent for gubernatorial elections. Elazar noted that many Texans inherited Southern racist attitudes, which for a century after the Civil War were reflected in state laws that discriminated against Blacks and other minority groups. Though Texas has in recent years removed more symbols of the Confederacy than any other state, and has increased the pace of removal in the wake of the protests following the murder of George Floyd, it still has the second highest number of Confederate memorials.[32]

A Changing Culture?

Since the mid-1970s Texas has experienced massive population influx from other countries and from states with more heavily moralistic political cultures. Since 2005, Texas has welcomed nearly twice the number of new arrivals as any other state. The addition of tens of millions of residents in a few decades raises important questions: Will individualistic and traditionalistic subcultures continue to dominate? Will population changes shift the state toward moralistic subculture? Texas's political culture, inherited largely from the 19th century, faces the transformative power of widespread urbanization, industrialization, education, communication, and population shifts. Change is inevitable, but the direction, scope, and impact of the change remain to be seen.

Jim Crow laws
Discriminatory laws that segregated Blacks and denied them access to public services for many decades after the Civil War.

✓ 1.2 Learning Check

1. Which two types of political subculture have traditionally been dominant in Texas?

2. What influences have been challenging Texas's traditionalistic-individualistic subculture?

Answers at the end of this chapter.

Image 1.3 Texas State Capitol Building

Courtesy of the Texas House of Representatives

— Competency Connection —
⊛ **SOCIAL RESPONSIBILITY** ⊛

In what ways is Texas's political culture (moralism, individualism, and traditionalism) reflected in politics, policies, and the people's attitudes about, and expectations of, government today?

⬕ The Land and Population Distribution

LO 1.3 Discuss the political implications of Texas's size in both geography and population, along with the geographic distribution of its residents.

Texas's politics and public policy have always been shaped by the state's size. With more than 267,000 square miles of territory, Texas is second only to Alaska (570,640 square miles) in area and is as large as the combined areas of Florida, Georgia, Alabama, Mississippi, and Tennessee. Connecting the more than 1,200 incorporated cities in Texas requires approximately 315,000 miles of roadways, including more than 80,000 miles of major highways constructed and maintained under the supervision of the Texas Department of Transportation. The state government is also responsible for more than 6,200 traffic signals, 1,000 dynamic message signs, and many programs to prevent and respond to accidents and damage to roads and bridges.[33] Texas's massive size has an impact on political campaigns. Running for statewide office—and in some instances for district-level office—requires a significant investment of financial resources. Despite the rise of social media as an inexpensive and effective campaigning and organizing tool, traveling the state for rallies and fundraisers while targeting 20 media markets with advertisements is an expensive undertaking that requires extensive fundraising.

Texas is large both physically and in population. In every decade since 1850, Texas's population has grown more rapidly than the overall population of the United States. According to the 2020 federal census, Texas's resident population totaled 29,145,505—a stunning increase of 40 percent from 2000. (The resident population of the United States in 2020 was 331,449,281—an increase of approximately 18 percent from 2000.) By 2020, Texas also had six of the top 13 fastest-growing large cities in the country.[34]

Urbanization

Although many people living outside of Texas may still associate the Lone Star State with lonesome cowboys on vast ranges, the great majority of the state's population growth has occurred in urban and metropolitan areas that are composed of one or more large cities and their surrounding suburban communities. Texas's four most populous counties (Harris, Dallas, Bexar, and Tarrant) have a combined population of almost 11.5 million people, larger than the population of 43 of the 50 states. Texas was 80 percent rural at the beginning of the 20th century, but today more than 88 percent of the state's population lives in Metropolitan Statistical Areas (MSAs) (those with populations greater than 50,000) in fewer than 20 percent of the state's 254 counties. It is politically significant that these 48 counties potentially account for about four of every five votes cast in state-wide elections. Thus, governmental decision-makers holding statewide office are primarily accountable to people living in one-fifth of the state's counties. Urban voters are consistently more supportive of the Democratic Party. Fort Worth voters were an exception to this trend until a majority of the city's voters cast their ballots for Democratic presidential candidate Joe Biden in 2020. Suburban voters tend more toward the Republican Party. Since metropolitan voters, as a whole, are rarely of one mind at the polls, they do not tend to overwhelm rural voters by taking opposing positions on all policy issues.

From 2010 to 2020, two Texas metropolitan statistical areas (Dallas-Fort Worth-Arlington and Houston-The Woodlands-Sugarland) added more than a million people each, making them the fourth and fifth most populous MSAs in the nation. The Texas Demographic Center projects that nearly 95 percent of the state's 2010–2050 population growth will be in its 82 metropolitan counties.[35] Most of these population concentrations are within the Texas Triangle, roughly outlined by segments of interstate highways 35, 45, and 10 that connect the cities of Houston, Dallas–Fort Worth, and San Antonio.

Suburbanization and Gentrification

Between 1980 and the present, Texas suburbs (relatively small municipalities, usually outside the boundary limits of a central city) experienced explosive growth and spread into rural areas. The early history of suburbanization was

redlining
A discriminatory rating system used by federal agencies to evaluate the risks associated with loans made to borrowers in specific urban neighborhoods. Today, the term also refers to the same practice among private businesses like banks and real estate companies.

marked by racial segregation, with Whites in more affluent suburbs and historical minority groups in the inner city and less affluent suburbs. Government policies were used purposefully to ensure residential segregation. The federal government used **redlining** to restrict lending in low-income neighborhoods. Because historical minorities are disproportionately included in lower socioeconomic groups, this practice barred lending to many minority borrowers. Additionally, the federal government used interstate highway designs and **urban renewal** projects to isolate and eliminate minority neighborhoods. Local policies like **exclusionary zoning** and federal policies requiring **racial covenants** prevented minorities from renting or buying homes in more affluent suburbs. In many White suburbs, the powers of city governments (including some police departments and inspectors' offices) and homeowners' associations were used to harass, intimidate, or neglect minority families or businesses that moved in. Even when laws and court decisions moved official policies away from racially discriminatory practices, integration was limited by economic inequality, the phenomenon of White flight, and the practice of some realtors and lenders to steer their clients into segregated neighborhoods. Today, *de facto* racial segregation (segregation by fact rather than by law) remains, especially in suburban areas, though to a lesser extent than in the past.[36]

Texas has seen large demographic movements from rural to urban areas and from large cities to the suburbs and back. Although the shift from rural to urban areas and the growth of exurbs (extra-urban areas beyond suburbs) have continued into the 21st century, a repopulation of inner cities has revitalized numerous downtown neighborhoods and attracted new residents. In a process called **gentrification**, middle-class and affluent people move into struggling inner city areas, investing in property improvement and new businesses. Gentrification can be controversial, as lower-income residents are often displaced by increases in

urban renewal
The relocation of businesses and people, the demolition of structures, and the use of eminent domain to take private property for development projects.

exclusionary zoning
The use of local government zoning ordinances to exclude certain groups of people from a given community.

racial covenants
Agreements written into real estate documents by property owners, subdivision developers, or real estate operators in a given neighborhood, binding property owners not to sell, lease, or rent property to specified groups because of race, creed, or color.

gentrification
A relocation of middle class or affluent people into deteriorating urban areas, often displacing low-income residents.

📊 How Do We Compare...

In Population?

2020 Resident Population as Reported by the U.S. Bureau of the Census

Most Populous U.S. States	Population	U.S. States Bordering Texas	Population
California	39,538,223	Louisiana	4,657,757
Texas	**29,145,505**	Oklahoma	3,959,353
Florida	21,538,187	Arkansas	3,011,524
New York	20,201,249	New Mexico	2,117,522

— Competency Connection —
☼ **CRITICAL THINKING** ☼

How does a large and rapidly growing population create both opportunities and challenges for Texas?

rent, property values, and tax rates. Locally owned small businesses are also frequently unable to compete with new competition from incoming businesses.[37] Local governments, however, may benefit from increased property tax revenue.

Rural Texas

Though Texas is primarily metropolitan, small-town Texas is still a reality for the more than 14 percent of Texans who live in rural areas, which cover 84 percent of the state's total land area. In rural Texas, a variety of challenges complicate the charms of small-town life. Hospital closures and the difficulty of recruiting doctors have increased the difficulty of accessing health care in rural communities. Roads, water systems, and other public infrastructure age and crumble as the cost of upgrades, repairs, and maintenance falls most heavily on local taxpayers. The same funding shortages have led to school closures and cutbacks in important educational services, including those for the increasing number of homeless rural students. The threat of natural disasters in the form of floods, fires, droughts, and tornadoes make farming a risky business, which many young people choose to avoid.

Farming and ranching communities tend to change slowly. Texas's least-populated county (Loving County) has remained at a population between 33 and 285 since 1900 (169 in 2019). Yet some rural areas in the Lone Star State experienced rapid population growth and development as a result of the resurgence in oil and natural gas production that reached a fever pitch after 2010 and again after 2015. In times of increased production, these boomtowns have explosive growth in employment, investment, and tax revenue as drilling operations move in. But booms also bring challenges to small communities in the form of environmental damage, crime, drugs, traffic, and soaring housing costs. Many such towns experience equally rapid economic decline following a rapid drop in oil prices as occurred in 2014 and again in 2020.[38]

The Regions of Texas

Because of the state's vast size and geographic diversity, many Texans have developed a concept of five areas—North, South, East, West, and Central Texas—as five potentially separate states. In fact, the United States congressional resolution by which Texas was admitted to the Union in 1845 specifies that up to four states "in addition to said state of Texas" may be formed out of its territory and that each "shall be entitled to admission to the Union." Various plans for carving Texas into five states have been proposed to the Texas legislature, but few Texans have taken these plans seriously. The Texas Comptroller's office identifies 13 separate economic regions in Texas; but for simplicity, we condense these 13 regions to 6 (Figure 1.1).

The West Texas Plains Agriculture is the economic bedrock of the West Texas Plains, from sheep, goat, and cattle production in its southern portions to cotton, grain sorghum, and feedlot cattle in the north. This area depends heavily on water from the continually depleting and environmentally sensitive Ogallala Aquifer. Formed almost 10 million years ago during the Pliocene epoch, this

Figure 1.1 The Six Regions of Texas

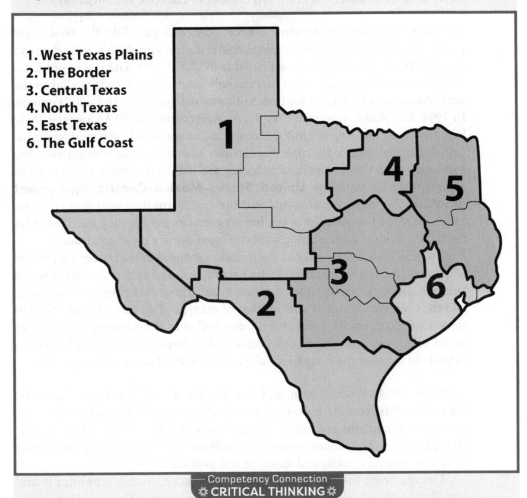

1. West Texas Plains
2. The Border
3. Central Texas
4. North Texas
5. East Texas
6. The Gulf Coast

— Competency Connection —
✿ **CRITICAL THINKING** ✿

How does Texas's large geographic size affect its politics and governance? How do the state's regions differ in culture, politics, and economy?

aquifer underlies eight states in the Great Plains, including the High Plains of Texas with the cities of Lubbock and Amarillo. Heavy agricultural demands are depleting the aquifer's water more rapidly than it is being replenished. Careful management of this underground water-bearing rock formation will be crucial to the region's future. South of the Cap Rock Escarpment, oil production forms the economic base of cities like Odessa and Midland. Though the recent boom in oil production in the Permian Basin lifted the local economy, a precipitous drop in oil prices due to the COVID-19 pandemic ushered in another economic bust in 2020 followed by a recovery in 2021.

From the Panhandle to Odessa, West Texas is known for social, economic, and political conservatism. Dominated by White evangelical Christians, agriculture, and oil, West Texas is fertile soil for the Republican Party. Democrats have little electoral success here, even in the larger cities of Lubbock and Amarillo.

The Border South and Southwest Texas border Mexico. Like the West Texas Plains, the western border region also benefited economically from the Permian Basin oil boom but saw that boom end due to COVID-19. The region produces citrus fruits and vegetables; but increasingly international trade is vital to the area's economy, which can thus be sensitive to swings in the Mexican economy. In 1994, the North American Free Trade Agreement (NAFTA) lowered trade barriers among Mexico, the United States, and Canada, which increased economic activity in the region. In 2018, the Trump administration renegotiated the agreement with the intention of reducing the U.S. trade deficit and moved to replace NAFTA with the **United States–Mexico–Canada Agreement (USMCA)**. All three countries adopted the agreement that went into effect on July 1, 2020. By that time, however, border counties were among the hardest hit by the coronavirus and resulting limits on cross-border travel and trade.[39]

From El Paso to Brownsville, many Texans living near the border are Latinos who have close ties with Mexico and are strongly linked to that country through family, friends, media, and trade. Spanish is the primary language for many here, and the Catholic Church is a major part of everyday life. Many Latinos tend to show strong support for government intervention in the economy, an extensive social safety net, and progressive taxation. The large Latino/a population has helped the Democratic Party have substantial electoral success in the region.

Central Texas Waco, Austin, and San Antonio are all in Central Texas. The region benefits from its universities and colleges, the high-tech sector, state government, tourism, and major military bases. It is also home to the German Hill Country, an agricultural region that holds onto its Central European (mostly German) cultural identity and its social and political conservatism.

Despite being the capital of a conservative state, Austin is politically and socially liberal and self-avowedly "weird." With a boom in the high-tech industry, a major university, and a thriving art and music scene, Austin has experienced rapid growth and in-migration from all over the country and the world. In particular, there has been an influx of highly educated former residents of the Northeast and West Coast. Austin also has the second highest concentration of Millennials in the nation. Since these groups tend to hold more progressive or liberal political values, the Democratic Party does well in Austin. San Antonio, home of the Alamo, is also one of the fastest-growing cities in the United States. Though San Antonio's numerous military installations and large Catholic population make it somewhat more conservative than Austin, the city has a relatively young population that is almost 65 percent Latino/a. Thus, San Antonio's voters are prone to electing Democratic candidates. Surrounding areas tend toward Republican conservatism.

North Texas The metropolitan area that contains Dallas, Fort Worth, and the more than 200 incorporated cities and towns that surround them is known popularly as the DFW Metroplex. This area has seen decades of explosive growth

United States–Mexico–Canada Agreement (USMCA) A trade agreement between the United States, Canada, and Mexico which revised and replaced the North American Free Trade Agreement (NAFTA). Major changes to NAFTA focus on the auto industry, new labor and environmental standards, intellectual property law, and some digital trade provisions.

and economic development as national and international corporations continue to move their headquarters to its cities. Observers often refer to Fort Worth as the place where the west begins and many residents still embrace their cowboy past. Dallasites seem to prefer diving headlong into the future. Both cities have become modern centers for high-tech industries, financial services, defense contractors, and food processing.

Dallas County Judge Clay Jenkins became nationally famous for his leadership in response to the coronavirus outbreak, taking a more active and aggressive approach than state leadership. The Democratic party's preference for more active government has increasingly found electoral success in the urban centers of the Metroplex in recent years. Suburban and rural parts of the Metroplex have generally remained conservative Republican strongholds. With many large corporations and wealthy residents, the Dallas–Fort Worth area is also a major source of funding for the Republican Party, with a sizeable number of the biggest political donors in the country living in the area.[40]

East Texas Cotton production has been a constant in East Texas since its settlement by White colonists and Black slaves, but recent years have been difficult for cotton farmers. In the past decade, the area's economy has also felt the impacts of both boom and bust in oil and gas production. Forestry and logging, along with production of wood and paper products in the area known as the Piney Woods, cattle and poultry farming, and some manufacturing helped fill the gap while other economic diversification has continued. A decline in demand for such products due to the coronavirus pandemic in 2020 caused a decline in the economy of the region, which already had a history of wages and employment lower than the state average and a poverty rate above the state average.

The westernmost extension of the Deep South, East Texas can seem a world apart, as references to life "behind the Pine Curtain" suggest. This area remains predominantly racially segregated, and it is dominated by evangelical Christianity and powerful families with deep historical roots. East Texas is now firmly a part of the Republican "Solid South."

The Gulf Coast The coast of the Gulf of Mexico stretches from the Louisiana border to the Rio Grande, though the region we focus on here surrounds Houston, the most populous city in Texas and the South, and the fourth most populous in the United States. Shipping and fishing are naturally important to the economy, but so are manufacturing and the presence of major corporate headquarters. Petrochemicals remain fundamental to the region's economy. It has thus been sensitive to oil booms and busts, including the recent fluctuations in fracking activity and in oil prices. In 2014, with fracking at its height, Houston's local economy was adding 100,000 jobs per year, far better than the nation as a whole. From 2015 through 2017, low oil and gas prices slowed job growth while unemployment rates exceeded the national rate. The city has continued to diversify its economy to cope with booms and busts. In 2018, Houston began a recovery that was halted by the 2020 coronavirus pandemic and the cold weather with power outages of February 2021 that had a devastating impact on the oil and gas industry and on international trade. Recovery resumed in spring of 2021.[41]

✓ **1.3 Learning Check**

1. What is the impact of the Lone Star State's size on Texas's politics?
2. True or False: All the regions of Texas are economically dependent on the same industries, and thus are nearly identical in culture and politics.

Answers at the end of this chapter.

The Beaumont–Port Arthur area has the highest concentration of union members in Texas. As a result of Houston's ethnic diversity and high levels of union membership in Beaumont–Port Arthur, Democrats have scored some electoral wins in the region. Suburban and rural parts of the Gulf Coast remain reliably Republican, however.

✚ **The Economy**

LO 1.4 Describe the industries that formed the historic basis for the Texas economy, the diversification of the modern Texas economy, and economic implications for Texas politics.

The Lone Star State's economic success has relied heavily on four land-based industries. These days, the Texas economy is vastly more diverse and includes a variety of 21st-century industries. Texas now produces more than 8 percent of U.S. GDP, second only to California.

The Texas Economy Through History

Much of Texas's early history was dominated by cattle, cotton, timber, and minerals (oil and gas). These four industries remain important sectors of the Lone Star State's economy and culture.

Cattle Plentiful land and minimal government interference encouraged cattle empires in Texas, established by politically powerful entrepreneurs such as Richard King and Mifflin Kenedy. During the 25 years after the Civil War, approximately 35,000 men, including many Black cowboys and Latino "vaqueros," drove nearly 10 million cattle and 1 million horses north to Kansas railheads. By the late 1880s, when railroads were built closer to Texas ranches, the cattle drives ended. In time, newly emerging industries diluted the economic impact of the beef business; but Texas still leads the nation in cattle production. Its inventory of approximately 13.1 million cattle is twice as many as that of Nebraska, the next largest cattle-producing state. Texas also leads the nation in production of horses, hay, sheep, goats, wool, and mohair.

Texas's $12.3 billion beef industry saw a 30 percent decrease in production as a result of meat-processing plant shutdowns due to coronavirus infections among workers in mid-2020.[42] Though plants began re-opening over the next several months and an industry rebound continued into 2021, damage to the Texas cattle industry was substantial.

Cotton Although popular culture romanticizes 19th-century cowboys and cattle drives, cotton formed the backbone of the state's economy in that era. This was particularly true in East and Central Texas, where soil and weather conditions resemble those in the Old South. Before the Civil War, slaves performed much of the field labor as cotton production spread. During that war, revenue from the export of Texas cotton (mostly shipped from Mexico to Europe) aided the Confederacy. As more frontier land was settled, cotton production moved westward and increased in volume.

Today, the Lone Star State produces almost a quarter of the nation's cotton and leads the country in exported cotton. Although cotton is grown throughout the state, the High Plains region of West Texas accounts for approximately 60 percent of the state's annual cotton yield. Since 2011, cotton production in West Texas has struggled to manage weather challenges that include drought, hail, blowing sand, flooding, and crippling storms. In addition, cotton farmers had to face a glut in global supply and elimination of federal price subsidies for the crop in 2014. Though the federal government announced new taxpayer-funded subsidies in early 2018, the U.S. government's trade war led China to enact retaliatory tariffs on U.S. cotton exports in the summer of that year. The 2020 coronavirus pandemic further reduced demand for cotton, cutting the market price per pound nearly in half. Year 2020 ended without demand and prices reaching pre-pandemic levels, but the industry continued to rebound into 2021.[43]

Timber East Texas includes the densely wooded Piney Woods and Big Thicket areas that were largely uninhabited until the 1800s. As the population grew, new towns and railroad lines increased demand for timber. By the mid-1800s, more than 200 sawmills were in operation from East to Central Texas. In the early 1900s, the timber industry was the state's largest employer, manufacturer, and revenue generator.[44]

The economic impact of timber declined in the 1920s, as clear-cutting by some logging companies and those exploring for oil depleted timber supply in many parts of East Texas. In 1933, the Texas legislature authorized the federal government to purchase more than 600,000 acres in East Texas for four national forests (Angelina, Davy Crockett, Sabine, and Sam Houston). In addition, the timber industry began to implement reseeding and sustainable logging practices. At the end of the 20th century, Texas was the nation's 10th largest timber producer, generating more than $12.9 billion annually.

In 2011, the beginning of a major drought, and to a lesser extent wildfires, resulted in the loss of between 100 and 500 million trees throughout the state, leading one Texas Parks and Wildlife Department official to predict that it would take more than half a century to recover fully from the loss. Precipitation increased in 2015; and by 2016 demand for timber in the housing, construction, and oil and gas industries fueled a Texas timber recovery. President Trump's trade war with China, coupled with the coronavirus pandemic, dramatically reduced exports and sent prices for the state's timber tumbling. By August 2020, mining and logging had seen the worst drop in employment of any sector of the Texas economy, with a striking 24 percent decrease in jobs. Though timber prices saw remarkable gains through the beginning of 2021, the volatility of the market makes predictions difficult even for experts.[45]

Oil and Gas In 1901, when the Spindletop Field was developed near Beaumont, petroleum ushered in the industry that dominated the state's economy for nearly a century. During the next 50 years, drilling, refining, and delivering oil and gas brought industrial employment on a grand scale to rural Texas. Several major oil companies were created, such as Humble (now ExxonMobil Corporation), Magnolia Petroleum Company, Sun Oil Company, Gulf Oil Corporation, and the Texas Company. (Gulf Oil Corporation and the Texas Company [Texaco] now are a part of Chevron.) Domination of the state by a single industry resulted in the rise of some of the most politically powerful businesses and individuals in

Texas history. In 1919, the Texas legislature gave the Railroad Commission of Texas limited regulatory jurisdiction over the state's oil and natural gas industry.[46] Because oil and gas producers were so economically and politically powerful, the commission quickly gained a reputation less for regulating the industry than for supporting and promoting it.

At its peak in the early 1980s, the Texas oil and gas industry employed half a million workers, who earned more than $11 billion annually. Oil and natural gas production and related industries accounted for almost one-third of the state's economy. That peak ended in an oil price crash that reached full swing in 1986 and ushered in an economic recession for the state. Over the next two decades, fluctuating prices reduced revenue and led Texas's leaders to seek diversification of the state's economy. Nevertheless, despite increased stability overall, the boom and bust cycle in oil and gas continues.

Discovery of major natural gas deposits in South, Central, and North Texas in the early 21st century, along with the newly profitable drilling method of **hydraulic fracturing** (fracking), launched an oil boom, but oil prices dropped from more than $100 a barrel in June of 2014 to $35 a barrel in early 2016.[47] Soaring production in the Permian Basin and new U.S. Geological Survey estimates of massive reserves of recoverable oil in that region started a second boom. Oil revenues were dealt a harsh blow when states and local governments issued stay-at-home orders for much of the country due to the coronavirus pandemic. In April 2020, the price for a barrel of oil went negative for the first time ever, forcing some producers to pay buyers to take their oil. Monthly oil and gas tax revenues plummeted. In July 2019, producers paid $440 million in oil and gas production taxes. In July 2020, they paid only $118 million; and revenues remained more than 40 percent lower than the previous year through the beginning of 2021.[48] Revenues from taxes on oil and gas help the Texas state government increase its Rainy Day Fund, complete highway construction and maintenance, invest in higher education through the Permanent University Fund, and finance the State Water Plans. Fluctuations in prices have a corresponding effect on the state's tax revenues.

The oil industry began 2021 on a rebound, and Texas remains the nation's top producer of oil and gas. The state accounts for approximately 30 percent of U.S. refinery capacity and 75 percent of U.S. petrochemical production.[49] If it were its own country, Texas would be the fourth largest oil and gas producer in the world.

Most oil and gas jobs pay relatively high wages and salaries, but employment in the industry rises and falls rapidly based on swings in oil prices and other factors. In the past decade, the number of jobs changed frequently, bouncing between a high of 306,300 in December 2014 and a low of 158,500 in September 2020. The industry ended 2020 with the largest drop in employment (29.7 percent) of any sector. Despite dramatic booms and busts in petrochemical industry revenue and jobs, because of the diversification of the state's economy, such cycles do not have the same impact on Texas's revenues or its overall economy as they once did. The oil and gas industry now accounts directly for around 1 percent of the state's jobs. Although industry officials continue to be politically powerful in Texas, they are not expected to regain their former level of political dominance.

hydraulic fracturing
Also known as "fracking," this method of extracting oil and natural gas involves forcing open fissures in subterranean rocks by introducing liquid at high pressure.

New Economic Directions

Devastation of plunging oil prices in the 1980s demonstrated the dangers of reliance on a single industry. Texas's business and government leaders subsequently pursued a restructuring and diversification of the state's economy. Texans launched new industries that quickly spread across the state, bolstering the Texas economy and playing an important role in the national economy. In 2006, for the first time, more *Fortune* 500 companies were headquartered in Texas than in any other state. In 2020, however, New York ranked first with 54 and Texas ranked third (behind California) with 50.[50] Until the economic downturn caused by the COVID-19 pandemic in 2020, the state was adding jobs in nearly all major nonagricultural industries. These areas included construction, manufacturing, trade, transportation, utilities, financial activities, professional and business services, education, health services, leisure and hospitality, government, and other services. The diversity of the Texas economy, its employer-friendly taxation and regulation policies, and other factors are believed to have combined to help Texas weather the Great Recession that began in 2008 better than most states. In 2019, Texas experienced the lowest unemployment rate since it began tracking that statistic in 1976, and the state added almost 1,000 jobs a day.[51] The coronavirus pandemic brought that growth to an abrupt halt and led to employment losses in all sectors of the Texas economy. Recovering from this economic reversal will require effective public policies, an educated and productive labor force, an adequate supply of capital, and sound business management practices.

Energy Thirty-nine of the forty-eight *Fortune* 500 companies headquartered in Texas in 2020 were energy-related. Texas is the country's leading producer not only of oil and gas but also lignite coal. In addition to the pandemic-induced downturn in the energy industry, awareness is growing of research results that establish fossil fuels as the world's principal source of air pollution that contributes to significant health problems. These fuels include oil, gas, and coal burned for industrial purposes and in automobiles, trucks, buses, and airplanes.[52] As a result, Texas is placing increased emphasis on new industries and opportunities, including the production of alternative energy, such as wind and solar power. In Texas, growth of renewable energy sources outpaced the growth of coal, natural gas, and other energy sources until the peak of the fracking boom. In 2019, Texas ranked only 44th out of 50 states in renewable energy production. Still, that was also the first year that Texas produced more energy from renewables than from coal.[53]

The overwhelming share of Texas's renewable energy comes from wind power, largely produced on West Texas wind farms. With 26 percent of its electricity generated by wind, Texas leads the nation in generation capacity from wind power and is well positioned to produce even more. The U.S. Department of Energy projects that Texas will have almost 20 percent of the nation's wind capacity by 2030.[54]

The Lone Star State also has abundant yearly sunshine. Though the solar industry has received little support from the Texas legislature, local governments and the private sector have increasingly turned to solar power to meet their energy needs. By 2020, Texas ranked fifth among the states in solar energy

Image 1.4 Texas leads the nation in energy production capacity from wind farms and continues to develop its solar energy potential.

Sarah Fields Photography/Shutterstock.com

— Competency Connection —
⚙ **CRITICAL THINKING** ⚙

What industries are essential to sustain and continue to develop the Texas economy in the 21st century?

production. Though solar accounts for only about 1 percent of electricity production in Texas, a recent study by Rice University researchers concluded that Texas has enough sun and wind combined to operate without coal. Texas also generates a small amount of energy from geothermal and hydroelectric plants.[55]

The Lone Star State already ranks second in the nation for employment in the renewable energy industry. Today, students in Texas can enroll in renewable energy programs and classes in wind and solar power at eight of Texas's public universities, Texas State Technical College, and community colleges in Austin, San Antonio, El Paso, Amarillo, Dallas County, and Tarrant County.

Despite some claims that reliance on renewable energy caused failure of the Texas power grid during winter storm Uri in February 2021, every type of generator in Texas (including nuclear, coal and natural gas) struggled to operate during subfreezing temperatures. Left largely unregulated, most Texas power companies had opted not to incur the costs of sufficiently "winterizing" generators.[56]

High Technology The term *high technology* applies to research, development, manufacturing, and marketing of a seemingly endless line of electronic products, such as computers, smartphones, and drones. High-technology businesses employ almost 8 percent of Texas's labor force and comprise just over 8 percent of the state's economy. Most high-tech jobs in Texas are in the fields of information technology and software services, engineering, research and development, testing, telecommunications, internet services, and technology manufacturing. The field is dominated by large firms, such as Motorola, Dell, Hewlett-Packard, Texas Instruments, and Applied Materials.

Salaries and wages in the Texas high-tech sector, averaging over $90,000 per year, are almost double average wages for the rest of the state's economy. The vast majority of these jobs are centered in Texas's major cities.[57] The number of technology companies either moving headquarters to or expanding operations in Texas in recent years has been high. Included are large companies like Amazon, Apple, Google, and Tesla, along with up-and-coming tech firms like Airtable, QuestionPro, Cloudflare, and Bold Commerce. Though COVID-19 damaged the overall economy, emphasis throughout the pandemic on digital working, shopping, and interacting created new opportunities. Even with a decline in job openings during the pandemic, Texas ranked second only to California in the number of high tech jobs available.[58]

In addition to efforts to expand the high-tech industry, the Texas government has also worked to develop **biotechnology** and the life sciences, which comprise a multibillion-dollar industry producing new medicines and vaccines, chemicals, and other products designed to benefit medical science, human health, and agricultural production. In the past two decades, biotech-related jobs have increased four times faster than the overall increase in employment in Texas. Home to more than 5,400 biotechnology firms, manufacturing companies, industry consortia, and research university facilities including 11 medical schools, Texas employs more than 106,000 workers in the biotech sector at an average annual salary of almost $84,000.[59]

Four areas of particular focus in Texas are biodefense and pandemic preparedness, personalized medicine, regenerative medicine, and vaccines. The Texas biotech industry spends approximately $5.6 billion annually on research and development projects. Almost $3.2 billion of that is spent at the state's research universities and colleges. The Texas A&M Center for Innovation in Advanced Development and Manufacturing, established in 2012 to lead the nation's biosecurity research efforts, is a public-private partnership likely worth $1.5 to $2 billion. An initial federal grant of more than $175 million is the largest sum of federal money awarded in the state since NASA (near Houston) in the 1960s.

Services Employing one-fourth of all Texas workers, in recent decades service industries provided new jobs more rapidly than all other sectors. Service businesses include healthcare providers (hospitals and nursing homes); personal services (hotels, restaurants, and recreational enterprises, such as water parks and video arcades); and commercial services (printers, advertising agencies, data processing companies, equipment rental companies, and consultants). Other service providers include education, investment brokers, insurance and real estate agencies, banks and credit unions, and merchandising enterprises. Most service jobs come with few or no benefits and pay lower wages and salaries than manufacturing firms that produce goods.

As local and state governments responded to the coronavirus outbreak by ordering non-essential face-to-face businesses to close or restrict services, unemployment in this sector soared. When many of the affected businesses were allowed to re-open with reduced capacity, the service sector experienced a moderate recovery. A subsequent resurgence of the virus sent the service sector back into a nosedive.[60] This industry remained sensitive to the fluctuations of coronavirus infections, experiencing a recovery as the pandemic receded in 2021.

biotechnology
Also known as "biotech," this is the use and/or manipulation of biological processes and microorganisms to perform industrial or manufacturing processes or create consumer goods.

Agriculture Texas ranks second in the nation in agricultural production (behind California) and sixth in agricultural exports. It leads the country in total acreage of agricultural land; numbers of farms and ranches; number of women and minority-owned farm operations; value of farm real estate; and production of beef, sheep, hay, goats, cotton, and mohair. Other important cash crops include corn, grain sorghum, rice, cottonseed, peanuts, soybeans, pecans, fresh market vegetables, and citrus. In 2019, the Texas Legislature passed and Governor Abbott signed HB 1325, legalizing the cultivation of industrial hemp in the state for the first time in more than 80 years. Industrial hemp had been banned because it is genetically identical to the marijuana plant, but contains 0.3 percent THC (the psychoactive compound that generates a "high") by weight or less. By mid-2020 more than 5,000 acres in Texas were licensed to grow the crop. By October of that year the first harvests had begun. Hemp cultivation requires little or no pesticides or herbicides and is used in products including paper, textiles, fuel, paint, detergent, varnish, oil, ink, building materials, food, medicine, and more. The economic impact of the industry remains to be seen. Farmers are optimistic but face challenges as they learn how to grow hemp in the climate and soil of Texas. They also face an oversaturated market, a pandemic, a lack of infrastructure to process the harvested plant, and a state government that lacks experience regulating the hemp market. Gross income from all of the products of Texas agriculture amounts to about $25 billion annually, making agriculture the second largest industry in the state. More than 408,000 Texas residents, including a large proportion of immigrants, are employed in agriculture-related jobs.[61]

Over the past eight decades, the number of farms and ranches in Texas has decreased from more than 500,000 to fewer than 250,000. This reduction largely reflects the use of labor-saving farm machinery and chemicals. Small family farms are also being rapidly replaced by large agribusinesses or sold for real estate development. When farm commodity prices are low (because of overproduction and weak market demand) or when crops are poor (as a result of drought or other weather conditions), many farmers end the year deeply in debt. Some must sell their land—often to larger farm operators, corporations, or wealthy investors. The federal government continues to support farmers and ranchers, whether small family farmers or agricultural corporations, with taxpayer-funded subsidies. This support has been a part of agricultural policy since the Great Depression. Through the U.S. Department of Agriculture, federal subsidies to Texas farmers and ranchers increased dramatically during the Trump administration—first, to compensate farmers for losses caused by the U.S. government's trade war and then for losses sustained as a result of the coronavirus. Even with government support, farm bankruptcies have risen in recent years. The trouble facing farmers intensified due to Winter Storm Uri in 2021, which caused an estimated $600 million in damage to Texas's agriculture industry.[62]

Trade By reducing and ultimately eliminating tariffs during the 15-year period from 1993 to 2008, the North American Free Trade Agreement (NAFTA) stimulated U.S. trade with Canada and Mexico. Because more than 60 percent of U.S. exports to Mexico are produced in or transported through Texas from other states, expanding foreign trade has produced jobs for Texans, profits for the state's businesses, and revenue for state and local governments. Nearly one million jobs in Texas depend directly or indirectly on American exports to Canada and Mexico. When the new United States–Mexico–Canada (USMCA) trade agreement replaced NAFTA in 2020, Texas's leaders were hopeful. They believed the new agreement would increase natural gas and agricultural goods exports, ease access to foreign markets for smaller businesses, provide greater intellectual property protections, and offer incentives to manufacture goods in Texas.[63]

Problems likely to remain despite the new agreement include increased trucking on highways between Mexico and Canada, which has contributed to air pollution and caused traffic congestion in Texas and elsewhere. Imports from Mexican **maquiladoras** will likely continue unabated. Work at these assembly facilities is usually low-paid and can be dangerous, with increasing reports of serious work-related injuries, illnesses from working with dangerous materials, and mental health problems from a stressful work environment.[64]

Though Texas has many trading partners, Mexico is its most important. Thus, a more prosperous and stable Mexico usually means more trade (and fewer jobless workers migrating to the United States), but a succession of crises in Mexico starting in 2006 raised serious questions concerning relations between the United States and Mexico. Ongoing efforts to contain criminal drug cartels with assistance from the U.S. government for the past 15 years have resulted in increased violence and a heightened military presence in Mexico. Violence reached record levels and continued to escalate.

Mexico's current president, Andrés Manuel López Obrador (known as "AMLO"), who was elected in 2018, has likewise attempted to rein in the violence and established a new National Guard to deal more forcefully with criminal organizations. He has worked cooperatively with the United States on some issues, including trade reform through USMCA. Still, Mexico's economic troubles reduced demand for American exports. In addition, continuing violence and cargo theft, combined with travel and trade restrictions due to the coronavirus pandemic, inflicted serious damage on Texas's cross-border trade.[65]

◩ Meeting New Challenges

LO 1.5 Identify four major policy challenges Texas faces in the 21st century.

Clearly, Texas has experienced rapid and dramatic change in recent decades, and the state has faced dramatic upheaval brought about by the coronavirus pandemic. Change and crisis present challenges, but they also present opportunities. Success will depend heavily on public policy decisions that address poverty and social problems, improve and finance the state's public schools and institutions of higher education, manage the state's increasing diversity, sustainably manage our natural resources, and protect the ecological system.

Poverty and Social Problems

By 2019, Texas had achieved its lowest poverty rate in a decade. Still, approximately one of every five children in Texas was living in poverty, the 11th highest child poverty rate of any state. Impoverished children are more likely to drop out

---

✔ **1.4 Learning Check**

1. What four industries were important to the Texas economy in the past?

2. True or False: The coronavirus pandemic had little impact on the diverse Texas economy.

Answers at the end of this chapter.

maquiladoras
Industrial plants on the Mexican side of the border which are partnered with American companies. Such plants typically use low-cost labor to assemble imported parts for a wide range of consumer goods and then export these goods back to the United States or to other countries.

of high school, become teenage parents, struggle with employment, be victims of crime or be arrested for criminal conduct, live in poverty as adults, draw on public assistance, and have poor health. As a result, many researchers argue that reducing childhood poverty is one of the most effective investments the state can make for its future prosperity, safety, and health. This investment will be even more challenging in the wake of the coronavirus pandemic.

Impacts of the coronavirus pandemic resulted in some 6.6 million Texans filing for unemployment assistance. Prior to the pandemic, estimates of the number of homeless people (including many children) varied widely, but at least 20,000—and perhaps more than 30,000—Texans could not provide themselves with shelter in a house or apartment. Not only did the pandemic increase the number of people without homes, but also it put those staying in homeless shelters at increased risk of contracting the virus.[66]

Health care is also a major issue for Texas. Of the 50 states, Texas has the highest percentage and largest number of uninsured residents. Uninsured people have less access to both critical and preventative care, receive poorer quality of care, and experience worse health outcomes than insured people. But a large uninsured population is also a burden on those who are insured. Public emergency rooms are required to treat patients regardless of ability to pay. Thus, a large uninsured population tends to increase medical costs, insurance premiums, emergency room crowding, and wait times. Uninsured people are also more likely to face bankruptcy, suffer worse health, miss or underperform at work, lose a job, and require government assistance programs. As a result, increasing the number and percentage of Texans with health insurance is believed to be important for improving health care for all and strengthening the state's economy.[67]

After implementation of the federal Affordable Care Act (also known as ACA or "Obamacare") began in 2010, the state's uninsured rate dropped from nearly 25 percent of the non-elderly uninsured to 16.6 percent in 2016. Texas, however, has continued to refuse federal funds to expand Medicaid coverage for adults under the Affordable Care Act and thus has lagged behind other states in increasing the number of people insured. Changes to the program by the Trump administration from 2017 through 2020 further increased the number of uninsured people in the state. Because the United States is the only advanced industrial democracy without universal health coverage, many Americans either pay out-of-pocket or receive insurance through their employer. Thus, the dramatic spike in unemployment due to COVID-19 resulted in the greatest increase in the uninsured population in recorded history. One study in mid-2020 noted that the percentage of non-elderly uninsured in Texas had reached nearly 30 percent.[68]

In addition to economic and health costs, poverty and social problems can damage democracy itself. Voting rates are low for those below the federal poverty level, and an increasing number of Texans fit that category. Citizens who do not vote or participate in political campaigns have less access to elected officials. The Lone Star State continues to rank near the bottom of the 50 states in governmental responses to poverty and social problems. Though there are different views of how to address these issues, development of innovative and effective solutions will be important for Texas's recovery.

Education

Research links higher levels of education in a society with improved economic performance, higher individual incomes, better health, political stability, higher tolerance levels, and less crime and violence. With a public-school student population that compares in size to the total population of Colorado, the future of Texas and its quality of life depend heavily on the quality of education. Texas faces significant challenges in this regard. Even prior to the pandemic, more than 60 percent of public school students were classified as economically disadvantaged, and more than 17 percent were English-language learners. A recent study that included 13 measures of chances for student success, 12 measures of K-12 achievement, and 8 measures of school finance, *Education Week* awarded Texas a "C-" and ranked the state's public school system 42nd among the 50 states.[69]

Funding education is a major controversy in Texas politics. Most public education revenue is derived from taxes on real estate within a school district's boundaries. Property values vary widely across Texas, so funding remains unequal. State and federal governments also provide some funding. For a more complete discussion of public school finance, see Chapter 11, "Finance and Fiscal Policy."

Teachers are the key element in any educational system, but from year to year, the Lone Star State is confronted with shortages of certified personnel to instruct its K-12 students. Although estimates of the severity of the teacher shortage vary, the Texas Education Agency reports that more than 10 percent of the state's 358,000 teachers quit teaching each year. The report indicates that even though some educators retire, most leave the profession for reasons that include inadequate pay and benefits, low prestige, conflicts with parents, and increasing time-consuming chores that often must be done at night and on weekends.

📋 Students in Action

Finding Purpose

Challenges in Jacob Peña's early life inspired his concern for those who struggle and his recognition of the importance of government. He and two siblings watched their single mother work full time while pursuing bachelor's and master's degrees in speech pathology. Though many in their community judged those who accepted government support, he saw how programs like federal student loans and WIC facilitated his mother's hard work and helped lift the family from needing help to being able to help others.

Despite his mother's example and a family that valued education, Jacob didn't take high school seriously and saw all his college applications rejected. But in his senior year at Allen High School, he joined his older brother at Collin College's Martin Luther King Breakfast and was introduced to Judge John Payton. The introduction led to an internship working with students facing truancy and other legal problems. By the time Jacob entered Collin College in 2014, he was helping run the program and discovering his potential for leadership and passion for serving his community.

Lift as You Climb

Collin College's chapter of the League of United Latin American Citizens (LULAC) provided additional avenues for service and leadership. His new sense of purpose led to academic excellence and awards that allowed him to transfer to UT-Austin —an exciting step for the grandson of one of UT's first Latino students. He continued with LULAC, majored in government, and earned an internship with State Senator Judith Zaffirini (D-Laredo) in the Texas Legislature. This intense but rewarding experience made his research come alive and increased his dedication to public service. An intensive 2017

(Continued)

summer program at the University of Michigan and
a visit to Washington, D.C., led him to apply for UT's
Archer Fellowship. This fellowship provided a full
semester of classes in D.C. and an internship at the
Center on Budget and Policy Priorities (CBPP).

After graduation, Jacob turned the CBPP
internship into a full-time job. He learned much,
but the importance of the upcoming presidential
election led him to leave CBPP and work with
Elizabeth Warren's campaign for the presidency in
Wisconsin. Though Warren's campaign ended in
March 2020, he continued to work in Wisconsin with
Voces de la Frontera Action organizing students
and immigrants for political action and then as an
electoral consultant in Georgia. Grateful to those
who facilitated these opportunities, he says "I want
to lift as I climb" and help empower others.

Senator Judith Zaffirini (D-Laredo) and Jacob Peña

Get Involved

Jacob's passion for civic engagement comes
from a deep belief in representative government
and recognition of how politics and policy shape
countless aspects of our lives. Representatives
make decisions that impact your life, he says, but
"politicians are not going to knock on everyone's
door" to understand your struggles and aspirations.
By getting involved, he emphasizes "you're
taking it into your own hands" to secure proper
representation for your family and community.[71]

Contributing to their decision to seek other careers is stress over classroom problems affected by the poverty and troubled home lives of many students. Additionally, teachers complain of burdensome government-mandated assessment and
accountability measures.[70]

The coronavirus pandemic upended education as dramatically as it upended
any facet of Texas life. Closed schools, waived accountability testing, and online
learning were among the changes faced by students, their families, and their
teachers. For a more in-depth discussion of public education and the effects of
the coronavirus, see Chapter 12, "Public Policy and Administration."

Increasing Diversity

Research demonstrates that diversity in groups leads to improvements in
problem-solving and innovation, resulting in better performance and better
results.[72] A multilingual and multicultural state is also better positioned to compete and cooperate in a global economy. As a result, Texas is well positioned to
use diversity to its advantage—if it can learn to manage that diversity produc-
tively. That means prioritizing the Constitutional guarantee of equal protection
under the law and handling immigration.

Equal protection under the law becomes slightly more complicated when it
comes to those who immigrate to Texas from foreign countries. While many follow all legal procedures, some immigrants are undocumented and enter the
United States in violation of federal immigration law or overstay legal visas. Most
come for work or to escape dangerous situations in their homeland. This raises
important questions: To what extent are legal residents and **undocumented
immigrants** entitled to the same protections as citizens? How does the state control the flow of immigrants and the type of labor nonresidents may perform?

**undocumented
immigrant**
A person who enters the
United States in violation
of federal immigration
law or overstays a legal
visa and thus lacks proper
documentation and
identification.

The impact of immigration on the Texas economy is complex. Because Texas relies largely on consumption and property taxes to fund state and local government services, even undocumented immigrants pay state taxes when they buy goods and services or rent or buy property. In fact, a Rice University study in 2020 discovered that for every dollar the state government spends on services for undocumented immigrants, it collects $1.21 in revenue. This confirms the findings of AngelouEconomics (an Austin-based consulting firm) in 2017, The Perryman Group in Waco in 2016, and the state comptroller's analysis a decade prior.[73] However, the comptroller's report also concluded that undocumented immigrants cost local governments about $1.44 billion in healthcare and law enforcement costs not reimbursed by the state. Costs and benefits of having an estimated 1.7 million undocumented immigrants are not distributed evenly among the Texas population. Employers in construction, agriculture, hospitality, and tourism benefit from an inexpensive supply of labor; and consumers who buy their products and services benefit from the resulting lower prices. Persons who hire undocumented domestic workers at low wages also benefit. American workers without high school diplomas lose out in competition for low-wage unskilled jobs and the accompanying depressed wages.[74]

Texas politicians often face the difficult task of balancing constituents' demands for increased border security against demands of a growing Latino/a constituency and a politically active business community pushing for immigration reforms. Despite increasing anti-immigrant sentiments nationally in the 1990s, in June 2001, a substantial bipartisan majority in the Texas legislature passed, and Governor Perry signed, the Texas DREAM Act. This law allows undocumented immigrants brought to Texas as children by their parents to pay in-state tuition at public colleges and universities if they graduated from high school or received a GED in the state. Available to those who have at least three years of residency and are seeking legal residency, this provision has benefited more than 25,000 Texas students. Republican legislators attempted to repeal the act during the 2015, 2017, 2019 and 2021 sessions of the Texas Legislature, but failed each time due in part to opposition from the business community. Opponents of the law argue that it provides incentives for more illegal immigration. Supporters contend that these young people who know only life in the United States should not be punished for actions of parents who brought them here illegally.

Republican legislators managed to pass a different anti-immigration bill during the 85th session of the Texas Legislature in 2017. The sanctuary cities bill, known as "SB 4," passed; and Governor Abbott signed it after much heated and emotional debate. The city of El Cenizo and Maverick County immediately sued to prevent implementation of the law. In March 2018, a panel of three U.S. Court of Appeals justices ruled in favor of most provisions of the bill, allowing the state to enforce SB 4 while the appeals process plays out. This statute allows law enforcement officers to question the immigration status of those they detain or arrest; and it requires local governments, including public colleges and universities, to cooperate with federal immigration officers. In November 2018, Texas Attorney General Ken Paxton sued the city of San Antonio for releasing 12 undocumented immigrants found in a tractor-trailer. Though most of the suit was set aside, the issue of whether the city has a general policy against cooperating with federal authorities regarding immigration laws continues to make its way through the courts.[75]

Texas executive officials have also attempted recently to limit immigration and to challenge benefits for undocumented immigrants. After President Obama directed the U.S. Department of Homeland Security to expand the Deferred Action for Childhood Arrivals (DACA) program to include their parents through the Deferred Action for Parental Accountability (DAPA) program, then-Attorney General Greg Abbott filed a lawsuit to block implementation. DACA provided two-year work permits and exemption from deportation to undocumented immigrants in Texas who were under the age of 16 at their time of arrival, had no criminal record, and met several other requirements. DAPA was initiated to provide temporary protection against deportation to undocumented immigrants whose children were citizens or lawful residents of the United States and who presented no criminal or terroristic threat to the country. In 2016, in a 4-4 split, the U.S. Supreme Court upheld an injunction blocking expansion of the program. In 2017, President Trump rescinded DACA altogether; but the next year, the U.S. Ninth Circuit Court of Appeals upheld lower court rulings that DACA must remain in place. In June 2020, the U.S. Supreme Court, concurring with *amicus* briefs filed by 200 major corporations in support of DACA, upheld the decision of the Ninth Court of Appeals and declared that the administration followed improper procedures in rescinding the program.[76]

Texas is also often at the center of controversy over state and federal efforts to prevent unauthorized attempts to cross the U.S. border with Mexico. Construction of fencing and other barriers along the United States–Mexico border began with the 2006 Secure Fence Act signed into law by President George W. Bush. Building the fence is an expensive undertaking, with some segments costing $6.5 million per mile. As of 2018, only about 115 miles of fencing had been completed along Texas's 1,254-mile border. Unable to secure funding for the wall from Mexico or from the U.S. Congress, President Donald Trump declared the construction of a border wall a national emergency in that year. The move, intended to facilitate the use of U.S. military troops and provide funds to seize land along the border through government condemnation and build a wall, met with immediate lawsuits and a Congressional resolution to end the emergency declaration. These efforts failed. During 2016–2021, the federal government repaired or replaced 452 miles of wall along nearly 2,000 miles of the U.S. border with Mexico. Only 47 miles were of new construction.[77]

Physical barriers like a wall are not the only attempts made to prevent border crossings. The same year that Texas sued to block President Obama's DACA expansion, Governor Rick Perry sent 1,000 National Guard troops to the border. The number of troops dropped to 100 by July 2015. Later in 2015, newly elected Governor Abbott extended their deployment, ordered more boat patrols on the Rio Grande, and increased air surveillance.[78] In 2018, Abbott expanded the number of Texas National Guard troops on the border to 1,145; and he praised President Trump's announcement that the United States would send as many as 15,000 active duty troops to prevent a caravan of thousands of Central American migrants from entering the United States. Only about 5,800 federal troops were actually deployed, 2,800 of whom were stationed in Texas. Because of the 1878 *Posse Comitatus* Act, these troops cannot actively engage in border patrol activities. Instead, they have assisted in setting up wire barriers and in transporting and protecting civil agents. What was left of the migrant "caravan" by the end of the year arrived at the California border rather than Texas. By that time, the federal deployment of troops had already cost an estimated $300 million dollars.

At the same time, the Texas government was spending $800 million per year on border security for a total cost approaching $2 billion since Governor Perry's initial deployment of National Guard personnel.[79]

In 2018, Texas also became the center of national attention regarding the treatment of people caught crossing the border without documentation. President Trump's "zero tolerance" policy instituted in that year separated immigrant children from their families. Outrage about psychological toll on the children and conditions in which they were held spread nationwide, sparking widespread political mobilization to end the policy. Texas's elected officials were divided on this issue. Attorney General Ken Paxton supported the policy. But Governor Abbott, along with members of the Texas delegation to the U.S. Congress, Speaker of the Texas House Joe Straus, and a variety of other Texas politicians sought policy changes to end family separation. In June, President Trump issued an executive order to end the separation of families, and a federal judge ordered the reunification of most separated families. Due to a confused bureaucratic reunification process, many families remained separated or were newly separated following the order. By 2019, the number of unaccompanied migrant children in Texas shelters reached its highest point ever (more than 8,500), comprising 60 percent of the nation's institutionalized minors. By early 2021 the parents of more than 600 children in detention still could not be located. Concerns were raised about sanitary and health conditions, deaths of at least seven children, and thousands of reports of sexual abuse. When the COVID pandemic hit Texas, it spread in immigrant detention centers where social distancing was not possible. Infection rates for detainees was 13 times that of the general population by mid-2020. In early 2021, President Biden began changing course at the border by ending zero-tolerance, creating a task force for family reunification, and reviewing other Trump-era policies for change.[80]

The coronavirus pandemic brought a large proportion of border crossings—both legal and illegal—to a halt. Travel bans on places deemed to be COVID hotspots reduced short-term travel to the United States. In March 2020, all Citizenship and Immigration Services offices closed, and Border Patrol agents began expelling people seeking asylum from persecution and torture. Green cards that allow documented immigrants to work and worker visas were severely restricted. As the impact of the coronavirus diminished and the Biden administration rolled back Trump-era policies, immigration increased and the issue of immigration reform has emerged again. So long as families seek to escape poverty and violence at home, and so long as jobs and safety are available in Texas, the state will continue to deal with people who wish to move here.

Sustainability

Ensuring a high quality of life for Texans into the future means managing the state's natural resources sustainably. With a tradition of electing pro-business, small-government politicians, regulations in Texas (including environmental restrictions) tend to be less exacting than in other states. According to a 2019 study, Texas ranked 42nd out of 50 states in air and water quality. In 2020, a total of 3,252 of the state's 7,052 public water systems violated the Environmental Protection Agency's water quality standards.[81] Water is a precious commodity that the state government has struggled to protect.

⊠ Point/Counterpoint

Should Texas expand regulations to protect the environment?

The Issue As part of its strategy of attracting industry to the state, the Texas government keeps regulation of industry to a minimum. The state regularly challenges federal environmental regulations in court.

For	Against
1. Texas ranks fourth among the states in total pounds of toxic chemicals released into the environment, with severe consequences for human and animal health.[82]	1. Regulation increases operating costs for businesses and can result in lower employment and higher prices for consumers.
2. Many studies show little or no economic damage to states resulting from environmental regulation. Businesses often overstate the costs of regulation and ignore the economic benefits of reduced healthcare costs and an improved housing market.	2. Environmental agencies frequently underreport the negative effect of regulations because they rely on a partial or direct analysis that looks only at the direct effect of a regulation on the affected industry and not at the indirect effect of a regulation on the economy as a whole, other industries, and consumer behavior.
3. Strict regulations spur innovation and technological advancement as industries develop cleaner and more energy-efficient ways of doing business and more sustainable ways of producing and delivering energy.	3. Many businesses seek to locate their operations where the cost of doing business is low. Texas's limited regulations bring economic activity and employment to the state, which has contributed to a state economy that is stronger than the national economy.

Source: This "Point/Counterpoint" is based in part on William Fulton, "Do Environmental Regulations Hurt the Economy?" *Governing*, March 2010, http://www.governing.com/columns/eco-engines/Do-Environmental-Regulations-Hurt.html.

Competency Connection
🖘 COMMUNICATION SKILLS 🖚

How might you communicate your views about the proper balance between economic growth and environmental protection to your elected representatives?

After a devastating drought in the 1950s, the Texas legislature created the Texas Water Development Board (TWDB) in 1957 and mandated statewide water planning. Since then, the TWDB and the Texas Board of Water Engineers have prepared and adopted 10 state water plans, including the most recent, *Water for Texas 2017*. This plan makes recommendations for development, management, and conservation of water resources and for better preparation for and response to drought conditions. Texas's water supply was severely depleted by drought that began in 2011. From that time until 2016, use of water per Texas fracking well increased 770 percent. This resulted in pumping an estimated 45 billion gallons of water.[83] In 2012, the Office of the Comptroller issued a report, "The Impact of the 2011 Drought and Beyond." It predicts that demand for water will rise 22 percent by 2060, while the state's current dependable water supply will meet only about 65 percent of the demand. Since 2011, Texas voters have ratified constitutional amendments authorizing state government loans to local governments for water, wastewater, and flood control projects. By 2021, the TWDB was providing approximately $31.4 billion in loan and grant programs for the planning, acquisition, design, and construction of water-related infrastructure and other water quality improvements across the state.[84]

Increased precipitation beginning in 2015 refilled many lakes and rivers. By June 2021, monitored water supply reservoirs in Texas were just over 85 percent full. Stream flow returned to normal across the state. Still, increased groundwater use for fracking (particularly on the Ogallala Aquifer), agriculture, and a growing population kept groundwater levels in many areas below normal. Increased rain and snow in the last five years has mostly been the result of a strong El Niño weather pattern (a cyclical event in the Pacific Ocean that only occurs every two to seven years) along with numerous and severe tropical storms in the Gulf of Mexico. Texas cannot rely on increased precipitation from El Niño. Its weather is predicted to be hotter and drier in the coming years than it has been in a millennium, due primarily to global climate change. Thus, the state must continue to prepare for future droughts and water shortages.

✔ 1.5 Learning Check

1. True or False: If current trends persist, demand for water will rise by 10 percent by 2060, and the state's current dependable water supply will meet that projected demand.

2. True or False: Texas has the highest rate and largest number of uninsured people in the nation.

Answers at the end of this chapter.

⊠ Keeping Current

Civic Engagement on the Rise

For decades, observers have predicted that rapid population growth and demographic changes in Texas would result in major political change. Despite a long history of low voter turnout and Republican dominance in the state, recent years have seen a dramatic increase in citizen involvement and increasingly close competition between Republican and Democratic candidates. The 2018 midterm elections saw exceptional levels of political activity and electoral gains for the Texas Democratic Party. With polls showing close races, many observers predicted even higher turnout and more success for Democrats in 2020. While there were no major gains for Democrats, observers were correct about gains in citizen participation.

An increase in civic engagement and voter turnout in Texas was not guaranteed. For much of its history the state's traditionalistic/individualistic political subculture meant less citizen involvement than in states with a moralistic political subculture. Protests, marches, strikes and the like have long been significantly more common in states like California and New York than in Texas. Still, protests spread across Texas cities large and small, both in response to restrictions imposed by government due to the COVID-19 pandemic and to incidents of police violence including the murder of George Floyd.

Polls showing competitive races in Texas's 2020 elections also sparked a continuation of the state's trend toward greater citizen involvement in campaigns. Both major parties saw increases in campaign contributions, volunteerism, and voter registration. Still, an increase in actual voter turnout could not be taken for granted. *Election Law Journal* recently ranked Texas 50th among the states for ease of voting.[85] In addition, voters faced fear of COVID-19, confusion about voting processes, misinformation, and more. Despite the obstacles, 66 percent of registered voters in Texas cast ballots. This was the state's highest voter turnout since 1992 (when incumbent president George H. W. Bush and independent candidate Ross Perot—both Texans—battled Arkansas Governor Bill Clinton for the presidency). Thus, turnout for 2020 was almost 7 percentage points higher than the 2016 presidential election.

It remains to be seen whether the recent increase in civic engagement in Texas was an aberration or if it signals a long-term shift toward a more moralistic political subculture.

Conclusion

With changing demographic, economic, social, and environmental conditions in the Lone Star State, Texas policymakers face several challenges. Both demographic and geographic diversities present myriad opportunities and problems. Because of its business-friendly policies, Texas has been successful in attracting new industries. Nevertheless, even when the Lone Star State's economy flourishes, many Texans live in poverty, while the state struggles to sustainably manage its natural resources. COVID-19 weakened Texas's economy, including most of its major industries. Both ordinary citizens and public officials must realize that their ability to cope with public problems now and in the years ahead depends largely on how well homes and schools prepare young Texans to meet the crises and demands of an ever-changing state, nation, and world.

Chapter Summary

LO 1.1 Describe the relationship between the social history of Texas and the political characteristics of the state's diverse population. Texas has a population of over 29 million. More than 88 percent of all Texans live in urban and suburban Metropolitan Statistical Areas. Texas's past was riddled with intergroup conflict. Racial and ethnic tensions remain, but the state has moved toward integration and cooperation. The three largest groups today are Whites, Latinos (the fastest-growing group by number), and Blacks. Texas has a small but growing population of Asians and approximately 320,000 Native Americans.

LO 1.2 Analyze how political culture has shaped Texas's politics, government, and public policy. The political culture of Texas is dominated by individualistic and traditionalistic subcultures. Individualistic subculture is rooted in the search for individual opportunity by the state's early settlers and is reflected in its constitutionally weak government and low spending on public programs. Traditionalistic subculture grew out of the Old South, where policies were designed to preserve the social order of a landed aristocracy, and the poor and minorities were often not allowed to vote. With an increasingly diverse population, some areas in Texas may be shifting toward an increase in the moralistic subculture, which favors government intervention to improve society.

LO 1.3 Discuss the political implications of Texas's size in both geography and population, along with the geographic distribution of its residents. With more than 267,000 square miles of territory and over 29 million people, Texas ranks second in both size and population among the 50 states. Infrastructure is therefore a major government issue. Cost of political campaigns in such a geographically large state and necessary fundraising are major political issues. Rapid population growth presents a variety of opportunities and challenges for the political system. Each of the six major regions in Texas is different in its economic and political climate.

LO 1.4 Describe the industries that formed the historic basis for the Texas economy, the diversification of the modern Texas economy, and economic implications for Texas politics. The Texas economy historically relied on cattle, cotton, timber, oil, and gas. Although each is still important, the Texas economy is now very diverse and includes many businesses that operate in renewable energy sources, high technology, the service sector, a variety of forms of agriculture, and international trade. Diversification decreased the political dominance of the four historical industries and helped stabilize the Texas economy, but the coronavirus pandemic severely damaged most Texas industries.

LO 1.5 Identify four major policy challenges Texas faces in the 21st century. Challenges to which Texas must respond include poverty and social problems, developing more effective educational programs, embracing increasing diversity, and sustainably managing the state's natural resources. Addressing these issues will require collection and spending of taxpayer money. The future of Texas depends on Texans' abilities to resolve problems and capitalize on human resources.

Key Terms

biotechnology, p. 29
Black Lives Matter, p. 9
exclusionary zoning, p. 19
gentrification, p. 19
government, p. 3
hydraulic fracturing, p. 26
Jim Crow laws, p. 16
Latin America, p. 5

maquiladoras, p. 31
political culture, p. 14
politics, p. 4
progressive, p. 14
public policy, p. 3
racial covenants, p. 19
redlining, p. 18
right-to-work laws, p. 15

social construct, p. 4
systemic racism, p. 9
Tejano, p. 7
Texian, p. 7
undocumented immigrant, p. 34
United States–Mexico–Canada
    Agreement (USMCA), p. 22
urban renewal, p. 19

Learning Check Answers

✓ 1.1

1. The Latino/a population is the fastest growing in the state in terms of size. This has led to increasing political influence for Texas Latinos at the local, state, and national level.

2. Systemic racism refers not to individual acts of discrimination, but to disadvantages inherited by people of color because of explicitly racist cultures, systems, and institutions that shaped the society we live in today.

✓ 1.2

1. Texas has historically been dominated by the individualistic subculture and the traditionalistic subculture.

2. Urbanization, industrialization, education, communication, and population shifts are changing the traditional political culture of Texas.

✓ 1.3

1. Texas's large size makes infrastructure a major budget item for state government and increases the cost of running for many offices, making campaign fundraising very important.

2. False. Each region of Texas has a distinctive economic base, social system, and political subculture.

1. Cattle, cotton, timber, oil, and gas were most important to the Texas economy in the past.

2. False. Decreased demand for goods and services and disruptions in international trade decreased employment and income in nearly every Texas industry.

 1. False. Demand for water is expected to rise by 22 percent by 2060, and the state's current dependable water supply will meet only about 65 percent of that projected demand.

2. True. Texas has a greater percentage and larger number of citizens without health insurance than any other state.

Federalism and the Texas Constitution

2

Learning Objectives

2.1 Analyze federalism and the powers of the state in a constitutional context.

2.2 Explain the origins and development of the state constitution.

2.3 Analyze the amendment process, focusing on recent constitutional amendment elections as well as attempts to revise the Texas Constitution.

2.4 Identify and differentiate the basic sections of the Texas Constitution.

Image 2.1 Pro-Trump Activists and Masked Anti-Trump protesters at Pro-Trump Rally at the State Capitol.

Visions of America, LLC/Alamy Stock Photo

Competency Connection
⭐ PERSONAL RESPONSIBILITY ⭐

How important is it for you to be politically engaged and convey your political views?

The Texas Constitution, adopted in 1876, serves as the Lone Star State's fundamental law. This document outlines the structure of Texas's state government, authorizes the creation of counties and cities, and establishes basic rules for governing. It has been amended frequently over the course of more than 15 decades. Lawyers, newspaper editors, political scientists, government officials, and others who consult this state constitution tend to criticize it for being too long and for lacking organization. Yet despite criticism, Texans have expressed strong opposition to, or complete lack of interest in, proposals for wholesale constitutional revision.

The Texas Constitution is the primary source of the state government's policymaking power. The other major source of its power is membership in the federal Union. Sometimes, tensions between the federal government and Texas may erupt, as illustrated by the state's ongoing challenges to the passage and implementation of the Affordable Health Care Act during the Obama Administration. Within the federal system, state constitutions are subject to the U.S. Constitution.

◘ The American Federal Structure

LO 2.1 Analyze federalism and the powers of the state in a constitutional context.

Federalism can be defined as a structure of government characterized by the division of powers between a national government and associated regional governments. The heart of the American federal system lies in the relationship between the U.S. government (with Washington, D.C., as the national capital) and the governments of the 50 states. Since 1789, the U.S. Constitution has prescribed a federal system of government for the nation; and since 1846, the state of Texas has been a part of that system.

Political scientist David Walker emphasizes the important role that states play in federalism: "The states' strategically crucial role in the administration, financing, and planning of intergovernmental programs and regulations—both federal and their own—and their perennial key position in practically all areas of local governance have made them the pivotal middlemen in the realm of functional federalism."[1] At the same time, the distribution of governmental power between national and state governments remains a constant tension within federalism. In his book, *Fed Up!*, in a chapter titled "Why States Matter," Rick Perry (the longest-serving governor in Texas history) asserts: "the very essence of America stems from a limited, decentralized government."[2] Yet, federal laws and court decisions often grant substantial power to the national government. American federalism has survived more than two centuries of stresses and strains. Among the most serious threats were the Civil War from 1861 to 1865, which almost destroyed the Union, and economic crises, such as the Great Depression, which followed the stock market crash of 1929. More recently, American federalism was tested again during the COVID-19 pandemic in addressing public health and the economic impact in the country and among the states.

Distribution of Constitutional Powers

Division of powers and functions between the national government and the state governments was originally accomplished by listing the powers of the national government in the U.S. Constitution and by adding the **Tenth Amendment**. The latter asserts that "the powers not delegated to the United States by the Constitution, nor prohibited by it to the States, are reserved to the States, respectively, or to the People." Although the Tenth Amendment may seem to endow the states with powers comparable to those delegated to the national government, Article VI of the U.S. Constitution contains the following clarification: "This Constitution, and the laws of the United States which shall be made in pursuance thereof; and all treaties made, or which shall be made, under the authority of the United States, shall be the supreme law of the land; and the judges in every State shall be bound thereby, anything in the Constitution or laws of any State to the contrary notwithstanding." Referred to as the **national supremacy clause**, this article emphasizes that the U.S. Constitution and acts of Congress, as well as U.S. treaties, must prevail over state constitutions and laws enacted by state legislatures.

Powers of the National Government Article I, Section 8, of the U.S. Constitution lists powers that are specifically delegated to the national government. Included are powers to regulate interstate and foreign commerce, borrow and coin money, establish post offices and post roads, declare war, raise and support armies, provide and maintain a navy, levy and collect taxes, and establish uniform rules of naturalization. Added to these **delegated powers** is a clause that gives the national government the power "to make all laws which shall be necessary and proper for carrying into execution the foregoing powers, and all other powers vested by this Constitution in the government of the United States, or in any department or officer thereof." Since 1789, Congress and the federal courts have used the "necessary and proper" clause as a grant of **implied powers** to expand the national government's authority.[3] Another way in which the federal government has expanded its powers is through the commerce clause in Article I, Section 8, of the U.S. Constitution. For instance, the U.S. Supreme Court, in a case originating in Texas, gave significant leeway to Congress under the commerce clause to legislate in matters traditionally reserved for the states. In this case, the Court allowed Congress to set a minimum wage for employees of local governments.[4]

Follow *Practicing Texas Politics* on Twitter **@PracTexPol**

Tenth Amendment
The Tenth Amendment to the U.S. Constitution declares that "the powers not delegated by the Constitution, nor prohibited by it to the States, are reserved to the States, respectively, or to the people."

national supremacy clause
Article VI of the U.S. Constitution states, "This Constitution, and the laws of the United States which shall be made in pursuance thereof; and all treaties made, or which shall be made, under the authority of the United States, shall be the supreme law of the land."

delegated powers
Specific powers entrusted to the national government by Article I, Section 8 of the U.S. Constitution (for example, regulate interstate commerce, borrow money, and declare war).

implied powers
Powers inferred by the constitutional authority of the U.S. Congress "to make all laws which shall be necessary and proper for carrying into execution the foregoing [delegated] powers, and all other powers vested by this Constitution in the government of the United States, or in any department or officer thereof."

Guarantees to the States The U.S. Constitution provides all states with an imposing list of **constitutional guarantees**, which include the following:

- A state may be neither divided nor combined with another state without consent of the U.S. Congress and the state legislatures involved. (Texas, however, did retain power to divide itself into as many as five states under the terms of its annexation to the United States.)

- Each state is guaranteed a representative government with elected lawmakers, also known as a republican form of government.

- Each state is guaranteed two senators in the U.S. Senate and at least one member in the U.S. House of Representatives.

- All states participate in presidential elections through the electoral college. Each state has a number of electoral college votes equal to the total number of U.S. senators and U.S. representatives from that state. (As of the start of 2021, Texas holds 38 electoral college votes, and is expected to gain as many as three seats after reapportionment takes place.)

- All states participate equally in approving or rejecting proposed amendments to the U.S. Constitution. Approval requires ratification either by three-fourths of the state legislatures or by conventions called in three-fourths of the states (only the Twenty-First Amendment, which repealed Prohibition and the Eighteenth Amendment, was not ratified in this way).

- Each state is entitled to protection by the U.S. government against invasion and domestic violence, although Texas has its own Army National Guard, Air National Guard, and State Guard units. For more information on the state's military forces, see Chapter 9, "The Executive Branch."

- Texas is assured that trials by federal courts for crimes committed in Texas will be conducted in Texas.

Another constitutional guarantee provided to the states is the authority to propose constitutional amendments to the U.S. Constitution. Such action requires two-thirds of the state legislatures (34 states) to call a national constitutional convention. Specifically, state legislatures must submit an application to Congress to call for a national convention of the states. This procedure, which has never been used, received considerable attention in 2016 when Texas Governor Greg Abbott called on states to convene a constitutional convention to propose several amendments as a means to restore states' rights.[5] In May 2017, the Texas Legislature became the 11th state in the country to pass a resolution calling for a national convention. As of 2020, another four states had passed similar resolutions, totaling 15 states.

Limitations on the States As members of the federal Union, Texas and other states are constrained by limitations imposed by Article I, Section 10, of the U.S. Constitution. For example, they may not enter into treaties, alliances, or confederations or, without the consent of Congress, make compacts or agreements with other states or foreign governments. Furthermore, states are forbidden to levy import duties (taxes) on another state's products. From the outcome of the Civil War and the U.S. Supreme Court's landmark ruling in *Texas v. White*, 74 U.S. 700 (1869),

constitutional guarantees
Rights and protections assured under the U.S. Constitution. For example, among the guarantees to members of the Union include protection against invasion and domestic uprisings, territorial integrity, a republican form of government, and representation by two senators and at least one representative for each state.

Texans learned that states cannot secede from the Union. In the *White* case, the Court ruled that the national Constitution "looks to an indestructible union, composed of indestructible states." In subsequent cases, the U.S. Supreme Court further restricted state power. For instance, a state legislature cannot limit the number of terms for members of the state's congressional delegation. The U.S. Supreme Court held that term limits for members of Congress could be constitutionally imposed only if authorized by an amendment to the U.S. Constitution.[6]

Other provisions in the U.S. Constitution prohibit states from denying anyone the right to vote because of race, gender, failure to pay a poll tax (a tax paid for the privilege of voting), or age (if the person is 18 years of age or older). The Fourteenth Amendment forbids states from denying to any persons the equal protection of the laws. For example, in a 1950 Supreme Court case (prior to the Thelma White case highlighted in the "Students in Action" segment), segregation on the basis of race at the University of Texas Law School was held to be in violation of the Fourteenth Amendment's equal protection clause. Although the state had established "a separate but equal law school" for African Americans, the Court held that it was grossly unequal to the University of Texas Law School. Therefore, the equal protection clause required Heman Sweatt's (the plaintiff in the case) admission to the University of Texas. This ruling opened the door to other qualified African Americans' admission to the law school.[7]

The Fourteenth Amendment also provides that no state may deprive persons of life, liberty, or property without due process of law. These protections include those rights covered in the U.S. Constitution's Bill of Rights. This expansion to the states has occurred primarily through a series of cases heard by the U.S. Supreme Court. Using a principle known as incorporation, the U.S. Supreme Court through a series of cases has selectively applied portions of the Bill of Rights to the states by virtue of the Fourteenth Amendment's due process clause. In effect, states are obligated to provide most of the protections covered in the Bill of Rights. For example, state and local law enforcement officers are required to inform anyone taken into custody of his or her right to remain silent (Fifth Amendment's right against self-incrimination) and the right to an attorney (Sixth Amendment's right to assistance of counsel). To ensure these protections, Congress has enforcement powers under the Fourteenth Amendment.

📋 Students in Action

Thelma White Case Forced College Integration

"In his court order no. 1616 issued July 25, 1955, Judge Robert E. Thomason prohibited Texas Western College from denying Thelma White 'or any member of the class of persons she represents, the right or privilege of matriculating or registering … because of their race or color.'"

—Veronica Herrera and Alan A. Johnson

How It All Began

On March 30, 1955, Thelma White filed suit in a U.S. District Court challenging the denial of her admission to Texas Western College (TWC; now University of Texas at El Paso [UTEP]). When she applied to TWC, officials rejected her application because of her race. The college was forced to obey

(Continued)

the state's segregation law. Black students could attend only two public colleges in Texas: Prairie View A&M or Texas Southern University, both in the Houston area and a considerable distance from El Paso.

Winning Her Case

While waiting for her lawsuit to go to court, White enrolled at New Mexico A&M (later New Mexico State University), where she continued her education. Before the case went to judgment, the University of Texas System decided that TWC could admit black students. [U.S. District] Judge R. E. Thomason [for the Western District of Texas] ruled that the state laws requiring segregation violated the U.S. Constitution, that White must be admitted, and that the entire University of Texas System, along with all other public universities, must admit black students to their undergraduate programs. Before this case, law and medical schools, as well as several graduate programs, had been opened to blacks, but all undergraduate schools had remained closed.

Fighting for Educational Rights

White felt that she and other black students were being denied their educational rights. TWC admitted White and 12 other black students for the 1955 fall semester. White's victory opened the door for the students, although she remained at New Mexico A&M. The next year several more black students came to TWC.

Leaving a Legacy

White's legacy lives on at UTEP to this day. In her memory, UTEP founded the Thelma White Network for Community and Academic Development. The

The University of Texas at El Paso

Shown above are seven of the Negro Freshman students as they come out of freshman orientation September 9. They are, from left to right: William Milner, Marcellus Fulmore, John English, Mable Butler, Clarence Stevens, Margaret Jackson, and Sandra Campbell.

White's victory opened the door for African American students to attend what would ultimately become UT El Paso.

network's single purpose is to assist black students with social and academic development at UTEP. Today, African American students are enrolled in virtually every academic program at UTEP, a fact made possible by White and her pioneering efforts to change the educational system in El Paso.

Edited excerpt from Veronica Herrera and Alan A. Johnson, "Thelma White Case Forced College Integration," *Borderlands* 14 (Spring 1996); abridged and reprinted by permission of the authors (Note: The original text and terminology were retained.) *Borderlands* is a collection of student-written articles on the history and culture of the El Paso–Juárez–Las Cruces border region. It is published annually by El Paso Community College. The website for this publication is http://epcc.libguides.com/borderlands.

Competency Connection
◉ **SOCIAL RESPONSIBILITY** ◉

What are your initial impressions regarding the student who believed so strongly in equality for African Americans? How essential is the 14th Amendment in our U.S. Constitution to our values of equality? How strongly do you support these values, and to what extent would you be willing to take action like Thelma White in this story?

Interstate Relations and State Immunities

Two provisions of the U.S. Constitution specifically affect relations between the states and between citizens of one state and another state. These provisions are Article IV and the Eleventh Amendment. Article IV of the U.S. Constitution provides that "citizens of each state shall be entitled to all privileges and immunities of citizens in the several states." This means that citizens of Texas who visit another state are entitled to all the **privileges and immunities** of citizens of that state. It does not mean, however, that such visiting Texans are entitled to all the privileges and immunities to which they are entitled in their home state. More than 200 years ago, the U.S. Supreme Court broadly defined "privileges and immunities" as follows: protection by government, enjoyment of life and liberty, right to acquire and possess property, right to leave and enter any state, and right to the use of courts. For some advocates of gun rights, this clause should extend to the right to keep and bear arms.

Article IV also states that "full faith and credit shall be given in each State to the public acts, records, and judicial proceedings of every other State." The **full faith and credit clause** means that any legislative enactment, state constitution, deed, will, marriage, divorce, or civil court judgment of one state must be officially recognized and honored in every other state. This clause does not apply to criminal cases. For example, a person convicted in Texas for a crime committed in Texas is not punished in another state to which he or she has fled. Instead, such cases are handled through extradition, whereby the fugitive would be returned to the Lone Star State at the request of the governor of Texas. Furthermore, for some felonies, the U.S. Congress has made it a federal offense to flee from one state to another for the purpose of avoiding arrest.

A controversy regarding the full faith and credit clause revolved around whether states must recognize same-sex marriages. In 1996, during President Bill Clinton's administration, Congress passed the Defense of Marriage Act (DOMA), prohibiting the national government from recognizing same-sex marriages and allowing states or political subdivisions (such as cities) to deny any marriage between persons of the same sex recognized in another state. In 2003, the Texas legislature passed a law prohibiting the state or any agency or political subdivision (such as a county or city) from recognizing a same-sex marriage or civil union formed in Texas or elsewhere. Then, in November 2005, Texas joined 15 other states in adopting a state constitutional amendment that banned same-sex marriage and defined marriage as "only the union of one man and one woman."[8] According to the National Conference of State Legislatures, 33 states had similar bans, either in their constitutions or by statutory law by 2015.

Although several challenges to the constitutionality of these state laws were presented to the U.S. Supreme Court, the Court was reluctant to review any such cases until 2012. Then in the 2013 case, *United States v. Windsor*, the U.S. Supreme Court struck down a provision of the Defense of Marriage Act that denied more than 1,000 federal benefits for same-sex married couples. The Court concluded that this provision deprived same-sex couples of rights and responsibilities protected by the due process clause of the Fifth Amendment and treated them differently in violation of equal protection principles.[9] Although the

privileges and immunities
Article IV of the U.S. Constitution guarantees that "citizens of each state shall be entitled to the privileges and immunities of citizens of the several states." According to the U.S. Supreme Court, this provision means that citizens are guaranteed protection by government, enjoyment of life and liberty, the right to acquire and possess property, the right to leave and enter any state, and the right to use state courts.

full faith and credit clause
Most government actions of another state must be officially recognized by public officials in Texas.

decision applied to federal laws and directives affecting legally recognized same-sex marriages performed in 17 states at the time, it left unclear whether states, like Texas, had to recognize legally sanctioned same-sex marriages performed in other states. In exercising its state's rights, Texas chose to refuse national directives in this area of law. For instance, the Texas National Guard initially refused to provide federal spousal benefits for same-sex couples despite a mandate by the U.S. Department of Defense. At least three federal lawsuits were filed as challenges to Texas's ban on same-sex marriage, claiming that the law subjected gay couples to unequal treatment in violation of the due process and equal protection clauses of the Fourteenth Amendment of the U.S. Constitution. In February 2014, U.S. District Judge Orlando L. García of the Western District in San Antonio struck down the Texas ban, ruling it did not have a "legitimate government purpose." Then the U.S. Supreme Court agreed to hear a case which directly challenged the marriage restrictions in Kentucky, Michigan, Tennessee, and Ohio. Kentucky's law was similar to the Texas law in declaring marriage to involve "one man and one woman." The U.S. Supreme Court ultimately ruled in 2014 in a 5–4 decision that the Fourteenth Amendment guarantees all couples the right to marry, regardless of sexual orientation, and that states must recognize same-sex marriages performed in other states.[10] Same-sex marriage bans in Texas and 12 other states were effectively struck down. Thus, same-sex marriages are now legal in all 50 states. However, the Texas Supreme Court, in 2017, held in a separate case that, while the nation's highest court ruled in favor of same-sex marriages, it did not require that Texas municipalities extend spousal benefits, such as health insurance, to the spouses of municipal employees. For many advocates of same-sex marriages, this ruling opened the door to further challenges.

The Eleventh Amendment also affects relations between citizens of one state and the government of another state. It provides, in part, that "The Judicial power of the United States shall not be construed to extend to any suit in law or equity, commenced or prosecuted against one of the United States by citizens of another state." U.S. Supreme Court rulings have ensured that a state may not be sued by its own citizens, or those of another state, without the defendant state's consent, nor can state employees sue the state for violating federal law.[11] This law, otherwise known as sovereign immunity, gives a tremendous shield to state governments. Yet this power is not absolute. For example, in 1993, several families whose children were eligible for Medicaid sued the state of Texas for its failure to provide these programs. A federal district court ordered the state to correct this problem. A consent decree was issued (an agreement of both parties to avoid further litigation). When the District Court ordered enforcement of the decree, the state appealed to the Fifth Circuit Court of Appeals arguing that the decree had many more requirements than the Medicaid law. Plaintiffs appealed to the U.S. Supreme Court, which held that the decree should be enforced even if it went beyond federal law. The Supreme Court ultimately held that this was not a sovereign immunity case, because the suit was not against the state but against state officials who had acted in violation of federal law. The Eleventh Amendment does not prohibit enforcement of a consent decree; enforcement by the federal courts is permitted to ensure observance of federal law.[12]

State Powers

Nowhere in the U.S. Constitution is there a list of state powers. As mentioned, the Tenth Amendment simply states that all powers not specifically delegated to the national government, nor prohibited to the states, are reserved to the states or to the people. **Reserved powers** of the states are, therefore, undefined and often very difficult to specify, especially when the powers are concurrent with those of the national government, such as the taxing power. Political scientists, however, view reserved powers in several broad categories:

- Police power: protection of the health, morals, safety, and convenience of citizens, and provision for the general welfare
- Taxing power: raising revenue to pay salaries of state employees, meet other costs of government, and repay borrowed money
- Proprietary power: public ownership of property, such as airports, energy-producing utilities, and parks
- Power of eminent domain: taking private property at a fair price for various kinds of public projects, such as highway construction

Needless to say, states today have broad powers, responsibilities, and duties. They are, for example, responsible for the nation's public elections—national, state, and local—because there are no nationally operated election facilities. State courts conduct most trials (both criminal and civil). States operate public schools (elementary and secondary) and public institutions of higher education (colleges and universities), and they maintain most of the country's prisons. Without a federal response under the Trump Administration, states also assumed more responsibility for protecting the public health of their residents during the COVID-19 pandemic.

One broad state power that has raised controversy is the power of eminent domain. Customarily, government entities have used the power of eminent domain to appropriate private property for public projects, such as highways, parks, and schools, as long as the property owners are paid a just compensation. In 2005, the U.S. Supreme Court expanded this power under the Fifth Amendment, allowing local governments to seize private property for private development. The Court, however, left the door open for states to set their own rules.[13] Then-Governor Rick Perry responded by calling a special legislative session in the summer of that year. As a result, statutory limits were imposed on government entities condemning private property where the primary purpose is for economic development. Exceptions were made, however, for public projects and to protect the city of Arlington's plan to build the Cowboys Stadium (now known as the AT&T Stadium), home of the Dallas Cowboys (a National Football League team).

To ensure constitutional protection of private property rights against abuses by governments, an amendment to the Texas Constitution was proposed and adopted in 2009. This amendment, however, does not bar energy companies from condemning private property for the construction of oil and gas pipelines. The pipeline owner must assure the Texas Railroad Commission that other companies will be able to use the pipeline. In doing so, the pipeline becomes a

reserved powers
Reserved powers are derived from the Tenth Amendment of the U.S. Constitution. Although not spelled out in the U.S. Constitution, these reserved powers to the states include police power, taxing power, proprietary power, and power of eminent domain.

"common carrier" that benefits the general public and not private individuals or companies. Controversy in East Texas surrounded the construction of the Keystone Pipeline, owned by TransCanada, a Canadian company. The northern portion of the pipeline was approved by President Trump after he took office in 2016 despite environmental concerns. In 2020, a federal judge from Montana revoked a permit to extend pipelines over bodies of water because of risks to endangered species and habitat, delaying the project. The southern portion from Cushing, Oklahoma, to Houston has been in operation since 2014. The Trans-Pecos pipeline, an intrastate pipeline intended to transport natural gas from the Ft. Stockton area in West Texas to Mexico, is even more controversial. The gas pipeline encountered growing resistance from landowners and conservationists for the potential damage to ranching, public safety, and Big Bend National Park. Nonetheless, in May 2016, the Federal Energy Regulatory Commission approved construction and the pipeline has been in operation (albeit slow in production) since 2017.[14] Other pipeline projects that could potentially impact other parts of Texas, especially the Hill Country in central Texas, pose new challenges to communities that rely on underground aquifers for their main water supply. Although most state powers are recognizable, identifying a clear boundary line between state and national powers often remains complicated. Once again, the U.S. Supreme Court has played a critical role in defining this balance of power. Take, for example, the constitutional provision of interstate commerce in the U.S. Constitution. Not until *United States v. Lopez* (1995), a case that originated in Texas, did the U.S. Supreme Court indicate that the U.S. Congress had exceeded its powers to regulate interstate commerce when it attempted to ban guns in public schools to address the increasing violence on school grounds. Operation of public schools has traditionally been considered a power of state and local governments, and the Supreme Court has used the *Lopez* case in later cases to rein in the federal government's power.[15] States have also become more willing to make claims of state sovereignty over federal authority in these cases.

The Supreme Court has limited state sovereignty with regard to the use of a certain type of products—specifically, marijuana for medical treatment of termi-nally ill patients. In *Gonzales v. Raich* (2005), the Court struck down a California initiative that made an exception to the illegalization of marijuana. It ruled that Congress has the sole power to regulate local and state activities that substantially affect interstate commerce.[16] Although the California measure would have pro-tected noncommercial cultivation and use of marijuana that did not cross state lines, the federal government contended that it would handicap enforcement of federal drug laws. In this regard, the Court ruled that the federal government is primarily responsible for regulating narcotics and other controlled substances. While the official position of the White House during the Obama administration was that it "steadfastly oppose[d] legalization of marijuana," the federal govern-ment did not fully enforce the U.S. restriction on marijuana in states that had decriminalized marijuana for either medicinal or recreational use. As of 2021, more than 36 states, plus Washington, D.C., have legalized the medical use of mar-ijuana and cannabis. As many as 15 states, such as Colorado, Washington, Oregon, and Illinois, including the District of Columbia, have legalized small amounts of marijuana and cannabis for recreational use. In effect, these states have ignored a limited area of federal law.[17] In 2015, Texas joined 15 states (at the time) that allowed limited use of cannabis oil to treat certain illnesses, such as epilepsy. Then, in 2019, the Texas legislature (in line with a 2018 federal law) legalized hemp, the plant from which cannabidiol (CBD) is derived. CBD contains only traces of the psychoactive compounds found in marijuana. This led to a booming industry of stores and dispensaries selling the product for a wide range of health issues.

Lawsuits against the federal government are another manifestation in the continuing fight for states' rights and a broad interpretation of state power under the Tenth Amendment. Under the Obama Administration, for instance, Texas led (or was part of) close to 50 lawsuits against the federal government. Many of these suits were led by Governor Greg Abbott, when he served as the state's Attorney General (2003–2015). Some of the legal challenges were filed under Abbott's successor, Attorney General Ken Paxton. The suits covered a variety of issues, including several challenges dealing with environmental standards and climate change, as well as funding for women's health programs and healthcare reform. Among these cases (which have been largely funded by taxpayer money), Texas had lost 12 cases and won seven (mainly around environmental regulations).[18] During the Trump Administration, Attorney General Paxton continued to file lawsuits, but many were either won or dropped because of President Trump's willingness to roll back several policies and regulations instituted under the Obama Administration, especially with regard to the environment.[19]

One area of law where Texas has both won and lost involves the Patient Protection and Affordable Care Act of 2010 (also known as Obamacare). Texas was one of 26 states led by Republican attorneys general and governors to challenge the constitutionality of this federal law. Contested provisions included congressional mandates requiring states to expand coverage and eligibility for Medicaid programs, as well as requirements that individuals purchase health insurance or face a penalty.

The U.S. Supreme Court ultimately heard *National Federation of Independent Business v. Sebelius*, concluding that it was within the Congress's taxing power to impose a penalty on individuals who failed to obtain health insurance. Nevertheless, the Court ruled that Congress could not withdraw existing Medicaid funding from states that failed to comply with the expanded coverage requirements for adults.[20] In response, Texas remained one of several states that did not expand Medicaid coverage. In a subsequent challenge to the Affordable Care Act, originating in the state of Virginia, the Supreme Court in 2015 refused to limit federal subsidies (in the form of tax credits) for eligible low-income individuals who obtained insurance through a federally administered healthcare exchange. Healthcare exchanges are online portals where insurance companies offer different health insurance plans to consumers. By forcing competition between the companies, federal government officials hoped insurers would lower healthcare premiums. The condition for federal subsidies was initially created as an incentive to encourage states to operate healthcare exchanges specifically designed for their residents. Texas and 35 other states chose not to establish state-run exchanges. The Court ultimately concluded that eligible residents of these states would also receive federal subsidies even though they purchased insurance through the federal exchange.[21] At the time, observers speculated that nearly one million Texans stood to lose these subsidies if the Supreme Court had decided differently. Litigation challenging the federal law continues. In December 2018, for instance, a federal district judge in Texas struck it down as being unconstitutional because Congress had repealed the individual mandate requirement, which imposed a tax penalty on consumers without coverage, making the entire federal law obsolete. In response, a coalition of Democratic Attorneys General, led by California, and the House of Representatives unsuccessfully appealed the case to the Fifth Circuit Court. In March 2020, the U.S. Supreme Court agreed to hear the case to determine if certain provisions of the federal law could essentially be "severed," yet retain the law as a whole. At the same time, the Supreme Court agreed to hear an appeal from Texas and other states that want the entire federal law to be invalidated. In November, the Supreme Court heard oral arguments in the case, *California v. Texas*, and was expected to decide the case in the summer of 2021, with the addition of a newly confirmed Supreme Court justice, Amy Coney Barrett.[22]

In another contentious area of law, immigration, Texas and 24 other states sued the federal government in 2014 granting temporary relief from deportation for more than four million undocumented immigrant parents of children who were U.S. citizens (known as DAPA). A federal district court said that the Department of Homeland Security under the Obama Administration had exceeded its administrative authority. A panel of three appellate justices on the U.S. Fifth Circuit Court of Appeals affirmed the lower court's decision, striking down Obama's immigration plan in November 2015. Under pressure from the White House, the U.S. Supreme Court agreed to hear the case. In June of 2016, the U.S. Supreme Court was evenly divided on the immigration program. Without a majority opinion to overturn the lower court's decision, the immigration plan was blocked from going into effect.[23] In May 2018, Attorney General Paxton led a coalition of 10 states to end the immigration program, DACA (Deferred Action for Childhood Arrivals) that grants lawful presence and work permits to roughly 700,000 (known as Dreamers) if they were under 17 when they arrived and if they arrived by 2007. The lawsuit, supported by President Trump, was ultimately reviewed by the U.S. Supreme Court during the 2019–2020 term. Although the Court did not address the constitutionality of the immigration program, the 5–4 decision by the Court concluded that the administration did not have the constitutional executive power to abruptly dismantle the program without the procedural requirement that requires "a reasoned explanation for its action."[24] In his first day as President, newly elected President Joe Biden declared in a memorandum that DACA would be "preserved and fortified."

Federal–State Relations: An Evolving Process

Since the establishment of the American federal system, states have operated within a constitutional context modified to meet changing conditions. At the same time, the framers of the U.S. Constitution sought to provide a workable balance of power between national and state governments that would sustain the nation indefinitely. This balance of power between federal and state governments has evolved over the years, with certain periods reflecting an expansion or decline of the involvement of the federal government, while also affecting Texas's resistance to increasing national control over traditional areas of state power. In certain areas of policy, such as regulating the legalized use of medicinal and recreational marijuana, as mentioned earlier, the federal government under the Obama administration left enforcement to state and local authorities. In 2020, President Trump appeared to shift gears during his presidential campaign, allowing federal funds to be used to prosecute persons for possession of marijuana legally prescribed for medical purposes under state law.

From 1865 until about 1930, Congress exercised power to regulate railroads and interstate commerce within and among states. In addition, with the onset of the Great Depression of the 1930s, the federal government extended its jurisdiction to areas traditionally within the realm of state and local governments, such as regulating the workplace. For example, expansion of federal law extended to worker safety, minimum wages, and maximum hours. This expansion occurred principally through broad interpretation of the interstate commerce clause by the U.S. Supreme Court, which, in a series of cases, expanded the national government's power to include these matters. Grants of money to the states from the federal government have also been used to influence state policymaking. The number and size of **federal grants-in-aid** grew while Congress gave states more financial assistance. As federally initiated programs multiplied, the national government's influence on state policymaking widened, and the states' control lessened in many areas. However, beginning in the 1980s and continuing through the presidential administration of George W. Bush (2001–2009), and during the Trump Administration, state and local governments gained more freedom to spend federal funds as they chose. In some areas, however, such as public assistance programs, they were granted less money to spend.

Decline in national control over state governments has often been identified as another development in federal–state relations called devolution. The underlying concept of devolution is to bring about a reduction in the size and influence of the national government by reducing federal taxes and expenditures and by shifting many federal responsibilities to the states. Because one feature of devolution involves sharp reductions in federal aid, states are compelled to assume important new responsibilities with substantially less revenue to finance them. Texas and other states have been forced to assume more responsibility for formulating and funding their own programs in education, highways, mental health, public assistance (welfare), and other areas. In some cases, federal programs are shared. States must match federal monies to benefit from a program, such as the Children's Health Insurance Program (CHIP), or risk losing the funds. (See Chapter 11, "Finance and Fiscal Policy," for a discussion of CHIP funding.)

An important feature of devolution is Congress's use of **block grants** to distribute money to state and local governments. Block grants are fixed sums of money awarded according to an automatic formula determined by Congress. Thus, states that receive block grants have greater flexibility in spending. Welfare policy is an excellent case. The country's welfare programs became primarily a federal responsibility during the Great Depression and the administration of

federal grants-in-aid
Money appropriated by the U.S. Congress to help states and local governments provide needed facilities and services.

block grant
Congressional grant of money that allows the state considerable flexibility in spending for a program, such as providing welfare services.

Franklin D. Roosevelt (1933–1945). Other federal responses to unemployment and poverty included such programs as food stamps and medical assistance for the poor as part of President Lyndon B. Johnson's Great Society. The Clinton administration (1993–2001) and a Republican-controlled Congress, however, eventually forced states to assume more responsibility for welfare programs and supplied federal funding in the form of block grants.[25] President George W. Bush continued these trends and added a new twist to devolution by giving federal financial assistance to faith-based organizations that provide social services to the poor. Devolution took on new meaning during the coronavirus pandemic under the Trump Administration, where states and municipalities were essentially left to determine testing and public health measures, such as mask-wearing requirements. However, Congress did provide economic relief funds. In the first round of relief funds, Congress passed in March of 2020 with bipartisan support and signed by President Trump, the CARES Act (Coronavirus Aid, Relief and

▣ Point/Counterpoint

Should Texas Support the Affordable Care Act?

The Issue In 2010, under the Obama administration, Congress passed the Patient Protection and Affordable Care Act, providing increased access to healthcare coverage for more people. Opponents and proponents of the law continued to debate the merits of the newly enacted law even after the U.S. Supreme Court upheld it twice. Opponents, such as former Governor Rick Perry and Governor Greg Abbott, argue that this law represents an overstepping of federal authority; whereas proponents argue that health care is an absolute necessity for all Texans. Whether to expand Medicaid in Texas has been contentious, especially with the rise of the coronavirus pandemic and healthcare access.

For	AGAINST
1. Expanding Medicaid would provide necessary health care for the state's low-income adults. This expansion is cost-effective for Texas because the federal government will cover 100 percent in the first few years and 90 percent thereafter.	1. The act is an intrusion on state sovereignty in an area of policy that has traditionally been a state power.
2. Texas will lose billions of dollars in federal funding if it opts out of the Medicaid expansion.	2. Even though the federal government will provide almost all of the funding for expanding Medicaid in the first few years, no guarantee exists that this level of funding will continue. If federal spending is reduced, the burden would shift to the states.
3. When fewer people are covered under health insurance, state and local governments will spend more on uncompensated medical care.	3. The law increases taxes and imposes a burden on the Texas economy.

— Competency Connection —
💬 COMMUNICATION SKILLS 💬

Should the federal government have the authority to require states to expand Medicaid coverage? Why or why not? How does this issue impact federal–state relations? How would you convey your views?

Economic Security Act) provided $150 billion, plus $272 billion of targeted funds, among the $2 trillion package, to state and local governments to address public health and the economic impact. In Texas, for instance, the CARES Act also provided a temporary $600 weekly benefit for Texas workers who filed for unemployment with the Texas Workforce Commission.[26] (See Chapter 11, "Finance and Fiscal Policy," for a discussion of funding to the states.)

As mentioned, Texas has challenged federal authority primarily through lawsuits. Less frequently, Texas has also refused some federal funds. Typically, more than one-third of the Lone Star State's biennial budget is funded by the federal government. Yet state officials have at times refused funding for Medicaid expansion, for instance, arguing that these funds required the adoption of national standards for state-run programs. State legislative actions or bills proposed in previous legislative sessions are part of the State Sovereignty Movement. This movement, which began gaining momentum in 2009, claims sovereignty under the Tenth Amendment against all powers not otherwise enumerated or granted to the federal government in the U.S. Constitution. Similar unsuccessful bills and resolutions were proposed in the Texas House in recent legislative sessions. For some observers, these actions continue to symbolize the polarization of national–state politics.

Governors, as the state's highest leaders, are also positioned to champion state's rights. During his 2012 and 2016 unsuccessful presidential bids, former Governor Perry advocated for state sovereignty and described the fight to defend the Tenth Amendment as the "battle for the soul of America." In *Fed Up! Our Fight to Save America from Washington*, Perry states that "the spirit and intent of the Tenth Amendment … is under assault and has been for some time. The result is that today we face unprecedented federal intrusion into numerous facets of our lives."[27] Talk of secession was even more pertinent in 2011 during the 150th anniversary of Texas's attempted secession from the Union at the onset of the Civil War. In a similar vein, Governor Greg Abbott, as mentioned earlier, called for a national constitutional convention to revisit state's rights. Among Abbott's nine recommendations are a constitutional amendment prohibiting "Congress from regulating activity that occurs wholly within one state" and allowing "a two-thirds majority of the states to override a federal law or regulation."[28] Governor Abbot outlined his proposal in his book, *Broken Not Unbowed: The Fight to Fix a Broken America*. As mentioned earlier, his call for a national convention gained some momentum.

> **✓ 2.1 Learning Check**
>
> 1. True or False: The Tenth Amendment specifically identifies states' powers.
> 2. Does devolution give states more or less freedom to make decisions?
>
> *Answers at the end of this chapter.*

⬢ The Texas Constitution: Politics of Policymaking

LO 2.2 Explain the origins and development of the state constitution.

As already mentioned, the current Texas Constitution is the main source of power for the Texas state government. Surviving for more than 140 years, this constitution establishes the state's government, defines governing powers, imposes limitations, and identifies Texans' civil liberties and civil rights. Political scientists and legal scholars generally believe that a constitution should indicate the process by which problems will be solved, both in the present and in the future, and should not attempt to solve specific problems. Presumably, if this principle is followed, later generations will not need to adopt numerous amendments. In many areas, however, the Texas Constitution mandates specific policies in great detail, which has required frequent amendments.

The preamble to the Texas Constitution states, "Humbly invoking the blessings of Almighty God, the people of the state of Texas do ordain and establish this Constitution." These words begin the 28,600-word document that became Texas's seventh constitution in 1876. By the start of 2021, that same document had been changed by no fewer than 507 amendments and contained about 92,000 words.

Framers of the Constitution spelled out policymaking powers and limitations in minute detail. This specificity, in turn, made frequent amendments inevitable as constitutional provisions were altered to fit changing times and conditions. For more than a century, the length of the Texas Constitution has increased through an accumulation of amendments, most of which are essentially statutory (resembling laws made by the legislature). The resulting document more closely resembles a code of laws than a fundamental instrument of government. To fully understand the present-day Texas Constitution, we will examine the historical factors surrounding its adoption, as well as previous historical periods and constitutions.

Historical Developments

The Texas Constitution provides the legal basis on which the state functions as an integral part of the federal Union. In addition, the document is a product of history and an expression of the dominant political philosophy of Texans living at the time of its adoption.

In general, constitution drafters have been pragmatic people performing an important task. Despite the idealistic sentiment commonly attached to constitutions in the United States, the art of drafting and amending them is essentially political in nature. In other words, these documents reflect the drafters' views and political interests, as well as the political environment of their time. With the passing of years, the Texas Constitution reflects the political ideas of new generations of people who amend or change it.

The constitutional history of Texas began with promulgation of the Constitution of Coahuila y Tejas within the Mexican federal system in 1827 and the Constitution of the Texas Republic in 1836. Texas has since been governed under its state constitutions of 1845, 1861, 1866, 1869, and 1876. Each of these seven constitutions has reflected the political situation that existed when the specific document was drafted.[29] In this section, we will see the political process at work as we examine the origins of these constitutions and note the efforts to revise and amend the current Texas Constitution.

The First Six Texas Constitutions In 1824, three years after Mexico gained independence from Spain, Mexican liberals established a republic with a federal constitution. Within that federal system, the former Spanish provinces of Coahuila and Tejas became a single Mexican state that adopted its own constitution. Thus, the Constitution of Coahuila y Tejas, promulgated in 1827, marked Texas's first experience with a state constitution.

Political unrest among Anglo Texans, who had settled in Mexico's northeastern area, arose almost immediately. Factors that led Texians (as Anglo Texans called themselves at the time) to declare independence from Mexico included, among others, their desire for unrestricted trade with the United States, Anglo attitudes of racial superiority, anger over Mexico's abolition of slavery, increasing numbers of immigrant settlers, insufficient Anglo representation in the 12-member Coahuila y Tejas legislature, and Mexico's failure to provide greater access to government in the English language.[30]

On March 2, 1836, at Washington-on-the-Brazos (between present-day Brenham and Navasota), a delegate convention of 59 Texians and Tejanos issued a declaration of independence from Mexico. Mexicans in Texas who also wanted independence and who fought for a free Texas state referred to themselves as Tejanos. Three Tejanos in particular served as delegates at the convention: Lorenzo de Zavala (representing Harrisburg [now a part of Houston]), Francisco Ruiz, and José Antonio Navarro (both representing Béxar). The delegates drafted the Constitution of the Republic of Texas, modeled largely after the U.S. Constitution.

During this same period, in an effort to retain Mexican sovereignty, General Antonio López de Santa Anna defeated the Texians (many of whom were not even from Texas) and some Tejanos in San Antonio in the siege of the Alamo, which ended on March 6, 1836. Shortly afterward, Sam Houston's troops, including a company of Tejanos who were recruited by Captain Juan N. Seguín, crushed the Mexican forces in the Battle of San Jacinto on April 21, 1836. Part of Texas's unique history in the United States is its existence as an independent nation for close to 10 years.

After Houston's victory over Santa Anna, Texas voters elected Houston as president of their new republic; they also voted to seek admission to the Union. Not until 1845, however, was annexation authorized by a joint resolution of the U.S. Congress. Earlier attempts to become part of the United States by treaty had failed. Texas's status as a slave state, as well as concerns that annexation would lead to war with Mexico, stalled the earlier efforts. Texas president Anson Jones ultimately called a constitutional convention. Its delegates drew up a new state constitution and agreed to accept the invitation to join the Union. In October 1845, after Texas voters ratified both actions of the constitutional convention, Texas obtained its third constitution. Then on December 29, it became the 28th member of the United States.

These events, however, set the stage for war between Mexico and the United States (1846–1848), especially with regard to where the boundary lines between the two countries would be drawn. Some historians suggest that U.S. expansionist politicians and business interests actively sought this war. When the Treaty of Guadalupe Hidalgo between Mexico and the United States was signed in 1848, Mexico lost more than half its territory and recognized the Rio Grande as Texas's southern boundary. Negotiations also addressed the rights of Mexicans left behind in Texas, many of whom owned land in the region. Under the treaty,

📊 How Do We Compare...

In State Constitutions?

Year of Adoption, Length of State Constitutions, and Number of Amendments (2019)

Most Populous U.S. States	Year of Adoption	Approximate No. of Words and Number of Amendments	U.S. States Bordering Texas	Year of Adoption	Approximate No. of Words and Number of Amendments
California	1879	77,000 (535)	Arkansas	1874	59,000 (108)
Florida	1968	49,000 (137)	Louisiana	1974	77,000 (196)
New York	1894	49,000 (229)	New Mexico	1911	33,000 (17)
Texas	1876	92,000 (507)*	Oklahoma	1907	85,000 (199)

Source: The Book of States, 2019, http://knowledgecenter.csg.org/kc/content/book-states-2019-chapter-1-state-constitutions.

*Includes results of November 2019 election.

Competency Connection
❖ CRITICAL THINKING ❖

Analyze this chart. What are your initial impressions regarding the number of words and number of amendments in the Texas Constitution in comparison to other state constitutions? In what way has adding amendments influenced the development of the Texas Constitution?

Mexicans had one year to choose to return to Mexico or to remain in the newly annexed part of the United States. It also guaranteed Mexicans all the rights of citizenship. For all intents and purposes, these residents became the first Mexican Americans of Texas and the United States. Many Mexican Americans, however, were soon deprived of most of their rights, especially their property rights.

The Texas Constitution of 1845 lasted until the Civil War began in 1861. When Texas voted to secede from the Union in that year, it joined with other southern states to form the Confederate States of America. At the time, secessionists argued that the U.S. Constitution created a compact (or agreement) among the states, and that each state had a right to secede. During this period, Texas adopted its Constitution of 1861, with the aim of making as few changes as possible in government structure and powers. The new constitution included changes necessary to equip the government for separation from the United States, as well as the maintenance of slavery.

After the Confederacy's defeat, however, the Constitution of 1866 was drafted amid a different set of conditions during Reconstruction. For this constitution, the framers sought to restore Texas to the Union with minimal changes in existing social, economic, and political institutions. Although the Constitution of

Image 2.2 The Tejano Monument on the Texas Capitol grounds, erected in 2012, symbolizes official recognition by the state of contributions by Tejanos in the state's development.

The Lyda Hill Texas Collection of Photographs in Carol M. Highsmith's America Project, Library of Congress, Prints and Photographs Division

Competency Connection
☼ **CRITICAL THINKING** ☼

Reflect on this photo. What are your impressions of the Tejano Monument and the images it represents especially in the development of our state's history?

1866 was based on the Constitution of 1845, as a necessary condition to rejoin the Union, it abolished slavery and recognized the rights of former slaves to sue in the state's courts, to enter into contracts, to obtain and transfer property, and to testify in court actions involving black citizens (but not in court actions involving white citizens). Although the Constitution of 1866 protected the personal property of African American Texans, it did not permit them to vote, hold public office, or serve as jurors.

The relatively uncomplicated reinstatement of Texas into the Union ended abruptly when the Radical Republicans gained control of the U.S. Congress after the election of November 1866. Refusing to seat Texas's two senators and three representatives, Congress set aside the state's reconstructed government, enfranchised (granted voting rights to) former slaves, disenfranchised anyone who had participated in or supported the Confederacy, and imposed military rule across the state. U.S. Army officers replaced civil authorities. As in other southern states, Texas functioned under a military government.

Under these conditions, delegates to a constitutional convention met in intermittent sessions from June 1868 to February 1869 and drafted yet another state constitution. Among other provisions, the new constitution centralized more power in state government, provided for compulsory school attendance, and guaranteed a full range of rights for former slaves. This document was ratified in 1869. The Fifteenth Amendment of the U.S. Constitution, granting voting rights to African American men, was also ratified in 1869.

Then, with elections supervised by federal soldiers, Radical Republicans gained control of the Texas legislature. At the same time, Edmund Jackson Davis (commonly identified as E. J. Davis), a former Union army general, was elected as the first Republican governor of Texas. Some historians (such as Charles William Ramsdell and T. R. Fehrenbach) described the Davis administration (January 1870–January 1874) as one of the most corrupt in Texas's history.[31] In recent years, however, revisionist historians (such as Patrick G. Williams, Carl H. Moneyhon, and Barry A. Crouch) have made more positive assessments of Davis and his administration.[32]

White Texans during the Davis administration tended to react negatively and with hostility to the freedom of former black slaves and to the political influence, albeit quite limited, that these freedmen exercised when they became voters. Violence and lawlessness were serious problems at the time; thus, Governor Davis imposed martial law in some places and used police methods to enforce his decrees. Opponents of the Davis administration claimed that it was characterized by extravagant public spending, property tax increases to the point of confiscation, gifts of public funds to private interests, intimidation of newspaper editors, and control of voter registration by the military. In addition, hundreds of appointments to various state and local offices were filled with Davis's supporters.

Although the Constitution of 1869 is associated with the Reconstruction era and the unpopular (with most whites) administration of Governor Davis, the machinery of government created by this document was quite modern. The new fundamental law called for annual sessions of the legislature, a four-year term for the governor and other executive officers, and gubernatorial appointment (rather than popular election) of judges. It abolished county courts and raised the salaries of government officials. These changes centralized more governmental power in Austin and weakened local government.

During the Davis administration, Democrats gained control of the legislature in 1872. In December 1873, Governor Davis (with 42,633 votes) was badly defeated by Democrat Richard Coke from Waco (with 85,549 votes). When Davis refused to leave his office on the ground floor of the Capitol, Democratic lawmakers and Governor-elect Coke are reported to have climbed ladders to the Capitol's second story where the legislature convened. When President Ulysses S. Grant refused to send troops to protect him, Davis left the Capitol under protest in January 1874. In that same year, Democrats wrested control of the state courts from Republicans. The next step was to rewrite the Texas Constitution.

Texas Grange
A farmers' organization, also known as the Patrons of Husbandry, committed to low levels of government spending and limited governmental powers; a major influence on the Constitution of 1876.

Drafting the Constitution of 1876 In the summer of 1875, Texans elected 75 Democrats and 15 Republicans (six of whom were African Americans) as delegates to a constitutional convention; however, only 83 attended the gathering in Austin. The majority of the delegates were not native Texans. More than 40 percent of the delegates were members of the **Texas Grange** (the Patrons of Husbandry), a farmers' organization committed to strict economy in government

Image 2.3 Some of the Constitutional Convention delegates of 1875.

Texas State Library and Archives Commission

Competency Connection
✿ **CRITICAL THINKING** ✿

How does Texas's constitutional history during the 1875 Constitutional Convention continue to influence the state's present-day constitution and government?

(reduced spending) and limited governmental powers. Its slogan of "retrenchment and reform" became a major goal of the convention.[33] So strong was the spirit of strict economy among delegates that they refused to hire a stenographer or to allow publication of the convention proceedings. As a result, no official record was ever made of the convention that gave Texas its most enduring constitution.

In their zeal to undo policies of the Davis administration, delegates on occasion overreacted. Striking at Reconstruction measures that had given Governor Davis control over voter registration, the overwrought delegates inserted a statement providing that "no law shall ever be enacted requiring a registration of voters of this state." Within two decades, however, the statement had been amended to permit voter registration laws.

As they continued to dismantle the machinery of the Davis administration, delegates restricted powers of the three branches of state government. They reduced the governor's salary, powers, and term (from four years to two); made all executive offices (except that of secretary of state) elective for two-year terms; and tied the hands of legislators with biennial (once every two years) sessions, low salaries, and limited legislative powers. All judgeships became popularly elected for relatively short terms of office. Justice of the peace courts, county courts, and district courts—all with popularly elected judges—were established. In addition, public services were trimmed to the bone. Framers of the new constitution limited the public debt and severely curbed the legislature's taxing and spending powers. They also inserted specific policy provisions. For example, they reinstated racially segregated public education and repealed the compulsory school attendance law, restored precinct elections, and allowed only taxpayers to vote on local bond issues. Texas's proposed constitution was put to a popular vote in 1876 and was approved by a more than two-to-one majority. Although Texans in the state's largest cities—Houston, Dallas, San Antonio, and Galveston—voted against it, the much larger rural population voted for approval. By the 1880s, the constitutional rights guaranteed to African Americans under the U.S. Constitution had begun to be curtailed, and by the 1890s, Jim Crow laws, which fostered segregation, also contributed to the limitation of their rights.

Distrust of Government and Its Legacy Sharing in the prevailing popular distrust of, and hostility toward, government, framers of the Texas Constitution of 1876 sought with a vengeance to limit, and thus control, policymaking by placing many restrictions in the state's fundamental law. The general consensus of the time held that a state government could exercise only those powers listed in the state constitution. Therefore, instead of being permitted to exercise powers not denied by the U.S. Constitution, Texas lawmakers are limited to powers spelled out in the state's constitution. In addition, the 19th-century Texas Constitution (even with amendments) provides only limited powers for the governor's office in the 21st century. As established by the Texas Constitution, it is still considered one of the weakest gubernatorial offices in the nation. (See Chapter 9, "The Executive Branch," for a discussion of the governor's office.)

Today: After More Than a Century of Usage

The structural disarray and confusion of the Constitution of 1876 compound the disadvantages of its excessive length and detail. Unlike the Texas Constitution, the U.S. Constitution has only 4,400 words and merely 27 constitutional amendments. With all its shortcomings, the **Texas Constitution of 1876** has lasted for more than 140 years. In actuality, it is quite common that state constitutions are lengthy documents, given the nature of state and local responsibilities. For one observer, the virtues of the Texas constitution are "its democratic impulses of restraining power and empowering voters." It is a "document of history as much as it is a charter of governance."[34]

Texas Constitution of 1876
The lengthy, much-amended state constitution, a product of the post-Reconstruction era that remains in effect today.

Filling the Texas Constitution with many details and creating a state government with restricted powers would inevitably lead to constitutional amendments and frequent alterations. In fact, many substantive changes in Texas government require an amendment. For example, an amendment is needed to change the way the state pays bills, to abolish certain unneeded state and county offices, or to authorize a bond issue pledging state revenues. Urbanization, industrialization, technological innovations, population growth, demands for programs and services, and countless social changes contribute to pressures for frequent constitutional change.

Most amendments apply to matters that should be resolved by statutes enacted by the Texas legislature. Notably, other states are able to handle most issues primarily through legislative action rather than through constitutional amendments. Instead, an often uninformed and usually apathetic electorate must decide the fate of many complex policy issues. In this context, special interests represented by well-financed lobbyists and the media often play influential roles in constitutional policymaking. They are also likely to influence the success or defeat of proposed amendments.

As the most visible policymaker in Texas, the governor can sway s public support or nonsupport of key propositions. Then-Governor Rick Perry, for instance, played a pivotal role in advocating specific constitutional amendment proposals. Signifying potentially a new direction in the substantive nature of constitutional amendments at the time, Rick Perry supported Proposition 2 in 2005. The controversial nature of this proposal, which sought to ban same-sex marriage, produced unprecedented media coverage and interest group activity. As mentioned previously, the proposed amendment defined marriage as consisting only of the "union of one man and one woman." It also prohibited the state and all political subdivisions from "creating or recognizing any legal status identical or similar to marriage." The measure overwhelmingly passed with 76 percent of the voters (more than 1.7 million) supporting it and 24 percent (more than 500,000) opposing it.[35]

Constitutional Amendment Elections Often, Texas voters are expected to evaluate numerous constitutional amendments. (Table 2.1 provides data on amendments proposed and adopted from 1879 through 2019.) Of the 690 constitutional amendment proposals presented to voters, 507 have been approved and 180 have been defeated. From 2003 to 2015, voters were presented with 86 constitutional amendment proposals, with as many as 22 in 2003, and voters approved 94 percent of these proposals. So, unless there is strong and vocal opposition, constitutional amendment proposals are increasingly likely to be approved.

One underlying theme among constitutional amendment elections centers on the legislative process. A notable example is the 2007 proposal that required state legislators to cast a recorded final vote on all substantive bills or constitutional amendment proposals and have it posted on the Internet for public review. Another major underlying theme relates to public finance. For instance, some constitutional amendments that have been approved provide property tax exemptions for different types of homeowners, such as surviving spouses of military personnel killed in action or deceased disabled veterans. One amendment increased the residential homestead exemptions for taxes supporting public schools. Voters have also approved temporary tax relief when property is damaged as a result from a natural disaster, such as Hurricane Harvey in 2019. Another subject area of constitutional amendments involves dedicating a portion of sales tax revenue for certain projects, such as using the state highway fund to build roads. In 2019, for instance, voters allowed revenue accumulated from the sale of sporting goods to be appropriated for support of the Texas Parks and Wildlife Department and the Texas Historical Commission. In that same year, another constitutional amendment allocated $800 million of Texas' Rainy Day Fund (the state's savings account) for flood mitigation efforts in response to the devastating impact of Hurricane Harvey along the Texas coast.[36]

Some of the more noteworthy constitutional amendments in recent years have had an impact on colleges and universities. For instance, in 2009, a proposal that received special attention by graduate students and faculty at state universities allowed Texas's public "emerging research universities" (including the University of Houston, University of Texas at El Paso, Texas Tech, and Texas State University at the time of the proposal) to compete for research money from the state's National Research University Fund. The objective was to raise the status of these schools to what are referred to as "Tier One" research institutions.[37] As of 2020, there were eight designated emerging research universities; but only two of Texas's public institutions (the University of Texas at Austin and Texas A&M University and one private institution (Rice University) were ranked as Tier One by all ranking authorities. (See Chapter 12, "Public Policy and Administration," for a discussion of higher education.) A 2009 proposal affected college students by authorizing the Texas Higher Education Coordinating Board to expand the state's ability to issue bonds for financing the College Access Loan program. This program provides low-interest loans to college students, irrespective of financial need. Private colleges and universities, who typically charge higher tuition rates, strongly supported this proposal. This amendment was proposed as lawmakers were making cuts in educational funding sources for students, specifically the Texas Grants Program and the Texas Equalization Program. (See Chapter 11, "Finance and Fiscal Policy," for a discussion of higher education funding.)

Table 2.1 Texas Constitution of 1876: Amendments Proposed and Adopted, 1879–2019

Year Proposed	Number Proposed	Number Adopted	Year Proposed	Number Proposed	Number Adopted
1879	1	1	1951	7	3
1881	2	0	1953	11	11
1883	5	5	1955	9	9
1887	6	0	1957	12	10
1889	2	2	1959	4	4
1891	5	5	1961	14	10
1893	2	2	1963	7	4
1895	2	1	1965	27	20
1897	5	1	1967	20	13
1899	1	0	1969	16	9
1901	1	1	1971	18	12
1903	3	3	1973	9	6
1905	3	2	1975	12	3
1907	9	1	1977	15	11
1909	4	4	1978	1	1
1911	5	4	1979	12	9

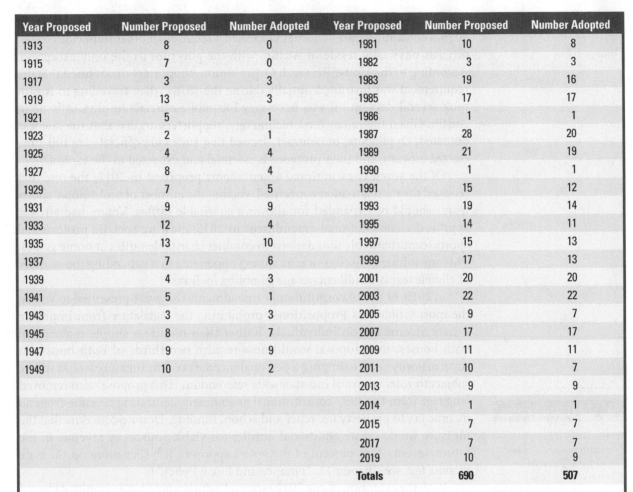

Year Proposed	Number Proposed	Number Adopted	Year Proposed	Number Proposed	Number Adopted
1913	8	0	1981	10	8
1915	7	0	1982	3	3
1917	3	3	1983	19	16
1919	13	3	1985	17	17
1921	5	1	1986	1	1
1923	2	1	1987	28	20
1925	4	4	1989	21	19
1927	8	4	1990	1	1
1929	7	5	1991	15	12
1931	9	9	1993	19	14
1933	12	4	1995	14	11
1935	13	10	1997	15	13
1937	7	6	1999	17	13
1939	4	3	2001	20	20
1941	5	1	2003	22	22
1943	3	3	2005	9	7
1945	8	7	2007	17	17
1947	9	9	2009	11	11
1949	10	2	2011	10	7
			2013	9	9
			2014	1	1
			2015	7	7
			2017	7	7
			2019	10	9
			Totals	**690**	**507**

Source: Research Division, Texas Legislative Council, Amendments to the Texas Constitution Since 1876, http://www.tlc.state .tx.us/pubsconamend/constamend1876.pdf.

— Competency Connection —
✿ **CRITICAL THINKING** ✿

Examine this table. What are your initial impressions of the number of constitutional amendments proposed by the Texas legislature and approved by the voters? Should voters be deciding so many constitutional amendments, especially when you consider the nature of some of these proposals?

Few constitutional amendments have expanded constitutional rights of individuals. Most notable of these was a proposal establishing a constitutional right to hunt, fish, and harvest wildlife, which was strongly supported by Governor Abbott in 2015. In an editorial opinion piece, he stated:

Texans have long lived off the bounty of the land and we know how to conserve our natural resources for future generations. It's so incredibly important that we protect our connection with the land. We need to act now so no special-interest group can come in and try to strip away your rights.[38]

Some constitutional amendments impact elected officials. For instance, in 2015, a constitutional amendment repealed a requirement that statewide elected officials physically reside in Austin, with the governor as the only exception. According to the House Research Organization, supporters maintained that the requirement was instituted initially during the 1870s when travelling to Austin took several days and it was necessary for public officials to physically be in Austin. Given the reliance on technology, supporters argued that the law was outdated. Opponents, in contrast, argued that statewide officials are full-time elected officials, and their presence is essential and expected in the capitol.[39]

Of the seven constitutional amendments proposed in 2017, the one that received the most attention concerned whether the number of professional sports teams should be expanded for allowing charitable raffles. Voters had already approved a constitutional amendment in 2015 allowing specific professional sports team charitable foundations to conduct charitable raffles at home games. This amendment raised concerns among opponents that expanding the number of eligible teams would encourage gambling in Texas.[40]

In 2019, of the 10 constitutional amendments that were presented to voters, the most visible was Proposition 4 prohibiting the legislature from imposing a state income tax on individuals. Rather than require a simple majority of both houses, the proposal would now require two-thirds of both houses (a supermajority vote) to impose a personal income tax. The measure would still be subject to voter approval in a statewide referendum. This proposal also removed language from the 1993 constitutional amendment dedicating revenue from an income tax to property tax relief and school funding. Despite concerns that the measure would create additional hurdles for viable sources of revenue in the future, seventy-four percent of the voters approved it.[41] (For more on the state income tax, see Chapter 11, "Finance and Fiscal Policy.")

With the exception of one 2019 proposal, which would have permitted elected municipal judges to serve multiple municipalities at the same time, all the other constitutional amendments were adopted, resulting in over 500 amendments to the state's constitution. By the end of the 2021 regular legislative session, 8 constitutional amendments passed both houses, and will be presented to voters in November.

✓ **2.2 Learning Check**

1. How many different constitutions has Texas had throughout its history?

2. True or False: Texas's present-day constitution has been amended just under 100 times.

Answers at the end of this chapter.

✪ Constitutional Amendments and Revision

LO 2.3 Analyze the amendment process, focusing on recent constitutional amendment elections as well as attempts to revise the Texas Constitution.

Each of the 50 American state constitutions provides the means for changing the powers and functions of government. Without a provision for change, few constitutions would survive long. A revision may produce a totally new constitution to replace an old one. Also, courts may alter constitutions by interpreting the wording of these documents in new and different ways. Finally, constitutions may be changed by formal amendment, which is the chief method by which the Texas Constitution has been altered.

Because Texas's registered voters have an opportunity to vote on one or more proposed amendments every two years—and sometimes each year—an understanding of the steps in the **constitutional amendment process** is important. Article XVII, Section 1, provides a relatively simple procedure for amending the Texas Constitution. The basic steps in that process follow:

- A joint resolution proposing an amendment is introduced in the House or in the Senate during a regular session or during a special session called by the governor.
- Two-thirds of the members in each chamber must adopt the resolution.
- The secretary of state prepares an explanatory statement that briefly describes the proposed amendment, and the attorney general approves this statement.
- The explanatory statement is published twice in Texas newspapers that print official state notices.
- A copy of the proposed amendment is posted in each county courthouse at least 30 days before the election.
- The voters must approve the proposed amendment by a simple majority vote in a regular or special election.
- The governor, who has no veto power in the process, issues a proclamation certifying the election results.

For a constitutional amendment to be considered by Texas voters, the legislature must adopt a joint resolution by a two-thirds vote in each chamber. Hundreds of constitutional amendment resolutions are considered every legislative session.

The Texas legislature decides whether a proposed amendment will be submitted to the voters in a **constitutional amendment election**, typically in November of an odd-numbered year. In some cases, a proposed amendment will be presented to voters in a special election scheduled for an earlier date. For instance, of the 17 amendments proposed in 2007, only one was presented to voters in May; the other proposals were presented in November of that same year. In 2014, voters were presented with (and approved) one proposal in the general election in November, diverting money from the "rainy day" fund to the State Highway Fund to pay for road construction and maintenance.

Part of the problem with frequent constitutional amendment elections is the typically low voter turnout in odd-numbered years, when no statewide offices are up for election. Generally, most constitutional amendment proposals are approved by a relatively small percentage of the voting population. The complex subject matter of most amendments is one explanation why voter interest and turnout is low. Constitutional amendment elections turnout is typically less than 10 percent. Turnout in 2011 was at an all-time low (less than 5 percent of the voting age population). In subsequent elections, voter turnout has remained

constitutional amendment process Process for changing the Texas Constitution in which an amendment is proposed by a two-thirds vote of each chamber of the legislature and approved by a simple majority of voters in a general or special election.

constitutional amendment election Election, typically in November of an odd-numbered year, in which voters are asked to approve one or more proposed constitutional amendments. An amendment must receive a majority of the popular vote to be approved.

below 10 percent, reaching 9 percent in 2019. Markedly, the 2013 constitutional election was also the first statewide election for which the voter photo ID law was implemented. (For more on the voter ID law, see Chapter 5, "Campaigns and Elections.")

Unlike voters in other states, Texans do not have the power of **initiative** at the state level; however, this power is exercised under some local governments. (See Chapter 3, "Local Governments," for a discussion of how these powers work locally.) If adopted, the initiative process would bypass the legislature and allow individual Texans or interest groups to gather the signatures required to submit proposed constitutional amendments and statutes (ordinary laws) for direct popular vote. According to the *Book of States*, there are only 18 states with some form of constitutional amendment procedure by initiative.[42] In recent years, no serious legislative efforts for amending the Texas Constitution to authorize the initiative process at the state level have emerged.

Constitutional Revision

Attempts to revise Texas's Constitution of 1876 began soon after its adoption. A legislative resolution calling for a constitutional revision convention was introduced in 1887 and was followed by others. Limited success came in 1969, when an amendment removed 56 obsolete constitutional provisions.

The only comprehensive movement to achieve wholesale **constitutional revision** began in 1971. In that year, the 62nd Legislature adopted a joint resolution proposing an amendment authorizing the appointment of a study commission and naming the members of the 63rd Legislature as delegates to a constitutional convention. Except for the state Bill of Rights, any part of the Texas Constitution of 1876 could be changed or deleted. Submitted to the voters in 1972 as a proposed constitutional amendment, the resolution was approved by a margin of more than half a million votes (1,549,982 in favor to 985,282 against).

A six-member committee (composed of the governor, the lieutenant governor, the speaker of the House, the attorney general, the chief justice of the Texas Supreme Court, and the presiding judge of the Court of Criminal Appeals) selected 37 persons to serve as members of the Constitutional Revision Commission. The commission prepared a draft constitution on the basis of opinions and information gathered at public hearings conducted throughout the state and from various authorities on constitutional revision. One-fourth the length of the present constitution, the completed draft was submitted to the legislature on November 1, 1973.

On January 8, 1974, all 181 members of both chambers of the Texas legislature met in Austin at a **constitutional revision convention**. Previous Texas constitutions had been drafted by convention delegates popularly elected for that purpose. When the finished document was put to a vote, the result was 118 for and 62 against, three votes short of the two-thirds majority of the total membership needed for final approval. (Approval required a total of at least 121 votes.) Attempts to reach compromises on controversial issues proved futile.

initiative
A citizen-drafted measure proposed by a specific number or percentage of qualified voters that becomes law if approved by popular vote. In Texas, this process occurs only at the local level, not at the state level.

constitutional revision
Extensive or complete rewriting of a constitution.

constitutional revision convention
A body of delegates who meet to make extensive changes in a constitution or to draft a new constitution.

The Constitutional Convention of 1974 provided perhaps the best demonstration of the politics surrounding Texas's constitution-making. First, the convention was hampered by a lack of positive political leadership. Then-Governor Dolph Briscoe maintained a hands-off policy throughout the convention. Former Lieutenant Governor Bill Hobby similarly failed to provide needed political leadership, and the retiring speaker of the House, Price Daniel Jr., pursued a noninterventionist course. Other members of the legislature were distracted by their need to campaign for reelection.

The primary reason that the convention failed to agree on a proposed constitution was the phantom "nonissue" of a right-to-work provision (which means people cannot be denied employment based on whether or not they are members of a labor union or labor organization). A statutory ban on contracts that require employers to hire only members of a labor union, known as shop labor contracts, was already in effect. Adding this prohibition to the constitution would not have strengthened the legal hand of employers to any significant degree. Nevertheless, conservative, anti-labor forces insisted on this provision, and a prolabor minority vigorously opposed it. The controversy aroused much emotion and at times produced loud and bitter name-calling among delegates on the floor and spectators in the galleries.[43] Stung by widespread public criticism of the 1974 convention's failure to produce a proposed constitution for public approval or rejection, the 64th Legislature resolved to submit a proposal to Texas voters. In 1975, both houses of the legislature agreed on a constitutional revision resolution comprising 10 articles in eight sections to be submitted to the Texas electorate in November of that year. The content of the articles was essentially the same as that of the final resolution of the unsuccessful 1974 convention.

The revision proposed in 1975 represented years of work by men and women well informed about constitution-making. Recognized constitutional authorities evaluated the concise and orderly document as one of the best drafted state constitutions ever submitted to American voters. Although new and innovative in many respects, the proposal did not discard all of the old provisions. In addition to retaining the Bill of Rights, the proposed constitution incorporated such basic principles as limited government, separation of powers, and bicameralism (a two-house legislature).

Nevertheless, Texas voters demonstrated a strong preference for the status quo by rejecting each proposition. In the end, voters in 250 of the state's 254 counties rejected all eight proposals. A mere 23 percent of the estimated 5.9 million registered voters cast ballots, meaning that only about 10 percent of the state's voting-age population participated in this important referendum. When asked to explain the resounding defeat of the eight propositions, Bill Hobby, then lieutenant governor, responded, "There's not enough of the body left for an autopsy."

More Revision Attempts

After the revision debacle of 1975, two decades passed before the next attempt to revise the constitution. In 1995, Senator John Montford (D-Lubbock) drafted a streamlined constitution that incorporated many of the concepts contained in the failed 1975 proposal. Montford's plan also called for a voter referendum every 30 years (without requiring legislative approval) on the question of calling a constitutional revision convention. But Montford resigned from the Texas Senate to become chancellor of the Texas Tech University System in 1996. With such issues as tax changes, welfare reform, and educational finance pressing for attention, the 75th Legislature did not seriously consider constitutional revision in 1997.

In 1998, Senator Bill Ratliff (R-Mount Pleasant) and Representative Rob Junell (D-San Angelo) launched another attempt to revise the constitution.[44] With assistance from Angelo State University students and others, they prepared a complete rewrite of the much-amended 1876 document. Subsequently, they introduced a draft for consideration by the 76th Legislature in 1999. It failed to muster enough support for serious consideration in committee and never received a floor vote in either legislative chamber.[45] This proposal would have cut the then 80,000-word document to approximately 19,000 words. Significant changes included expanding the powers of the governor, repealing the current partisan election method of selecting state judges, and increasing salaries of the House speaker and the lieutenant governor.

Another proposal, created by a bipartisan group of private citizens, represented an attempt to make the constitution more accessible and readable. Led by Roy Walthall (a retired instructor at McLennan Community College in Waco) in 2010, the team set out to reorganize the constitution. Rather than make substantive changes, which would provoke political opposition, the team claimed that they did not change the content or legal meaning. According to Walthall, the bulk of their work was rearranging many of the existing provisions into more logical sections. The governor would have to appoint a commission to study the reorganized constitution, and it could take several legislative sessions before the constitutional proposal would be presented to the state's voters. If approved, a new state constitution would enable Texas to join the other 49 states that have updated their constitutions since the beginning of the 20th century.

During the 21st century, the legislature has ignored or delayed action on the issue of constitutional revision. A series of budget crises, redistricting issues, school funding demands, and natural disasters (to name a few reasons), has dominated the legislative agenda. As a result, large-scale constitutional reform remains an problem. However, some individuals in the legislature have attempted to keep the subject on the agenda. In 2011 and again in 2013, Representative Charles Anderson (R-Waco), for instance, unsuccessfully introduced a resolution asking the leadership in the legislature to create a joint study committee to examine a nonsubstantive reorganization of the state constitution similar to Walthall's proposal.[46]

Constitutional revision attempts have not gained momentum. Today, the Texas Constitution, despite its flaws, remains the "supreme law of the State of Texas."

Piecemeal Revision

Because extensive constitutional reform has proved futile, Texas legislators have sought to achieve some measure of government reform by other means, including legislative enactments and piecemeal constitutional amendments. In 1977, for example, the 65th Legislature enacted into law two parts of the 1975 propositions defeated at the polls. One established a procedure for reviewing state administrative agencies; the other created a planning agency within the Office of the Governor. In 1979, the 66th Legislature proposed six amendments designed to implement parts of the constitutional revision package rejected in 1975. Three were adopted by the voters and added to the Texas Constitution. They accomplished the following:

- Established a single property tax appraisal district in each county (discussed in Chapter 3, "Local Governments")
- Gave criminal appellate jurisdiction to 14 courts of appeals that formerly had exercised civil jurisdiction only
- Allowed the governor restricted removal power over appointed statewide officials[47]

Other proposals for important constitutional changes have been unsuccessful in the House and the Senate. Instead, for the last twenty years, the state legislature has been unwilling to make significant constitutional changes. For example, during the regular session of the 77th Legislature in 2001, Representative Rob Junell (D-San Angelo) submitted a proposal that was considered and approved by the House Select Committee on Constitutional Revision. Among other items, the proposal would have changed the terms of office for state senators and House members. It also would have created a Texas Salary Commission to set salaries for elected and appointed officials of the executive, judicial, and legislative branches. This proposal, however, was never brought up for a floor vote in the legislature.[48]

To modernize the Texas Constitution, one constitutional amendment (adopted in 1999) authorized elimination of certain "duplicative, executed, obsolete, archaic and ineffective provisions of the Texas Constitution." Among resulting deletions were references to the abolished poll tax and the governor's authority "to protect the frontier from hostile incursions by Indians." Another constitutional amendment in 2007 eliminated the constitutional county office of inspector of hides and animals, which had been created in the 1880s. Nevertheless, the Texas Constitution still has problems.

> ✓ **2.3 Learning Check**
>
> 1. When was the last time voters were presented with a wholesale constitutional revision proposal from the state legislature?
>
> 2. True or False: Amending the Texas Constitution requires two-thirds of the members of each chamber of the state legislature voting for a proposed amendment and three-fourths of the voters approving it in a constitutional amendment election.
>
> *Answers at the end of this chapter.*

⚡ The Texas Constitution: A Summary

LO 2.4 Identify and differentiate the basic sections of the Texas Constitution.

A widely accessible published text of the constitution has been unavailable for the past 20 years, chiefly because of its length (over 200 pages). The last major source of the printed text, the *Texas Almanac*, now refers readers to the Internet and websites, such as the Texas Legislature Online, to review the document.

Although *Practicing Texas Politics* does not include the entire text of the Texas Constitution, each chapter looks to Texas's basic law for its content. The rest of this chapter presents a brief synopsis of the document's 17 articles.[49]

The Bill of Rights

We begin by examining Article I, the Texas Constitution's Bill of Rights. The **Texas Bill of Rights** is similar to the one found in the U.S. Constitution. Composed of 30 sections, it guarantees protections for people and their property against arbitrary actions by state and local governments. Included among these rights are freedom of speech, press, religion, assembly, and petition; the rights of accused and convicted criminals and victims of crime; and equal rights for women. Article I also includes philosophical observations that have no direct force of law.

Constitutional Rights Against Arbitrary Governmental Actions

Eleven of Article I's sections provide protections for people and property against arbitrary governmental actions. Guarantees, such as freedom of speech, press, religion, assembly, and petition, are included. The right to keep and bear arms, prohibitions against the taking of property by government action without just compensation, and protection of contracts are also incorporated. Most of these rights found in the Texas Constitution are also protected under the U.S. Constitution. Thus, with their basic rights guaranteed in both national and state constitutions, Texans, like people in other states, have a double safeguard against arbitrary governmental actions.

One of these constitutional rights, protected for Texans by both state and federal constitutions, centers on freedom of religion. A constitutional right to freedom of religion is essentially the same in both the Texas Constitution and the U.S. Constitution, yet when one examines the actual wording, it is different. The Texas Bill of Rights, Section 6, states, "All men have a natural and indefeasible right to worship Almighty God according to the dictates of their own conscience. No man shall be compelled to attend, erect or support any place of worship, or to maintain any ministry against his consent … and no preference shall ever be given to any religious society or mode of worship." Under the U.S. Constitution, the First Amendment (as applied to the states under the Fourteenth Amendment) provides that states "shall make no law respecting an establishment of religion, or prohibiting the free exercise thereof."

Cases on religious freedom stemming from the U.S. Constitution have gone from Texas all the way to the U.S. Supreme Court. Included among these are two cases that yielded different results: one centered on student-led prayer before a school football game; the other involved a Ten Commandments monument placed on the Texas state Capitol grounds. The U.S. Supreme Court, interpreting the establishment clause of the U.S. Constitution to require a separation of church and state, struck down school prayer before public school football games, contending that the message conveyed amounted to an endorsement of religion on school grounds.[50] In contrast, the U.S. Supreme Court upheld the Ten Commandments display, concluding that it is a historical monument among other historical monuments on state grounds.[51]

Texas Bill of Rights
Article I of the Texas Constitution guarantees protections for people and their property against arbitrary actions by state and local governments. Protected rights include freedom of speech, press, religion, assembly, and petition.

Rights of Criminals and Victims Thirteen sections of the Texas Constitution's Bill of Rights relate to the rights of persons accused of crimes and to the rights of individuals who have been convicted of crimes. For example, one section concerns the right to release on bail; another prohibits unreasonable searches and seizures; and a third declares that "the right to trial by jury shall remain inviolate." These provisions relate closely to similar language in the national Bill of Rights.

The Texas Constitution is even more protective of certain rights than is the U.S. Constitution. An additional set of rights added by constitutional amendment in 1989 protects crime victims. This provision was developed in the early 1980s in response to findings of a presidential task force that explored the inequality of rights for crime victims. In general, the state constitution now gives victims rights to restitution, information about the accused (conviction, sentence, release, etc.), protection from the accused throughout the criminal justice process, and respect for the victim's privacy.

Equal Rights for Women Another example of the Texas Constitution's providing more protection than the U.S. Constitution relates to equal rights for women. Attempts nationwide to add a proposed Equal Rights Amendment (ERA) to the U.S. Constitution failed between 1972 and 1982 (even though the amendment was approved by the Texas legislature). Nevertheless, the **Texas Equal Legal Rights Amendment (ELRA)** was added to Article I, Section 3, of the Texas Constitution in 1972. It states: "Equality under the law shall not be denied or abridged because of sex, race, color, creed, or national origin." This constitutional amendment was proposed and adopted after several unsuccessful attempts dating back to the 1950s.[52] Interestingly, despite the ELRA, the Texas Constitution still has a provision that states, "All free men have equal rights."

Additional Protections Additional protections in the Texas Constitution include prohibitions against imprisonment for debt, outlawry (putting a convicted person outside the protection of the law), and the punishment of transportation (punishing a convicted citizen by banishment from the state). Monopolies are prohibited by a provision of the Texas Bill of Rights but not by the U.S. Constitution, although federal statutory law does prohibit monopolies. Some of these added gurantees have been achieved through constitutional amendments. For instance, in 1993, taxpayers were provided constitutional protection by prohibiting the establishment of a state income tax without voter approval. To ensure stricter guidelines, another constitutional amendment addressing a state income tax was adopted in 2019. In 2009, property homeowners were provided additional protection from the government's taking of private property for the primary purpose of economic development. As mentioned earlier, since 2015, Texans have had constitutional protection to hunt, fish, and harvest wildlife; but this right is limited because of the state's conservation laws.

Interpretation of the Texas Constitution by the Texas Supreme Court has also provided additional rights, such as the court's interpretation of Article VII, Section 1 (titled Education), which requires the state legislature to provide support and maintenance for "an efficient system of free public schools." In 1989,

Texas Equal Legal Rights Amendment (ELRA)
Added to Article I, Section 3, of the Texas Constitution, it guarantees that "equality under the law shall not be denied or abridged because of sex, race, color, creed, or national origin."

the high court first held that the state legislature had a constitutional requirement to create a more equitable public school finance system. The Texas Supreme Court revisited school finance in 2005 and declared the school finance system unconstitutional. Rather than focusing on the system's continued and persistent inequities, however, the court focused on whether the state-imposed property tax cap amounted to a statewide property tax, which the Texas Constitution forbids. (Property taxes can be collected only at the local level.) Because more than 80 percent of all school districts had reached this cap and state funding had continued to decline, the court held that school boards had effectively lost control of tax rates. Equally important, the Court rejected the claim that more money in the system was necessary to comply with the Texas Constitution's requirement to provide for the "general diffusion of knowledge."[53] Challenges to school funding in the courts continued. In 2015, district court judge John Dietz considered more evidence in the case after the 84th Legislature restored $3.7 billion (out of the $5.4 billion) of the cuts made to school funding in 2011. He ruled that the school finance system was still unconstitutional. Then, the Texas Supreme Court heard oral arguments in an appeal in September 2015. This Court overturned the lower court's decision in May 2016, when it held that the state's funding system met "minimum constitutional standards" despite being "a Band-Aid on top of Band-Aid" reform effort.[54] School funding was revisited during the 2019 legislative session, with nominal salary increases for school teachers and librarians. (For more on school finance, see Chapter 11, "Finance and Fiscal Policy.")

Philosophical Observations Three sections of the Texas Bill of Rights contain philosophical observations that have no direct force of law. Still stinging from what they saw as the "bondage" years of Reconstruction, the angry delegates to the constitutional convention of 1875 began their work by inserting this philosophical statement: "Texas is a free and independent state, subject only to the Constitution of the United States." They also asserted philosophical theories that all political power resides with the people and is legitimately exercised only on their behalf and that the people may at any time "alter, reform, or abolish their government." To guard against the possibility that any of the rights guaranteed in the other 28 sections would be eliminated or altered by the government, the framers also proclaimed in Section 29 that "everything in this 'Bill of Rights' is excepted out of the general powers of government, and shall forever remain inviolate."

The Powers of Government and Separation of Powers

separation of powers
The assignment of lawmaking, law-enforcing, and law-interpreting functions to separate branches of government.

Holding fast to the principle of limited government and a balance of power, the framers of the Constitution of 1876 firmly embedded in the state's fundamental law the familiar doctrine of **separation of powers**. In Article II, they assigned the lawmaking, law-enforcing, and law-adjudicating powers of government to three separate branches, identified as the legislative, executive, and judicial departments, respectively.

Article III is titled "Legislative Department." Legislative powers are vested in a bicameral legislature, composed of the House of Representatives with 150 members and the Senate with 31 members. A patchwork of more than 60 sections, this article provides vivid testimony of the many decades of amendments directly affecting the legislative branch. For example, in 1936, an amendment added a section granting the Texas legislature the authority to levy taxes to fund a retirement system for public school, college, and university teachers. Today, public school teachers and personnel employed by public universities and community colleges benefit from pension programs provided by the state.

Article IV, "Executive Department," states unequivocally that the governor "shall be the Chief Executive Officer of the State" but then shares executive power with four other popularly elected officers independent of the governor: the lieutenant governor, the attorney general, the comptroller of public accounts, and the commissioner of the General Land Office. Originally, a state treasurer was included in this list, but a constitutional amendment abolished the office. Additionally, the state's secretary of state is part of the Executive Department, but this official is appointed by the governor. With these and other provisions for division of executive power, some observers consider the Texas governor no more than first among equals in the executive branch of state government.

Through Article V, "Judicial Department," Texas joins Oklahoma as one of only two states in the country with a bifurcated court system that includes two courts of final appeal: one for civil cases (the Supreme Court of Texas) and one for criminal cases (the Court of Criminal Appeals). Below these two supreme appellate courts are other courts authorized by the Texas Constitution: intermediate appellate courts (14 courts of appeal) and more than 1,500 courts of original jurisdiction (trial courts), including district courts, county courts, and justice of the peace courts. The legislature is allowed to create any other courts it deems necessary. Thus, by statute, it has created county courts-at-law and probate.

Suffrage

Article VI, titled "**Suffrage**" (the right to vote), is one of the shortest articles in the Texas Constitution. Before 1870, states had the definitive power to conduct elections. Since that time, amendments to the U.S. Constitution, acts of Congress such as the Voting Rights Act of 1965, and U.S. Supreme Court rulings have vastly diminished this power. In addition, amendments to the Voting Rights Act of 1975 require Texas to provide bilingual ballots. For more than 35 years, Texas had to receive federal preclearance for any changes to voting laws or district boundary lines for elected officials. In 2013, however, mandatory preclearance was eliminated when the U.S. Supreme Court found the requirement unconstitutional in a separate case originating in Alabama, *Shelby County v. Holder* (2013).[55] During this time, a lawsuit was filed against Texas under Section 2 of the Voting Rights Act. It challenged one of the strictest ever photo voter ID laws approved by the 82nd Legislature (2011) from going into effect, claiming that the law

suffrage
The right to vote.

discriminated against minority voters. Rather than wait for a court decision, then-Attorney General Gregg Abbott interpreted the *Shelby* decision to allow immediate implementation of the voter ID photo requirement beginning with the constitutional amendment election in 2013. Litigation led the Texas Legislature to ultimately revise the photo ID law to allow voters without one of the acceptable forms of ID to sign an affidavit confirming their identity and provide acceptable documents verifying their identity, such as utility bills. In April 2018, a panel on the 5th Circuit Court of Appeals upheld the revised law as constitutionally acceptable, despite concerns among many that it disproportionately discriminates against racial and ethnic minorities.[56] (For more on voting, see Chapter 5, "Campaigns and Elections.")

Within the scope of current federal parameters, the Texas Constitution establishes qualifications for voters, provides for citizen voter registration, and governs the conduct of elections. In response to federal-level changes, this article has been amended to abolish the payment of a poll tax or any form of property qualification for voting in the state's elections and to change the minimum voting age from 21 to 18.

Image 2.4 Governor Greg Abbott speaks at a campaign rally with U.S. President Trump for Senator Ted Cruz in Houston.

Bloomberg/Getty Images

Competency Connection
☼ **CRITICAL THINKING** ☼

How important do you think it is for the Texas governor to participate in a campaign rally with the President in support of one of the U.S. Senator's re-election campaign? What are the implications for federal–state relations?

Local Governments

The most disorganized part of the Texas Constitution concerns units of **local government**: counties, municipalities (cities), school districts, and other special districts. Although Article IX is titled "Counties," provisions concerning county government are scattered through four other articles. Moreover, the basic structure of county government is defined not in Article IX on counties but in Article V on the judiciary. Article XI on municipalities is equally disorganized. Only four of the sections of this article relate specifically to municipal government. Other sections deal with areas that concern county government, taxation, public indebtedness, and forced sale of public property.

Along with counties and municipalities, the original text of the Constitution of 1876 referred to school districts but not to other types of special districts. Authorization for special districts, however, crept into the Texas Constitution with a 1904 amendment that authorized the borrowing of money for water development and road construction by a county "or any defined district." Since then, special districts have been created to provide myriad services, such as drainage, conservation, urban renewal, public housing, hospitals, and airports.

local government
Counties, municipalities, school districts, and other special districts that provide a range of services, including rural roads, city streets, public education, and protection of persons and property.

Other Articles

The nine remaining articles also reflect a strong devotion to constitutional minutiae: Education, Taxation and Revenue, Railroads, Private Corporations, Spanish and Mexican Land Titles, Public Lands and Land Office, Impeachment, General Provisions, and Mode of Amendment. The shortest is Article XIII, "Spanish and Mexican Land Titles." The entire text was deleted by amendment in 1969 because its provisions were deemed obsolete. The longest article is Article XVI, "General Provisions." Among other stipulations, it prohibits the bribing of public officials and authorizes the legislature to regulate the manufacture and sale of intoxicants.

✔ **2.4 Learning Check**

1. True or False: The Texas Constitution contains constitutional rights not found in the U.S. Constitution.
2. Article II of the Texas Constitution assigns powers to which branches of government?

Answers at the end of this chapter.

Conclusion

As a member of the United States, Texas is provided with certain constitutional guarantees as well as limitations on its powers. The U.S. Constitution plays a significant role in defining federal–state relations. This balance of power between the federal government and the state government is constantly evolving. The Texas government derives most of its powers from the Texas Constitution. Understanding Texas's constitutional history explains to a large degree the characteristics of its present-day constitution. Amending the Texas Constitution occurs frequently through constitutional amendment elections, but recent attempts to revise the constitution have not been successful. As a result, the structure of the Constitution of 1876 remains essentially unchanged.

Chapter Summary

LO 2.1 Analyze federalism and the powers of the state in a constitutional context. The American federal system features a division of powers between a national government and 50 state governments. As a member of the Union, Texas has certain constitutional guarantees and limitations. Several constitutional provisions in the U.S. Constitution affect interstate relations and state immunity. Controversy may arise when uniformity in certain areas of policy among the states does not exist. Powers not delegated (nor implied, as interpreted by federal courts) to the federal government are reserved to the states or to the people under the Tenth Amendment. These state powers have largely formed around several broad categories, and identifying a clear boundary between state and national powers (or responsibilities) is often complicated. Striking a balance of power between the national and state governments is constantly shifting and evolving over time.

LO 2.2 Explain the origins and development of the state constitution. Today's Texas Constitution is the country's second longest and, by 2020, had 507 amendments. Most amendments are statutory in nature, so the document resembles a code of laws. Texas has had seven constitutions, each reflecting the political situation that existed when the specific document was drafted. The Constitution of 1876 has endured, despite its excessive length, confusion, and statutory detail.

LO 2.3 Analyze the amendment process, focusing on recent constitutional amendment elections as well as attempts to revise the Texas Constitution. Changing the Texas Constitution requires an amendment proposed by a two-thirds majority vote of the members in each legislative chamber and approved by a simple majority of the state's voters in a general or special election. Despite efforts to conduct a wholesale revision of the Texas Constitution, only piecemeal revisions have occurred.

LO 2.4 Identify and differentiate the basic sections of the Texas Constitution. The Texas Constitution is the fundamental law that sets forth the powers and limitations of the state's government. It is composed of 17 articles. Included are the Bill of Rights, an article on suffrage, articles on the three branches of state government, and provisions concerning the powers of state and local governments.

Key Terms

block grant, p. 55
constitutional amendment
    election, p. 69
constitutional amendment process,
    p. 69
constitutional guarantees, p. 46
constitutional revision, p. 70
constitutional revision
    convention, p. 70

delegated powers, p. 45
federal grants-in-aid, p. 55
full faith and credit clause, p. 49
implied powers, p. 45
initiative, p. 70
local government, p. 79
national supremacy clause, p. 45
privileges and immunities, p. 49
reserved powers, p. 51

separation of powers, p. 76
suffrage, p. 77
Tenth Amendment, p. 45
Texas Bill of Rights, p. 74
Texas Constitution of 1876, p. 64
Texas Equal Legal Rights
    Amendment (ELRA), p. 75
Texas Grange, p. 62

Learning Check Answers

 2.1   1. False. The Tenth Amendment does not specifically identify the powers of the states.

2. Devolution gives the states more freedom to make decisions, especially with funding.

 2.2   1. Texas has had seven constitutions throughout its history.

2. False. The present-day Texas Constitution has been amended almost 500 times.

 2.3   1. November 1975 was the last time that voters were presented with a wholesale constitutional revision proposal from the state legislature; more recent attempts have failed.

2. False. Amending the Texas Constitution requires two-thirds of the members of each chamber of the state legislature to vote for a proposed amendment but only a simple majority of the voters to approve it in a constitutional amendment election.

 2.4   1. True. The Texas Constitution does contain additional constitutional rights, such as the Equal Legal Rights Amendment, not found in the U.S. Constitution.

2. The Texas Constitution assigns power to the legislative, executive, and judicial branches.

3 Local Governments

Learning Objectives

3.1 Explain the relationships that exist between a local government and all other governments, including national, state, and other local governments.

3.2 Describe the forms of municipal government organization.

3.3 Identify the rules and social issues that shape local government outcomes.

3.4 Analyze the structure and responsibilities of counties.

3.5 Explain the functions of special districts and their importance to the greater community.

3.6 Discuss the ways that local governments deal with metropolitan-wide and regional issues.

Image 3.1 The overwhelming majority of Texans live in metropolitan areas such as El Paso, pictured below. They and their rural neighbors depend heavily on local governments for a multitude of services affecting their daily lives.

Source: City of San Antonio

— Competency Connection —
☼ **CRITICAL THINKING** ☼

How has local government affected your life? (You may want to revisit this question after reading the chapter.)

When Texans think about government, most think about the national or state government, but not about the many local governments. Yet of all three levels of government, local government has the greatest impact on citizens' daily lives. Most people drive every day on city streets or county roads, drink water provided by the city or a special district, attend schools run by the local school district, play in a city or county park, eat in restaurants inspected by city health officials, and live in houses or apartments that required city permits and inspections to build.

All governments, including local, involve both cooperation and conflict. Many citizens' contacts with local governments are positive. Potholes are filled, trash is picked up, ball fields are groomed for games—but other experiences are negative. Streets and freeways are increasingly congested, many schools are over-crowded, and the property taxes to support them seem high. In addition, people of good will often disagree about public policy, for example, putting money into freeways or public transportation, the amount and use of standardized testing in schools, and where to locate public housing.

Commonly, the sharpest divisions in Texas local government are between central cities, suburbs, and small town/rural Texas. In urban areas, local governments face a growing list of demands for more and better traditional services (such as streets and safety) and newer services (such as skate parks, public housing, and pre-kindergarten). Many needs, such as transportation and hospital access, cross government boundaries. Central cities and their suburbs often fight over what kinds of services are needed and who will pay for them. Suburbanites, for example, tend to prefer more freeways, while central city residents often want more public transportation. Many rural Texans prefer that government provide only the most minimal services, regulate little, and collect few taxes. But even they want roads maintained, a good education for their kids, and safety for their families and businesses.

A common problem facing almost all local governments is that there is not enough money to satisfy all the demands citizens make. Tax revenue doesn't grow as fast as demands, and the state and national governments have been relatively stingy. The Great Recession of 2007–2009 with recovery taking through 2016, the fluctuation in oil prices during 2014–2020, and the recession caused by the 2020 covid-19 pandemic added to the financial woes of local governments. The result is that local governments have had to limit services and go heavily into debt. For years, local governments in Texas have had one of the highest per capita debt levels among the 50 states, while Texas state government's per capita debt has been among the lowest. (See "How Do We Compare. . . .")

To confront problems successfully and make local governments more responsive to our needs, we have to understand how these governments are organized and work. The organization of governments is important because it affects who has influence over what the government does and how efficiently it works. Local government comes in many forms. Texas has municipalities (more than 1,200 city and town governments), counties (254), and special districts (almost 3,900). The special district that most students know best is the school district (about 1,100), but there are also special districts for water, hospitals, conservation,

Follow *Practicing
Texas Politics* on
Twitter **@PracTexPol**

housing, and a multitude of other services (about 2,800). Each local government covers a certain geographic area and has legal authority to carry out one or more government functions. Most collect revenue such as taxes or fees, spend money to provide services, and are controlled by officials ultimately responsible to voters. These local, or **grassroots**, governments affect our lives directly.

★ Local Politics in Context

LO 3.1   Explain the relationships that exist between a local government and all other governments, including national, state, and other local governments.

Local government and politics are greatly affected by the context within which they operate—the federal system. In Texas and elsewhere, local governments were created by the state, and what they do is often shaped by the actions of other governments—national, state, and local.

Local Governments and Federalism

In the 19th century, two opposing views emerged concerning the powers of local governments. **Dillon's Rule**, named after federal judge John F. Dillon and still followed in most states (including Texas), dictates that local governments have only those powers granted by the state government, those powers implied in state grants, and those powers indispensable to their functioning.[1] The opposing Cooley Doctrine, named after Michigan judge Thomas M. Cooley and followed in 10 states, says "Local Government is a matter of absolute right; and the state may not take it away."[2]

Texas's local governments, like those of other states, are at the bottom rung of the governmental ladder, which makes them politically and legally weaker than the state and federal governments. In addition, Texas is among those states that more strictly follow Dillon's Rule.[3] Cities, counties, and special district governments are creatures of the State of Texas. They are created through state laws and the Texas Constitution, and they make decisions permitted or required by the state. Local governments may receive part of their money from the state or national government, and they must obey the laws and constitutions of both. The influence of the national government over Texas's local governments is significant in some areas, such as non-discrimination, rights of the accused, and the environment, but the federal government's influence is far smaller than that of the state.

States often complain about unfunded mandates (requirements placed on states by the federal government without federal money to pay the costs). Local governments face mandates from both the national and state governments. Some of these mandates are funded by the higher levels of government, but some are not. Examples of mandates at the local level are as diverse as improving the quality of the air, providing access for people with disabilities (both federal mandates), meeting state jail standards, and prohibiting cities from banning plastic grocery bags (state mandates). For some years, state officials have been more willing than

grassroots
Local (as in grassroots government or grassroots politics).

Dillon's Rule
A legal principle, still followed in the majority of states including Texas, that local governments have only those powers granted by their state government.

in the past to usurp local policy making when they disagree with the policies. For more discussion, see the Point/Counterpoint discussion.

Both the national and Texas state governments provide funding to local governments, sometimes to assist and other times to encourage the recipients to follow policies desired by the donor. Threats to withhold aid are also used to affect the recipients' actions. In Texas, the state government commonly provides one-fourth of local government general revenue; however, there is great variation. Cities get around two percent, while school districts average close to 40 percent. State agencies also often receive federal funds to distribute to local governments, which they may use for leverage over local officials. Federal assistance is a major part of Texas state government revenue (commonly around one-third of general revenue) but a small part of local government funding (three percent, and much of that for schools and in recent years, medical care).

In times of natural disaster, Texas often turns to the national government for help. From 1953 to 2020, Texas led the nation in the number of federally declared disasters (360) and major disasters (100), mostly from wind, floods, droughts, and fire plus the covid-19 pandemic in 2020.[4] Getting federal help requires a great deal of interaction between the three layers of government. Formally, the governor asks for a declaration of disaster, supported in practice by other state and local leaders. If a declaration is made, the Federal Emergency Management Agency (FEMA) can provide some funds, but if the damage is great, local and state leaders will lobby congress for additional funding (and try to raise money locally).

The response to Hurricane Harvey illustrates the process. Harvey hit Houston and the Texas Gulf Coast in August 2017. A federal aid package was quickly put together, followed over the next half year by two more, with members of congress from Texas playing a major role. However, two sets of problems quickly became apparent. First, while the aid totaled $28 billion,[5] Harvey had done $125 billion damage. Most individuals received only part of their losses. Others were turned down for aid. Second, the distribution of the money by federal, state, and local agencies was slow. By three years after Harvey, only one-third of the assistance had been outlaid. The federal General Accounting Office criticized both national and Texas agencies for weak procedures and slowness in providing aid. Help was also slowed by conflict between the state's General Land Office (GLO) and local governments. For example, using federal money, home repairs were to be assisted by the City of Houston within its boundaries, by Harris County in the remainder of the county, and by the GLO in the rest of the Gulf Coast. However, disputes including the speed of work led to the GLO demanding to take over the entire program. In 2020, Harris County ceded its program to the GLO, which sued Houston to take its program as well.

At the local level, federalism is more than just dealing with the state and national governments. Local governments have to deal with each other as well. Texas has over 5,300 local governments. Bexar County (home of San Antonio) has 65 local governments, Dallas County has 61, and Travis County (Austin) has 147. The territories of local governments often overlap. Your home, for example, may be within a county, a municipality, a school district, a community college district, and a hospital district—all of which collect taxes, provide services, and hold elections.

Local governments generally treat each other as friends but occasionally act as adversaries. For example, the city of Houston and Harris County worked together, as well as with state and national officials, to respond to Hurricanes Katrina, Rita, Ike, and Harvey. On the other hand, in 2014, the small border city La Villa shut off the local school district's water in a dispute over rates, and in 2018, the Texas Supreme Court decided a dispute between Nueces and San Patricio Counties over which could tax piers in Corpus Christi Bay.[6] Clearly, federalism and the resulting relationships between and among governments, (**intergovernmental relations**), are important to how local governments work. (For more on federalism, see Chapter 2, "Federalism and the Texas Constitution.")

Grassroots Challenges

Local governments face a multitude of challenges. About 85 percent of all Texans reside in cities and towns, and they have concerns they want addressed: fear of crime and, recently, the role of police; decaying infrastructure, such as streets and bridges; controversies over public schools; and healthcare, including in 2020 how to respond to the pandemic.

Texas cities are also becoming increasingly diverse, with more Black and Latino Texans now seeking access to public services and local power structures long dominated by Whites. Making sure that all communities receive equal access to public services is a key challenge for grassroots-level policymakers and community activists. Opportunities to participate in local politics begin with registering and then voting in local elections. (See Chapter 5, "Campaigns and Elections," for voter qualifications and registration requirements under Texas law.) Some citizens will decide to run for city council, county commissioners court, school board, or other local policymaking body. Others volunteer to serve on appointed advisory boards that make recommendations to the elected board. However, having an impact doesn't require seeking or holding office. Additional opportunities include homeowners' or neighborhood associations, community or issue-oriented organizations, voter registration drives, election campaign work, speaking at hearings, and volunteer work with community groups. Internships provide work experience while building contacts and knowledge of the process. By gaining influence in city halls, county courthouses, and special district offices, individuals and groups are in a better position to address grassroots problems.

Grassroots government faces the challenge of widespread voter apathy. Frequently, fewer than 10 percent of a community's qualified voters participate in a local election. The good news is that involvement increases when people understand that they can deal with problems in Texas through participation.

✪ Municipal Governments

LO 3.2 Describe the forms of municipal government organization.

Perhaps no Texas government influences the daily lives of citizens more than **municipal (city) government**. Whether taxing residents, arresting criminals,

---

✔ 3.1 Learning Check

1. Do local governments have more flexibility to make their own decisions under Dillon's Rule or the Cooley Doctrine? Which one does Texas follow?

2. Are intergovernmental relations marked by conflict, cooperation, or both?

Answers at the end of this chapter.

intergovernmental relations
Relationships between and among different governments that are on the same or different levels.

municipal (city) government
A local government for an incorporated community established by law as a city.

collecting garbage, transporting water and sewer, providing libraries and parks, regulating construction and restaurants, or repairing streets, municipalities determine how millions of Texans live. Knowing how and why public policies are made at city hall requires an understanding of the organizational and legal framework within which municipalities function.

Legal Status of Municipalities

City government powers are outlined and restricted by municipal charters, state and national constitutions, and statutes (laws). Texas has two legal classifications of cities: **general-law cities** and **home-rule cities**. A community with a population of 201 or more may become a general-law city by adopting a charter prescribed by a general law enacted by the Texas legislature.[7] A city of more than 5,000 people may be incorporated as a home-rule city, with a locally drafted charter adopted, amended, or repealed by majority vote in a citywide election. Once chartered, a general-law city does not automatically become a home-rule city just because its population increases to greater than 5,000. Citizens must vote to become a home-rule city, but that status does not change if the municipality's population decreases to 5,000 or fewer.

Texas has almost 900 general-law cities, most of which are fairly small in population. Although some of the about 350 home-rule cities are small, most larger cities tend to have home-rule charters. The principal advantage of home-rule cities is greater flexibility in determining their organizational structure and how they operate. Citizens draft, adopt, and revise their city's charter through citywide elections. The charter establishes the powers of municipal officers; sets salaries and terms of offices for council members and mayors; and spells out procedures for passing, repealing, or amending **ordinances** (city laws).

The ordinance-making power of Texas municipalities is not unlimited. Under Dillon's Rule, the state creates and can limit local government authority. For example, in November 2014, voters in Denton, located north of Dallas–Fort Worth, approved an ordinance banning hydraulic fracturing (fracking) within city limits. However, the following May, the Texas legislature responded to oil and gas industry lobbying by prohibiting cities from regulating underground oil and gas operations, which includes fracking.[8] This began a period of increased limitations on Texas local governments by state leaders. (For a discussion of how much authority the state should have over city ordinances, see this chapter's Point/Counterpoint feature.)

Home-rule cities may exercise three powers not held by the state government or general-law cities: recall, initiative, and referendum. **Recall** provides a process for removing elected officials through a popular vote. In May 2016, a recall election was held in Crystal City, a small community in South Texas, after federal agents arrested the mayor, two city council members, and the city manager on bribery and kickback charges. After the city clerk rejected a citizen-initiated recall petition saying there were not enough signatures, five Crystal City residents filed a lawsuit to force approval of the petition. In February 2016, State District Judge Amado Abascal ordered the clerk to verify the signatures, and if valid, move forward with the election. In that vote, citizens removed the mayor, the mayor

general-law city
A municipality with a charter prescribed by the legislature.

home-rule city
A municipality with a locally drafted charter.

ordinance
A local law enacted by a city council or approved by popular vote in a referendum or initiative election.

recall
A process for removing elected officials through a popular vote. In Texas, this power is available only for home-rule cities.

pro-tempore, and a councilman.[9] Recall is used less in Texas than in many states and often involves hot-button issues. During 2018–2020, there were recall petitions involving a gay councilman in a small Southeast Texas town, a controversial Black councilman in a heavily White Dallas suburb, and a councilman who had made anti-Islam posts on social media.

An **initiative** is a citizen-drafted measure proposed by a specified number or percentage of qualified voters. If approved by popular vote, an initiative becomes law without city council approval, whereas a **referendum** approves or repeals an existing ordinance. Ballot referenda and initiatives require voter approval and, depending on city charter provisions, may be binding or nonbinding on the city.

Initiatives and referenda can be contentious. For example, in 2014, the Houston City Council enacted the Houston Equal Rights Ordinance (HERO) banning discrimination in a number of areas, including sexual orientation and gender identity. Controversy arose because the ordinance would allow transgender people to use facilities such as restrooms consistent with their gender identity rather than their biological sex. It quickly became known as the "bathroom bill." Opponents raised a petition calling for a vote to repeal the ordinance. In November, voters rejected the ordinance by a vote of 61–39 percent. A proposed statewide bathroom bill requiring use of facilities consistent with the sex listed on one's birth certificate failed in the 2017 legislature. In 2019, the state's top three leaders rejected trying again.[10]

Across the nation, conflict has arisen over how to regulate ridesharing services such as Uber and Lyft. In 2016, a political action committee supported by the two companies obtained 65,000 signatures calling for a referendum to prevent an Austin ordinance from going into effect. The ordinance required fingerprint-based background checks for ridesharing drivers, a process similar to that used for taxi drivers. Proponents of fingerprinting argued that it was necessary for public safety. Opponents said that it was unnecessary and costly.[11] Uber and Lyft spent nearly $9 million on the campaign, the most expensive referendum campaign in the city's history. In May 2016, Austin voters defeated Proposition 1, allowing the city council ordinance to take effect. Days after the election, Lyft and Uber pulled out of Austin, and local companies quickly filled the gap. Uber and Lyft immediately lobbied the legislature to pass statewide regulations preempting local regulations. Many legislators saw the issue in terms of liberal Austin versus free enterprise. The legislature passed a bill giving the state the power to regulate ridesharing and requiring a background check without fingerprints. Both companies were back in Austin, a year after leaving.

initiative
A citizen-drafted measure proposed by a specific number or percentage of qualified voters, which becomes law if approved by popular vote. In Texas, this process occurs only in home-rule cities.

referendum
A process by which issues are referred to the voters to accept or reject. Voters may also petition for a vote to repeal an existing ordinance. In Texas, this process occurs at the local level in home-rule cities. At the state level, state constitutional amendments and bonds secured by taxes must be approved by the voters.

Forms of Municipal Government

How a government is organized has important consequences, among them who has access to decision-makers, what kinds of policies are likely to be enacted, and how efficiently the government works. The four principal forms of municipal government used in the United States and Texas—strong mayor-council, weak mayor-council, council-manager, and commission—have many variations. The council-manager form prevails in almost 90 percent of Texas's home-rule cities, and variations of the two mayor-council systems operate in many general-law cities. In practice, various combinations of the forms are permissible under a home-rule charter, as long as they do not conflict with state law. Informal practice also may make defining a city's form difficult. For example, the council-manager form may work like a strong mayor-council form if the mayor has a strong personality and the city manager is timid.

Strong Mayor-Council Among larger American cities, the **strong mayor-council form** continues as the predominant governmental structure. Among the nation's 10 largest cities, Dallas, San Antonio, Phoenix (Arizona), and San Jose (California) operate with a council-manager) rather than strong mayor-council system. In New York City, Los Angeles, Chicago, Philadelphia, and San Diego, the mayor is the chief administrator and the political head of the city. Of Texas's 25 largest cities, however, only Houston and Pasadena still have the strong mayor-council form of government. Many people see the strong mayor-council system as the best form for large cities because it allows strong leadership and is more likely than the council-manager form to be responsive to the full range of the community. In the early 20th century, however, the strong mayor-council form began to fall out of favor in many places, including Texas, because of its association with the corrupt political party machines that once dominated some cities. Now most of Texas's home-rule cities have chosen the council-manager form.

In Texas, cities operating with the strong mayor-council form have the following characteristics:

- A council traditionally elected from single-member districts, although many now have a mix of at-large and single-member district elections
- A mayor elected at large (by the whole city), with the power to appoint and remove department heads
- Budgetary power (preparation and execution of a plan for raising and spending city money) exercised by the mayor, subject to council approval before the budget may be implemented
- A mayor with the power to veto council actions

Houston's variation of the strong mayor-council form features a powerful mayor aided by a strong appointed chief of staff and an elected controller with budgetary powers (Figure 3.1). Most Houston mayors have delegated administrative details to the chief of staff, leaving the mayor free to focus on the larger picture. Duties of the chief of staff, however, vary widely depending on the mayor currently in office.

Weak Mayor-Council As the term **weak mayor-council form** implies, this model gives the mayor limited administrative powers. The mayor's position is weak because the office shares appointive and removal powers over municipal government personnel with the city council. Instead of being a chief executive, the mayor is merely one of several elected officials responsible to the electorate. In elections, voters choose members of the city council, some department heads,

strong mayor-council form
A type of municipal government with a separately elected legislative body (council) and an executive head (mayor) elected in a citywide election with veto, appointment, and removal powers.

weak mayor-council form
A type of municipal government with a separately elected mayor and council, but the mayor shares appointive and removal powers with the council, which can override the mayor's veto.

Figure 3.1 Strong Mayor-Council Form of Municipal Government: City of Houston

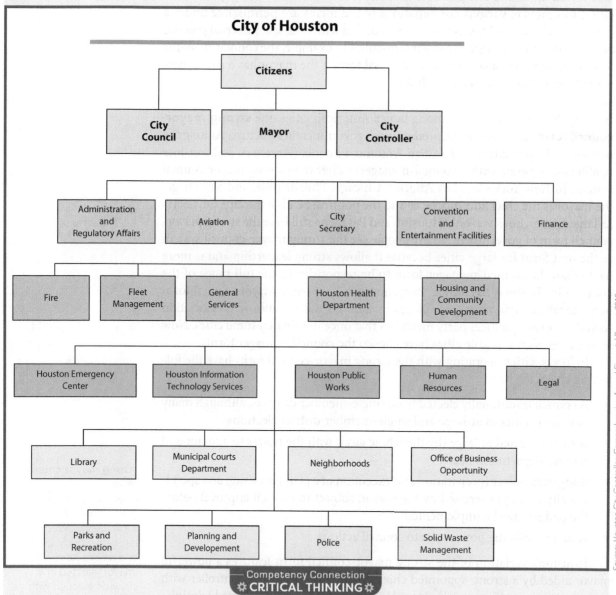

Source: Houston City Controller, Comprehensive Annual Financial Report 2019, http://www.houstontx.gov/controller/cafr.html.

Competency Connection
☼ CRITICAL THINKING ☼

What are the differences between strong mayor-council and weak mayor-council forms of government?

and other municipal officials. The city council has the power to override the mayor's veto.

The current trend is away from the weak mayor-council form. None of the largest cities in Texas has this form, though some small general-law and home-rule cities in Texas and other parts of the country use it. For example, Conroe, a city with a population of more than 91,000 in Montgomery County (north of Houston), describes itself on its website as having a mayor-council form of government. The mayor's powers are limited, and the city administrator manages city departments on a day-to-day basis. The mayor, however, maintains enough status and power to serve as a political leader.

Council-Manager When the cities of Amarillo and Terrell adopted the **council-manager form** in 1913, a new era in Texas municipal administration began. Today, most of Texas's almost 350 home-rule cities follow the council-manager form (sometimes termed the commission-manager form).

Figure 3.2 illustrates how this form is used in San Antonio. The council-manager form has the following characteristics:

- A mayor, elected at large, who is the presiding member of the council but who generally has few formal administrative powers
- City council or commission members elected at large or in single-member districts to make general policy for the city
- A city manager who is appointed by the council (and can be removed by the council) and who is responsible for carrying out council decisions and managing the city's departments

Under the council-manager form, the mayor and city council make decisions after debate on policy issues, such as taxation, budgeting, annexation, and services. The city manager's actual role varies considerably; however, most city managers exert strong influence. City councils generally rely on their managers for the preparation of annual budgets and policy recommendations. After a policy is made, the city manager's office directs an appropriate department to implement it. Typically, city councils hire professional managers, who usually possess graduate degrees in public administration and earn competitive salaries. In 2019, city manager annual salaries for Texas's five largest council-manager cities were $341,000 (El Paso) to $575,000 (San Antonio). The highest salary in Texas was $880,000 (Laredo).

Obviously, a delicate relationship exists between appointed managers and elected council members. In theory, the council-manager system has a weak mayor and attempts to separate policymaking from administration. Councils and mayors are not supposed to "micromanage" departments. However, in practice, elected leaders sometimes experience difficulties in determining where to draw the line between administrative oversight and meddling in departmental affairs.

A common weakness of the council-manager form of government is the lack of a leader to whom citizens can bring demands and concerns. The mayor is weak; the city council is composed of a number of members (anywhere from 4 to 16 individuals, with an average of 8, among the 25 largest cities in Texas); and the city manager is supposed to "stay out of politics." Thus, council-manager cities tend to respond more to elite and **middle-class** concerns than to those of the **working class** and ethnic minorities. (The business elite and the middle class have more organizations and leaders who have access to city government and know how to work the system.) Few council-manager cities have mayors who regularly provide strong political and policy leadership. One of these exceptions is San Antonio, where mayors, due to tradition and personality, generally are strong leaders. The council-manager form seems to work well in cities where

council-manager form
A system of municipal government in which an elected city council hires a manager to coordinate budgetary matters and supervise administrative departments.

middle class
Social scientists identify the middle class as those people with white-collar occupations (such as professionals and small business owners).

working class
Social scientists identify the working class as those people with blue-collar (manual) occupations.

Figure 3.2   Council-Manager Form of Government: City of San Antonio (2018)

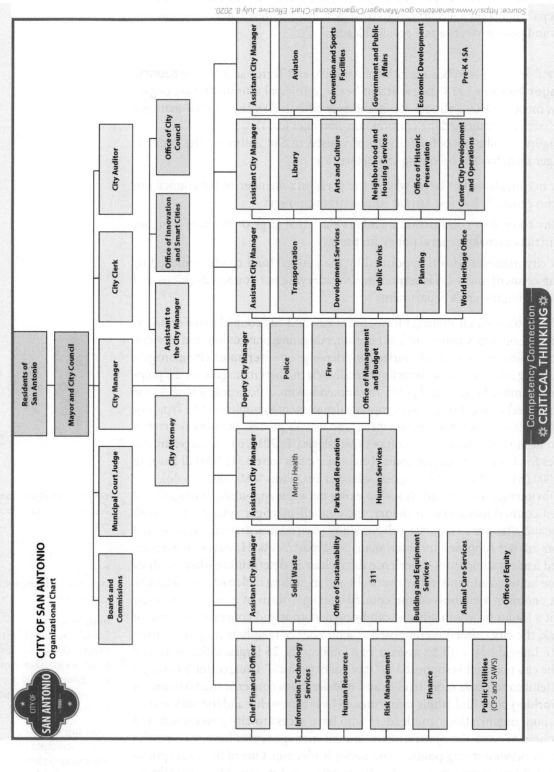

Source: https://www.sanantonio.gov/Manager/Organizational-Chart. Effective July 8, 2020.

— Competency Connection —
✿ CRITICAL THINKING ✿

What advantages does the city manager have in this form of government over the mayor? What concerns should citizens have about this form of government and why?

most people are of the same ethnic group and social class and thus share many common goals. Few central cities fit this description, but many suburbs do.[12]

Commission Today, none of Texas's cities operates under a pure **commission form** of municipal government. First approved by the Texas legislature for Galveston after a hurricane demolished the city in 1900, this form lacks a single executive, relying instead on elected commissioners that form a policymaking board.

In the pure commission form known as the Galveston Plan, each department (for example, public safety, finance, public works, welfare, or legal) is the responsibility of a single commissioner. Most students of municipal government criticize this form's dispersed administrative structure and lack of a chief executive. No home-rule city in Texas uses the commission form, and general-law cities are prohibited from using the Galveston Plan. Therefore, the few Texas municipalities that have a variation of the commission form operate more like the mayor-council form and designate a city secretary or another official to coordinate departmental work.

✪ Municipal Politics

LO 3.3 Identify the rules and social issues that shape local government outcomes.

Election rules and socioeconomic forces make a difference in who wins and what policies are more likely to be adopted. This section examines several election rules that affect local politics and then looks at social and economic factors that affect the nature of local politics in Texas.

Rules Make a Difference

Under Texas law, home-rule cities have the option to allow partisan elections in which a candidate's political party affiliation is included on the ballot.[13] Nonetheless, all city and special district elections in Texas are **nonpartisan elections**. That is, candidates are listed on the ballot without party labels in order to reduce the role of political parties in local politics. This rule has been effective in most local Texas governments, where political parties play little to no role. However, they often play some role in the metropolitan areas, particularly around Houston and Dallas.

While the parties do not officially run candidates in city elections, local party activists may recruit candidates, argue issues, and raise money and campaign workers. State level leaders may endorse candidates or become candidates themselves. Long-time democratic state representative Sylvester Turner was elected mayor of Houston in 2015 and re-elected in 2019, while democratic state senator Leticia Van de Putte lost in her 2015 race for San Antonio mayor. While serving as San Antonio mayors, Henry Cisneros and Julián Castro gained national prominence and became democratic leaders after leaving office.

Nonpartisan elections have at least two negative consequences. First, without political parties to stir up excitement, voter turnout tends to be low compared with state and national elections. Voting in the United States and Texas tends to

commission form
A type of municipal government in which each elected commissioner is a member of the city's policymaking body and heads an administrative department (e.g., public safety with police and fire divisions).

nonpartisan election
An election in which candidates are not identified on the ballot by party label.

be racially polarized (that is, people are likely to vote for candidates of their own race or ethnicity).[14] Because those who do vote in low turnout elections are more likely to be White and middle class, the representation of ethnic minorities and the working class is reduced. San Antonio, for example, has a majority Latino population, but because of greater White voter turnout, only three of 14 mayors from 1970 to 2020 were Latino. Exceptions have been Mexican American candidates who appealed to both Whites and Latinos (Henry Cisneros, Edward Garza, and Julián Castro). In 2014, Ivy Taylor became the city's first Black mayor by appointment and then was elected with a coalition of Blacks and conservative Whites. She was defeated in 2017 by Ron Nirenberg (of Eastern European Jewish and Asian background), who ran as the more progressive candidate.

A second problem of nonpartisan elections is that they tend to be more personal and less issue-oriented. Being well known is an advantage in almost any campaign, but without a party for a guide, voters focus even more on personalities, not issues. In smaller communities, local elections are often decided by who has more friends and neighbors.

The two most common ways of organizing municipal elections are the **at-large election**, in which council members are elected on a citywide basis, and the **single-member district election**, in which voters cast a ballot only for a candidate who resides within their district. Texas municipalities long used at-large elections. However, this system was challenged because it tends to overrepresent the majority White middle class population and underrepresent ethnic minorities. In at-large elections, the city's majority voting bloc tends to be the majority in each electoral contest, which works to the disadvantage of ethnic minorities. Dividing a city into single-member districts tends to create some districts with a majority of historically excluded ethnic minorities, thereby increasing the chance of electing a Latino, Black, or Asian American candidate to the city council. District elections also help White working class representation.

Prompted by ethnic conflict, lawsuits, and sometimes generational change, Texas cities are moving away from reliance on at-large elections. By 2020, only three of Texas's 25 largest cities used only at-large elections for their council. The rest used only district election (13) or a combination of district and at-large election (9). Increased use of single-member districts has led to more ethnically and racially diverse city councils.[15] Low voter turnout by an ethnic group, however, can reduce the effect of single-member districts.

Throughout the country, representative bodies whose members are elected from districts (such as the state legislature, city councils, county commissioners court, and school boards) must **redistrict** (redraw their district boundary lines) after every 10-year census. If at-large or cumulative voting (described below) is used, redistricting is not necessary. After the 2010 census, Texas's city councils had to redraw districts to reflect shifts in population within cities and between districts. The process is being repeated as a result of the 2020 census.

In 1975, because of its long history of racial discrimination, all Texas governments were placed under a provision of the federal Voting Rights Act that required governments to receive preclearance from the U.S. attorney general or the Federal District Court for the District of Columbia for changes affecting voting. However, the U.S. Supreme Court in the case of *Shelby v. Holder* (2013) found Section 4 of the Voting Rights Act unconstitutional, making preclearance much less likely.

at-large election
Members of a policymaking body, such as a city council, are elected on a citywide basis rather than from single-member districts.

single-member district election
Voters in an area (commonly called a district, ward, or precinct) elect one representative to serve on a policymaking body (e.g., city council, county commissioners court, state House and Senate).

redistricting
Redrawing of boundaries after the federal decennial census to create districts with approximately equal population (e.g., legislative, congressional, commissioners court, and city council districts in Texas).

The city of Pasadena (a Houston suburb), which is two-thirds Latino, has long been dominated by its minority White population, which received the majority of city spending but felt threatened by increasing Latino council membership. Without the threat of federal preclearance, the city changed the council from eight district seats to six district and two at-large, which made continued Anglo dominance likely. In 2015, five Anglos and three Latinos were elected. In 2017, in a suit filed by Latino leaders, a Houston federal district judge threw out the at-large seats and ordered the 2017 elections to be held with eight district seats. Because of low turnout, Latinos continued to be a minority on the council but believed that the all-district system would reward get-out-the-vote efforts. The 2017 election and term-limiting of the former mayor led to a unanimous council decision to drop the city's appeal of the order, accept being under federal preclearance until 2023, and pay plaintiffs' court costs ($1.1 million).

In recent decades, the major controversy over redistricting at the local level has been the issue of the representation of Texas's major ethnic groups—particularly Latinos, who were the main source of the state's population growth in the 2010 census and since. Expansion of the Latino population in urban areas has increased the number of Latino opportunity districts. These districts are drawn to include a large enough population of Latinos to give a Latino candidate a good chance of winning.[16] Low Latino turnout, however, has limited the number of Latino council members actually elected. (For a discussion of minority opportunity districts, see Chapter 5, "Campaigns and Elections.")

As of 2018, to increase minority representation, 50 Texas local governments, including 34 school districts and 16 cities, used **cumulative voting**. In this election system, voters cast a number of votes equal to the positions available and may cast them for one or more candidates in any combination. For example, if eight candidates vie for four positions on the city council, a voter may cast two votes for Candidate A, two votes for Candidate B, and no votes for the other candidates. By the same token, a voter may cast all four votes for Candidate A. In the end, the candidates with the most votes are elected to fill the four positions.

Where racial minority voters are a numerical minority, cumulative voting increases the chances that they will have some representation. The largest government entity in the state to use cumulative voting is the Amarillo Independent School District, which adopted the system in 1999 in response to a federal Voting Rights Act lawsuit. The district was 30 percent minority but had no minority board members for two decades. With the adoption of cumulative voting, Black and Latino board members were elected. In 2020, the seven-member board included two Blacks (one of whom was president of the board) and one Latina.

Home-rule cities may also determine whether to institute **term limits** for their elected officials. Proponents of term limits argue that they make officials more responsive to the public and bring fresh ideas. Opponents say that inexperienced representatives have to rely on lobbyists and the bureaucracy for information and then have to leave about the time they know how things work.

Beginning in the 1990s, many Texas cities amended their charters to institute term limits for their mayor and city council members. By 2020, five of Texas's six largest cities had adopted term limits (most commonly to 8 years total service). Fort Worth was the one exception, with no limits. In 2019, Betsy Price won a fifth two-year term and became the longest serving mayor in Fort Worth history.

cumulative voting
When multiple seats are contested in an at-large election, voters cast one or more of the specified number of votes for one or more candidates in any combination. It is designed to increase representation of historically underrepresented ethnic minority groups.

term limit
A restriction on the number of terms officials can serve in a public office.

When officials are denied re-election, they frequently call for overturning term-limits. However, gaining support to eliminate established term limits is difficult. A more successful compromise has been to increase the number of terms or to lengthen the terms of office for elected officials. In 2008, San Antonio changed its limits from two to four terms, with two-year terms for its mayor and city council members. This move was expected to give time for Latino city council members to build the support necessary to run for mayor. Houston extended terms of office for all city officeholders to two terms of four-years each in 2015. Four-year as opposed to two-year terms can give officials a longer time perspective on public issues and allow them to devote more time to public business rather than spending every other year campaigning. By 2020, four of the six largest cities had four-year terms, and two had two-year terms.

Socioeconomic and Demographic Changes

It should be clear that election rules make a difference in who is elected. Historical, social, and economic factors make a difference as well. Texas's increasing levels of urbanization, education, and economic development have made the state more economically, culturally, and politically diverse (or more pluralist). Local politics reflect these changes. Many Texas city governments were long dominated by elite business organizations, such as the Dallas Citizens Council and the San Antonio Good Government League. But greater pluralism and changes in election rules have given a say to a wider range of Texans in determining how their local governments function.

Social and economic changes have a profound effect on local government. Growth in population size, increased amounts of citizen organization, and higher levels of personal income tend to increase demands on local government and produce higher public spending. The kind of economic growth also affects politics. The Houston-Galveston-Beaumont area (or upper Gulf Coast) is the one area of the state that had any significant amount of heavy industry. Large plants with concentrations of unskilled and semi-skilled workers increase the amount of union organization, which tends to give workers not just higher wages but more say in local government. While heavy industry has declined and unions have faced substantial state restriction, the traditions and mechanisms of working class participation have persisted in the upper Gulf Coast.

Economic development in other parts of the state makes working class organization more difficult. Plants tend to have fewer working class people and to be more dispersed. Services, such as finance and information, tend to have more middle class employees. Dallas's growth fits this pattern. It was long dominated by business elites supported by a substantial middle class. However, as many of the middle class moved to the suburbs and more working class people entered, Dallas's politics changed significantly.

Houston has long been Texas's most diverse local political system. It has a strong business community, many labor union members, a Black community with almost a century's experience in fighting for its views and interests, a growing and increasingly organized Latino community, an expanding Asian American community that is becoming more active, and an activist gay community. Black churches and White evangelical churches are divided on policy, but both push their members to vote. Multiethnic and cross-class coalitions have been the norm in Houston's mayoral races for decades; and nonbusiness interests have significant, if variable, access to city hall.

Dallas has long had serious Black–White racial tensions. Although these conflicts have not been eliminated, changes in election rules and demographics have increased the number of racial minorities on the city council. In 1995, Ron Kirk became the first Black in modern times elected mayor of one of Texas's largest cities. Since 1976, three women have served as mayor. In 2020, Dallas had a Black mayor and a city council composed of four Latinos, three Blacks, and seven Whites. There were four women and ten men.

▣ Point/Counterpoint

Should the State of Texas have more control over city government decisions?

The Issue The 2015 legislature considered more than 1,600 bills affecting the authority of cities. The three following legislatures continued to reduce local decision-making, generally by giving the state government authority in an area and thus preempting local decisions. Among the bills considered were attempts to bar sanctuary cities, ban red light cameras, limit cities' taxing and borrowing power, reduce cities' annexation authority, and prohibit local regulation of fracking, knives, tree removal, small honey operations, plastic bags, and straws. During the 2020 pandemic, the governor added restrictions on local responses. The Texas Municipal League called it a "philosophical attack on local control."

For	Against
1. For efficiency, regulations should be consistent throughout the state. A patchwork of regulations that vary across local governments is costly for businesses.	1. Different communities have different needs. Allowing local governments to address these differences is more appropriate than applying the same regulatory scheme statewide.
2. Some city ordinances, such as prohibitions against fracking, interfere with individuals' property rights because they effectively destroy the right to exploit one's property for financial gain.	2. Texas law already provides that if a government takes someone's property, the property owner must be compensated. However, use of one's own property to damage others' property should not be protected.
3. Texas is being "Californiazed" by local officials with unnecessary regulations.	3. When problems develop, local officials are more accessible to citizens than state officials. Limiting local control gives too much influence to powerful special interests.

Competency Connection
⊛ SOCIAL RESPONSIBILITY ⊛

It seems ironic that the conservative Republicans attacking local control once championed it, while liberal Democrats defending Texas's cities once preferred national action. The reality is that policy preferences (and the groups they benefit) generally trump philosophical preferences. In practice, leaders tend to prefer dominance by the level they control. Do you, as a citizen, support increasing the state's authority over local governments? Why?

Racial and ethnic discrimination and conflict are a part of Texas history and remain a problem today. Communities are working to resolve their issues, albeit in differing ways and to different degrees. One way has been to increase the number of minority Texans in leadership positions, a long and difficult process. Table 3.1 shows the first Black, Latino, and women mayors of major Texas cities in the modern era. Note that their election did not begin until the 1970s and continued through 2014. In smaller cities, the election of "firsts" continues, and all three groups are still underrepresented. In 2020, among the mayors in the 25 largest Texas cities, 18 were White, 3 Latino, 3 Black, and 1 Other. Three were women and 22 were men.

Table 3.1. First Mayors in Texas By Ethnicity and Sex

(Elected unless appointment indicated*)

City	Year	Latino/a	Black	Woman
Waco	1974		Oscar DuConge#	
Dallas	1976			Adlene Harrison (appointed)
San Antonio	1981	Henry Cisneros (first since 1842)		
Houston	1981			Kathy Whitmire
Austin	1983	John Treviño, Jr.** (appointed)		
Waco	1986			LaNelle McNamara#
Dallas	1987			Annette Strauss (first elected)
Fort Worth	1991			Kay Granger
Dallas	1995		Ron Kirk	
Houston	1997		Lee Brown	
Laredo	1998	Betty Flores (first Latina)		Betty Flores (first woman)
Austin	2001	Gus Garcia		
Waco	2004		Mae Jackson (first Black woman)	Mae Jackson
Houston	2009			Annise Parker (second woman; one of first openly gay mayors of a major U.S. city)
San Antonio***	2014		Ivy Taylor (first Black, 2014 appointed, 2015 elected)	Ivy Taylor (first Black woman)

*All appointments were by vote of the city council.

#Waco did not have direct popular election of the mayor during 1948–1988.

**First Mexican American council member in Austin (1975–1988).

***Ron Nirenberg, elected mayor of San Antonio in 2017, is of Eastern European Jewish and Asian ancestry.

Source: Compiled by author.

— Competency Connection —
☼ CRITICAL THINKING ☼

Does the ethnicity or gender of leaders make a difference? In what ways? Why?

Since at least 2004, Texas has had the largest number of Latino elected officials in the nation (over 40 percent of the total). In 2019, Non-Whites were 20 percent of elected Texas officials (Latinos 15 percent and Blacks 4 percent). Women were 34 percent. There were only 8 Asian Americans. Most Texas ethnic minorities and women are elected at the local level: more in municipalities, followed in order by school boards, law enforcement/judicial offices, and counties.[17]

Beginning in the 1960s and 1970s, South Texas's majority Latino population elected Latino (and some non-Latino) leaders at all levels. In the rest of the state, central cities and some near-in suburbs tend to have a majority of Latinos, Blacks, and Asian Americans, which gives these groups more electoral clout. Suburbs farther from the center tend to be predominantly White and often heavily middle class, which produces more middle-class White leaders. In Texas, as throughout the United States, an increasing number of ethnic and racial minority populations are moving to the suburbs. For example, in Fort Bent County, southeast of Houston, Latinos, Blacks, and Asian Americans are each over 20 percent of the population. Clearly, the face of local government has changed as a result of increased use of single-member districts; greater pluralism; and the growing number, organization, and political activity of minority Texans.

The changes just described have had two consequences that a casual observer might not notice: the increased number, range, and role of interest groups and lobbyists in local government and an increase in civil society. Interest groups and their lobbyists don't just work at the state and national level. Cities, counties, and special districts tax, spend, and make policy decisions that cost or benefit businesses and groups. Not surprisingly, those affected want to influence (and benefit from) decisions.

Businesses and their associations are the most powerful interest groups at both the state and local level, while organized labor is relatively weak in Texas. However, police and fire unions have considerable bargaining power with their local governments and often play an important role in election campaigns and lawsuits. Both police and fire unions have had considerable success in collective bargaining, particularly in the area of pensions. Police unions have been outspoken in defense of their members accused in police shootings and the handling of protests. They have been politically adept in opposing efforts to provide more oversight of police. In recent years, city leaders of San Antonio and Houston have succeeded in somewhat reducing pension costs but have been much less successful in increasing police oversight. See the Chapter 7 on "The Politics of Interest Groups" for more information.

Civil society refers to organizations, groups, and networks outside of government, such as universities, churches, Little League, veterans groups, and clubs such as Rotary and Lions. They better our lives independent of government but also provide us with information and tools for influencing government and the private sector. Texas is not as rich in civil society as some states, but it has grown substantially over time and provides Texans more access and influence in local government. Sports fans may have noted the increase in the number of softball and soccer fields provided by local governments, community associations, and private individuals. Natural disasters such as fires and hurricanes bring out a

civil society
Organizations, groups, and networks outside of government that better lives independently of government but also provide tools for influencing government and the private sector.

strong community response and substantial interaction between governments on the one hand and groups (both formal and informal) on the other.

Municipal Services

Most citizens and city officials believe city government's major job is to provide basic services that affect people's day-to-day lives: police and fire protection, streets, water, sewer and sanitation, and perhaps parks and recreation. These basic services tend to be cities' largest expenditures, though the amounts spent vary from city to city. Austin tends to spend the most per capita, with other major Texas cities spending considerably less. Police and fire protection is consistently over 50 percent of general expenditure, with other expenditures varying considerably from one city to another. San Antonio, for example, spends a higher proportion of its budget on housing and community development, while Austin spends a higher proportion on health and human services. Over the last 30 years, parks and recreation have seen a marked drop in funding as other demands have taken precedence.[18]

Police-ethnic minority conflict and suspicion have a long history in Texas. The deaths of Michael Brown in Ferguson, Missouri, in 2014 and of Sandra Bland in Texas in 2015 produced demonstrations and calls for police reform. The death of George Floyd in Minneapolis in 2020 followed by police-involved shootings in Texas and elsewhere renewed protest. All of Texas's major cities and many smaller cities have seen protests and renewed demands for reform, which would have to be implemented by cities and counties. Mayors, police chiefs, sheriffs, and some prosecutors had to take the lead (or work to avoid the spotlight). Suggested reforms included removing the few "bad apples" among police, additional training on defusing situations, changing police culture, and making police more accountable (through civilian review, easing restrictions on firing for cause, and making it easier to prosecute police bad behavior).

In 2020, the Black Lives Matter movement began to call for "defunding the police" in response to a spate of deaths of Blacks at the hands of police caught on video. What most advocates meant was to move some of the duties and funding of police to alternative public safety programs and social service providers who are better suited to deal with problems such as mental illness. In Austin, there were months of criticism of the city's police over the killing of an unarmed Black and Hispanic man, use of force against anti-police-brutality protestors, and questions about the investigation of a demonstrator's killing by another citizen. The city council eventually cut the police budget $150 million, about one-third, and shifted the funds to other safety related services. Governor Abbott and Attorney General Paxton immediately condemned the decision and threatened state action. Limits on cuts were passed by the 2021 legislature.

Beyond traditional basic services, Texas cities also wrestle with demands for convention centers and sports facilities, airports, economic development, historic preservation, arts and culture, child and elder care, low income housing, regulation or help for the homeless, and response to gentrification (both for and against). Recently, cities have faced demands for police reform and removal of confederate statues. These competing demands for municipal action often require elected officials to make difficult decisions. When cities were short of funds because of the Great Recession, low oil prices, or the 2020-2021 pandemic, the traditional services tended to be cut less than newer services.

Municipalities also regulate important aspects of Texans' lives, notably construction, food service, sanitation, and zoning (regulating the use of land by separating residential and commercial areas). Houston is often cited as the only large American city without zoning. However, it uses a variety of measures such as the city enforcing deed restrictions, density and lot size regulation, and rules on communities near airports (which under federal law is much of Houston). The result is that Houston looks much like other sprawling Texas cities that have zoning.[19]

Regulation became a major issue during the 2020 covid-19 pandemic, with cities and counties having to make decisions concerning closure and reopening of businesses, mask wearing, public gatherings, and access to facilities (such as convention centers, parks, and beaches). In March, the mayor of Austin issued a local state of disaster declaration, which led to cancellation of the annual SXSW festival (South by Southwest Music, Film, and Interactive Festival), and in July Houston's mayor took actions that cancelled the Republican State Convention scheduled to meet in person in the city. After much recrimination and a court suit, the convention was held virtually.

Local response to the pandemic became more complex and conflictual when Governor Abbott preempted local response authority but vacillated on what local officials could actually do. On March 22, the Governor invited local officials to respond to local conditions by implementing stricter standards where needed. Some mayors and county judges issued orders mandating wearing masks in public. In late April, the Governor forbade local officials from penalizing failure to wear a mask. When illness increased, the Governor accepted the approach taken by Bexar County Judge Nelson Wolf. Cities and counties could require businesses to require customers to wear masks. The Governor later issued a statewide order requiring people not in essential business or service to stay at home, with enforcement by fine or jail. Another order covering much of the state mandated mask wearing. However, when Dallas officials ordered a hairdresser (a non-essential business) to close, she refused and was fined. When she refused to follow a court order, she was jailed, which produced great publicity. The Governor retroactively dropped the penalties.

During the pandemic, local officials, particularly mayors and county judges, had to coordinate or facilitate testing, hospital space, efforts to assist those laid off because of business closings, and informing the public. Along the Gulf Coast, local officials were simultaneously grappling with how to prevent future flooding such as that created by Hurricane Harvey—issues such as buying out homes in frequently flooded areas, dealing with builders who wanted to build in floodplains, improving drainage, and concerns about reservoirs and dams.

A concern for many Texas local governments, especially cities, is increased liability for employee pensions and other retirement benefits. Firefighters, police, and other municipal employees can participate in defined-benefits pension plans. While they are working, employees contribute a portion of their salaries to the pension plan. Each year, the city funds an amount equal to a percentage of the department's payroll to the plan. When an individual city worker retires or becomes disabled, the retirement plan is obligated to make monthly payments for the remainder of the former employee's life regardless of the city's financial condition.

The conflict over pensions in Houston since 2015 illustrates many aspects of the municipal policy process when there are strong disagreements—the role of elections in highlighting issues, the role of politically skilled city leaders, the strength of interest groups, the use of referenda, the interplay with the state level, the regular threat and use of court suits, and the long timeline. In the 2015 Houston mayoral election, dire predictions regarding the city's economic future because of its pension obligations were a major campaign issue. The city contributed more than $350 million to its three pension funds in 2015, almost twice its spending for libraries, trash pickup, and parks combined. The city reported a $3.2 billion gap between pension assets and future liabilities, an amount equal to more than its entire city budget. The concern is that as more city revenue is dedicated to funding pensions, less will be available to provide city services.

This problem is not unique to Houston. There are at least 99 major pension funds in the state. Scarce financial resources available to local governments, pressures from employees and citizens, growing health costs, longer life expectancies, and frequent over-optimism have created similar problems across the country. When Moody's listed the 15 cities with the largest unfunded pension gaps, four Texas cities made the list: Dallas second, Houston fourth, Austin ninth, and San Antonio twelfth.

To resolve the issue in Houston, Mayor Turner negotiated a plan requiring city employees to contribute more to their pension funds and accept benefit cuts in exchange for an infusion of money to maintain the pension funds. The city had to persuade the 2017 legislature to pass a bill authorizing the deal and then win approval of a $1 billion bond by city voters later that year. Firefighters, who had opposed the compromise, filed suit and supported a successful 2018 charter amendment to grant firefighters pay parity with police. In 2019, the state court of appeals declared the proposition unconstitutional, giving the city the advantage, but conflict continued.

Municipal Government Revenue

Most city governments in Texas and the nation face a serious financial dilemma: they barely have enough money to provide basic services; thus, they must reject or shortchange new services. Cities' two largest tax sources—sales and property taxes—are limited by state law. These taxes produce inadequate increases in revenue as the population grows. Moreover, Texas voters are increasingly hostile to higher property taxes. Adding to the problem are low levels of state assistance to Texas cities as compared to those of many other states. As a result, Texas cities are relying more heavily on fees (such as liquor licenses, franchise fees for cable television companies, and water rates) and are going into debt. Per capita local government debt in Texas was the fourth highest in the nation in 2020. (Texas state government, by comparison, was seventh lowest.)[20]

Although Texas has diversified its economy, the revenue of Texas governments at all levels has long been tied to the ups and downs of the oil and gas industry. Between 2008 and 2014, local governments in Texas benefited from a flourishing oil and gas market. Property and sales tax receipts grew in areas with oil and gas drilling or refining. But since 2014, the fluctuation in the price of crude oil has been substantial,[21] which has made municipal revenue often low and planning difficult. The fluctuations also reduce state assistance. The covid-19 pandemic added to the difficulties.

With less revenue, municipalities try to reduce costs. Conservatives argue for privatization, that is, hiring private companies to provide services such as issuing building permits and cleaning. Liberals point out the serious problems in state efforts to privatize prisons, Medicaid, and Child Protective Services. Research indicates that the profit motive works well "if the task is clear-cut and it's possible to define concrete goals and reward those who meet them."[22] But if the objectives are complex and diffuse, as is often the case in public services, it is difficult to align profit and public goals. Thus, privatization has a mixed record, sometimes saving local governments money and sometimes reducing the quality of service.

Taxes The state of Texas permits municipalities to levy taxes based on the value of property (**property tax**). The tax rate is generally expressed in terms of the amount of tax per $100 of the property's value. This rate varies greatly from one city to another. In 2019, rates varied from 7 cents per $100 valuation to $1.57, with an average of 54 cents. A problem with property taxes is that poorer cities with low

Image 3.2 Denton residents object to the state law that denies cities the right to ban fracking.

Tribune Content Agency LLC/Alamy Stock Photo

─ Competency Connection ─
★ PERSONAL RESPONSIBILITY ★

Should you protest? What would you protest? And how can you make your protest more effective?

property tax
A tax that property owners pay according to the value of real estate and other tangible property. At the local level, property owners pay this tax to the city, the county, the school district, and often other special districts.

property values must charge a high rate to provide minimum services. In Dallas County, for example, in 2019, Highland Park (near downtown Dallas) had an annual median family income of $207,000 and set a property tax rate of 23 cents per $100 in valuation. Glenn Heights (south of Dallas) had an annual median family income of $65,000 and set its tax rate at 83 cents per $100 in valuation. The result was that the more affluent city received $1,640 per capita in revenue, while the less affluent city received $336 per capita.[23] This inequity affects all local governments and has been the basis of lawsuits over school funding.

In an attempt to slow the growth of property taxes, the 2019 legislature mandated that if a city or county's tax rate will increase revenue by 3.5 percent or more, there must be a citizen vote to approve. The previous "rollback" limit was 8 percent, which remains in effect for community colleges and hospital districts. The rule for school districts is different and will be explained in the section on Public School Districts.

The other major source of city tax revenue is an optional 1.25 to 2 percent sales tax that is collected along with the state sales tax. Local governments are in competition for sales tax dollars. The sum of city, county, and special district government sales taxes cannot exceed 2 percent. For example, a city might assess 1 percent; the county, 0.5 percent; and a special district, 0.5 percent. In order to prevent going over the cap of 2 percent, state law sets up the order in which sales taxes are required to be collected: first the city, second the county, and third special districts. Further, voters must approve the imposition of a local sales tax within their jurisdiction. An additional problem is that sales tax revenues fluctuate with the local economy, making it difficult to plan how much money will be available. For example, from August 2019 to August 2020, oil-dependent Odessa suffered a 17 percent decline in sales tax revenue, while McKinney (in the Dallas suburbs) saw a 14 percent increase. The hotel occupancy tax is another significant source of revenue for cities with tourism; professional sports teams; major sports events, such as the NFL Super Bowl or Grand Prix racing; or international festivals like South by Southwest Music, Film, and Interactive Festival (SXSW).

Fees Lacking adequate tax revenues to meet demands, Texas municipalities have come to rely more heavily on fees (charges for services and payments required by regulations). Cities levy fees for such things as beer and liquor licenses and building permits. They collect traffic fines and may charge franchise fees based on gross receipts of public utilities (for example, telephone and cable television companies). A 2019 law reduced the ability of cities to charge telecom companies for the use of city rights-of-way, one of several acts by the 2019 legislature reducing city revenues. Texas municipalities are authorized to own and operate water, electric, and gas utility systems that may generate a profit for the city. (Seventy-two cities and towns own an electric utility.) Charges also are levied for such services as sewage treatment, garbage collection, hospital care, and use of city recreation facilities. These user fees may allow a city to provide some services with little or no subsidy.

Bonds and Certificates of Obligation Taxes and fees normally produce enough revenue to allow Texas cities to cover day-to-day operating expenses. Money for capital improvements (such as construction of city buildings or parks) and emergencies (such as flood or hurricane damage) often must be borrowed. This money is obtained through the sale of municipal **bonds**, which may be redeemed over periods of 1 to 30 years. The Texas Constitution allows cities to issue bonds, but any bond issue to be repaid from taxes (called a general obligation bond) must be approved by the voters. In 2019, there were 71 municipal bond elections in Texas, with voters approving 58. Amounts ranged from $800,000 to $413 million (the latter, El Paso for police and safety facilities).

There are several other types of indebtedness. Revenue bonds do not require voter approval because they are not secured by taxes but rather by the revenue they generate. Round Rock and Sugar Land, for example, use revenue bonds for sewer and water projects and pay them off using income from the utilities. During the recent recession, local governments made more use of certificates of obligation, which do not require voter approval and typically are used for smaller amounts and short-term financing. Some local governments now issue capital appreciation bonds that require no repayment for years. However, they have higher interest rates.

Property Taxes and Tax Exemptions Property owners pay taxes on the value of their homes, businesses, and land to the city as well as to the county, the school district, and often other special districts. When property values or tax rates go up, the total tax bill goes up as well. The Lone Star State has one of the highest property tax rates in the nation (seventh among the 50 states in 2018).[24] To offset the burden of higher taxes resulting from reappraisals of property values, local governments (including cities) may grant homeowners up to a 20 percent homestead exemption on the assessed value of their homes. Cities may also provide an additional homestead exemption for disabled veterans and their surviving spouses, for homeowners 65 years of age or older, or for other reasons, such as adding pollution controls.

Cities, counties, and community college districts may also freeze property taxes for senior citizens and the disabled. Property tax caps (or ceilings) can be implemented by city council action or by voter approval. The dilemma is that cities can help their disadvantaged citizens, but doing so costs the city revenue. In 2015, exemptions cost Texas cities an estimated $44 billion in revenue. As baby boomers reach retirement age, exemptions and property tax caps will reduce revenue even further. Local governments are also losing revenue from challenges to the appraised value of property by both businesses and individuals, often represented by firms specializing in such challenges.

The Bottom Line Because of pressure against increasing property tax rates, municipal governments sometimes refrain from increased spending, cut services or programs, or find new revenue sources. Typically, city councils are forced to opt for one or more of the following actions:

- Create new fees or raise fees on services such as garbage collection and water
- Impose hiring and wage freezes for municipal employees
- Cut services, particularly newer, non-traditional services and those that serve politically weaker citizens
- Contract with private firms for service delivery
- Improve productivity, especially by investing in technology

bond
A mechanism by which governments borrow money.

tax increment reinvestment zone (TIRZ)
Also called a Tax Increment Finance District (TIF). An area in which municipal tax incentives are offered to encourage businesses to locate in and contribute to the development of a blighted urban area. Commercial and residential property taxes may be frozen.

✓ 3.3 Learning Check

1. What are two methods to increase the number of elected officials who are members of historical racial or ethnic minority groups?

2. What are the two largest tax sources that provide revenue to local governments? Do these taxes usually provide enough revenue for local governments to meet the demands placed on them?

Answers at the end of this chapter.

Generating Revenue for Economic Development

Inner cities face the challenge of rundown housing, abandoned buildings, poorly maintained infrastructure (such as streets), and shortages of grocery stores. This neglect blights neighborhoods and may contribute to social problems. Texas cities have the local option of a half-cent sales tax for infrastructure upgrades, such as repaving streets and improving sewage disposal. The increased sales tax, however, must stay within the 2 percent limit the state imposes on local governments.

Following a national trend, some Texas cities are trying to spur development by attracting businesses through tax incentives. The Texas legislature authorizes cities to create **tax increment reinvestment zones (TIRZs)**, often called tax increment finance (TIF) districts. A TIRZ uses tax breaks such as freezing taxes to attract private investment in blighted areas. Cities using TIRZs/TIFs include Houston, Dallas, Fort Worth, Austin, San Antonio, El Paso, Waco, Arlington, and Wichita Falls. Whether such plans work is controversial. Many observers argue that companies attracted by tax breaks often make minimal actual investments and leave as soon as they realize a profit from tax subsidies. Yet, because TIRZs sometimes work, many cities starved for resources are willing to take the gamble. In addition, attempts to develop or improve neighborhoods often disrupt established communities and eliminate or raise the cost of housing for residents, complaints made in all of Texas' larger cities in recent years.

🏢 How Do We Compare...

in Local Debt?

Local Debt per Capita

Most Populous U.S. States	Per Capita Debt	U.S. States Bordering Texas	Per Capita Debt
California	$8,274	Arkansas	$3,674
Florida	$4,506	Louisiana	$4,058
New York	$11,563	New Mexico	$4,559
Texas*	**$8,459**	Oklahoma	$2,970

*Texas state government per capita debt: $1,818,

Source: USGovernmentSpending.Com, "Government Spending Details for 2020," https://www.usgovernmentspending.com/year_spending_2020TXdn_22ds2n#usgs302. Amounts are projections.

Competency Connection
◉ **SOCIAL RESPONSIBILITY** ◉

Should the state provide more funding to local governments to lower local debt?

✪ Counties

LO 3.4 Analyze the structure and responsibilities of counties.

Texas **counties** present an interesting set of contradictions. These local entities are technically an arm of the state, created to serve its needs, but both county officials and county residents see them as locally controlled governments and resent what many view as state interference. Counties collect taxes on both urban and rural property but focus more on the needs of rural residents and people living in unincorporated suburbs, who do not have city governments to provide services. This 19th-century form of government serves 21st-century Texans.

Texas is divided into 254 counties, the most of any state in the nation. There would be another county in the Panhandle if the U.S. Supreme Court had not awarded Greer County to Oklahoma in 1896. The basic form of Texas counties is set by the state constitution, though their activities are heavily shaped by whether they are in rural or metropolitan areas. As an agent of the state, each county issues state automobile licenses, enforces state laws, registers voters, conducts elections, collects some state taxes, and helps administer the law. In conjunction with state and federal governments, counties conduct health and welfare programs, maintain records of vital statistics (such as births and deaths), issue various licenses, collect fees, and provide a host of other public services. Yet state supervision of county operations is minimal. Rural counties generally try to keep taxes low and provide minimal services. They are reluctant to take on new responsibilities, such as regulating septic systems and residential development. In metropolitan areas, however, counties have been forced by citizen demands—and sometimes by the state—to take on varied urban tasks, such as providing ballparks and recreation centers, hospitals, libraries, airports, and museums.

Politics in Texas's larger counties is changing. Outer suburbs and rural and small town areas in much of the state remain Republican, while Democrats are gaining in central cities and close-in suburbs. Following both the 2018 and 2020 elections, Democrats held a majority on the commissioners court in four of the state's five largest counties. (Republicans held a 3-2 advantage in Tarrant County [Fort Worth] after both elections.) Since 2006, Dallas County has tended to be Democratic, with a major victory in 2018. In Harris County (Houston), both parties were competitive (depending on turnout) in 2008–2016, but in 2018, Democrat Lina Hidalgo ousted longtime Republican county judge Ed Emmett, as Democrats won all seven countywide races. Seventeen Black women were elected as judges. At the same time, in Nueces County (Corpus Christi), a Latina, Barbara Canales, became the first woman and the first Democrat in a decade to win the county judge race, giving the Democrats a majority on the commissioners court.

Structure and Operation

As required by the state constitution, all Texas counties have the same basic governmental structure, despite wide demographic and economic differences between rural and urban counties. (Contrast Figure 3.3, Harris County, the most populous Texas county with more than 4.7 million residents in 2019, with Figure 3.4, Loving County, the least populous with 169 residents in that year.)

county
Texas is divided into 254 counties that serve as an administrative arm of the state and provide important services at the local level, especially in rural areas.

Figure 3.3 Harris County Government (County Seat: Houston).

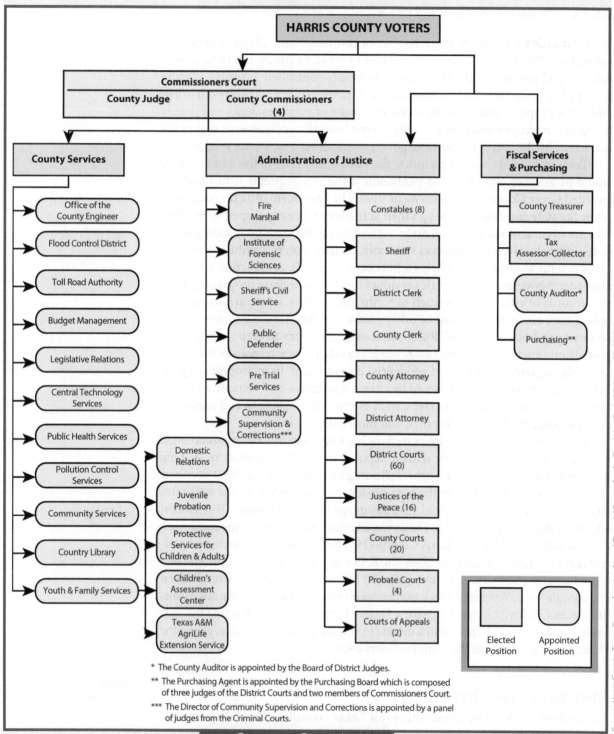

Source: Harris County, Texas, Comprehensive Annual Financial Report for the Fiscal Year Ended February 28, 2019, August 23, 2019, p. 8, https://www.harriscountytx.gov/Portals/49/Documents/Harris%20 County%20FY2019.pdf?ver=2020-02-10-153417-900.

Do most citizens know the role of their county commissioners court? Why is it important for more citizens to understand its role?

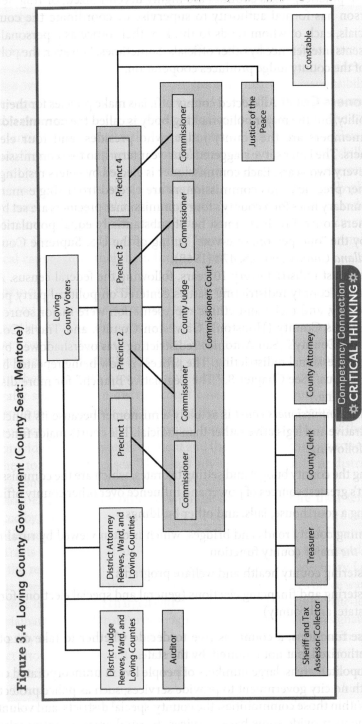

Figure 3.4 Loving County Government (County Seat: Mentone)

Source: Compiled by authors from multiple sources.

— Competency Connection —
✿ **CRITICAL THINKING** ✿

How does a county's population size change the job of the county commissioners court? Compare Figure 3.3 (Harris County) to Figure 3.4 (Loving County).

Judges The number of officials in the county justice system varies greatly with the size of the county. The judicial role of the constitutional county judge also varies. In counties with a small population, the county judge may exercise important judicial functions, such as handling probate matters, small civil cases, and serious misdemeanors. In counties with a large population, constitutional county judges are so involved in their political, administrative, and legislative roles that they have little time for judicial functions. Instead, **statutory county courts** have often been established with lawyers for judges and more formal procedures. The kinds of cases they decide (such as civil, criminal, probate, or family law) vary greatly and are set by the statute creating the particular court.

Bail reform has been an issue in Texas for several years, particularly in the large counties. The problem is that a defendant can pay to be released prior to trial if they have enough money for bail but if not must stay in jail till trial. In 2017, a federal appeals court sped up the bail process but did not resolve the issue. The 2018 elections saw the defeat of the mostly Republican statutory county judges who had presided over misdemeanor cases in Harris County and who had fought the change. The new Democratic judges changed the policy and allowed most misdemeanor defendants to avoid posting cash bail. The decision and a federal report finding the change did not lead to reoffending animated the movement for change in the other large counties.[26]

Each county has from one to eight justice of the peace precincts. The number is decided by the commissioners court, which may also abolish courts (often to save money), as happened in Brazos and McLennan Counties in 2014 and Bexar County in 2016. **Justices of the peace** (commonly called JPs) handle minor civil and criminal cases, including small claims court cases. JPs hear a large volume of legal actions, with traffic cases representing a substantial part of their work. In some counties, they also serve as coroner (to determine cause of death in certain cases) and as a magistrate (to set bail for arrested persons). Similar to the constitutional county judge, they do not have to be lawyers but are required to take some legal training.

County Sheriff and Constables

The **county sheriff**, as the county's chief law enforcement officer, appoints deputies and oversees the county jail and its prisoners. In practice, the sheriff's office works with city police but commonly focuses on crime in unincorporated areas and leaves law enforcement in cities primarily to the municipal police. In a county with a population of fewer than 10,000, the sheriff may also serve as tax assessor-collector. In a few rural counties, the sheriff may be the county's most influential leader.

Constables assist the justice court by serving subpoenas and other court documents and maintaining order in JP courts as the court's bailiff. They and their deputies are peace officers who commonly play a law enforcement role in rural areas and unincorporated communities. A county's commissioners court may abolish the office, and there are calls for moving constables into the generally better trained and disciplined sheriff's departments.

statutory county court
Court created by the legislature at the request of a county; may have civil or criminal jurisdiction or both, depending on the legislation creating it.

justice of the peace
A judge elected from a justice of the peace precinct who handles minor civil and criminal cases, including small claims court.

county sheriff
A citizen popularly elected as the county's chief law enforcement officer; the sheriff is also responsible for maintaining the county jail.

constable
An official elected to assist the justice of the peace by serving papers and in some cases carrying out security and investigative responsibilities.

County Clerk, District Clerk, and County Tax Assessor-Collector

A **county clerk** keeps records and handles various paperwork chores for both the county court and the commissioners court. In addition, the county clerk files legal documents (such as deeds, mortgages, and contracts) in the county's public records and maintains the county's vital statistics (birth, death, and marriage records). The county clerk may also administer elections, but counties with larger populations often have an elections administrator. The **district clerk** maintains records for the district courts.

One of the responsibilities of Texas's county clerks is to issue marriage licenses. In 2015, the U.S. Supreme Court ruled in *Obergefell v. Hodges* that same-sex marriage was legal in all 50 states. State Attorney General Ken Paxton said after the Court's decision that county clerks with religious convictions against gay marriage did not have to issue the license themselves but could have an employee who was not opposed issue the license. Eventually, tiny Irion County was the only county in the nation refusing to issue marriage licenses to same-sex couples. The noncompliant county clerk was elected county judge in 2018. In a related action in 2020, the State Commission on Judicial Conduct issued a Waco Justice of the Peace a public warning over her refusal to perform same-sex ceremonies because of religious objections. Since performing marriages is optional rather than required for JPs, the commission's opinion suggested she could officiate all marriages or no marriages, but not selectively choose one type.

A county office that has seen its role decline over time is the **county tax assessor-collector**. The title is partially a misnomer. Since 1982, the countywide **tax appraisal district** has assessed (determined) property values in each county. The tax assessor-collector still collects county taxes and fees and certain state fees, including the license tag fees for motor vehicles and fees for handicapped parking permits. The office commonly handles voter registration, although some counties have an elections administrator.

Treasurer and Auditor

The **county treasurer** receives and pays out all county funds authorized by the commissioners court. Some counties have eliminated the position, but this requires a constitutional amendment approved by a statewide vote. If the office is eliminated, the county commissioners assign treasurer duties to another county office. When voters allowed Tarrant and Bexar Counties to eliminate the office, these counties authorized the county auditor to deal with responsibilities that were once held by the county treasurer. A county of 10,000 or more people must have a **county auditor**, appointed by the county's district court judges. The auditing function involves checking the account books and records of officials who handle county funds. Some observers worry that allowing the county auditor to be both auditor and treasurer eliminates necessary checks and balances.

County Finance

Although urban counties spend substantial amounts, they generally provide fewer services and thus spend less than the cities within them. Overall, Texas counties spend less and have less debt than municipalities or school districts. In

county clerk
An official elected to perform clerical chores for the county courts and commissioners court, keep public records, maintain vital statistics, and administer public elections, if the county does not have an administrator of elections.

district clerk
A citizen elected to maintain records for the district courts.

county tax assessor-collector
This elected official no longer assesses property for taxation but does collect taxes and fees and commonly handles voter registration.

tax appraisal district
The district appraises all real estate and commercial property for taxation by units of local government within a county.

county treasurer
An elected official who receives and pays out county money as directed by the commissioners court.

county auditor
A person appointed by the district judge or judges to check the financial books and records of other officials who handle county money.

significant part, this is because the county's power to tax and, to a lesser extent, to spend is limited by the state constitution and laws. Citizens and county leaders also tend to see the county's role as limited. Like cities, counties faced increased financial problems because of the Great Recession, the fluctuating price of oil, and the pandemic. Nevertheless, increasing demands for services impose an ever-expanding need for money on both urban and rural counties.

Taxation The Texas Constitution authorizes county governments to collect taxes on property, and that is usually their most important revenue source. Although occupations may also be taxed, no county implements that provision. Each year the commissioners court sets the county tax rate, which is subject to a rollback election if it will produce more than a 3.5 percent increase in revenue. Counties may also add 0.5 to 1.5 cents onto the state sales tax, which is 6.25 cents on the dollar. (Remember, however, that the add-on by all local governments may not exceed 2 cents on the dollar.) Just under half of Texas counties (primarily those with relatively small populations) impose a sales tax, and most set the rate at 0.5 cents.

Revenues from Nontax Sources Counties receive small amounts of money from various sources that add up to an important part of their total revenue. All counties may impose fees on the sale of liquor, and they share in state revenue from liquor sales, various motor vehicle taxes and fees, and traffic fines. Like other local governments, counties are eligible for federal grants-in-aid; but over the long term, this source continues to shrink. With voter approval, a county may borrow money through sale of bonds to pay for capital projects, such as a new jail or sports stadium. The Texas Constitution limits county indebtedness to 35 percent of a county's total assessed property value.

Tax Incentives and Subsidies Like cities, a commissioners court may grant tax abatements (reductions or suspensions) on taxable property, reimbursements (return of taxes paid), or tax increment financing (TIF; the use of future gains in property value to finance current development projects) to attract or retain businesses. For instance, in 2003, Bexar County offered a $22 million tax abatement for a Toyota factory to be built to produce pickup trucks in San Antonio. The offer was part of a complex incentive package put together by state, county, city, and other officials that totaled an estimated $133 million in tax breaks and infrastructure spending. The plant went into operation in 2006, creating more than 2,000 high-paying jobs and contributing to economic development. As with the experience of cities, some projects work well, many do not.

The Bottom Line Despite various revenue sources, Texas counties, like other units of local government, are pressured to increase property taxes or to balance their budgets by eliminating or reducing programs and services. Although administrative costs and demands for expanded public services continue to increase, sources of county revenue are not expanding as quickly as demand.

Expenditures The state restricts county expenditures in certain areas and mandates spending in others, yet patterns of spending vary considerably from county to county. The greatest variation is between rural and metropolitan counties. Hospitals and health care, public safety, and roads (in that order) are the largest expenditures for Texas counties. This expenditure pattern holds for Texas's largest counties, which also spend smaller, but still significant, amounts on urban amenities (such as parks) and social services (such as housing and welfare). Rural counties tend to spend a large portion of their budget on public safety and roads but little on social services and urban amenities. On what services money is spent makes a difference. A study of local government spending in Texas published in the *Southern Medical Journal* found that spending in four categories "were associated with significant improvements in health outcomes: fire and ambulance, community health care and public health, housing and community development, and libraries."[27] These services are provided by municipalities, counties, and special districts.

Although the county judge, auditor, or budget officer prepares the budget, the commissioners court is responsible for final adoption of an annual spending plan. Preparation of the budget generally enhances the commissioners court's power within county government. Counties do not have complete control over their spending because state and federal rules mandate some county services and regulatory activities. Examples include social services, legal assistance and medical care for poor people, and mental health programs. Over the last decade, almost all counties have passed resolutions calling for a state constitutional amendment to ban unfunded mandates, but through 2021, none has had any success in the legislature.

County jails must follow regulations imposed by the state legislature and the Texas Commission on Jail Standards. In 2015, the legislature required at least two face-to-face visitation periods per week for each county inmate. Fiscal notes to the proposed bill warned that some counties might incur significant costs. Travis County was exempt from the requirement because it spent a significant amount of money on a video system for inmate visits. Two of the facilities, however, used a Skype-like video-based system furnished by a private contractor, who made money from those who used the system. For that reason, the state Commission indicated it might disapprove Travis County's exemption. To avoid controversy, Travis County reinstated face-to-face visits. Additional software, personnel, and physical space were required to accommodate in-person visits.[28] Thus, these additional expenditures constituted an unfunded mandate.

County Government Reform

Texas counties have various problems: rigid structure and duties fixed in the state constitution and statutes, inefficiency related to too many elected officials and the lack of merit systems (hiring and promoting based on competence rather than who they know), and too little money. Counties with larger populations may establish merit employment systems, and half of those eligible have done so. One often-suggested reform is county home rule to give counties more ability to organize and operate in accordance with local needs and wishes. Research suggests that although county home rule better meets community demands, it also tends to expand county spending.

Different states allow varying degrees of county home rule. Texas is among the states that are most strongly opposed.[29] Until 1969, Texas actually had a home-rule provision for counties in the constitution, but it was too difficult to implement. Reviving a workable version today would be hard to achieve. Many (probably most) county officials prefer the present system, as do many constituents, particularly in those counties outside metropolitan areas.

Border Counties

The population of counties near the lower Rio Grande has grown markedly because of immigration and trade. Unfortunately, population growth has outstripped economic growth, and the traditionally impoverished region now has even more poor people. Many of the poor live in **colonias** (depressed housing settlements, often without running water or sewage systems).[30] Current estimates identify about 2,300 colonias in Texas, where as many as 500,000 Texans live in substandard conditions. Hidalgo County has more colonias than any county in Texas or elsewhere in the United States.

Image 3.3 Colonias lack infrastructure or utilities.

Lisa Wiltse/Corbis/Getty Images

Competency Connection
✿ **CRITICAL THINKING** ✿

How should county governments along the border improve the conditions of colonias? Why?

colonia
A low-income community, typically located in South Texas and especially in counties bordering Mexico, that lacks running water, sewer lines, and other essential services.

Minimal efforts have been made by the state and local governments to deal with problems of the colonias. Activists and self-help have played an important role in the small victories achieved. Security and public safety are a major concern for residents. For example, Hidalgo County's colonia residents petitioned for streetlights for several decades. Nearly 85 percent of neighborhoods lacked streetlights. In 2007, legislation gave the county authority to install streetlights, but it did not set up a process for collecting fees. In 2015, House Bill 3002, passed without Governor Abbott's signature, allowed Hidalgo County to collect fees to pay for streetlights in colonias. In 2016, streetlights were installed in eight of Hidalgo County's 900 colonias, increasing safety and evening activity. By 2019, the number had only grown to 26.

Another major issue for colonias is drainage. Extreme storms have devastated areas in the Rio Grande Valley, particularly in colonias where drainage is lacking and there is nowhere for water to go. Colonias have to wait for counties to bring in pumps after a flood, which takes time. Activists put together a design for a drainage system specific to the needs of colonias. Spanish Palms, located in Hidalgo County, used the system and connected it to the county's drainage ditch, which allowed water to empty out of the colonia. Activists urged other colonia residents to build drainage systems designed for their communities, but funding has lagged. The 2017 legislature cut several programs that benefit the colonias, and Governor Abbott vetoed another. The 2019 legislature proposed and voters approved a constitutional amendment that provides funds for water and wastewater infrastructure in areas such as the colonias.

Border Security In recent years, the flow of undocumented immigrants, combined with the continuing violence by drug gangs on the Mexican side of the border, has created great controversy. The national government has responsibility for border security, but Texas has supplemented the federal effort, spending over $2.4 billion from 2008 to 2019. By 2020, Texas had over 1,000 Department of Public Safety (DPS) personnel and 1,100 national guard troops on the border. Sheriffs and police departments have received federal and state money to increase their own capabilities.

Surveys show that a majority of border residents distrust the Border Patrol, and many complain of intimidation by DPS officers from outside the region and the "military occupation." Some welcome the spending they bring. Although violence in Mexico occasionally spills over the Rio Grande, the Texas side remains relatively safe. In spite of great growth in population (usually accompanied by higher crime rates), border cities have lower crime rates than the state's largest cities and cities of similar size to those on the border. Only higher income suburban cities tend to be safer. Anecdotal evidence suggests, however, that safety in some rural areas has declined.[31]

The national government's decision to build a physical wall along major portions of the border has created problems. Walls divide communities, separate families, and cause environmental dislocation. Experts tend to believe that other measures would be more effective in impeding border crossing. Since the 2016 presidential campaign, completion of the border wall has been a major issue.

Surveys consistently indicate that the majority of border residents, both in Texas and the rest of the border, oppose completing the wall. Texans as a whole are split evenly, dividing strongly along party lines (Republicans supporting, Democrats opposing).[32]

✚ Special Districts

LO 3.5 Explain the functions of special districts and their importance to the greater community.

Among local governments, the least known and least understood are special districts, yet they represent the fastest-growing form of government. They fall into two categories: school districts and noneducation special districts. Created by an act of the legislature or, in some cases, by local ordinance (for example, establishing a public housing authority), a **special district** usually has one function and serves a specific group of people in a particular geographic area. Districts can cover more than one county and commonly overlap other local governments, such as municipalities and other special districts.

Public School Districts

Citizen concerns about education cause local school systems to occupy center stage among special district governments. There are about 1,100 Texas **independent school districts (ISDs)**, created by the legislature and governed by popularly elected, nonsalaried boards of trustees. The school board selects the superintendent, who by law and practice makes most major decisions about the district's educational programs and who tends to influence other decisions as well. It is the superintendent who is responsible for leading the school district. Major functions of the superintendent include preparing a budget for approval by the board, day-to-day operations, and acting as chief communicator with legislators, media, and parents. Board members, generally local businesspeople and professionals, tend to focus on money issues, such as taxes, budgets, and salaries.

School board elections in Texas are nonpartisan (officially and usually in practice) and generally have low voter turnout. In smaller districts, they tend to be friends-and-neighbors affairs, but in larger districts, campaigns often are more organized and intense. When school elections become heated, it is generally because of sharp divisions within the community over volatile cultural issues, such as sex education or prayer in schools, racial and ethnic conflict, athletic programs (especially football), or differences over taxing and spending.

Texas has long had a highly centralized educational system in which the Texas Education Agency (TEA) places significant limitations on local district decisions. In 1995, the legislature gave school boards increased autonomy but left the TEA with substantial direct and indirect power over local decisions. National influence has been far more limited and targeted than that of the state.

special district
A unit of local government that performs a particular service, such as providing schools, hospitals, or housing, for a particular geographic area.

independent school district (ISD)
Created by the legislature, an independent school district raises tax revenue to support its public schools. Voters within the district elect a board that hires a superintendent, determines salary schedules, selects textbooks, and sets the district's property tax rate.

📋 Students in Action

Changing School District Policies

Students commonly think of government policy as something imposed on them, not as something they can change. But some San Antonio students found that they can change policy. Ruby Polanco, a senior at San Antonio ISD's Young Women's Leadership Academy noticed that the district's nondiscrimination statement did not include sexual orientation and gender identity. She soon found that while "not straight" identities were not a problem at the academy, coworkers at her afterschool job and friends from nearby Lanier High School saw a different experience. Her research found that a majority of LGBTQ+ students experienced discrimination.

Derek Davis/Portland Portland Press Herald/Getty Images

A key to Polanco's success is that she understood and followed established protocol. She started with a teacher and worked her way up to the district superintendent, the school board president, the area's state senator, and then the school board. "I talked to literally anyone I could get my hands on." She also started an online petition and enlisted the support of other students. The leader of Equality Texas, which for years had lobbied the district unsuccessfully, said that "The fact that [this time] it was a student-led initiative speaks volumes."

The district board unanimously agreed to add sexual orientation, gender identity, and gender expression to its nondiscrimination policies and applied the protections to both students and teachers. Polanco is not sure how much the nondiscrimination policy will change student culture, but she hopes that those affected will feel the support of the district and those who came together to change the policy.

Source: Bekah McNeel, "How One Student Brought LGBTQIA Protections to SAISD," *San Antonio Report*, August 24, 2017, https://sanantonioreport.org/how-one-student-brought-lgbtqia-protections-to-saisd/.

Competency Connection
◉ SOCIAL RESPONSIBILITY ◉

Is there a public policy in your community you would like to see changed?
How would you go about changing it?

Federal involvement has focused on improving the situation of groups historically neglected or discriminated against in Texas education. Districts must comply with federal regulations in areas such as racial and gender nondiscrimination and treatment of students with disabilities.

Money is also a source of influence. In academic year 2018–2019, school districts raised an average of 51 percent of their revenue locally; the state contributed 37 percent; and the federal government added 12 percent.[33] Federal aid has particularly targeted the children of the poor and language minorities. Thus, school districts make local educational policy in the context of substantial limits, mandates, and influences from the state and federal governments.

The covid-19 pandemic of 2020 highlighted the difficulties of decision-making in a system of local management under substantial state control. On March 4, Texas's first confirmed case of the virus was reported. On March 11, two school districts, acting on their own, were the first to close. On March 19, Governor Abbott issued an executive order temporarily closing all schools, an order that was extended over time to the end of the academic year. Schools scrambled to provide remote learning, relying primarily on the Internet, an effort that most agree produced a significant decline in learning. Most teachers and their schools were not experienced in remote teaching, many students lacked computers or home Internet, and most parents didn't know how to help. A significant number of students were "lost," not becoming a part of remote learning.

Between March and August, local districts were frustrated by changing and confusing decisions by the governor and the TEA over when the new school year could begin, what kind of instruction could be used, and who could make decisions. Most school districts eventually offered parents variations on remote and in-person learning, and many began the school year with a delayed start and/or a transition period of on-line learning to be followed, hopefully, by in-class instruction. Some observers saw this episode as local decision-makers muddling forward knowing that state leaders would be reluctant to enforce their decisions and would have to bow to the reality of varying local conditions.

The shared control of public education has been highlighted in recent years by conflicts over state and federal requirements for accountability testing of students. Districts have been forced to spend more time and money on preparing students for standardized tests. Supporters say that testing has improved student performance and made local schools more accountable. Critics charge that although students are now better at taking tests, they learn less in other areas.

A second challenge for local education is the increasing ethnic and economic diversity of Texas's schoolchildren. For two decades, traditional minorities have been a majority in Texas schools, and for a decade, a majority of Texas students have come from economically disadvantaged families. Meeting their needs is important not only for the children but for the economic health of the entire state.

A third challenge facing Texas schools is finance, which actually has two faces: equity (that is, equal access to similar revenue per pupil) and amount (how much should be spent). In 1987, a state district court (later affirmed by the Texas Supreme Court) held that the state's system for school finance violated the Texas Constitution. The basic problem was that poor districts, relying on property taxes, had to tax at a high rate to provide minimum expenditures per pupil. Wealthier districts, on the other hand, could spend much more with significantly lower tax rates. After various attempts to resolve the problem, the issue continues today.

The other school finance issue is the conflict between the increased need for services and the slow growth of funding. Clearly, demands on the schools to do more (and therefore to spend more) have increased. Yet the two major sources of funding for school districts (state appropriations and the property tax) have expanded more slowly than demand. The proportion of education funding provided by the state has remained at 40 percent or below, and property tax revenue tends to grow slowly and to fluctuate. In the face of the Great Recession, the 2011 legislature (for the first time in 60 years) reduced the actual amount appropriated for schools. The results were more than 10,000 teacher and staff layoffs, larger classes, and cuts in programs. Although most of this funding was restored in 2013 and 2015, school enrollment had increased so that the available dollars per student was less.

The property tax is the only local source of tax revenue for Texas public schools. Unlike other local governments, school districts cannot use the sales tax for revenue. Not surprisingly, school districts receive more than 50 percent of property taxes collected in the state. As we saw with other local governments, state laws exempt part of a property's value from taxation for a number of groups. In 2019, school districts lost $14 billion to exemptions, 31 percent of what they could have collected.

In 2019, legislators increased school funding and sought to slow the growth of property taxes. They increased the state portion of school funding from 38 to 45 percent and added another $5.1 billion to lower property taxes. Previously, the state attempted to limit school property tax increases by requiring voter approval of increases over 4 percent. From 2009 to 2018, however, voters approved the increase in 82 percent of the 434 rollback elections. With new funding, it was hoped that school districts could lower tax rates. Beginning in 2021, the state would limit school property taxes. While the increased funding was widely welcomed, many worried whether the increases would be sustained over time. (The 2021 legislature did maintain funding levels.)

As discussed above, Texas schools are significantly more indebted than cities and counties. This is in largest part because of the cost of facilities that have to be paid for over time, but it is also because of the squeeze between demands and revenue. For more detailed discussions of education policy and finance, see Chapter 11, "Finance and Fiscal Policy" and Chapter 12, "Public Policy and Administration."

Junior or Community College Districts

Another example of a special district is the **junior college or community college district**, which offers two-year academic programs beyond high school, as well as various technical and vocational programs. The latter two may be part of the regular degree and certificate programs or special nondegree training programs to meet local worker and employer needs. Each district is governed by an elected board that has the power to set property tax rates within limits established by the state legislature, issue bonds (subject to voter approval), and adopt an annual budget.

There are 50 districts, and many have multiple campuses. For example, in 2020 Austin Community College (ACC) had 11 campuses. In addition to the community college districts, the Texas State Technical College System (TSTC) has ten campuses across the state, and the Texas State University System (TSUS) has three two-year colleges in southeast Texas. Unlike community colleges, neither the TSUS' two-year schools nor the TSTC campuses receive financial support from local property taxes. However, in 2019, the legislature appropriated

junior college or community college district
Establishes one or more two-year colleges that offer both academic and vocational programs.

funds that were used to lower tuition at the three TSUS colleges. Together, Texas's public two-year colleges enroll almost 760,000 students, which is 100,000 more than the state's public universities. (See Figure 3.5 for the locations of these districts.)

Community colleges, like state universities and technical colleges, are funded by state appropriations, student tuition and fees, and small amounts of federal aid and private donations. Where they differ from public universities is the support that community colleges receive from property taxes raised by the local district. Because of these funds, community colleges are able to charge lower tuition rates than four-year schools. However, as a result of the Great Recession, community college enrollment increased markedly, while

Figure 3.5 Texas Community, Technical, and State Colleges

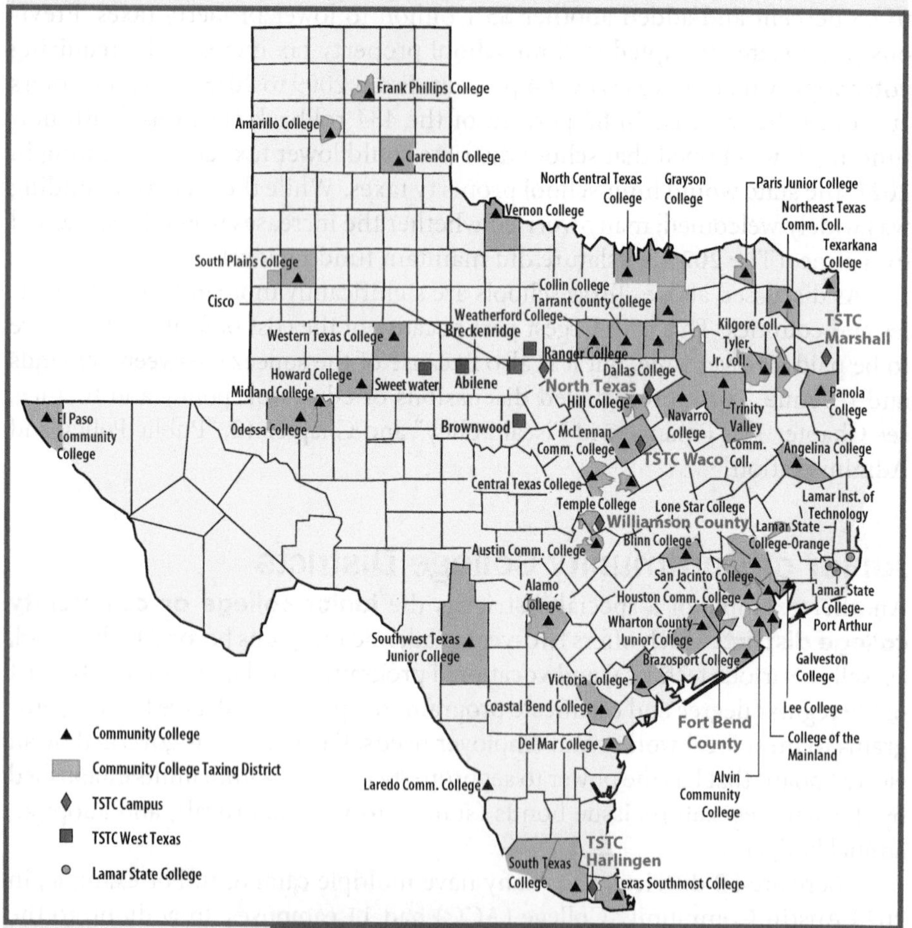

Community College
Community College Taxing District
TSTC Campus
TSTC West Texas
Lamar State College

Competency Connection
◉ SOCIAL RESPONSIBILITY ◉

How will tuition increases affect student access to and success in higher education?

revenues from local taxes and state appropriations slowed. In response, the two-year schools raised tuition, and some considered limiting enrollment. Tuition costs remain below that of universities. Community college enrollment reached a peak in 2011, followed by a small decline but had largely recovered by 2019.

Research has consistently shown that community colleges stimulate local economies and provide training vital to a region's economic development. They are also positively associated with improvements in health and reductions in crime, welfare costs, and unemployment.[34]

Noneducation Special Districts

Texas has almost 2,800 **noneducation special districts** handling a multitude of problems—water, sewage, parks, housing, irrigation, fire, and other emergency services to name a few. Among reasons that Texas has so many special districts, three stand out. First, many local needs—such as mass transit, hospitals, and flood protection—cut across the boundaries of cities and counties. Second, in other cases, restrictive state constitutional provisions or the unwillingness of local government leaders make it difficult for existing governments to take on new tasks. Hospital districts have been created for both reasons. The closing of many rural/small town hospitals throughout the state, the financial difficulties of most that remain, the large number of uninsured Texans needing healthcare, and the covid-19 pandemic have put pressure on hospital districts and made them more visible to officials and the public. In a few recent cases, their board elections have generated heated contests.

Third, in some cases, individuals create special districts to make money for themselves. For example, real estate entrepreneurs in metropolitan areas have often developed subdivisions in unincorporated areas through the creation of municipal utility districts (MUDs). The developer is reimbursed for street, water, and sewage system construction costs with bond proceeds. Homeowner property taxes are used to repay bondholders. Therefore, the developer is reimbursed for initial investment costs and homeowners ultimately repay these amounts through high property taxes. In 2019, Harris County (Houston) had 360 MUDs and Travis County (Austin) 63.

The late oilman T. Boone Pickens illustrates a common way in which special districts can be manipulated for private gain. In 2007, Pickens created a public water district on eight acres outside of Amarillo. He sold the land to five employees. Two of them, the couple who managed his ranch (and the only residents of the eight acres), voted approval of the district. Under Texas law, water could then be extracted and sold regardless of the impact on neighbors and the aquifer. The water district met serious political and legal challenges because it used a public entity for private gain, promoted the unpopular taking of land for rights-of-way, and involved extraction of large amounts of water from the troubled Ogallala Aquifer, which the Panhandle's agriculture and cities depend upon. Others, however, followed this model because it made them money.

noneducation special districts
Special districts, other than school districts or community college districts, such as fire prevention or municipal utility districts, that are units of local government and may cover part of a county, a whole county, or areas in two or more counties.

The structure and powers of special districts vary. Most are governed by a board, collect property taxes and fees, can issue bonds, and spend money to provide one or more services. Mass transit authorities, such as Houston's Metro or Dallas's DART, rely on a 1 percent sales tax. Depending on the board, members may be elected or appointed, or they may automatically sit on the board because of another position they hold. Most special districts are small and hardly noticed by the general public. Only a few receive continuing public attention.

Special districts will remain important because they provide many necessary services. Unfortunately, because they are invisible to most voters, they are the local government most subject to corruption and abuse of power.

✪ Metropolitan Areas

LO 3.6   Discuss the ways that local governments deal with metropolitan-wide and regional issues.

About 88 percent of Texans live in metropolitan areas, mostly central cities surrounded by growing suburbs. People living in a metropolitan area share many problems, such as traffic congestion, crime, pollution, and a need for health care. Yet having so many different governments makes effectively addressing problems affecting the whole area difficult. The situation is made worse by differences between central city residents and suburbanites. Most people who live in central cities need and use public facilities, such as bus and rail lines, parks, and public hospitals, whereas many suburban residents have less interest in public services, particularly public transportation. Class and ethnic differences also divide metropolitan communities, especially the central city from the suburbs.

One way to deal with area-wide problems is **metro government** (consolidation of local governments into one "umbrella" government for the entire metropolitan area). Examples include Miami–Dade County, Florida; Louisville–Jefferson County, Kentucky; and Nashville–Davidson County, Tennessee. By 2020, there were 44 consolidated governments of varying combinations around the country, including four in neighboring Louisiana (e.g., the Parish of Orleans and New Orleans). However, there is no significant movement for consolidation in Texas. In 2013 and 2015, bills to allow San Antonio and Bexar County governments to consolidate were introduced in the legislature but had no success.

Municipal Annexation

To assist cities grappling with suburban sprawl, the 1963 legislature gave Texas cities **extraterritorial jurisdiction (ETJ)**, or limited authority outside their city boundaries. ETJ was ended in 2019. But during its half century of life, it

metro government
Consolidation of units of local government within an urban area under a single authority.

extraterritorial jurisdiction (ETJ)
The limited authority a city has outside its boundaries. The larger the city's population size, the larger the reach of its ETJ.

profoundly affected Texas's metropolitan areas. Within its ETJ, a home-rule city could regulate aspects of development and make contiguous unincorporated areas part of the city (**annex**) without a vote by those who live there. (Incorporated areas could not be annexed without consent of their residents.) In fiscal year 2018, 51 cities annexed and one deannexed territory.

Texas's larger cities, particularly central cities, strongly supported ETJ. In most states, central cities are surrounded by incorporated suburbs and cannot expand. Because of ETJ, however, Texas's central cities are much larger in physical size than cities in other states. By capturing part of the revenue growth of Texas's expanding metropolitan areas, they were also financially healthier than those in many other states. Attitudes of people living in a city's ETJ varied. Communities with few urban services (such as police, fire, and sewer) were often happy to be annexed. However, established communities generally objected strenuously to being "gobbled up" without their permission. The result was a long, central, city-suburb conflict fought in the courts and legislature.

The 2017 and 2019 legislatures made unilateral annexation unlikely. In 2019, the legislature allowed annexation only under four circumstances: (1) on request of the landowner; (2) of an area with less than 200 people by petition; (3) of an area with over 200 residents by election; and (4) certain narrowly-defined situations (such as a city-owned airport or navigable stream). With the changes, annexation is likely only for communities wanting city services. The major cities worry about problems with regional planning and revenue. Opponents of annexation emphasize freedom, property rights, and maintaining their communities. Likely losers are suburban poor and ethnic minority communities.[35]

Councils of Governments

The one thriving, if somewhat minimal, approach to coordinating metropolitan efforts in Texas is provided by councils of government. Looking beyond city limits, county lines, and special district boundaries requires expertise from planners who think regionally. In the 1960s, the Texas legislature created the first of 24 regional planning bodies known as **councils of governments (COGs)** or, in some areas, planning/development commissions/councils (Figure 3.6).

COGs are voluntary associations of local governments. Staff employees do regional planning and provide services requested by member governments or directed by federal and state mandates. Their expertise is particularly useful in applying for and implementing state and federally funded programs. COGs also provide a forum where local government leaders can share information with each other and coordinate their efforts. The value of COGs is to provide a mechanism and resources for coordination and planning for those who want to work together.

annex
To make an outlying area part of a city. Now, this must be done by vote or petition of those to be annexed.

council of governments (COGs)
A voluntary association of local governments to assist in regional planning, development, and cooperation. Provides expert assistance on federal and state grants.

✔ **3.6 Learning Check**

1. What were the two primary ways that Texas dealt with problems in metropolitan areas?
2. Which groups want to be annexed? Which do not?

Answers at the end of this chapter.

Figure 3.6 Texas Councils of Governments

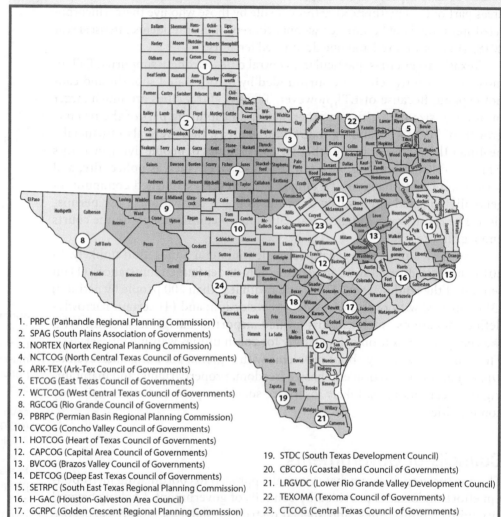

1. PRPC (Panhandle Regional Planning Commission)
2. SPAG (South Plains Association of Governments)
3. NORTEX (Nortex Regional Planning Commission)
4. NCTCOG (North Central Texas Council of Governments)
5. ARK-TEX (Ark-Tex Council of Governments)
6. ETCOG (East Texas Council of Governments)
7. WCTCOG (West Central Texas Council of Governments)
8. RGCOG (Rio Grande Council of Governments)
9. PBRPC (Permian Basin Regional Planning Commission)
10. CVCOG (Concho Valley Council of Governments)
11. HOTCOG (Heart of Texas Council of Governments)
12. CAPCOG (Capital Area Council of Governments)
13. BVCOG (Brazos Valley Council of Governments)
14. DETCOG (Deep East Texas Council of Governments)
15. SETRPC (South East Texas Regional Planning Commission)
16. H-GAC (Houston-Galveston Area Council)
17. GCRPC (Golden Crescent Regional Planning Commission)
18. AACOG (Alamo Area Council of Governments)
19. STDC (South Texas Development Council)
20. CBCOG (Coastal Bend Council of Governments)
21. LRGVDC (Lower Rio Grande Valley Development Council)
22. TEXOMA (Texoma Council of Governments)
23. CTCOG (Central Texas Council of Governments)
24. MRGDC (Middle Rio Grande Development Council)

Source: Reprinted by permission of the Texas Association of Regional Councils. http://www.txregionalcouncil.org.

— Competency Connection —
☼ **CRITICAL THINKING** ☼

Why does Texas have so many governments? Are COGs really necessary?

Conclusion

Local governments deliver a substantial number of government services directly to their residents. The success of these governments depends heavily on the actions and cooperation of other local governments and the two levels above them (state and national). What local governments do is largely shaped by three forces: formal rules (such as laws, the way governments are organized, and election rules), socioeconomic forces (such as economic power, social class, and ethnic/racial cooperation and conflict), and the efforts of individuals and groups. Texas has three kinds of local government (municipalities, counties, and special districts) with differences in structure and behavior both within each type and among types. Understanding the basic forces at work in local government helps those who want to make a difference apply the principles of government organization and citizen participation to the issues affecting their own community.

Chapter Summary

LO 3.1 Explain the relationships that exist between a local government and all other governments, including national, state, and other local governments. Local governments are part of the federal system and thus are affected by decisions made by state, national, and other local governments. Under Texas law and its constitution, local governments are largely limited to what is required or permitted by the state. Even with these limits, however, local governments traditionally make a wide range of important decisions. In recent years, state leaders have reduced local authority in many areas.

LO 3.2 Describe the forms of municipal government organization. Texas has two legal classifications of municipalities: general-law cities and home-rule cities. Large municipalities have home-rule charters that spell out the structures and powers of the individual city, whereas a smaller municipality is prescribed a charter by the legislature. Texas law allows four forms of municipal government: strong mayor-council, weak mayor-council, council-manager, and commission. The council-manager form is used by a majority of home-rule cities.

LO 3.3 Identify the rules and social issues that shape local government outcomes. Although local governments provide the most direct contact between residents and their government, voter apathy at this level remains a problem. This situation is unfortunate because local governments are important to most Texans' day-to-day lives. Election rules for local governments and the way they are organized make a difference in who is elected and who benefits from government.

Elections for cities and special districts are nonpartisan, and most are organized as either at-large or single-member districts. The increased use of single-member districts; greater pluralism; and the growing number, organization, and political activity of minority Texans are changing the face of local governments. Formal rules and socioeconomic change help shape the way government works, including who wins and who loses. City governments focus primarily on delivering basic services—police and fire protection, streets, water, sewer and sanitation, and often parks and recreation. They also regulate important aspects of our lives, such as construction and food service sanitation. The two major sources of revenue for cities are property taxes and the sales tax. Counties rely primarily on property taxes. Both cities and counties are having a difficult time as they face increasing demands for services from their citizens, the state, and the national government. As a result, local governments are utilizing fees and taking on debt because of limited revenue sources. Economic fluctuations, the covid-19 pandemic, protests, and natural disasters have provided challenges to all local governments.

LO 3.4 Analyze the structure and responsibilities of counties. County governments have fragmented organizational structures and powers restricted by the Texas Constitution. Counties must provide an array of services, conduct elections, and enforce state laws. Actual governmental activities vary greatly between metropolitan and rural counties. Various county officials are policymakers, but the major policymaker is the commissioners court, composed of the county judge (who generally leads) and four elected commissioners.

LO 3.5 Explain the functions of special districts and their importance to the greater community. The many special district governments provide public schools, community colleges, and a multitude of other services such as hospitals and mass transit. School districts are locally managed by an elected school board and an appointed superintendent but are heavily regulated by the state. Although noneducation special districts are important for the many services they provide, many voters are unaware of them. This lack of public attention allows some to be subject to fraud and manipulation.

LO 3.6 Discuss the ways that local governments deal with metropolitan-wide and regional issues. Dealing with metropolitan-wide problems is a difficult task. To do so, Texas relies heavily on councils of governments that are designed to increase cooperation. Annexation remains a controversial process and is now largely voluntary and much less likely to be used. Presently, metro government is unlikely to be adopted.

Key Terms

annex, p. 125
at-large election, p. 94
bond, p. 105
civil society, p. 99
colonia, p. 116
commission form, p. 93
commissioners court, p. 110
constable, p. 112
council of governments (COGs), p. 125
council-manager form, p. 91
county, p. 107
county attorney, p. 111
county auditor, p. 113
county clerk, p. 113
county judge, p. 111
county sheriff, p. 112
county tax assessor-collector, p. 113
county treasurer, p. 113
cumulative voting, p. 95

Dillon's Rule, p. 84
district attorney, p. 111
district clerk, p. 113
extraterritorial jurisdiction (ETJ), p. 124
general-law city, p. 87
grassroots, p. 84
home-rule city, p. 87
independent school district (ISD), p. 118
initiative, p. 88
intergovernmental relations, p. 86
junior college or community college district, p. 121
justice of the peace, p. 112
metro government, p. 124
middle class, p. 91
municipal (city) government, p. 86
noneducation special districts, p. 123

nonpartisan election, p. 93
ordinance, p. 87
property tax, p. 103
recall, p. 87
redistricting, p. 94
referendum, p. 88
single-member district election, p. 94
special district, p. 118
statutory county court, p. 112
strong mayor-council form, p. 89
tax appraisal district, p. 113
tax increment reinvestment zone (TIRZ), p. 106
term limit, p. 95
weak mayor-council form, p. 89
working class, p. 91

Learning Check Answers

 3.1
1. Local governments have the greatest flexibility under the Cooley Doctrine. Under Dillon's Rule, which is followed closely in Texas, local governments can do only those activities permitted by the state.

2. The relations among the three levels of government and among the various local governments are marked by both cooperation and conflict.

 3.2
1. The two legal classifications of cities in Texas are general-law and home-rule cities. A home-rule city has more flexibility because it establishes its own charter, which specifies its form and operation. A general-law city adopts a charter set in law by the Texas legislature.

2. The council-manager form of municipal government is most common in Texas's larger home-rule cities, although the strong mayor-council form is most common in the U.S.'s largest cities.

✓ **3.3**
1. Single-member districts and cumulative voting are most likely to increase the representation of minorities in government. Redistricting may help or hurt, depending on how lines are drawn.

2. Most revenue of local governments comes from property taxes and sales taxes, but these two sources are frequently inadequate to meet the demands.

✓ **3.4**
1. False. The structure of county governments is determined by the state constitution.

2. The major policymaking body in each Texas county is the commissioners court.

✓ **3.5**
1. The two categories of special districts in Texas are school districts and noneducation districts.

2. Many local needs cut across boundaries of cities and counties; and limitations in the state constitution and the unwillingness of some officials to act make it difficult to take on new tasks. Special districts can take on these responsibilities.

✓ **3.6**
1. The two primary ways Texas dealt with problems in metropolitan areas were through councils of government and annexation, which is now weakened.

2. Unincorporated communities lacking services, such as police and sewers, often want to be annexed. Established communities with existing services generally oppose annexation.

4 Political Parties

Learning Objectives

4.1 Evaluate the role of political parties in Texas.

4.2 Compare and contrast the different political ideologies found in the Lone Star State.

4.3 Identify electoral trends in Texas, including realignments, third parties, and independent candidates.

4.4 Trace the evolution of political parties in Texas.

4.5 Describe the political party system in Texas.

Image 4.1 Julián Castro, former Mayor of San Antonio and Secretary of Housing and Urban Development, campaigning for the Democratic Party.

Paul Steinhauser/Foster's Daily Democrat/AP Photo

Competency Connection
★ PERSONAL RESPONSIBILITY ★

Attachments to political parties have become stronger for Americans and Texans over the past decade. Is it better for democracy when we have strong attachments to political parties, or when we are independents and do not have attachments to parties?

For the past two decades, the Republican Party has dominated Texas elections and politics. No Democratic candidate has been elected to a statewide office since 1998. In addition, every Republican presidential nominee has carried the Lone Star State since 1980. Political commentators often refer to red states as those in which the Republican Party is dominant and blue states as those in which the Democratic Party prevails. Although Texas is a red state, Democrats believe that they had an opportunity to become competitive after enjoying success in the 2018 Blue Wave election. In that year they gained seats in the Texas legislature and the U.S. House of Representatives, while Beto O'ourke ran a close but unsuccessful campaign for a U.S. Senate seat. Texas Democrats were less successful in their 2020 campaigns, and Republicans remain in control of state government. This chapter examines the features of political parties in Texas, their evolution, recent electoral trends, voting coalitions, and changing demographics.

⬧ Role of Political Parties

LO 4.1 Evaluate the role of political parties in Texas.

Although neither the U.S. Constitution nor the Texas Constitution mentions political parties, these organizations are an integral part of the American governmental process. A **political party** can be defined as a combination of people and interests whose primary purpose is to gain control of government by winning elections. Whereas interest groups tend to focus on influencing governmental policies, political parties are chiefly concerned with the recruitment, nomination, and election of citizens to governmental office. (For a discussion of interest groups, see Chapter 7, The Politics of Interest Groups.)

In Texas, as throughout the United States, the Democratic and Republican parties are the two leading political organizations. When someone refers to themself as a Republican or a Democrat, they are referring to their **party identification**. This is a psychological identification that individuals have with a political party.[1] It is an important concept in understanding political preferences. Party identification can be thought of as a lens that affects how one views politics. For example, the Centers for Disease Control began recommending individuals wear face masks to reduce the risk of transmitting or being infected by COVID-19 (prior to the development of vaccines). Figure 4.1 presents an analysis of the percent of those wearing face masks by party identification (Texas Poll, June 2020), and there are stark differences between Democrats and Republicans. Seventy percent of Republicans indicated they wear face masks while 95 percent of Democrats wear faces masks—a 25-point difference.

State and county level elected officials are elected as Democrats or Republicans, and their party affiliations affect how they govern. Parties also have organizations that work to recruit and elect candidates for public office. This is why political scientists consider functioning political parties to be an essential component of democracy.

Follow *Practicing Texas Politics* on Twitter **@PracTexPol**

political party
An organization with the purpose of controlling government by recruiting, nominating, and electing candidates to public office. Those who share the same beliefs and values often identify with a specific political party.

party identification
A psychological identification individuals have with a political party. It is an important concept in understanding political preferences.

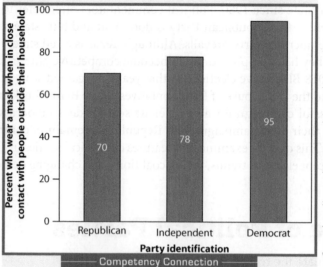

Figure 4.1 Percent Wearing Masks for COVID-19 by Party Identification, June 2020

Source: https://texaspolitics.utexas.edu/research-data-archive. Figure created by authors.

— Competency Connection —
⚖ PERSONAL RESPONSIBILITY ⚖

Are you surprised there was a partisan difference with how often people report wearing masks? Is it an individual right to decide, or do we have a personal responsibility to wear masks during a pandemic?

third party
A party other than the Democratic Party or the Republican Party. Sometimes called a "minor party" because of limited membership and voter support.

Duverger's Law
Plurality single member district systems favor a 2-party system, and proportional electoral (PR) systems favor multiparty systems.

In Texas, as throughout the United States, the Democratic and Republican parties are the two leading political parties. Americans commonly apply the term **third party** (or minor party) to any political party other than the Democratic or Republican Party. Why does the USA (and Texas) have a two-party system? Nations that have a multiparty system (more than two parties that win elections) typically have a proportional representation (PR) system. This system allocates legislative seats to parties based on percentage of the vote received by a party during the election. In a simplified system with a 100-seat legislature, a party that receives 12 percent of the vote in an election, for instance, wins 12 legislative seats. In the PR system, parties that receive a small percentage of the vote can still win seats. Texas uses the single member district (SMD) plurality system for legislative elections. In SMD plurality systems, candidates run to represent a legislative district, with the candidate receiving the most votes (a plurality) winning. Parties with candidates receiving a small percentage of the vote will not win any seats in a plurality system.

The influence that electoral systems have on the number of parties is understood with **Duverger's Law**. According to this rule, governments with SMD plurality systems (used extensively in the U.S.A) favor a 2-party system; but PR systems (common in Europe) favor multiparty systems.[2]

In addition, Texas election laws make it difficult for third parties to qualify for places on the ballot. In 2019 the Texas legislature passed House Bill (HB) 2504, which made changes for third party ballot access. Previously there was a threshold of 5 percent of the vote, by any of the party's statewide candidates, for the party to qualify automatically for the ballot. HB 2504 lowered the threshold to 2 percent, thus seemingly making it easier for third parties, such as the Green Party, to qualify. However, the law requires third parties that nominate candidates by conventions also to pay filing fees, or gather signatures. This requirement is $5000, or 5000 signatures, for statewide candidates. These are the same fees or number of signatures required by the Democratic and Republican party for their candidates. In 2020, several Green Party and Libertarian candidates almost did not appear on the general election ballot, after being challenged in court by the Democratic and Republican parties, because they did not pay filing fees or gather the required signatures to appear on the ballot. Eventually, they qualified to appear on the ballot after prevailing in lawsuits that reached the Texas Supreme Court.[3]

✪ Political Ideology

LO 4.2 Compare and contrast the different political ideologies found in the Lone Star State.

Political ideology can be defined as a collection of beliefs about the appropriate order of society and how to achieve it.[4] Ideology, traditions, and culture influence the issues on which political parties align. Demands and expectations change over time, and this leads to political parties evolving to reflect new expectations and issues. Political parties cannot remain static and survive, nor can politicians win elections unless they are in step with the opinions of a large percentage of voters. Although individuals do not need to have an ideological orientation, ideology is an important concept in politics; and it helps with understanding the issues on which political parties align. In fact, political science research has found that, at most, 20 percent of Americans pay attention to ideological themes.[5]

From the 1930s to the early 2000s, the terms *liberal* and *conservative* have meant more to many Texas voters than have the actual names of political parties. This is because Texas was dominated by a Democratic party with liberal and conservative factions. Terms liberal and conservative are difficult to define because each label has varying shades of meaning for different people. Whereas the Republican Party tends to be dominated by right-wing social conservatives, the Democratic Party is influenced (but not dominated) by left-wing liberals. Origins of the terms *left* and *right* to refer to political affiliation can be traced back to the time of the French Revolution (1789–1799), when monarchists sat to the right side of the president in the French National Assembly and supporters of a republic sat to his left side. Ideology, in contemporary American politics, is largely defined by the preferred role of government.

✓ **4.1 Learning Check**

1. True or False: Political parties are specifically mentioned in the U.S. Constitution.
2. Is there a difference in the percentages of Republicans and Democrats who report they wear masks when in close contact with people outside of their households?

Answers at the end of this chapter.

political ideology
A collection of beliefs about the appropriate order of society and how to achieve it.

Conservatism

Conservatism today has a belief in a minimal role of government in regulating the economy and business. In addition, conservatism is typically associated with an emphasis on traditional social values. While conservatives generally advocate a minimal role for government on economic matters, they tend to favor a more active role for government on social issues (but not on civil rights). Conservatives have often opposed actions to promote civil rights for racial/ethnic groups and sexual orientation. **Conservatives**, therefore, are generally opposed to government-managed or government-subsidized programs, such as assistance to low-income families with dependent children, unemployment insurance, the Affordable Care Act ("Obamacare"), environmental regulations, and civil rights legislation. Conservatives are also opposed to laws regulating firearms. Nevertheless, conservatives support a more active role for government with regard to restriction of reproductive rights for women (such as birth control included in health insurance plans) and opposition to marriage equality.[6]

There are different subsets of conservatives—fiscal conservatives and social conservatives. Today's fiscal conservatives give the highest priority to reduced taxing and government spending, and minimizing government regulations of business. For example, fiscal conservatives oppose raising the minimum wage. Social conservatives (such as those associated with the Christian right) stress the importance of traditional family roles, along with opposition to abortion and homosexuality. They support school vouchers that would provide government-funded assistance to parents who choose to send their children to private schools, especially church-affiliated schools.[7] Teaching of creationism and intelligent design in public schools is also favored by social conservatives.[8]

The 2019 legislative session illustrates concerns of conservative factions. Social conservatives expressed frustration that they were unable to pass their high priority legislation such as Senate Bill 17. This bill would have allowed state-licensed professionals (doctors, counselors, child care providers) to refuse to provide services on the basis of their deeply held religious beliefs. The concern was that this could lead to anti LGBTQ+ (lesbian, gay, bisexual, transgender, questioning, and allied) discrimination. The bill passed the Texas Senate with support from social conservatives, including Lieutenant Governor Dan Patrick. Nevertheless, it did not pass in the Texas House, where fiscal conservative Republicans expressed concern that the social conservative agenda was a reason they lost 12 seats in the 2018 midterm election. Thus, they wanted to avoid social conservative controversial issues in 2019.[9]

Liberalism

Liberals favor an active role for government regulation in economic areas. They claim that government is obligated to aid unemployed people and to alleviate poverty (especially for the benefit of children), and favor laws to raise the minimum wage. In addition, liberals favor government action to protect the environment, regulate firearms, and to guarantee equal rights for racial/ethnic minorities, women, and LGBTQ+. Liberalism seeks a limited role for

conservative
A person who advocates minimal intervention by government in economic matters and who gives a high priority to reducing taxes and curbing public spending, while supporting a more active role for government in traditional social issues.

liberal
A person who advocates government support in social and economic matters and who favors political reforms that extend democracy, achieve a more equitable distribution of wealth, and protect individual freedoms and rights. Liberals tend to favor less government regulation in the private lives of individuals.

government involvement with regard to other social issues, especially those related to morality or religion. Liberals are more likely to oppose prayer in public schools, government subsidies for religious institutions, and church involvement in secular politics. Many Texas Democrats have a **neoliberal** ideology. This position incorporates a philosophy of less government regulation of business and the economy while adopting a more liberal view of greater government involvement in social programs.[10]

Beyond Liberal and Conservative: Thinking about Ideology

Is a binary liberal/conservative dimension for political ideology reflective of Texas politics? What about individuals who are economically liberal (favor raising the minimum wage) and socially conservative (oppose marriage equality), or those who are economic conservatives (oppose raising the minimum wage) and social liberals (favor marriage equality)? In addition, there are people who prefer to identify as moderate or middle of the road, meaning they take a position between conservative and liberal. The liberal/conservative dimension may also ignore the experiences of different groups. For example, research on Latinos indicate that many are economically liberal and socially conservative.[11] Similarly, analyses of Black Democrats find they identify as moderate.[12] This suggests that the traditional view of political ideology may not be reflective of political reality. While ideology is an essential concept for understanding politics, it is important to remember that it is not necessary for individuals to fit neatly into conservative or liberal categories.

Libertarianism is the ideology for those who believe in a minimal role for government in economic matters and social issues. A libertarian would oppose a government-mandated minimum wage as an intrusion in economic matters. Likewise, libertarians oppose laws making marijuana possession illegal, because they believe such restrictions are unnecessary intrusions into private lives. Furthermore, libertarians also profess to be strong advocates of civil liberties, and thus would be expected to be skeptical of law enforcement powers that violate individual rights.

In 2009, some conservatives within the Republican Party formed the Tea Party movement. Taking their name from the Boston Tea Party, an event that led to the American Revolution, Tea Party activists have argued that the size and scope of government have grown out of control. Starting in the 2010 Republican Primary and in subsequent primaries, Tea Party-backed Republicans have defeated several mainstream Republican candidates, and they helped elect Ted Cruz to the U.S. Senate. Tea Party–backed Republicans are noted for being more conservative than mainstream Republicans, and their success made the Tea Party a strong faction in the Texas Republican Party. Initial analyses of the Tea Party indicated it had a libertarian economic ideology, focused on such fiscal issues as government debt reduction, less spending, and tax cuts.[13] Subsequent analyses have questioned the libertarian economic ideology of the Tea Party, arguing that it was more about opposition to President Obama than libertarian economics.[14]

neoliberal
A political ideology that advocates less government regulation of business and supports governmental involvement in social programs.

libertarianism
The concept of advocating minimal government intervention in both economic and social issues.

✓ 4.2 Learning Check

1. Do conservatives or liberals favor raising the minimum wage?
2. True or False: It is important for individuals to clearly identify as liberals or conservatives?

Answers at the end of this chapter.

✪ Electoral Trends

LO 4.3 Identify electoral trends in Texas, including realignments, third parties, and independent candidates.

When studying electoral trends in Texas, one notices that parties change over time and they are changing today. Level of competitiveness, issues they stand for, and their supporters are continuously evolving. During the past 40 years, competition between Texas's Democratic and Republican parties has brought a more diverse group of women, Latinos (Latinas, Latinx), Black Americans, Asian Americans, Muslim Americans, and LGBTQ+ into the state's political system. Native American populations in Texas are quite small, and thus have not received much attention from either party. Compared with the politics of earlier years, Texas politics today is more partisan (party centered).

Parties change over time because the major issues on which they align tend to evolve. In the 1930s, during the Great Depression, economic issues and the role of government in the economy were major alignment issues. The 1960s was an era of civil rights protests, environmental movements, and antiwar protests. These were new issues that parties needed to respond to. Responses that parties made have had electoral consequences. Political science research indicates the Civil Rights movement brought racial issues to the forefront of American (and Texas) politics. As racial issues evolved, the positions that parties took on issues related to race led to a transformation of the parties and the groups that support them.[15]

Republican electoral victories throughout the 1990s and into the 21st century, in Texas and across the South, demonstrate that there was a regional **realignment** among White voters (Latinos Asian Americans, and African Americans tend to remain Democratic Party supporters).[16] Realignments indicate that there has been a major change in support for political parties. The change in Texas and other southern states from solidly Democratic states to solidly Republican states is evidence of a regional realignment. A **dealignment** occurs when voters no longer identify with a political party.

Realignment in Texas was gradual, with Republicans making incremental gains beginning in the 1960s, big gains in the 1980s, and then statewide control by 2002. Looking at election trends, Republican candidates carried Texas in 14 of the 18 presidential elections between 1952 and 2020, including all of the elections since 1980. Jimmy Carter, in 1976, was the last Democratic presidential candidate to win Texas. Republican candidates also won eight of 10 gubernatorial elections between 1978 and 2018.

Republican strongholds are in West Texas including the Panhandle–South Plains; some small towns and rural areas in East Texas; and the exurbs of Dallas, Fort Worth, Houston, San Antonio, and Austin. With the exception of Democratic El Paso, West Texas Republicanism is predominant from the Permian Basin (Midland–Odessa) through the Davis Mountains and the Hill Country. This West Texas region, like the Panhandle–South Plains area to the north, is populated

realignment
Occurs when there is a major change in the support of political parties.

dealignment
Occurs when citizens have no allegiance to a political party and become independent voters.

primarily by conservative farmers and ranchers, as well as people connected with the oil and gas industry in Midland–Odessa and other parts of the Permian Basin. White Texans (especially older white people) are more likely to identify as Republicans than Democrats.

Although the Democratic Party has been unsuccessful in statewide election contests in recent years, it still controls many county offices and made gains in the legislature and U.S. House in 2018. Democrats hoped to win additional legislative and congressional seats in 2020, but that did not happen. They won only one additional seat in the Texas Senate while holding onto the gains made in 2018. Democratic voting strength is concentrated in El Paso, South Texas, the Golden Triangle (Beaumont, Port Arthur, and Orange), and portions of the diverse Central Texas region. Democrats have had increasing success in cities and counties with large populations and in their surrounding suburbs. In addition, the Democratic Party continues to receive support from Latinos and especially African Americans. Asian Americans, particularly in the Houston area, have also begun emerging as a Democrat-leaning group. Additionally, there is a growing education divide, as those with higher levels of education are more likely to identify as Democrats than Republicans. Finally, LGBTQ+ Texans are also more likely to identify as Democrats.

Straight-ticket voting means voting for all the candidate of one party. Texas general election ballots used to have an option for voters to make one selection to vote straight-ticket. Thus, if a voter voted straight-ticket Republican, it meant every Republican candidate on the ballot, from president to county commissioner, received a Republican vote. Republicans benefited from straight-ticket voting from the 1980s into the 2000s. An increase in straight ticket voting for Democratic candidates from the late 2000s to the late 2010s in the urban counties (such as Harris and Dallas) led to an increase in Democratic victories. In response, a law was passed during the 2017 legislative session to eliminate the straight-ticket voting option after the 2018 general election.

Third Parties

A major party's success is measured by its ability to win elections. By this measure, third parties are unsuccessful. Instead, third parties' successes can be better measured by their ability to make the public aware of their issues, persuade the major parties to adopt those issues, or compel the major parties to bring those issues into a coalition (temporary alliance). When judged by these measures, third parties in Texas have enjoyed occasional success. Third parties can also play the role of "spoilers" in elections if they are able to win some votes that may have gone to a major party, and hence potentially change the outcome in the election. The Green Party is thought to potentially take votes from Democrats and the Libertarians from Republicans.

Looking back historically, during the 1890s, the Populist Party successfully promoted agricultural issues and displaced the Republicans as the "second" party in Texas.[17] In the 1970s, La Raza Unida Party fielded and elected candidates to

straight-ticket voting
Voting for all the candidates of one party.

Image 4.2 Green Party of Texas Tweet

Source: Twitter

Competency Connection
💬 **COMMUNICATION SKILLS** 💬

What political issues are not being addressed by the major parties but could provide an opening for a third party to increase its vote share?

local offices in South Texas (principally Crystal City, Zavala County, and school board offices) by campaigning to combat the discrimination that the Mexican American community was experiencing. This third-party activity began drawing votes from the Democratic Party.[18] The dominant conservative faction of the Democratic Party was accused of ignoring Mexican American issues, and La Raza Unida won votes at the expense of the Democrats in the early 1970s. This put pressure on the Democratic party to address issues raised by the La Raza Unida party in order to win back the voters it was losing.

The Libertarian Party (a party that advocates minimizing government involvement at all levels while maximizing individual freedom and rights) has nominated candidates for national, state, and local offices throughout Texas. The Green Party has advocated environmental protection and government reform policies. However, Green candidates (like Libertarians) rarely received more than 3 percent of the vote. In the 2020 Texas presidential election, Green Party candidate Howie Hawkins received .3 percent of the vote, and Libertarian Jo Jorgensen received 1.12 percent. A few Libertarian and Green affiliated candidates have been elected to local offices.

Lacking the financial resources available to the two major parties to purchase expensive airtime on television or radio stations, third parties and third-party candidates often rely on social media (for example, Facebook or Twitter) to share their messages. The screenshot shown in Image 4.2 of the Green Party of Texas's Twitter account is an example of a political tweet and the use of hashtags to generate attention for the party at little to no financial cost.

📖 How Do We Compare...

Which Party Controls the Statehouses in 2021

Most Populous U.S. States	Governor/Senate/House	U.S. States Bordering Texas	Governor/Senate/House
California	Democrat/Democrat/Democrat	Arkansas	Republican/Republican/Republican
Texas	**Republican/Republican/Republican**	Louisiana	Democrat/Republican/Republican
Florida	Republican/Republican/Republican	New Mexico	Democrat/Democrat/Democrat
New York	Democrat/Democrat/Democrat	Oklahoma	Republican/Republican/Republican

Source: https://www.ncsl.org/legislators-staff/legislators/legislative-leaders/2020-state-legislative-leaders.aspx.

— Competency Connection —
✿ CRITICAL THINKING ✿

What criteria would you use to assess if it is better to have one party control a statehouse instead of having divided control?

Independents

The term **independent** applies to candidates who have no party affiliation. It is difficult for independent candidates to win because they do not have the affiliation of a political party to help with campaigning and fundraising. Also, they do not have the benefit of receiving support from voters based on party affiliation. In addition, independents have difficulty in gaining ballot access. For instance, the Texas Election Code requires independent candidates to file by gathering signatures on a petition. The number of signatures required for a statewide office is "one percent of the total vote received by all candidates for governor in the most recent gubernatorial general election."[19] Based on this criterion, to qualify for statewide ballot access in 2020, an independent candidate was required to gather 83,717 signatures from registered voters who had not voted in either the Democratic or Republican primary elections, or in the primary runoff elections, and who had not signed another candidate's petition for that office that year.[20]

No one has succeeded in winning the governorship without affiliation with one of the two major political parties since Sam Houston was elected governor in 1859. In 2006, songwriter, author, and humorist Richard S. "Kinky" Friedman and former state comptroller Carole Keeton Rylander Strayhorn ran for governor as independents. Despite Friedman's celebrity status and Strayhorn's previous statewide electoral success as a Republican, their results were the same as that of most independent candidates: they lost. Strayhorn received slightly more than 18 percent of the vote, and Friedman a little more than 14 percent. Democratic gubernatorial candidate Chris Bell got 30 percent, and Governor Rick Perry, the Republican candidate, was reelected with a plurality of 39 percent.

independent
A candidate who runs in a general election without party endorsement or selection.

✓ 4.3 Learning Check

1. Texas went from a solid Democratic state to a solid Republican state? Why do political parties change over time?

2. Which third party affected the Texas Democratic Party in the 1970s?

Answers at the end of this chapter.

⊡ An Overview of Texas Political History

LO 4.4 Trace the evolution of political parties in Texas.

How did the current political parties in Texas get to the point where they are today? Parties evolve over time in response to political issues. The following section traces evolution of the party system and addresses the major issues that have impacted the party system. While the party names remained the same over time, the issues and their supporters definitely have changed.

1840s to 1870s: The Origin of the Party System

Before Texas's admission into the Union in 1845, its political parties had not fully developed. Political factions during the years that Texas was an independent republic tended to coalesce around personalities. The two dominant factions were the pro-(Sam) Houston and the anti-Houston groups (Houston was opposed to secession). Even after the Lone Star State's admission into the Union, these two factions remained. By the 1850s, the pro-Houston faction began referring to itself as the Jackson Democrats (Unionists), whereas the anti-Houston faction called themselves the Calhoun Democrats (after South Carolina senator John C. Calhoun, a proslavery advocate). In the course of the Civil War, after Texas seceded from the Union, White Texans became firmly aligned with the Democratic Party and Republicans (Abraham Lincoln's party) were viewed as a disloyal minority.

During the period of Reconstruction (1865–1873) that followed the Civil War, the Republican Party controlled Texas politics. The Reconstruction Acts passed by the U.S. Congress purged all officeholders with a Confederate past. Congress also disenfranchised all Southerners who had ever held a state or federal office before secession and who later supported the Confederacy. Republican governor Edmund J. Davis, a former Union army general, was elected in 1869 during this period of Reconstruction. The Davis administration quickly became unpopular with Texas's White majority. During his tenure in office, Davis took control of voter registration and appointed more than 8,000 public officials. From Texas Supreme Court justices to state police to city officials, Davis placed Republicans (including some Black Americans) in office throughout the state. Opposed by former Confederates, Davis's administration was condemned by most White Texans for corruption, graft, and high taxation.[21] After Davis's defeat for reelection in 1873 by a newly enfranchised electorate, Texas voters did not elect another Republican governor for more than 100 years.

1870s to 1970s: A One-Party Dominant System

From the end of Reconstruction until the 1970s, Texas and other former Confederate states had a one-party identity in which the Democratic Party was dominant. During those years (when a gubernatorial term in Texas was two years),

Democratic candidates won 52 consecutive gubernatorial elections, and Democratic presidential nominees carried the state in all but three of the 25 presidential elections. It was the era of the "yellow-dog Democrats." This term has been applied to people whose party loyalty is said to be so strong that they would vote for a yellow dog if it were a Democratic candidate for public office.

Democratic party dominance in the south (including Texas) resulted from the lingering divide in the nation from the Civil War. Texas and Southern Democrats dominated state politics and worked to segregate and disenfranchise Black Americans. In the latter part of the 19th century, Democrats faced a greater challenge from the Populist Party than they did from Republicans. The Populist (or People's) Party formed in Texas as an agrarian-based party, winning local elections throughout the state. This party was a response to what many viewed as corruption, too much corporate power, and growing income inequality. From 1892 to 1898, its gubernatorial nominees received more votes than did Republicans. Although its ideas remained influential in Texas (for example, protection of common people by government regulation of railroads and banks), the Populist Party became less important after 1898. In large measure, the Populist Party declined because the Democratic Party adopted Populist issues, such as government regulation of railroads and banks. The Texas Department of Banking, for example, was established in 1905 by the state legislature to provide bank supervision.[22] Rural Texans continued to be active in politics, but most farmers and others who had been Populists shifted their support to Democratic candidates.[23]

In the early 20th century, the Democratic Party strengthened its control over state politics. Having adopted Populist issues, Democratic candidates faced no opposition from Populist candidates. During the next five decades, two factions emerged within the Democratic Party: conservatives and liberals. Fighting between these two factions was often as fierce as between two separate political parties. For example, conservative Democrats were considered probusiness and pushed for right-to-work laws (laws that weakened labor unions), whereas liberals were associated with New Deal policies (and the Roosevelt Administration), including support for organized labor.[24]

By the late 1940s and early 1950s, Civil Rights was emerging as a major issue in American politics, it also impacted Texas, as the national Democratic Party began to advocate for Civil Rights legislation.[25] During this era Republican presidential candidates began enjoying greater support from the Texas electorate. With the backing of conservative Democratic governor Alan Shivers, Republican presidential nominee Dwight D. Eisenhower successfully carried Texas in 1952 and 1956. In addition, in 1961, Texas Republican John Tower, a political science professor at Midwestern State University in Wichita Falls, won election to the U.S. Senate. Tower won a special election to fill the vacancy created when Lyndon Johnson left the Senate to become vice president (later president) of the United States. Johnson was the Majority Leader in the U.S. Senate and a legendary, powerful, political leader. Tower was the first Republican to win statewide office in Texas since 1869, and he won successive elections until his retirement in 1984.

During the 1960s, Texas Latinos and Black Americans became more active in Texas politics and began having a growing impact on the Democratic Party.

In particular, they had the potential to strengthen the liberal faction of the party. Viva Kennedy Clubs were created in Texas as Latinos (primarily Mexican Americans) worked to elect John Kennedy as President during his 1960 election campaign. Overwhelming Latino support (estimates of 85 percent) helped Kennedy win Texas and the presidency.[26] During the late 1960s and early 1970s, La Raza Unida, as mentioned earlier in the chapter, emerged in South Texas and won some local races, defeating Democratic candidates.[27]

President Lyndon Johnson signed the Civil Rights Act into law in 1964 and the Voting Rights Act in 1965. Johnson's passage of these laws, after intense lobbying from Civil Rights leaders such as Dr. Martin Luther King Junior and John Lewis, is credited with increasing Black support for the Texas Democratic Party. This was a major change because the Democratic Party of Texas and the South had fought against civil rights for Black and Latino Americans. Many Black Americans had historically supported the Republican Party because it was the party of Abraham Lincoln. The Voting Rights Act passed with congressional Republican support. After signing the Civil Rights Act into law, President Johnson is reported to have said to an aide, "We (Democrats) have lost the South for a generation."[28] What Johnson meant was that he knew Texan and southern White Democrats would abandon the Democratic party because of the pro-Civil Rights issues the party was championing. The next section indicates Johnson was correct.

1970s to 1990s: An Emerging Two-Party System

Mexican American (Latino) political activism increased into the 1970s and continued to have an impact on the Democratic Party, in particular, the liberal faction of that party. In 1972, Ramsey Muñiz was nominated as La Raza Unida Party's (LRUP) gubernatorial candidate. Muñiz got 6 percent of the vote and denied the winner of the election, Democrat Dolph Briscoe, a majority of votes (Briscoe won with a plurality of votes). Briscoe's election marked the first time in the 20th century that the winner of a gubernatorial election did not win a majority of votes. The last statewide general election contested by LRUP was in 1978.

With passage of the Voting Rights Act, Black political participation increased. In 1972, Democrat Barbara Jordan, of Houston, was the first Black woman from a southern state elected to the U.S. Congress. Jordan rose to national prominence in 1974, as a member of the House Judiciary Committee, during the Nixon impeachment hearings. She also delivered the keynote address at the 1976 Democratic National Convention, and she was awarded the Presidential Medal of Freedom in 1994.[29]

The year 1978 was a watershed year for Republican success in Texas elections. When William P. ("Bill") Clements was elected governor of the Lone Star State that year, he became the first Republican to hold this office since Reconstruction. In the 1980s, voters elected growing numbers of Republican candidates to the U.S. Congress, the Texas legislature, and county courthouse offices. Moreover, Republican-elected officials began to dominate local politics in suburban areas around the state.

During the 1980s, Latinos, Blacks, female candidates, and candidates from the liberal faction began to have more success in the Democratic Party and won several statewide elections. In 1986, Democrat Raul Gonzalez was elected to the Texas Supreme Court, becoming the first Latino (Mexican American) to win a statewide election in Texas. Democrat Dan Morales was elected as Attorney General in 1990 and reelected in 1994. Democrat Ann Richards became the second woman elected governor in 1990, defeating Clayton Williams for an open seat. Democrat Morris Overstreet was elected to the Court of Criminal Appeals, becoming the first Black Texan to win a statewide office. The conservative Democratic faction was in decline.

Texas Republicans continued to make substantial gains throughout the 1990s. The Republican victory of U.S. senatorial candidate Kay Bailey Hutchison in 1993 signaled a series of "firsts" for the Texas Republican Party: the first woman to represent Texas in the U.S. Senate and the first representation of Texas by two Republican U.S. senators since Reconstruction.

The election of 1994 was a preview of future elections. This election was the last one in which any Democrat won a statewide office. Republican George W. Bush defeated Ann Richards, and Rick Perry was reelected agriculture commissioner. Democrats won four executive offices: lieutenant governor, attorney general, comptroller of public accounts, and commissioner of the general land office. All other statewide positions were won by Republicans.

2000 to 2016: Republican Dominance

Realignment of conservative white Texans was completed in the early 2000s. As the Republican Party emerged as a viable conservative option, it began to attract support from conservative Texans, and eventually their historic ties to the Democratic Party were cut. Recall that conservative Democrats had been in the party with liberal Democrats. Now with the conservative Democrats gone, the Democratic Party became more liberal than it had been compared to the party of the 1950s, 1960s, and 1970s.[30] Today's Republican Party is dominated by conservatives, many of whom remain loyal to former president Donald Trump.[31]

In the closest presidential election of modern times, former Texas Governor George W. Bush defeated Democratic nominee Al Gore by four electoral votes (271 to 267) in 2000, even though Gore won the national popular vote. After controversial recounts and protracted court battles over Florida's 25 electoral votes, Bush was ultimately declared the victor in Florida (by 537 votes) in mid-December 2000 after a 5–4 ruling by the U.S. Supreme Court. After Bush's election as president, he was succeeded as governor by Lieutenant Governor Rick Perry. For the third straight election, all statewide Republican candidates won.

In 2002, Democrats selected what was dubbed the "dream team" for the three highest statewide offices: Laredo businessman Tony Sanchez Jr., a Mexican American, for governor; former Dallas mayor Ron Kirk, a Black American, for U.S. senator; and former state comptroller John Sharp (White) for lieutenant governor. The expectation was that a multiracial Democratic ticket would encourage higher levels of voter participation by members of minority groups. Texas Democrats

📋 Students in Action

Working in Political Campaigns

Michelle Hargrove, a foster child, was raised in Texas and graduated from Gregory-Portland High School in Portland, Texas. After high school, Michelle attended Texas A&M University-Kingsville, majoring in engineering and minoring in political science. After taking political science classes, Michelle realized she would rather major in political science, and decided to change her major to political science and transfer to Texas A&M University-Corpus Christi.

Her involvement in politics began when she volunteered to work on an independent candidate's campaign for Congress. She liked his stances on issues that were important to the Corpus Christi area and she gained political experience.

Political Party Action

Michelle became active with party politics when she joined the campaign of a Democratic candidate for state representative district 32 as a part of an internship during her senior year at Texas A&M University-Corpus Christi. The candidate needed campaign workers to knock on doors and call potential voters, and the candidate's campaign consulting firm hired college students to work as interns. Michelle found she was very good at this and enjoyed the work. In addition, with her undergraduate research methods training she was able to conduct data analyses for the campaign to identify potential Democratic voters.

She was originally attracted to the Libertarian party. Then, as she learned more about politics, she came to support the Democratic party because of their emphasis on issues she thought were important to Corpus Christi. Among these issues were the ways the party wanted to engage and mobilize voters by expanding vote by mail options and making it easier to register to vote.

Michelle Hargrove

Photo Courtesy of Michelle Hargrove

Michelle graduated in December 2020 and went to work full-time for the campaign consulting company that she had interned with while in college. Her recent assignment was field manager for a city council candidate in San Antonio. In this job she did data analysis for the campaign so they knew where to send campaign volunteers to knock on doors and reach potential voters.

Her advice to students seeking to get involved with political parties is to volunteer with a party or candidate because they need workers. Also look to see if there are any internship opportunities. Michelle found that that she enjoyed talking to potential voters. She noted working on campaigns was a great way to make connections. She also noted that the research skills students learn in college are valuable when working for a political party or candidates.

— Competency Connection —
⚙ CRITICAL THINKING ⚙

If you were an intern for a candidate, what kind of issues or characteristics would you look for in a candidate? Could you work for a candidate if you do not agree with them on issues?

ran with a full slate of candidates for other statewide offices. On election night, however, the Republicans swept all statewide races. The 2002 election increased Republican control over the Texas Senate from a one-seat majority to a seven-seat majority (19 to 12). For the first time since Reconstruction, Republicans gained control of the Texas House of Representatives, winning 88 of 150 seats. Thus, the stage was set to elect a Republican speaker of the Texas House in the 78th regular legislative session in January 2003.

Because of redistricting efforts in 2003 that redrew districts to be more favorable for election of Republicans, the Texas congressional delegation has been majority Republican since 2005. In addition to gaining a majority of Texas congressional seats in the 2004 general election, Republicans won all statewide elections, maintained control of the Texas Senate and the Texas House, and picked up approximately 200 more county and district-level offices. Benefiting many of the Republican candidates was the fact that at the top of the ballot, President George W. Bush carried the state with more than 61 percent of the popular vote, compared with Senator John Kerry's 38 percent. Bush's strong showing also benefited Republicans running for other races down the ballot.

In the presidential election of 2008, Barack Obama became the second Democratic presidential candidate in history to be elected without winning Texas. Republican nominee John McCain carried the state with almost one million more popular votes than Obama (4,479,328 to 3,528,633). Although Obama did not win the state, Democrats could point to gains in several areas. The 2008 election marked the first presidential election in more than a quarter of a century in which the Democratic nominee carried at least four of the state's five most populous counties. One reason Obama fared so well in these counties was the support he received from Latino and Black voters. Democratic candidates also won a majority of countywide offices in Harris County for the first time in more than 20 years. In addition, for the third straight general election cycle, Democrats gained seats in the Texas House of Representatives.

In the 2010 Republican primary, incumbent Rick Perry's victory over U.S. Senator Kay Bailey Hutchison and Tea Party activist Debra Medina set up a general election showdown with popular three-term Houston mayor and former Texas Democratic Party chair Bill White. Many believed White to be the most viable Democratic gubernatorial nominee since Ann Richards in 1990. In the general election, however, White lost to Perry, receiving 42 percent of the vote to Perry's 55 percent. In 2010, Republican candidates were once again elected to all statewide offices and gained additional seats in the Texas delegation to the U.S. House of Representatives. The Republican Party continued to maintain its majority in the Texas Senate (19 Republicans to 12 Democrats) and extended its majority in the Texas House of Representatives, winning 99 seats (to the Democrats' 51 seats). The Republican Party increased its membership in the Texas House of Representatives to 101, when two Democratic state representatives switched to the Republican Party after the November election.

In the presidential election of 2012, Barack Obama was reelected president without carrying the Lone Star State. Republican nominee Mitt Romney won Texas by 57 percent to Obama's 41 percent and received over 1.2 million votes more than the president (4,569,843 to 3,308,124). Although President Obama received fewer votes in 2012 than he had in 2008, he again carried four of the state's five most populous counties (Harris, Dallas, Bexar, and Travis). Following the 2012 general election, the Republican Party remained firmly in control of all three branches of state government (Table 4.1).

Table 4.1 Number of Selected Republican Officeholders, 1974–2020

Year	U.S. Senate	Other Statewide Offices	U.S. House	Texas Senate	Texas House	S.B.O.E.*	Total
1974	1	0	2	3	16	—	22
1976	1	0	2	3	19	—	25
1978	1	1	4	4	22	—	32
1980	1	1	5	7	35	—	49
1982	1	0	5	5	36	—	47
1984	1	0	10	6	52	—	69
1986	1	1	10	6	56	—	74
1988	1	5	8	8	57	5	84
1990	1	6	8	8	57	5	85
1992	1	8	9	13	58	5	94
1994	2	13	11	14	61	8	109
1996	2	18	13	17	68	9	127
1998	2	27	13	16	72	9	137
2000	2	27	13	16	72	10	140
2002	2	27	15	19	88	10	161
2004	2	27	21	19	87	10	166**
2006	2	27	21	20	79	10	159***
2008	2	27	20	19	77	10	155***
2010	2	27	20	19	77	10	155***
2012	2	27	23	19	101	10	182***
2014	2	27	25	20	98	10	182***
2016	2	27	25	20	94	10	179***
2018	2	27	23	19	83	10	164***
2020	2	27	23	18	83	9	162***

*State Board of Education
**Data for 1974–2004 reprinted by permission of the Republican Party of Texas.
***Data for 2006–2020 were compiled by the authors.

Competency Connection
COMMUNICATION SKILLS

Looking at this data, when would you argue that Texas became a Republican state? Has Republican control of the state legislature peaked?

In July 2013, Governor Rick Perry announced that he would not seek reelection in 2014. In December of that year, Texas Court of Criminal Appeals Judge Larry Meyers, a Republican member of that court since 1993, switched parties and filed as a Democrat in a special election for the Texas Supreme Court against Republican Justice Jeff Brown, who had been appointed to fill a vacancy in 2013. Because Meyers was not required to resign from the Texas Court of Criminal Appeals to run unsuccessfully for the Texas Supreme Court, his switch gave Democrats their first incumbent statewide officeholder since 1998. Meyers's last term on the Court of Criminal Appeals expired at the end of December 2016, after he was defeated by Republican Mary Lou Keel in the November general election.

More than 4.7 million Texas voters cast their ballots in the 2014 general election. This turnout represented approximately 35 percent of the 14 million registered voters at that time. Following the election, the Republican Party retained control of all three branches of government. Republican nominee Greg Abbott defeated Democratic nominee Wendy Davis by more than 950,000 votes (2,790,227 to 1,832,254). Abbott won 59 percent of the vote compared to Davis's 39 percent. The remaining 2 percent was split among the Libertarian Party, Green Party, and write-in candidates. Republicans held on to all 27 statewide offices (plus two U.S. Senate positions), with no candidate receiving less than 58 percent of the vote. Of the 36 U.S. congressional seats, Republicans won 25, and Democrats won 11. In legislative races, the Republican Party extended its margin of control in the Texas Senate by picking up a seat previously held by a Democrat and holding 20 out of 31 seats. In Texas House contests, Republicans won 98 seats and Democrats 52.

2016 and Beyond

What happened to the Democrats? A similar realignment pattern of moving from Democratic to Republican dominance occurred across the southern states. Changes in Texas are consistent with those that occurred elsewhere in the South. How did the realignment of White Texans happen? Did individuals switch their party identification from Democrat to Republican, or is there another explanation?

One explanation for understanding how Texas realigned (and how another realignment may be on the horizon) is to consider impressionable years and generational change.[32] Party identification is formed during the young adult period, which is referred to as the impressionable years. After individuals move out of the impressionable years, and identify with a party, it becomes less likely that their party identification will change. Generations that went through their impressionable years prior to the Civil Rights movement developed their party identification in an era when issues of race did not divide the parties like it does today. They became Democrats because that was the dominant party in Texas. Generations that experienced their impressionable years during and after the Civil Rights movement had a very different experience. In this era, racial issues came to divide the parties. The Democratic Party moved in a liberal direction, particularly on civil rights, while the Republican Party moved in a conservative direction.

Research concerning the southern realignment finds that from 1960 to 2008, southern Whites who went through their impressionable years during and after the Civil Rights movement were more likely to identify as Republican than those who had their impressionable years prior to the Civil Rights movement. In addition, all White age cohorts experienced declines in Democratic party identification over this time period. These patterns explain how Republicans made gradual gains in Texas—over time the older generations of White Democrats were replaced by younger generations that were more Republican.[33] Southern Blacks and Latinos remained Democratic. By 2002 the realignment was complete.

Results from the 2016, 2018, and 2020 elections have given Democrats some hope. Texas was one of the few states that voted more Democratic in the 2016 presidential election compared to 2012. The 2018 midterm election brought national attention to Texas as Beto O'Rourke mounted a strong challenge to incumbent Senator Ted Cruz. Nevertheless, Cruz wound up winning reelection by a margin of 2.5 percent, a much narrower margin compared to past elections that saw Republicans winning by large margins. Several other statewide races also had close margins, though Governor Abbott easily defeated Democrat Lupe Valdez by a large margin in the gubernatorial contest. The Republican Party won all statewide elections and retained control of the state legislature. Democrats gained two seats in the Texas Senate, 12 seats in the Texas House, and two seats in the U.S. House. At the same time, Republicans maintained their areas of strength throughout the state. Democrats continued to do best in South Texas and the urban counties of El Paso, Bexar, Dallas, Travis, and Harris. Democrat O'Rourke also won in Nueces County and in reliably Republican Tarrant County. Democrats won convincingly in Harris County, winning control of the county government. Overall, Democrats did particularly well in the counties of the state's largest cities with their more diverse populations. An analysis of the Latino electorate found that voter mobilization efforts in Texas continue to not be as effective compared to other states.[34]

Democrats went into the 2020 election with expectations of building on the gains from 2018 and winning control of the Texas house, additional congressional seats, and maybe even a statewide win by Joe Biden in the presidential election. Instead, the statewide losing streak continued. Joe Biden closed the gap with Donald Trump and Democrats held onto the gains from 2018, yet there were signs that Democratic mobilization efforts were ineffective as Donald Trump did better than expected in heavily Democratic counties in the Rio Grande Valley. (Figure 4.2).

According to political strategist Molly Beth Rogers, future Democratic gains will require mobilization of Latino and Asian American voters, retaining support of Black Texans, and an increase in support from White voters. Rogers argues that Democrats need to win at least 35 percent of the White vote to be competitive. Wendy Davis, 2014 Democratic gubernatorial candidate, received 25 percent of the White vote while Beto O'Rourke received 31 percent in 2018.[35]

Figure 4.2 Texas Counties won by Joe Biden (in blue) and by Donald Trump (in red) in the 2020 Presidential Election

Size of Lead — Trump 0-5% 5-10% 10%+ — Biden 0-5% 5-10% 10%+

Source: https://www.cnn.com/election/2020/results/state/texas

Competency Connection
COMMUNICATION SKILLS

Donald Trump continued the Republican winning streak in Texas presidential elections. Looking at the map, are there counties where Democrats may win in the future, or are Republicans likely to expand the counties they win?

Are the recent good results for Democrats an aberration (the Republicans still control state government) or is this an indicator of change? Perhaps a similar process that led to Texas becoming a Republican state is occurring, but this time will lead to Texas Democrats becoming more competitive. Analyses of Texas public opinion survey evidence from 2009 to 2019 (Figure 4.3) indicates there are generational and demographic changes occurring in Texas that provide an opportunity for Democrats among younger Texans and people of color (POC).[36] The x-axis of the line graphs represents the year when the survey was administered. The y-axis measures party identification, which is measured as the percent who identify as Democrats.[37] For this analysis, POC includes those who did not identify as White, with the three largest groups

Figure 4.3 Percent Identifying as Democrats by Age, and Race/Ethnicity

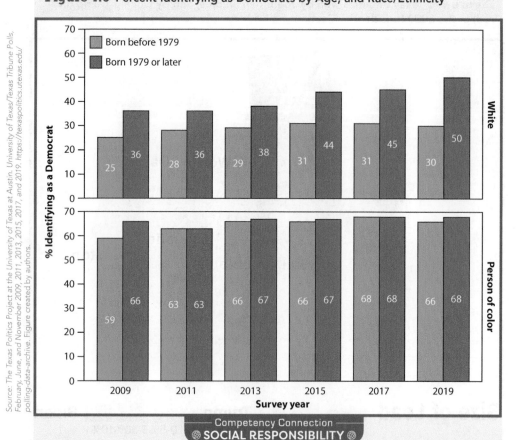

Source: The Texas Politics Project at the University of Texas at Austin. University of Texas/Texas Tribune Polls, February, June, and November 2009, 2011, 2013, 2015, 2017, and 2019. https://texaspolitics.utexas.edu/polling-data-archive. Figure created by authors.

— Competency Connection —
◉ SOCIAL RESPONSIBILITY ◉

Can you think of reasons why younger Texans are more likely to identify as Democrats? Are younger Texans likely to begin identifying as Republicans as they get older?

being Latinos, Blacks, and Asian Americans. Figure 4.3 has two panels – one with findings for POC and one for Whites – and it indicates younger White Texans (those born 1979 or later) are more likely to identify as Democrats than older White Texans (born before 1979). For example, in 2019, 50 percent of Whites born 1979 or later identify as Democrats compared to 30 percent for those born before 1979. Findings in Figure 4.3 indicate that POC consistently identify as Democrats at rates of 60 percent or higher, and there are only small differences between the two age categories.

Implications of findings presented in Figure 4.3 suggest conditions may be present for party change in Texas as a result of generational replacement. Those most likely to identify as Republican are older Whites. The younger cohort replacing them in the electorate is less likely to identify as Republican. With each passing year the cohort of Whites born 1979 or earlier becomes a smaller percentage of the Texas electorate. Those born 1979 and later had their impressionable years during the Iraq War, Great Recession, 2008 election of President Obama, and the President Trump era. They also experienced change on social issues such as marriage equality, LGBTQ+ rights, civil rights, immigration, the Me Too movement (against sexual abuse and harassment committed by men), and the Black Lives Matter movement. Finally, government's response to COVID-19 may have a lasting impact for young adult populations and their evaluations of political parties.

In addition, POC are growing as a percentage of the state's population (and electorate) and are more likely to identify as Democrats than any generation cohort of Whites. Thus, as older Texans are replaced in the electorate by younger Texans who are less Republican, it is possible that the thresholds to be a competitive political party identified by Rogers may be met, leading to a more competitive Democratic party. Nonetheless, change is not inevitable, and the increase in support Donald Trump received in the Rio Grande Valley Democratic stronghold provides a strong reminder that mobilization and outreach matter. Texas could follow the path of Arizona, Nevada, and New Mexico by moving in a Democratic direction, or the path of Florida that has been trending in a Republican direction.

✓ 4.4 Learning Check

1. Is there a generational difference in party identification compared to those born before 1979 and those born 1979 and later?
2. What has been the impact of Latino and Black support in urban counties?

Answers at the end of this chapter.

✚ Party Structure

LO 4.5 Describe the political party system in Texas.

American political parties exist on four levels: national, state, county, and precinct (the division of an area into smaller units within which voters cast their ballots at the same location). In part, these levels correspond to the organization of the U.S. federal system of government. Whereas a corporation is typically organized as a hierarchy, with a chain of command that makes each level directly accountable to the level above it, a political party is organized as a **stratarchy**, in which power is diffused among and within levels of the party organization.[38] Each major party is loosely organized so that state and local party organizations are free to decide their positions on party and policy issues. State and local-level organizations operate within their own spheres of influence, separate from one another, though there are some party governance rules that they must adhere to. Although these levels of the two major parties are encouraged to support national party policies, this effort is not always successful. As mandated by the Texas Election Code, Texas's two major parties are alike in structure. Each has permanent and temporary organizational structures (Figure 4.4).

stratarchy
A political system in which power is diffused among and within levels of party organization.

temporary party organization
Primaries and conventions that function briefly to nominate candidates, adopt resolutions, adopt a party platform, and select delegates to party conventions at higher levels.

Temporary Party Organization

The **temporary party organization** consists of primaries and conventions. These events are temporary because they are not ongoing party activities. Through primaries, members of the major political parties participate in

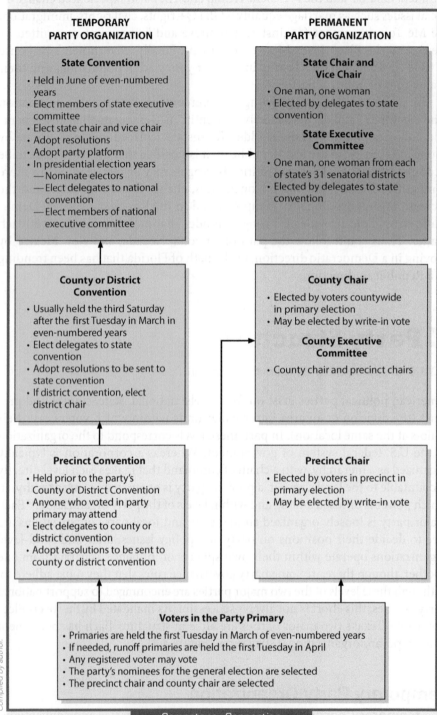

Figure 4.4 Texas Political Party Organization

TEMPORARY PARTY ORGANIZATION

State Convention
- Held in June of even-numbered years
- Elect members of state executive committee
- Elect state chair and vice chair
- Adopt resolutions
- Adopt party platform
- In presidential election years
  — Nominate electors
  — Elect delegates to national convention
  — Elect members of national executive committee

County or District Convention
- Usually held the third Saturday after the first Tuesday in March in even-numbered years
- Elect delegates to state convention
- Adopt resolutions to be sent to state convention
- If district convention, elect district chair

Precinct Convention
- Held prior to the party's County or District Convention
- Anyone who voted in party primary may attend
- Elect delegates to county or district convention
- Adopt resolutions to be sent to county or district convention

PERMANENT PARTY ORGANIZATION

State Chair and Vice Chair
- One man, one woman
- Elected by delegates to state convention

State Executive Committee
- One man, one woman from each of state's 31 senatorial districts
- Elected by delegates to state convention

County Chair
- Elected by voters countywide in primary election
- May be elected by write-in vote

County Executive Committee
- County chair and precinct chairs

Precinct Chair
- Elected by voters in precinct in primary election
- May be elected by write-in vote

Voters in the Party Primary
- Primaries are held the first Tuesday in March of even-numbered years
- If needed, runoff primaries are held the first Tuesday in April
- Any registered voter may vote
- The party's nominees for the general election are selected
- The precinct chair and county chair are selected

Compiled by author.

Competency Connection
◉ SOCIAL RESPONSIBILITY ◉

Is participating in party politics an effective way to engage in local and state politics?

▣ Point/Counterpoint

What Are the Positions of the Two Major Political Parties on Key Issues?

The Issue The two major parties, as identified in their platforms, differ substantially on many social and economic issues. The following excerpts, taken from each party platform as adopted at their respective state conventions in 2020, illustrate several of these different points of view. The complete texts of the parties' platforms are available on their websites.

Democratic Platform	Republican Platform
1. **Voting Rights:** "Protect voting rights by enforcing the Texas Voting Rights Act and the federal Voting Rights Act with restored preclearance provisions."	1. **Voting Rights:** "We urge that the Voting Rights Act of 1965, codified and updated in 1973, be repealed and not reauthorized."
2. **Marriage Equality:** "Protect the U.S Supreme Court decisions which guaranteed marriage equality and the full benefits of marriage to all couples."	2. **Marriage Equality:** "We oppose homosexual marriage, regardless of state of origin."
3. **Affordable Care Act:** "Protect and improve the Affordable Care Act to further reduce disparities in health coverage and outcomes, as we move toward universal healthcare."	3. **Affordable Care Act:** "We demand the US Congress to repeal the ACA and pass healthcare reform that results in more affordable healthcare through a market- based, competitive, and transparent healthcare system . . . ."
4. **Minimum Wage:** "Ensure that the minimum wage in Texas is a living wage that is at least $15 per hour, indexed to inflation."	4. **Minimum Wage:** "Minimum Wage: We believe the Minimum Wage Act should be repealed."

Sources: Texas Democratic Party 2020 – 2022 Platform, https://www.texasdemocrats.org/our-party/texas-democratic-party-platform/; Report of 2020 Platform & Resolutions Committee, https://www.texasgop.org/platform/.

— Competency Connection —
⚖ PERSONAL RESPONSIBILITY ⚖

We often hear that there is no difference between the Democrats and Republicans. After reading these platform excerpts, do you believe that statement is true? Why or why not?

elections to select candidates for public office and local party officers. Primary election voting may involve a runoff primary. For a discussion of party primaries and runoff primaries, see Chapter 5, Campaigns and Elections.

Conventions elect state-level and senate-district party officers; and conventions can be scheduled at precinct, county, state senatorial district, and state levels. Each convention lasts a limited time, from less than an hour to one or two days. At the state level, conventions select party leaders chosen by delegates elected at the local level. Rules of the Texas Democratic and Republican parties mandate that party policy be determined at their conventions. These policy decisions are evidenced by resolutions that are adopted in both local and state conventions, and by party platforms adopted at the state conventions. A **platform** is a document that sets forth the party's position on current issues. State parties and national parties each draft and approve their own platforms.

platform
A document that sets forth a political party's position on public policy issues, such as income tax, school vouchers, or the environment.

The national Republican party broke from this tradition, however, and chose to not adopt a new platform at its 2020 national convention. Instead, it decided to support then President Trump's policies in lieu of approving a traditional party platform.

In presidential election years, state-level conventions select delegates who attend a party's national convention. In addition, state delegates nominate a slate of electors to vote in the electoral college if their party's presidential candidate wins a plurality of the general election vote. At a national party convention, candidates are officially chosen to run for president and vice president of the United States. All Texas political conventions must be open to the media, according to state law.

Precinct Conventions In Texas, **precinct conventions** have traditionally occurred every even-numbered year on the first Tuesday in March, which is the day of the first primary. The state executive committee of each party establishes rules governing the determination of the time and place for precinct conventions and whether the party will hold precinct conventions separate from county and senatorial district conventions. If a political party decides to conduct separate precinct conventions, this event serves as the lowest level of temporary political party organization. There, participants adopt resolutions and select delegates to a county (or district) convention. In recent years, only the Republican Party has chosen to conduct separate precinct conventions, while Democrats have been hosting precinct meetings on the same day as the county/senate district conventions.

precinct convention
A convention, held at the voting precinct level, to adopt resolutions and to select delegates to the party's county or senatorial district convention.

By state law, if a political party decides to conduct precinct conventions, any citizen who voted in the party primary or has completed an oath of affiliation with a political party is permitted to attend and participate in that party's precinct convention as a delegate (Figure 4.4). For the Republican Party, each county organization chooses the date and location of the precinct convention.[39] The main business of the Republican precinct convention is to elect delegates to the county or district convention (one for each 25 votes cast in the precinct for the most recent Republican gubernatorial nominee). Delegates to the Republican precinct convention are also allowed to submit and debate resolutions. These resolutions express the positions of precinct convention participants on any number of issues, ranging from immigration and abortion to the national debt. If adopted, a resolution will be submitted to a county or district convention for consideration.

county convention
A party meeting of delegates held in even-numbered years on a date and at a time and place prescribed by the party's state executive committee to adopt resolutions and to select delegates to the party's state convention.

Democratic Party precinct conventions are held the day of the county or senatorial district convention. The precinct convention is used to begin the process of selecting delegates to the state convention. Each precinct nominates delegates for the state convention, but precincts with only a few voters are combined.[40]

senatorial district convention
Held in even-numbered years on a date and at a time and place prescribed by the party's state executive committee in counties that have more than one state senatorial district. Participants select delegates to the party's state convention.

County and Senatorial District Conventions State law requires that **county conventions** and **senatorial district conventions** occur on the date selected by the party's state executive committee. A senatorial district convention is held when there are two or more state senatorial districts in a county. These conventions are held after precinct conventions The main business of county and district conventions is to elect delegates to the state convention. Delegates attending a county or district convention also consider and adopt resolutions. These resolutions then go to the party's state convention for consideration.

Under the rules for each party, county and district conventions select delegates to their respective state conventions. Both Republicans and Democrats may select one delegate to the state convention for every 300 votes cast in the county or district for the party's gubernatorial nominee in the most recent general election. In addition, in selecting delegates at all levels, rules of the Democratic Party require delegations to reasonably reflect presidential preferences (in presidential years), to include young people and people with disabilities, and to reflect diversity in race, sex, gender identity, ethnicity, and sexual orientation.

State Conventions In accordance with the Texas Election Code, in even-numbered years, each political party must hold a biennial **state convention** to conduct party business. State conventions occur during a two-day period. Delegates conduct the following tasks:

- Certify to the secretary of state the names of party members nominated in the primaries for Texas elective offices (or by convention if no primary was held)[41]
- Write the rules that will govern the party
- Draft and adopt a party platform
- Adopt resolutions that express the official position of the party
- Select members of the party's state executive committee

In presidential election years, state convention delegates also perform the following three functions:

- Elect delegates to the national presidential nominating convention (the total number for Texas is calculated under national party rules)
- Elect members from Texas to serve on the party's national committee
- Elect a slate of potential presidential electors to cast Texas's electoral votes if the party's ticket wins a plurality of the state's popular presidential vote

Texas cast 38 electoral votes in 2020. A state's electoral vote equals the total of its senators and representatives in the U.S. Congress. Each state has 2 senators, and Texas had 36 representatives apportioned according to the state's population based on the 2010 census. However, in accordance with Article II, Section 1, of the United States Constitution, "no Senator or Representative, or Person holding an Office of Trust or Profit under the United States, shall be appointed an Elector." Texas will have 40 electoral votes in 2024.

state convention
Convenes every even-numbered year to make rules for a political party, adopt a party platform and resolutions, and select members of the state executive committee; in a presidential election year, it elects delegates to the national convention, names members to serve on the national committee, and elects potential electors to vote if the party's presidential candidate receives a plurality of the popular vote in the general election.

In 2020, both the Democratic and Republican state conventions were held virtually because of the COVID-19 pandemic. Large, indoor gatherings of delegates at conventions was viewed by public officials in the host cities as being a public health risk. Texas Democrats had planned for their convention to be held in San Antonio, but instead held it virtually from June 1 to June 6.

The 2020 Republican state convention was originally scheduled for Houston from May 11 to 16. This convention was rescheduled for July 13 to 18, 2020, with hope that the COVID-19 situation would improve by then. However, as the convention date neared, COVID-19 cases were on the rise in Houston; and there were calls for the Republican Party to have a virtual convention. The party decided against a virtual convention and proceeded to plan for an in-person, mask optional, convention at the Houston Convention Center. Eventually, Houston Mayor Sylvester Turner took steps to stop the convention from meeting in the city in order to prevent the spread of COVID-19. The Texas Republican Party responded by filing, and ultimately losing, lawsuits in state and federal courts. The convention was then convened virtually; but it experienced technical difficulties, delaying the start of the convention by a day.[42]

Image 4.3 Republican Party of Texas Convention Moved Online After Unsuccessful Lawsuits to Meet in Houston Convention Center

Source: Twitter

KHOU 11 News Houston ✔ @KHOU · Jul 18, 2020   ...
UPDATE: Houston Mayor @SylvesterTurner tweeted overnight that an appeals court has stayed a federal judge's ruling, meaning the GRB will not be open for the @TexasGOP **convention**.

'The doors remain locked' | Appeals court stops possible in-person T...
Overnight, Houston Mayor Sylvester Turner tweeted that an appeals court has stayed a federal court ruling which would have allowed an i...
🔗 khou.com

💬 18   🔁 76   ♡ 312   ⬆

— Competency Connection —
⚙ CRITICAL THINKING ⚙

Do political parties still need to meet in person to hold conventions, or will virtual conventions replace the traditional in-person conventions?

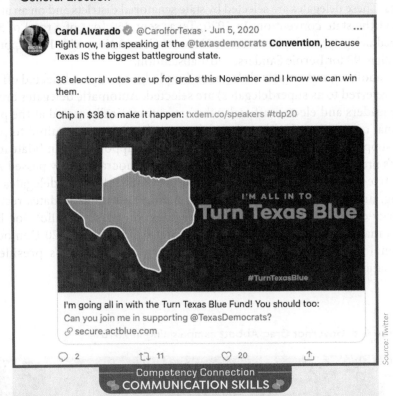

Image 4.4 Texas Senator Carol Alvarado, Democrat of Houston, Encouraging Democrats to Donate for the Fall 2020 General Election

Carol Alvarado ✔ @CarolforTexas · Jun 5, 2020 ...
Right now, I am speaking at the @texasdemocrats **Convention**, because Texas IS the biggest battleground state.

38 electoral votes are up for grabs this November and I know we can win them.

Chip in $38 to make it happen: txdem.co/speakers #tdp20

I'M ALL IN TO
Turn Texas Blue

#TurnTexasBlue

I'm going all in with the Turn Texas Blue Fund! You should too:
Can you join me in supporting @TexasDemocrats?
🔗 secure.actblue.com

💬 2   ↻ 11   ♡ 20   ⬆

Source: Twitter

— Competency Connection —
💬 **COMMUNICATION SKILLS** 💬

Are tweets, with links to donate online, an effective means of communication for political parties to raise money for elections?

Selection of National Convention Delegates

Selection of delegates to a national party convention depends on the delegates' support of particular candidates for the party's presidential nomination. In a **presidential preference primary**, individual party members can vote directly for the presidential candidates of their choice.[43] Delegates to the party's national convention are chosen according to the results of the primary vote. The respective national conventions nominate the parties' candidates for president and vice president.

Texas uses primaries; but in some states, such as Iowa, parties select delegates to a national convention in **caucuses**. Party members assemble in caucuses (meetings) at the respective precinct, county, and state levels. Here, they choose national convention delegates who either are pledged to support a particular presidential candidate or are uncommitted.

presidential preference primary
A primary in which the voters indicate their preference for a person seeking nomination as the party's presidential candidate.

caucus
A meeting at which members of a political party assemble to select delegates and to make policy recommendations at the precinct, county, or state senatorial district, and state levels.

Democratic Selection Presidential candidates are awarded delegates to local and state conventions in proportion to the number of their supporters in attendance. In Texas, national delegates are selected based on primary election results. These delegates are selected by state senatorial districts and on an at-large basis at the state convention. In 2020, Texas sent 260 (out of a total of 3,979) pledged delegates to the Democratic National Convention, with 161 supporting Joe Biden, 98 for Bernie Sanders, and 1 abstention.[44]

In addition, **automatic delegates** (unpledged party and elected officials, often referred to as superdelegates) are selected. Automatic delegates are state party leaders and elected officials who are automatically seated at the party's national convention. Unlike other delegates, they are not required to pledge their support for a particular candidate and may support any candidate for the party's presidential nomination. In 2016, the Democratic Party passed a rule (effective for the 2020 nomination) that prevents automatic delegates from voting, unless there is a contested nomination and no candidates receive a majority of pledged delegates (1991 delegates) on the first ballot. Joe Biden won a majority of delegate votes on the first ballot at the 2020 Democratic National Convention, and hence formally won the party's presidential nomination.[45]

Image 4.5 Governor Greg Abbott campaigning in 2018

Bloomberg/Getty Images

automatic delegate
An unpledged party official or elected official who serves as a delegate to a party's national convention.

Competency Connection
🔹 **COMMUNICATION SKILLS** 🔹

What kinds of communication skills are most effective in a political campaign?

Republican Selection The Republican Party selects national delegates proportionally from the results of the presidential preference primary for those candidates who finish above 20 percent of the vote statewide. Three delegates are awarded in each congressional district (total of 36 districts in 2020). A candidate wins all three delegates if they clear 50 percent of the vote in the district. If no candidate exceeds 50 percent per district, the first-place candidate receives two delegates and the second-place finisher receives one.[46] Others are chosen on an at-large basis by the entire convention. A nominating committee selects all at-large delegates. State convention delegates approve all national delegates. In 2020, Texas sent 155 (out of a total of 2,551) delegates to the Republican National Convention. All delegated were pledged for Donald Trump.[47]

Permanent Party Organization

Each major political party in the United States consists of thousands of nearly autonomous executive committees at the local, state, and national levels. These committees are given great latitude in their operating structures. For Democrats and Republicans alike, the executive committees across the nation are linked only nominally. For example, several Republican Party county chairs shared a conspiracy on Facebook about George Floyd's death. The Texas Republican Party chair, plus Governor Abbott and other elected Republicans, called on the county chairs to resign. However, the chairs refused to resign, and the Republican Party of Texas leadership did not have authority to force their resignations.[48]

At the highest level, each party has a national committee. In Texas, the precinct chairs, together with the county, district, and state executive committees, make up the permanent organization of the state parties. The role of the **permanent party organization** is to recruit candidates, devise strategies, raise funds, distribute candidate literature and information, register voters, and turn out voters on Election Day.

Precinct Chair In Texas, the basic party official is the **precinct chair**, who is elected for a two-year term by precinct voters in the party primaries. A party precinct chair's duties and responsibilities include registering and persuading voters within the precinct, distributing candidate literature and information, operating phone banks within the precinct on behalf of the party and its candidates, and getting people to the polls. A precinct chair is an unpaid party official who also arranges for the precinct convention (in the Republican Party) and serves on the county executive committee.

County and District Executive Committees A **county executive committee** comprises all the precinct chairs and the county chair, who are elected by county party members in the primaries. The county chair heads the party's countywide organization. County executive committees conduct primaries and arrange for county conventions. At the local level, the **county chair** is the key party official and serves as the party's chief strategist within that county. Duties of the county chair include recruiting local candidates for office,

permanent party organization
In Texas, the precinct chairs, county and senatorial district executive committees, and the state executive committee form the permanent organization of a political party.

precinct chair
The party official responsible for the interests and activities of a political party in a voting district.

county executive committee
Composed of a party's precinct chairs and the elected county chair.

county chair
Elected by county party members in the primaries, this key party official heads the county executive committee.

raising funds, establishing and staffing the party's campaign headquarters within the county, and serving as the local spokesperson for the party.

A **senatorial district executive committee** consists of precinct chairs who reside within the senatorial district. Senatorial district committees may be called upon to select a nominee for a vacancy in a districtwide office. Committee members also perform any other statutory or party responsibilities that may be required of them.

State Executive Committee For each major political party, the highest permanent party organization in the state is the **state executive committee**. As mandated by Texas law, an executive committee is composed of one man and one woman from each of the 31 state senatorial districts, plus a chair and a vice chair, one of whom must be a woman and the other a man. For both the Democratic and Republican Parties, a state executive committee with 64 members is elected at the party's state convention. At the same time, convention delegates choose the chair and vice chair at large. The party's state chair serves as its key strategist and chief spokesperson. In addition to the 64 statutory members of the party's state executive committee, party rules may allow "add-on" members. An add-on member may represent recognized statewide auxiliary organizations that have voting power within the party, such as women's groups (Texas Democratic Women, Texas Federation of Republican Women), racial groups (Texas Coalition of Black Democrats, Hispanic Caucus, Republican National Hispanic Assembly), House and Senate caucus chairs, youth groups (Texas Young Democrats, Texas College Republicans), and county chairs associations (Texas Democratic County Chairs Association and the Texas Republican County Chairmen's Association).

The party's state chair works with the party's state executive committee to recruit candidates for statewide and district offices, plan statewide strategies, and raise funds for the party at the state level. At its 2012 state convention, the Democratic Party chose the first Latino chair of a major political party in Texas when it selected Rio Grande Valley native and former court of appeals judge Gilberto Hinojosa as its state chair. Hinojosa was reelected state party chair in 2014 and 2018 at the Democratic state conventions in June of those years for four-year terms. The Texas Republican Party chose the first Black chair of the party when retired Army Lt. Col. Allen West defeated incumbent party chair James Dickey at the 2020 Texas Republican Convention. West resigned in June 2021.[49]

The state executive committee of each party must also canvass (or count) statewide primary returns and certify the nomination of party candidates. It also conducts the state convention, promotes party unity and strength, maintains relations with the party's national committee, and raises some campaign money for party candidates (though most campaign funds are raised by the candidates themselves).

Political parties often place several nonbinding propositions on the primary ballot for voters to decide upon. These proposals are used to express party primary voters' opinions and have no legal effect. In 2020, the Texas Democratic Party placed 11 proposals on the Texas Democratic primary ballot.[50]

senatorial district executive committee
Composed of a party's precinct chairs who reside within a senatorial district.

state executive committee
Composed of a chair, vice chair, and two members from each senatorial district, this body is part of a party's permanent organization.

A sample of proposals includes the following:

- Should every eligible Texan have the right to vote, made easier by automatic voter registration, the option to vote by mail, guaranteed early and mobile voting stations, and a state election holiday—free from corporate campaign influence, foreign and domestic interference, and gerrymandering?

- Should everyone in Texas have the right to a fair criminal justice system that treats people equally, uses proven methods for de-escalating situations instead of excessive force, and puts an end to the mass and disproportionate incarceration of people of color for minor offenses?

The 2020 Republican ballot had 10 propositions, including the following two:

- Texas should support the construction of a physical barrier and use existing defense-grade surveillance equipment along the entire southern border of Texas.

- Texas election officials should heed the directives of the Office of the Governor to purge illegal voters from the voter rolls and verify that each new registered voter is a U.S. Citizen.[51]

All proposals were overwhelmingly approved by each party's primary voters.

> ✓ **4.5 Learning Check**
>
> 1. What role does a party's temporary organization have with the presidential nomination system?
> 2. True or False: A political party platform refers to the stage and podium that candidates use while giving speeches at a political convention.
>
> *Answers at the end of this chapter.*

✪ Keeping Current

Challenges Facing the Parties

The Republican and Democratic parties each have different challenges going forward. For the Republicans, one challenge is the influence of former president Trump (Trumpism) on the party. While the former president has loyal supporters among many in the Republican base, he also did worse statewide in 2020 compared to 2016, and Republicans lost seats in the Texas legislature and congressional seats in the 2018 midterms. In addition, the presence of white nationalist organizations at his campaign events and at the January 6, 2021 insurrection attack on the U.S. Capitol brought scrutiny to the campaign and questions about how the party can reach out to non-White voters. Trump has threatened to support primary election challenges to Republican officeholders who do not support him. Thus, as Texas experiences changing demographics and generational change, how will the Republicans adapt?

Democrats continued their statewide losing streak and failed to win control of the Texas House of Representatives. An internal analysis found that the party did a poor job at engaging and mobilizing potential voters in the 2020 election. While Democrats can point to Biden's narrower loss in 2020 (compared to Clinton in 2016) and support in the populous counties, John Cornyn defeated M.J. Hegar by almost 10 percent of the vote. The question then is Cornyn's or Trump's margin a better indicator of where Democrats stand statewide? In addition, the 2022 election will be conducted after redistricting in 2021, and the Republican controlled process is likely to result in favorable districts for Republicans.

In June of 2021 organizers announced the formation of the Save America Movement (SAM) Party of Texas. The SAM party aspires to be a non-ideological party focused on problem solving and electoral reform, arguing that the Democrats and Republicans are too ideologically polarized. Several leaders of the SAM Party are former Republicans. Are there enough voters in Texas who are disillusioned with the Democrats or Republicans to consider the SAM Party at the expense of a major party, or will they perform like most third parties?

Conclusion

Historically, Texas politics has been characterized by prolonged periods of one-party domi-nation—first the Democrats and later the Republicans. Party identification has become more important in Texas politics. With changing demographic and generational patterns, however, the nature of partisan politics in Texas and the struggle for control of public office by political parties continue to evolve. Shifts in voting alignments will change how both parties develop campaign strategies and target groups of voters. The biggest question remains whether Texas will continue to be a solidly Republican state, or if Democrats are poised to begin making it competitive.

Chapter Summary

LO 4.1 Evaluate the role of political parties in Texas. Political parties are considered an integral part of the American governmental process and are defined as a combination of people and interests whose primary purpose is to gain control of government by winning elections. In Texas, and across the United States, the Democratic and Republican parties are the two leading parties, thus creating a two-party system. Nations that have two-party systems tend to have single member district plurality electoral systems (the type used in the United States) while nations with multiparty systems typically have proportional rep-resentation systems. Party identification is an attachment individuals have with a political party, and it has a major impact on how individuals evaluate politics and in making voting decisions.

LO 4.2 Compare and contrast the different political ideologies found in the Lone Star State. Texas voters and political parties represent various political ideologies, including conservatism and liberalism. Conservatives believe in a minimal role of government in regulating the economy and business, while emphasizing traditional social values and an active role for government on social issues. However, they are further divided between fiscal conservatives and social conservatives. Fiscal conservatives tend to give the highest priority to reduced taxing and spending. Social conservatives support greater government intervention in social issues (for example, laws against abortion and same-sex marriage) to support their family values. Liberals generally favor government regulation of the economy to achieve a more equitable distribution of wealth and favor a limited role for government in social issues. In Texas, many Democrats have a neoliberal ideology, which incorporates a philosophy of less government regulation of business and the economy while adopting a more liberal view of greater government involvement in social programs.

LO 4.3 Identify electoral trends in Texas, including realignments, third parties, and independent candidates. Beginning in the late 1970s, competition between Texas's Democratic and Republican parties has brought more women, Latinos, Black Americans, Asian Americans, and LGBTQ+ into the state's political system. As a result, party politics has become increasingly competitive and tied to national trends. Compared with the politics of earlier years, Texas politics today is more partisan (party centered). However, both the Democratic and the Republican parties experience internal feuding (factionalism) among competing groups. Political scientists assert that the success of the Republican Party throughout the 1990s and into the 21st century demonstrates that many White Texans who were previously Democrats have switched their political affiliation and loyalty to the Republican Party in a realignment of voters. A dealignment occurs when voters no longer identify with a political party. Minor (or third) parties and independents have never enjoyed the same success as the two principal parties. Their victories are generally limited to their ability to make the public aware of their issues or persuade the major parties to adopt those issues.

LO 4.4 Trace the evolution of political parties in Texas. Before Texas's admission into the Union in 1845, its political parties had not fully developed, and political factions tended to form around personalities. During the Civil War, as Texas seceded from the Union, politics became firmly aligned with the Democratic Party. However, during the period of Reconstruction (1865–1873) after the Civil War, the Republican Party controlled Texas politics. From the end of Reconstruction until the 1970s, Texas was dominated primarily by one political party: the Democratic Party. In the 1970s and 1980s, Texas moved toward a competitive two-party structure. By the 1990s and into the 21st century, the Lone Star State had seemingly become a one-party state with the Republican Party in control. As Texas voters become younger and more racially and ethnically diverse, the Democratic Party may become more competitive. Beto O'Rourke's 2018 Senate race and gains Democrats made in the legislature and U.S. House have raised the possibility that Texas could become a competitive state. However, results from the 2020 election demonstrated that Texas remains a Republican state.

LO 4.5 Describe the political party system in Texas. Political parties are organized as stratarchies in which power is diffused among and within levels of the party organization. The temporary party organization consists of primaries and conventions. Through primaries, members of the major political parties participate in elections to select candidates for public office and local party officers. Conventions elect state-level and senate-district party officers and are scheduled at precinct, county/state senatorial district, and state levels. At the state level, conventions also write party rules, adopt party platforms, and (in presidential election years) select delegates to national conventions and presidential electors.

Key Terms

automatic delegate, p. 158

caucus, p. 157

conservative, p. 134

county chair, p. 159

county convention, p. 154

county executive committee, p. 159

dealignment, p. 136

Duverger's Law, p. 132

independent, p. 139

liberal, p. 134

libertarianism, p. 135

neoliberal, p. 135

party identification, p. 131

permanent party organization, p. 159

platform, p. 153

political ideology, p. 133

political party, p. 131

precinct chair, p. 159

precinct convention, p. 154

presidential preference
   primary, p. 157

realignment, p. 136

senatorial district convention, p. 154

senatorial district executive
   committee, p. 160

state convention, p. 155

state executive committee, p. 160

straight-ticket voting, p. 137

stratarchy, p. 151

temporary party organization, p. 151

third party, p. 132

Learning Check Answers

✓ 4.1 **1.** False. Political parties are not mentioned in the U.S. Constitution, even though they are now considered essential in democracies.

2. Yes, there are differences between Republicans and Democrats in the precent who report they wear masks when in close contact with those not in their household.

✓ 4.2 **1.** Liberals favor raising the minimum wage. Conservatives oppose it because it is an example of government regulation of the economy.

2. False. While it is important that individuals understand ideology, it is not necessary for individuals to fit neatly into conservative or liberal categories.

✓ 4.3 **1.** The major issues political parties align or evolve over time. New issues emerge, and other issues become less relevant and this can affect party support.

2. The La Raza Unida Party affected the Democratic Party in the 1970s by winning votes that would have traditionally gone to the Democrats, and thus leading Democrats to become more responsive to Mexican American concerns in order to win back the votes.

✓ 4.4 **1.** Yes, there is a generational difference among White Texans, with those born 1979 and later more likely to identify as Democrats compared to those born before 1979. Among people of color, there is not a generational difference.

2. In several urban counties, such as Harris, Bexar, and Dallas, strong support from Blacks and Latinos has led to Democratic Party victories in those counties.

✓ 4.5 **1.** The temporary party organization consists of primaries and conventions in which delegates for presidential candidates are selected.

2. False. The party platform is a document that sets forth a political party's position on public policy and political issues.

5 Voting and Elections

Learning Objectives

5.1 Explain how individual characteristics and the voting process promotes and inhibits voter participation.

5.2 Analyze how voters choose which candidates to vote for and the role of campaigns.

5.3 Describe the impact of Texas's changing demographics on voting and elections.

5.4 Describe the evolving role of women and LGBTQ+ in Texas politics.

5.5 Understand election administration, including differences among primary, general, and special elections.

Image 5.1 Voters waiting in line to vote during the COVID-19 pandemic

Callaghan O'Hare/Bloomberg/Getty Images

— Competency Connection —
★ PERSONAL RESPONSIBILITY ★

Voting is fundamental to democracy. Texas did not require voters to wear masks while voting in person. Is it ethical for individuals to not wear masks, while in public, during a pandemic? What are the consequences to others of voting in public without a mask?

he fundamental principle on which every representative democracy is based is citizen participation in the political process. Yet in Texas, even with record high national turnout for the 2020 presidential election, voter turnout remains low. An analysis of 2020 turnout finds Texas ranked 45th in turnout compared to the other states and the District of Columbia. Among the voting eligible population (citizens and those not disqualified from voting), 60 percent of Texans voted in the 2020 presidential election while the national average was 66 percent. Minnesota had the highest turnout at 79.6 percent and Oklahoma the lowest at 54.8 percent.[1] This chapter focuses on understanding why Texans vote the way they do, campaigns, group differences in voting, voting administration, and different types of elections.

⭐ Voting

LO 5.1 Explain how individual characteristics and the voting process promotes and inhibits voter participation.

The U.S. Supreme Court has declared the right to vote the "preservative" of all other rights.[2] For most Texans, voting is their principal political activity. For many, it is their only exercise in practicing Texas politics. Casting a ballot brings individuals and their government together for a moment and reminds people anew that they are part of a political system.

Elections in Texas allow voters to decide whether state and local governments can borrow money by issuing bonds; make some public policy decisions; and choose officials to fill national, state, county, city, and special district offices. With so many electoral contests, citizens are frequently besieged by candidates seeking votes and asking for money to finance election campaigns. The democratic election process, however, gives Texans an opportunity to influence public policymaking by expressing preferences for candidates and issues when they vote.

Just over 11.3 million Texans voted in the November 3, 2020 general election. This was the largest number of Texans to ever vote. Nonetheless, there were vast differences in turnout among registered voters across the state's 254 counties, with some approaching 80 percent turnout and others as low as 44 percent.[3] How do voters make the decision to vote, and then how do they decide which candidate to support? Political science research offers answers to these questions by examining individual level characteristics and the impact of the electoral system.

Voter Turnout

voter turnout
The percentage of voters (either voting age population, voting eligible population, or registered voters) casting a ballot in an election.

One of the first issues political scientists face when studying voter turnout is how to calculate it. Sometimes the number of people who voted is reported as turnout. Political scientists are typically interested in the percent of eligible or potential voters who voted instead of simply the number of voters. The number of voters is readily available (numerator), but the number of potential voters (denominator) is more difficult to define. Frequently used definitions of **voter turnout** are the percentages of the voting-age population (adults 18 or older), registered voters, or voting-eligible population (estimate of persons eligible to vote) casting ballots. Not all adults 18 or older are eligible to vote. Researchers at the *United States Election Project* estimated that 12.6 percent (almost 2.78 million) of Texas's population was ineligible to vote in 2020 because of citizenship status. Another 2 percent (492,390) of Texans were ineligible to vote because of their status as convicted felons who had not completed serving their sentences. The right to vote is restored upon the felon's completion of a prison sentence. Texas had an estimated 2020 voting age population of 22,058,260 and a voting eligible population of 18,784,280.[4]

A third way to measure voter turnout is by including only registered voters. A reason this method is used is because the number of registered voters in states, counties, and cities is easily obtainable—there are lists of registered voters and the number of registered voters is often reported with election results. Data for the voting age population and voting eligible populations are not as readily available. One must locate data from the U.S. Census or use estimates (such as *United States Election Project*), but this data may not be accessible at the county or city level.

Hence, when examining voter turnout results, it is important to note the method of calculation. Turnout from the presidential race in the 2020 Texas General Election was 51.3 percent of the voting age population, 60.2 percent for the voting eligible population, and 66.7 percent of registered voters.[5] The denominator makes a difference when calculating percentages and can lead to different conclusions.

Voter turnout in state and local elections is usually lower than in presidential elections. For instance, the 2018 Texas midterm election yielded a 46.3 percent turnout of the voting-eligible population.[6] Turnout in the Texas 2014 midterm election was 28.3 percent. The higher turnout in 2018 is attributed to the Senate race (Cruz vs. O'Rourke) and voter reaction to the Trump presidency. In local elections at the city or school district level, a turnout of 20 percent is relatively high. In 2019, registered voter turnout in the San Antonio mayoral election runoff was 14.3 percent.[7] These figures illustrate one of the ironies in politics: people are less likely to participate at the level of government where they can potentially have the greatest influence. In an effort to increase turnout, cities such as El Paso and Corpus Christi moved their city elections from the spring of odd years to the November general election date in even-numbered years. Corpus Christi had a registered voter turnout rate of 8.3 percent for the May 2011 mayoral election (last one in an odd year), compared to 55 percent registered voter turnout in the November 3, 2020 mayoral election.[8]

Understanding Why People Vote

Political science has extensive research examining whether or not someone votes. This research has identified individual level characteristics and voter mobilization as important to understanding voter turnout.[9] In addition, the electoral system, such as laws that disenfranchise voters, or laws that make voting easier or more difficult, also affect voter turnout (discussed in the Electoral Systems and Keeping Current sections of the chapter).

Individual Level Characteristics Individual socioeconomic factors (such as education, income, and age) are related to voter turnout. As education increases, so does the likelihood of voting. Education enhances one's ability to learn about political parties, candidates, and issues. Figure 5.1 presents a bar chart with the relationship between education and the percent of respondents who report voting in every election, using survey data from the October 2020 *Texas Poll*.[10] The X axis has education level measured by whether or not the respondent has a 4-year college degree and the Y axis represents the percentage of respondents who report that they vote in every election. Findings demonstrate 54 percent of those with a college degree report they vote in every election, while 43 percent of those without a college degree vote in every election.

Age also affects voting behavior. In the United States and Texas, young voters have lower turnout than older voters. Highest voter turnout is among Americans 60 years of age and older.[11] The explanation for the lower turnout among young adults (including college students) is there is a life cycle when it comes to voting. Young adults are not yet as engaged in their communities and politics because they are focused on other activities such as attending college or entering the workforce. As they age, and become more deeply engaged in a community, they become more likely to vote. Figure 5.2 examines different age generations and those who report voting in every election. Generation Z (25 percent) and Millennials (27 percent) have the lowest reported voter turnout

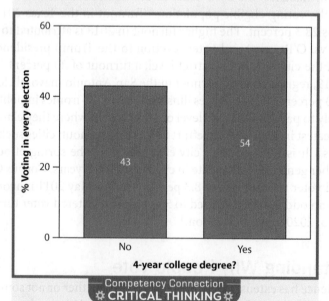

Figure 5.1 Percent Voting in Every Election by College Degree

Competency Connection
☼ **CRITICAL THINKING** ☼

Do the inquiry, critical thinking, and analytical skills developed in college explain why those with college degrees are more likely to vote than those without college degrees? Why or why not?

Figure 5.2 Percent Voting in Every Election by Generation

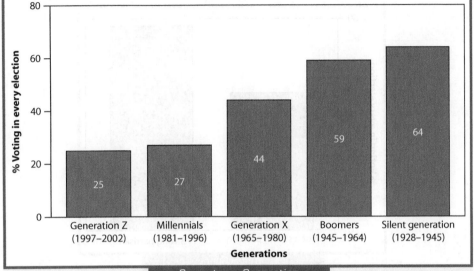

Competency Connection
⦿ SOCIAL RESPONSIBILITY ⦿

Do individuals develop knowledge of civil responsibility and the ability to engage in political communities as they get older; and does this explain why voter turnout increases among the older generations?

of any age group. Boomers and the Silent Generation have the highest reported turnout. This is not to state young adults will not participate—analyses of the 2020 election indicate that the increase in overall turnout in Texas was driven by voters aged 18–29.[12]

People decide to vote or not to vote in the same way they make most other decisions, on the basis of anticipated consequences. A strong impulse to vote may stem from interest in politics, peer pressure, self-interest, or a sense of duty toward country, state, local community, political party, or interest group. People also decide whether to vote based on costs measured in time, money, experience, information, job, and other resources, such as political efficacy. External political efficacy (that is the belief that elected officials respond to attempts to influence them) and strength of party identification are additional factors for explaining voter turnout.[13] Texans with high levels of political efficacy are more likely to vote, while those with low levels are less likely. Those who identify as strong Republicans or strong Democrats are more likely to vote than those with weaker attachments. Figure 5.3 presents findings from the October 2020 *Texas Poll* examining the relationship between strength of partisanship and voting in every election. Strength of partisanship is on the X axis and compares strong partisans (citizens who identify themselves as strong Democrats or strong Republicans) to those who are not strong partisans. According to the analysis, 58 percent of strong partisans responded they vote in every election compared to 39 percent of those who are not strong partisans.

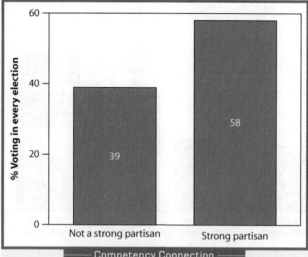

Figure 5.3 Percent Voting in Every Election by Strong Partisans

Competency Connection
◉ **SOCIAL RESPONSIBILITY** ◉

Do you think strong partisans are more likely to vote than those who are not strong partisans because an attachment to a party raises levels of civic responsibility? Why or why not?

Race and ethnicity also influence voter turnout. Political scientist Bernard L. Fraga has identified a persistent "turnout gap" when comparing voter turnout of Blacks, Latinos, and Asian Americans to Whites.[14] His research, that includes Texas, finds that even when taking education, income, and age into account, turnout is lower for these groups (especially for Latinos and Asian Americans) compared to Whites. Fraga finds that the turnout gap shrinks for Blacks, Latinos, and Asian Americans when their numbers become large enough to affect election results and when they are voting in elections where their votes can make a difference for the final outcome.

The U.S. Census Bureau has information on Texas demographics and voter registration numbers that can be used to calculate the percent of the population that is registered to vote by racial and ethnic groups for the 2018 general election.[15] Results are presented in Table 5.1. The total population column has the percent of those 18 and older for Whites, Blacks, Asian Americans, and Hispanics (Latinos). It demonstrates Whites are a plurality of the adult populations at 45 percent followed by Hispanics at 36.4 percent, Blacks at 12.5 percent, and Asian Americans at 5.2 percent. The next column presents the percent of the citizen adult population. Notice the percent citizen drops for Hispanics and Asian Americans. This is because both populations have immigrant populations who are not citizens, and hence are ineligible to vote. Whites are a majority of the adult citizen population. The third data column presents the percent for racial/ethnic group among registered voters. Whites comprise 57.5 percent of registered voters,

Hispanics 24.4 percent, Blacks 13.6 percent, and Asian Americans 3.4 percent. The final column presents the percentages of registered voters who vote by racial/ethnic group. These results find 60.7 percent of voters are White and 13.5 percent are Black. Whites comprise three-fifths of voters and just over one half of the citizen population, while Blacks are about even with their numbers of voters and citizens. Asian Americans and Hispanics vote at lower percentages than their citizen populations, with a 9 percent difference among Hispanics. These findings indicate the racial/ethnic group with a percent citizen and percent voters close to equal are Blacks. Whites comprise a larger percentage of voters than their percent of adult citizens, while voters lag for both Hispanics and Asian Americans. These findings corroborate the presence of the turnout gap in Texas.

Nonetheless, there are indications that turnout rates of Blacks, Hispanics (Latinos), and Asian Americans are increasing. Increased turnout among Black, Latino, and Asian American Texans in the 2018 elections, compared to their turnout in the 2014 and 2016 elections, is credited with contributing to Democratic Party gains in 2018.[16] For the 2020 general election, estimations are that the number of Asian Americans voting tripled compared to 2016.[17]

Mobilization A key factor in understanding voter turnout is **Mobilization**. This refers to actions such as voter registration drives, calling potential voters, using social media, knocking on doors, and holding campaign rallies that political organizations, political parties, and candidates take to get individuals to turn out and vote. Voters who are contacted about voting are more likely to vote; thus, mobilization is an important concept to understand voting. Some of these efforts are led by non-partisan organizations seeking to increase turnout, such as the League of Women Voters of Texas and MOVE Texas (focusing on underrepresented youth), and some focus on mobilizing members of groups with low voter turnout (Voto Latino).[18] Candidates and parties also work to mobilize supporters. The role of parties and candidates will be further discussed in the Political Campaigns section of this chapter. Individuals who are contacted by an organization, candidate, or party are more likely to vote than those who are not contacted.

mobilization
Actions such as voter registration drives, making phone calls, using social media, knocking on doors, and holding campaign rallies that political organizations, political parties, and candidates take to get individuals to turn out and vote.

Table 5.1 Turnout Gap

Racial/Ethnic Group	Percent Adult	Percent Citizen	Percent Registered Voters	Percent Voters of Registered Voters
White	45.1	50.1	57.5	60.7
Black	12.5	13.6	13.6	13.5
Asian American	5.2	4.0	3.4	3.2
Hispanic (Latino)	36.3	30.5	24.4	21.6
Total number (in thousands)	21,064	18,374	11,634	8,886

— Competency Connection —
★ PERSONAL RESPONSIBILITY ★

What kinds of consequences are there for Texas if a persistent turnout gap remains?

✦ Electoral Systems

Electoral systems affect who can vote and levels of participation. The right to vote has not always been as widespread in the United States as it is today. **Universal suffrage**, meaning almost all citizens 18 years of age and older can vote, did not become a reality in Texas until the mid-1960s. Although most tactics used to prevent people from voting have been abolished, their legacy remains, and voting rights violations still occur. Federal laws and constitutional amendments have eliminated many features of electoral systems that disenfranchised voters, yet states can still take actions to make voting easier or more difficult. Such actions affect voter turnout.

Obstacles to Voting

Adopted after the Civil War (1861–1865), the Fourteenth and Fifteenth Amendments to the U.S. Constitution were intended to prevent denial of the right to vote based on race. For the next 100 years, however, Black citizens in Texas and other states of the former Confederacy, as well as many Latinos (in Texas, primarily Mexican Americans), and Asian Americans were prevented from voting by one barrier after another—legal or otherwise. For example, the white-robed Ku Klux Klan and other lawless groups used terrorist tactics to keep Blacks from voting. Northeast Texas was the focus of the Klan's operations in the Lone Star State.[19] Disenfranchisement of Black Americans began at the end of the Reconstruction era (1873 in Texas) via violence, intimidation, and harassment.[20]

universal suffrage
Voting is open for virtually all persons 18 years of age or older.

poll tax
A tax levied in Texas from 1902 until voters amended the Texas Constitution in 1966 to eliminate it; failure to pay the annual tax made a citizen ineligible to vote in party primaries or in special and general elections.

white primary
A nominating system designed to prevent Black Americans and some Latinos from participating in Democratic primaries from 1923 to 1944.

Poll Tax Beginning in 1902, Texas required that citizens pay a special tax, called the **poll tax**, to become eligible to vote. The cost in 1966 (last year it existed for state election in Texas) was $1.75 ($1.50, plus 25 cents that was optional with each county). This amount would have been equal to about $14 in 2021. For the next 64 years, many Texans—especially low-income persons, including disproportionately large numbers of Blacks and Mexican Americans—failed to pay their poll tax during the designated four-month period from October 1 to January 31. This failure, in turn, disqualified them from voting during the following 12 months in party primaries and in any general or special election. As a result, Black voter participation declined from approximately 100,000 in the 1890s to about 5,000 in 1906. With ratification of the Twenty-Fourth Amendment to the U.S. Constitution in January 1964, the poll tax was abolished as a prerequisite for voting in national elections. Then, in *Harper v. Virginia State Board of Elections*, 383 U.S. 663 (1966), the U.S. Supreme Court invalidated all state laws that made payment of a poll tax a prerequisite for voting in state elections and in 1966 the Texas Constitution was amended to eliminate it.

All-White Primaries The so-called **white primary**, a product of political and legal maneuvering within the southern states, was designed to deny Blacks and some Latinos access to the Democratic primary.[21] Texas's White Primary law, passed in 1923, designated the Democratic Party primary to be a private party function, thus not protected by the Fourteenth and Fifteenth Amendments. This law allowed the Democratic Party to ban nonwhites from voting in the primary. Because the winner of the Democratic primary would win in the general election (Texas was a one-party Democratic state at that time), the white primary effectively disenfranchised nonwhite voters. In *Smith v. Allwright*, 321 U.S. 649 (1944), the U.S. Supreme Court overturned an earlier ruling that had allowed the white primary. The *Smith* decision came out of efforts from Houston's organized and active Black community.[22] As a result of this action, the white primary was disallowed in 1944.

Literacy Tests Beginning in the 1870s, as a means to prevent Blacks from voting, some southern states (although not Texas) began requiring prospective voters to take a screening test that conditioned voting rights on a person's literacy. Individuals who could not pass these **literacy tests** were not allowed to vote. The tests consisted of difficult and abstract questions concerning a person's knowledge of the U.S. Constitution or understanding issues supposedly related to citizenship. In no way, however, did these questions measure a citizen's ability to cast an informed vote—the purpose was to disenfranchise. The federal Voting Rights Act of 1965 made literacy tests illegal.

Grandfather Clause Another device, not used in Texas but enacted by other southern states to deny suffrage to minorities, was the **grandfather clause**. Laws with this clause provided that persons who could exercise the right to vote before 1867, or their descendants, would be exempt from literacy, property, or tax requirements for voting. Because Blacks had not been allowed to vote before adoption of the Fifteenth Amendment in 1870, grandfather clauses prevented Blacks from voting. The U.S. Supreme Court, in *Guinn v. United States*, 238 U.S. 317 (1915), declared the grandfather clause unconstitutional because it violated the equal voting rights guaranteed by the Fifteenth Amendment.

Diluting Minority Votes Drawing boundaries of a district, such as a state senatorial or representative district, to include or exclude certain groups of voters and thus affect election outcomes is called **gerrymandering**. While gerrymandering in and of itself is not discriminatory against minorities, there are situations where it has been used to dilute minority voting strength. Minority candidates have a difficult time getting elected from districts that do not have a sizeable minority population. For example, Latino representatives are unlikely to be elected from districts with small Latino populations.[23] Thus, one method for minimizing the impact of a minority community is to spread out the population among several districts so there is not a majority of the minority population in any district (known as cracking or splintering). This reduces the likelihood of a minority group candidate winning an election. Another tactic, packing, concentrates minority voters into a few districts with very large percentages of minorities. Thus, a minority population in a state may be large enough to elect several representatives if they are distributed more evenly across districts, instead of being concentrated into a few districts. Although racial gerrymandering that

literacy tests
Although not used in Texas as a prerequisite for voter registration, the test was designed and administered in ways intended to prevent Black Americans from voting.

grandfather clause
Although not used in Texas, the law exempted people from educational, property, or tax requirements for voting if they were qualified to vote before 1867 or were descendants of such persons.

gerrymandering
Drawing the boundaries of a district, such as a state senatorial or representative district, to include or exclude certain groups of voters and thus affect election outcomes.

discriminates against minority voters is disallowed, federal law allows **affirmative racial gerrymandering** that results in the creation of "majority–minority" districts (also called minority-opportunity districts) favoring election of more racial and ethnic minority candidates. These districts must be reasonable in their configuration and cannot be based solely on race. Research finds that minority opportunity districts provide a means to boost minority voter turnout, and hence reduce the turnout gap.[24] For a further discussion of gerrymandering, see Chapter 8, The Legislative Branch.

Another way minority voting strength may be diluted is through creation of **at-large districts**. In these districts, representatives are elected from an entire entity, such as a city. Thus, an at-large member of a city council is elected in a citywide election, instead of a single-member district election. Under this scenario, the votes of a minority group can be diluted when combined with the votes of a majority group. Even though a minority group, such as Latinos or African Americans, can comprise a numerical majority, from a political power standpoint they are still considered minorities. In a city like San Antonio, where Latinos are a numerical majority, they are still considered to be a minority group from a political perspective. Federal courts have declared at-large districts unconstitutional where representation of ethnic or racial minorities is diminished.[25] San Antonio abolished at-large city council seats and replaced them with seats for 10 single member districts (and a mayor elected at-large) in 1977. This action was taken after the U.S. Department of Justice informed the city that the at-large system was in violation of the Voting Rights Act.[26] For a comparison of at-large and single-member districts in local elections, see Chapter 3, Local Governments.

Federal Voting Rights Legislation The Voting Rights Act (VRA) of 1965 expanded the electorate and encouraged voting. This act has been renewed and amended by Congress four times. The 2006 extension had overwhelming bipartisan support as it renewed protection until 2031. The law (together with federal court rulings) now does the following:

- Abolishes use of all literacy tests in voter registrations
- Prohibits residency requirements of more than 30 days for voting in presidential elections
- Requires states to provide some form of absentee or **early voting**
- Allows individuals (as well as the U.S. Department of Justice) to sue in federal court to request that voting examiners be sent to a particular area
- Requires states and jurisdictions within a state with a significant percentage of residents whose primary language is one other than English to use bilingual ballots and other written election materials, as well as provide bilingual oral assistance. In Texas, this information must be provided in Spanish throughout the state and in Vietnamese and Chinese in Harris County and Houston.

In *Shelby County v. Holder*, 570 U.S. 529 (2013), the U.S. Supreme Court declared unconstitutional Section 4(b) of the Voting Rights Act (VRA) of 1965, which established a formula for determining which jurisdictions were required

affirmative racial gerrymandering
Drawing the boundaries of a district designed to favor representation by a member of a historical minority group (for example, Black Americans) in a legislative chamber, city council, commissioners court, or other representative body.

at-large district
An area in which representatives are elected from an entire entity, and not a single-member district.

early voting
Conducted at the county courthouse and selected polling places before the designated primary, special, or general election day.

to obtain preclearance from the U.S. Department of Justice before making any alterations to their election laws. Preclearance meant that voting jurisdictions, including states, counties, and cities, with a history of violating minority voting rights had to obtain approval before making changes for elections, such as drawing boundaries for state legislative districts. The State of Texas was among the governmental entities that had such a history. Writing for a 5–4 decision, Chief Justice John Roberts invalidated the provision because the coverage formula was based on 40-year-old data, making the formula no longer responsive to current needs and "an impermissible burden on the constitutional principles of federalism and equal sovereignty of the states." In dissent, the late Supreme Court Justice Ruth Bader Ginsburg wrote, "Throwing out preclearance when it has worked and is continuing to work to stop discriminatory changes is like throwing away your umbrella in a rainstorm because you are not getting wet."[27] Other parts of the VRA are still in effect, including Section 2 which "… prohibits voting practices or procedures that discriminate on the basis of race, color, or membership in one of the language minority groups…."[28]

The National Voter Registration Act (1993), or **motor-voter law**, permits registration by mail; at social services, disability assistance, and motor vehicle licensing agencies; or at military recruitment centers. People can register to vote when they apply for, or renew, driver's licenses or when they visit a public assistance office. Motor vehicle offices and voter registration agencies are required to provide voter registration services to applicants, using an appropriate state or federal voter registration form. If citizens believe their voting rights have been violated, federal administrative and judicial agencies, such as the U.S. Department of Justice, are available for assistance.

Amendments to the U.S. Constitution also eliminated obstacles to voting and expanded the American electorate. In addition to the previously mentioned protections of the Fourteenth, Fifteenth, and Twenty-Fourth Amendments, the Nineteenth Amendment (1920) precludes denial of suffrage on the basis of gender and the Twenty-Sixth Amendment (1971) forbids setting the minimum voting age above 18 years.

Trends in Contemporary Voting Rights

Voting rights have steadily expanded to include virtually all persons who are 18 years of age or older. Additionally, the Voting Rights Act and the Motor Voter Act have led toward uniformity of voting policies among the 50 states. However, there is still variation in institutional electoral system practices among the states. Some policies potentially increase turnout. Others are claimed to be necessary to combat voter fraud but may make voting more difficult and hence lead to lower voter turnout (the Keeping Current section has additional information).

Making Voting More Convenient

Institutional practices that make voting more convenient are associated with higher voter turnout. Examples of these practices are ballots by mail for all voters (as in Washington, Oregon, and California) and same-day or online voter registration. In 2000, Oregon became the first state to adopt voting by mail for all voters. Registered voters are sent a ballot that they then mark and return. There are no traditional voting

motor-voter law
Federal legislation requiring certain government offices (for example, motor vehicle licensing agencies) to offer voter registration applications to clients.

sites. The expectation was that this would make voting more convenient, and hence increase turnout. Research examining the impact of Oregon's change to vote by mail found that it led to a 10 percent increase in voter turnout (among registered voters) in both mid-term and presidential elections.[29] Texas offers voting by mail for some voters, and the Elections section of this chapter provides information about eligibility.

Forty states and the District of Columbia (as of October 2020) offer online voter registration.[30] Pre-registration is a system that allows citizens under 18 years of age to add their names to the list of registered voters before they are eligible to vote (such as when applying for a driver's license at 16). After they turn 18, they will be registered. Research on online registration and pre-registration find that these procedures lead to an increase in voter turnout for young adults.[31] Fourteen states allow pre-registration for 16-year-olds, and four states have authorized it for 17-year-olds.[32] Texans can register to vote when they reach the age of 17 years, 10 months old.

A federal judge ordered Texas, in late August 2020, to offer a limited version of online registration. The federal National Voter Registration Act (motor voter law) requires states to offer voter registration when individuals apply for or renew driver's licenses. Texas was not offering an online voter registration option for individuals who renewed their driver's licenses online with the Texas Department of Public Safety (DPS). When selecting the option to register to vote, individuals were directed to a webpage for printing a form to be mailed, but they were not automatically registered. In late September 2020, Texas complied with the judge's order. Now Texas citizens who use the DPS website to renew a driver's license can automatically register to vote online.[33]

One step taken by Texas to increase turnout was to reduce the number of election dates. The concern was that Texas voters were suffering from "turnout burnout" because of the frequency of elections. In 2015 a law was passed that limits most elections to two uniform election dates each year; the second Saturday in May and the first Tuesday after the first Monday in November. Evidence concerning uniform election dates is mixed on the turnout impact for constitutional amendment elections that average 8.5 percent turnout among the voting age population. For instance, in 2013, statewide voter age population turnout was 6 percent for the constitutional amendment election, 4 percent in 2017, and 9 percent in 2019.[34]

Making Voting More Difficult States can take actions that make voting more difficult. In 2011 the Texas legislature passed a bill that required voters to provide photo identification (ID) in order to cast a ballot. It failed to obtain preclearance by the Department of Justice (DOJ) in August 2012. The DOJ determined the law violated the VRA. Following the U.S. Supreme Court's decision in *Shelby County v. Holder* (invalidating the preclearance provision), the law went into effect in 2013.

Proponents argue that voter ID laws protect against voter fraud. The Texas law enhances the penalties for illegal voting from a third-degree felony to a second-degree felony. Attempted illegal voting is a state jail felony instead of a

Class A misdemeanor (for descriptions of penalties see Chapter 13, The Criminal Justice System). Acceptable forms of photo identification include a driver's license, passport, military ID card, concealed handgun license, or state-issued ID card from the DPS. Student ID cards are not an acceptable form of photo identification. Opponents of the voter ID law argue that individuals without a driver's license, such many who are elderly or poor, may not be able to vote because they lack documents (original or certified copy of birth certificate) required for getting the state-issued ID card.[35]

In October 2014, shortly before early voting began, a U.S. District Court judge in Corpus Christi ruled the ID law violated the VRA and was unconstitutional. This decision (*Veasey v. Abbott*, No. 14-41127) held that the Texas law was effectively a poll tax. Nevertheless, because the election was imminent, the Fifth Circuit Court of Appeals and the U.S. Supreme Court allowed the general election to proceed with the voter ID law in effect.

On July 20, 2016, the full Fifth Circuit Court of Appeals ruled against Texas, declaring that the voter ID law violated the Voting Rights Act because it has a discriminatory effect against Black and Latino voters. On August 10, 2016, U.S. District Judge Nelva Gonzales Ramos (the judge who originally ruled against the Texas voter ID law) signed an agreement among the civil rights plaintiffs, Texas, and the federal government. It allows voters to cast a ballot without a photo ID if they have a "reasonable impediment" to acquiring one of the acceptable forms detailed in the law. In 2017, the Texas Legislature passed Senate Bill 5, which revised the photo ID law to include changes agreed upon (and approved by Judge Ramos) by the plaintiffs, Texas, and the federal government. On April 27, 2018, a divided three-judge panel of the federal Fifth Circuit Court of Appeals upheld Senate Bill 5, ruling that the opponents of the revised photo ID law did not prove it had a discriminatory effect. This ended the legal challenge against Texas's photo ID law.[36]

Texas maintained that the voter ID law was necessary to protect the integrity of elections by preventing voter-impersonation fraud, whereby a person gives the name of another voter and then votes under that voter's name. Critics of the law note that the type of voter fraud that the voter ID bill is intended to prevent is very rare. An analysis of elections from 2000 to 2014, with 72 million votes cast, found only four cases of in-person voter-impersonation fraud. Thus, the chance of in-person voter fraud is only 1 in 18 million.[37]

Voter registration drives, by volunteers with organizations such as the League of Women Voters, are a common means to get individuals registered to vote. Texas has several certification requirements for volunteers to become deputized registrars. These requirements are considered more restrictive than those found in other states.[38] For example, deputized registrars are only allowed to register voters in the county where they are deputized. Hence, if there is a voter registration drive in Harris County, and someone from neighboring Brazoria County is visiting and attempts to register to vote, the deputized registrar from Harris County is unable to register the Brazoria County resident to vote in Brazoria County. These extra requirements can make voter registration drives less effective, resulting in fewer registered voters.

📋 Students in Action

A Duty to Participate

José Gonzales (They/Them) grew up in Corpus Christi, Texas. After graduating from Carroll High School José attended Del Mar College, graduating with an Associate of Arts degree in psychology. They are currently a student at Texas A&M University-Corpus Christi, pursuing a double major in psychology and art.

José's interest in politics began when they were a child due to their family's presence in local politics. They remember accompanying family members while campaigning for a congressional candidate. One of their aunts also spent time visiting with José about the importance of politics, and taught them the necessity of building alliances and holding onto one's values. She also taught José the worth of working toward the common good. José learned that we are part of community and connected, and that voting is the foundation for future actions. José notes that voting can begin the process of change, yet it can also be difficult for students to vote because of burdensome registration requirements.

Taking Action

At the encouragement of a professor, José began taking action when they became a deputized voter registrar while at Del Mar College and registered students to vote. José remained politically active in Corpus Christi when a friend suggested applying to work for MOVE Texas – a non-partisan organization, founded by students at the University of Texas at San Antonio, to politically engage underrepresented youth (movetexas.org).

One of José's roles with MOVE Texas is to increase voter registration among young adults. José reaches out to professors to show presentations on voter registration and help college students get registered. The COVID-19 pandemic made it difficult for organizations, such as MOVE Texas, to conduct traditional on-campus voter registration drives, and José is hopeful that those can return once the pandemic has ended, so voter participation of students and young adults can increase.

To José, participation begins with registering to vote and voting. Thus, voting is the first step in political engagement and the next step is to begin working to improve communities. To do this, one must understand community needs, and then begin advocating to address those needs. This is done by building political coalitions that can then work to influence government to take action. Thus, while José wants to increase voter turnout among students and young adults, their larger goal is to build political engagement and improve people's lives.

After graduation from Texas A&M University-Corpus Christi, José is considering attending graduate school or law school. If they pursue graduate school, José would like to do research on the trauma immigrants can suffer from. In addition to this, José also wants to expand the art community in Corpus Christi to make it more accessible for QTBIPOC+ (Queer, Trans, Black, Indigenous People of Color+).

— Competency Connection —
❖ CRITICAL THINKING ❖

Young adults, including college students, typically have lower rates of voter participation than older adults. What actions can organizations, such as the one José works for, take to increase student political participation and engagement?

In summary, steps that simplify voting are associated with higher voter turnout, yet political scientists and observers have noted that Texas does not make registering and voting easier for citizens.[39] Some steps Texas has taken, such as requiring photo identification to vote and adding additional requirements for groups that seek to register voters, have potentially made it more difficult to vote. The effort to standardize election dates may help increase turnout.

✓ 5.1 Learning Check

1. Is there a difference in voting turnout between those without a college degree and those with a college degree?
2. True or False: Texas offers online voter registration for all Texans who wish to register to vote.

Answers at the end of this chapter.

★ The Vote Choice

LO 5.2 Analyze how voters choose which candidates to vote for and the role of campaigns

The previous section of this chapter discussed factors that explain whether or not citizens choose to vote. After the decision to vote is made, the question then is understanding why voters choose certain candidates over others. Political science research on voting decisions is extensive, and students who are interested in learning more about how voters make their choices are encouraged to take a political science or government class focused on voting and elections. Despite increasing technological access to information about candidates and issues, a minority of Texans, and indeed other Americans, are actively engaged with politics. To many voters, character and political style of candidates have become more important than issues. For others, however, party affiliation and issues are most important.

One way to evaluate character and political style, as an explanation of the vote choice, is to examine favorability ratings of candidates and the candidate voters intend to support. Political science research has found that those with favorable views of a candidate are more likely to support that candidate, while those with unfavorable views are less likely to support them. In the October 2020 *Texas Poll*, respondents were asked if they had a favorable view of Senator Cornyn and if they intended to vote for him or for Democratic challenger M.J. Hegar. Figure 5.4 presents a bar chart of this relationship. The Y axis displays the percentage of respondents who indicated they would vote for John Cornyn in the 2020 general election and the X axis is the category of favorability ranging from very favorable to very unfavorable. The relationship is clear: 97 percent of those with a very favorable view of Sen. Cornyn indicate they will vote for him compared with only 2 percent of those with very unfavorable views.

Some voters pay more attention to issues when choosing a candidate to support. COVID-19 was a top issue in Texas and the nation during the 2020 general election. Figure 5.5A examines the relationship between how well Texas is handling the COVID-19 response and the 2020 U.S. Senate election in Texas. Among those who responded that they viewed the Texas response to COVID-19 as going "very well," 93 percent reported they intended to vote for John Cornyn, compared to 5 percent voting for Cornyn who rated the COVID-19 response as going badly. An additional way to examine issue

Figure 5.4 Percent Supporting Cornyn by Favorability

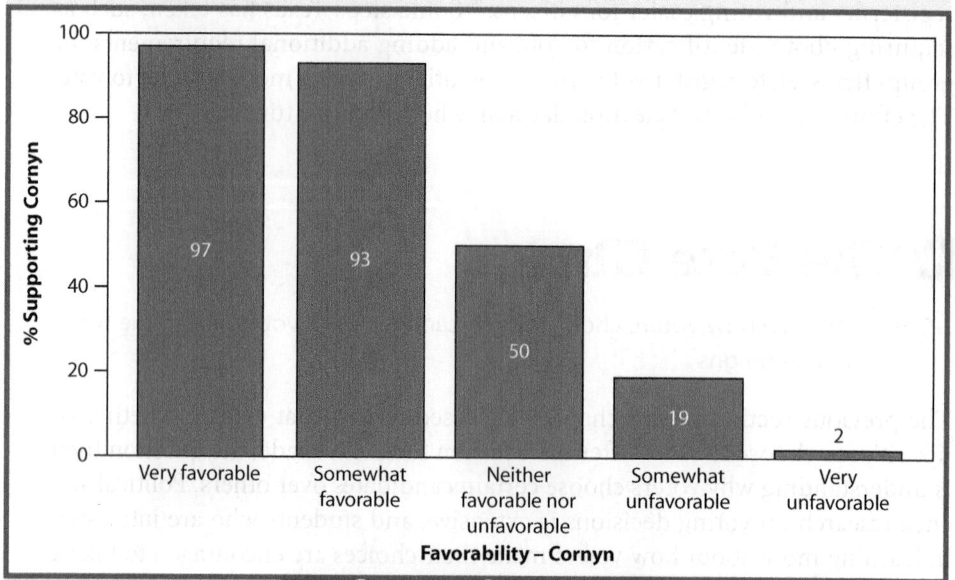

Competency Connection
★ COMMUNICATION SKILLS ★

Looking at this bar graph, what can you interpret about the relationship between favorability of Cornyn and supporting Cornyn?

voting is to ask voters if they approve of the job an incumbent has done. Job approval is considered a form of issue voting because voters are being asked to assess the overall job performance an incumbent has done in handling issues. Figure 5.5B presents an analysis of job approval for Senator Cornyn and the percentage of those reporting they will vote for Cornyn in the 2020 general election. Only 1 percent of those who strongly disapprove of Cornyn's job performance indicate they would vote for him, while 98 percent who strongly approve do plan to vote for Cornyn.

As mentioned in Chapter 4, perhaps the best predictor of the vote choice is party identification. Those who identify as Democrats are much more likely to support Democratic candidates, and those who identify as Republicans support Republican candidates. An analysis of party identification and the vote for Cornyn, in Figure 5.6, substantiates this. Three percent of Democrats indicate they plan to vote for Cornyn, whereas 94 percent of Republicans plan to vote for him. Party identification is even more important for vote choice in lower profile races, such as judicial and county level races. In many of those contests, voters have less information about the candidates. Thus, they may not be able to make a vote choice based on candidate favorability or issues. With less information about candidates, voters often use party affiliation of the candidate when making their vote choice. In higher profile races (for example governor, senator, and president), voters are more likely to be familiar with candidates and can

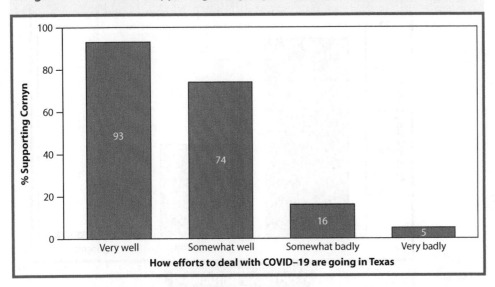

Figure 5.5A Percent Supporting Cornyn by COVID-19 Efforts in Texas

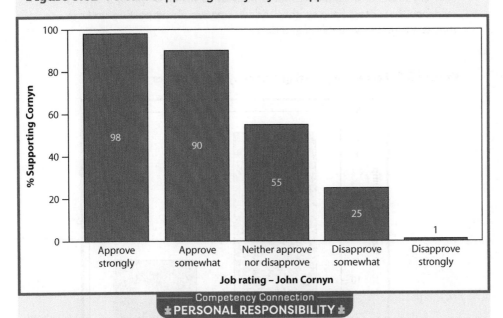

Figure 5.5B Percent Supporting Cornyn by Job Approval

Competency Connection
★ **PERSONAL RESPONSIBILITY** ★

Would it be better if more Texans voted on issues instead of candidate favorability? Are there consequences of not voting on issues?

make decisions based on that information instead of relying on the candidate's party affiliation.

Research has also found that there are group differences in voting behavior.[40] For example (according to Figure 5.7), 45 percent of older Texans (those born before 1981) reported they planned to vote for Trump's re-election compared to

Figure 5.6 Percent Supporting Cornyn by Party Identification

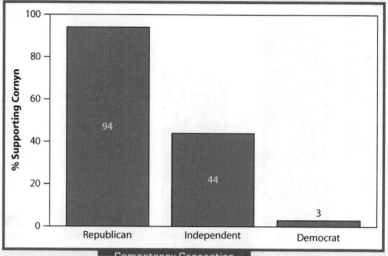

Competency Connection
⚙ **CRITICAL THINKING** ⚙

When voters rely on party identification to make vote choices, are they not carefully evaluating candidates? Alternatively, is voting on party identification evidence that voters have synthesized information about parties, and can use that as a tool for evaluating candidates?

Figure 5.7 Percent Supporting Trump by Born 1981 or Later

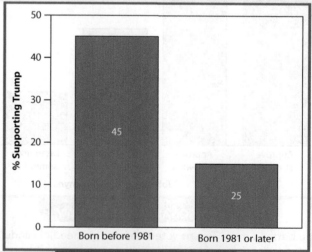

Competency Connection
⊚ **SOCIAL RESPONSIBILITY** ⊚

Based on what you know, how would you explain the differences in support? Are the different age groups engaging with different issues? Are there cultural differences between the two groups that help explain the differences in support?

25 percent of younger Texans (those born 1981 or later). A rural/urban divide has been emerging in national and Texas politics. In the 2020 election, Biden won the five counties with the largest populations (Harris, Dallas, Tarrant, Bexar, and Travis) while Trump did best in rural counties.[41] The roles of racial/ethnic groups and women are discussed later in this chapter.

✪ Political Campaigns
Conducting Campaigns in the 21st Century

Election results from 2020 reveal there are variations in the victory margins among winning statewide candidates in Texas. Donald Trump won over Joe Biden by 5.6 percentage points while Senator Cornyn defeated M. J. Hegar by 9.6 percentage points. This variation helps illustrate that voters have different motivations for their vote choices. If party identification were the only predictor of the vote choice, then Trump and Cornyn would have won by the same margins. The fact that they did not is evidence that factors such as favorability and issues also influence the vote choice for some voters, meaning campaigns matter.

Campaigns are no longer limited to speeches by candidates on a courthouse lawn or from the rear platform of a campaign train. Today, potential voters are more likely to experience a barrage of campaign publicity involving television and radio broadcasting, yard signs, bumper stickers, newspapers, social media posts, text messaging, and billboards. Moreover, voters may encounter door-to-door canvassers, receive political information in the U.S. mail, and be asked to answer telephone inquiries from professional pollsters or locally hired telephone bank callers. In recent years, the array of available social media tools has altered political campaigns in Texas and other states. Candidates and politicians set up Twitter, Facebook, TikTok, YouTube, and Instagram accounts, and they continuously experiment with using the latest social media tools.

Importance of the Media Since the days of W. Lee "Pappy" O'Daniel, the media have played an important role in Texas politics. In the 1930s, O'Daniel (with his band, the Light Crust Doughboys of Burnet Mills) gained fame as a radio host for Light Crust Flour and later his own Hillbilly Flour Company. On his weekly broadcast show, the slogan "Pass the biscuits, Pappy" made O'Daniel a household name throughout the state. In 1938, urged by his radio fans, O'Daniel ran for governor and attracted huge crowds. With a platform featuring the Ten Commandments and the Golden Rule, he won the election by a landslide.[42]

By the 1970s, television and radio ads had become a regular part of every gubernatorial and U.S. senatorial candidate's campaign budget. Radio became the medium of choice for many "middle-of-the-ballot" (statewide and regional candidates for offices other than governor or senator) and local candidates. The

Follow *Practicing Texas Politics* on Twitter @PracTexPol

prohibitive cost of television time, with the exception of smaller media markets and local cable providers, forced the use of radio to communicate with large numbers of Texans. To visit every county personally during a primary campaign, a candidate must go into an average of four counties per day, five days a week, from the filing deadline in January to the first primary in March (the usual month for party primaries). Such extensive travel leaves little time for speechmaking, fundraising, and other campaign activities. Although some candidates for statewide office, including 2018 Democratic senatorial candidate Beto O'Rourke, have traveled to each county in the state, none has won an election. Therefore, Texas statewide campaigners must rely more heavily on television, radio, and social media exposure than do candidates in other states.

Most Texas voters learn about candidates through television commercials that range in length from 10 seconds for a **sound bite** (a brief statement of a candidate's campaign theme) to a full minute. Television advertisements allow candidates to structure their messages carefully and avoid the risk of a possible misstatement that might occur in a political debate. Therefore, the more money a candidate's campaign has, the less interest the candidate has in debating an opponent. Usually, the candidate who is the underdog (the one who is behind in the polls) wants to debate.

Political campaigns rely increasingly on social media, email, and text messages to communicate with voters. Campaigns must remain current when using social media, because different platforms attract different types of users. Texts and email are inexpensive and easy to send; however, there is a risk that these messages will be ignored or flagged as spam. Campaigns must be savvy and understand how to best use social media to reach potential supporters and mobilize supporters to vote.

Issues with using social media include limited use and understanding of this type of media by the older (over 65) voting population. Additional complexities include access to smartphones and computers, hyperlinks to inappropriate websites, and "cybersquatting" (individuals other than a candidate purchasing domain names similar to the candidate's name and then selling the domain name to the highest bidder). In Texas Senator Ted Cruz's quest for the Republican presidential nomination in 2016, his campaign did not own the domain name tedcruz. com. Instead, it was used by someone endorsing President Obama's immigration reform plan.[43]

While social media are popular, candidates are also learning that past social media posts can be used against them. Opposing campaigns and news organizations will review old social media posts for incriminating statements. In the 2020 sheriff election in Brewster County, reports of racist tweets from 2013 emerged. The sheriff candidate initially suggested their twitter account had been sabotaged and denied making the posts, but then dropped out of the race.[44] In addition, comments and replies on social media posts made and received by candidates can become toxic, and social media companies have come under criticism for not addressing this issue.[45] Users of social media need to be mindful that they are reaching a candidate's verified account instead of a parody account.

sound bite
A brief statement intended to be easily quotable by the news media that is designed to convey a specific message that a campaign wishes to make.

Negative Campaigns Political observers often lament the amount of negative campaigning and attack ads, arguing that by attacking their opponents, candidates avoid discussing critical public issues. Campaigns employ negative advertising and make exaggerated claims. The media emphasize poll results and the horserace appearance of a contest, rather than basic issues and candidate personalities that relate to leadership potential.

Senator Cornyn and challenger M. J. Hegar, along with groups supporting them, engaged in negative campaigning during the 2020 U.S. Senate election. Cornyn ran ads accusing Hegar of wanting to dismantle police departments, destroy the oil industry, and defund Medicare. At the same time, Hegar accused Cornyn of caring more about lobbyists and special interests as well as being under the control of then Senate Majority leader Mitch McConnell. In addition, organizations that supported these candidates, but were independent of the campaigns, also contributed to the negative ads.[46]

There is a concern negative campaigns lower electoral participation by turning voters off to politics. Political science research on negative campaigning finds negative campaign messages that focus on irrelevant material, presented in an uncivil fashion, are most likely to discourage voters. Negative messages

Image 5.2 Ratioed Tweet (indicating a negative reaction to the tweet) from U.S. Senator Ted Cruz distributing water in Houston, Texas, in the aftermath of the February 14–17, 2021, winter storm. Cruz's tweet was "ratioed" as he received criticism for taking a trip to Cancun, Mexico, while millions of Texans suffered in the cold after having lost electricity.

Source: Twitter, Inc.

— Competency Connection —
⊚ **SOCIAL RESPONSIBILITY** ⊚

While widely used by politicians, does social media provide a means to effectively engage in regional, national, and global communities? Is ratioing (a negative reaction to a tweet indicated by receiving more comments to the tweet than likes) an effective means for the public to engage?

addressing relevant topics, presented civilly, may lead to greater political participation.[47] Because candidate character is an important consideration for many voters, negative campaigning remains prominent.

Campaign Finance

On more than one occasion, President Lyndon Johnson bluntly summarized the relationship between politics and finance: "Money makes the mare go." Although most political scientists would state this differently, it is obvious candidates need money to pay expenses of election campaigns. Unlike the federal government, however, Texas has few laws that limit political contributions. Laws that exist only apply to some judicial races.

Texas's 2018 U.S. Senate contest between Cruz and O'Rourke was the second-most expensive campaign in the nation (after Florida), with a total of $138,562,773 spent on the election. Of that amount, $124,712,559 was spent by the candidates, and $13,850,214 was spent by outside groups supporting one of the candidates. Cruz's campaign raised $45,260,806 and O'Rourke's raised $78,979,726.[48] Spending for the 2020 U.S. Senate campaign did not rank in the country's top 10.

Many Texans are qualified to hold public office, but relatively few can afford to pay their own campaign expenses (as 2014 lieutenant gubernatorial candidate David Dewhurst did). Others are unwilling to undertake fundraising drives designed to attract significant campaign contributions. Candidates need to raise large amounts of funds at local, state, and national levels to compete. Successful Houston City Council candidates often require from $150,000 (for district races) to $300,000 (for at-large races). Houston mayor Sylvester Turner won re-election against challenger Tony Buzbee in 2019, when candidates spent about $19 million combined. Turner raised and spent $7.2 million while Buzbee spent $12 million of his own money in a losing effort.[49]

Some individuals and **political action committees (PACs)**, which are organizations created to collect and distribute contributions to political campaigns, donate because they agree with a candidate's position on the issues. Motivations of others, however, may be questionable. Certainly, there is an appearance that money is influencing votes. However, it is very difficult to demonstrate that campaign contributions cause elected officials to vote in favor of the contributor. For example, the payday-loan industry has grown in Texas, while the state legislature has not updated laws to tighten regulations. Payday loans are high interest, high fee, short-term cash advances that individuals typically use to get money until their next paycheck. Texans who obtain these loans can find themselves paying very high interest and fees as they attempt to pay off their obligations. The Federal Trade Commission warns consumers about the risks of payday loans.[50] In 2014, the payday-loan industry donated $2.5 million to Texas legislative candidates. Did the money cause the legislature to not pass laws to regulate the payday-loan industry, or was the payday-loan industry helping to elect lawmakers that support free markets?[51]

Both federal and state laws have been enacted to regulate various aspects of campaign financing. Texas laws on the subject, however, are relatively weak and

political action committee (PAC)
An organization created to collect and distribute contributions to political campaigns.

tend to emphasize reporting of contributions with few limits on the amounts of donations. Federal laws, most prominently the Federal Election Campaign Act, are more restrictive, featuring both reporting requirements and limits on contributions to a candidate's political campaign by individuals and PACs.

In 1989, chicken magnate Lonnie "Bo" Pilgrim handed out $10,000 checks on the Texas Senate floor, leaving the "payable to" lines blank, as legislators debated reforming the state's workers' compensation laws. Many were surprised to find that Texas had no laws at that time prohibiting such conduct. Two years later, the Texas legislature passed laws prohibiting political contributions to members of the legislature while they are in session; and in 1993, Texas voters approved a constitutional amendment establishing the **Texas Ethics Commission**.

Administration and enforcement of the Texas Election Code as it relates to campaign fundraising, expenditures, advertising, and ethics of government officials and state employees are responsibilities of the Texas Ethics Commission. Some key responsibilities include collecting and maintaining political fundraising and spending activity reports. Lobbyists are required to file reports of their activities (see Chapter 7, The Politics of Interest Groups, for more information about lobbyists). State officials, including elected and appointed officials, and the executive heads of state agencies, also file personal financial disclosure reports with the Commission. The Commission is constitutionally mandated to be comprised of four Republicans and four Democrats. The power of the Commission is its authority to levy fines for violations, such as a candidate's failure to report campaign fundraising donations.[52]

Large amounts of money and concerns about its influence led to calls for reform. However, success in this area has been fairly limited. In 2002, the U.S. Congress passed the long-awaited **Campaign Reform Act**, signed into law by President George W. Bush. This federal law prohibited **soft money** (money used to fund election activities that is not directly donated to a political campaign); increased the limits on individual **hard money** (or direct) contributions; and restricted corporations' and labor unions' ability to run "electioneering" ads that feature names or likenesses of candidates close to Election Day.[53]

Plaintiffs challenged the constitutionality of the Campaign Reform Act. They claimed it was an unconstitutional restraint on freedom of speech. In a sharply divided decision, the U.S. Supreme Court upheld the constitutionality of the soft money ban in *McConnell v. FEC*, 540 U.S. 93 (2003). Seven years later, however, in a 5–4 decision, the U.S. Supreme Court in *Citizens United v. Federal Election Commission*, 558 U.S. 50 (2010), overturned a provision of the act that banned unlimited **independent expenditures** made by corporations, unions, and nonprofit organizations in federal elections. This decision was widely criticized by Democrats and by some members of the Republican Party as judicial activism that would give corporations unlimited power in federal elections.

That same year, a nine-judge federal appeals court unanimously ruled in *SpeechNow.org v. Federal Election Commission*, 599 F. 3rd 686 (2010), that campaign contribution limits on independent organizations, using the funds only for independent expenditures, are unconstitutional. The U.S. Supreme Court refused to hear this case on appeal, letting the lower court's decision stand. Decisions in

Texas Ethics Commission
A state agency that enforces state standards for lobbyists and public officials, including registration of lobbyists and reporting of political campaign contributions.

Campaign Reform Act
Enacted by the U.S. Congress and signed by President George W. Bush in 2002, this law restricts donations of soft money and hard money for election campaigns, but its effect has been limited by federal court decisions.

soft money
Unregulated political donations made to national political parties or independent expenditures on behalf of a candidate that are used to fund election activities but are not directly donated to a political campaign.

hard money
Campaign money donated directly to candidates or political parties and restricted in amount by federal law.

independent expenditures
Expenditures that pay for political campaign communications and expressly advocate the nomination, election, or defeat of a clearly identified candidate but are not given to, or made at the request of, the candidate's campaign.

these cases led to creation of **super PACs**, which are independent, expenditure-only committees that may raise unlimited sums of money from corporations, unions, nonprofit organizations, and individuals. Super PACs are then able to spend unlimited sums to openly support or oppose candidates. By January 2021, a total of 2,276 super PACs reported having spent more than $2.1 billion (nationally) on the 2019–2020 election cycle.[54]

Although the *Citizens United* decision removed limits on how much money can be given to or spent by outside groups on behalf of federal candidates, it did not address limits on campaign contributions to candidates or committees by individual donors. In another sharply divided decision, the U.S. Supreme Court in *McCutcheon v. Federal Election Commission*, 572 U.S. 185 (2014), struck down aggregate limits on the amount an individual may contribute during a two-year period to all federal candidates, parties, and political action committees combined. By a vote of 5–4, the Court ruled that the aggregate limit an individual could donate to candidates for federal office, political parties, and political action committees per election in an election cycle was unconstitutional under the First Amendment. The amount that can be donated to a specific candidate, political party, or PAC is limited, however. As with the *Citizens United* decision, several groups criticized this ruling as a further erosion of protections against undue influence in elections by a small portion of the electorate.

As noted above, Texas places few limitations on the amount of money contributors may donate to a candidate's political campaign. Texas's state campaign finance laws have focused on making contributor information more easily available to citizens. Restrictions on the amount of donations apply only to some judicial candidates. Individual contributions to judicial candidates are limited to $5,000 for candidates for the Supreme Court of Texas and the Texas Court of Criminal Appeals. This same limitation applies to courts of appeals, district courts, and county courts if the population of the judicial district is more than one million. The limit is $2,500 for candidates if the population of the judicial district is from 250,000 to one million and $1,000 for candidates if the population of the judicial district is less than 250,000.[55] Treasurers of campaign committees and candidates are required to file periodically with the Texas Ethics Commission. With limited exceptions, these reports must be filed electronically. Sworn statements list all contributions received and expenditures made during designated reporting intervals. Candidates who fail to file these reports are subject to a fine (usually around $500 per violation).

In 2003, the Texas legislature passed a law requiring officials of cities with a population of more than 100,000 and trustees of school districts with enrollments of 5,000 or more to disclose the sources of their income, as well as the value of their stocks and real estate holdings. In addition, candidates for state political offices must identify the employers and the occupations of donors contributing $500 or more to their campaigns. Furthermore, they are required to publicly report cash on hand.[56] The law also prohibits state legislators from lobbying for clients before state agencies, like the Railroad Commission.

Recent court decisions and loopholes in disclosure laws have opened the door for **dark money**. This is political spending by nonprofit groups, with the money coming from anonymous sources because the nonprofits do not need to

super PAC
Independent expenditure-only committees that may raise unlimited sums of money from corporations, unions, nonprofit organizations, and individuals.

dark money
Political spending by nonprofit groups, with the money coming from anonymous sources because the nonprofits do not need to disclose the sources of their contributions.

disclose sources of their contributions. These groups claim to be social-welfare organizations, and their contributions go toward independent expenditures instead of candidates.[57] In 2013, then-Governor Rick Perry vetoed a bill that would have required nonprofit organizations spending $25,000 or more on political campaigns to publicly disclose contributors who donate more than $1,000. The Texas Ethics Commission adopted a rule in 2015 to require some disclosure of dark money contributors if they spend money on advertising within 30 days of an election.[58] The Texas Ethics Commission is currently engaged in a lawsuit against the dark money group Empower Texans over a fine imposed on the group in 2014. In this case, the Texas Supreme Court ordered Empower Texans to divulge financial records to the commission, providing insight into the sources of the dark money.[59] Opponents of dark money disclosures have filed lawsuits (not yet decided) in an attempt to defeat the dark money regulation, arguing the Texas Ethics Commission does not have the authority to regulate dark money.[60]

Federal and state campaign finance laws have largely failed to regulate transfers of large amounts of money from donors to political campaigns in the form of campaign contributions. Rulings from the U.S. Supreme Court, equating campaign contributions and spending with free speech, have hindered legislation that the Court will consider constitutional. In addition, donors wishing to make large contributions find legal means (loopholes) to evade the intent of existing laws.

★ Racial and Ethnic Politics

LO 5.3 Describe the impact of Texas's changing demographics on voting and elections.

Racial and ethnic factors strongly influence Texas politics and shape political campaigns. Latinos (Hispanics), Black Americans, and Asian Americans are the three largest racial/ethnic minority groups in Texas. They comprise 57 percent of Texas's total population (other non-White groups including Native Americans, account for 2 percent).[61] Numerically, it appears the state's ethnic and racial minorities would wield enough voting strength to decide any statewide election and determine the outcomes of local contests in areas where their numbers are concentrated. However, as was noted in the turnout section of this chapter, racial and ethnic minorities do not comprise a majority of the state's voters. Black and Latino voters are more likely to participate in Democratic primaries and vote for Democratic candidates in general elections. Asian Americans have also been trending toward supporting Democratic candidates, and White Texans are the group most likely to support Republican candidates.

Latinos

In the 2018 and 2020 elections, candidates for elective office in Texas, and most other parts of the United States, recognized the impact of the Latino vote. When discussing the Latino vote in Texas and throughout the United States, one must

5.2 Learning Check

1. True or False: Party identification is a poor predictor of understanding why voters choose to vote for candidates because issue voting is more important.
2. Under which conditions is negative campaigning most effective?

Answers at the end of this chapter.

remain aware of the diversity of the Latino population and the resulting political implications. Latinos (Mexican Americans in El Paso, Central Americans in Houston, Cuban Americans in south Florida, and Puerto Ricans in New York) have vastly different experiences. This can affect voting preferences. For example, a media narrative from the 2020 presidential election was that Latinos shifted to Trump because he won the Latino vote in Miami-Dade County, Florida, by a 2 to 1 margin. However, in the rest of Florida Biden won the Latino vote by a 2 to 1 margin, and nationally Biden won the Latino vote by a 3 to 1 margin. A similar narrative emerged in Texas because Trump did well in the Rio Grande Valley and won Zapata county—a county that traditionally heavily favored Democratic presidential candidates. Nonetheless, Latinos in the larger population counties in Texas favored Biden 2 to 1 over Trump.[62] Thus, while there are similarities among Latinos, there are also substantial political differences within the population.

Chapter 4, Political Parties, has information about how the Kennedy campaign in 1960 mobilized Mexican American voters via Viva Kennedy Clubs and in the 1970s how the emergence of La Raza Unida Party compelled the Democratic Party to pay more attention to Latinos. Most candidates now use Spanish phrases in their speeches, advertise in Spanish-language media (television, radio, social media, and newspapers), and voice their concern for issues important to the Latino community. During presidential elections, candidates from both major political parties traditionally include appearances in Latino communities and before national Latino organizations, like the League of United Latin American Citizens (LULAC) and the National Council of La Raza. This is a part of their campaign strategies. Such appearances recognize the political clout of Latinos in the Republican and Democratic presidential primaries, as well as in the general election.

Communities and counties with large Latino populations, and electoral districts with majority Latino populations, tend to vote for Democratic candidates. Thus, there is an anticipation that because the majority of Latinos are more likely to support Democratic candidates, increasing Latino voter turnout will elect more Democrats to office. Registering and turning out voters among the growing Latino population is a focus for Democratic strategists who hope to turn Texas into a competitive state for Democrats again.

In 2002, Laredo businessman Tony Sanchez, Jr. became the first Latino candidate nominated for governor by a major party in Texas. Challenged for the Democratic nomination by former Texas attorney general Dan Morales, on March 1, 2002, the two men held the first Spanish-language gubernatorial campaign debate in U.S. history. Underscoring its strategy to attract more Latino voters, in 2012 the Democratic Party selected the first Latino state chair of a major political party in Texas when it chose Gilberto Hinojosa for that position. In 2018, Democrats Sylvia Garcia of Houston and Veronica Escobar of El Paso became the first Mexican American Latinas elected to the U.S. House from Texas, while Lupe Valdez became the first female Mexican American candidate for governor after winning the Democratic nomination.

In 2020, former San Antonio mayor and Cabinet Secretary Julián Castro sought the Democratic Party nomination for U.S. president. Castro hoped that Texas Latinos would be a source of support and help him win the nomination and make Texas a competitive state.[63] While Castro's campaign was historic, he was unable to generate enough support to remain in the race, so he dropped out before the Texas Democratic primary on March 3, 2020. Republican Tony Gonzalez won his party's nomination against Raul Reyes for an open seat in the 23rd congressional district. Then he defeated Democrat Gina Ortiz Jones in the 2020 general election. This competitive district stretches from San Antonio to El Paso and borders Mexico. Gonzalez's victory, in a district that includes many Latino voters, is a reminder that a large Latino population does not assure victory for Democratic candidates.

By July 2021, a substantial number of Latinos held elected office, including the following:

- Two statewide positions (commissioner of the general land office and one supreme court justice)[64]
- One U.S. senator
- Seven U.S. representative seats in Texas's congressional delegation
- Forty-five seats in the Texas legislature
- More than 2,650 of the remaining elected positions in the state[65]

With a growing, and Democratic-leaning, Latino population, why are Texas Democrats unsuccessful in statewide elections? Republicans have had success, yet this success has come despite growth of the Latino voting age population. Analysis of a 2020 election-eve public opinion survey estimated 67 percent of Latinos favored Joe Biden and 29 percent favored Donald Trump.[66] This is a large margin, though not as large as in 2016 when 80 percent of Texas Latinos supported Clinton and 16 percent supported Trump (also an election eve poll).[67] In the 2018 Senate race, 74 percent of Latinos indicated support for O'Rourke compared to 24 percent for Cruz.[68] From 2012 to 2016, Latino turnout increased by 30 percent while the population increased by 15 percent, indicating that the increase in Latino turnout is outpacing the increase in population growth. Latinos are favoring Democratic candidates, yet it has not yet led to statewide wins for Democrats.

The 2020 election results indicate a great deal of variation among the Texas Latino population in voting preferences. While Trump improved in the heavily Mexican American Rio Grande Valley (RGV), Biden prevailed with Latinos across most of Texas, and especially in the most populous counties. About 15 percent of Texas Latinos reside in the RGV, meaning the vast majority of Latinos live in other parts of the state. The question of how Trump did well in the RGV, but not in the rest of the state is one political scientists will research. There are several potential explanations. It has been suggested that the growing rural/urban divide in American politics may also be influencing Latinos in Texas. While the population of the RGV is growing, it does not have large cities such as Houston, San Antonio, Dallas, and Austin. Hence, it is possible that there is an electoral divide between Latinos in the large cities compared to those not living in large cities. Another potential explanation is the impact COVID-19 had on traditional campaigning. Democrats chose to avoid face-to-face campaign techniques such as block walking (knocking on doors and speaking with voters) and holding large in-person rallies. Instead, they relied on virtual campaigning. Republicans continued to use traditional face-to-face campaign strategies. Thus, a possible explanation for Trump's improved performance (compared to 2016) is that his Republican mobilization and campaign efforts were more effective than those of the Biden/Harris campaign and Democratic Party.

In addition, there is a growing evangelical Protestant movement in Latino communities. Prior research has found Latino evangelical Protestants are more likely to vote Republican than Latinos who are not evangelical Protestant.[69] The U.S. Border Patrol increased the number of agents during the Trump administration and became a major source of employment in the RGV. The oil and gas industry is also a major employer in south Texas. It is conceivable that voters in the RGV and south Texas viewed a Biden administration as less supportive of the Border Patrol and oil and gas industry, leading to fewer jobs.[70]

Overall, the pattern is Texas Latinos favor Democratic candidates, and the vast majority of Latino elected officials are Democrats. Republican Latinos have had success at the statewide level with Senator Ted Cruz, Land Commissioner George P. Bush (his mother was born in Mexico), and former Supreme Court Justice Eva Guzman. Supreme Court Justice Rebeca Aizpuru Huddle was appointed to a vacancy on the Texas Supreme Court in October 2020. There is one Latino Republican in the state legislature and the other 44 are Democrats.

Latinos have demonstrated their electoral potential in recent elections and are poised to become the state's largest racial/ethnic group, yet the electoral potential remains unrealized. Democrats were optimistic heading into 2020 that Latinos would help their party win a majority of the Texas House of Representatives, but it did not happen. Democrats have been criticized for not doing enough to engage Latino voters in a sustained manner by having a continuous presence and investing enough resources for turning out the potential Latino vote.[71] Arizona went from supporting Trump in 2016 to voting for Biden in 2020, and the Latino vote was decisive. In Arizona there was a sustained effort by Latino Democratic Party activists to engage and mobilize voters. This could provide a template for Texas.[72]

Republicans have been strategizing about how to win support from more Latinos. Yet, with a few exceptions, GOP candidates have not gained much support. In 2012, the Republican National Committee launched the Growth and Opportunity Project, with a list of recommendations and strategies designed to expand the base of the party and win more elections. Among recommendations, this report encouraged the Republican Party to focus messaging, strategy, outreach, and budget efforts to gain new supporters and voters in the Latino community (as well as in other racial/demographic communities, including Pacific Islanders, African Americans, Asian Americans, Native Americans, women, and youth). Political observers have noted that the outreach envisioned in the project was not implemented by the Republican Party in the 2016 election.[73] In the 2020 election, Republicans pursued a conservative agenda that included emphasizing issues such as border security, social conservatism, and the economy.

The Texas Republican Party has pursued policies that are popular with many conservatives, such as legislation to repeal in-state tuition for undocumented immigrants at public institutions of higher education. The GOP thus has a number of activists and elected officials who wish to take a hard line on immigration-related legislation, such as former President Trump's border wall. Hispanic Republicans have noted that proposals attacking the citizenship of Hispanics are perceived as anti-Hispanic and put support for the Republican Party at risk.[74]

The sheer number of Texas Latinos causes politicians to solicit their support because Latino voters can represent the margin of victory for a successful candidate. Lower levels of political activity than the population at large, however, both in registering to vote and in voting, limit an even greater impact of the Latino electorate. Nationally, nearly 20 percent of all Latinos in the United States live in Texas. In the 2020 census report, Texas Latinos are expected to outnumber Whites in Texas and by 2040, Latinos will be a majority of the state population.[75] Consequently, mobilization, political engagement, and electoral preferences of Texas Latinos appear to be the key to winning future elections in the Lone Star State.[76]

Black Americans

In April 1990, the Texas State Democratic Executive Committee filled a candidate vacancy by nominating Potter County court-at-law judge Morris Overstreet, a Black Democrat, for a seat on the Texas Court of Criminal Appeals. Because the Republican candidate, Louis Sturns, was also Black, this historic action guaranteed Texas voters would elect the first Black American to statewide office. Overstreet won in 1990 and again in 1994. Governor George W. Bush appointed Republican

Image 5.3 Democratic Vice President Nominee Kamala Harris campaigned in Texas during the 2020 presidential election. Harris identifies as Black and Indian American, and is the daughter of immigrant parents. The campaign was hopeful she could mobilize Black, Asian American, and Latino voters.

KRIS 6 News ✔ @KRIS6News · Oct 28, 2020
Democratic Vice Presidential candidate **Kamala Harris'** campaign has announced she has added a stop in McAllen during her **Texas** swing on Friday.

WATCH LIVE: Kamala Harris visiting McAllen
Kamala Harris' trip to Texas on Friday will include another stop as she plans to visit the Rio Grande Valley, her campaign announced.
🔗 kristv.com

♡ 36

Source: Twitter, Inc.

Competency Connection
COMMUNICATION SKILLS

Are candidates who share experiences with voters (such as race/ethnicity, or generation) more effective at communicating with those voters? Why or why not?

Michael Williams to the Texas Railroad Commission in 1999. Williams was elected to a six-year term in 2002 and again in 2008. He was appointed by Governor Perry as commissioner of education in 2012 but resigned in 2015.

Wallace Bernard Jefferson's appointment by Governor Perry to the Texas Supreme Court in 2001 made him the first Black to serve on that court. Jefferson and another Black, Dale Wainwright, were elected to the Texas Supreme Court in 2002 and reelected in 2008. Jefferson again made history in 2004 when Governor Perry appointed him as chief justice. In 2002, former Dallas mayor Ron Kirk became the first Black nominated by either major party in Texas as its candidate for U.S. senator. Although unsuccessful in the general election, Democrat Kirk's candidacy appeared to many political observers as an important breakthrough for Black politicians. Houston (current mayor Sylvester Turner), Dallas, and San Antonio have all elected Black mayors. In 2014, no Black from either party was a candidate for statewide office. Only one was a candidate in 2016 and 2018. In 2020, Kamala Harris was a statewide candidate for Vice President. In that year, state Senator Royce West sought the Democratic nomination for the U.S. Senate in 2020, but he lost the primary run-off to M. J. Hegar.

Since the 1930s, most Black Texans have identified with the Democratic Party. After national civil rights legislation was enacted in the 1960s under the leadership of President Lyndon Johnson, a Texan, Democratic party identification of Blacks strengthened. An election-eve public opinion poll for the 2020 presidential election found 86 percent of Black Texans supported Biden/Harris, while 10 percent supported Trump/Pence.[77] In a survey for the 2018 Senate race, 86 percent of Blacks intended to vote for O'Rourke and 10 percent for Cruz.[78] According to 2018 data, Blacks make up 12.5 percent of the total population of Texas and 13.6 percent of registered voters (see Table 5.1). Black voters were pivotal in the 2020 presidential election, helping Joe Biden to win in the crucial states of Pennsylvania, Michigan, Wisconsin, and Georgia. In Texas, Black voters contributed to Biden's win in Tarrant County (Fort Worth and Arlington), as the county voted Democratic for president for the first time since 1964.[79]

Black voters also contributed to Democratic Party gains in the 2018 mid-term elections, especially in Harris County where Democrats won control of county government and numerous judicial positions. Also in 2018, Democrat Colin Allred defeated an incumbent Republican to win the 32nd congressional district (northeastern Dallas County area); and he won re-election in 2020. Fort Bend County has been transitioning from reliably Republican to competitive, and in 2020 two Black Democrats were elected to countywide positions. Eric Fagan was elected as the county's first Black sheriff since the Reconstruction era, and Brian Midddleton was elected as the county's first Black district attorney.[80]

Republican prospects with most Black voters in Texas will likely depend on the direction the party takes in the post-Trump presidency. Former President Trump's responses to Black Lives Matter, the presence of Confederate flags at his rallies, and the allegations (without evidence) that he lost the 2020 presidential election because of massive voter fraud in states with large Black populations (Michigan, Pennsylvania, Georgia, and Wisconsin) create a difficult climate for Republican candidate outreach to Black voters. If the GOP should change its platform and procedures in the post Trump era, there might be new opportunities for Republican candidates to gain support by Black voters.

In early 2021, many Black Texans held elected office, including the following:

- Five U.S. representative seats in Texas's congressional delegation
- 19 seats in the Texas legislature
- More than 500 of the remaining elected positions in the state

Asian Americans

Asian Americans are a diverse and fast-growing group that is experiencing an increase in political attention and electoral influence in key districts where there are sizable Asian American communities.[81] At times, discussions of Asian Americans include Pacific Islanders, with references to the group as Asian Americans and Pacific Islanders (AAPI). Indian and Pakistani Americans comprise about 34 percent of the total Asian American population in Texas. The three counties with the highest Asian American and Pacific Islander populations are Harris, Dallas, and Fort Bend.[82]

The Asian American community is comprised of many different national origin groups with different political preferences. Indian Americans lean Democratic, Vietnamese Americans lean Republican, and Filipino Americans are more evenly divided. In public opinion polls, Republicans have lost some support from Chinese Americans. Former President Trump's references to COVID-19 as the "Chinese virus" and other comments blaming China for the pandemic were thought to be factors in increasing Asian American support for Democrats.[83] Blaming the pandemic on China led to an increase in reports of attacks and harassment of Asian Americans.[84] Anti-communism is an issue that has influenced Vietnamese Americans to support Republicans, and former President Trump's hardline approach to China was thought to be appealing to Taiwanese Americans who view China as a threat to Taiwan.

Asian American candidates in the 2020 election included Kamala Harris (Indian American) for the office of Vice President. Harris campaigned in Texas during that year with the hope of mobilizing Asian Americans to vote Democratic and help Democratic candidates win elections in districts where Asian American voters could affect the outcome. Sri Kulkarni ran competitive campaigns as the Democratic nominee in the 22nd congressional district (Fort Bend county, southwest Houston area) in 2018 and 2020. He sought to build a coalition of Asian Americans in a very diverse, and traditionally Republican district. After losing by 5 percentage points in 2018, there was speculation he could win in 2020 in the rapidly changing district, but he lost by 6.9 percentage points in 2020. Kulkarni's Republican opponent, Troy Nehls, launched an Asian American advisory board as part of his campaign's outreach efforts.[85] In the 2020 election, K. P. George was the first Indian American elected as judge in Fort Bend County.[86] In the Texas House there are four Asian American representatives (2 Democrats and 2 Republicans), all representing districts with sizable Asian American communities in the Houston and Dallas areas. As a fast-growing diverse group, Asian Americans are poised to increase their political influence in districts where their population is large enough to affect election outcomes. It is also important to remember that demographic changes in Texas will not inevitably lead to political change.

✓ 5.3 Learning Check

1. True or False: Among Latinos, Blacks, and Asian Americans, Black voters are the least likely to support Democratic candidates.

2. Why are Latinos considered to be an important group in Texas elections?

Answers at the end of this chapter.

✪ Women and LGBTQ+ in Politics

LO 5.4 Describe the evolving role of women and LGBTQ+ in Texas politics.

Race and ethnicity are not the only changes affecting Texas politics. Women and men are voting differently and LGBTQ+ Texans are also influencing elections. When studying women and politics, it is also important to consider socio-economic status, race, and ethnic differences. Women cannot be treated as one homogeneous group. Analyses that claim women prefer a specific candidate may find there are vast differences when taking race/ethnicity or education level into consideration.[87]

Women

Texas women did not begin to vote and hold public office for three-quarters of a century after Texas joined the Union. Until 1990, only four women had won a statewide office in Texas, including two-term governor Miriam A. ("Ma") Ferguson (1925–1927 and 1933–1935). She owed her office to supporters of her husband, Jim, who had been impeached and removed from the governorship in 1917. By 1990, Texas female voters outnumbered male voters, and Ann Richards was elected governor. After 1990, the number of women elected to statewide office increased dramatically.

In the early 1990s, Texas women served as mayors in about 150 of the state's towns and cities, including the top four in terms of population (Houston, Dallas, San Antonio, and El Paso). Mayor of Dallas Annette Strauss (1988–1991) was fond of greeting out-of-state visitors with this message: "Welcome to Texas, where men are men and women are mayors." As of July 2021, of the 10 largest cities in Texas, only Corpus Christi (Paulette Guajardo) and Fort Worth (Mattie Parker) had female mayors.[88] In 2018, Lina Hidalgo (Harris) and Barbara Canales (Nueces) won elections for county judge. Guajardo and Canales represent a historic first for Texas (and nationally) because the concurrent leaders of the state's 8th largest city, in the 12th largest county (Corpus Christi is in Nueces County), are Mexican American Latinas.

The impact of women's voting power was also evident in several elections early in the 21st century, when women (U.S. Senator Kay Bailey Hutchison in 2000 and state comptroller Carole Keeton Rylander Strayhorn in 2002) led all candidates on either ticket in votes received. Democratic primary results in 2014 marked the first election in which female candidates held the top two positions on a party's ticket in Texas, with Wendy Davis for governor and Leticia Van de

Image 5.4 Mexican American Latinas County Judge Barbara Canales and Mayor Paulette Guajardo lead the Nueces County/Corpus Christi Region.

Source: Twitter, Inc.

> **Tweet**
>
> **Caller.com** ✔
> @callerdotcom
>
> 'This is the power of women': Here's why these two women made history for Corpus Christi
>
> 'This is the power of women': Here's why these two women made history f...
> caller.com
>
> 7:44 AM · 2/26/21 · SocialNewsDesk

— Competency Connection —
◉ **SOCIAL RESPONSIBILITY** ◉

How do different experiences and knowledge help leaders engage and lead their communities?

Putte for lieutenant governor. In the 2020 general election, Democrats had seven female candidates for statewide office and Kamala Harris for U.S. vice president. Republicans candidate Jane Bland (for Texas Supreme Court) was the only one who won.

Female candidates have succeeded in winning an increasing number of seats in legislative bodies. In 1971, no women served in Texas's congressional delegation, and only two served in the Texas legislature. In the 2020 congressional elections, women were candidates in 19 of the 36 races, with 12 Democrats and 7 Republicans. The race for the 24th Congressional District featured two female candidates—Republican Beth Van Duyne and Democrat Candace Valenzuela, who sought to become the first Black Latina elected to Congress. Van Duyne won by a margin of 1.3 percent.

As a result of the 2020 election, in 2021 the number of women in Texas's congressional delegation was seven. The number of women in the Texas legislature was 48 (10 in the Senate and 38 in the House of Representatives), an increase of seven compared to the 86th Legislature (2019). The expanded presence of women in public office does have a positive impact on the success of legislation affecting women. Research has found a positive relationship between women holding legislative seats and the gender orientation of public policy. While more women in office can make a difference, there is also evidence that party affiliation and political ideology remain major influences on passing legislation concerning issues considered important for women.[89]

Despite their electoral victories in Texas and elsewhere across the nation, fewer women than men seek elective public office. Female candidates face numerous obstacles that may prevent them from campaigning. Although women enjoy increasing freedom, they still shoulder more responsibilities for family and home than men do (even in two-career families). Some mothers feel obliged to care for children in the home until their children finish high school. Such parental obligations, together with age-old prejudices and sexism, deny women their rightful place in government. For example, female candidates have been criticized for pursuing professional careers. In the 2014 gubernatorial election, Democratic candidate Wendy Davis was accused of "abandoning her children" because she left them with extended family while she attended Harvard Law School in Massachusetts.[90] The negative way that news media can cover female leaders is also cited as a barrier to women running for office.[91]

In the 2020 general election there was much speculation about the electoral impact of women because there was a gender gap in pre-election surveys indicating women were more likely to prefer Democratic candidates while men preferred Republicans. This illustrates the importance of not just analyzing political preferences of women, but also examining the race/ethnicity of women to understand differences. For example, Democrats hoped to make electoral gains in suburban areas, building on their suburban gains in 2018, because suburban women indicated a preference for Democrats. Upon investigation, an explanation for why suburban women seemed more likely to support Democrats was because the suburbs had become much more racially and ethnically diverse; and it was the Black, Latina, and Asian American women who preferred Democrats.[92] An election-eve poll illustrates differences among White women, Black women, and Latinas. Black women supported Biden at 89 percent, Latinas at 75 percent, and White women at 38 percent.[93]

LGBTQ+

In 2010, when Annise Parker was sworn in as mayor of Houston, she made history as the first openly gay mayor of a major U.S. city. Although Parker had been public about her sexual orientation during her previous elections as the city's comptroller and, before that, as a city council member, her November 2009 election as mayor of the country's fourth-largest city received national media attention.

The 2018 election was dubbed the "rainbow wave" in Texas because 35 gay, bisexual, and transgender candidates (a record) ran for office and 14 won. Among the 2018 winners were three for the state legislature from the Dallas area and five judicial candidates from Harris County. Lupe Valdez, the Democratic nominee for governor in 2018, was the first Latina and openly gay candidate to win a party's nomination for governor in Texas. Gina Ortiz Jones (of Filipino descent, an Air Force and Iraq War veteran and also a lesbian candidate) almost won the 23rd Congressional district in 2018, losing to Republican incumbent Will Hurd by just under 1,000 votes.[94] Bruno Lozano was elected mayor of Del Rio in 2018. The five legislators who formed the LGBTQ Caucus in the state legislature were all re-elected in 2020. In addition, several non-LGBTQ+ candidates, who were endorsed by LGBTQ+ organizations for being pro-equality, won their 2020 election contests. Gina Ortiz Jones returned as a congressional candidate for the 23rd district in 2020, although she lost again in the general election.[95]

Passing non-discrimination laws to protect the rights of the LGBTQ+ community remains a top priority for LGBTQ+ elected officials and organizations. Legislators introduced bills in the 2021 session to provide sexual orientation and gender identity protection in the state's non-discrimination laws, and to prevent discrimination in housing and public spaces (the bills did not become law). Advocates argue that the non-discrimination laws will provide an economic boost by making Texas more competitive in attracting a wider range of talent and corporate investment.[96] While legislative gains have been made, there are still efforts to pass legislation that would discriminate against the LGBTQ+ community; and anti-LGBTQ+ campaigning continues to occur.[97] A partisan divide remains with attitudes towards the LGBTQ+ community. For example, the Texas Republican Party rejected a request by Log Cabin Republicans (a LGBTQ+ Republican group) to have a booth at the party's 2020 state convention.[98]

✅ 5.4 Learning Check

1. True or False. Half of state legislators are female.
2. Why was the 2018 election referred to as the Rainbow Wave?

Answers at the end of this chapter.

✛ Elections

LO 5.5 Understand election administration, including differences among primary, general, and special elections.

In Texas, as in other states, determining voting procedures is essentially a state responsibility. The Texas Constitution authorizes the legislature to provide for the administration of elections. This term refers to the various individuals and officials who have a role in running, or administering, elections. State lawmakers, in turn, have made the secretary of state the chief elections officer for Texas but have left most details of administering elections to county officials. Thus, administration of elections in Texas is decentralized.

All election laws currently in effect in the Lone Star State are compiled into one body of law, the **Texas Election Code**.[99] In administering this legal code, however, state and party officials must protect voting rights guaranteed by federal law.

Qualifications for Voting To be eligible to vote in Texas, a person must meet the following qualifications:

- Native-born or naturalized citizen of the United States
- At least 18 years of age on Election Day
- Resident of the state and county for at least 30 days immediately preceding Election Day
- Resident of the area covered by the election on Election Day
- Registered voter for at least 30 days immediately preceding Election Day
- Not a convicted felon (unless sentence, probation, and parole are completed)
- Not declared mentally incompetent by a court of law[100]

Voter registration is intended to determine in advance whether prospective voters meet all the qualifications prescribed by law. Most states, including Texas, use a permanent registration system. Under this plan, voters register once and remain registered unless they change their mailing address and fail to notify the voting registrar within three years or lose their eligibility to register in some other way.

The Texas Election Code provides for voter registration centers in addition to those sites authorized by Congress under the motor-voter law. Thus, Texans may also register at local marriage license offices, in public high schools, with any volunteer deputy registrar, or in person at the office of the county voting registrar. Students away at college may choose to reregister using their college address as their residence if they want to vote locally, or they must request an absentee ballot or be in their hometown during early voting or on Election Day if they wish to vote.

Between November 1 and November 15 of each odd-numbered year, the registrar mails to every registered voter in the county a registration certificate that is effective for the succeeding two voting years. A Texan can legally cast a ballot without a certificate by providing some form of identification (such as a driver's license) and signing an affidavit of registration at the polls. However, under the state's law requiring a voter to show a valid photo identification for casting a ballot, the voter's name on the photo identification must appear exactly as it appears on the elections department's registration list. If the name on the photo ID doesn't match exactly but is "substantially similar" to the name on the registration list, the voter will be permitted to cast a ballot after signing an affidavit stating that he or she is the same person as the one on the list of registered voters.

Voting Early Opportunities to vote early in Texas are limited to in-person early voting, voting by mail, and facsimile machine voting (for military personnel and their dependents in hostile fire or combat zones). Texas law allows voters to vote "early"—that is, beginning 17 days before a November general election,

Texas Election Code
The body of state law concerning parties, primaries, and elections.

12 days before a March primary election or runoff, and 10 days before runoffs in all other elections. Early voting ends, however, four days before any election or primary. In less populated rural counties, early voting occurs at the county courthouse. In more populous urban areas, the county's election administrator's office accommodates voters by maintaining additional sites for early voting, including at malls, schools, and college campuses. According to figures from the Texas Secretary of State's office, more than 57 percent of registered voters voted early in the 2020 general election, up from nearly 40 percent in 2018.

Due to the COVID-19 pandemic, Governor Abbott issued an executive order adding a week of early voting for the July 14 primary runoff election and November 3, 2020 general election. The extra week of early voting was intended to reduce crowds and lines of people waiting to vote, thus reducing the risk of spreading and contracting COVID-19. Republican party officials sued Abbott for adding the extra week, claiming he exceeded his authority. However, the Texas Supreme Court ruled in favor of the extra week.[101] This extra week, plus concerns about avoiding crowds on election day during a pandemic, likely caused the increase in the number of Texans voting early in 2020.

Registered voters who qualify may vote by mail during an early voting period. Voting by mail has been available for decades to elderly Texans and those with physical disabilities. Today, anyone meeting any of the following qualifications can vote by mail-in ballot:

- Will not be in his or her county of residence during the entire early voting period and on Election Day
- Is at least age 65
- Is, or will be, physically disabled on Election Day, including those who expect to be confined for childbirth on that day
- Is in jail (but not a convicted felon) during the early voting period and on Election Day
- Is in the military or is a dependent of military personnel and has resided in Texas[102]

Concerns about the COVID-19 pandemic led to calls to expand voting by mail for the 2020 elections. Those advocating for expansion of voting by mail (Democrats and voting rights activists) argued that the concern for catching COVID-19 while voting counted as a disability. Most Republicans were opposed. After winning an initial victory in state district court, the Texas Supreme Court ruled against expanding the disability qualification to include concern about catching COVID-19. Nonetheless, the numbers of individuals requesting ballots to vote by mail increased. Meanwhile, the United States Postal Service was in the news because of delays in mail delivery. Voters were urged to mail their ballots early or drop them off in person. Several counties proceeded to add additional locations for voters to drop off ballots. Governor Abbott opposed adding drop-off locations, and he ordered counties to have one location. Larger counties challenged the order, arguing that in heavily populated counties (such as Harris) it was impractical and unfair to voters to have only one location. Nevertheless, a federal appeals court upheld Abbott's order to limit counites to a single location.[103]

Image 5.5 Sample General Election Ballot for Val Verde County, Texas

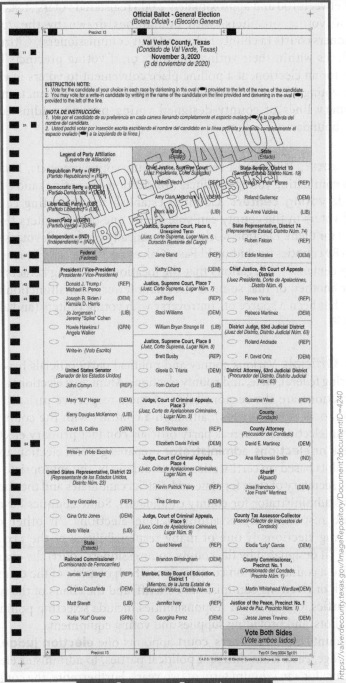

Competency Connection
★ PERSONAL RESPONSIBILITY ★

Straight ticket voting was not available for the 2020 general election. Do voters have a personal responsibility to learn about each race and candidate, or is voting for a party a responsible action because there are too many candidates for voters to learn about?

Voting Precincts The basic geographic area for conducting national, state, district, and county elections is the **voting precinct**. Each precinct usually contains between 100 and approximately 2,000 registered voters. Texas has more than 8,500 voting precincts, with boundaries drawn by the 254 county commissioners courts (a county judge and four commissioners). Citizens vote at polling places within their voting precincts or, if voting precincts have been combined for an election, at a polling place convenient to voters in each of the combined voting precincts. Municipal and special district precincts must follow the boundary lines of county-designed voting precincts adjusted to their respective boundaries.

Voting Centers While most Texas counties use voting precincts, Texas election law allows eliminating voting precincts (for election day voting) and establishing countywide **voting centers**. Counties establish several voting centers, and registered voters in the county can vote at any one of the centers that is most convenient for them. Election workers electronically verify each voter's eligibility. More than 80 counties (including El Paso, Galveston, Collin, and Brazos counties) use voting centers.[104] Allegations that the locations of voting centers favor one party over another, or that some centers have fewer (or malfunctioning voting machines) has been a source of controversy with voting centers (and also voting precincts).[105]

Election Officials Various county and political party officials have a role in administering federal, state, and county elections. Municipal elections and special district elections are the responsibility of their respective jurisdictions (see Chapter 3, Local Governments), although a contract with the county may be made to run elections. Whereas party officials conduct primary elections, the county clerk or **elections administrator** prepares general election and special election ballots based on certification of candidates by the appropriate authority (that is, the secretary of state for state and district candidates and the county clerk or elections administrator for county candidates). Some counties have officials whose sole responsibility is administering elections. In other counties, administering elections is one of many responsibilities of the tax assessor-collector or (if designated by the county commissioners court) the county clerk. There is also a county election commission, which consists of the county judge, county clerk or elections administrator, sheriff, and the chairs of the two major political parties. Commission responsibilities include selecting polling places, printing ballots, and providing supplies and voting equipment.

Each county commissioners' court appoints one **election judge** and one alternate judge, each from different political parties, to administer elections in every precinct for a maximum term of two years. Furthermore, the commissioners court canvasses and certifies election results. The election judge selects as many clerks as will be needed to assist in conducting general and special elections in a precinct. Clerks must be selected from different political parties. In city elections, the city secretary (some cities call them municipal clerk) appoints election judges, unless the city contracts with the county to administer an election.

voting precinct
The basic geographic area for conducting primaries and elections; Texas is divided into more than 8,500 voting precincts.

voting center
A countywide voting system that allows voters to vote, after being electronically verified, at any voting center in a county.

elections administrator
Person appointed to supervise voter registration and voting for a county.

election judge
Official appointed by the county commissioners court to administer an election in a voting precinct.

▶ Point/Counterpoint

Should Texas Switch to a Ranked Choice Voting System?

The Issue The Single-Member District Plurality (SMDP) system is widely used in the United States and Texas to elect members of Congress and state legislators. In this system, candidates compete in an electoral district, and the candidate receiving the most votes (a plurality) wins the election. However, winning by a plurality means it is possible to win with less than a majority. When this happens, a majority of voters preferred other candidates to the winner. The state of Maine adopted ranked choice voting (RCV) and used it for the first time in 2018. In this system, voters rank the candidates in order of choice. Hence, in a race with four candidates, voters can rank their top choice as number one and their least preferred as number four. If one candidate receives a majority of the first-choice votes, they win. If no candidate has a majority of first-choice votes, the process proceeds to the "instant run-off phase." The candidate with the fewest first-choice votes is eliminated, and for voters who ranked the eliminated candidate first, their second choice is now counted. If one of the remaining candidates now has a majority of votes after including the second choice from voters who had the eliminated candidate ranked first, that candidate wins, and if no candidate has a majority, the process repeats until a candidate wins a majority.

For	Against
1. The winning candidate will win a majority of the vote with RCV, unlike the plurality system when a candidate can win with less than a majority.	1. Stating that winning by a majority is "better" than winning by a plurality is a judgment call.
2. RCV eliminates the "spoiler" effect that minor parties can have in an election.	2. Voters who do not rank candidates, and only vote for their top choice, may not have a vote if the ballot goes to second choices.
3. Supporters of minor party candidates are not wasting their votes when they rank a minor candidate as their first choice.	3. Counting RCV ballots can be complicated, especially when there is a large number of candidates. Election administrators need suitable technology for the counting, and that is an additional expense.
4. RCV includes an "instant" run-off and eliminates the need for a separate run-off election.	4. Voters may not understand RCV since they are used to voting for a single candidate instead of ranking them.

Sources: National Conference of State Legislatures, "Ranked-Choice Voting," NCSL.org, https://www.ncsl.org/research/elections-and-campaigns/ranked-choice-voting636934215.aspx; "Ranked Choice Voting 101" FairVote.org, https://www.fairvote.org/rcv#where_is_ranked_choice_voting_used.

Competency Connection — SOCIAL RESPONSIBILITY

Do you recommend Texas switches to a Ranked Choice Voting system to insure that candidates win with a majority and encourage voting for minor party candidates? Why or why not?

Voting Systems In general elections, Texas uses three voting systems: paper ballot; optical scan (similar to a scantron); and direct recording electronic (DRE), also known as a touch screen. In every county, the county commissioners court determines which system will be used. Each system has advantages and disadvantages in such matters as ballot and equipment costs, ease of use by voters, accuracy of counting, labor cost, and time required to count the votes. For example, paper ballots are relatively cheap and easy to use, but counting is slow. Some sparsely populated counties continue to use paper ballots, which must be counted by hand. Some optical scan and DRE systems automatically count each vote as the ballot is cast. Optical scan and DRE systems require mechanical and electronic voting equipment, which is expensive to purchase and store but can reduce election costs when many voters are involved. Under Texas law, anyone on a space flight on Election Day can vote by electronic ballot that is transmitted from the astronaut-voter's home county through NASA.

On general election ballot forms, lists of candidates for national office appear first, followed by state, district, and local offices, in that order. (Image 5.5 shows a sample ballot used in a recent general election.) A list of all write-in candidates who have filed an appropriate declaration is posted in each polling place on the day of an election. Legislation passed in 2017 eliminated straight ticket voting that allowed voting for all of a party's candidates with a single mark. The 2020 election was the first without straight ticket voting. In some instances, candidates for nomination or election to an office may request a recount of ballots if they believe vote tabulations were inaccurate. The Texas Election Code also provides detailed procedures for settling disputed elections.

Since the 1960s, several changes in voting procedures by both federal and state governments have been made to encourage full, informed participation in elections. As a result of the 1975 extension of the federal Voting Rights Act, registration and election materials used in all Texas counties must be printed in both English and Spanish. In Harris County and the City of Houston, materials in Chinese and Vietnamese must also be provided. Texas voters can take voting guides, newspaper endorsements, and other printed material into a voting booth, although wireless communication devices such as cell phones and tablet computers are prohibited.[106]

Disabled voters are ensured access to polling places and an opportunity to cast a secret ballot. One option is curbside voting, with election workers taking a ballot to voters who have difficulty entering the voting location. Harris County set up drive through voting locations for the 2020 election. All voters could use these locations during the early voting period. Republicans challenged this procedure, alleging it was an illegal expansion of curbside voting (which is only allowed for voters with a disability). There was also a Republican-led lawsuit to toss out nearly 127,000 drive through votes in Harris County. A federal judge denied this effort to reject votes. Due to the legal challenges, Harris County decided to use only one drive through voting location on election day.[107]

Primary, General, and Special Elections

The electoral process includes nomination and election of candidates through primary, general, and special elections. This section will focus on state and county elections. Local elections are discussed in Chapter 3, Local Governments. A clear distinction must be made between party primaries and general elections. **Primary** elections are party functions that allow party members to select nominees to run against the candidates of opposing parties in a general election for national, state, and county offices. **General elections** determine which candidates will fill government offices. These electoral contests are public and are conducted, financed, and administered by state, county, and municipal governments as well as by special districts.

Thus, even though the state regulates and largely finances primaries, they serve only as a means for political parties to nominate candidates. The general election ballot also includes the names of **independent candidates**, space for write-in candidates, and names of candidates nominated by party convention because the law does not require nomination by direct primary.

Primary Elections

Political parties conduct primaries to select nominees for public office. In Texas, party primaries are held in even-numbered years. Presidential primaries occur every four years and provide a means for Democrats and Republicans to select delegates to their parties' national conventions, where candidates for president and vice president are nominated. Other primaries occur every two years, when party members go to the polls to choose candidates for the U.S. Congress and for many state, district, and county offices. If a political party's candidate receives more than 20 percent of the total gubernatorial vote, the party must use primaries to select its nominees in the following even-numbered year. Political parties may use primaries for selecting their nominees "... if the party's nominee for governor in the most recent gubernatorial election received at least two percent but less than 20 percent of the total number of votes received by all candidates for governor."[108] Even minor parties that reach this threshold, along with those that fail to do so, use conventions to select their nominees.

Development of Direct Primaries A unique product of American politics, the **direct primary** was designed to provide a nominating method that would avoid domination by party bosses and allow wider participation by party members. This form of nomination permits party members to choose their candidates directly at the polls. For each office (except president and vice president of the United States and some local officials), party members select by popular vote the person they wish to be their party's candidate in the general election, in which candidates of all parties compete. In Texas, an absolute majority of the vote (more than 50 percent) is required for nomination. If the primary fails

primary
An election conducted within the party to nominate candidates who will run for public office in a subsequent general election.

general election
Held in November of even-numbered years to elect county, state, and federal officials from among candidates nominated in primaries or (for minor parties) in nominating conventions.

independent candidate
A candidate who runs in a general election without party endorsement or selection.

direct primary
A nominating system that allows voters to participate directly in the selection of candidates for public office.

to produce such a majority, a **runoff primary** is held the fourth Tuesday in May to allow party members to choose a candidate from the first primary's top two vote-getters. Due to the COVID-19 pandemic, Governor Abbott ordered the May 26, 2020, runoff primary postponed until July 14, 2020, with early voting beginning July 6.[109]

Four basic forms of the direct primary have evolved in America. Most states use some form of **closed primary**, which requires voters to declare a party affiliation when registering to vote. They must show party identification when voting in a primary election and can vote only in the party primary for which they are registered. Other states use an **open primary**, which does not require party identification of voters. At the polls, voters in an open primary can choose a ballot for any party, regardless of their party affiliation. Texas uses a combination of open and closed primaries.

Some states use a variation of the open primary, called the **top-two primary** (California and Washington) or jungle primary (Louisiana). Here voters receive the same ballot, on which are printed all candidate names. Candidates from all parties run in a single election. If a candidate receives more than 50 percent of the vote, he or she is declared the winner. If no candidate receives more than 50 percent, the top two vote-getters will participate in a runoff election. A criticism of the open primary is that it gives voters of one party an opportunity to sabotage the primary of another party. This can occur when voters who normally affiliate with one party try to nominate a "fringe" candidate from another party who has little chance of victory in the general election. Criticisms of top-two and jungle primaries include (1) they may produce two candidates from the same party competing for the same office in the general election, and (2) they limit the possibility of a third-party or independent candidate's ability to win the nomination.

Texas Primaries Before 1905, various practices had been used to select a party's nominees for public office. With the enactment of the Terrell Election Law in 1905, however, Texas political parties gained the opportunity to conduct primaries. The Texas Democratic Party has held primaries since that year, but the Republican Party did not begin conducting primaries until 1926.

Beginning in the early 1950s, it became common practice for Texans to participate in the primaries of the Democratic Party and then legally cross over to vote for Republican candidates in the general election, a practice known as **crossover voting**. Historically, Texas Republicans were more likely to engage in crossover voting. As the number of Republican candidates increased, however, the number of crossover Republican voters correspondingly declined. Today, Democrats in Republican-dominated counties (such as Collin, Denton, Midland, and Montgomery) are likely to participate in crossover voting.

Texas does not register voters as Democrats or Republicans. The Texas Election Code requires voters to identify their party affiliation at the time of voting when they choose to vote in the Democratic or Republican primaries. This makes Texas a combination of a closed primary state and an open primary state. Voter registration certificates may be stamped with the party name when

runoff primary
Held after the first primary to allow party members to choose a candidate from the first primary's top two vote-getters if no candidate received a majority vote.

closed primary
A primary in which voters must declare their support for a party before they are permitted to participate in the selection of its candidates.

open primary
A primary in which voters are not required to declare party affiliation.

top-two primary
A nominating process in which voters indicate their preferences by using a single ballot on which are printed the names and respective party labels of all persons seeking nomination. A candidate who receives more than 50 percent of the vote is elected; otherwise, a runoff between the top two candidates must be held.

crossover voting
A practice whereby a person participates in the primary of one party, then votes for one or more candidates of another party in the general election.

voters participate in a primary. Qualified voters vote in the primary of any party, as long as they have not already voted in another party's primary or participated in another party's convention in the same year.

Administering Primaries In most states, political parties sponsor and administer their own primaries. The Texas Election Code allocates this responsibility to each party's county executive committee. The primary normally occurs on the first Tuesday of March. In 2020, the primary was held on March 3; and in 2022, it is scheduled for March 1.

Individuals who want to run in a direct primary for their party's nomination for a multicounty district office or a statewide office must file necessary papers with their party's state chair. This party official certifies the names of these persons to each county chair in counties in which the election is administered. Prospective candidates who want their names placed on the primary ballot for a county or precinct office must file with their party's county chair. County executive committees for each political party supervise the printing of primary ballots. If the parties conduct a joint primary, the county elections administrator or the county clerk administers the election. If each party conducts its own primaries, county chairs arrange for voting equipment and polling places in the precincts or voting centers. Together with the state executive committee, the county executive committee determines the order of names of candidates on the ballot and **canvasses** (that is, confirms and certifies) the vote tally for each candidate.

canvass
To scrutinize the results of an election and then confirm and certify the vote tally for each candidate.

Financing Primaries Major expenses for running party primaries include renting facilities for polls (the places where voting is conducted), printing ballots and other election materials, and paying election judges and clerks. In recent years, approximately 30 percent of the cost of holding Texas primaries has come

📊 How Do We Compare...

In Types of Primaries?

Most Populous U.S. States	Primary Type	U.S. States Bordering Texas	Primary Type
California	Top-two primary	Arkansas	Open
Florida	Closed	Louisiana	Jungle (two-round system)
New York	Closed	New Mexico	Closed
Texas	**Combination (open/closed)**	Oklahoma	Closed

Source: FairVote, http://www.fairvote.org/primaries#congressional_primary_type_by_state.

— Competency Connection —
☼ **CRITICAL THINKING** ☼

Is it fair, in a primary election, for only members of a party to choose their nominee, or should all registered voters have the opportunity to participate?

from filing fees paid by candidates. The balance of these expenses is usually paid by the State of Texas. For example, candidates for the office of U.S. senator pay a $5,000 filing fee, and candidates for governor and all other statewide offices pay a $3,750 filing fee. Candidates for the Texas Senate and the Texas House of Representatives pay $1,250 and $750, respectively.[110]

In lieu of paying a fee, a candidate may file a nominating petition containing a specified number of signatures of people eligible to vote for the office for which that candidate is running. A candidate for statewide office must obtain 5,000 signatures. Candidates for district, county, or precinct office, and for offices of other political subdivisions, must obtain either 500 signatures or the equivalent of 2 percent of the area's votes for all candidates for governor in the last general election, whichever is less.

General and Special Elections

The date prescribed by Article I of the U.S. Constitution for congressional elections is the first Tuesday following the first Monday in November of even-numbered years (for example, November 3, 2020 and November 8, 2022). Presidential elections take place on the same day in November every four years (for example, November 3, 2020 and November 5, 2024).

In Texas's general elections involving candidates for state, district, and county offices, the candidate who receives a plurality (the largest number of votes) in a contest is the winner. Even if no candidate wins a majority, because of votes received by third-party or independent candidates, the state does not hold a runoff election. Thus, Beth Van Duyne (R-Irving) was elected to Congress in 2020 after receiving 48.8 percent of the vote to Candace Valenzuela's (D) 47.5 percent (the rest of the vote went to the Libertarian candidate and two independent candidates). Elections for governor and other statewide officers serving terms of four years are scheduled in the off year. These **off-year or midterm elections** are held in November of the even-numbered years between presidential elections (for example, November 6, 2018 and November 8, 2022). Along with most other states, Texas follows this schedule to minimize the influence of presidential campaigns on the election of state and local officials. Elections to fill offices for two-year or six-year terms must be conducted in both off years and presidential years.

In addition, **special elections** are called to vote on constitutional amendments and local bond issues, as well as fill interim vacancies in legislative and congressional districts. If no candidate obtains a majority in a special election, a runoff contest between the top two contenders must be conducted to determine the winner. On September 29, 2020, voters participated in a special election to fill a vacancy for Senate District 30. Six candidates filed to fill the north Texas area Senate seat, but no candidate emerged with a majority. This led to a runoff election held December 19, 2020. Drew Springer (R-Muenster) won with 56.5 percent of the vote. Vacancies in state judicial and executive offices are filled by gubernatorial appointment until the next general election, special elections are not required. Special elections for local governments (cities and counties) are discussed in Chapter 3, Local Governments.

off-year or midterm election
A general election held in the even-numbered year following a presidential election.

special election
An election called by the governor to fill a vacancy (for example, U.S. congressional or state legislative office) or to vote on a proposed state constitutional amendment.

✓ 5.5 Learning Check

1. True or False: Political parties are responsible for conducting general elections.

2. What is the difference between open and closed primaries?

Answers at the end of this chapter.

✠ Keeping Current

Aftermath of 2020 Election and Looking Forward

The 2020 election wound down on January 20, 2021, when Joe Biden and Kamala Harris were sworn in as president and vice-president, respectively, two weeks after a violent insurrection at the U.S. Capitol to prevent Congress from counting electoral college votes. Former president Trump and his allies claimed, without evidence, that he had won and that the election was stolen because of massive voter fraud. However, former President Trump and his allies lost their legal challenges.

Nonetheless, many states, including Texas, have proposed legislation to make voting more difficult, on the basis that election fraud must be stopped. Voting rights advocates counter that the proposed legislation is unnecessary, because there was no evidence of massive voter fraud in 2020, and that the legislation is really an effort to suppress voter turnout. Democrats in Congress have proposed legislation to protect voting rights and President Biden issued an executive order to expand voting access.

Texas Republicans attempted to pass Senate Bill (SB) 7 during the 2021 (87th) regular session. SB 7 included provisions to require proof when claiming a disability to vote by mail, reduced early voting opportunities, and made it easier for a judge to overturn an election. SB 7 failed when House Democrats broke quorum by leaving the chamber late in the evening on May 30, 2021 as the midnight deadline to approve the bill was approaching. The House must have 100 members present to conduct business, so by leaving, House Democrats prevented a vote on SB 7 before the deadline. Governor Abbott called a Special Session for July 2021 to make another attempt at changing voting laws (similar to SB 7).

The legislature must also address redistricting. Texas gained two seats to the U.S. House, and the boundaries for U.S House seats must be re-drawn to add the new seats. Furthermore, house and senate districts for the Texas Legislature also must be re-drawn to reflect shifts in population. Allegations of gerrymandering and legal challenges to the redistricting for voting rights violations are inevitable. Texas Republicans control redistricting, and are likely to draw districts that are friendly for Republican candidates. Governor Abbott is expected to call a Special Session in fall of 2021 for redistricting.

Conclusion

Texas continues to have low voter turnout compared to other states. Individual level characteristics, such as education and age affect voter turnout, as well as institutional features of the electoral system, such as the ease or difficulty of voting. The vote choice is influenced by candidate evaluations, issues, and party identification. In addition, there are differences in voting preferences for different racial/ethnic groups, as well as for women and LGBTQ+.

Chapter Summary

LO 5.1 Explain how individual characteristics and the voting process promotes and inhibits voter participation. Individual characteristics such as education, age, and strength of partisanship can help explain voter turnout. Federal voting rights legislation has expanded the electorate, simplified voter registration, and encouraged voting. Nonetheless, states can implement practices that make voting easier, and that tends to lead to higher turnout. Texas has not implemented many practices associated with higher turnout.

LO 5.2 Analyze how voters choose which candidates to vote for and the role of campaigns. Voters chose which candidate to support based on character, issues, and party identification. Group differences, including race and ethnicity, women, and LGBTQ+ also affect the vote choice. Political campaigns seek to mobilize voters and use political advertising and social media. Campaigns are expensive, and money must be raised to run viable ones. Regulations on campaign finance have been weakened by U.S. Supreme Court rulings.

LO 5.3 Describe the impact of Texas's changing demographics on voting and elections. Racial and ethnic factors are strong influences on Texas politics and shape political campaigns. The increasing size of the Latino population makes Latinos an important factor in elections. A majority of Latino voters and super majorities of Black voters participate in Democratic primaries and vote for Democratic candidates in general elections, while Asian Americans have begun to trend toward Democrats. Lower levels of political activity than in the White population limits the impact of the Latino and Asian American electorates.

LO 5.4 Describe the evolving role of women and LGBTQ+ in Texas politics. Before 1990, only four women had won a statewide office in Texas. Since then, women have made notable gains statewide, in the legislature and at the local level. Despite their electoral victories in Texas and elsewhere across the nation, fewer women than men seek elective public office. Women continue to confront sexism when seeking public office. The 2018 general election was called the "rainbow wave" because of the success of LGBTQ+ candidates.

LO 5.5 Understand election administration, including differences among primary, general, and special elections. The Texas Election Code is the body of election laws for the state. Primary elections are elections conducted within a political party to nominate candidates who will run for public office in a subsequent general election. General elections are conducted in November of even-numbered years to elect county, state, and federal officials from among candidates nominated in primary elections (or for small parties, in nominating conventions). Special elections are called by the governor to fill a vacancy (for example, U.S. congressional or state legislative office) or to vote on a proposed state constitutional amendment.

Key Terms

affirmative racial gerrymandering, p. 174

at-large district, p. 174

Campaign Reform Act, p. 187

canvass, p. 207

closed primary, p. 206

crossover voting, p. 206

dark money, p. 188

direct primary, p. 205

early voting, p. 174

election judge, p. 202

elections administrator, p. 202

general election, p. 205

gerrymandering, p. 173

grandfather clause, p. 173

hard money, p. 187

independent candidate, p. 205

independent expenditures, p. 187

literacy tests, p. 173

mobilization, p. 171

motor-voter law, p. 175

Learning Check Answers

5.1
1. Yes, those with college degrees are more likely to report voting than those without a college degree.
2. False. Only Texans renewing their driving licenses online have an opportunity to register to vote online.

5.2
1. False. Party identification is a very good predictor of understanding why voters choose candidates.
2. Negative campaigning is most effective when it helps to inform voters and is civil

5.3
1. False. Black voters are more likely to support Democratic party candidates than Latinos or Asian Americans
2. Latinos are an important group because the size of the population, and their electoral impact, is growing.

5.4
1. False. There are 10 females (31 seats) in the Texas Senate and 38 (150 seats) in the Texas House.
2. The 2018 was referred to as the Rainbow Wave because several openly LGBTQ+ candidates were elected to the legislature and local offices.

5.5
1. False. Political parties are responsible for primary elections. Government officials are responsible for conducting general elections.
2. Closed primaries are restricted to registered members of a political party. Any registered voter can participate in an open primary.

6

The Media and Politics

Learning Objectives

6.1 Compare the ways in which Texans get their information today with past patterns.

6.2 Describe the roles of the media in Texas politics.

6.3 Discuss the roles of the media in modern Texas election campaigns and citizen movements.

6.4 Analyze the issue of bias in the Texas media.

6.5 Discuss the representation of women and ethnic minorities in Texas media.

6.6 Distinguish how print and electronic media are regulated by government.

6.7 Discuss the positive and negative effects of changes the media are undergoing in Texas.

Image 6.1 Students in a computer lab at the University of Texas Rio Grande Valley, Brownsville Campus.

Robert Daemmrich Photography Inc/Corbis/Getty Images

Competency Connection
☆ **CRITICAL THINKING** ☆

Texans who want to stay informed are transitioning from reliance on newspapers and television to the Internet and social media. How well are you served by this change? Why? After reading the chapter, think about whether you would give the same answer.

In February 2021, Winter Storm Uri brought a week of arctic temperatures to Texas, creating major problems for all of the state. Half of Texans lost their water, 70 percent lost power, a third reported water damage to their home, and 200 died. Losses were estimated at $195 to $295 billion (potentially greater than hurricanes Harvey and Ike). Once water was restored, it had to be boiled to be safe to drink. Transportation of goods and commuting to work were limited. Hoarding was a problem, with water and many food items disappearing from grocery shelves. At Governor Abbott's request, President Biden made a federal disaster designation.

News media covered the approaching storm but were disrupted as power was lost. Social media, the Internet, local television and radio news, and texts all became sources for the latest weather, the status of power and water, road conditions, and sources of help. Many local governments took quick action to try to deal with the loss of power and water but were slow in keeping their citizens informed. The media also began to play its traditional role of questioning those in charge. The largest issue was the failure of the power industry to be prepared for the extreme cold. The state's deregulated power industry had not been required to winterize, and the power grid was not linked to the national power network so as to be able to draw power from outside the state. State leaders quickly began to politicize the issue, trying to place blame on the other side. The media debunked some of the obviously false charges (such as solar and wind energy being the source of the failure) and began looking at abuses such as price gouging, huge spikes in bills coming from some energy plans, and the suffering caused for people dependent on electrical devices or transportation for dialysis or similar treatments.

The **media** have long had a major impact on politics in Texas and the nation. They play a key role in maintaining our democracy: informing citizens and leaders about what governments and politicians are doing and the debates about those actions, sometimes reporting information officials would rather we didn't know; affecting the issues that governments consider seriously; and, to some degree, shaping public opinion. In carrying out these roles, the media both affect and are affected by the other political actors—government and political leaders, interest groups, and the public. Because of the importance of the media, serious debate surrounds whether and what kinds of bias exist, the rapidly changing nature of the media, and the role of women and racial and ethnic minorities. These topics are explored in this chapter.

In many ways, Texas is a unique state. However, as we will see, the media and their role in politics are similar to national patterns in most respects—with a few important exceptions. This chapter compares national and Texas patterns and explores how they play out in Texas.

This text distinguishes between three types of media: The term *print media* is generally accepted for newspapers and news magazines. Here, we refer to radio and television as *electronic media* and distinguish between broadcast and cable television. The Internet and social media are commonly referred to as *digital media*. Second, note that the word *media* is plural; for example, "The media *have* long had a major impact."

media
Major means of mass communication.

★ Where Do We Get Our Information?

LO 6.1   Compare the ways in which Texans get their information today with past patterns.

The simple answer to the question of where we get our information is that it comes from newspapers, news magazines, television, radio, the Internet, social media, and people we know. However, the complete answer is more complex. Most people get news from more than one source (commonly three or four), and whether they remember the information depends on the trust they have for the source and other factors.

Change in news sources is ongoing. Newspapers were once the dominant source of news. Today, however, newspapers are in decline in both numbers and readership, although they remain very important for Texas and national leaders. Television news is widely watched but is thin in content and is being overtaken by the Internet and social media. Newer platforms are helping sustain older platforms. Newspapers and television stations boost their audience with their own internet news sites. Social media is changing as high school and college age Texans move away from Facebook to other internet platforms, while senior Texans are increasing their use of Facebook. Two-thirds of Texans now get news on their smartphones, the same proportion as those that use a desktop or laptop.

Family and friends are another important source of news for many people. The most common way that people begin the process of understanding a news story is, not surprisingly, from conversations—in person or over the phone (voice or text). For example, over two-thirds of Texans got news about the COVID-19 pandemic from family and friends. A majority of people follow up the information from family and friends by seeking the story in the news media—traditional or new. Texans still count more on news organizations than family and friends for information, but they tend to be suspicious of both sources.[1]

Tables 6.1 and 6.2 provide two different looks at how Texans learn about news. (They are based on scientific surveys by Texas universities.) Table 6.1 simply asks people how they got their news in the last two weeks and allows multiple answers. Several things stand out. Texans and the national population are quite similar in their news sources across the various platforms. Individuals commonly get their news from more than one source. Local television news gets the most viewers, but network news, cable news, local newspapers, and social media inform similar percentages of the state and national populations. Table 6.2 asks Texans their *main* source of news. Television in its various forms is most important for three in four Texans, followed by social media, newspapers, and radio. Nationally, television is still the largest source of news but is losing ground to the Internet and social media faster than in Texas.

These and other surveys suggest that Texans still think of television as their biggest source of news in general, but the most important source may depend on the subject of the news. When Texans were asked how often they followed the

Follow *Practicing Texas Politics* on Twitter @PracTexPol

Table 6.1 Sources of News in Past 14 Days for Texas and the United States (percent)

Broadcast TV	TX	U.S.
Local television news	57	51
Network evening news	26	27
NewsHour on PBS	5	5
Cable TV		
CNN	25	22
Fox News Cable	21	19
MSNBC	13	12
Newspapers		
Local newspaper	25	30
Washington Post	10	10
New York Times	9	11
Wall Street Journal	6	6
Radio		
National Public Radio	10	13
Rush Limbaugh Show	6	4
Online News Sites		
The Huffington Post	8	8
Drudge Report	3	2
Breitbart	3	1
Social Media		
Facebook	28	24
YouTube	12	8
Twitter	7	6
Instagram	3	3
Reddit	1	2
Snapchat	1	2

Question: "From which sources did you get news IN THE PAST 14 DAYS, two weeks ago through today?" Multiple answers permitted. Field dates: May 16–31, 2018. Number of respondents: Texas 1,004; U.S. 1,062.

Source: Annette Strauss Institute for Civic Life, Moody College of Communication, University of Texas at Austin, *2018 Texas Media & Society Survey: Topline Results*, https://moody.utexas.edu/centers/strauss/texas-media-society-survey.

— Competency Connection —
✿ CRITICAL THINKING ✿

The table shows few major differences in sources of news between the Texas and national samples. Why do you believe this similarity exists?

Table 6.2 Main Source of News for Texans

Television	%
Cable News (CNN, Fox, MSNBC)	28
National broadcast television (ABC, CBS, NBC, PBS)	25
Local television news	20
Spanish news (Telemundo, Univision, etc.)	2
Social media	**11**
Newspapers	
National newspapers (*NY Times, Wash. Post*, etc.)	4
Local newspapers (Texas examples)	3
Radio (NPR, Talk Radio)	3
Other	5
TOTAL	101

Question: "What is your main source of news?" Field dates: June 29–July 7, 2020. Number of people responding: 1,883. Adds to 101 percent because of rounding.

Source: Dallas Morning News/UT Tyler, *Texas Registered Voter Sample*, 2020, https://www.uttyler.edu/politicalscience/pollingcenter/.

— Competency Connection —
☼ **CRITICAL THINKING** ☼

There are many sources of news. Can you rank them in terms of which are better sources? What factors did you consider in your ranking?

2016 election campaign in each of the media, slightly more followed the campaign on the Internet than TV—both ahead of newspapers. But when Texans were asked their sources of information about COVID-19 in 2020, "local news" and "family and close friends" were the largest sources. "Newspaper and journalism online outlets" and television followed, with a significant drop off to social media.[2]

In Texas and the nation, people tend to value local news. When asked how closely they paid attention to "local news," 76 percent of Texans said "very closely" or "somewhat closely," more attention than national, international, or sports news received. Only attention to weather topped local news.[3] A survey of views on local news in major metropolitan areas, including six in Texas—Dallas-Fort Worth, Houston, Austin, San Antonio, El Paso, and Corpus Christi—found great similarities among all six. In each, substantial majorities felt attached to their community and followed local news; television and Internet topped print and radio as preferred sources of local news; local journalists were seen as in touch with the community and as reporting accurately and fairly; but only a minority of people found it "easy to stay informed about government and politics." When asked if government and politics were "important for daily life," only a minority of each metro thought so. (This helps explain why most people are satisfied with the minimal coverage of public affairs available on television, radio, and much of social media.) Of eleven topics covered as news, people in each metro ranked government and politics fifth (behind weather, traffic, and crime but ahead of sports, arts and culture, and restaurants and bars).[4]

On the other hand, a few differences stood out. For five of the areas, television was the most preferred source of local news. In Austin, however, the Internet (news websites/apps and social media) was preferred by a majority. Corpus Christi and El Paso residents were most likely to prefer TV, least likely to prefer the Internet, and most likely to praise local journalists.

Digital Media: The Internet and Social Media

In comparison to the other media, the Internet is a recent phenomenon with its roots in the 1960s. The blooming of what we think of as the Internet and **social media** came in the period 1994–2004. Since that time, there has been an explosive growth of websites, both in number and function. By at least 2010, internet news sites and social media had become important sources of political news for Texans, and the proportion of users has grown ever since. Successful candidates and political movements now rely heavily on the Internet. Social distancing and restrictions on meeting size because of the 2020 pandemic increased reliance on digital campaigning.

The pandemic also highlighted a problem in Texas's digital infrastructure. When schools closed, students had to rely on the Internet for instruction. But many students in rural and poorer urban areas lacked computers and internet access. (See "How Do We Compare…") Schools tried to provide computers, but some students gathered around stores, libraries, and other hot spots to pick up Wi-Fi or simply missed out.

> About 2 million people across the state lack access to fixed broadband. Rural areas are especially hard-hit: 31 percent of rural Texans do not have any access to basic broadband service…. The problem of a digital divide isn't limited to rural areas. Five major Texas cities—Dallas, Houston, San Antonio, El Paso, and Corpus Christi—rank among the top 25 large U.S. cities with the "worst connections," according to census data. That means a quarter or more of their populations do not subscribe to fixed broadband services due to cost or other factors.[5]

In response, bills were filed in the 2021 legislature, and plans were announced by the Texas Education Agency to give all students access.

Today, **news websites** and political **blogs** are increasingly important outlets for news. It is now uncommon for a Texas newspaper of any size (including many weeklies) or television station not to have a website providing news and often blogs. In the words of one executive, "We are not a TV station anymore as much as a provider of news on multiple platforms."[6] Newspapers with large print circulation and those owned by chains are most likely to have extensive websites. In terms of traffic, the website of the *Houston Chronicle* was ranked seventh in the nation among newspaper sites in 2019. *The Dallas Morning News* was 23rd and the three other major Texas dailies were 64th to 70th.[7] Texas's major cities also

social media
Websites and computer applications that allow users to engage in social networking and create online communities. Social media provide platforms for sharing information and ideas through discussion forums, videos, photos, documents, audio clips, and the like.

news websites
Internet sites that provide news. These sites are often affiliated with a newspaper or television station, but increasingly, many are independent.

blogs
Websites or web pages on which a writer or group of writers record opinions, information, and links to other sites on a regular basis.

have alternative media that are relying increasingly on their websites. Texas is home to 7 of the 100 news websites with the most traffic. (See "How Do We Compare…")

The connection of news to social media is also strong. Social media carry news and encourage its discussion, while traditional media report what is trending and policy positions announced on Twitter. (See the three logos in Image. 6.2)

The Internet has spawned news sites independent of print news. Since 2009, the *Texas Tribune* has been a high-quality nonprofit online newspaper that reaches a wide range of people, including most of the state's political elite. Since 2014, *Breitbart News* has had a *Texas Edition*, which, like its parent site, provides far right commentary, conspiracy theories, and news stories that frequently don't hold up under fact checking (examination for accuracy by specialists). Similarly, in 2018, former state senator and Tea Party leader Konnie Burton founded *The Texan* to be "both right-wing and unbiased." Unfortunately, it relies heavily on sources fact checkers find questionable for "extreme bias, consistent promotion of propaganda/conspiracies, [and] poor or no sourcing."[8]

Texas has long had political newsletters that cover major issues and happenings—generally for a fee. The *Quorum Report*, for example, has been a self-described source of "information and gossip" since 1983 and went online in 1998. *Capitol Inside* has provided news and analysis since 2003. Their audiences are small but influential.

Over the last decade, political blogs (regularly updated websites providing information and/or opinion) have become increasingly important in Texas politics. They tend to provide opinion (from diatribes to serious analysis) and news (commonly with the author's spin). They entertain, provide information, reinforce views, bring together like-minded citizens, and sometimes coordinate action.

Texas's two major political parties, most statewide and some local candidates, and a multitude of interest groups maintain blogs, along with authors from both the left and right. Examples of ideological blogs on the left include *Off the Kuff*

Image 6.2 Symbols of the new media: Facebook, Twitter, and the Tumblr site for Texas's online newspaper, *The Texas Tribune*.

Competency Connection
⬤ SOCIAL RESPONSIBILITY ⬤

How have the Internet and social media influenced the reliability of news?

(self-described as Texas's longest running progressive political blog) and *Grits for Breakfast* (postings focused on criminal justice reform and available since 2004). Examples on the right include *Texas Conservative Review* (by a longtime Republican activist, published since 2002), *Big Jolly Politics* (with a range of conservative views sprinkled with humor, published since 2009), and *Texas Insider* (with coverage of national and state issues for 175,000 readers and posted daily since 2003). Part-time blogs often come and go, and recently because of problems with advertising revenue, some established Texas political blogs have effectively ceased or changed platforms, particularly to podcasts or Twitter. Podcasts (digital audio files available on the Internet) are now used by about a fourth of Texans.

Texas politics is found in the full range of social media. The two major parties, for example, use Facebook, Twitter, YouTube, and Instagram, in addition to long time use of email and texts. While only about a fifth of Texans and Americans report using Twitter, its impact has grown enormously in recent years. Most Texas political figures are fairly cautious in what they post. However, a few use it frequently and loudly. They include Governor Greg Abbott, Senator Ted Cruz, former Congressman Beto O'Rourke, and Lieutenant Governor Dan Patrick. In the words of *Texas Monthly* writer Sean O'Neal, "because the media and political beasts comprise an outsized proportion of … [users], Twitter is credited with 99 percent of 'The Discourse,' midwifing the daily gaffes and scandals that feed our news and fostering the partisan sniping through which we process it."[9]

Over time, the use of social media has grown considerably among all demographic groups. Today, over 80 percent of Texas adults use social networking sites such as Facebook and Twitter. (See Table 6.3.) Social network

Table 6.3 Use of Social Media (%)

	TX	US
Facebook	67	64
YouTube	46	37
Instagram	25	24
Twitter	18	16
Snapchat	12	13
Reddit	5	4
Does not use social networking	18	24

Question: "Which of the following social networking sites, if any, do you use?" Survey conducted May 16–30, 2018.

Source: Annette Strauss Institute for Civic Life, Moody College of Communication, University of Texas at Austin, *2018 Texas Media & Society Survey: Topline Results*, 2018, https://moody.utexas.edu/centers/strauss/texas-media-society-survey.

Competency Connection
✿ CRITICAL THINKING ✿

What do you think of the quantity and quality of news provided through social media?

usage is little affected by gender, race/ethnicity, or place of residence (urban, suburban, or rural). Education and income make some difference. Only age makes a substantial difference. While the young are still more likely than older Texans to use social media in general, there have been two important changes. Facebook is still the most used social media platform in Texas and the nation, but younger people are moving heavily to other sites. By 2020, use of Facebook for news was related positively to age. That is, as age increased, so did Facebook usage. The opposite was true for other social media sites. For example, Texans ages 18–24 were most likely to use Twitter, while those over 65 were least likely. A second change is that because many Texans have grown up with social media, the big divide in social media use tends to be between those above and below age 40.[10]

In this hyper-partisan age, party identification tends to affect a multitude of opinions and actions. However, in Texas, being a Republican or Democrat appears to have little to do with media preference other than a Republican preference for consciously conservative Fox News.

Many people get news from social networking sites. For example, in 2016, 70 percent of Texans reported learning campaign news from social media,[11] and in 2020 over a fourth got information on coronavirus from social media. However, news exposure is often incidental to searching for other information. Thus, social media users have more exposure to news but may disregard or forget the message because it was not their primary focus. Also, the range of news topics users find is broad. For example, entertainment news about celebrities is the most common kind of information accessed on Facebook. News about national government and politics is fourth, and local government is seventh. Those who rely on social media for news tend to be less informed and more likely to get the facts on coronavirus and other issues wrong.[12]

Those who learn about a news story on social media may then access a news site. About two out of five Texans reported doing so in 2020. However, those who go directly to a news website spend three times as long there as those who arrive through social media. Twitter is particularly important for following news as it happens and seeing comments on the event. However, research shows that social media does not always facilitate discussion of important topics on-line or in person. Many users are reluctant to discuss topics when they perceive that their audience might disagree with them.[13]

Individuals also contribute to news reporting by posting photos or video they took at an event. Videos of incidents involving police have had a major impact on public discussion of police practice. Witnesses, for example, videoed the deaths of two unarmed Black men at the hands of police—Eric Garner in New York in 2014 by an illegal chokehold and George Floyd in 2020 in Minneapolis from an officer kneeling on his neck. The visual impact of the videos contributed to mass demonstrations nationally and in Texas, gave resonance to the Black Lives Matter movement, and produced calls for changes at both the state and local level in police discipline, training, and funding. Videos not only show (and therefore discourage) bad police behavior; they also can clear police acting properly. Both incentives have played a role in police officials requiring more use of dashboard and body cameras by their officers.

Groups also make use of online videos to further their cause. In 2015, a California anti-abortion group posted secretly taped videos of a conversation with a Planned Parenthood representative in Houston. In the discussion, group members asked about the possibility and cost of obtaining fetal tissue from aborted fetuses for research. A firestorm of reactions in Texas and Washington, D.C., followed. The effect of the incident carried into proposals made in the 2019 legislature. The videos proved a major blow to Planned Parenthood even though a Harris County grand jury cleared the organization of any violation of the law and indicted the videographers for tampering with a government document (a driver's license) and purchase or sale of human organs (the charge they attempted to make against Planned Parenthood). Both charges were later dropped.

Another ruse used to affect public opinion and political outcomes through media coverage took place during the 2020 pandemic. A Dallas salon owner was jailed briefly for violating Governor Abbott's order closing non-essential businesses to fight the spread of the coronavirus. The publicity over the incident made Shelley Luther a hero of the anti-closing movement and propelled her into a race for the Texas Senate. (In a special election to fill a vacant seat, Luther made it into the runoff before losing to another Republican.) She made Governor Abbott a special target for not being sufficiently anti-closing. It was later found that the incident was staged. A Tea Party faction had trolled the Internet to find an effective martyr to oppose the closings, and a GoFundMe account that raised over $500,000 for Luther was begun the day before she reopened her salon.[14] Although many staged political stunts don't work in Texas, this one did.

A problem with the increasing role of blogs, ideological "news" sites, and ordinary citizens in generating and disseminating news is frequent lack of honesty and vetting (checking for accuracy). Blogs and social media can quickly spread false or distorted information. Fortunately, fact-checking for both traditional and digital media is increasing. PolitiFact.com has a Texas-specific section, and other sites such as FactCheck.org, Snopes.com, OpenSecrets.org, and PunditFact.com cover Texas along with the rest of the nation. Other sites rate news outlets for bias and factual reporting: Media Bias/Fact Check and AllSides.com. Like the claims they check, these fact-checkers should not be taken as definitive. The reader should examine how the site decided something was true or false.

Print Media: Newspapers and News Magazines

Newspapers were for a long time *the* news media for Americans. Nationally, newspapers began in the colonies in the early 1700s and had become important sources of political news by 1750. After 1800, they grew in number and news content. However, facing competition from television and later the Internet, U.S. newspaper circulation peaked in the mid-1980s, and both circulation and revenue fell by half in the first two decades of the present century. The table "How Do We Compare…" shows the marked drop in per capita circulation in Texas and other states from 2010 to 2019.

From the first newspaper in Texas, the *Gaceta de Tejas* (which may have published only one or two editions in 1813), to Texas's independence, few newspapers were actually published in the state. By 1860, there were 82. Most ceased publication during the Civil War, but the number of newspapers increased soon after the war and into the 20th century.

By 1965, Texas ranked third in the nation in number of daily newspapers, and 80 percent of Texas households subscribed to at least one newspaper. However, competition from television slowed the growth of newspapers, and the advent of the Internet put them into decline. Newspapers have been particularly harmed by loss of advertising to internet sites such sites as Craigslist. The business closings and uncertainty of the COVID-19 pandemic cut further into revenue.

The number of Texas newspapers has declined precipitously since 2000. By 2020, the state's 41 daily newspapers represented just over a third of the number that had been available in 1975; there were also 101 that published 2–6 days a week and 476 that published weekly. Nevertheless, the five largest Texas cities had newspapers that ranked in the top 52 of the nation in circulation in 2019. Two are in the top ten—the *Houston Chronicle*, followed by the *Dallas Morning News*, which had long been the state's most-read newspaper. Only 13 Texas dailies have a paid circulation over 30,000. Traffic on the websites of major and many smaller papers has partially compensated for the decline in print circulation. Like those in the rest of the country, surviving Texas newspapers have reduced staff and news pages and in some cases number of days they publish.

Weeklies provide local social and political news but little state or national news. (Lots of pictures of kids, awards, and weddings greatly help circulation.) They tend to serve small towns and counties, suburban areas, college campuses, and communities with common interests, such as business, legal, military, and ethnic groups. There are at least 29 college newspapers and six serving military bases.

Decline of the major dailies has given an opening to alternative newspapers in larger cities, such as the *Dallas Observer*, *Houston Press* (online-only beginning in 2017), *Austin Chronicle*, *Fort Worth Weekly*, *San Antonio Current*, and *What's Up, El Paso*. Alternative newspapers vary greatly in quality and focus, but they commonly provide investigative reporting, commentary, culture, and entertainment. During 2020, survival became a serious concern for Texas's alternative media. Facebook and Google were siphoning off advertising dollars, while dealing with the pandemic caused businesses to be uncertain about how much advertising to do. Although digital traffic was up during the pandemic, all alternative media were affected. There were major staff layoffs, cuts in salaries, less frequent publication, and donation requests.

Availability of print news has been boosted to some extent by the rise of several newspapers to national circulation, particularly the *New York Times*, *Wall Street Journal*, *Washington Post*, *USA Today*, and *Los Angeles Times*. These dailies, of course, carry little Texas state and local news, but at least 10 percent of Texans report reading them and 4 percent see them as their main source of news (Tables 6.1 and 6.2).

News magazines have always been fewer in number and read by fewer people. However, these periodicals are quite influential because they tend to be read by elites. Because news magazine reporters have more time to gather information and study it, their stories often provide more perspective than those published

Image 6.3 Delivering newspapers on a bike: A vanishing piece of Americana.

Vstock LK/Alamy Stock Photo

— Competency Connection —
☼ **CRITICAL THINKING** ☼

Will local newspapers survive the internet challenge? Why or why not?

in newspapers. With its large population, Texas would seem a likely candidate for several competing news magazines. However, this competition has not emerged. Progressives and liberals have read the *Texas Observer* since 1954, but there is not a comparable conservative news magazine. *Texas Monthly*, an award-winning magazine, covers some politics but since its 2016 ownership change, the print edition focuses more on social and cultural stories. Its website still carries influential stories and commentary. Its article on the best and worst legislators after each biennial session of the Texas legislature is watched with trepidation by legislators up for reelection. (In 2019, it moved to the website.)

Print media have been particularly important sources of political information for at least four reasons. First, compared with television and radio, print media have the space to cover more stories and to develop these stories in greater detail. Although many in the general public are satisfied with only headlines and highlights, opinion leaders and those actually involved in government and politics need more detail and more complete coverage. Hence, the second reason for the importance of newspapers is that they are the major source of news for the elite (the better educated, more affluent population and political leaders). Websites of major print media and independent news websites have these same two advantages. They have the space, and they are utilized by elites, particularly younger to now middle-aged leaders.

Third, newspapers in Texas and the nation remain the largest gatherers of news. Print media have more reporters to find news and are more often the ones who break stories (that is, initially report them). Major national newspapers and two wire services—New York City–based Associated Press (AP) and London-based Reuters—provide much of the national and international news that appears in newspapers, on television and radio, and on internet news sites and blogs.

On their own, television and radio stations tend to report sensational accidents, crime, and human interest stories, along with weather, traffic, and sports. For local politics and government, they rely heavily on statements from local officials and local newspaper stories. TV stations and the few news radio stations often follow up on stories broken by the local paper but less commonly originate the story. For state and national news, they rely on wire services and feeds from their parent company. Texas internet newsletters are mostly behind a pay wall and focused on news for the state's political elite. Texas blogs occasionally break news but seldom on an ongoing basis. Newspapers, thus, tend to set the news agenda for broadcast news and the Internet in both Texas and the nation.

Finally, major print media today require that stories be vetted (checked) for accuracy and attempt to follow standards of objectivity in reporting. To make their reporting reliable, national newspapers and major Texas dailies all practice vetting beforehand and also retract or correct stories they later find to be in error. The respected Media Bias/Fact Check rates all five major Texas dailies, the online *Texas Tribune*, *Texas Monthly*, and *Texas Observer* as "High" for factual reporting. Until recent decades, Texas media often were not objective when reporting on Blacks, Latinos, Asian Americans, poor Whites, gays, liberals, and organized labor. Many observers say that although today the major Texas dailies uphold standards of objectivity, there are still problems of objectivity in reporting on these groups. Some would add the homeless, undocumented workers, California, and others to the list. Vetting and objectivity are only gradually developing on many internet news sites not connected with print journalism. Professional standards also vary considerably among Texas's weekly and semi-weekly newspapers.

The decline of local newspapers in Texas and elsewhere is important for at least two additional reasons. First, local newspaper reporters are often responsible for exposing corruption and graft in public life. (See the later section, "Investigative Journalism.") Second, when cities had competing newspapers, their presence facilitated public debate because editorial boards commonly took opposing stances on political issues. Through 1995, Houston had two dailies, the *Chronicle* (sometimes called the *Comical*) and the now defunct *Post* (sometimes called the *Pest*). Editorial positions changed somewhat with ownership, but editors' views for each paper often conflicted. In the mid-1980s, San Antonio's *Express* and *News* combined to form the *Express-News*, and in 1993, the *San Antonio Light* went out of business. The Dallas–Fort Worth Metroplex is currently served by two major newspapers. On their editorial pages, the *Dallas Morning News* often reflects center-right (moderate conservative) and conservative views. The *Fort Worth Star-Telegram* is sometimes said to reflect center-left (moderate liberal) and centrist perspectives. However, Media Bias/Fact Check rates both papers' editorial position as center-right.

Electronic Media: Television and Radio

Television In the 20th century, television went from humble beginnings to become Texans' major source of news, a position it still holds. However, since the turn of this century, it has fought a battle with the Internet it will probably lose in the long run.

Regularly scheduled television broadcasting in the United States began in 1928. However, Texas did not have commercial television until after World War II, when the industry began to flourish nationally. In 1948, WBAP-TV, the first television station in Texas and the South, was opened by Amon G. Carter, publisher of the *Fort Worth Star-Telegram* and a pioneer in Texas radio. In the 1950s, television flourished in the state. Texas paralleled the nation in the expansion of television. Nationally, the number of households with television expanded from 9 percent in 1950 to 97 percent in 1975, a percentage that has held steady to the present. Today, 80 percent of households have cable or satellite, although the proportion is declining among younger viewers. As of 2020, there were 140 full power television stations in Texas, 11 of which are nonprofit Public Broadcasting Service (PBS) stations, covering 90 percent of the state's population. Houston's TV 8 (affiliated with the University of Houston) was the nation's first public broadcasting station and a founding member of PBS in 1969.

Television news today comes in five major formats: local news, cable news (particularly Fox, MSNBC, and CNN), network news (NBC, CBS, ABC, and PBS), political talk shows, and late night comedy shows. Only the first of these, local news, has significant Texas content, and as we noted earlier, that coverage tends to lack depth. Local public television and radio stations tend to provide somewhat more depth on public issues, but they, too, are limited in airtime.

Radio Commercial radio in the United States began in the 1920s and by the 1930s entered its two-decade "Golden Age." Radio, however, did not penetrate Texas and the rest of the South in the 1930s to the degree that it did elsewhere. In Texas and other states, coverage of the war fronts during World War II enhanced the standing of radio, as did its value as a distraction from the horrors of war. Nationally and in Texas, radio remains pervasive. Ninety-nine percent of American homes have one or more radios receiving broadcasts from almost 15,500 radio stations. In Texas, there are almost 2,400 stations.[15]

Radio is an important source of entertainment, particularly music, but it has limited value as a source of political news. Texas radio stations usually provide five minutes of news on the hour—headlines without much detail. For state and national news, most stations have at best a small news staff and depend on stories from the news services, their parent company, or feeds from such sources as the Texas State Network or, more recently, Fox News Radio. Local news tends to lack substance, and politics must compete with local social, cultural, and sports events for the short time available.

Two developments have increased the news impact of radio: the rise of talk radio and the development of radio focused on news. In the 1980s, politically oriented radio call-in talk shows became popular. Two decisions by the federal government had a major impact on this phenomenon in Texas and elsewhere. In 1987, the Federal Communications Commission (FCC) abolished the Fairness Doctrine that required stations to provide both sides of controversial topics they chose to air. Under the Fairness Doctrine, stations effectively had to provide both liberal and conservative commentators. Without the Doctrine, conservatives, with a bigger audience, quickly outpaced the liberals.

In a second change, the federal Telecommunications Act of 1996 facilitated the development of large chains of radio stations, which in turn made easier the syndication of popular talk radio programs. This made talk radio available to more stations and their listeners. iHeartMedia, Inc. (formerly Clear Channel Communications), headquartered in San Antonio, for example, has become a major player in talk radio. It is a holding company involved in radio and television, outdoor advertising, and online programming. It is the largest owner of radio stations in the country (over 850), including 72 in Texas. iHeartMedia's eight news and talk radio stations in Texas cover four of the five largest metropolitan areas in the state (not Austin).

In Texas, nationally syndicated talk show hosts have substantial followings, along with hosts who have Texas ties, such as Dan Patrick, Alex Jones, Michael Berry, Neal Boortz, Joe Pagliarulo, and Glenn Beck. Patrick's popularity led to a state senate seat and then his election as lieutenant governor in 2014 and 2018. Pundit Allen West, a Texan since 2015, was elected chair of the state Republican Party in 2020. Austin-based Alex Jones mixes conspiracy theories and far right views. His denial of the Sandy Hook School shooting led to lawsuits, and in 2018, he was banned from four major online platforms, including YouTube and Facebook, for "promoting violence and hate speech."

Talk radio provides an opportunity for its predominantly conservative audience to air their views and create a sense of community. Talk shows generally are a mix of opinion and entertainment with some news. Opinion and entertainment often taint the news, which is seldom fact-checked. More than half of listeners simply reinforce their preexisting views. Nevertheless, research also shows that regular listeners are influenced by the views they hear.[16]

The political role of radio has also been enhanced by the availability of all-news stations—some local, some part of large chains, and some from satellite radio, which provides a variety of news formats. In addition, public radio provides substantial coverage of local, state, and national news. Examples include KERA in Dallas, Houston Public Media, Austin's KUT, and Texas Public Radio, which operates three stations in San Antonio and the Hill Country. All offer internet programming, and the first two public television. In Austin, KUT's coverage is enriched by a partnership with the online newspaper *The Texas Tribune*. Over time, public radio stations in different Texas cities have combined resources for special reporting projects such as TXDecides, StateImpact, and Texas Standard (to which one of the authors, Carlos Huerta, contributes).

✓ 6.1 Learning Check

1. From which media do most Texans get their news today?
2. From which medium did most Texans get their news in the early 20th century?

Answers at the end of this chapter.

◪ The Media's Roles in Politics

LO 6.2 Describe the roles of the media in Texas politics.

The media are commonly said to fill four roles in politics: provide information for the public and decision makers, help citizens maintain democracy, help shape the public agenda (what government does and doesn't do), and influence citizens' views.

Providing Information

The first role, providing information, is basic and sounds simple. For example, three out of four Texans say they follow local news "somewhat" or "very closely." However, transfer of information to the public is complex. Most people are not involved in politics and at best care only marginally about what is happening politically. They are more likely to hear and remember important but unexciting information if it comes from someone they trust. This source may be a trusted newscaster such as Walter Cronkite (1916–2009), the Texan who was anchor for CBS's nightly news program for 19 years, or local news anchors such as Houston's Bill Balleza, who anchored Houston's KPRC 2 for 39 years; Dallas-Fort Worth's Clarice Tinsley, dean of area news anchors (42 years); and San Antonio's Randy Beamer (31 years). Bloggers and talk show hosts also may fill this role.

Trusted opinion leaders are often friends or relatives who pay close attention to the news and pass on the information to people they know. Because these leaders are known and trusted, the information they provide is more likely to be heard, remembered, and further explored. A majority of people who hear about a story from friends and family follow up by seeking a full news story.

Knowing something about an issue increases the probability that related media stories will be heard and remembered. Thus, members of the political elite are more likely to pay attention to the news and to get more out of it than the general public. They know more initially, and because of their knowledge, they feel a greater incentive to become aware of what is happening. Research shows that a substantial, long-term difference exists between ordinary citizens and political leaders in understanding the news and in levels of knowledge (remembering and putting it into context). Many scholars see a growing knowledge divide between the informed and the less informed.

An impediment to gaining information for both an interested public and the elite is the softening of the news. Growth in the number and range of alternatives to newspapers and network evening news has produced a sharp increase in competition for advertising dollars, which are closely connected to audience size. To gain more readers/listeners, news providers have increased the amount of entertainment in news broadcasts (often referred to as **soft news**). Concomitantly, they have decreased the quantity of news focused on facts and affecting public policy (referred to as **hard news**). Local television news in Texas and elsewhere has long focused on accidents, crime, and the reaction of local residents to

soft news
News that is more entertaining, sensationalized, covers only the surface, and has little connection to public policy.

hard news
News that focuses on the facts, provides more depth, and commonly has implications for public policy.

national events. As a result, although crime has tended to decline over time, regular viewers of local news often believe that crime is increasing. Similarly, followers of talk radio, the ideological cable television networks, or ideological internet blogs may develop more political knowledge but also come to accept inaccurate or incomplete versions of reality.

Digital media make important contributions to the flow of information to the public. They remove filters put in place by traditional media that limit direct access to information and allow the public to communicate directly. Friends and family now have a major role in contributing and disseminating news. Not only do stories get posted on social networking sites, but users have the chance to include their own views and experiences.

The site Reddit, for example, allows users (rather than media professionals) to select the most important stories of the day. Unfortunately, the news role of social media has a fundamental conflict without an easy answer. On the one hand, few people use sites such as Reddit (5 percent of Texans), and for those users, entertainment value often trumps substantive value in the news chosen. On the other hand, considerable evidence supports the charge that news selection by professional journalists is elitist in nature and does not resonate with a large part of the public.

Government, interest groups, and the elite want to get the word out to the public. This goal, for a long time, has meant trying to get the print and electronic press to cover their concerns as news. Today, the Internet and social media provide an array of direct outlets for users that avoid the filtering by professional journalists: their own internet sites; advertisements on others' sites; blogs; and social media sites like Facebook, Twitter, and Instagram. If someone "likes" or "follows" a politician or interest group on a social media site, it is possible to contribute directly to the news feed and help spread the "news" by sharing a post.

Most Texas state officials make substantial use of the Internet to connect directly with citizens. The official website of the Office of the Governor, for example, lists (and uses professionally) Facebook, Twitter, Flickr, Email, YouTube, LinkedIn, Instagram, and RSS Feed. Chapter 9, "The Executive Branch," gives examples of how governors Perry and Abbott used the new media to enhance their informal powers.

Maintaining Democracy

Historically, the media have played a key role in protecting democracy. Without the media reporting what is happening, citizens and leaders alike would be unable to make intelligent decisions about public policies and candidates. We would be dependent on what government and interest groups tell us. We also rely on the media to investigate and dig out information that government officials and special interests wish to hide. Unfortunately, the ability of the press to fill these roles has fluctuated greatly over time.

The Partisan Past Throughout the 19th century, newspapers in Texas and the nation were highly partisan, often scurrilous, and not addicted to the truth. For example, newspapers around the state were strongly divided on the personality of Sam Houston in both the editorial and news pages. When newspapers reemerged after the Civil War, they divided sharply over Reconstruction's Governor Edmund J. Davis. At the close of the 19th century, some newspapers followed the lead of the Hearst and Pulitzer newspapers, publishing sensationalist and exaggerated stories, known as "**yellow journalism**." In any event, the *Galveston News* in the second half of the 19th century began to move away from harsh partisanship, and by the end of the century most Texas newspapers were following suit.

Two factors seem to have contributed to this movement toward more even-handed reporting. One was the growth of news services such as the Associated Press, which meant that newspapers were sharing the same story. The other was the increasing reliance on advertising revenue. Technological changes made possible the publication of large runs of a newspaper, which increased circulation. Publishers had to become more moderate and professional because they could not afford to alienate either advertisers or subscribers. Advertisers then and now look at circulation numbers to determine whether to buy advertising space and how much to pay.

Professionalism and Democracy In the 20th century, **professionalism** gradually became the standard for American and Texas journalists. To be professional, reporting should be objective, neutral, and accurate, not based on partisanship, ideology, or the economic interest of reporters or owners. Professional journalism has long been seen as important to democracy. Citizens and leaders gain a fuller and more accurate picture of events, and government and special interests get away with less. However, there are other perspectives.

Advocacy journalists strive for accuracy but reject objectivity (presenting both sides well). Ideological publications, such as the *Texas Observer*, practice advocacy. It is rated "Left Biased" for story selection and "High" for factual reporting because it never failed a fact check and uses proper sourcing.[17] In newspapers, the distinction generally is easy to see. It is on the news pages that professionalism—objectivity and neutrality—should apply. Advocacy is practiced on the editorial pages or in pieces labeled "analysis" or "commentary."

The working of professionalism can be seen in the way newspapers endorse candidates for election. The *Houston Chronicle* follows common practice. An editorial board researches and interviews candidates and then decides who to recommend to voters. To separate editorial opinion from news reporting, editorial staff report directly to the publisher, not through the news editor. As a result, on the same day in 2020, the business columnist from the newsroom strongly criticized Congressman Dan Crenshaw's stand on renewable energy, while the editorial board endorsed him for reelection. The editor said he laughed out loud. In television and internet news, the news and opinion segments tend to be less clearly separated.

Professionalism requires honesty in reporting. In 2018, a *Houston Chronicle* reporter raised questions with the editor about the accuracy of a colleague's stories. The *Chronicle* hired an independent journalist to review the stories, which led to the retraction of eight stories, correction of 64 more, and the resignation of the accused reporter.

yellow journalism
Journalism that is based on sensationalism and exaggeration.

professionalism
Reporting that is objective, neutral, and accurate.

Professionalism is, of course, an ideal, and most suppliers of news are judged by how closely they come to the ideal, not by whether they are perfect. Several trends have chipped away at the standards of professionalism. Critics have noted that professional journalists tend to see official sources (that is, government officials and other powerful people) as reliable, legitimate, and knowledgeable. Thus, professionals may over report views of the government and the elite while neglecting the views of others. For example, many reporters seem to have long taken at face value the bragging by legislative leaders about their balancing of the Texas state budget when the federal government has not been able to do so. The fuller picture is that the state constitution makes it virtually impossible for the legislature to appropriate more than the comptroller predicts the state will have available to spend. Also, the legislature has often used an array of accounting maneuvers or tricks.

Similarly, being objective means presenting multiple perspectives on an issue. However, if there is no debate among the powerful, concerns by ordinary citizens may be neglected. For example, in 2004, the Texas Education Agency effectively capped the number of special education students schools could serve. The public and, apparently, top state officials were unaware of this until a 2016 investigation by the *Houston Chronicle* reported the policy and that as many as 250,000 students may have been denied help. Public outcry and a 2018 federal report reversed the policy. However, news reports questioned the effectiveness of the changes, concerns that were reflected in a 2020 letter from the U.S. Department of Education to the Texas Education Agency.

An issue also may have two sides among political leaders and a third position held by the public that goes unreported in the news. For example, in the debate over anti-abortion legislation passed by the legislature since 2013, most of the reporting focused on the two extremes—prolife and prochoice. However, for years the largest segment of the public has tended to reject the two extremes—no abortion at all or abortion for any reason. Texans and Americans are more likely to believe that abortion should be available, but only under certain circumstances.[18] The independent nature of internet and social media interactions gives hope that citizen views not reflected in elite opinion will be heard.

In recent years, the national media have become more **adversarial**. The sharp conflict between President Trump and the press reinforced this trend at the national level. In Texas, social media, talk shows, and blogs are often adversarial. However, the state's traditional news media (print and broadcast) have not followed the national pattern. Instead, from the time of Democratic Party dominance to today's Republican dominance, critics have complained that the media are too friendly to state leaders and seldom seriously challenge their policies. However, during the COVID-19 pandemic, the state press became more aggressive and questioning of state leaders about apparent waffling in decision-making and the lack of cooperation with, and aid to, local officials. The greater assertiveness of the press was aided by the loud criticism of Governor Abbott's pandemic policies by both the left and right.

During the pandemic, several governors gained political capital from their well-done regular press conferences. However, Governor Abbott appears to be uncomfortable with press conferences and confrontation. After a few attempts, he focused on short interviews with local news outlets broadcast from a studio

adversarial
Reporting featuring opposition and a combative style. Also called *attack journalism*.

in Austin. In two months, he did over 200. This approach allowed him to choose his audience and tailor his message. Importantly, local anchors doing the live interviews were less likely to challenge or fact-check the governor than would the Austin press corps. Editors of the five largest newspapers sent a letter to the governor asking that he make himself more available for questioning.[19] He did not. Avoiding hard questions by going directly to local outlets is not a new tactic, and it has been enhanced by social media.

Many observers believe that the national media are more partisan today than during most of the last century. Clearly, some forms of media in Texas are partisan: blogs, social media, and talk radio/television. But the traditional media tend not to be heavily partisan. In terms of newspapers, differences are more a matter of degree than absolute. For example, the editorial policy of the *Fort Worth Star-Telegram* and of the *Dallas Morning News* is center-right (moderately conservative), while the *Texas Tribune* and the major newspapers in San Antonio, Austin, and Houston, are rated center-left (moderately liberal). All five major print newspapers endorsed favorite son George W. Bush for president in 2004. In five presidential elections from 2004 to 2020, all five endorsed at least one Republican and one Democrat. In 2012, of Texas's 12 largest newspapers, eight endorsed Republican Mitt Romney and two Democrat Barack Obama.

In 2016, newspapers in the state and nation overwhelmingly rejected Republican Donald Trump. In Texas, eight endorsed Democrat Hillary Clinton, one Trump, and one "not Trump." That year, the *Dallas Morning-News* endorsed a Democrat for president for the first time since before World War II, while recommending five Republicans, one Libertarian, and one Democrat for statewide office. In 2020, only six of the largest papers in the nation endorsed President Trump. In Texas, three major papers endorsed Democrat Joe Biden, and two (Dallas and Fort Worth) gave no endorsement.

Endorsements of candidates in the primary elections may give an indication of ideological orientation. In the 2016 Democratic presidential primary, the major newspapers in Dallas, Houston, and San Antonio endorsed the moderate liberal Hillary Clinton over the more liberal Bernie Sanders. In the Republican primary, these three, along with the *Fort Worth Star-Telegram* and the *Waco Tribune-Herald*, split their endorsements among Jeb Bush, John Kasich, and Marco Rubio, who were generally considered more mainstream Republican candidates. The *Austin American-Statesman* did not endorse presidential candidates in 2012 or 2016 but summarized the message of the major Texas papers making endorsements in the 2016 primary as: "Please, please … don't pick Ted Cruz or Donald Trump, and let pragmatism prevail." Trump, the victor, was far from a conventional candidate and strongly anti-Republican establishment. Cruz, a U.S. Senator from Texas, was the most ideological conservative among the viable candidates. In 2020, only one of the five largest Texas papers endorsed a presidential candidate in the Democratic primary and none did so in the Republican primary.

In 2018, the major newspapers in Dallas, Fort Worth, Houston, and San Antonio each endorsed Republican Greg Abbott for governor and Democrat Beto O'Rourke for the U.S. Senate. In 2020's state and local races, the three papers that endorsed Biden recommended more Democrats than Republicans, while the Dallas and Fort Worth dailies each supported more Republicans.

The take-away is that today major Texas newspapers endorse candidates from both parties on a case by case basis but have some preference for competent incumbents, conventional candidates, and those closer to their own editorial perspective.

Investigative Journalism We look to the media to keep our public officials honest by asking hard questions and investigating suspicious actions. Unfortunately, the ability of Texas and national media to conduct investigations has declined. A reduction in number of reporters is the major reason. Texas's traditional media commonly have a reporter who investigates complaints from individuals mistreated by public or private actions. Beyond that, given limited funds and personnel, most Texas media concentrate on a few investigations of major public problems.

An important tool for the watchdog role of the Texas media is use of open meetings and open records. Many government officials in Texas are reluctant to share information about how public money is spent, how decisions affecting the public interest are made, or what information was used in making decisions. Failing to share information with the public may hide self-serving decisions or avoid opposition to policies preferred by decision-makers. Government officials sometimes argue that they want to protect the public or that compiling information is difficult and costly. Some agencies, (notably, the Texas Commission on Environmental Quality and the Railroad Commission) are said to have a culture of hostility to the idea of public information.

In the past, meetings of school boards and other public boards were often closed to the public. However, during the 1973 session of the legislature, in the aftermath of the Sharpstown scandal (see later discussion), the public interest group Common Cause received strong support from other public interest groups and the media to push through **open meetings** and **open records** legislation. (A weak open meetings law was passed in 1967. The open records act is now officially the Public Information Act.)

When the laws were first passed, many observers saw them as among the strongest in the nation. However, the legislature has added a multitude of exceptions, and state courts have weakened a number of provisions. The 2019 legislature corrected some of these problems, but non-compliance and obstruction by some state and many local agencies create a checkerboard effect. Some follow the spirit of the act; others do not. In 2012 and 2015 reports, researchers from different groups gave the state an F in public access to information. In the 2015 report, Texas ranked 48th among the states. In 2019 in a simplified test, Texas was one of 15 states ranked "good" (the highest of three rankings).[20]

open meetings
Meetings of public entities that are required by law to be open to the public.

open records
Government documents and records that are required by law to be available to the public.

Under open meetings law, government boards must discuss proposals and make their decisions in meetings open to the public. There are exceptions, such as personnel matters, contracts, and real property purchases or sales that can be discussed in executive (closed) session, but even then, actual decisions generally must be made in sessions open to the public. Ordinary citizens can attend, but it is reporting by the media that makes information widely available.

The 84th Legislature (2015) required larger school districts, cities, and counties to video record their public meetings and post them online. For example, the city of Victoria posts its city council meetings on YouTube.

Most reports, communications, and paperwork generated within executive agencies may be requested by citizens, and the agency must respond within 10 working days or ask the Attorney General whether they have to divulge the information. It must then provide the information "within a reasonable time, without delay." If the information is not provided, the requestor may sue, but lawsuits are expensive and thus more likely to be filed by organizations, businesses, or affluent individuals. In 2013, the legislature updated requirements to clarify the inclusion of emails under open records laws. No reason need be given for an open records request, and there is no restriction on use of the information.

We only have anecdotal evidence of who makes open records requests in Texas; however, the pattern here appears to be similar to the federal pattern. The Texas and federal open records acts were proposed to allow the press more ability to inform the people. But in practice, over half of federal record requests are made by businesses and attorneys and a fifth by individuals. Journalists and nonprofits ask for 8 percent each.[21] Many of these nonprofits are advocacy or public interest groups, and many of the individuals are activists. But we don't know what proportion.

As with open meetings laws, open records laws include restrictions as to what can be released, and this limitation can lead to difficulties obtaining information. For example, in 2020, in the face of public information requests, the Texas Health and Human Services Commission (HHSC) refused to release the names of nursing homes with cases of COVID-19 for four months, even though many were virus hotspots. They cited patient privacy concerns. HHSC had to give in when the Attorney General ruled against them because the requests were for the names of facilities, not patients. This and other clashes highlight the legitimate conflict between, on the one hand, protecting our privacy and keeping information from those who would do us harm and, on the other hand, the public's need to know such things as where it is safe to live and work. Cynics add that public safety and privacy also provide broad cover for officials hostile to releasing public information.

Non-compliance with open records law appears to be a greater problem with local governments than with many state agencies. In a year-long study of open records compliance in North Texas, the *Dallas Morning News* sent five requests each to 113 local governments and found:

Inconsistent treatment of the release of public information, giving rise to systemic violations of the law …

- Widely varied costs for basic information, ranging from free to thousands of dollars.
- Routine flouting of the law's response time deadlines.
- An inability or refusal to provide some or all information about public expenditures in a searchable, electronic format.[22]

The media not only report information they gather from open meetings and open records requests, but they also report information obtained by others using data the state requires to be reported. For example, candidates, lobbyists, and officeholders are required to report financial information, such as campaign contributions and expenditures, to the Texas Ethics Commission, which places the information online but not always in a readily usable form. Public interest groups, such as Texans for Public Justice, often compile the information to make patterns clearer. (In recent years, they reported on campaign contributions in Austin city elections and oil and gas industry contributions to legislators and regulators.) Media also compile public information from government sites and make it accessible. For example, the online *Texas Tribune* has developed several searchable databases, including salaries of public employees, the Texas Public Schools Explorer, higher education outcomes, prison information, and the COVID-19 pandemic.

Political Scandals and the Texas Media One of the roles often portrayed for the press is investigating wrongdoing by government and its leaders. Texas has a long history of political scandals in which the media have played a significant but seldom leading role. The Texas press more commonly spreads the word and keeps the pot boiling, which allows time for concerned citizens and leaders to seek reforms. The classic case is the Sharpstown stock fraud scandal of the early 1970s in which federal prosecutors filed charges that resulted in criminal convictions. The media gave substantial coverage to the scandal and the subsequent actions of the "Dirty Thirty," a group of legislators who forced public discussion of the issues involved. As a result, Governor Preston Smith (named as an unindicted coconspirator), Lieutenant Governor Ben Barnes (who was not a participant in the conspiracy), and a large majority of the legislature were swept from office. A flurry of mild reforms followed.

In four other prominent cases, media investigations uncovered corruption. In the mid-1950s, the managing editor of the *Cuero Record* won a Pulitzer Prize for exposing the defrauding of veterans by the state land commissioner, Bascom Giles, who went to prison. Following up on Sharpstown, in the 1970s, the media and prosecutors found widespread corruption, such as illegal hiring of relatives and theft of legislative stamp allotments. In 2020, Jeffrey Gerritt, editor of the *Palestine Herald Press* (in Southeast Texas) won a Pulitzer Prize for exposing medical neglect that led to deaths of pre-trial inmates in the local county jail, bringing attention to a statewide problem.

Scrutiny of the Texas Supreme Court began when two San Antonio newspapers questioned decisions by justices that favored their campaign contributors. That led to a fuller investigation by *Texas Monthly* and then a national story in 1987 by the investigative television program *60 Minutes*. In a rare move, the Texas Commission on Judicial Conduct publicly reprimanded two justices. Three justices took early retirement. Tenacious reporting changed personnel on the court and contributed to its moving from all Democrats to all Republicans. But this did not change the fundamental problem: Judges still have to raise money for their election campaigns. (In 2020, for example, three incumbent Supreme Court justices spent a combined $4.2 million to win reelection.) In 1998, *60 Minutes* revisited the high court and found the same problem. Before, Democratic justices had favored their contributors: plaintiffs' attorneys. Now, Republican justices were favoring their contributors: business and insurance. (For further discussion of this issue, see Chapter 10, "The Judicial Branch.")

In both the Sharpstown and Texas Supreme Court cases, the changes were in personnel, not fundamental changes in the system. Because the system remains unchanged, so too does the likelihood of future abuses. Serious reform is a hard sell in Texas.

The national press sometimes finds abuses by Texans in Washington. In 2016, the *New York Times* found that Senator Ted Cruz of Texas had failed to report borrowing $1 million for his 2012 campaign (the majority from the often-criticized investment bank, Goldman Sachs, where his wife worked). In 2019, the Federal Election Commission fined his campaign $35,000 for the violation.

Setting the Public Agenda

A third major role of the media is its substantial contribution to setting the public agenda (called **agenda setting**)—that is, influencing which issues are dealt with by government. There is a multitude of problems affecting the public, but if public officials are not aware of them, nothing happens. In addition, officials may be aware of problems but not want to act. For example, low funding for mental health resources in Texas has created major problems for many Texans, but strong resistance to spending money to increase social services has long left Texas among the lowest states in per capita mental health expenditures. Without the public's becoming aware and highly concerned, state leadership can ignore the problem. When a substantial segment of the public or major leaders become aware of issues, action is more likely. It often takes a major event or outside pressure to produce change. The killing of 10 people and the wounding of 10 more at Santa Fe High School in 2018 led Governor Abbott to propose more spending on mental health, which did produce increased funding from the 2019 legislature.

An example of media influence on policy took place in early 2014. The plan of the Texas Department of Transportation (TxDOT) to build a bypass around the town of Snook (near Bryan/College Station) would have required cutting down several trees and damaging others in a stand of 200- to 300-year-old live oaks. When residents protested in the nearby Bryan/College Station media, TxDOT promised an attempt to save some but not all of the trees. A Facebook page and an online petition were created. Then, within days of the story's appearing in a major daily, the *Houston Chronicle*, TxDOT devised a new plan that would move traffic safely, save the trees, and stay within budget.

The Texas media have a limited influence on agenda setting. Competing with the media in setting the public agenda are the governor, legislative leaders, and interest groups, who have more power and resources. In addition, the decline in the number of reporters, the fragmented nature of the state's executive branch, the large number of local governments (particularly thousands of special districts

agenda setting
Affecting the importance given issues by government and public leaders.

and multiple county offices), and reliance on non-local and out-of-state collectors of information make it likely that many possible agenda items will be missed by the Texas media. Although the Texas press influences major state-level agenda items and many local issues, it has too few resources to cover, let alone influence, the majority of state agencies, county offices, and special districts.

Even if the press gives substantial coverage to an issue over time, the power of other forces often means that the issue is ignored or dealt with only marginally. The *Dallas Morning News* and *Houston Chronicle* have done major studies of the multiple abuses in Texas nursing homes that produced a flurry of attention without a major fix. Similarly, the lack of funding of mental health, the rapid draining of the Ogallala aquifer (providing irrigation and drinking water for Texas's High Plains), the death and suffering caused by the failure to take advantage of federal money to expand Medicaid coverage, and the long term problems with Child Protective Services (CPS) have all been covered extensively by the press without the legislature taking serious action.

The elitist nature of the state political system and the power of special interest groups assure that non-elites face substantial competition for media attention. Grassroots movements, such as the Tea Party, the #MeToo Movement, and

📋 Students in Action

Learning Campaign Communications

When Quinn Kobrin began college at Sam Houston State, he had a passion for writing but thought he needed a real job to pay the bills. Being a high school English teacher would meet both needs. He majored in English with minors in Political Science and Communication Studies and became an "ambassador" in the university's Center for Law, Engagement, and Politics (LEAP), which allowed him to meet leaders from a variety of areas and levels. It also prepared him to seek internships and work experience.

While still a student, he worked for two political campaigns. In the first, a small longshot campaign, he began as a volunteer doing research and gradually worked up to a paid position as communications director. He created graphics, ran ads and posted on social media, and wrote emails, press releases, and drafts of speeches. The second campaign was larger and already had a developed volunteer program, which made it harder to establish a niche for himself. But in time he was invited to write a

Monkey Business Images/Shutterstock.com

messaging calendar both for a social media account he would run and the official campaign account. Finally, Quinn worked as an intern for Huntsville's Old Town Theatre, responsible for the website and social media. After the internship, he was asked to serve on the board of the nonprofit.

(Continued)

Quinn had three takeaways from his experience. First, "getting a role on a campaign requires timing and luck." The interviewer for an internship referred him to the first campaign. For the second, he completed a "campaign boot camp" with the Annette Strauss Institute for Civic Life at the University of Texas and, unknown to him, was recommended to the campaign. Second, "I would say that the most important lesson I learned through LEAP is not being afraid to take risks, especially when opportunities present themselves. The leaders we heard all emphasized the importance of taking advantage of opportunity, of putting in work, and of staying committed to what you want to do." Third, he learned that he didn't want to make a career of campaign work. He didn't relish a life of constantly moving to the next campaign. "My passion for politics falls more on the side of shaping the message and policy."

Like most of his generation, Quinn grew up with social media and the Internet. His classes honed his writing and analysis skills, and his experience outside of class gave him a chance to apply his skills in a variety of ways. "The most important skill," he says "is flexibility. You have to be ready to try things you aren't comfortable with, volunteer to do something you don't know how to do."

Competency Connection
💬 COMMUNICATION SKILLS 💬

What preparation is needed by journalists and others in the media? Would you prefer that journalists have more preparation in the techniques of the trade (such as research, investigation, writing, and speaking) or in the field on which they report (such as politics, business, or sports)?

Black Lives Matter, had to learn to use social media combined with methods such as rallies and demonstrations to gain the attention of the public and leaders. However, the ability of ordinary citizens to come together over an issue of concern to them and use the new media sources to add their cause to the public agenda still appears to be in its infancy (but an infancy with possibilities of healthy growth).

Shaping Our Views?

A fourth role often attributed to the media is to shape our perceptions of events and issues. Many people believe that the media tell us what to believe—that is, they create opinion. Research finds little evidence for this view. Rather, it finds a much more complex process in which the media play important roles. We have seen that the media are a major source of information. However, this effect is reduced because we are more likely to perceive an issue and its importance if we already know something about the topic or if the information comes from a trusted source, such as a friend or favorite newscaster. Then, we are more likely to "hear" the news. Similarly, students in an introductory political science class are likely to find the news makes more sense (and therefore remember it) as they learn more background and context from the course.

Do the media change our minds? If we actually have a developed opinion, the answer is "not often." The reason is found in the concept of selective perception and retention. As a general rule, we tend to hear and remember those ideas that support what we already believe and to reject those views that conflict with our own. Consistently, when a group of Republicans and Democrats gather in the same room to listen to their parties' gubernatorial candidates debate issues, most of the group come away thinking that their candidate made the stronger arguments and won the debate. This tendency means that the media are unlikely to change the minds of those who strongly support candidates or issues, but they may have an effect on marginal supporters. Attack ads are a case in point.

Attack Ads Scurrilously attacking your opponent was a common practice in 18th- and 19th-century politics. Though generally less mean-spirited and less common today, **attack ads** (personal attacks) are still an important part of national and state politics. Advertisements that are negative toward the opponent are quite common and can rise to sharp attacks. A major reason that candidates run attack ads is that they work—on two levels. Negative ads tend to influence the tone and content of news coverage. Said another way, they often generate free media coverage. Second, votes may be won by negative ads. The public tends to accept accurate attacks on the issues, and negativity is often more interesting (and thus more memorable) than positive ads.

People regularly complain about negative campaign ads, but the importance of the political race and the repetition of the ads cause many to "hear" the charges. Convinced supporters will tend to reject the charges made in the ads, but marginal supporters may become less certain and abstain from voting for the candidate. This result seems to be the strongest electoral effect of attack ads. Research shows that as the number of negative ads increases, news coverage tends to become more negative, which lowers participation and trust in government. Hearing and seeing negative or disrespectful behavior in the media increases the likely impact on our emotions and therefore on our view of politics.[23]

The 2014 governor's race between Republican State Attorney General Greg Abbott and Democratic State Senator Wendy Davis included a great deal of mudslinging. One fight focused on the compelling life narratives each used. (Davis' biography was that of a divorced teenage mother living in a trailer who worked her way to Harvard and political success. Abbott's life story was one of perseverance—the victim of a freak accident that put him in a wheelchair, who persevered to serve on the state Supreme Court and as Attorney General.) Abbott's campaign accused Davis of exaggerating her hardships, while Davis' campaign accused Abbott of winning $10.7 million in a lawsuit over his injury but then as a public official blocking suits by others who were injured.

Campaign ads are financed by both the candidate and outside groups, particularly PACs (political action committees) and the parties' campaign committees. Attack ads by outside groups are usually the harshest and least constrained by facts. This was true in the 2020 cycle in Texas. The closing weeks of the U.S. Senate race saw attack ads increase substantially. In one outside-sponsored ad, Democrat M. J. Hegar was accused of being a radical for having tattoos on her arms. The military veteran replied that they covered war wounds with beauty.

attack ads
Advertisements meant as a personal attack on an opposing candidate or organization.

In Texas and nationally, five themes stood out in attack ads: Democrats as threats to law and order, Republicans as threats to health care and coverage of preexisting conditions, Democrats as radical on healthcare (Medicare-For-All), Democrats supporting Speaker Nancy Pelosi and other liberals, and Republicans as the corrupt party of special interests.[24] (Note the national focus of the themes.)

Anti-LGBTQ ads appeared to increase in 2020. In one of a number of examples, a PAC sent a mailer to San Antonio voters describing a male school board candidate as "'married' to same-sex man" with "no children" in the district, while his opponent was a "wife and mother of 6" (true statements but quite loaded). The candidate had been appointed to the board and won reelection. He said the attack revitalized his campaign and brought in workers and contributions.

Priming and Framing Two related concepts are important in understanding the impact of the news on our views: priming and framing. Most issues can be seen in different ways. The idea of **priming** is that the issues emphasized by the media frequently become the issues the public uses to evaluate leaders and policies. A classic example happened in the 1990 gubernatorial election between liberal Democrat Ann Richards and conservative Republican Clayton Williams. Through much of the campaign, the focus was primarily on the ideological differences between the two. As the conservative candidate in a conservative state, Williams maintained a comfortable lead. But then Williams told a joke to a group of reporters comparing rape to the weather and later refused to shake Richards's hand over charges she had made. As a result, his persona suddenly became the major focus for the press and many voters. (What kind of Southern man won't shake a woman's hand, and is he an insensitive sexist?) Poll results began to change, and Richards was narrowly elected.

Framing identifies which aspects of a problem are relevant and important (and which are not). Framing is based on the assumption that how an issue is characterized by the media can influence how it is understood by audiences. The clash over how to deal with the COVID-19 pandemic is an example of framing. Two traditional methods for fighting pandemics—wearing masks and social distancing (which closed or reduced service in many businesses)—were presented (framed) by public health professionals as temporary and proven measures to reduce sickness and death. They presented the issue as very important in order to get people to accept the inconveniences. However, the president, the lieutenant governor, the Texas Tea Party, and the new chair of the state Republican Party sought to frame the measures as government intrusion into personal freedom and as destructive of the economy. Playing down the seriousness of the disease, they argued that it only affects the old; we've turned the corner; and it will be over soon.

Public acceptance of the competing framing broke strongly along partisan lines, with Republicans more likely to see the pandemic as less serious and the economy as more important and threatened.[25] Most local Texas news, by its nature, emphasized the human tragedy—deaths, suffering, and tearful families. This reinforced the framing by health professionals. National media tended to split along ideological lines: conservatives vs. non-ideological professionals, centrists, and liberals.

priming
Issues emphasized by the media frequently become the issues the public uses to evaluate leaders and policy.

framing
Identifies which aspects of a problem are relevant and important.

Another conflict in 2020 illustrates (1) that social movements often face real difficulty translating activism into policies that can be enacted and (2) that many people respond to nuances in framing. The racial protests against police misconduct in 2020 produced a call to "Defund the Police." Some were so angered by police abuse that they wanted to dismantle police departments. But most meant that some money given to police departments should be redirected to programs that reduce the causes of crime and that the police should deal with fewer non-criminal matters. The problem is that the slogan "Defund the Police" has resonance in a protest but frames the issue for opponents and those outside the movement as "eliminate the police." Governor Abbott quickly adopted this framing, saying crime would run rampant and calling for penalties against cities, like Austin, that redirected police funding.

The issue quickly became partisan. Republican leaders overwhelmingly followed Abbott's framing, while Democratic leaders were divided. When Texans were asked in 2020 if they supported or opposed "defunding police," only about a quarter supported defunding. In the same survey, people were asked about cutting "some funding from police departments to increase spending on social services in your community." With this wording, the two sides were close to evenly split.[26] Thus, even though Texans are reluctant to limit the police, they do respond to nuances that in the long run could produce incremental changes.

So, Does the Media Shape Our Views? Our understanding of the influence of the media has undergone substantial change over time. Today, researchers find considerable evidence for a *subtle effects* model. The media are not all-powerful but are influential in important ways. In the words of Professors Rosalee Clawson and Zoe Oxley, "This tradition argues that the media influence citizens through agenda setting, priming, and framing; the media influence what citizens think about, which issues or traits citizens bring to bear when evaluating political leaders, and which considerations shape their thinking on political issues."[27]

Who is most likely to be influenced by the media? Research suggests the media have the most influence on those who lack background information or developed opinions, on people who rely on only one news source or news from one ideological viewpoint, and on issues that are far removed from daily life, such as false teeth or air conditioning for prison inmates.

✓ **6.2 Learning Check**

1. Are the media today becoming more or less able to investigate government wrongdoing?
2. What is the difference between soft and hard news?

Answers at the end of this chapter.

⭐ Campaigns and Citizen Participation

LO 6.3 Discuss the roles of the media in modern Texas election campaigns and citizen movements.

The media play a major role in campaigns for public office and citizen attempts to be heard. With the decline in the ability of political parties to mobilize voters, television and newspapers were the major mechanism for candidates to reach potential voters. In a state as large as Texas, this is an extremely expensive undertaking and one that is not always successful. The rise of the Internet and social media has given candidates more ability to reach out directly to voters and to target specific messages to specific groups. The new media have also provided new tools for citizen groups to organize and to try to sell their message.

Campaigns and the Traditional Media

In the past, candidates relied on rallies and mobilization by local leaders and party organizations. With the advent of television and decline of political parties, candidates for national, state, and many local offices came to rely on the mass media to get their message out. They seek press coverage of their events, generate situations and issues they hope the media will cover, and buy ads. For years, the ads have made heavy use of television, although by 2008 the Internet was gaining ground.

Texas has 20 media markets, eight more than California. (A **media market** is an area in which people receive the same traditional media—television and radio stations and newspapers.) As a result of so many markets, the cost of a traditional media campaign is substantial. For example, in the hotly contested 2018 and 2020 U.S. Senate races in Texas, candidates and supporters spent $139 and $90 million, respectively. Not surprisingly, candidates seek as much free media coverage as possible. Campaign events are designed more to gain news coverage than to involve those citizens attending, who are often more backdrop than participants.

The relationship between candidates and the press is often testy. Both need each other, but they have different goals. The candidate wants free and friendly coverage; the press wants entertaining news stories—controversy, scandals, and candidate mistakes. Candidates at both the state and national level want to control or at least influence the news. In Texas, the news environment makes it easier for the candidates to exercise control. There are fewer reporters; many of them know the candidate; and there is less of a press culture of asking challenging questions. This environment led to problems for Governors George W. Bush and Rick Perry, who went directly from working only in Texas state politics to running for president. They were not used to the rough-and-tumble aspects of national news, and as a result fared poorly in public debates and other encounters with reporters. Opportunities for direct contact with citizens through social media have enhanced the ability of candidates to bypass traditional media. Facebook and Twitter are now used extensively by candidates and office holders.

One of the complaints about news coverage of campaigns is that it tends to be **horserace journalism**; that is, it focuses more on who is winning than on the issues. Even after officials are elected, stories continue to focus on competition. For example, would Governor Abbott run for president in 2024? Once again, entertainment appears to triumph over content. A strong reason for horserace coverage is that news management wants a large audience and prefers stories that alienate neither side.

Digital Campaigning

The 2008 and 2012 presidential campaigns saw the Internet and social media come of age as a part of campaigning. Mainstream media provided blogs and online news coverage. YouTube, Facebook, and other social media provided outlets for candidates and citizens alike. Candidates began to use the Internet in a

media market
Area in which people receive the same traditional media—television and radio stations and newspapers.

horserace journalism
News that focuses on who is ahead in the race (poll results and public perceptions) rather than policy differences.

How Do We Compare...

In Media Access?

Most Populous States	Number of Media Markets (2020)	Newspaper Circulation Per Capita (2010)	(2019)	Number of Top 100 News Websites (2020)	Percentage of Households with Broadband Connection (2019)
California	12	0.16	0.06	17	89
Florida	10	0.14	0.06	8	86
New York	10	0.31	0.17	24	85
Texas	**20**	**0.08**	**0.04**	**7**	**86**
States Bordering Texas					
Arkansas	4	0.15	0.08	0	79
Louisiana	7	0.12	0.05	0	79
New Mexico	2	0.12	0.08	0	78
Oklahoma	4	0.13	0.08	0	83

Sources: "Nielsen DMA Rankings 2020," *Media Tracks Communication*, 2020, https://mediatracks.com/resources/nielsen-dma-rankings-2020/; Amy Watson, "Paid Circulation of Daily Newspapers in the United States in 2018, by State," *Statista*, March 3, 2020, https://www.statista.com/statistics/660219/paid-circulation-us-daily-newspapers-by-state/; "Top 100 USA News Websites on the Web," *Feedspot*, December 9, 2020, https://blog.feedspot.com/usa_news_websites/; S. O'Dea, "Home Broadband Connection Usage in the United States in 2019, by State," *Statista*, November 9, 2020, https://www.statista.com/statistics/185535/us-household-broadband-internet-connection-usage-by-state/.

— Competency Connection —
☼ **CRITICAL THINKING** ☼

Leaving aside number of media markets, what patterns do you see among the larger states? Between Texas and the smaller, less affluent states? Why?

major way, putting up high-quality campaign sites and using social media to get out their message. Digital advertising is cheaper than television and can be more readily targeted to specific audiences. Moreover, it can harness the powerful force of friendship. Both Barack Obama's use of social media to target younger voters and Donald Trump's tweets contributed significantly to their victories.

In Texas, statewide and local campaigns make heavy use of the Internet and social media. In his highly successful 2010 gubernatorial campaign, Governor Perry adapted established campaign practices to modern-day reality, while his primary and general election opponents ran more traditional campaigns. Rather than use direct mail, phone banks, and knocking on the doors of strangers, the Perry campaign asked volunteers to identify 12 friends and turn them out to the polls. Facebook messages to friends were encouraged.[28]

Ted Cruz's upset victory in the 2012 Republican primary for the U.S. Senate was fueled in significant part by skillful use of the Internet and social media. Among other efforts, the campaign advertised and raised funds on a multitude of platforms, targeted people who "liked" those who had endorsed Cruz, manipulated key words for Google searches, and used "promoted Tweets" (paid ads on Twitter that show up first in search results). Cruz's opponent in 2018, Beto O'Rourke, also made extensive use of the Internet, social media, and texting. O'Rourke appears to have spent more than any other candidate in the nation on social media advertising.

Because of the COVID-19 pandemic, the 2020 election campaigns relied heavily on television and social media. Limits on large gatherings and personal contact outside one's "bubble" made it difficult to hold rallies and go door to door, while telemarketers had made phone banks less effective.

By the 2014 elections, the Internet and social media were a standard part of Texas campaigns, particularly for statewide and congressional races. However, many local and traditional candidates were caught unaware by the new media, suffering embarrassment and sometimes defeat.

Inappropriate posts, cell phone pictures, and videos of off-the-cuff remarks are common on social media. Some go viral. In June 2020, five GOP country chairs were under fire for sharing social media posts with racist tones, and the *Texas Tribune* quickly found seven more with similar posts. (Readers should remember that comments and pictures posted on the Internet are seen by more than the intended audience and are likely to outlive you.)

Citizen Participation in the Digital Age

One of the charges against digital media is that use of the Internet and social media contributes to lower **civic engagement** (citizen actions to address issues of public concern). The idea is that because digital communication is not face-to-face, users are not well connected to other people and society. However, as younger people have grown up with the Internet and as the net has permeated modern society, some of the forms of engagement are changing. The young, for example, are more likely to be politically active on social networking sites.

In the past, studies consistently showed Texans as low in civic engagement compared to the rest of the nation. Texas is still below the national average in such areas as the proportion of people voting, donating to charity, and volunteering. However, some of this may be changing. By 2018, Texans were similar to national proportions of those who "discuss politics with family and friends," "follow what's going on in government and public affairs," belong to groups such as neighborhood associations and sports leagues, and take such actions as contacting a local government or signing a petition.[29]

Like candidates, citizens on both the left and right have learned to use digital media to increase their influence in the political arena. The Texas Tea Party's success in organizing grassroots campaigns, for example, is commonly attributed to the aggressive use of social media. Protestors have found social media to be an excellent tool for organizing events, fundraising, and recruiting participants. Extremist groups and individuals also troll (plant false or inflammatory stories) to disrupt protests and provoke confrontation—for example, in 2020 calling for the defense of monuments they falsely claimed BLM protestors were going to deface.

civic engagement
Actions by citizens to address issues of public concern.

Although not covered extensively in the news media, Texas has a variety of extremist groups that use protest and digital media to organize, recruit members, and sell their ideology, The Southern Poverty Law Center tracked 54 hate groups in the state in 2020 (up from 38 in 2000). Their messages include neo-Nazi, anti-Muslim, anti-Semitic, Ku Klux Klan, white nationalist, black nationalist, anti-LGBTQ, and anti-immigrant views. Two of these Texas-based groups that have received some notoriety are the Proud Boys and the Patriot Front. Proud Boys was heavily involved in a variety of violent actions around the country, including the January 6, 2021, insurrection at the U.S. Capitol (for which they were designated a terrorist group by the Canadian government). Patriot Front is most noted for distributing racist and anti-Semitic propaganda on college campuses. Their actions are taken with the publicity value in mind. Both make substantial use of the Internet and social media.[30]

Image 6.4 Mourners hold a candlelight vigil as a memorial to those slain and wounded by a sniper at a peaceful Dallas march, 2016.

Anadolu Agency/Contributor/Getty Images

Competency Connection
◉ **SOCIAL RESPONSIBILITY** ◉

Is the growth of the Internet and social media making protests less necessary or more effective tools of citizen action?

Protests: Getting the Public's Attention

Political insiders, such as party and interest group leaders, generally have ready access to policy makers and the media. For outsiders, such as ethnic minorities and working class or poor people, such access commonly is more difficult. One tool is protest. The hope is that media will cover the protest and make the public and leaders sufficiently aware of the problem to do something about it. That is a messy and long-term effort that is likely to suffer many failures along the way. Common examples of eventual successes are the women's suffrage movement and the civil rights movements of Blacks and Latinos, all of which had a Texas component.

To be effective, protests must capture the attention of the media (both traditional and digital), and even then, a major problem is the inability to control events and how the actions will be interpreted. In July 2016, out-of-state police-involved shootings of Blacks sparked demonstrations in Dallas, which received local, state, and national coverage on both traditional and new media. Then, at a peaceful march, a heavily armed sniper killed five police officers and wounded seven others and two civilians. This produced even greater coverage, much of which was not helpful to the movement.

Texas has a long history of attacks by Whites against minority Texans that the media of the time ignored or reported from the White perspective. In more recent times, violence against ethnic and racial minorities has received greater media coverage, and videos of incidents posted on the Internet and run on television news have had far greater impact on public and elite opinion than stories based on police reports and witness reports. The killing of unarmed Black men by police in 2014 and 2020 set off strong protests against police brutality in Texas and the nation.

Protests have had an impact in Texas, although not as much as organizers would wish. While most Texas protests were peaceful, protests appear threatening to many, and there was some violence, which, regardless of who was to blame, worked to the disadvantage of protestors. Surveys show the difficulty of changing minds through protest. In 2020, Texans were asked if "recent street protests made you more likely or less likely to support the goals of the Black Lives Matter movement." (BLM was the major organizer of anti-racism protests at the time.) A third of respondents said "no change," while slightly more said they were "less likely" than said they were "more likely." The responses broke heavily along partisan lines, with a majority of Republicans reporting "less likely" and a majority of Democrats saying they were "more likely" to support the goals of the movement.[31] Today, political party identification is one of the lenses through which we perceive news.

If recent Black protests produced little net change in public opinion among Texans, were the protests more successful in changing public policy? The answer is mixed. The call to defund the police had little success outside of Austin, but the movement to reduce symbols of the Confederacy and white supremacy in public space has had significant success in Texas. Surveys show a shift in Texans' opinion from 2017 to 2020 to majority support of removing or moving the monuments. Nationwide, through 2018, 114 statues and symbols had been removed or changed, 33 of which were in Texas (the most of any state).[32] With the extensive protests in the state in 2020, twelve more were removed. In response to complaints from Native Americans, San Antonio removed a statue of Columbus and renamed Columbus Park near downtown to Piazza Italia Park.

> ## ✔ 6.3 Learning Check
>
> 1. Why are statewide election campaigns so expensive in Texas?
> 2. Are political campaigns using the Internet and social media more effectively?
>
> *Answers at the end of this chapter.*

✪ Bias?

LO 6.4 Analyze the issue of bias in the Texas media.

Given the important roles played by the media, it is not surprising that activists of all persuasions often believe the media are biased against them. President Trump did not invent the term "fake news" but certainly popularized it. Today, "misinformation, spin, conspiracy theories, mistakes, and reporting that people just don't like" may be labeled fake news by some.[33] Certainly, in the 19th century, bias was the norm. However, growth of journalistic professionalism in the 20th century increased public confidence. Through the mid-1980s, the majority of the American public believed the press was relatively unbiased. Since that time, however, substantial majorities have come to perceive bias in the media.

Like most public institutions in the last half century, the media have seen a drop in public trust. In 2020, a majority of Texans did not trust the news media "to give you accurate information about the coronavirus." Again, trust broke along party lines. (Three out of five Democrats trusted the news media, while four out of five Republicans did not.) Among Texans and nationally, social media are less trusted than television and newspaper news.[34] Contrary to the decline in public trust in the media, research indicates that while some types of media have become more partisan and ideological, most of the mainstream media still adhere to standards of objectivity and neutrality. To understand this conclusion requires explanation.

It is well established by research that over the last 30 years a larger proportion of reporters are more liberal and aligned with the Democratic Party than is the general population,[35] while newspaper management has long tended to be more conservative and Republican. Many from both groups do not fit these tendencies, but the pattern is strong and persistent. Owners and publishers tend to be more conservative, possibly because of their greater affluence and business position. Newspapers have traditionally endorsed candidates for public office, and the choices (particularly for the top offices) generally reflect the position of owners and managers. Nationally, in the 23 presidential elections from 1932 to 2020, Republicans received more newspaper endorsements (17 elections) than Democrats (5). (In 1996, some 70 percent of newspapers made no presidential endorsement.)

Texas's pattern is more complex. In the long period of Democratic Party dominance, both parties generally nominated conservative candidates; but in the Democratic primary, there was often a contest between a liberal and one or more conservatives. Texas newspapers, with some exceptions, generally supported conservatives. The more mixed pattern today is discussed above in the section on "Professionalism and Democracy."

Media Bias and the News

Do personal preferences of reporters and publishers affect coverage of the news? The answer is "yes" in countries with a partisan press, as was the case in the United States until the 20th century. Today, traditions of professionalism are the standard for journalists. These professional standards hold that the press should report the facts as they are, not the way journalists want them to be, and that opinion should be clearly separated and identified as such. This view has dominated major Texas newspapers and television since the early 1900s with, of course, some exceptions. However, the pattern was challenged at the national level during the Trump presidency.

Over a fourth of Texans describe cable news as their "main source" of news (Table 6.2). Two of the major cable news networks are consciously ideological in their orientation—Fox to the right (conservative) and MSNBC to the left (liberal). CNN (Cable News Network), the pioneer in cable news, began with a tradition of objective reporting but recently has been rated Left Bias by Media Bias/Fact Check. The site rates all three as "Mixed" on factual reporting.[36]

Almost half of Texans report listening to talk radio regularly or sometimes. Talk radio has long been dominated by conservatives at both the local and national level. On the Internet, a wide range of blogs make it easy for users to get their information from congenial sources that entertain and reinforce the reader's views. Texas has popular blogs on both the right and left, with fewer in the center.

Seven of ten Texans use social media (Table 6.3). The growth of social media increases the role of friends and opinion leaders in originating and framing issues. Availability of sites such as YouTube and Twitter increases self-selection of what news and views to receive. This practice leads to confirmation bias in which people become more fixed in their beliefs and attitudes because they seek out information that supports their beliefs.[37]

Objective reporting still remains the standard for the three major television broadcasting networks (CBS, NBC, and ABC), the public networks (NPR, PRI, and PBS), and the major newspapers of Texas. At times, the media deviate from objectivity.

From his arrival in the U.S. Senate, Texan Ted Cruz used blunt, combative rhetoric and showed an unwillingness to follow many of the informal rules of the Senate aimed at reducing open conflict. This attitude resonated with his supporters but created a variety of enemies among other senators. The negativity was reflected in his coverage by the media. In his 2016 presidential bid, he tended to be viewed negatively by the press but received substantial coverage because extreme statements by the former Princeton debater provided entertaining sound bites. Since 2016, Senator Cruz has been somewhat less abrasive and is now in his second term, both of which have softened somewhat his treatment by the press. However, taking his family to a resort in Mexico during the February 2020 arctic storm in Texas launched a firestorm of criticism by both the public and the press. His quick return and admission the trip was a "mistake" did little to quiet the censure.

So, Is There Bias in the Media?

Is there partisan or ideological bias in the media? The findings are clear but nuanced. There is little objective evidence of systematic ideological or partisan bias in the reporting of news in the mainstream media.[38] Major newspapers and network television news generally adhere to the standards of objectivity and journalistic professionalism. In the words of media scholar Timothy E. Cook, "Newsmaking is a collective process more influenced by the uncritically accepted routine workings of journalism as an institution than by attitudes of journalists."[39] With some notable exceptions, reporters and managers tend to act professionally and not let their ideological preferences dictate their choice of stories or direct the tone of their reporting. The ideological divide between reporters and managers probably also tends to reduce ideological or partisan bias, as each group moderates the views of the other.

Nevertheless, today more debate occurs between "talking heads" representing differing interpretations on cable television, and more analysis stories are in newspapers and on the Internet. Many examples of biased coverage of issues and events can be found; however, they balance out over the long run. Where media have become highly partisan and ideological is in areas in which consumers can choose their source of information and entertainment—Fox or MSNBC, which blog, which talk show?

Two other forms of bias are also noted in the media: a bias toward entertaining over important news, and a commercial bias. Both are discussed later in the chapter in the section "Change in the Media."

✓ 6.4 Learning Check

1. Do studies find that there is a bias in the media to the left or right?

2. In which area of the media is partisanship increasing?

Answers at the end of this chapter.

⬆ Latinos, Blacks, and Women in Texas Media

LO 6.5 Discuss the representation of women and ethnic minorities in Texas media.

Although Black and Latino Texans have a rising middle class, they are still underrepresented among decision-makers and those who influence decisions, including the media. In 2019, for example, racial and ethnic minorities were 40 percent of the U.S. population but only 22 percent of journalists and 18 percent of newsroom leaders. These proportions have changed little over the last two decades. For the last decade, ethnic minorities graduated from journalism schools in similar proportions to Whites but were less likely to be hired. Diversity tends to be lowest at small local newspapers and TV stations, the places where journalists traditionally seek their first job. Women, who are slightly more than half the population were 41 percent of both newsroom journalists and managers in 2019. As in much of the economy, women journalists tend to make less than their male colleagues.[40]

Data for Texas journalists are less systematic but seem to follow the national pattern. Similarly, a study of the political pundits quoted by Texas media during the 2014 campaign found that seven political scientists (all White males) were the dominant sources—quoted 1,331 times. In Texas's 2020 U.S. Senate primaries, 71 percent of quoted sources were White; 72 percent were male.[41]

Why do these numbers matter? In addition to issues of equity, traditional racial and ethnic minorities are now a majority of Texas's population. Critics observe that to cover all Texans requires people who are familiar with the state's various communities and who speak the same language as the audience. Otherwise, reporting may be "incomplete, tone-deaf, or biased." Black and Latino journalists also often try to correct colleagues' negative or stereotypical portrayals. What seems most effective in increasing coverage and accuracy of historical minority issues is the combination of diversity in the newsroom and a large Black and Latino audience.

Today, non-White Texans are portrayed more often than in the past, with fewer stereotypes, and in a wider variety of contexts than was previously true. However, critics see continuing, if sometimes subtle, stereotypes and stories focusing on family problems, crime, and traditional subordinate roles (such as maid, gardener, or unskilled labor). Two recurring positive themes found in coverage of Latinos are achievement and culture. Researchers disagree as to whether media coverage of minority group success counterbalances the negative reporting.[42]

An example of the limited attention to minority Texans is the cover page of the state's leading monthly magazine—*Texas Monthly*. (Editors commonly see the cover page as the most important page.) From its founding in 1973 through 2020, of 555 covers, Blacks appeared 22 times, 13 of those as a major focus. Included were two maids serving white women, a hustler, athletes, and two members of

Congress. Latinos appeared 10 times (3 were of the singer Selena). There were no Asian Americans.

The small number of racial and ethnic minorities in newsrooms may also affect how events are interpreted. Critics, for example, report a difference in the view of racial groups reflected in the news coverage of the 2015 biker shoot-out in Waco and treatment of violence by Blacks. (In Waco, a meeting of rival motorcycle gangs led to shooting within the meeting and with police that killed 9 and injured 20. It received extensive news coverage.) A commentator noted: "The biker shoot-out saw no extended conversation about gun control, mental illness, 'White thug life' nor family breakdown. The latter typically comes up specifically when news media covers Black-on-Black homicides."[43]

How do people feel the media treat racial and ethnic minorities? A Ford Foundation survey looked at this question for Whites, Blacks, Latinos, and Asian Americans. All four groups thought that Blacks were more negatively portrayed in the media than the reality and that Asian Americans were accurately portrayed. Nearly half of minorities thought that White Americans were more *positively* portrayed in the media than the reality. Blacks and Latinos believed that Latinos were portrayed negatively, while White and Asian Americans thought the portrayal was accurate.[44]

A small but significant number of ethnic news media outlets can be found in Texas and across the nation. One site's listing of media outlets in Texas included 26 Latino-, 9 Black-, 9 Asian American-, and one Russian-oriented newspaper. In the past, the author found listings of 50 newspapers in the state serving Latinos, Blacks, or Asian Americans. However, searches in 2019–2020 suggest that the number regularly publishing may be closer to 25. Just as English-language newspapers are in decline, so too are Spanish-language publications. The number varies somewhat over time, but in late 2020 there were four full-power and 22 low-power Spanish-language television stations in the state, plus Mexican stations along the border aimed at Texas audiences. In a listing of Spanish language weeklies publishing in 2015, *La Voz de Houston* had the third largest circulation in the nation at 190,000. Four weeklies had circulation over 100,000 each, and the eight Texas weeklies listed had a total circulation over 720,000.[45]

Univision, the largest Spanish-language network in the United States, began in San Antonio and Los Angeles in 1962. The second largest, *Telemundo*, started its Texas operations in Dallas in 2002. With the growth of the Latino population in metropolitan areas, Spanish-language television has done well in Texas. Since at least 2018, Spanish-language newscasts during primetime in Houston, Dallas, and San Antonio have frequently topped English-language news broadcasts in audience share. A problem for Texas's Spanish-language television is that it depends heavily on an influx of immigrants to maintain its audience. As Latinos become bilingual or unilingual-English, they make less use of Spanish-language media.

Availability of Spanish-language news produces a trade-off in attitudes. Research indicates that when Whites see a political article in Spanish, there tends to be a small increase in resentment, whereas Spanish-speakers tend to show an increase in sense of belonging.[46]

Nationally, Black-oriented media have a long history and are still the most prevalent, although the traditional Black media have lost audience in recent years. In Texas, with a smaller Black population, African American media are second to Latino media. Of 12 Black-owned television stations in the nation, there is one in Texas, KPEJ in Odessa.[47] Blogs and internet websites are more common but not as well established as in some other parts of the country.

Neither ethnicity nor gender makes a large difference in media preferences. In a 2020 survey by the University of Texas at Austin, respondents were asked how much they relied on eight different kinds of media for information on the coronavirus. White, Latino, and Black Texans gave similar responses. For all three groups, 70–73 percent relied on local news sources "a lot" or "some." As is true for national data, Black Texans had a slightly greater use of television (broadcast and cable) than did Whites and Latinos. Women and men had similar media usage with a few small differences.[48] Survey research also shows that Black adults are more trusting of local news organizations than are other racial/ethnic groups. They also are more likely to see the media's watchdog role as necessary.[49]

✪ Regulation

LO 6.6   Distinguish how print and electronic media are regulated by government.

In many countries, the media are owned or heavily regulated by government. In the United States, the First Amendment to the U.S. Constitution protects freedom of the press, which has meant little regulation of newspapers. Broadcast media (radio and television) were long regulated under federal law to ensure they "serve the public interest, convenience, and necessity." In comparison to regulation in other Western nations, regulation in the United States has been minimal.

Regulation of Print and Broadcast Media

U.S. courts have been particularly suspicious of **prior restraint** or censorship before information can be made available to the public. The key idea is that government should not restrict the free flow of ideas beforehand, although certain kinds of statements may lead to punishment after publication or speech. For example, in *New York Times Co. v. United States*, 402 U.S. 713 (1971), the U.S. Supreme Court allowed publication of a highly classified government study of the Vietnam War popularly known as *The Pentagon Papers*, even though government officials argued that their publication might damage national security.

Protection against prior restraint also applies to the Internet. In a 2014 case (*Kinney v. Barnes*, 443 SW3d 87), the Texas Supreme Court held that authors of existing defamatory online posts (statements that are untrue and damaging) may be required to take them down. However, courts cannot prohibit future similar posts because that would be prior restraint.

One of the ironies in legal treatment of the media is the difference in governmental responses to criticism of government and obscenity. U.S. courts have

✓ 6.5 Learning Check

1. Today, are women and ethnic minorities found in the news media in similar proportions to their numbers in the state's population?

2. In the news, are minority Texans portrayed in a fashion similar to Whites?

Answers at the end of this chapter.

prior restraint
Suppression of material before it is published, commonly called censorship.

protected the right of the media to criticize government more than is the case in most other countries. The Federal Communications Commission (FCC), however, has regulated obscenity more tightly than have most other Western nations.

At the national level, the FCC is responsible for media regulation. Today, the FCC still regulates broadcast television. Radio and cable television were deregulated in 1996. Media are subject to general laws, such as those regulating business practices and monopolies. The Internet has not experienced the degree of regulation faced by the broadcast media and cable but has had to deal with a number of legal issues over time: copyright protection, pornography, cybersecurity, harvesting of personal information from the Internet, government spying, and censorship by internet platforms.

Internet Regulation

Perhaps the most significant regulatory issue facing the Internet today is **net neutrality**, which means that internet service providers must treat all data on the Internet equally, not providing faster connection speeds for a premium price and not curbing access or slowing transmission of lawful content. Opponents of net neutrality argue it stifles innovation, while supporters fear censorship, pay-to-play, and harm to small business. In 2015, under pressure from President Obama, a reluctant FCC approved rules favoring net neutrality. However, two years later under President Trump, the FCC repealed the rules. Some states are moving to require net neutrality within their boundaries, but this appears unlikely in Texas.

State and Local Regulation

State and local governments may regulate the media in areas not covered by FCC rules. In Texas, regulation has been minimal, although issues over franchises for cable outlets have been a source of considerable conflict. A long-standing free press issue was resolved in 2009 when Texas became the 37th state to pass a **shield law** protecting journalists from having to reveal certain confidential sources.

The Free Flow of Information Act, allows reporters to protect their sources by not having to testify or produce notes in court (unless they witness a felony). Journalists argued that they were not able to carry out their investigative role if they could not protect the identity of their sources. Prosecutors opposed such measures because they believed protection of sources impeded evidence gathering. Both sides finally agreed to a compromise that protects most sources, unaired video, and the identity of anonymous posts on news websites. Reporters generally agree that the law works as intended, except that it is not clear that the law has increased the number of whistleblowers willing to speak with journalists.

A tactic used by companies, organizations, and wealthy individuals to deter negative comments in the media has been to sue for libel, thus saddling defendants with heavy costs to defend themselves. These "strategic lawsuits against public participation" or **SLAPP** have often had a chilling effect on public discussion of misdeeds. In 2011, Texas joined the majority of states in passing anti-SLAPP legislation. Together with amendments in 2013 and state court decisions through

net neutrality
A legal principle that internet service providers and government officials should treat all data on the Internet equally, not discriminating or charging differentially and not blocking content they do not like.

shield law
A law protecting journalists from having to reveal confidential sources to police or in court.

SLAPP
Strategic lawsuits against public participation are suits filed primarily to silence criticism and negative public discussion.

2018, Texas's law prohibiting frivolous defamation lawsuits was one of the strongest in the country. However, because of the way the law was applied, industry representatives became concerned about protecting trade secrets and non-compete agreements.

Over the strong objection of reporters and free speech advocates, business interests made a major effort in the 2019 legislature. While some of the harsher provisions in the original bill were softened, the scope of the SLAPP law was significantly reduced by the legislation. Opponents fear that new provisions will discourage whistleblowers.

Under American common law, and now much statutory law, **defamation** of a person is a civil (not a criminal) wrong. That is, anyone who says or prints untrue information that damages a person's reputation may be subject to a civil lawsuit. If the comment is written, it is called **libel**; if spoken, it is **slander**. Because of the protection of freedom of the press and of speech in the First Amendment to the U.S. Constitution, libel and slander are much more difficult to prove than is the case in Europe and much of the rest of the world. What constitutes defamation varies from state to state and in federal law. In all cases, the statement's being true is an absolute defense. Since a 1964 U.S. Supreme Court case (*New York Times Co. v. Sullivan*, 376. U.S. 254), public figures suing for defamation have a heavier burden than do ordinary citizens. In addition to proving that a statement is false and harmful, public figures must prove that it was made with "actual malice." (Public figures include political leaders, celebrities, and some others who may have received unwanted notoriety.)

Defamation suits arising from statements on the Internet are increasing. Information on the Internet, including social media, tends to be permanent and searchable. Whether anonymous or not, many find it easier to make negative comments on the Internet than in person. Although the right to post comments anonymously is protected by the First Amendment, libel is not. Under a Texas case, providers may be forced to identify the "speakers."[50]

defamation, libel, and slander
Communicating something untrue that damages a person's reputation (defamation) may be subject to a civil lawsuit. If the comment is written, it is called libel; if spoken, it is slander.

✓ **6.6 Learning Check**

1. Which medium is most regulated today?
2. Which level of government has traditionally regulated media the most?

Answers at the end of this chapter.

⬧ Change in the Media: More Participation, More Sources, but Less News?

LO 6.7 Discuss the positive and negative effects of changes the media are undergoing in Texas.

The nature of the media is changing rapidly. From the 19th century through the first half of the 20th century, newspapers were the major source of news for Texans. But in the second half of the 20th century, television came to be the dominant source of information for Americans and Texans alike. Now, in the 21st century, the Internet and social media are challenging television news for viewers, particularly among the young. Many see these changes as positive: People now have a wider range of choices for their news and can get it according to their own schedule and wishes. Through the Internet, people have more opportunity to participate in collection and distribution of news. Others see the changes as fraught with dangers for citizens' level of accurate information.

What do we know? First, newspapers remain the major gatherers of news. Television and internet news depends heavily on major newspapers for originating stories. In the case of internet news, an ongoing debate continues as to whether enough people will pay for news on the Internet and whether enough advertisers can be obtained to finance the level of news-gathering now provided by newspapers. Fifteen percent of Texans say they paid for a newspaper subscription in the last year; 5 percent paid for digital news. A fundamental problem is that as digital advertising increases, news organizations are competing for a smaller share. Second, the need to draw audiences by being more entertaining has decreased the amount of hard news across the media. Third, a proliferation of channels on television and blogs on the Internet has led to increased **niche journalism** (also called **narrowcasting**) that appeals to a narrow audience, which often leads to more extreme ideological and partisan views.

Concentration of Ownership

Another change profoundly affecting the media is a growing concentration of ownership. Today, fewer than 10 corporations (depending on the latest mergers) own most of the national newspapers, news magazines, broadcast television networks, and cable news networks, as well as publishing houses, movie studios, telephone companies, and internet service providers.[51] Corporations that own media outlets tend to be conglomerates; that is, they own companies that make or sell a variety of products, not just entertainment and information. A major concern is that they will pressure their own media to avoid negative reporting on the other companies in the conglomerate.

In Texas, local ownership of the media has declined sharply, and corporate ownership has become complex. Of the major Texas newspapers, only the *Dallas Morning News* is still owned by a Texas company, the Dallas News Corporation, which also owns the *Denton Record-Chronicle*. (In March 2021, the A. H. Belo Corporation, created in 1885, changed its name to separate from its founder, who was a Confederate colonel and slave holder.) All other major dailies are owned by out-of-state media giants, such as McClatchy Company (owner of 29 dailies in 14 states) and Gatehouse Media (owner of 260 dailies and 300 weeklies around the country). Fifteen of the state's television stations, including stations in the state's largest metropolitan areas, are owned by TEGNA, a broadcast company based in Virginia. Of San Antonio's iHeartMedia's 850 radio stations, 72 are in Texas.

The Spanish-language television network, *Univision,* has 47 television stations with 7 in Texas. In 2020, Searchlight Capital Partners, headquartered in New York bought 64 percent of the company. Mexico City media giant Grupo Televisa, which had been instrumental in *Univision*'s origins, retained its 36 percent stake. *Telemundo*, owned by NBCUniversal, has 18 affiliates in Texas.

niche journalism (narrowcasting)
A news medium focusing on a narrow audience defined by concern about a particular topic or area.

Homogenization Concentration of media ownership has four consequences that worry critics. The first is **homogenization of news**—the increased likelihood that the same stories will be presented in the same way, stories that in the past might have been affected by local and regional culture and concerns. Other critics refer to the *illusion* of choice—many ways to get the same news. Chains tend to provide the same feed to all the radio or television stations they own, for example. Ownership concentration has combined with tendencies of both newspapers and the electronic media to respond to their limited resources by reducing (or eliminating) reporters who gather news. Instead, media outlets rely on wire services, outside networks (such as Texas State Network News), or corporate feeds and stories. A quarter of the 952 U.S. television stations that air newscasts do not produce their own news programs. No comparable data is available for Texas, but an examination of websites indicates the pattern's existence in Texas. Additional stations have sharing arrangements under which much of their content is produced outside their own newsrooms.

In a state as large and diverse as Texas, homogenization represents a considerable change. Although the Internet provides more diversity in the presentation of news, so far the lack of revenue, reporters, and professional standards makes it more reactive and opinion-oriented than traditional news reports. A study by the Pew Trust found that 99 percent of the stories covered by blogs originated in the traditional media and were then rebroadcast through bloggers.

Occasionally, however, the blogosphere does generate news and forces the traditional media to take notice. For example, in 2011, *TheAustinBulldog.org*, an essentially one-person operation, and the *Austin American-Statesman* newspaper used Texas's open records law to request personal emails by Austin city council members discussing city business. In 2016, a Texas appeals court ruled that the city had to provide the emails.

Soft News A second consequence of growing concentration of ownership is the decline in the amount of news and its "softening." Prior to the 1980s, the news departments of the three major television networks (NBC, CBS, and ABC) were substantially shielded from profit expectations, and their evening news broadcasts were *the* national news, most of it hard news. However, in the mid-1980s, new ownership took over the three networks and demanded more advertising revenue from news. In this period, technological change allowed the emergence of competition from cable television. (CNN debuted in 1980, and a wide array of new and entertaining programs and networks soon followed.) Having to compete for audience share, network news executives sought more entertainment value by reducing the amount of hard news and increasing the emphasis on scandal, horserace coverage of political campaigns, and controversial sound bites. Eventually, softer coverage of news would come to CNN, NPR, and PBS. The ideological networks, Fox and MSNBC, have made their staple a minimum of hard news combined with entertaining spin and drawing in the ideological faithful as viewers.

Local television news in Texas and elsewhere is often cited as an example of soft news. Local news coverage prioritizes weather, traffic, sports, crime, accidents, and human interest. Soft or not, local television news is watched

homogenization of news
Making news uniform regardless of differing locations and cultures.

regularly by half of Texans, almost twice the number that watch network news. Perhaps the reason is captured by Pew researchers:

> Local TV news *is* more likely than other media we studied to try to portray regular people from the community and how they feel about things, rather than just officials. The reporting was straightforward and mostly strictly factual, with little of the journalist's opinion thrown in. . . . Viewers got straight news from their local TV stations, and it was certainly about the community.[52]

Less State and Local News Part of the accepted wisdom in Texas and elsewhere is that "All politics is local." However, an examination of candidate speeches and partisan and ideological blogs shows traditional state and local issues being overwhelmed by national issues. Columnist Erica Grieder noted that in the 2016 elections, "Transportation and water, two of the biggest issues facing the state, have been largely sidelined in favor of the same set of issues that animated voters in the Iowa [presidential] caucuses … : immigration and sanctuary cities [and] the correct way to refer to radical Islamist terrorism …"[53] The pattern continued in the 2018 and 2020 election cycles.

In 2020, polls consistently showed Texans most concerned about health/the pandemic, the economy/jobs, and border security/immigration, all of which were also national concerns).[54] Driving the relative importance of these issues were party identification and views about President Trump. Issues specific to Texas did not make the cut for most Texans. Part of the reason for this nationalization of Texas politics is the nationalization of the news—in 2020, the focus of national reporting on President Trump and the strong division between the two parties.

Additionally, non-local owners of the state's newspapers have shown little interest in state and local news. Publishers have cut staff, and, very importantly, reduced the size of the **Capitol press corps**. The number of reporters assigned to cover state news in Austin by Texas news outlets dropped from 66 in 1991 to about 50 in 2000 and then to 32 in 2016. At the opening of the 2021 legislature, there were 85 reporters credentialed by the House of Representatives. A major reason for the recent uptick is that the number of television reporters increased to become a majority.

When the decline of the Capitol press corps first became obvious, some observers were optimistic that the Internet would fill the void.[55] So far, however, there are no signs of this happening. The Capitol press corps is declining in most large states. The decline in full-time reporters covering state government means fewer hard questions and less investigative journalism to provide oversight of what our state government does and doesn't do.

Commercial Bias A final concern arising from the growing concentration of media ownership is commercial bias and conflict of interest—that is, favoring the owners' company by presenting favorable stories or ignoring the bad the company does.[56] Traditionally, advertising provides 80 percent of newspaper revenue and subscriptions 20 percent. Highly dependent on advertisers and needing to be

Capitol press corps
Reporters assigned to cover state-level news, commonly working in Austin.

responsive to corporate owners, reporters and editors face pressure to avoid angering either. Thus, "[i]n a survey of 118 local news directors, more than half report that advertisers try to tell them what to air and not to air—and they say the problem is growing." One-third of newspaper editors report that they would not feel free to publish news that might harm their parent company.[57] The problem is not restricted to newspapers. According to reports, several employees of ABC who were critical of Disney practices were fired when the company acquired control of ABC. In Texas, Clear Channel (predecessor of iHeartMedia) was accused of censoring reporters' opinions. As corporations invest more heavily in digital sites, some observers fear that commercial bias will intrude further into the Internet.

Beyond concerns about protecting parent companies, concentration of media ownership has raised issues about an elitist bias in news (a tendency to present topics and views congenial to the wealthy and powerful but not necessarily to the rest of the population). Additional potential biases sometimes argued include those favoring large corporations and their executives' opposition to organized labor.

In authoritarian countries, publicly owned media commonly reflect government's views. However, in democratic societies, publicly supported media are more often independent and of high quality. National Public Radio (NPR), the Public Broadcasting System (PBS), and local public radio and TV stations receive a small amount of public financing. These entities raise most of their money from individual and corporate donors. Public stations in Texas and the nation tend to attract a more liberal audience. MediaBias/FactCheck rates both PBS and NPR as left center (moderately liberal), while Ad Fontes Media scores both as centrist. Both services give the two public networks high ratings for factual reporting and reliability. The non-profit online *Texas Tribune* attempts to avoid partisan or ideological bias. It is rated left center in orientation and high for factual reporting by MediaBias/FactCheck. Nevertheless, its reliance on contributions from individuals and corporations has raised some claims of conflict of interest.[58]

✓ 6.7 Learning Check

1. Are the changes in the news media trending toward more or less news being gathered?

2. Are people using social media as a news source?

Answers at the end of this chapter.

🖹 Point/Counterpoint

Will the Internet and Social Media Be Able to Replace the Quantity and Quality of News Now Provided by Traditional Media?

The Issue For more than a half century, the print media, radio, and television have provided a substantial amount of news in a relatively unbiased, professional manner. However, the Internet and social media are rapidly changing the pattern. Newspapers, the major gatherers of news, are in sharp decline, and television news has become softer and, in the case of cable news, more ideological. Internet news sites are increasing in number, and social media are becoming more diverse and more important sources of news.

The greater number of media options for both news and entertainment has increased competition between news and entertainment, in many ways melding the two together. At the same time, competition for advertising dollars has reduced revenue. As a result, less money has been available to hire reporters. Some claim this competitive environment and fewer professionals have had a negative effect on the quantity and quality of Texans' news.

(Continued)

For	Against
1. Throughout its history, the media have been in constant change. This shift to digital media is simply another step in its evolution.	1. With so many choices, the present trend will continue. People will tend to choose entertaining news over hard and professional news. Soft news will be competing with partisan news.
2. Ultimately, advertising dollars will move to internet news sites, and social media will continue to adapt to meet people's needs.	2. Audience size is key. Advertising dollars will go to entertainment over news and try to censor reporting when advertisers sponsor news.
3. Social media are producing a new approach to news by providing information while entertaining, eliminating traditional news media filters that limit direct access to information, and giving ordinary people tools to uncover and report the news.	3. Amateurs will not be able to produce the quantity and quality of news now provided by professionals even with new tools.

— Competency Connection —
✿ CRITICAL THINKING ✿

Over the next decade, what will be lost and what will be gained as we move to more dependence on the Internet and social media for our news?

⊠ Keeping Current

Election 2020 in Texas

State media coverage of the 2020 election in Texas was more substantial than in recent years, even more than the hotly contested 2018 U.S. Senate race. Although Texas did not receive the attention of battleground states, national media took more notice of the state. Social media and the Internet were particularly important for campaigns because of past success and the limitations imposed to fight the pandemic. The top two races and to a lesser extent the threat to Republican dominance of legislative seats drove the coverage. The other statewide races—Railroad Commission and judges—drew little coverage. Reporting of local races varied greatly.

As usual, horserace coverage (who's ahead) was dominant over issues. With 2020 being a difficult year, together with harsher partisanship, it was feared that campaigns would be mean and full of attack ads. In Texas, with a few exceptions, harsh rhetoric and attack ads did not appear to be more common than in other recent campaigns. To the degree that Texas candidates and media focused on issues, much of the discussion was again on national issues, with major state problems getting short shrift. The one partial exception was border security, which was also a national issue. As was the case nationally, polls underestimated the Trump vote and his coattails, which affected coverage. This was particularly noticeable in South Texas, where Democrats won overall but by lower margins among Latinos.

Texas newspapers continued to cut staff and number of pages, while local television news provided local color but little depth. On the other hand, internet news and social media were spurred by the campaign.

Conclusion

In many areas, Texas has patterns that differ significantly from those of the nation, but the media at both levels have remarkably similar histories and patterns. Newspapers have long been the major outlet for news and remain important today, particularly as gatherers of news and as the source of the details of the news for the elite. Today, television is being overtaken by the Internet and social media as the major source of news for Texans, particularly among the young. Soft news and the decline in the number of reporters are major concerns. Growth in the number of ways to receive news provides the elite and news junkies a wealth of information. Potentially, social media provide more opportunity for ordinary Texans to participate in the reporting of news and to select how and what they receive. The concern is that the rise of social media is making news softer and more ideological.

The media continue to play a number of vital roles, albeit playing some better than others: informing citizens and leaders, maintaining democracy, setting the public agenda, and influencing our views. Diversity remains a major challenge. Changes in ownership of the media, availability of better campaign techniques for office seekers and citizen groups, and movement toward predominance of the Internet and social media portend both challenges and opportunities.

Chapter Summary

LO 6.1 Compare the ways in which Texans get their information today with past patterns. The sources of news for Texans are changing. Newspapers were most important in the 1800s and the first half of the 20th century. Today, the interested public gets news from multiple sources. Newspapers are still important, particularly for the elite. Television remains the major source for most Texans, but we are following the national trend of increased preference for the Internet and social media. A major concern with the changes is the decline in the amount of actual news received by the public.

LO 6.2 Describe the roles of the media in Texas politics. There are many platforms from which to receive news, but the content of the news appears to be in decline. Absorbing the news requires some effort and certain conditions, which means that interested citizens and leaders are likely to gain much more from the news than the average citizen. Historically, the press was highly partisan and often an unreliable source of accurate information. In the 20th century, the press became a more professional provider of information in Texas and the nation, although in recent years the national media have become more adversarial. The media have used the state's open meetings and open records laws to provide more information about public policy-making. In Texas and the nation, the ability to investigate is in decline because of lack of money and corporate influence, but the state's press has generally played a positive role in exposing political scandals. The media, together with political leaders and interest groups, participate in setting the agenda of what government will or will not consider. Texas media have worked at this role but face difficulties and are not always successful. The media seldom change people's minds, but they do affect public opinion through priming and framing. They help to shape what we think about and the evaluations we make.

LO 6.3 Discuss the roles of the media in modern Texas election campaigns and citizen movements. The media play a significant role in campaigns through the ads they run and the coverage they give candidates. Because the media and the candidates have different goals but need each other, the relationship is often conflictual. Each tries to manipulate the other. Use of the Internet and social media in campaigns has become very important and more sophisticated beginning in 2008. Digital campaigning accelerated during the 2020 pandemic. Citizens are also learning to use the media, particularly social media, to organize protests and lobby government leaders. Protests remain a major tool for Texans who are "outsiders," with both successes and failures.

LO 6.4 Analyze the issue of bias in the Texas media. Research indicates that there is not a net bias in the media toward one party or ideology, although many parts of the media— talk shows, the ideological cable networks, and blogs—have become more partisan. Researchers have found evidence of a commercial bias and a frequent preference for soft news, which is entertaining rather than important but boring or difficult to understand.

LO 6.5 Discuss the representation of women and ethnic minorities in Texas media. In Texas and the nation, women and ethnic minorities are underrepresented in journalism, and the proportions are even lower in management positions. One consequence is less representation in the news provided. Texas does have a tradition of ethnic news media, which may become more prevalent on the Internet.

LO 6.6 Distinguish how print and electronic media are regulated by government. The national government has taken primary responsibility for regulation of the media. Newspapers have never faced substantial regulation, and today only broadcast television is still heavily regulated. The major legal issue facing the Internet is whether and how to apply the idea of net neutrality. In Texas, defamation, particularly through the Internet, remains an important topic, along with the state's shield law and the recent weakening of the anti-SLAPP law.

LO 6.7 Discuss the positive and negative effects of changes the media are undergoing in Texas. Newspapers have long been the major gatherers of news. Their decline has meant fewer reporters actually gathering news for other forms of media to use. The growth of cable news and the increasing role of internet blogs and social media are giving impetus to softer news and more opportunities for partisanship. Digital media provide more opportunity for citizen participation and innovation and will probably become the dominant media outlet for news. How that will affect news is the subject of a major debate.

Key Terms

adversarial, p. 230
agenda setting, p. 235
attack ads, p. 238
blogs, p. 217
Capitol press corps, p. 255
civic engagement, p. 243
defamation, libel, and slander, p. 252
framing, p. 239
hard news, p. 227

homogenization of news, p. 254
horserace journalism, p. 241
media, p. 213
media market, p. 241
net neutrality, p. 251
news websites, p. 217
niche journalism (narrowcasting), p. 253
open meetings, p. 232

open records, p. 232
priming, p. 239
prior restraint, p. 250
professionalism, p. 229
shield law, p. 251
SLAPP, p. 251
social media, p. 217
soft news, p. 227
yellow journalism, p. 229

Learning Check Answers

 6.1
1. Texans get news from a variety of sources, but television is still most used. Like national patterns, the Internet and social media are gaining.

2. In the early 20th century, most Texans got their news from newspapers.

 6.2
1. With fewer reporters, the media are less able to investigate government wrongdoing.

2. Soft news is more entertaining but has less substance. Hard news has more depth and is commonly connected to public policy.

6.3
1. The biggest factor in the high cost of Texas political campaigns is having to advertise in so many media markets.

2. Yes, political campaigns are using the Internet and social media more effectively.

6.4
1. No, examples of bias tend to balance out.

2. Partisanship tends to appear most consistently in areas in which consumers can choose their preferred ideological presentation, such as blogs, talk shows, and cable television.

6.5
1. No, women, and more so racial and ethnic minorities, are currently underrepresented in Texas newsrooms.

2. Reporting on minority Texans has improved but is still different in important ways, such as less coverage and some continued stereotyping.

6.6
1. Broadcast television is the most regulated medium.

2. The federal government has regulated media more than has the state.

6.7
1. With fewer reporters and the decline of newspapers, less news is being gathered.

2. Yes, many people rely on social media for their news, although other forms of media are more important overall.

7

The Politics of Interest Groups

Learning Objectives

7.1 Explain what interest groups are, why they form, and what their essential characteristics are.

7.2 Describe types of interest groups and analyze the characteristics of a powerful interest group.

7.3 Evaluate the kinds of activities that interest groups use to influence Texas government.

7.4 Assess how interest groups are regulated and evaluate the effectiveness of these laws.

Image 7.1 Black Lives Matter protesters rally against police brutality after Mike Ramos was killed by police in Austin.

Vic Hinterlang/Shutterstock.com

Competency Connection
COMMUNICATION SKILLS

What are your views with regard to the use of excessive force by the police of unarmed suspects? How would you convey your position to others?

The typical focus of politics is on nomination and election of citizens to public office. There is, however, much more to politics than politicians and elections. Politics is perhaps best understood as the process of influencing public policy decisions in order to protect and preserve a group, to achieve the group's goals, and to distribute benefits to the group's members. Organized people demand policies that promote their financial security, education, health, welfare, and protection.

Because government makes and enforces public policy decisions, it is not surprising that people try to influence officials who make and apply society's rules or policies, nor is it surprising that one important approach is through group action. History shows that people who organize for political action tend to be more effective in achieving their goals than persons acting alone. This principle is particularly true if a group is well financed. Money plays a major role in state government and elections, so groups often achieve their goals after helping to finance campaigns.

⊡ Interest Groups in the Political Process

LO 7.1 Explain what interest groups are, why they form, and what their essential characteristics are.

When people attempt to influence political decisions or to select men and women who make such decisions, they usually turn either to political parties (examined in Chapter 4), the media (examined in Chapter 6), or interest groups (the subject of this chapter). Interest groups participate in a variety of activities to obtain benefits, along with favorable laws and policies, for their members.

What Is an Interest Group?

An **interest group** may be identified as a pressure group, a special interest group, or a lobby. It is an organization whose members share common views and objectives. To promote their interests, such groups participate in activities designed to influence government officials and policy decisions for the benefit of group members or their cause. When a group or individual communicates directly with a government official to influence that official's decision on a policy matter, this activity is called **lobbying**. For example, during every regular legislative session, the Independent Colleges and Universities of Texas (ICUT), an organization of more than 40 private colleges and universities (like The University of Incarnate Word in San Antonio and Southern Methodist University in Plano) lobbies the legislature against appropriation cuts affecting Texas Equalization Grants (TEG). This is a state government program that provides financial assistance to college students attending private institutions of higher education in Texas.

interest group
An organization that seeks to influence government officials and their policies on behalf of members sharing common views and objectives (for example, labor unions or trade associations).

lobbying
Communicating with legislators or other government officials for the purpose of influencing decision-makers.

Follow *Practicing Texas Politics* on Twitter
@PracTexPol

Different types of businesses and industries also seek to influence government officials. For instance, oil and gas production has been an important part of the Texas economy for more than 100 years. During the 84th legislative session (2015), the Texas Independent Oil Producers and Royalty Owners aligned against environmental groups (like the Sierra Club) that supported a bill prohibiting local governments from banning hydraulic fracturing (fracking) in oil and gas production. Legislators passed the bill.

Although political parties and interest groups both attempt to influence policy decisions by government officials, they differ in their methods. The principal purpose of party activity is to increase the number of a party's members who are elected or appointed to public offices. Each party wants to gain control of government and achieve party goals. In contrast, an interest group seeks to influence government officials (regardless of their party affiliation) to the advantage of the group. In general, an interest group wants government to create and implement policies that benefit the group, without necessarily placing its own members in public office.

Part of the purpose of economic groups (for example, the Texas Association of Business) and professional groups (such as the Texas Trial Lawyers Association) is to make their policy preferences known to government officials. Interest groups act as intermediaries for people who share common interests but reside throughout the state. Essentially, interest groups add to the formal system of geographic representation used for electing most officeholders. Such organizations serve the interests of their members by providing functional representation within the political system. They offer a form of protection by voicing interests of groups like businesspeople, religious groups, racial/ethnic groups, teachers, physicians, healthcare professionals, and college students across the state. These groups are composed of people who have similar interests but who may not constitute a majority in any city, county, legislative district, or state.

The Reasons for Interest Groups

Growth and diversity of interest groups in the United States continue unabated. An increasingly complex society has much to do with the rate of growth of interest groups throughout the country and within states. Political scientists Allan Cigler and Burdett A. Loomis contend that growing numbers, plus high levels of activity, distinguish contemporary interest group politics from that of previous eras.[1] Interest groups proliferate in Texas and throughout the country for several reasons.

Legal and Cultural Reasons In *NAACP v. Alabama*, 357 U.S. 449 (1958), the U.S. Supreme Court recognized the **right of association** as part of the right of assembly guaranteed by the First Amendment in the U.S. Constitution. This decision greatly facilitated the development of interest groups, ensuring the right of citizens to organize for political, economic, religious, and social purposes.

Political culture has traditionally encouraged American people to organize themselves into a bewildering array of associations—religious, fraternal, professional, and recreational, among others. They have responded by creating literally

right of association
The U.S. Supreme Court has ruled that this right is part of the right of assembly guaranteed by the First Amendment to the U.S. Constitution and that it protects the right of people to organize into groups for political purposes.

thousands of such groups. During the 1960s and 1970s, for example, social movements sparked interest group activities on issues concerning civil rights, women's rights, student rights, and opposition to the Vietnam War. In Texas, controversies over social issues (such as same-sex marriage), education policy issues (such as school finance), immigration reform, police reform, and gun rights have sparked new groups and revitalized existing interest groups. For instance, in 2012, Texans for Real Efficiency and Equity in Education, an education group, was formed to intervene in public school finance lawsuits. This group's solution to problems in the school system was to establish charter schools as an alternative to public schools. In 2013, the Reform Immigration for Texas Alliance (RITA) was formed as a statewide network dedicated to building support for comprehensive immigration reform. It sought to promote fair, humane, and sensible policies, as well as to advocate for preservation of allowing undocumented people to attend public institutions of higher education at in-state tuition rates. Other interest groups, such as Texas Carry, were formed to advocate for the right to keep and bear arms, especially the right to carry handguns openly. In 2015, the Texas legislature approved Texans' right to do so. That bill was signed into law by Governor Abbott at an indoor gun range. Some organizations, (such as Black Lives Movement Houston) were formed after the recent killing of George Floyd by police in Minneapolis. Objectives of these organizations include racial justice, criminal justice reform, and police reform.

Decentralized Government In a **decentralized government**, power is not concentrated at the highest level. Decentralization is achieved in two principal ways. First, the federal system divides power between the national government and the 50 state governments (as explained in Chapter 2, "Federalism and the Texas Constitution"). In turn, each state shares its power with local governments: counties, cities, and special districts. Second, within each level of government, power is separated into three branches or departments: legislative, executive, and judicial. Separation of powers is especially apparent at national and state levels.

A decentralized structure increases opportunities for interest groups to organize and influence government. It provides different access points for groups to fight their battles at different levels of government and within different branches at each level. For instance, Equality Texas, formed in 2006 to advocate for the rights of the LGBTQ+ community, has been unsuccessful in passing statewide legislation. Yet, the organization has made considerable progress at the municipal level. Some cities, such as San Antonio, Dallas, Plano, and Austin, have passed ordinances protecting against discrimination on the basis of sexual orientation or gender identity in private and public employment, housing, and public accommodations.

decentralized government
Decentralization is achieved by dividing power between national and state governments and separating legislative, executive, and judicial branches at both levels.

Strength of the Party System and Political Ideologies Among factors that have precipitated the influence of interest groups are strength (or weakness) of the party system and political ideologies. First, absence of unified and responsible political parties magnifies opportunities for interest group action. Lack of strong, organized parties can particularly affect policymakers (both state and local). In such cases, public officials are less likely to vote along party lines and therefore are more susceptible to pressure from well-organized interest groups (particularly if candidates rely on campaign contributions from these groups). In recent years, the Republican Party has been dominated by leaders in the Texas legislature and statewide elective and appointive officials. At the same time, factions have developed within the Republican Party. For example, the Texas Tea Party became a powerful faction within the Texas GOP. It has exercised considerable influence in Republican primaries and state conventions, especially in 2018 (see Chapter 4, "Political Parties"). Such factions tend to weaken party unity. Liberal and conservative ideologies are distinct orientations of political, social, and economic beliefs, especially about the preferred role of government. Nevertheless, Texas public officials tend to rely more on their constituents or on issues and less on ideology. In the end, however, public officials are susceptible to the pressures of interest groups.

Characteristics of Interest Groups

Citizens may join an interest group for different reasons, whether financial, professional, or social. Students who graduate from college often find themselves joining a professional or occupational group (Table 7.1).

In some cases, people join an interest group simply because they want to be part of a network of like-minded individuals working for a cause. Interest groups often provide members with information and benefits, while trying to involve them in the political process. Such a description suggests that any organization becomes an interest group when it influences or attempts to influence governmental decisions.

There are almost as many **organizational patterns** as there are interest groups. This variety arises from the fact that most interest groups perform nonpolitical functions that are of paramount importance to their members. Texas Impact, for example, is a centralized religious grassroots network that represents several faith communities. It emphasizes charitable and spiritual activities, such as assisting low-income people in applying for social-welfare benefits, but also undertakes interfaith legislative advocacy. This organization was especially active during the pandemic in 2020, advocating for healthcare access and expanding Medicaid for underserved communities.

Some interest groups are highly centralized organizations that take the form of a single controlling body. An example of such a group currently operating in Texas is the National Rifle Association. Other groups are decentralized, consisting of loose alliances of local and regional subgroups. Their activities may be directed at either the local, state, or national level. Many trade associations (such as the Texas Mid-Continent Oil and Gas Association) and labor unions (such as those affiliated with the American Federation of Labor-Congress of Industrial Organizations [AFL-CIO]) are examples of decentralized organizations active in Texas politics. Other types of decentralized interest groups, including the National Women's Political Caucus (a women's rights organization) and Common Cause (a public interest group dedicated to government reform), have both state and local chapters in Texas.

Interest groups are composed chiefly of persons from professional and managerial occupations. Members of interest groups tend to have greater resources than most individuals possess. For instance, members are more likely to be homeowners with high levels of income and formal education who enjoy a high standard of living. Participation in interest groups, especially active participation, varies. Many citizens are not affiliated with any group, whereas others are members of several. Technology provides individuals easier access to interest group membership, unlike the

organizational pattern
The structure of a special interest group. Some interest groups have a decentralized pattern of organization. Others are centralized.

Image 7.2 TCCTA's website shows one approach of how interest groups attract new members.

New to TCCTA?

Just a few reasons TCCTA is right for you!

>> High quality, high value
professional development

>> Low cost professional liability insurance

>> Effective advocacy before the Texas Legislature
and state agencies

>> A robust, statewide network of colleagues

Join Now!

Competency Connection
☼ CRITICAL THINKING ☼

Review the resources that TCCTA provides only for its members. If you were a college professor at a community college, which of these resources would convince you to join?

Filemaker Central

group leadership
Individuals who guide the decisions of interest groups. Leaders of groups tend to have financial resources that permit them to contribute money and devote time to group affairs.

✓ **7.1 Learning Check**

1. Name at least two factors that motivate interest group formation.
2. True or False: Most interest groups have an active membership.

Answers at the end of this chapter.

registration paper forms of the past. For example, the Texas Community College Teachers Association (TCCTA) gives potential members an opportunity to join and register for conferences online. This site includes several resources, web links, and access to financial and liability insurance benefits. In addition, TCCTA maintains Facebook and Twitter accounts, and a blog on topics such as resources for teaching equity and inclusion, as well as information on use of social media in the classroom and online teaching. Prompted by the COVID-19 pandemic, many interest groups (like the Texas Classroom Teachers Association) also offered members informative webinars and virtual events. Some individuals, however, will not join an interest group—especially when they believe that they still benefit without actually having to join and pay the costs of membership.[2] People who receive benefits without paying for membership, either in time or money, are sometimes referred to as "free riders."

An organized group of any size usually comprises an active minority and a passive majority. As a result, decisions are regularly made by relatively few members. These decision makers may range from a few elected officers to a larger body of delegates representing the entire membership. Organizations generally leave decision-making and other leadership functions to a few people. Two factors may explain limited participation in most group decisions: widespread apathy among rank-and-file members and the difficulty of removing entrenched leaders. Factors that influence **group leadership** include the group's financial resources (members

Table 7.1 Texas Professional and Occupational Associations*

Health Related

Texas Dental Association

Texas Health Care Association

Texas Hospital Association

Texas Medical Association

Texas Ophthalmological Association

Texas Nurses Association

Texas Physical Therapy Association

Texas Counseling Association

Law Related

Texas Criminal Defense Lawyers Association

Texas Civil Justice League

Texas Trial Lawyers Association

Mexican American Bar Association of Houston

Texas Women Lawyers

Texas Young Lawyers Association

Texas Association of Consumer Lawyers

Education Related

Texas American Federation of Teachers

Texas Association of College Teachers

Texas Classroom Teachers Association

Texas PTA (Parent Teacher Association)

Texas Community College Teachers Association

Texas State Teachers Association

Texas Library Association

Texas Association of College and University Student Personnel

Texas Faculty Association

Texas School Counselor Association

Texas Association of School Administrators

Miscellaneous

North Texas Association of Environmental Professionals

Texas Society of Architects

Texas Society of Certified Public Accountants

Intelligent Transportation Society (ITS) Texas

All organizations listed can be found on the Internet.

Competency Connection
★ PERSONAL RESPONSIBILITY ★

Review Table 7.1 on professional interest groups. Given your professional goals, which interest group might you join? What, do you suppose, would be the advantages of joining a professional interest group?

who contribute most heavily usually have greater weight in making decisions), time-consuming leadership duties (only a few people can afford to devote much of their time without compensation), and the personality traits of leaders (some individuals have greater leadership ability and motivation than others).

⬢ Types of Interest Groups

LO 7.2   Describe types of interest groups and analyze the characteristics of a powerful interest group.

Increasing diversity of American interest groups at national, state, and local levels of government permits groups to be classified in several ways. Not only can interest groups be studied by organizational patterns (such as centralized versus decentralized, as discussed earlier), but they can also be categorized according to level or branch of government to which they direct their attention. Some groups exert influence on public officials and other policymakers at all levels of government and in different branches of government. Others may try to spread their views among the general public and may best be classified according to the subject matter they represent. Other groups do not fit readily into any category, whereas a few fit into more than one. In this section, we examine various types of interest groups: economic groups, professional and public employee groups, social groups, and public interest groups.

Economic Groups

economic interest group
An interest group that exists primarily to promote their members' economic self-interest. Trade associations and labor unions are classified as economic interest groups because they are organized to promote policies that will maximize profits and wages.

Many interest groups exist primarily to promote their members' economic self-interest. These organizations are the most common in Texas and are known as **economic interest groups**. Traditionally, many people contribute significant amounts of money and time to obtain the financial benefits of group membership. Thus, some organizations exist to further the economic interests of a broad group, such as trade associations, whereas others seek to protect the interests of a single type of business, such as restaurant associations. The Texas Association of Business (generally identified as TAB) is an example of a broader type of interest group that is known as an umbrella organization. Such a group represents smaller groups and coordinates their state and national government activities. Businesses from a variety of industries and the state's local chambers of commerce are members of TAB. Individual corporations, such as communications giant AT&T, use the political process to promote a company's particular economic interests.

business organization
An economic interest group, such as a trade association (for example, Texas Gaming Association), that lobbies for policies favoring business.

Business Groups Businesspeople understand they have common interests that may be promoted by collective action. They were among the first to organize and press national, state, and local governments to adopt favorable public policies. **Business organizations** typically advocate lower taxes, lessening or elimination of price and quality controls by government, minimal concessions to labor unions. Recently, business organizations sought financial assistance from the state and federal government during the COVID-19 pandemic. At the state level, business organizations most often take the form of trade associations (groups that act on behalf of an industry. The Texas Gaming Association (a group that favors the creation of destination casino resorts in the state) is an interest group that has lobbied the Texas legislature in support of gambling interests. One of the many other Texas trade associations is the Texas Association of Builders (TAB), which is a group that focuses on creating a positive environment for the housing industry. Another trade association is the Texas Good Roads and Transportation Association composed of highway construction contractors, chambers of commerce members, professionals, transportation experts, and others dedicated to ensuring efficient transportation and increased funding for highways).

In past legislative sessions, Texas businesses and their representatives have succeeded in enacting many of their policy preferences into law. One notable case study is the impact of campaign contributions on the transfer of power to a GOP-controlled 78th Legislature (2003). Some reports indicate that TAB, along with Texans for Lawsuit Reform, contributed more than $2.6 million to support Republican candidates in key legislative races in 2002. Subsequently, the newly GOP-controlled Legislature passed several "business friendly" bills. One of the more significant bills limited lawsuits against manufacturers, pharmaceutical companies, and retailers.[3] Big business (such as oil and gas, banking and finance, and insurance) has also been successful in defending tax breaks and corporate subsidies in past legislative sessions. One tax that businesses pay is the franchise tax, a special tax charged for the privilege of doing business within the state. (For a discussion of the franchise tax, see Chapter 11, Finance and Fiscal Policy.) In past legislative sessions, small businesses were effective in adding a permanent minimum $1 million deduction to the small business franchise tax exemption. The franchise tax rate was further reduced by 25 percent. This reduction resulted in estimated annual savings to Texas businesses of approximately $1.3 billion. The Texas Restaurant Association strongly advocated for economic relief, especially for small businesses, during the COVID-19 pandemic.

Labor Groups Unions representing Texas workers, though relatively active, are not as numerous or powerful as business-related groups. The state's **labor organizations** seek, among other goals, government intervention to increase wages, especially the state's minimum wage. In addition, labor groups work to obtain adequate health insurance coverage, provide unemployment insurance, and promote safe working conditions. Although Texans are traditionally sensitive to the potential political power of organized labor, certain industrial labor organizations are generally regarded as significant in Texas government. These groups are the Texas affiliates of the AFL-CIO (comprising 1,300 local unions and more than 240,000 members), the Communication Workers of America, and local affiliates of the International Brotherhood of Teamsters. For a highly industrialized state with a large population, union membership in Texas is small compared with that of most other states.

Texas is one the few states with union membership rates less than 5 percent. As of 2019, only 4.0 percent of Texas's wage and salary workers belong to a union, which accounts for close to 500,000 union members, according to the U.S. Bureau of Labor

labor organization
A union that supports public policies designed to increase wages, obtain adequate health insurance coverage, provide unemployment insurance, promote safe working conditions, and otherwise protect the interests of workers.

Statistics. With the pending legislative cuts in education, healthcare, and state jobs in 2011, several unions began relying on rallies as a means of expressing opposition. The Texas State Employees Union was a leading organizer of the "Save Our State Rally," one of the largest recorded rallies, with an estimated 6,000 to 7,000 people participating at the steps of the state Capitol. Although this rally brought considerable media attention, unions were unsuccessful in preventing budgetary cuts made during the legislative session. The Texas State Employees Union has held a "lobby day" rally of their members and supporters during subsequent legislative sessions. In addition, this union has organized a series of mini-lobby days for different state employee groups, such as retirees, parole officers, and university workers. Although successful in obtaining a 2.5 percent pay raise for state workers in the 84th legislative session (2015), the pay raise was allocated to mandatory employee contributions to the state retirement fund. Thus, the pay raise did not put more money in employees' pockets.

Professional/Public Employee Groups

Closely related to economic interest groups are groups dedicated to furthering the interests of a profession, such as physicians or attorneys. Teachers have been especially active in their efforts to influence government decisions.

Image 7.3 United Auto Workers went on strike at the General Motors Assembly Plant in Arlington as part of a national strike to draw attention to their jobs, pay and benefits in place of temporary workers.

Jim West/Alamy Stock Photo

— Competency Connection —
⦿ **SOCIAL RESPONSIBILITY** ⦿

Rallies and strikes are often powerful strategies to mobilize the members of an interest group. How important are these tactics for conveying their message to policymakers or employers?

Professional Groups Standards of admission to a profession or an occupation, as well as licensing of practitioners, concern **professional groups**. Examples of Texas professional and occupational associations are the State Bar of Texas (attorneys), the Texas Health Care Association, and the Texas Society of Certified Public Accountants. (See Table 7.1 for a list of some of the more important Texas professional and occupational associations.) Professionals are more effective if they organize in groups that advocate for their interests. Physicians won a significant victory in the 76th Legislature in 1999, when Texas became the first state to allow doctors to bargain collectively with health maintenance organizations concerning fees and policies. The Texas Medical Association (TMA) successfully lobbied for passage of a constitutional amendment, Proposition 12, which authorized the state legislature to impose a $250,000 cap for noneconomic damages in medical malpractice cases. TMA also won approval in the state legislature for a new medical school in the Rio Grande Valley and an increase in the state's cap on student loans for young physicians in order to increase the number of primary care doctors. In 2019, TMA successfully lobbied legislators to raise the minimum age for purchasing tobacco products to 21. In addition, TMA was unsuccessful in persuading lawmakers in 2021 to expand Medicaid so that compensated care would be available to more Texas patients. Medicaid funding was especially critical during the healthcare crisis of COVID-19, when inequities in healthcare were even more apparent.

Responding to pressure from teacher groups and their supporters, the 86th legislature (2019) enacted a law requiring schools to spend a percentage of their new per-student funding toward compensation increases for teachers as well as librarians, school nurses, and counselors. This legislation emphasized higher pay for more-experienced personnel. The last time teachers were successful in significantly increasing salaries and improving health packages was in 1999. At that time, they persuaded the legislature to increase pay for every public school teacher, librarian, and registered school nurse in Texas. Legislators also fully or partially funded state-supported health insurance for public school teachers and other school employees, both active and retired. Teacher organizations, such as the Texas American Federation of Teachers, have continued to lobby for higher levels of school funding, as well as to oppose school finance legislation that they believe provides inadequate funding and would intrude on local control of school matters. Teacher organizations unsuccessfully opposed a 2019 constitutional amendment proposal that imposes additional restraints against the possibility of a state income tax. Organized teachers were concerned that this amendment would reduce or eliminate potential sources of future school funding. (For more on school finance, see Chapter 11, Finance and Fiscal Policy.) Teacher organizations have also been vocal with regard to changes in curriculum requirements by the State Board of Education and high-stakes standardized testing mandates set by the legislature and the Texas Education Agency. (For more on education policy affecting public schools, see Chapter 12, Public Policy and Administration.) During the COVID-19 pandemic, the Texas Classroom Teachers Association expressed concerns about reopening schools too soon. Several recommendations by this association were posted on its website.

professional group
An organization of physicians, lawyers, accountants, or other professional people that lobbies for policies beneficial to members.

Public officer and employee groups of state and local governments organize to obtain better working conditions, higher wages, more fringe benefits, and better retirement packages. The Texas State Employees Association, for instance, lobbies for legislation that prevents job cuts but increases pay and healthcare benefits as well as unemployment benefits.

Among government workers, the oldest and largest group is the Texas Public Employees Association with more than 15,000 active and retired employees. City government groups include the Texas City Management Association and the Texas City Attorneys Association. Through their organizational activities, these groups resist efforts to reduce the size of state and local governmental bureaucracies (though not always with success). The County Judges and Commissioners Association of Texas and the Justices of the Peace and Constables Association of Texas, for example, have been instrumental in assuring that measures designed to reform Texas's justice of the peace courts and county courts reflect their members' interests.

Two of Texas's largest police unions are the Texas Municipal Police Association (TMPA) and the Combined Law Enforcement Associations of Texas (CLEAT). TMPA represents more than 30,000 local, county, and state law enforcement officers and CLEAT has more than 24,000 members. When the 2015 legislature was in the final stages of the open-carry bill (a law that allows licensed gun owners to openly display their weapons), TMPA took the position that the organization supported open carry but had concerns with an amendment that prevented police officers from asking to see a person's handgun license simply because he or she was openly carrying a handgun. The amendment was not included in Texas's open-carry law that went into effect in January 2016. In addition, Texas police organizations went on record in support of legislation that bans texting while driving. Subsequent to the Black Lives Matter Movement, the Blue Lives Matter Movement developed to protect the rights of police officers in the face of increased scrutiny, as well as to counter attempts by some local governments to defund police departments.

Social Groups

Texas has a wide array of **social interest groups**. These include racial and ethnic organizations, civil rights organizations, women's organizations, groups representing the LGBTQ community, religious-based organizations, and several public interest groups.

Racial and Ethnic Groups Leaders of Texas's **racial and ethnic groups** recognize that only through effective organizations can they hope to achieve their cherished goals. Examples of these goals include promoting racial justice at various levels, eliminating racial discrimination in employment, improving public schools, increasing educational opportunities, and obtaining greater representation in the state legislature, city councils, school boards, and other policymaking bodies of government.

One formidable group, the National Association for the Advancement of Colored People (NAACP), is an effective racial interest group. According to the

public officer and employee group
An organization of city managers, county judges, law enforcement, or other public employees or officials that lobbies for public policies that protect group interests.

social interest group
A group concerned primarily with social issues, including organizations devoted to civil rights, racial and ethnic matters, religion, and public interest protection.

racial and ethnic groups
Organizations that seek to influence government decisions that affect a particular racial or ethnic group, such as the National Association for the Advancement of Colored People (NAACP) and the League of United Latin American Citizens (LULAC), which seek to influence government decisions affecting African Americans and Latinos, respectively.

Texas State Historical Association, chapters of the Texas NAACP were established during the World War I era, with the first chapter forming in El Paso in 1915. This organization has been successful in influencing public policies relating to school integration and local government redistricting. The NAACP also effectively fought for hate crimes legislation that enhances penalties for crimes based on race, color, disability, religion, national origin, gender, or sexual preference.[4] In addition, this organization continues to advocate strict enforcement against racial profiling. Texas law defines racial profiling as an action by law enforcement personnel on the basis of an individual's race, ethnicity, or national origin as opposed to the individual's behavior or information identifying the individual as being engaged in criminal activity.

Beginning in 2011, the Texas NAACP actively opposed making a Confederate battle flag image available on specialty Texas license plates. The association appealed successfully to the Texas Department of Motor Vehicles to prevent legitimizing a symbol that, in its view, represents brutality and fear. Moreover, the Texas NAACP argued that the Confederate "Stars and Bars" is used by hate groups to promote a racist ideology. The U.S. Supreme Court ultimately struck down these specialty license plates, concluding that the state did not create a "limited public forum" that allowed an individual's freedom of expression. Instead, the Court held in *Walker v. Sons of the Confederate Veterans* (2015) that license plates signified "government speech" and the state had a right to reject these plates.[5] In addition, the NAACP has opposed Confederate monuments in public places. Along with Latino groups, it has strongly advocated against Texas's controversial voter ID law. (For more on this issue, see Chapter 5, Campaigns and Elections.) The NAACP has been affiliated with the Black Lives Matter Movement in advocating for racial justice by law enforcement, especially following the death of Michael Ramos at the hands of Austin police.

Asian Americans have formed organizations and political action committees (PACs) that raise and distribute money to political candidates. One of these PACs is the Network of Asian American Organizations, which serves the interests of Asian American communities in Central Texas.

In Texas, Latino groups, especially Mexican American organizations, are more numerous than African American interest groups in certain regions. The oldest Latino group, the League of United Latin American Citizens (LULAC), was founded in 1929 in Corpus Christi.[6] LULAC has worked for equal educational opportunities for Latinos, as well as for full citizenship rights. It continues to advocate for adequate public school funding, Mexican American Studies curriculum in public schools, and bilingual education. In higher education, LULAC supports policies like the "Top Ten Percent Rule" and affirmative action, both of which are designed to ensure diversity of college and university student populations. In addition, LULAC successfully pressed for state funds to open the school of pharmacy at Texas A&M–Kingsville, which was named after the late state legislator and strong advocate for higher education, Irma Rangel.[7] LULAC brought attention to the importance of the 2020 U.S. Census as well as voter suppression of Latinos during the 2020 election cycle involving primary and presidential elections.

Another organization, the Mexican American Legal Defense and Education Fund (MALDEF), formed in 1968 in San Antonio, uses court action in pursuit of political equality, equal education, immigration rights, representation for Latinos, and most recently, attempts of voter suppression for recently naturalized citizens. Both LULAC and MALDEF have been instrumental in addressing redistricting, especially when it comes to voting rights. On behalf of a statewide coalition of Texas Latino organizations called the Texas Latino Redistricting Task Force, MALDEF has successfully challenged redistricting plans created by the Texas legislature for the U.S. House of Representatives and the Texas House. The Task Force aims to ensure fair representation for Latinos. In 2012, a three-judge federal court allowed creation of two out of the four newly established congressional seats as Latino-majority districts. This court also created an additional Latino-majority district in the Texas House of Representatives, thus increasing the number of Latino-majority districts to 34. MALDEF continues to challenge, with some success, the drawing of some congressional and state legislative districts that dilute the voting strength of ethnic and racial minorities. With redistricting on the agenda for the Texas Legislature in 2021, more court battles are expected.

MALDEF has successfully advocated against anti-immigrant legislative proposals in recent years. However, it was unsuccessful in challenging the ban on "sanctuary cities" (municipalities with policies that prohibit local law enforcement officers from inquiring into the immigration status of a person or report violations to federal immigration enforcement officials). The Texas law was passed by the legislature in 2017. This chapter's Students in Action features another pro-immigrant rights organization, RAICES, which provides volunteer and internship opportunities for college students who have a passion for the safety and dignity of undocumented immigrants.

Women's Groups The Texas Women's Political Caucus is an example of a **women's organization** that promotes equal rights and greater participation by women in the political arena. The League of Women Voters of Texas is a nonpartisan organization advocating greater political participation and public understanding of governmental issues. It also assists voters in becoming better informed by publishing *The Texas Voters Guide*, which provides information about elections, candidates, and candidates' positions on various issues. The year 2020, which marked the one hundred year anniversary of the U.S. Constitution's 19th Amendment, prompted many women's organizations to galvanize the women's vote in various state and congressional races, as well as the presidential race.

women's organization
A women's group, such as the League of Women Voters, that engages in lobbying and educational activities to promote greater political participation by women and others.

The Texas Federation of Republican Women, a partisan interest group with more than 10,000 members and more than 164 local clubs, provides resources for women to influence government actions and policies. This organization actively encourages Republican women to run for public office. Another organization that formed in 2003, in response to the dwindling number of Democratic women in the Texas legislature, is Annie's List. This organization recruits, trains, and supports progressive female candidates; and it raises campaign money for them. Two of the List's most notable endorsements were made in 2014, when it supported Democratic candidates Wendy Davis for governor and Leticia Van de Putte for lieutenant governor. This was the first time that two women candidates ran for the top two positions on the Texas ballot, but both were defeated. In recent elections, Annie's List endorsed several Latina and African American candidates for seats in the Texas Senate and Texas House of Representatives. The organization provides supporters with an opportunity to "Join our Movement" on its website. In the 2020 election cycle, the organization endorsed more than 50 women candidates, primarily for state legislative races. Other interest groups, such as the Hispanic Women's Network of Texas, focus on the concerns and needs of Latinas. This statewide organization is dedicated to advancing the interests of Latinas in public, corporate, and civic arenas. The Texas Latina List, which has its origin in Fort Worth, is a political action committee that recruits and funds Latina candidates for offices at all levels. In 2018, it endorsed one of the two first two Texas Latinas elected to the U.S. Congress, Veronica Escobar from El Paso.

Religion-Based Groups The Christian Coalition is an example of a **religion-based group**. With millions of Texans identifying themselves as conservative Christians, the organization continues to be one of the state's most influential political forces, though it had more momentum in the 1990s than it does now. This interest group engages in political action, primarily within the Republican Party. Issues that precipitated the Christian Coalition's entrance on the political scene are abortion, homosexuality, limits on prayer in public schools, and decline of the traditional nuclear family.[8]

Image 7.4 Annie's List is an example of a women's organization that focuses on electing women to public office.

Source: https://annieslist.com

ENSURING WOMEN'S VOICES ARE HEARD FROM THE BALLOT BOX TO THE HALLS OF POWER.

— Competency Connection —
⊚ SOCIAL RESPONSIBILITY ⊚

What are your impressions of this image of women candidates? How important do you think it is for women candidates to have the support of women's organizations like Annie's List?

religion-based group
An interest group, such as the Texas Freedom Network, that lobbies for policies to promote its religious interests.

Other organizations have formed, such as Texas Values, which was founded in 2012, to educate the public about religious liberty and expression. In 2014, this group established Texas Values Action, a lobbying and advocacy organization. Its purpose is to support openly both candidates and legislation promoting religious freedom without government interference or workplace retribution. This group raises money, endorses candidates, and sponsors activities promoting its agenda. In 2015, for instance, Texas Values Action claimed success in a citizen-initiated referendum that repealed Houston's antidiscrimination ordinance. This municipal regulation prohibited discrimination based on a number of factors, including sexual orientation and gender identity. Texas Values was a strong proponent of the "bathroom bill," which would require public school students to use only bathrooms and lockers designated for the gender shown on their birth certificates.

The Texas Freedom Network was formed in the 1990s to oppose the increasing presence of the Christian Coalition. This network monitors activities of right-wing conservatives, musters liberal and mainstream voters, and provides an alternative voice on current political issues.[9] *Texas Faith Network*, the official blog of the Texas Freedom Network, monitors religious leaders who represent the religious right and who attempt to influence political conservatives (usually Republicans). In recent decades, the Texas Freedom Network has sought to defend civil liberties, strengthen public schools, and especially to maintain separation of church and state. This organization is also vocal in its opposition to social conservatives on the State Board of Education who influence the public school curriculum and the content of textbooks. It was especially vocal in its opposition in 2015 when Governor Greg Abbott appointed Donna Bahorich (R-Houston), a social conservative with ties to the Tea Party, to chair the State Board of Education. Confirmed by the Texas Senate, she served in this role for four years.

Another religion-based organization, the Texas Industrial Areas Foundation, operates in cities such as Dallas and Houston and in the Rio Grande Valley. It supports increased funding for parent training, easier access for children to qualify for Medicaid benefits, and extending Children's Health Insurance Program (CHIP) eligibility to more families.[10] The organization sought to educate communities, especially immigrant communities, concerning the necessity to complete the U.S. Census in 2020. Valley Interfaith, made up primarily of churches and private schools, has successfully lobbied the Brownsville school district to increase wages for employees. In addition, it has indirectly influenced other public institutions and companies to provide a living wage for their workers so they can live above the poverty level. In past legislative sessions, the organization has actively lobbied legislators, demanding restoration of funds cut from CHIP, expansion and increases in Medicaid funding, and more state funding for public schools, as well as an equitable tax system that does not burden the poor.

Communities Organized for Public Service (COPS) in San Antonio has been active since the 1970s. Working with an affiliated organization, Metro Alliance, it has successfully lobbied the legislature to allow cities to use sales tax revenue to create job training and early childhood development programs.[11] In recent years, COPS/Metro leaders succeeded in raising wages for more than 5,000 low-paid employees of local governments and area hospitals. The city of San Antonio, for instance, voted in 2018 for a living wage of $15.00 per hour.

Public Interest Groups

Unlike most other interest groups, **public interest groups** claim to promote the general interests of society, rather than narrower private or corporate interests. Environmental, political participation, education-related, and public morality (not directly associated with established religion) organizations are often identified as public interest groups.

Public interest organizations pursue diverse goals. Common Cause Texas, for example, focuses primarily on governmental and institutional reform. It advocates open meeting laws, public financing of political campaigns, and stricter financial disclosure laws. During the 2020 presidential cycle, Common Cause, along with several civil rights organizations, joined forces to advocate for greater access to mail-in ballots during the time of the pandemic. Texans for Public Justice supports efforts toward campaign finance reform, such as limitations on campaign contributions by political action committees and individuals. The Texas League of Conservation Voters uses a scorecard to monitor voting records of state lawmakers who support environment-friendly "green" bills. These public interest organizations also use social media technology, such as Twitter and Facebook, to keep supporters connected. (See Table 7.2 for a partial list of Texas public interest groups.)

Texas Power Groups

Texas legislators readily identify the types of interest groups they consider most powerful: business-oriented trade associations (representing oil, gas, tobacco, chemical manufacturers, insurance, and railroads), professional associations (physicians, lawyers, and teachers), and labor unions. Other groups wielding considerable influence include brewers, truckers, automobile dealers, bankers, and realtors. Some of the most influential interest groups operating not only in Texas but also nationwide are general business organizations (for example, chambers of commerce), schoolteacher organizations, utility companies, insurance companies, and various associations like hospital and nursing home associations along with bar associations for lawyers.[12]

Interest groups typified as **power groups** have several common traits. For one, these groups maintain strong links with both legislators (whose policy decisions affect group interests) and bureaucrats (whose regulatory authority controls activities of group members). Power groups often are repeat players in Texas politics, meaning they have been influencing politics in consecutive legislative sessions for a long time. Another indication of power group influence is having headquarters in Austin. Many business-related associations, for example, own a

public interest group
An organization claiming to represent a broad public interest (such as environmental, consumer, political participation, or public morality) rather than a narrow private interest.

power group
An effective interest group strongly linked with legislators and bureaucrats for the purpose of influencing decision-making and having a continuing presence in Austin as a repeat player from session to session.

headquarters building in the capital city. Others lease or rent buildings and office suites there. This proximity to the Texas Capitol and the main offices of state agencies provides regular contact with state officials and gives such associations a path to influence in state government.[13] In some cases, according to watchdog organizations, interest groups have received free use of meeting rooms in the Texas Capitol building for receptions.

One of the most influential power groups is the Texas Medical Association (TMA), formed in 1853. With a well-organized grassroots network, a skilled lobbying team, and more than 53,000 licensed physicians and medical students in Texas, TMA is one of the state's most powerful professional groups. According to TMA's data, this group succeeded in passing as much as 90 percent of its agenda items in the late 1990s.[14] Although TMA was not able to persuade the Texas legislature in 2013 to restore funding cuts in Medicaid from previous legislative sessions, the organization succeeded in preventing severe cuts to physicians' Medicaid payments so that doctors would continue seeing needy patients. In 2015, TMA successfully lobbied for a significant expansion of funding for

Table 7.2 Texas Public Interest Groups*

Civil Rights Related
Texas Civil Rights Project
Lawyers Committee for Civil Rights
Environmental
Texas Campaign for the Environment
Texas Wildlife Association
Environment Texas
Sierra Club, Lone Star Chapter
Public Participation and Social Justice
Texas Association of Community Action Agencies
Communities Organized for Public Service
Public Citizen/Texas
Equality Texas
Public Morality
Mothers Against Drunk Driving
Texas Right to Life Committee
National Abortion and Reproductive Rights Action League Pro-Choice Texas

All organizations listed can be found on the Internet.

— Competency Connection —
⦿ **SOCIAL RESPONSIBILITY** ⦿

Review Table 7.2, which provides a sample of public interest groups. If given the opportunity, what central issue/concern would you create a public interest group around?

medical education, especially for medical residencies at hospitals. (For more on Medicaid funding, see Chapter 11, Finance and Fiscal Policy.) Yet the TMA, like other interest groups, is not always successful. In recent legislative sessions, TMA members and their lobbyists were unsuccessful in expanding Medicaid in Texas under the Affordable Care Act. In light of the healthcare crisis in 2020, TMA, along with more than 30 other organizations, advocated for expansion of Medicaid (government health insurance for low income families) to fight the COVID-19 pandemic.

✔ 7.2 Learning Check

1. True or False: All interest groups have one objective in common: to promote their self-interest.
2. Which are generally more powerful in Texas, business interest groups or labor groups?

Answers at the end of this chapter.

✚ Interest Group Activities

LO 7.3 Evaluate the kinds of activities that interest groups use to influence Texas government.

When interest groups urge their members and others to become actively involved, they encourage people to participate in the political process. In some cases, interest groups even encourage members to consider running for public office. Groups benefit from having their supporters serve in decision-making positions, especially on influential boards and commissions. Local property taxpayers' associations, for example, frequently put forward candidates for public school boards and municipal offices in an effort to keep property taxes low. Likewise, when organizations of real estate agents or developers successfully lobby for placing their members in appointed positions on local planning and zoning commissions, they gain a distinct advantage. Because government officials need support for their policies, interest groups seek to mobilize and build that support, particularly for policies that form part of a group's goals and interests. Having the support or opposition of certain interest groups may determine the success or failure of bills, proposed budgets, appointments, and other policy matters.

Interest groups also are an outlet for discussions concerning policy issues; they shape conflict and consensus in society. Conflict is the more usual outcome because each group is bent on pursuing its own ends. This commitment, in turn, leads to clashes with other groups seeking their own ends. Conflict is even more likely when addressing controversial issues, such as school finance, abortion, environmental protection, same-sex marriage, voter identification, redistricting, or immigration reform. More recently, issues that center around racial justice and police reform animated the Black Lives Matter Movement and interest group activity.

In some cases, however, certain issues may galvanize coalitions among various interest groups. For instance, groups representing teachers, parents, religious organizations, and civil rights organizations have rallied around the need for increased school funding. Even business organizations, such as the Texas Association of Business, joined forces. In recent years, many groups organized rallies called Save Texas Schools, which were centered on the issue of increased school funding and using the Rainy Day Fund (the state's savings account) to cover budgetary shortfalls. (For more on the rainy day fund, see Chapter 11,

Finance and Fiscal Policy.) In another unlikely coalition, the Texas Association of Business joined forces with the pro-immigrant rights group, Reform Immigration for Texas Alliance (RITA). Their objective was to support legislation providing undocumented immigrants with an opportunity to obtain a state driver's license or a state resident driver's permit in order to make them eligible to buy car insurance. During the COVID-19 pandemic, the Children's Healthcare Coverage Coalition (CHCC), a statewide coalition of over 20 organizations strongly advocated leaders to ensure children healthcare coverage and healthcare access at a time when many families faced the loss of job-based health insurance.

Political scientists know that interest groups use a wide range of techniques to influence policy decisions. These **interest group techniques** may be classified as lobbying; personal communication; giving favors and gifts; grassroots activities; electioneering; campaign financing by political action committees; and, in extreme instances, bribery and other illegal or unethical practices.

interest group technique
An action (such as lobbying, personal communication, giving favors and gifts, grassroots activities, electioneering, campaign financing by political action committees, and, in extreme instances, bribery and other unethical practices) intended to influence government decisions.

Image 7.5 Along with tourists who visit the Capitol and government employees, lobbyists walk through the rotunda and halls as they seek to speak to state legislators.

Bernie Epstein/Alamy Stock Photo

Competency Connection
◆ COMMUNICATION SKILLS ◆

Lobbyists are an important component for the success of interest groups in the Texas Legislature. What do you think are some of the qualities of an effective lobbyist?

Lobbying

Lobbying is perhaps the oldest, and certainly the best-known, interest group tactic. According to Texans for Public Justice's last report in 2014, "special interests spent up to $3 billion over the past decade on more than 72,000 Texas lobby contracts."[15] Identifying interest groups that hire lobbyists is one way to determine which interests are being represented before the state legislature and which are not. Lobbyists are individuals who are hired by an interest group. These full-time professional lobbyists attempt to influence government decision-makers on behalf of special interests. Lobbying is most often directed at legislators and the lawmaking process, although it is also practiced within state agencies.

Not all lobbyists are full-time professionals. Most work for businesses and only occasionally go to Austin to speak to lawmakers about their concerns. Some lobbyists represent cities and counties. Among the most successful lobbyists are former state legislators, legislative aides, and gubernatorial aides. In recent years, Texas has ranked second in the country, after California, in money spent on lobbying the state government. At the same time, lobbyists generally outnumber the 181 Texas legislators by a ratio of roughly nine to one. Typically, the number of registered lobbyists increases during an election cycle. For the 2020 election cycle, there were more than 1,500 registered lobbyists. At the start of the 87th legislative session in 2021, the number stood at more than 2,700 lobbyists.[16]

Some interest groups, such as the Texas Motorcycle Rights Association claiming to represent as many as 900,000 licensed motorcycle riders in Texas, will typically travel to Austin and hold a "lobby day" at the Capitol to confer with lawmakers about preserving bikers' rights. Even college students have their "lobby day." Some students dedicate a lot of time to planning and strategy development as they prepare to be effective advocates in Austin. Another organization, Texas Interfaith Center, provides members and supporters with information on its website on "faithful participation" and tips for meeting and interacting with legislators.

Personal Communication One of the main interest group techniques is personal communication by lobbyists. The immediate goal of lobbyists is to inform officials concerning their group's position on an issue. Because professional lobbyists are often experts in a specific field (and in some cases are former state officials), their tools of influence are the information and research they convey to public officials. The first task of the lobbyist is to gain access to legislators and other government decision-makers. Once the lobbyist has made personal contact with a policymaker and captured the desired attention, he or she may use a variety of techniques to make that government official responsive to the group's demands, preferences, and expectations.

Because the process requires careful strategy, the lobbyist chooses the most appropriate time and place to speak with an official and determines how best to phrase arguments in order to have a positive impact. For maximum effectiveness in using this technique, a lobbyist must select the proper target (for example, a key legislative committee chair, regulatory agency administrator, county commissioner, or city zoning board member). Successful lobbyists rely heavily on a variety of technology, including smart phones, iPhones, iPads, and social media platforms such as FaceTime, Instagram, Pinterest, and Twitter. In fact, an important early study of interest group politics in Texas concluded that lobbying in the Lone Star State had shifted from an emphasis on personal argument to information-based communications.[17] A former Texas legislator compared lobbyists with pharmaceutical salespeople who explain new medicines to doctors who are too busy to keep up with the latest developments. In the same way, lobbyists provide data, information, and expertise about complex public policy issues to decision-makers. For instance, lobbyists representing the Texas Medical Society recruited Dr. Thomas Kim, a telehealth physician, to provide testimony to the House Public Health Committee on ways to regulate this new form of healthcare delivery.[18] To perform their jobs effectively, successful lobbyists should clearly indicate the group they represent, define their interests, make clear what they want to do and why, answer questions readily, and provide enough accurate information for politicians and other officials to make judgments.

Successful lobbyists befriend as many legislators as possible, especially influential legislative leaders such as committee chairs; and these lobbyists discover the interests and needs of the officials. Relationships are formed over time. Lobbyists also put pressure on sympathetic legislators to influence other legislators.

At present, no effective laws prohibit former Texas legislators (including former committee chairs and presiding officers) from becoming lobbyists and immediately lobbying former colleagues. As of 2020, according to the National Conference of State Legislatures, at least 41 states required by statute some kind of mandatory waiting period, ranging from six months to as much as two years after leaving office.[19] These lobbyists, and the interest groups that contract with them, are more likely to have connections in the state legislature than most other lobbyists. Proposals in the Texas legislature to address this "revolving door" problem have not been successful.[20] In 2019, however, the legislature enacted restrictions on registered lobbyists who were formerly candidates or public officials. They cannot use political contributions to make or authorize political contributions or expenditures.[21] In 2017, Governor Abbott, a strong advocate of ethics reform when first elected, signed into law the requirement that state elected officials doing business with cities, counties, and other governmental entities must disclose to the Texas Ethics Commission their contracts. For many supporters, this law provides more government transparency and addresses potential conflicts of interests.[22]

Favors and Gifts Another lobbying technique used by interest groups, and especially by lobbyists, involves giving favors and gifts to legislators and other government decision-makers. Common favors include arranging daily or weekly luncheon and dinner gatherings; providing free liquor, wine, or beer; furnishing tickets for entertainment events, air transportation, and athletic contests; and giving miscellaneous gifts.

For female lawmakers, gifts often include flower bouquets and spa treatments; but male lawmakers are likely to get gifts like guns, knives, and deer processing services. Free tickets for Cowboys and Texans games, along with free access to some of the biggest collegiate football games across the state, are also commonplace and legal gifts for lawmakers from lobbyists, so long as the value of freebies for any legislator from an individual lobbyist does not exceed $500 per calendar year. There are limits on the value of "travel gifts" for public officials and candidates, as well as for state agency employees.[23] In addition, public officials must report gifts valued at more than $250 to the Texas Ethics Commission.

Grassroots Activities Yet another influential technique used by interest groups is grassroots lobbying. Interest groups rely heavily on pressure from a grassroots network of organization members and sympathizers. These groups attempt to create an image of broad public support for an organization's goals, mobilizing support when it is needed. The Internet has emerged as a significant forum for grassroots lobbying. Interest groups and lobbyists are increasingly using social media, such as Facebook, Twitter, Instagram, text alerts, and blogs. Such communication methods are designed to generate information favorable to an interest group's cause and to spread that information widely among legislators, other policymakers, and the general public. Interest groups create Facebook pages to connect with supporters, gather signatures on petitions, or announce events. Another tactic, called "astrotweeting," uses fake social media accounts to provide a false impression of the number of supporters or opponents an issue actually has. Petition websites are also becoming more common for interest groups to demonstrate support for their positions, although some groups argue this approach is much less effective than letters and face-to-face contact with elected officials. The Texas State Teachers Association (TSTA) is very effective at communicating its agenda to members through Flickr and Facebook. Another education-related organization, the Texas Public Charter School Association, advocates and promotes charter schools and online virtual schools. Also, it tweets to inform the public and its supporters about issues. The Texas legislature has increased the maximum number of charter schools in Texas, while also increasing school funding. (For more on charter schools, see Chapter 12, "Public Policy and Administration.")

📋 Students in Action

What is RAICES and what do they do?

Based in San Antonio, Texas, the Refugee and Immigrant Center for Education and Legal Services (RAICES) is a 501(c)(3) non-profit organization serving immigrants and refugees through advocacy initiatives, free and low-cost legal services, and social programs. Initially, RAICES was a small organization founded in 1987 in San Antonio, Texas-as the Refugee Aid Project by a group of activists to aid Central American refugees arriving in the United States. The non-profit agency garnered national attention after a Facebook fundraiser launched by a Californian couple raised over 20 million dollars in June of 2018, during the zero-tolerance policy, which charged any individual caught entering the United States with criminal prosecution and separated children from their parents.

Today, RAICES is the largest provider of immigration legal services in Texas with offices located throughout the state and with over 292 pro bono attorneys and 37,863 cases concurred in 2018. In addition, the non-profit organization has paid over $4.7 million to reunite families (as a result of the zero-tolerance policy). It created a national hotline for immigrants and refugees. It also advocates for Dreamers through their citizenship services and against the inhumane treatment of children and adults in immigration retention centers through social media campaigns.

Maria "Lupita" Partida pictured in front of the St. Mary's campus.

Immigration While Growing Up in a Latinx Community

As a first-generation Latina, who was born and raised in Laredo, Texas, a border town, I have witnessed the political ramifications in my community with shifting presidential administrations and policies on immigration—from my parents' fervent resolution to migrate to the United States, to witnessing family separations at the South Texas border during the 2018 zero-tolerance policy, to several of my friends' legal status in the United States as DACA recipients. The issue of immigration has varied widely with immigration

Electioneering

electioneering

Active campaigning by an interest group in support of, or in opposition to, a candidate; actions urging the public to act on an issue.

Participating in political campaign activities, or **electioneering**, is widespread among interest groups. These activities usually center on particular candidates but may also revolve around issue advocacy. If a candidate who favors a group's goals can be elected, the group has a realistic expectation that its interests will be recognized and protected once the candidate takes office. Interest group participation in the election process takes various forms. Publishing or otherwise publicizing the political records of incumbent candidates on a group's website is one of the simplest and most common forms of interest group participation. In recent years, an explosion of YouTube videos has helped interest groups build support for candidates and issues. Providing favored candidates with group membership information, mailing lists, and email lists are other valuable ways that help candidates solicit money and votes. In addition, groups may allow candidates to waves and presidential administrations. In particular, the Deferred Action for Childhood Arrivals (DACA)—developed in 2012 under the Obama Administration—was established to protect individuals that arrived in the United States as children, from deportation and granted them a work authorization. This evoked significant triumphs to thousands of Dreamers (the name that DACA recipients use to refer to themselves), many of which include St. Mary's students.

After the implementation of DACA, post-secondary enrollments and graduation rates among DACA recipients heightened—ensuring new avenues for opportunity. However, DACA was temporarily rescinded in 2018 under the Trump Administration. Processing new applications was halted and thousands of Dreamers confronted a state of limbo. The Supreme Court reviewed the legality of terminating DACA during the summer of 2020 and held that DACA applications were to resume. Over 100,000 Dreamers from Texas were protected from deportation following the Court's ruling.

Internship with RAICES

After a representative from RAICES visited St. Mary's and held a presentation about their initiatives and work, I was inclined to learn more about immigration in the United States. It propelled me to apply as an intern. During the summer of 2019, I served as the data and reporting intern at one of the San Antonio offices. Through this internship, I was provided with resources and workshops. I learned about U.S. immigration law and policy, as well as development and fundraising strategies that permit a nonprofit organization to prosper. I also obtained skills in data analytics and entry. Working with the staff at RAICES invigorated my passion for advocacy, public service, and immigration law.

RAICES holds a number of internship and volunteer opportunities in diverse departments including advocacy, community outreach, law, and others. This grants students hands-on experience and knowledge at an immigrant and refugee organization. If you are interested in learning more about RAICES, or would like to intern or volunteer with them, visit their website at http://www.raicestexas.org.

About the author: Maria "Lupita" Partida graduated in 2020 with a degree in Political Science from St. Mary's University in San Antonio, Texas.

Competency Connection
◉ SOCIAL RESPONSIBILITY ◉

How important do you think it is for college students to volunteer or serve as interns for organizations that work and advocate for social justice?

---

speak at their meetings, thus giving them opportunities for direct contact with voters and possible media coverage or Facebook coverage. Public endorsements can also benefit candidates, sending a cue to the group's membership and other interested voters with regard to which candidates they should support. Facebook pages and Twitter accounts are also created to generate "likes" for candidates and can facilitate garnering campaign contributions. New apps, such as Influence Texas which was unveiled in 2019, tracks campaign finance records of Texas lawmakers and the role of money in politics. New forms of social media, such as webinars and Zoom sessions, were center stage for the 2020 election cycle during the COVID-19 pandemic.

Another type of group participation in electioneering involves "Get Out the Vote" (GOTV) campaigns—that is, the favorable vote. Typically, increasing favorable voter turnout entails mailing campaign propaganda, making phone calls to members, registering voters, transporting voters to the polls, and door-to-door canvassing (soliciting votes). Social media, again, provide significant tools for rallying a candidate's base. For instance, Texas's controversial abortion bill, passed in the 2013 legislative session, generated unprecedented activity on the internet from groups on both sides of the issue. Former Senator Wendy Davis 11-hour filibuster against a bill restricting access to abortion on the Senate floor resulted in what some observers called a "tweetstorming" tactic. Proposed gun legislation during the 2015 legislative session prompted record-breaking discourse on social media for both sides of the issue on Twitter.[24] The Official Hashtag of the Texas Legislature, #Txlege was passed during the 84th legislative session.[25] Controversial issues, such as the "bathroom bill" in 2017, dominated social media.

Campaign Financing by Political Action Committees

Because political campaigns are becoming more expensive with each election, contributions from interest group members constitute an important form of participation in both federal and state elections. Although individuals continue to make personal financial contributions to candidates, some campaign funds also come from political action committees (PACs) (see Chapter 5, "Campaigns and Elections"). The Texas Ethics Commission defines a PAC as "a group of persons that has a principal purpose of accepting political contributions or making political contributions."[26] Texas statutes prohibit direct political contributions by corporations and labor unions to individual candidates. These and other groups, however, may form PACs composed of their employees or members. In 2019, the Texas legislature gave additional leverage to corporations by allowing them to match partial or full charitable contributions to federally exempt, non-profit organizations. Political watchdogs, such as Common Cause, opposed this measure that would expand the political influence of corporations.

PACs have the task of raising funds and distributing financial contributions to candidates who are sympathetic to their cause. A PAC may also influence political campaigns involving issues that affect the group's vital interests. Currently, Texas imposes no limits on what PACs (or individual citizens for that matter) can raise or contribute to candidates running for statewide offices or a legislative seat, except in judicial races. However, state law prevents legislators and statewide officeholders from accepting campaign donations during a legislative session. The Texas Ethics Commission enforces a moratorium (starting in December, before a regular legislative session begins, and ending in June) whereby officeholders may not accept campaign contributions.

Proposals to place limits on amounts that citizens and PACs can contribute to candidates have not been given serious consideration by the legislature, although some limits and deadlines have been placed on campaign contributions to judicial candidates. In addition, current state law does not prohibit accepting campaign contributions during special sessions of the legislature called by the governor. This omission allows legislators and the governor to raise significant funds during one or more special sessions, each session with a maximum duration of 30 days.

⬚ Point/Counterpoint

Should Campaign Contributions Be Limited?

The Issue Most observers of Texas politics would agree that money plays a big role in political campaigns. Unlike the federal government, except for judicial elections, Texas law does not restrict the amount anyone can contribute to a state political campaign. That campaign donations are unregulated appears to enhance the role of money in elections. Yet the ability to donate money to election campaigns is also a form of political expression and free speech protected by both the Texas Constitution and the U.S. Constitution.

For	Against
1. In states with no campaign contribution limits, it is difficult for anyone to successfully challenge an incumbent.	1. Campaign contributions to political candidates are a form of freedom of expression protected by the First Amendment of the U.S. Constitution.
2. Without a cap on campaign contributions, money controls politics, and wealthy individuals and PACs have tremendous influence in public policymaking.	2. Campaign contributions to candidates and public officials guarantee only access, not policy outcomes.
3. Disclosure of campaign contributions under current laws does not convey a complete picture of the role of money in elections.	3. Limits on campaign contributions have a chilling effect on the right to participate in the democratic process.

Source: Edwin Bender, "Evidencing a Republican Form of Government: The Influence of Campaign Money on State-Level Elections," *Montana Law Review,* 74, no. 1 (2013): 165–82.

— Competency Connection —
✿ CRITICAL THINKING ✿

Campaign contributions by PACS are a major way that interest groups participate in elections. Do you believe there should be reasonable limits, if any, on political campaign contributions?

PAC activities and their influence continue to increase. According to the Texas Ethics Commission, more than 2,000 active PACS registered at the start of 2020.[27] (See Table 7.3 for a list of some of the top Texas contributors during the 2020 election cycle.) Typically, PAC contributions have been dominated by interests representing the business sector, ideological groups (which have partisan affiliations), single-interest groups (which have only one interest, such as the Texas Right to Life PAC), and labor. During the 2018 and 2020 election cycles, for instance, one PAC that supports Democratic candidates, ACTBlue Texas, was one of the top 10 contributors.[28]

Perhaps the best indication of power among interest groups is the connection between the election campaign contributions of PACs and lobbying activities. It takes a coordinated effort by an interest group to influence one part of the political process (the campaign) while also affecting policy decisions in other areas (the legislative and executive branches). In this way, interest groups can exercise far greater control over the output of Texas legislators and other officials than their numbers would indicate.

How Do We Compare...

Total Contributions in U.S. Congressional Races (2019–2020)

Most Populous U.S. States	Total Contributions*	Percent Given to Democrats	Percent Given to Republicans	Ranking** to Democrats	Ranking** to Republicans
California	$ 836,998,804	67.4	29.4	13	38
Texas	$ 370,106,050	35.6	62.4	40	10
Florida	$ 307,159,179	38.3	59.3	37	14
New York	$ 486,153,112	71.9	23.8	10	44
U.S. States Bordering Texas					
Arkansas	$ 40,845,155	30.9	67.0	45	6
Louisiana	$ 35,775,626	23.5	71.9	50	2
New Mexico	$ 29,781,742	63.2	35.4	18	33
Oklahoma	$ 34,272,964	31.9	63.5	44	9

*This figure includes PAC contributions to candidates, individual contributions to candidates and parties, and soft money contributions to parties in federal elections. (Soft money contributions are unlimited funds spent independently by supporters to benefit a candidate or by a party to educate voters.)

**Refers to how the state compares with all 50 states. For example, Texas's percentage of contributions to Republicans ranked 18th highest in the nation.

Source: "Open Secrets," Center for Responsive Politics, data reported as of September 21, 2020, http://www.opensecrets.org/states/.

— Competency Connection —
☼ CRITICAL THINKING ☼

Analyze this table. What are your initial impressions regarding the amount and percentage of PAC contributions by interest groups to Texas congressional candidates for Democrats versus Republicans in comparison to the other states?

Bribery and Unethical Practices

Bribery and blackmail, though not common in Texas, nevertheless have occurred in state and local government. One of the most notorious examples of corruption took place in the 1970s. Called the Sharpstown Bank scandal, it rocked the legislature. House Speaker Gus Mutscher (D-Brenham) and others were convicted of conspiring to accept bribes for passing deposit insurance bills as requested by Houston banker Frank Sharp. After the scandal, the state legislature passed a law prohibiting candidates for the office of Speaker of the House of Representatives from giving supportive legislators anything of value for their help or support in a campaign for the speakership. The law now requires separate campaign finance committees for election as a representative and for the Speaker's race. Contributions, loans, and expenditures received and made by a House Speaker candidate must be reported to the Texas Ethics Commission.

Table 7.3 Top Texas Contributors, (including PACs) in Spending by Category, 2020 Election Cycle

Donor	Spending	Category
1. ActBlue Texas	$11,607,357	Supports Democrats
2. Texas Association of Realtors	$4,686,421.69	Business group
3. Texans for Lawsuit Reform	$4,278,222.75	Focuses on lawsuit restrictions
4. Forward Majority Action	$3,268,000.00	Supports Democrats
5. Forward Majority Action Texas	$3,030,473.01	Supports Democrats in Texas
6. Powered by People	$1,705,325.59	Supports Democrats
7. Future Now Fund Texas	$1,548,421.63	Supports progressive Democrats
8. Texas Organizing Project PAC	$1,074,633.51	Supports progressive Democrats in support of Latino and Black Texans
9. Texan Federation of Children PAC	$932,378.60	Focuses on education reform and school choice
10. Texans for Insurance Reform	$921,732.44	Focuses on tort reform

Note: List includes only interest groups. Period includes yearly total, the two-year election cycle ending in December 2019.

Source: Search "Campaign Finance Reports, Cumulative PAC Only Yearly Totals," "Total Contributions and Expenditures Texas Ethics Commission, https://www.ethics.state.tx.us/search/cf/cANDelists2020-2016.php#2020

— Competency Connection —
✿ CRITICAL THINKING ✿

Analyze this chart. What are your initial impressions regarding the types of interest groups that are among the top donors in Texas elections? In your opinion, what motivated more pro-Democrat interest groups and their PACs to contribute to campaigns in 2020?

In 1980, an FBI investigation revealed that Texas House Speaker Billy Clayton (D-Springlake) accepted (but did not spend) $5,000 intended to influence the awarding of a state employee insurance contract. Because he had not cashed the checks, a federal district court found Clayton innocent of all bribery charges. In January 1981, he was elected to a fourth term as Speaker of the House. After eight years as Speaker, Clayton left the House to become an influential lobbyist.

In 1991, five-time Texas House Speaker Gib Lewis (D-Fort Worth) was indicted on two misdemeanor ethics charges by a Travis County grand jury. Rather than face the possibility of a trial, subjecting him to a stiffer penalty, Lewis agreed to a plea bargain, was fined $2,000, and announced his decision not to seek reelection to the House of Representatives in 1992. He became a successful lobbyist.

Behavior of candidates for House speaker has not been immune from public scrutiny. Although Texas law prohibits a speaker candidate from donating money to House candidates' election campaigns, in 2002 state Representative Tom Craddick (R-Midland) donated $20,000 from his reelection campaign to Campaign for Republican Leadership, a political action committee. In turn, the PAC gave all of its $176,500 to eight Republican candidates for the Texas House of Representatives. After Republicans won a majority of House seats for the first time since Reconstruction, Craddick was elected as the first Republican Speaker in January 2003. Controversy also swirled around Republican Speaker Dennis Bonnen in 2019, when a taped conversation between the Speaker and Michael Quinn Sullivan of a conservative group, Empower Texas, revealed the Speaker was indirectly requesting Mr. Sullivan to help defeat (in the next election) several Republican representatives that he found objectionable. In exchange, the organization would receive media credential access, granting Sullivan's employees access to the house floor. Amidst questions of ethical and campaign financial violations, Bonnen announced he would resign when his term ended in November 2020, yet maintained his role as House Speaker.[29]

Political action committees have also been orchestrated by influential policymakers in the U.S. Congress with ties to Texas. One notorious case study took place during the 2002 election. Texans for a Republican Majority (TRMPAC), was organized under the patronage of former U.S. House member Tom DeLay (R-Sugar Land). TRMPAC was involved in raising money for GOP candidates seeking seats in the Texas House in this election cycle. Later, in cooperation with DeLay, former Speaker Craddick played a major role in the 2003 congressional redistricting effort. (For more on redistricting, see Chapter 8, The Legislative Branch.) Craddick was not charged with violation of any law, but DeLay and three associates involved with TRMPAC were indicted in 2005 by a Travis County grand jury for money laundering and conspiracy to launder $190,000 of campaign contributions from corporate contributors to Republican candidates.[30] After indictment, DeLay was forced to step down as majority leader in the U.S. House of Representatives, and ultimately resigned from his seat while awaiting trial. Convicted and given a three-year sentence in 2011, DeLay remained free on bond during his appeal. His conviction was ultimately overturned in 2014 by the Texas Court of Criminal Appeals. In the end, DeLay's political career was ruined, but Republicans were successful in gaining a majority of congressional seats in Texas's delegation for the first time since Reconstruction.

★ Power and Regulation in Interest Group Politics

LO 7.4 Assess how interest groups are regulated and evaluate the effectiveness of these laws.

Clearly, interest groups play a significant role in Texas politics. They have access to a number of strategies and tactics to influence elections and policy decisions. So, how are interest groups regulated? Are these regulations effective? Do interest groups have too much political influence in shaping public policy?

Regulation of Interest Group Politics

Prompted by media reports of big spending by lobbyists and a grand jury investigation into influence peddling, in 1991 the 72nd Legislature proposed a constitutional amendment to create the eight-member **Texas Ethics Commission** to

7.3 Learning Check

1. Name two techniques lobbyists use to influence legislators.
2. Does Texas place limits on PAC contributions to state candidates, as the federal government does on federal candidates?

Answers at the end of this chapter.

Texas Ethics Commission
A state agency that enforces state standards for lobbyists and public officials, including registration of lobbyists and reporting of political campaign contributions.

enforce legal standards for lobbyists and public officials. Voters approved the amendment in November of that year, thereby allowing the eight commission members to be appointed by the governor (four members), the lieutenant governor (two members), and the House Speaker (two members).[31] This legislation was initially designed to increase the power of public prosecutors to use evidence that some contributions to lawmakers by lobbyists and other individuals are more than mere campaign donations. This legislation also expanded disclosure requirements for lobbyists and legislators, and it put a $500 annual cap on lobbyist-provided food and drink for a lawmaker. Additionally, the law bans honoraria (gratuitous payments in recognition of professional services for which there is no legally enforceable obligation to pay) and lobby-paid pleasure trips (unless a legislator makes a speech or participates in a panel discussion). Furthermore, state law requires public officials to disclose and describe any gifts valued at greater than $250.

The ethics law defines as illegal any campaign contribution accepted with an agreement to act in the contributor's interest. The problem, however, is the difficulty in proving that a candidate or public official has intentionally accepted a campaign contribution from a particular interest group in exchange for policy benefits. The law also prohibits a candidate or official from receiving a contribution in the Capitol building itself.

Detailed records of political contributions and how this money is spent must be filed with the Texas Ethics Commission between two and seven times each year. These records are open to the public and are available on the commission's website. Candidates for legislative and statewide office are required to file electronic campaign disclosure reports, so that this information can be made instantly available. Current law requires that all candidates file semiannual reports. In contested elections, however, candidates must file itemized contribution and expenditure reports every six months, and 30 days and eight days before the election.

Generally, contributions and expenditures made by candidates in the last two days prior to an election campaign need not be disclosed until the next semiannual report is due. At present, there are no laws in Texas preventing these last-minute contributions by interest groups. Therefore, interest groups can potentially alter the outcome of key races in the few days before the election. It is also not uncommon for special interests to make campaign contributions after the election takes place. Current law prohibits lawmakers and other elected state officials from raising money during the regular legislative session. However, these postelection, or "late train," donations typically take place immediately following the November election until early December.

On its website, the Texas Ethics Commission lists the names of lobbyists and their clients, as well as payments received by each lobbyist. The commission's records, however, do not give a complete picture. Lobbyists do not have to report exact dollar amounts for their contracts; they only need to indicate ranges. For example, compensation from each client is reported as less than $10,000, and then in $15,000 increments up to more than $500,000. For anything over $500,000, the exact amount is required. In addition, lobbyists are required to notify their clients if they represent two or more groups with competing interests, as well as notify the Texas Ethics Commission about any possible conflicts. This information, however, is not made available to the public or lawmakers.

The Texas Ethics Commission (TEC) is also authorized to hear ethics complaints, brought by a third party, against state officials, candidates for office, and state employees, although its budget and staff are typically very small and allow only a limited number of reviews each year. For the year 2020, there were 24 sworn complaints, around the same average as 2019.[32] Most infractions center on penalties against campaign and PAC treasurers who failed to file reports; missed filing deadlines; or provided faulty reports on contributions, earnings, or expenditures. These types of infractions center on violations of the Texas Election Code. Fines are then assessed by the Ethics Commission on any infractions. On rare occasions, the TEC reviews complaints by state officials against organizations.

On occasion, the TEC may also issue subpoenas. Beginning in 2014, the Texas Ethics Commission, in response to an official complaint by two Republican lawmakers, issued a subpoena to a Tea Party—affiliated conservative group, Empower Texas. This action sought release of a donor list and communication records with lawmakers, after the group refused to register as a lobbyist and allegedly abide by ethics rules. Empower Texas continues to challenge the central authority of the TEC to enforce campaign finance laws in the courts.

When the names of donors are not disclosed by an interest group, donations are referred to as secret money—some observers also call this "dark money." This phenomenon has become increasingly present in campaign contributions by organizations. One of the more contentious legislative proposals during the 2013 legislative session would have required nonprofit organizations that spend money on political campaigns to disclose the names of their donors. Although the legislature passed the bill, Governor Perry vetoed it.[33] Another failed attempt to regulate dark money was proposed during the 84th legislative session by Representative Byron Cook (R-Corsicana). This action was opposed by Lieutenant Governor Dan Patrick and Governor Abbott. In the 85th legislative session (2017), Cook was unsuccessful in proposing a constitutional amendment to require nonprofit organizations to disclose the names of their contributors.[34]

Reform advocates and others contend that staff members with the Ethics Commission are restricted from investigating complaints because of strict confidentiality rules. In addition, a complainant must be a Texas resident and demonstrate proof of residency. The complaint must be filed on a form provided by the commission and include information about the respondent and the complainant. Once the complaint has been filed, the TEC must immediately attempt to contact the respondent.[35] The Texas Ethics Commission is required to dismiss any Election Code complaint if the respondent claims that the violation was a clerical error and corrects the mistake within two weeks. This requirement also effectively weakens the ability of the agency to impose fines for most infractions.[36]

Some political reform groups, such as Common Cause Texas, claim that although some ethics laws are in place, they remain ineffective. Furthermore, questionable connections between lobbyists and legislators are largely unchecked. There have also been instances where governors have hired former lobbyists as senior staff personnel, or former staff of the governor leave their employment to become highly paid lobbyists. For many observers, this marks how special interests enter the governor's office through a revolving back door.

Although Texas law prohibits corporations and unions from providing campaign contributions directly to candidates, soft money can be directed to state Republican and Democratic party coffers for "administrative expenses." In light of the U.S. Supreme Court decision in *Citizens United v. Federal Election Commission* (2009), the Texas Ethics Commission issued an advisory opinion stating that corporations and unions are allowed to make expenditures independent of a political candidate, such as paying for political advertising that calls for the election or defeat of candidates, so long as they do not coordinate with the candidate's campaign. In February 2014, the TEC adopted another rule requiring PACs, *before* they receive donations from corporations or unions, to provide an affidavit that they intend to "act exclusively as a direct expenditure committee."[37]

As a result of *Citizens United*, a proliferation of super PACs was created, especially at the federal level. Super PACs raise unlimited sums of money from corporations, unions, associations, and individuals. Then PACs are allowed to spend unlimited amounts to directly target and advocate for or against specific political candidates. In 2014, Texas's prohibition of super PACs for state elections was overturned by the U.S. Fifth Circuit Court of Appeals. Now, similar to federal law, state super PACs raise unlimited sums for independent expenditures. Federal law requires a super PAC to report the names of its donors, unless a nonprofit organization is involved. State law requires the disclosure of the names of all donors regardless of the involvement of a nonprofit organization. During the 2020 presidential election, a super PAC, Forward Majority, targeted several state house legislative races with the hopes of gaining a Democrat majority.

A powerful relationship continues between campaign contributions and policy decisions. For some observers, little has changed since creation of the Texas Ethics Commission, because the system is still set up to favor incumbents.[38] All attempts to significantly reform campaign finance have been defeated. Proposed reforms have included contribution limits for individuals and PACs in legislative and statewide races, as well as full disclosure laws. As the late journalist Molly Ivins observed, "Texas is the Wild Frontier of campaign financing."[39] Campaign contributions are also connected to influential political appointments for state boards and commissions made by the governor. Although the regulatory authority of the Texas Ethics Commission was strengthened in 2003 as a part of a review by the Sunset Advisory Commission, many observers argue that the commission's powers are inadequate for the job it is intended to perform.[40] (For more information on the Sunset Advisory Commission, see Chapter 9, "The Executive Branch.")

Interest Group Power and Public Policy

The political influence of interest groups is determined by several factors. Some observers argue that a group with a sizable membership, above average financial resources, a knowledgeable and dedicated leadership, and a high degree of unity (agreement on and commitment to goals among the membership) will be able to exert virtually limitless pressure on governmental decision-makers. Others point out that the more the aims of an interest group are consistent with broad-based public beliefs or stem from issue networks (coalitions that form around a particular policy issue), the more likely the group is to succeed and wield significant power. They also observe that if interest groups are well represented in the structure of the government itself, their power will be enhanced materially. Also, it is noted that a structure of weak governments will ordinarily produce strong interest groups.

From a different point of view, others insist that factors external to the group are also highly relevant. Research indicates that a strong relationship exists between the larger socioeconomic conditions in a state and the power of interest groups. These findings have led some observers to conclude that states with high population levels, advanced industrialization, significant per capita wealth, and high levels of formal education are likely to produce relatively weak interest groups and strong political parties. Interestingly, despite a large population, Texas is among the states with strong interest groups and relatively weak political parties. Compared with other states, scholars ranked Texas as one of 26 states where interest groups dominate or fluctuate in power over time.[41] The Center for Public Integrity (CPI), in its last analysis of transparency and accountability of state governments in 2015, graded Texas below a D; only 3 states received better than a D+.[42] The Lone Star State received a grade of F in eight of the 13 categories, including lobbying disclosure, political campaign financing, and accountability for all three branches of government. According to the Center, the lower the grade the greater the likelihood of corruption in a state.

Three circumstances explain why states such as Texas may not fit the expected pattern. First, many Texas interest groups are readily accepted because they identify with free enterprise, self-reliance, and other elements of the state's individualistic political culture. The influence of the state's traditionalistic political culture suggests a reliance on a political elite to control governmental decisions and limited involvement by the general public. As a result, many Texans are predisposed to trust interest groups (especially business interest groups) and their lobbyists. Second, the century-long, one-party Democratic tradition in Texas and the subsequent one-party Republican trend have rendered interparty competition negligible in many counties and districts. Furthermore, low levels of political participation, along with the absence of strong parties and meaningful competition between parties, has made Texas government vulnerable to the pressures of strong interest groups and their lobbyists. Finally, the Texas Constitution of 1876 and its many amendments have created state and local governments beset by weak, uncoordinated institutions. Faced with a government lacking sufficient strength to offer any real opposition, interest groups often obtain decisions favorable to their causes.

Pinpointing Political Power

Assessing the political power and influence that interest groups have in American government is difficult, and determining the extent of their power in Texas is especially complex. There is no simple top-down or bottom-up arrangement. Rather, political decisions (especially policy decisions) are made by a variety of individuals and groups. Some of these decision-makers participate in local ad hoc (specific purpose) organizations; others wield influence through statewide groups. Ascertaining which individuals or groups have the greatest influence often depends on the issue or issues involved.

The political influence of any interest group cannot be fairly calculated by looking at only one political asset, whether it be money, status, knowledge, organization, sheer numbers, or in today's world, social media capabilities. Nevertheless, we may safely conclude that organized interest groups in Texas often put the unorganized citizenry at a great disadvantage when public issues are at stake.

Conclusion

As we have learned, there are numerous interest groups in Texas. They exert tremendous influence over public decisions at all levels and in all branches of government. Some interest groups, however, have more influence than others. They participate in an assortment of activities and use a variety of techniques to influence government. What's more, few, if any, regulations effectively control the power of interest groups in Texas. These factors suggest that interest groups will continue to play a significant role in Texas politics for years to come.

Chapter Summary

LO 7.1 Explain what interest groups are, why they form, and what their essential characteristics are. Interest groups act on behalf of their members to influence policy decisions made by government officials. Various factors foster interest group formation or effectiveness, such as legal and cultural reasons, a decentralized government, the strength of the party system, and political ideologies. Interest group participation influences public policy at all levels and within each branch (legislative, executive, and judicial) of Texas government. Involvement in an interest group provides members with information and opportunities to become active in the political process. Interest groups vary by organizational pattern, membership, and leadership.

LO 7.2 Describe types of interest groups and analyze the characteristics of a powerful interest group. In general, all interest groups at all levels of government can be classified according to their interests, membership, and the public policies they advocate. Among the types of interest groups that are trying to influence government policies and policymakers are those interested in economic issues, the professions, public employment matters, social issues, and the public good. Some interest groups are more powerful than others when one considers their financial resources and success rates within the legislature.

LO 7.3 Evaluate the kinds of activities that interest groups use to influence Texas government. Interest groups are involved in all types and areas of political activity. They serve various functions, which include recruiting candidates for public office, shaping consensus on issues, and providing an outlet for concerned citizens. To influence policy decisions, interest groups use several techniques, including lobbying, personal communication, giving favors and gifts, grassroots activities, electioneering, campaign financing by political action committees (PACs), and in extreme cases, resorting to bribery and other unethical or illegal practices.

LO 7.4 Assess how interest groups are regulated and evaluate the effectiveness of these laws. An eight-member Texas Ethics Commission is charged with enforcing legal standards for lobbyists and public officials. Although money is a powerful influence over policy decisions, the state only limits campaign contribution amounts for judicial candidates and places few other restrictions on donations. Texas's campaign finance laws are best characterized as involving public disclosure by public officials, lobbyists, and PACs.

Key Terms

business organization, 268
decentralized government, 264
economic interest group, 268
electioneering, 284
group leadership, 266
interest group, 262
interest group technique, 280
labor organization, 269

lobbying, 262
organizational pattern, 265
power group, 277
professional group, 271
public interest group, 277
public officer and employee group, 272

racial and ethnic groups, 272
religion-based group, 275
right of association, 263
social interest group, 272
Texas Ethics Commission, 290
women's organization, 274

Learning Check Answers

 7.1
1. Legal decisions, political culture, a decentralized government, the strength of the party system, and political ideologies are among the factors that contribute to the formation of interest groups.
2. False. Active membership will vary, depending on the organization and leadership of the organization.

7.2
1. False. Unlike most interest groups, public interest groups are interested in promoting the public interest.
2. In Texas, business groups are generally more powerful than labor groups.

7.3
1. Lobbyists use personal communication as well as favors and gifts to influence legislators.
2. Unlike federal law, Texas law does not limit campaign contributions by PACs to candidates for a state office (with the limited exception of judicial candidates).

7.4
1. True. Texas's campaign finance laws often involve disclosure by public officials and lobbyists, though critics would argue that current disclosure requirements are not sufficient to reform the system.
2. True. The Texas Ethics Commission is the primary state agency regulating the political contributions and expenditures by lobbyists and public officials.

8 The Legislative Branch

Learning Objectives

8.1 Describe the structure of the Texas legislature.

8.2 Describe the membership of the Texas legislature.

8.3 Compare the organization of the Texas House of Representatives and the Texas Senate.

8.4 Outline the responsibilities of the Texas legislature.

8.5 Explain the influences on legislators' voting decisions.

Image 8.1

Texas state Representative Kyle Biedermann (R-Fredricksburg), facing the camera, as he observed protesters in Washington, DC, on January 6, 2021.

Kolten Parker ✔ @KoltenParker · Mar 22 · · ·
NEW: Video shows Texas lawmaker @KyleBiedermann near steps of U.S. Capitol as rioters clashed with officers

Before this footage was unearthed, Biedermann was confirmed in DC but his exact whereabouts during siege were unknown.
ksat.com/news/local/202... with @dilloncollier #txlege

💬 33   🔁 400   ♡ 446   ⬆️

Source: Twitter, Inc

Competency Connection
⊛ SOCIAL RESPONSIBILITY ⊛

Should Representative Kyle Biedermann have joined protesters whose march led to invasion of the Capitol by rioters?

Most Texans know their state legislators propose bills that may pass and become laws, if not vetoed by the governor. Also, they know that bills may be passed over the governor's veto; but only a few bills get much publicity. On January 26, 2021, however, Representative Kyle Biedermann (R-Fredericksburg), a German American, attracted attention when he filed House Bill 1359. Known for an occasion when he masqueraded as a "gay Hitler," Biedermann stated on his website that it is time to decide if Texas should depart from the Union. His bill calls for a referendum on November 2, 2021, so that Texas voters can determine if the Lone Star State should take steps to secede from the United States and become an independent republic within five years.[1] Biedermann's bill was referred to the House State Affairs Committee, but died there because of lack of support by Speaker Dade Phelan, House State Affairs Committee members, and most other House members.

At the time this bill was filed, both House and Senate members were struggling to do their work under restrictions imposed because of the COVID-19 pandemic. Posted on "Texas Legislature Online" (https://capitol.texas.gov) with thousands of other bills and resolutions filed from 1991 to the present, House Bill 1359 was introduced only three weeks after Biedermann, Attorney General Ken Paxton, and Paxton's wife, state Senator Angela Paxton, participated in the Washington demonstration that preceded the Capitol riot on January 6, 2021. Although a strong supporter of President Donald Trump, Biedermann insisted that he was not involved with the violent invasion of the Capitol. Nevertheless, a video shows him near the steps of the Capitol when rioters were attacking the police barricade. Among the first 329 rioters to be indicted, 30 were from Texas (more than any other state).[2]

At home, Biedermann's business is Ace Hardware in Fredericksburg. During the Civil War, many German Americans in the Hill Country area around Fredericksburg supported Abraham Lincoln and the Union. Some of them were killed by Confederate secessionists.

Enacting legislation by any elected representative body is a slow, frustrating, and often disappointing process. Multiple sessions and good political skills are required to make many laws. Most citizens are impatient with political tactics and procedural delays, even if their policy objectives are eventually achieved. They dislike the inevitable compromises involved in the legislative process. Nevertheless, Texas legislators perform work of vital importance. They make laws that affect the life, liberty, and property of every person in the state. (For an example of how students are affected, see **Point/Counterpoint** for arguments for and against the law on concealed carry of handguns on the campuses of Texas's colleges and universities.)

Follow *Practicing Texas Politics* on Twitter @ **PracTexPol**

⊠ Point/Counterpoint

Should Concealed Carry of Handguns on Campuses Be Retained?

The Issue In 2015, the Texas Legislature passed, and Governor Greg Abbott signed, Senate Bill 11 authorizing licensed persons to carry handguns on the campuses of institutions of higher education. This controversial legislation is an example of how state laws can have an impact on students and others.

For	Against
1. Holders of handgun licenses are armed to defend themselves and others.	1. Concealed handguns distract students from learning and promote a culture of fear.
2. Private institutions can opt out of allowing handguns on campus.	2. Law enforcement officers will have difficulty distinguishing between criminal shooters and licensed handgun bearers.
3. Institutions can be flexible in creating rules to regulate campus carry.	3. Guns on campus could result in fatal accidents and more suicide.
4. The number of licensed carriers is relatively small, because a large majority of students are under age 21 or cannot qualify at ages 18 to 20 because they are not active or former military personnel.	4. Institutions of higher education could have difficulty recruiting faculty and staff as well as attracting students.

Source: Major Issues in the 84th Legislature, Focus Report 84-7 (Austin: House Research Organization, Texas House of Representatives, September 22, 2015), 112–113, https://hro.house.texas.gov/pdf/focus/major84.pdf.

— Competency Connection —
❖ CRITICAL THINKING ❖

What are reasons for and against allowing private colleges and universities to opt out of campus carry?

After years of research, Professor Alan Rosenthal (1932–2013) of Rutgers University concluded: "[Legislatures] are far from perfect, yet they are the best we have, and preferable to any conceivable alternative. Not only that, they actually work, albeit in rather messy and somewhat mysterious ways—representing, lawmaking, and balancing the power of the executive."[3] After reading this chapter on the Texas legislature, you can decide whether Rosenthal's conclusions apply to the Lone Star State.

✪ Legislative Framework

LO 8.1 Describe the structure of the Texas legislature.

In Texas's Declaration of Independence (1836), delegates complained that the Mexican government "had dissolved, by force of arms, the state Congress of Coahuila and Texas, and obliged our representatives to fly for their lives from the seat of government, thus depriving us of the fundamental right of representation."

That fundamental right was subsequently established in the Constitution of the Republic of Texas (1836) and in all of Texas's five state constitutions, wherein Texans have entrusted the power to enact bills and adopt resolutions to popularly elected legislators. These powers are the essence of representative government. Other legislative functions include proposing constitutional amendments, adopting budgets for state government, levying taxes, redistricting, impeaching and removing executive and judicial officials if warranted, and investigating issues.

In Texas and 40 other states, the larger chamber of a **bicameral** (two-chamber, or two-house) legislature is called the House of Representatives. Some states use the terms Assembly, House of Delegates, or General Assembly. Only Nebraska has a **unicameral** (one-chamber, or one-house) legislature with 49 senators. In the 49 states with bicameral legislatures, the larger chamber ranges in size from 40 members in Alaska to 400 members in New Hampshire. Texas has 150 members in its House of Representatives. The smaller legislative chamber is called the Senate. Alaska has the smallest Senate with 20 members; Minnesota has the largest with 67. The Texas Senate has 31 members.

Election and Terms of Office

Voters residing in representative and senatorial districts elect Texas legislators. Representatives are elected for two years. Senators are usually elected for four years. Terms of office for members of both houses begin in January of odd-numbered years. Under the current Texas Constitution, legislators elected in 1876 convened in regular session as the 1st Legislature in January 1877. After 144 years, members of the 87th Legislature were elected in 2020 and convened for a regular session in January 2021.

Legislative redistricting for both the Texas House and the Senate occurs in the first odd-numbered year in a decade based on the results of the federal decennial census. In each even-numbered year, voters elect a new House of Representatives, as will happen in 2022. That is also the year for electing a new Senate. Because Senate terms are four years, however, in January of the next odd-numbered year (for example, 2023), senators draw lots by choosing from 31 numbered pieces of paper sealed in envelopes. The 16 who draw odd numbers get four-year terms, and the 15 who draw even numbers get only two-year terms. Thus, in 2024, elections will be held for 15 positions in the Senate. Approximately one-half of the senators (that is, 15 or 16) are then elected for four-year terms in each even-numbered year through 2030.

A legislator may be expelled by a two-thirds majority vote of the membership of the legislator's chamber. If a senator or representative dies, resigns, or is expelled from office, the vacancy is filled in a special election called by the governor. A legislator called to active military duty for more than 30 days retains the office if he or she appoints a qualified temporary replacement who is approved by the appropriate chamber. Some male legislators called to military duty have appointed their wives as temporary replacements.[4]

bicameral
A legislature with two houses or chambers, such as Texas's House of Representatives and Senate.

unicameral
A one-house legislature, such as the Nebraska legislature.

Sessions

Texas law requires **regular sessions** to begin on the second Tuesday in January of each odd-numbered year (for example, January 12, 2021, and January 10, 2023). In practice, these regular biennial sessions always run for the full 140 days (including weekends and eight state holidays), as authorized by the Texas Constitution (for example, through May 31, 2021, and through May 29, 2023). Nevertheless, some cynics have insisted the intent of the constitution drafters was that the legislature would convene for a two-day session every 140 years! Like Texas, the legislatures of Montana, Nevada, and North Dakota convene for biennial sessions. All other state legislatures have annual sessions. A beneficiary of the Texas legislature's sessions is the Austin economy, because legislators and lobbyists spend millions of dollars for housing, food, beverages, and entertainment during each session.

When the 87th Legislature convened in January 2021, its work was overshadowed by the recent Washington riot that brought death and destruction to the national Capitol. Some Texans feared that there might be a similar riot in Austin. At the same time, appearance of legislators and staff personnel wearing facemasks showed that lawmaking would be affected by the coronavirus pandemic. In the days that followed, at least five legislators became ill with COVID-19; guided tours of the Capitol for visitors were ended; Zoom and texting took the place of face-to-face communication; and social distancing was mandated for everyone in House and Senate chambers and committee rooms. In an effort to protect people entering the Capitol, new air cleaning units were installed throughout the building.[5]

The governor may call **special sessions**, lasting no longer than 30 days each, at any time. During special sessions, the legislature may consider only those matters placed before it by the governor. Special sessions are unpopular with legislators and costly to taxpayers. In 2021, the total per diem cost to cover travel and living expenses for all of the 181 legislators was about $42,000 per day or about $1,260,000 for a 30-day special session.

Governor Abbott called a special session in 2017 to consider 19 items. Included were abortion issues, use of bathrooms by transgendered people, and school finance.[6] Because he did not call a special session to deal with the COVID-19 pandemic in 2020, Senate Joint Resolution 33 (SJR 33) was introduced at the beginning of the 87th regular session. If it had been adopted by the Senate and House, and then approved by a majority of voters as a constitutional amendment, it would have allowed a special session to be called by joint action of the speaker and the lieutenant governor. They would have determined the subject or subjects for consideration.

Districting

Providing equal representation in a legislative chamber involves dividing a state into districts with approximately equal numbers of residents. The Texas Legislature performs this task with assistance from the nonpartisan Texas Legislative Council and its Red Apple (short for Redistricting Application) software. Population distribution changes constantly as the result of migration, births, and deaths. (For example, between 2010 and 2020 the population of the Capital Region around Austin grew rapidly, while the population of the

regular session
A session of the Texas legislature that is constitutionally mandated and begins on the second Tuesday in January of odd-numbered years and lasts for a maximum of 140 days.

special session
A legislative session called by the governor and limited to no more than 30 days.

Image 8.2 Representative Eric Johnson (D-Dallas) led the effort to remove the "Children of the Confederacy" plaque from the Texas Capitol. Johnson was elected as mayor of Dallas in June 2019.

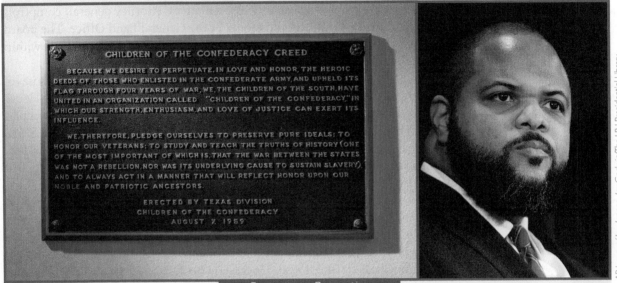

CHILDREN OF THE CONFEDERACY CREED

BECAUSE WE DESIRE TO PERPETUATE, IN LOVE AND HONOR, THE HEROIC DEEDS OF THOSE WHO ENLISTED IN THE CONFEDERATE ARMY, AND UPHELD ITS FLAG THROUGH FOUR YEARS OF WAR, WE, THE CHILDREN OF THE SOUTH, HAVE UNITED IN AN ORGANIZATION CALLED "CHILDREN OF THE CONFEDERACY," IN WHICH OUR STRENGTH, ENTHUSIASM, AND LOVE OF JUSTICE CAN EXERT ITS INFLUENCE.

WE, THEREFORE, PLEDGE OURSELVES TO PRESERVE PURE IDEALS; TO HONOR OUR VETERANS; TO STUDY AND TEACH THE TRUTHS OF HISTORY (ONE OF THE MOST IMPORTANT OF WHICH IS, THAT THE WAR BETWEEN THE STATES WAS NOT A REBELLION, NOR WAS ITS UNDERLYING CAUSE TO SUSTAIN SLAVERY), AND TO ALWAYS ACT IN A MANNER THAT WILL REFLECT HONOR UPON OUR NOBLE AND PATRIOTIC ANCESTORS.

ERECTED BY TEXAS DIVISION
CHILDREN OF THE CONFEDERACY
AUGUST 7, 1959

Competency Connection
◉ **SOCIAL RESPONSIBILITY** ◉

Why do you believe the Children of the Confederacy plaque is controversial?

Northwestern Region in the Panhandle declined slightly.) Therefore, legislative district boundaries must be redrawn periodically to ensure equitable representation; but each legislator wants a district with a safe majority of supporting voters.[7]

In Texas, the first legislative and congressional elections in districts determined by 2020 census data were scheduled for November 2022. During the previous decade, the 2010 census was the basis for legislative and congressional representation.

State Legislative Districts Our Texas Constitution requires **reapportionment** (allotment of seats according to population) every decade. **Redistricting** features drawing new district lines to reflect apportionment and population change. Populations of districts should be equal or almost equal and must not be drawn so as to deny or abridge the right to vote based on color, language, or race.[8]

Redistricting by politically motivated Texas legislators is a slow, painful, and expensive process. Moreover, often their district maps are rejected by courts. In contrast, David Bradlee claims that high school students, and even some middle school students, can produce good maps by clicking on his website, https://davesredistricting.org.

Prior to 1948, the legislature often failed to redistrict the state after each census. In that year, legislative districting inequities led to adoption of a state constitutional amendment designed to pressure the legislature to remedy this situation. Now, the legislature's failure to redistrict during the first regular session after a decennial

reapportionment
Allotment of legislative seats according to population.

redistricting
Redrawing of boundaries after the federal decennial census to create single-member districts with approximately equal population (for example, legislative and congressional districts in Texas).

AP Images/Jay Janner, Jay Godwin/The LBJ Presidential Library census (or the governor's veto of a redistricting plan that is not overridden by the legislature) brings the Legislative Redistricting Board into operation. This board consists of five *ex officio* (that is, "holding other office") members: the lieutenant governor, speaker of the House of Representatives, attorney general, comptroller of public accounts, and commissioner of the General Land Office. The board must meet within 90 days after the legislative session and redistrict the state within another 60 days. Otherwise, a state or federal court will perform this task.

Although the legislature drew new legislative districts after the federal censuses of 1950 and 1960, the Texas Constitution's apportionment formulas for the Texas House and Senate discriminated against heavily populated urban counties. These formulas were not changed until the U.S. Supreme Court held in *Reynolds v. Sims*, 377 U.S. 533 (1964) that "the seats in both houses of a bicameral state legislature must be apportioned on a population basis." This "one person, one vote" principle was first applied in Texas by a federal district court in *Kilgarlin v. Martin*, 252 F. Supp. 404 (1965).

Attempts to redefine the "one person, one vote" principle have been based on only considering the voter-eligible population rather than the total apportionment population in determining a district's population. Such a definition would exclude children, prisoners, and noncitizens. The U.S. Supreme Court rejected this argument in the Texas case *Evenwel v. Abbott*, 136 S. Ct. 1120 (2016), noting that all 50 U.S. states use total population as the basis for redistricting. Nevertheless, the Court left unclear whether total population is the only basis for determining population for state legislative districts. Speaking for the Project on Fair Representation, which supported the lawsuit, Edward Blum (a politically conservative legal strategist) expressed disappointment with the decision. He asserted, "the issue of voter equality is not going to go away."[9]

Redistricting by the Texas legislature often sparks complaints about **gerrymandering**, a practice that involves drawing districts to include or exclude certain groups of voters in order to favor one group or political party. Usually, gerrymandered districts are oddly shaped rather than compact. This term "gerrymander" originated to describe irregularly shaped districts created under the guidance of Elbridge Gerry, governor of Massachusetts, in 1812. One gerrymandering tactic involves "packing" supporters of one party into a district in order to reduce that party's strength in adjoining districts. Another gerrymandering tactic features "cracking" a district by adding parts of its territory to one or more other districts. A third gerrymandering tactic "highjacks" or "pairs" two or more incumbents in the same district, so that only one can be reelected. The political party holding the most seats in a legislature often benefits in elections conducted after redistricting. Many state and federal court battles have been fought over the constitutionality of Texas's legislative and congressional districting arrangements.[10]

Members of the Texas Senate have always represented **single-member districts**—that is, the voters of each district elect one senator. Redistricting according to the 2020 federal census provided for an ideal population of 941,396 (the total state apportionment population of 29,183,290 divided by 31) in each senatorial district. Many of the 31 senatorial districts cover several counties, but a few big-city senatorial districts are formed from the territory of only part of a county. Figure 8.1 shows senatorial district maps used for the 2020 election. Compare these maps with senate district maps drawn in 2021 for the 2022 election. (See District Viewer at https://dvr.capitol.texas.gov/.)

gerrymandering
Drawing the boundaries of a district, such as a state senatorial or representative district, to include or exclude certain groups of voters and thus affect election outcomes.

single-member district
An area that elects only one representative to a policymaking body, such as a state House, a state Senate, or the U.S. Congress.

Until 1971, a Texas county with two or more seats in the House was a **multimember district** in which voters elected representatives at-large to represent the whole county. Voters in these counties voted in all House races in the county. In 1971, however, single-member districts were established in Harris, Dallas, and Bexar counties. Four years later, single-member districting was extended to

multimember district
A district in which all voters participate in the election of two or more representatives to a policymaking body.

Figure 8.1 Court-Ordered Texas State Senate Districts as used in the 2020 election. The accompanying map shows districts wholly or partially within Harris County. Compare with the map created in 2021, as shown in Texas Legislature Online, district viewer (dvr.capitol.texas.gov).

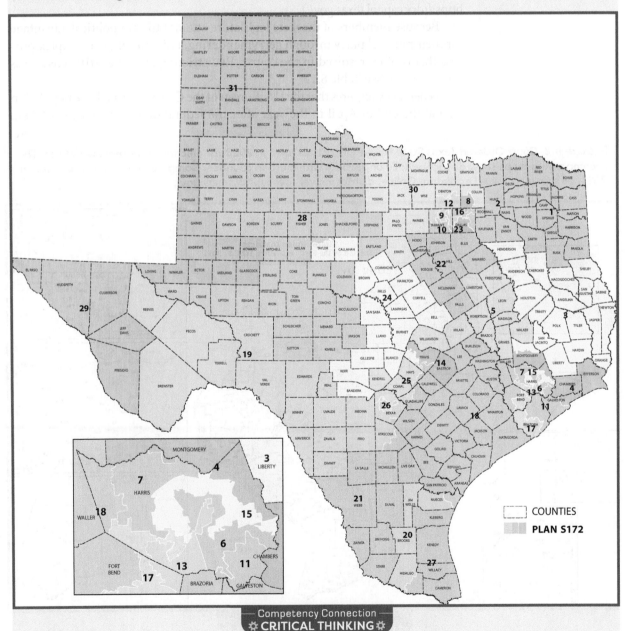

Competency Connection
☼ CRITICAL THINKING ☼

Should drawing maps that favor the election of members from a specific political party (partisan gerrymandering) be illegal?

all counties in which voters elected more than one representative. This change to single-member districts was largely a result of court actions. Election results demonstrate that single-member districts reduce campaign costs and increase the probability that more Black and Latino candidates will be elected. As a result of the federal census of 2020, redistricting gave each state representative's district an ideal population of 194,555 (state apportionment population divided by 150); but districts commonly vary in population by as much as 10 percent. Figure 8.2 shows house district maps for the 2020 election of 36 U.S. representatives. Compare these maps with house district maps drawn in 2021 for the 2022 election. (See District Viewer at https://drv.capitol.texas.gov/.)

Because members of the state legislature attempt to gain political advantage for their political party through gerrymandering, redistricting is a complex process that is often resolved in the courts. Redistricting after the 2010 census was no exception. See Table 8.1.

Federal law requires that the U.S. Bureau of the Census must release population data at the end of April in the year after the federal decennial census is taken.

Figure 8.2 Court-Ordered Texas State House Districts as used in 2020 for electing state representatives. The accompanying maps show districts wholly or partially within urban counties. Compare with the map created in 2021, as shown in Texas Legislature Online, district viewer (dvr.capitol.texas.gov).

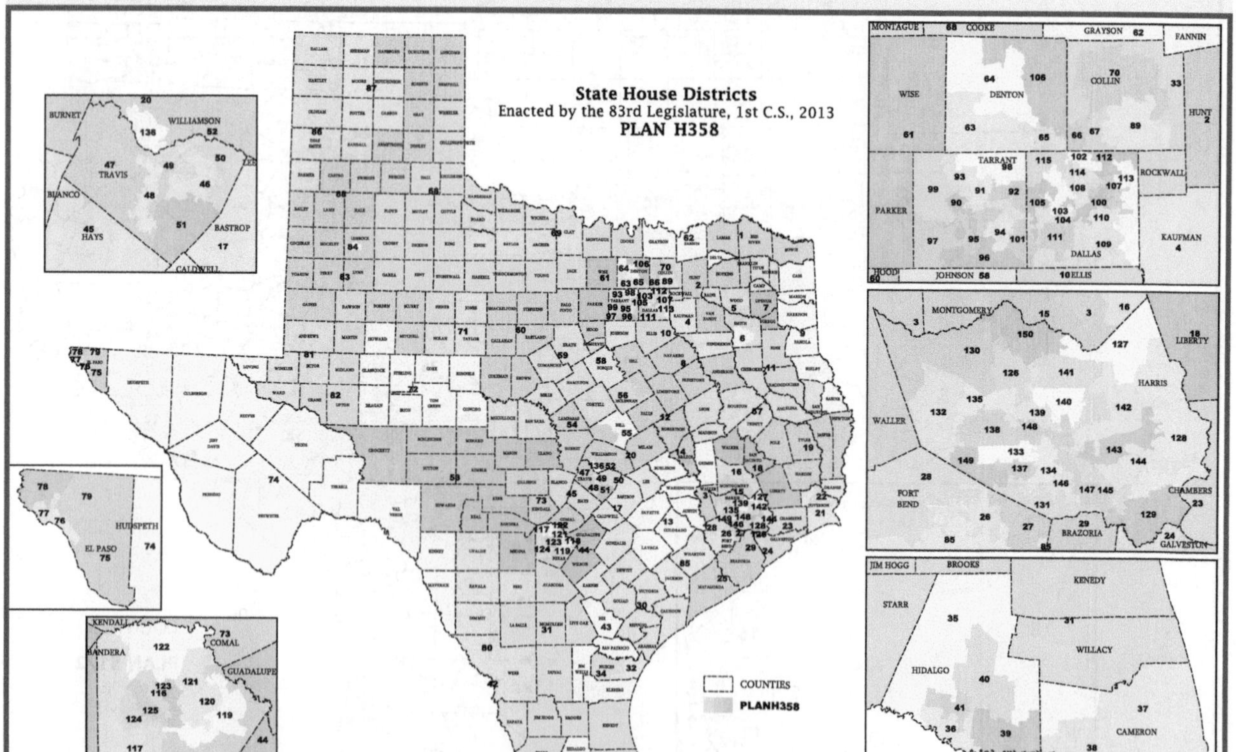

Competency Connection
★ PERSONAL RESPONSIBILITY ★

Should the courts be able to redraw boundary lines approved by the state legislature? Why or why not?

Nevertheless, the COVID-19 pandemic and political confusion caused by President Trump's failed attempt to put a citizenship question in the census caused postponement of release of these data until September 2021. Because the regular session of the Texas Legislature ended in May, this delay meant that redistricting for legislative and congressional districts would require action in a special session called by the governor.

U.S. Congressional Districts As with districts for state legislators, congressional districts cannot be drawn so as to deny or abridge the right to vote on the basis of color, language or race. Figure 8.3 shows Texas congressional

Table 8.1 History of Texas Redistricting Plans (2010 Census)

Year	Action	Elected Offices Affected	Effects	Results
2011	82nd Legislature adopts plans	U.S. House of Representatives Texas Senate Texas House of Representatives	Favored election of Republicans Appeared to reduce influence of Black and Latino voters	Plan rejected under provisions of federal Voting Rights Act *Perez v. Perry* filed by private citizens challenging fairness
2012	Federal district court redraws interim maps	U.S. House of Representatives Texas Senate Texas House of Representatives	Republicans argue maps favor Democrats	Maps challenged in U.S. Supreme Court and Court orders they be redrawn Federal District court redraws maps Primary elections held in late May rather than March Republicans win approximately 2/3 of U.S. House, Texas Senate and Texas House of Representatives positions
2013	83rd Legislature redraws maps	U.S. House of Representatives Texas Senate Texas House of Representatives	U.S. House and Texas Senate maps follow District Court's plan Texas House of Representatives' map changes boundaries for four multidistrict counties	After Voting Rights Law modified by Supreme Court in *Shelby County v. Holder*, new lawsuit filed challenging U.S. House of Representatives and Texas House of Representatives maps
2014–2018	Federal District court orders use of interim maps	U.S. House of Representatives Texas House of Representatives	Private citizens file *Abbott v. Perez* challenging maps.	U.S. Supreme Court holds that boundaries of one House district in Tarrant County result in racial gerrymandering that is not permitted.
2018–2020	Federal district court orders legislature to redraw map affecting state House District 90 in Tarrant County	Texas House of Representatives	86th Legislature fails to redraw map	Federal district court redraws House of Representatives map for Tarrant County's District 90 and adjoining Districts 97 and 99.

— Competency Connection —
☼ **CRITICAL THINKING** ☼

Which elected offices were affected by all of the redistricting actions from 2011 to 2020?

Figure 8.3 Court-Ordered Interim U.S. Congressional Districts for electing U.S. representatives in 2020. Accompanying map shows districts wholly or partially within Harris County. Compare with the map created in 2021, as shown in Texas Legislature Online, district viewer (dvr.capitol.texas.gov).

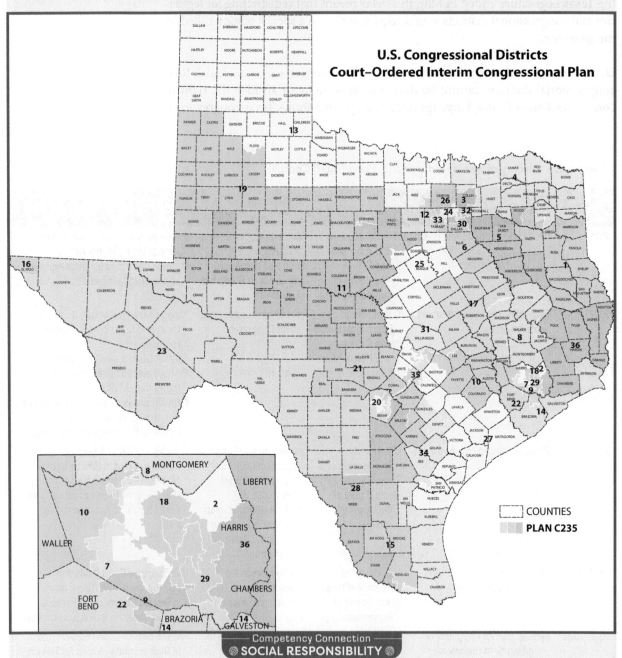

U.S. Congressional Districts
Court–Ordered Interim Congressional Plan

COUNTIES
PLAN C235

Competency Connection
◉ SOCIAL RESPONSIBILITY ◉

If a particular ethnic or racial group is primarily responsible for an increase in population in a state, should that group be entitled to the possibility of more representation in the U.S. Congress for members from their ethnic or racial group?

district maps for the 2020 election of 36 U.S. representatives. Compare these maps with congressional district maps drawn in 2021 for the 2022 election of 38 U.S. representatives with an ideal apportionment population of 767,981. (See District Viewer at https://drv.capitol.texas.gov/.)

⬦ Legislators

LO 8.2 Describe the membership of the Texas legislature, including legislators' formal and informal qualifications and compensation.

Texas is a representative or indirect democracy with state legislators elected by citizen voters. These representatives and senators make laws on behalf of the people who elect them. The concept of **descriptive representation** is that lawmakers have the same characteristics as their constituents. For instance, a female representative representing females or a Latino representative representing Latinos are examples of descriptive representation. The idea of **substantive representation** is that lawmakers will work on behalf of individuals and groups without regard for social and economic characteristics. Thus, substantive representation in the Lone Star State describes lawmakers who promote the interests of a particular group, such as an older representative focusing on issues that affect young adults. Evidence from political science research indicates that increasing descriptive representation for a group leads to improved substantive representation for that group.[11]

Members of the Texas legislature may not hold another government office. Furthermore, they must meet specific state constitutional qualifications concerning citizenship, voter status, state and district residence, and age. Despite such restrictions, millions of Texans possess all legal (constitutional and statutory) qualifications to serve in the legislature. These are the formal qualifications for an office. As is true of the memberships in other state legislatures, however, biographical data for members of recent Texas legislatures suggest many informal qualifications that restrict opportunities for election.

Qualifications and Characteristics

The Texas Constitution specifies the formal qualifications for House and Senate members. Age requirements differ between the Texas House (21 years) and Senate (26 years); and residency immediately before an election is two years for representatives and five years for senators. Qualifications are the same for citizenship (United States and Texas), voter status (qualified Texas voter), and residence in the district to be represented (one year). If a question arises concerning constitutional qualifications or if a dispute develops over election returns, each legislative chamber determines who will be seated.

To be elected, the typical Texas legislator also meets a number of informal qualifications. These informal qualifications include being a White Protestant male between 40 and 60 years of age, a native-born Texan, a college graduate, and an attorney or a businessperson who has served one or more previous terms of office. Although such characteristics do not guarantee any predetermined reaction to issues and events, legislators tend to be influenced by their family, occupation, and environment. Because these factors can have policy consequences, any study of the legislature must account for the biographical characteristics of legislators.[12] Table 8.2 provides data for both chambers of the 87th Legislature in 2021, as well as for the Texas delegation to the U.S. Congress.

Table 8.2 Texan Lawmakers 2021: Party, Gender, and Ethnicity

	Texas House 150 members	Texas Senate 31 members	U.S. House 435 members	U.S. Senate 100 members
Republicans				
White Men	73	12	18	1
White Women	6	6	3	0
Latino Men	1	0	1	1
Latino Women	0	0	0	0
Black Men	1	0	0	0
Black Women	0	0	0	0
Asian Men	1	0	0	0
Asian Women	1	0	0	0
Republican Totals	**83**	**18**	**22***	**2**
Democrats				
White Men	6	2	1	0
White Women	6	2	1	0
Latino Men	22	5	4	0
Latino Women	15	2	2	0
Black Men	6	2	3	0
Black Women	10	0	2	0
Asian Men	2	0	0	0
Asian Women	0	0	0	0
Democrat Totals	**67**	**13**	**13**	**2**

*Republican total will be 23 after a July run-off involving a Republican man and a Republican woman.
Sources:
1. Texas House of Representatives 87th Legislature, https://www.house.texas.gov/members/
2. Texas Senate 87th Legislature, https://www.senate.texas.gov/members/
3. Vote USA, Current U.S. House Members, https://vote-usa.org/officials.aspx?report=u3
4. Vote USA, Current U.S. Senate Members, https://vote-usa.org/officials.aspx?Report=U2

Competency Connection
☼ **CRITICAL THINKING** ☼

What do you believe are the most important results of legislative and judicial actions concerning Texas redistricting plans since 2011?

Gender and Ethnic Classifications White men dominate the Texas legislature, and almost all White legislators are Republicans. Only 16 of the 181 legislators in the 87th Legislature were White Democrats (8 men and 8 women), but the Texas legislature has become more diverse. For example, it included many more women and members of historical minority groups in 2021 than it did half a century earlier. Nevertheless, slightly over half the state's population are women, but only 48 state legislators in 2021 (26.5 percent) were women (22 White, 10 Black, 15 Latina, and one Asian).

Representation of members of historical racial and ethnic minorities has increased substantially since the late 1960s, but Blacks, Latinos, and Asian Americans have been underrepresented in the Texas legislature. In 2021, however, members of the 87th Legislature included 19 Blacks (11 percent), 46 Latinos (26 percent), and four Asian Americans (2 percent). Only one Black representative and one Latino representative were Republicans in that year. Texans elected the first Asian American legislator in the 1960s, but they did not elect another Asian American for almost 40 years. An Asian American has never been elected to the Texas Senate.

Political Party Affiliation In 1961, no Republican held a seat in the Texas legislature, but when the legislature convened 36 years later (1997), the GOP had a Senate majority. Beginning in January 2003, Republicans have controlled both the Senate and the House. Since that year, each chamber has produced many "party line" votes, with all Democrats voting on one side and all Republicans voting on the other side.

In 2011, Republicans achieved supermajority status (two-thirds of total membership) in the Texas House of Representatives, with 101 Republican representatives compared to 49 Democrats. Republican representation in the Texas Senate has fluctuated between 18 and 20 of the 31 senate seats since 2007. Most of the increase in Republican strength resulted from election victories. Between 2009 and 2012, however, four representatives switched to the GOP after having been elected as Democrats. In regular and special elections from 2012 to 2021, Democrats increased their numbers in the House of Representatives, resulting in 67 Democratic House members in the 86th and 87th Legislatures. Numbers remained fairly constant in the Senate, where Democrats won from 12 to 14 seats in elections from 2012 to 2020.

Central city residents usually elect Black and Latino Democrats, whereas Republican senators and representatives receive their strongest support from rural and suburban White voters. Nevertheless, these practices are changing. (See Chapter 4, "Political Parties," and Chapter 5, "Voting and Elections," for discussions of parties and voting.) Residents of South Texas districts largely elect Latino Democrats, although the number of Republican voters in that area increased in 2020.

Education and Occupation In government, as in business, most positions of leadership call for college credentials. Although not a formal constitutional requirement for election to the Texas legislature, in recent years nearly all

Image 8.3 Lieutenant Governor Dan Patrick (left) and Speaker Dade Phelan (center) with Governor Greg Abbott (right). Photo from Elizabeth Conley/ *Houston Chronicle*

Elizabeth Conley/Houston Chronicle/AP Photo

Competency Connection
COMMUNICATION SKILLS

Which of these three Texas officials has the most legislative power?

members have attended one or more institutions of higher education. Most of them could claim a bachelor's degree, and many had graduate or professional degrees (especially in law).

Traditionally, Texas legislators have included many attorneys and business owners or managers. Lesser numbers of real estate and insurance people, as well as some farmers, ranchers, and teachers, also have served. Healthcare professionals, engineers, and accountants have held few legislative seats, although five of the members of the 87th Legislature were physicians (three senators and two representatives). Over the last 75 years, laborers have won few legislative seats. One exception was plumber-pipefitter Lloyd W. Criss, Jr, who wrote a book that covers his 12 years as a member of the House of Representatives (1979–1991) and his life as a laborer and union official.[13]

Lawyer-legislators may receive retainers (payments) from corporations and special interest groups, with the understanding that legal services will be performed if needed. Some critics question whether lawyer-legislators are hired for their legal abilities, to delay a court proceeding with a continuance, or to influence legislation. An attorney who serves in the legislature can obtain a continuance (that is, a postponement) of any case set for trial during a period extending from 30 days before to 30 days after a legislative session. To avoid abuse of this privilege, judges can deny a continuance if a lawyer was hired to assist with a case within 10 days of trial or any related legal proceeding. Payments received for obtaining a continuance must be disclosed. A legislator may not represent paying clients before state agencies, such as the Railroad Commission. (For information about state agencies, see Chapter 9, The Executive Branch.)

Religious Affiliation The Texas Constitution requires that public officials must "acknowledge the existence of a Supreme Being." Nevertheless, it guarantees freedom of religion and prohibits use of public funds to benefit a sect or religious group. Even though most Texas legislators profess recognition of the principle of separation of church and state, a lawmaker's religious beliefs may play a critical role in formulating public policy. This factor is especially important when considering legislation involving issues related to moral behavior (such as abortion or gambling) and some economic matters (such as state aid to church-related schools). Although the religious affiliation of each legislator is not a matter of record, a review of self-reported religious preferences indicates that Catholic legislators are most numerous in Texas, followed by Baptists.

Legislative Experience In a legislative body, experience is measured in terms of turnover (that is, first-termers replacing experienced members who have retired or lost an election) and tenure (years served in a legislative chamber). For the five most recent Texas legislatures (83rd–87th), the average turnover in the House was about 18 percent of the membership every two years. In the Senate, it was about 15 percent. Turnover tends to be greater for the first legislature after redistricting or in the event of a scandal.

The average length of service by legislators in the most recent legislatures was more than six years in both the House and the Senate. In 2021, nine of the 31 senators in the 87th Legislature had served as representatives. After a term in office, an incumbent is more likely to win an election than is an inexperienced challenger.

As a general rule, lawmakers become most effective after they have spent two or more years learning procedural rules related to enacting legislation and working with constituents, bureaucrats, lobbyists, fellow legislators, and other elected officials. Some representatives and senators have held their current positions for decades. The most senior member of the House, Tom Craddick (R-Midland), was first elected in 1968. The most senior member of the Senate, John Whitmire (D-Houston), was first elected to that chamber in 1982. (Senator Whitmire was in the House of Representatives for 10 years prior to his service in the Senate.) Texas is one of 35 states that does not have term limits for legislators. Even though some Democrats and Republicans have worked to achieve term limits for state-level officeholders (including legislators), these efforts have failed. Although some Texas legislators want term limits, political science has an extensive literature about why term limits are not a good idea. For example, Seth Musket concludes, "The overall summary of the literature is that term limits weaken legislatures (to the benefit of governors, parties, and lobbyists), increase polarization, and fail to achieve much of their good government goals."[14]

Compensation

The lowest-paid state legislators in the nation are from New Hampshire. These elected officials are paid $200 per year with no per diem (compensation to cover expenses). Although New Mexico does not pay members of its legislative bodies any annual salary, legislators receive $161 per diem for each day the legislature is in session. In contrast, California's annual salary of $110,459 is more than any other state pays its legislators. Texas's state senators and representatives receive low pay, reasonable allowances, and a relatively generous retirement pension after a minimum period of service.

Pay and Per Diem Allowance Originally, Texas legislators' salaries and per diem (daily personal allowances during a regular or special session) were specified by the state constitution and could be changed only by constitutional amendment. Now, as authorized by a constitutional amendment, the Texas Ethics Commission sets the per diem expense allowance. In addition, this commission may recommend salary increases for legislators and even higher salaries for the speaker and the lieutenant governor. Texas voters, however, must approve all such recommendations and therefore make the ultimate decision. The $600 monthly salary ($7,200 per year) has not increased since 1975.

For the 87th Legislature, which convened in January 2021, the per diem allowance to cover meals, lodging, and other personal expenses was $221 for senators, representatives, and the lieutenant governor. This per diem amounted to a total of $30,940 per official for the 140-day regular session. When the legislature was not in session, members could receive a maximum of 12 per diem payments of $206 during each month if they were working on state business.

In view of these facts, each Texan should ponder the following: Are our legislators, each receiving a total of less than $50,000 for salary and living expenses (if there isn't one or more special sessions), compensated adequately for a two years term in office? After all, they make laws affecting every Texan, authorize a multi-billion-dollar biennial state budget, and levy taxes to pay for it. Per capita cost of all state government operations for two years is about $425, including $8.50 for the legislative branch.

Expense Allowances At the beginning of a session, each chamber authorizes contingent expense allowances. For example, during the 87th regular session, the House authorized every representative's operating account to be credited monthly with $20,000. House members use money in this account to cover the cost of official work-related travel within Texas, postage, office operations, and staff salaries. Representatives can also use money from campaign contributions to supplement their assistants' salaries and their own travel allowances.

For the 87th regular session, each senator had a monthly allowance of $43,000. Other expenses for carrying out official duties (for example, subscriptions, postage, telecommunications, and stationery) were paid from the Senate's contingent expense fund. Like representatives, senators can supplement staff salaries with money from campaign contributions.

Staff members assist legislators with office management, research, constituent service (assist district residents with their government problems), and communication. Although assistance in responding to postal mail and email is a staff function, communications via social media, especially Twitter, is of increasing importance for legislators. Many legislators have staff to manage these accounts, but some elected officials prefer to handle their social networking accounts directly. Early in the 87th legislative session, 141 of the state's representatives and 30 senators had active Twitter accounts.

Retirement Pension Under terms of the Texas State Employees Retirement Act of 1975, legislators contribute 8 percent of their state salaries to a retirement fund. Retirement pay for senators and representatives amounts to 2.3 percent of the state-funded portion of a district judge's annual base salary ($140,000 in fiscal years 2022 and 2023) for each year served and cannot exceed this amount. For example, should Representative Tom Craddick or Senator John Whitmire retire, he would be eligible for the maximum $140,000 in annual retirement benefits.

Legislators with a minimum of 12 years of service may retire at age 50 with an annual pension of $38,640. Those with at least eight years of service may retire at age 60 with a pension of $25,760 per year. Many legislators do not serve long enough to qualify for a pension; but for those who are eligible, payments can begin while they are relatively young.

In 2017, the 85th Legislature enacted Senate Bill 500, which directs withholding retirement pensions for legislators and other elected officials convicted of crimes while in office. Included are bribery, embezzlement, tampering with a government record, and perjury.[15]

📖 How Do We Compare...

In Salary of Legislators?

Annual Salary of Legislators for the Year of the Last Regular Session

Most Populous U.S. States	Annual Salary	U.S. States Bordering Texas	Annual Salary
California	$110,459	Arkansas	$41,394
Florida	$ 29,697	Louisiana: Senate/House	$35,384/$28,820
New York	$ 110,000	New Mexico	$0*
Texas	**$ 7,200**	Oklahoma	$35,021

*Legislators in New Mexico receive a $161 per diem allowance but no annual salary.

Source: "Comparison of State Legislative Salaries," *Ballotpedia,* https://ballotpedia.org/Comparison_of_state_legislative_salaries.

Competency Connection
☼ **CRITICAL THINKING** ☼

How do you account for the wide range of salaries for state legislators? Is the salary of Texas legislators adequate or should they be paid more or less?

Legislative Organization

LO 8.3 Compare the organization of the Texas House of Representatives and the Texas Senate.

Merely bringing legislators together in the Capitol does not ensure the making of laws or any other governmental activity. Gathering people to transact official business requires organized effort. Formal organization of the Texas legislature features a presiding officer and several committees for each chamber. Informal organization involves various caucuses that do not have legal status but must register with the Texas Ethics Commission.

Presiding Officers

The Texas Constitution establishes the offices of president of the Senate and speaker of the House of Representatives. It designates the lieutenant governor (informally called the "lite" governor) as president of the Senate and provides for the election of a speaker to preside over the House of Representatives. Important powers exercised by these presiding officers include appointing standing committee members and chairs, breaking tie votes, directing bills to committees, interpreting rules of procedure, scheduling and controlling floor action, recognizing members for points of order and bill amendments, and appointing members of conference and joint committees.

President of the Senate: The Lieutenant Governor The most important function of the lieutenant governor of Texas is to serve as **president of the Senate**.[16] Just as the vice president of the United States is empowered to preside over the U.S. Senate but is not a member of that national lawmaking body, so too the lieutenant governor of Texas is not a member of the state Senate. The big difference between them is that the lieutenant governor presides over most sessions and plays a leading role in legislative matters (see Table 8.3 for powers). The vice president, however, had seldom presided or become involved in the daily business of the U.S. Senate—until 2021. At that time, 50 Republican senators and 50 Democrat senators could produce a deadlock requiring a tie-breaking vote by Vice President Kamela Harris.

Chosen by the people of Texas in a statewide election for a four-year term, the lieutenant governor is first in line of succession in the event of the death, resignation, or removal of the governor. When the governor is absent from the state, the lieutenant governor serves as acting governor and receives the gubernatorial salary, which amounted to slightly more than $400 per day at the beginning of 2021. Ordinarily, however, the lieutenant governor's salary is $600 per month. That amounts to about $20 per day.

president of the Senate Title of the lieutenant governor in his or her role as presiding officer for the Texas Senate.

Most of the lieutenant governor's powers are granted by the Senate Rules rather than by the Texas Constitution. Nevertheless, this official is perhaps the most powerful elected officer in the state, especially when the legislature is in session. At the end of the 84th regular session, Dan Patrick told reporters, "I will

Table 8.3 Comparison of Powers of Presiding Officers

Lieutenant Governor (President of the Senate)	Speaker of the House
Issues interim charges to standing committees for subjects to be studied in the interim between regular sessions	Same as Lieutenant Governor
Creates and abolishes committees	Same as Lieutenant Governor
Appoints Senate committee and subcommittee chairs and vice chairs	Same as Lieutenant Governor
Appoints all members of Senate committees and subcommittees	Appoints most members of House committees and subcommittees (limited by seniority rules)
Determines the Senate committee to which a bill will be sent after introduction	Same as Lieutenant Governor
Recognizes senators who wish to speak on the Senate floor or make a motion	Same as Lieutenant Governor
Votes only to break a tie vote	Votes (rarely) on bills and resolutions
Serves as joint chair of the Legislative Council, the Legislative Budget Board, and the Legislative Audit Committee	Same as Lieutenant Governor

— Competency Connection —
☼ **CRITICAL THINKING** ☼

How important is it for representatives and senators to be political allies of the presiding officers? Are there consequences to being an opponent of the presiding officers?

never be running against Greg Abbott for governor." Then he added, "I will be lieutenant governor. This will be my last job in Texas. I love this job. This is where the action is. It's a lot of fun."[17]

If the lieutenant governor dies, resigns, or assumes another office, the Senate elects one of its members to serve as acting lieutenant governor. At the beginning and end of each session, the Senate elects a president pro tempore, who presides when the lieutenant governor is absent or disabled. Senator Brian Birdwell (R-Granbury) was elected president pro tempore when the legislature convened in January 2021 for its 87th regular session. Donna Campbell (R-New Braunfels) was elected at the end of that session as president pro tempore.

Speaker of the House The presiding officer of the House of Representatives is the **Speaker of the House**, a representative elected to that office for a two-year term by the House in an open (that is, not secret) vote by the House membership.[18] A speaker has use of an apartment in the Capitol. Proceedings in the House are controlled by the speaker (see Table 8.3), who may vote on any bill but seldom does. Many observers argue the speaker is the second most powerful official in state government. Like the president of the Senate, most of the speaker's powers are outlined in House Rules. One rule authorizes the speaker to name another representative to preside over the chamber temporarily. The speaker may also

Speaker of the House
The state representative elected by House members to serve as the presiding officer for that chamber.

name a member of the House, who is typically a strong supporter of the speaker, to serve as permanent speaker pro tempore for as long as the speaker desires. At the beginning of the 87th session, Speaker Dade Phelan (R-Beaumont) appointed Joe Moody (D-El Paso) to this position. A speaker pro tempore performs all the duties of the speaker when that officer is absent.[19]

Because of the speaker's power, filling this House office involves intense political activity. Lobbyists make every effort to ensure the election of a speaker sympathetic to their respective clients and causes. Potential candidates for the position begin to line up support several months or even years before a speaker's race begins. Long before this election, anyone aspiring to the office of speaker will attempt to induce House members to sign cards pledging their support. House rules, however, prohibit soliciting written pledges during a regular session. After being elected, a speaker usually finds it easier to obtain similar pledges of support for reelection to the speakership.

Speaker candidates must file with the Texas Ethics Commission. No limitations on donations exist. According to a judicial decision, any attempts to limit spending are unconstitutional because such restrictions would "significantly chill political speech protected by the First Amendment" of the U.S. Constitution.[20] In 2019, Dennis Bonnen (R-Angleton) was elected unanimously as speaker at the beginning of the 86th regular session. Bonnen did not seek reelection to the House in 2020 after the release of a recording of a meeting in which he made disparaging comments about fellow Republicans. In January 2021, a coalition of House Republican and Democrat representatives elected a new speaker, Dade Phelan (R-Beaumont).

Bonnen's downfall resulted from a secretly taped meeting on June 12, 2020, with Representative Dustin Burrows (R-Lubbock) and conservative activist Michael Quinn Sullivan (known around Austin as MQS and nicknamed "Mucus" by critics). At that time, Sullivan headed Empower Texans, a conservative advocacy group funded largely by Midland oil tycoon Tim Dunn and comprising a web of nonprofit organizations and political action committees. In July 2020, Sullivan publicized the content of his recording. Then on October 19, 2020, he released the tape that features scurrilous statements by Bonnen concerning both Republican and Democrat representatives. This tape reveals that Speaker Bonnen offered press credentials for media access to the House chamber for Empower Texans personnel in return for helping to defeat 10 Republican representatives who displeased him. At the same time, Bonnen offered to take press credentials away from Scott Braddock, a reporter for *Quorum Report*. This daily nonpolitical newsletter had criticized Empower Texans. Subsequently, Sullivan left Empower Texans and became president of Texas ScorecardMedia and editor of the *Texas Scorecard* blog.[21] In an unrelated case, an Austin judge supported the Texas Ethics Commission that fined Sullivan $10,000 for failing to register as a lobbyist.[22]

Committee System

Presiding officers appoint committee members, designate committee chairs and vice chairs, and determine the standing committees to which bills will be referred. (See Table 8.4 for number of members on the 87th Legislature's House and Senate standing committees, along with party affiliation for members and the name of

Table 8.4 Committees (with numbers of members, party affiliations [Republican, R; Democrat, D], and chairs), 87th Texas Legislature, January 2021–January 2023

House Standing Committees (substantive committees in regular print, *procedural committees* in italics)

1. Agriculture & Livestock, R5+D4/Dewayne Burns (R-Cleburne)
2. Appropriations, R16+D11/Gregg Bonnen (R-Friendswood)
3. Business & Industry, R5+D4/Chris Turner (D-Dallas)
4. *Calendars*, R11+D4/Dustin Burrows (R-Lubbock)
5. Corrections, R6+D3/Andrew Murr (R-Junction)
6. County Affairs, R5+D4/Garnet Coleman (D-Houston)
7. Criminal Jurisprudence, R5+D4/Nicole Collier (D-Fort Worth)
8. Culture, Recreation & Tourism, R5+D4/Ken King (R-Canadian)
9. Defense & Veterans' Affairs, R5+D4/Richard Peña Raymond (D-Laredo)
10. Elections, R5+D4/Briscoe Cain (R-Houston)
11. Energy Resources, R6+D5/Craig Goldman (R-Fort Worth)
12. Environmental Regulation, R5+D4/Brooks Landgraf (R-Odessa)
13. *General Investigating*, R3+D2/Matt Krause (R-Fort Worth)
14. Higher Education, R5+D6/Jim Murphy (R-Houston)
15. Homeland Security & Public Safety, R6+D3/James White (R-Hillister)
16. *House Administration*, R6+D5/Will Metcalf (R-Conroe)
17. Human Services, R5+D4/James Frank (R-Wichita Falls)
18. Insurance, R5+D4/Tom Oliverson (R-Cypress)
19. International Relations & Economic Development, R5+D4/Angie Chen Button (R-Garland)
20. Judiciary & Civil Jurisprudence, R5+D4/Jeff Leach (R-Plano)
21. Juvenile Justice & Family Issues, R5+D4/Victoria Neave (D-Dallas)
22. Land & Resource Management, R5+D4/Joe Deshotel (D-Beaumont)
23. Licensing & Administrative Procedures, R6+D5/Senfronia Thompson (D-Houston)
24. *Local & Consent Calendars*, R6+D5/Charlie Geren (R-Fort Worth)
25. Natural Resources, R6+D5/Tracy O. King (D-Uvalde)
26. Pensions, Investments, and Financial Services, R5+D4/Rafael Anchia (D-Dallas)
27. Public Education, R7+D6/Harold V. Dutton, Jr. (D-Houston)
28. Public Health, R7+D4/Stephanie Klick (R-Fort Worth)
29. *Redistricting*, R8+D7/Todd Hunter (R-Corpus Christi)
30. *Resolutions Calendars*, R6+D5/Ryan Guillen (D-Rio Grande City)
31. State Affairs, R8+D5/Chris Paddie (R-Marshall)
32. Transportation, R7+D6/Terry Canales (D-Edinburg)
33. Urban Affairs, R3+D6/Philip Cortes (D-San Antonio)
34. Ways & Means, R6+D5/Morgan Meyer (R-Dallas)

Senate Standing Committees

1. Administration, R4+D3/Charles Schwertner (R-Georgetown)
2. Business & Commerce, R6+D3/Kelly D. Hancock (R-N. Richland Hills)
3. Criminal Justice, R4+D3/John Whitmire (D-Houston)
4. Education, R7+D4/Larry Taylor (R-Friendswood)
5. Finance, R12+D3/Eddie Lucio, Jr. (D-Brownsville)
6. Health & Human Services, R6+D3/Lois W. Kolkhorst (R-Brenham)
7. Higher Education, R5+D4/Brandon Creighton (R-Conroe)
8. Jurisprudence, R3+D2/Joan Huffman (R-Houston)
9. Local Government, R5+D4/Paul Bettencourt (R-Houston)
10. Natural Resources & Economic Development, R5+D4/Brian Birdwell (R-Granbury)
11. Nominations, R5+D4/Dawn Buckingham (R-Lakeway)
12. State Affairs, R6+D3/Brian Hughes (R-Tyler)
13. Transportation, R5+D4/Robert Nichols (R-Jacksonville)
14. Veterans Affairs & Border Security, R4+D3/Donna Campbell (R-New Braunfels)
15. Water, Agriculture & Rural Affairs, R5+D4/Charles Perry (R-Lubbock)

Other Senate Committees

Select Committee on Ports, R4+D3/Brandon Creighton (R-Conroe)

Special Committee on Redistricting, R10+D7/Joan Huffman (R-Houston)

Sources: Texas Legislature Online, including websites for the House (*https://house.texas.gov/committees*) and Senate (*https://senate.texas.gov/committees.php*); and *Texas Legislative Handbook: 2021–2022 Legislative Roster with Committees* (Austin: Texas State Directory Press, 2021).

— Competency Connection —
☼ **CRITICAL THINKING** ☼

How could serving on a specific committee benefit a legislator?

substantive committee
With members appointed by the House speaker, this permanent committee considers bills and resolutions related to the subject identified by its name (such as the House Agriculture and Livestock Committee) and may recommend passage of proposed legislation to the appropriate calendars committee.

procedural committee
These permanent House committees (such as the Calendars Committee and House Administration Committee) consider bills and resolutions relating primarily to procedural legislative matters.

select committee
This committee, created independently by the House speaker or the lieutenant governor, may consider legislation that crosses committee jurisdictional lines or may conduct special studies.

interim committee
A House or Senate committee appointed by the speaker or lieutenant governor to study an important policy issue between regular sessions.

standing committee
A permanent Senate or House committee whose members are appointed by the president of the Senate or the speaker for the purpose of considering proposed bills and resolutions before possible floor debate and voting.

each committee chair.) To consider legislation that crosses the jurisdictional lines of standing committees, presiding officers may appoint select committees. These are temporary committees that may include members who are not legislators. For example, in 2021 Dan Patrick appointed the Select Committee on Ports. In addition, presiding officers may appoint members of joint interim study committees composed of senators and representatives (and in some cases, private citizens). Joint committees make recommendations for consideration by both the House and the Senate. Because House and Senate committees play important roles in the fate or fortune of all bills and resolutions, selection of committee members goes a long way toward determining the amount and type of legislative output during a session. Permanent staff members are available to assist legislators with standing committee work on a continuing basis. Usually, these staff members also work with interim study committees created to examine legislative issues between regular sessions.

House Standing Committees In the Texas House of Representatives, **substantive committees** consider bills and resolutions relating to the subject identified by a committee's name (for example, elections or transportation). Substantive committees sometimes have subcommittees in which a few of the committee's members focus more closely on specific issues under the committee's jurisdiction. Seniority, based on years of service in the House of Representatives, determines a maximum of one-half the membership for substantive committees, excluding the chair and the vice chair. When a regular session begins, each representative, in order of seniority, designates three committees in order of preference. A representative is entitled to become a member of the committee of highest preference that has a vacant seniority position. The speaker appoints other committee members.

Seniority does not apply to membership on **procedural committees**, each of which considers bills and resolutions relating primarily to an internal legislative matter (for example, the Calendars Committee, which determines when a bill will be considered by the full House). The speaker appoints all members of procedural committees. Despite protests by strong GOP partisans, Speaker Dade Phelan appointed 13 Democrats to head standing committees in 2021. See Table 8.4.

Although substantive and procedural committees are established under House rules adopted in each regular session, the speaker independently creates **select committees** and **interim committees**. In addition, the speaker appoints all members of these committees. A speaker usually creates select committees during a session to consider legislation that crosses committee jurisdictional lines or during an interim (between regular sessions) to conduct special studies.

Senate Standing Committees Senate rules provide for **standing committees** (though the rules do not identify them as substantive or procedural committees), select committees, interim committees, and special committees like the 17-member Special Committee on Redistricting appointed by Lieutenant Governor Dan Patrick in 2021. Standing committees sometimes have subcommittees. As president of the Senate, the lieutenant governor appoints all committee members and designates the chair and vice chair of each committee. Lieutenant Governor Dan Patrick exercised this power by naming only one Democratic senator, John Whitmire, to chair a standing committee for the 87th Legislature.

Legislative Caucus System

Legislative caucuses are organized on the basis of partisan, philosophical, racial, ethnic, or other special interests. Until the 1990s, Democratic leadership in the Texas House of Representatives and the Senate absorbed potential opponents within their teams and discouraged caucuses. By March 2021, however, 37 caucuses were registered with the Texas Ethics Commission as required by law. Although increasingly important for legislators and interest groups, legislative caucuses are prohibited from receiving public money. These groups stay connected to voters through social media such as Facebook, Twitter, Pinterest, and RSS feeds. Some groups attempt to heighten the impact of their messages by subscribing to services such as ShareThis. Supporters become a distribution network sending press releases and other information through their social networks. Some caucuses do not have web pages. They rely solely on Facebook and other social media platforms to engage voters who share their interests.

Party Caucuses Strengthened party caucuses in each chamber of the Texas legislature is one indication that Texas has become a two-party state. The House Democratic Caucus was organized in 1981. In recent years, all Democratic legislators have been reported as belonging to their party's House or Senate caucuses. Under the leadership of Tom Craddick (R-Midland), the House Republican Caucus was organized in 1989. For the 87th Legislature, Jim Murphy (R-Houston) served as chair of that caucus; and Democrats elected Chris Turner (D-Arlington) for his third term as chair of the House Democratic Caucus.

Although they have no formal organizational role in either chamber, party caucuses take policy positions on some issues and promote unity among their members. Strong party caucuses increase party-line votes. In recent years, Republican legislators have become more conservative and Democratic legislators have tended to be more liberal. This growing partisanship makes cooperation across party lines more difficult. It is a reflection of the political polarization that has widened political space between Republicans and Democrats throughout Texas. In the legislature, it causes problems for many lawmakers trying to muster support for their bills and resolutions.

Racial/Ethnic Caucuses Racial and ethnic groups also organize and form voting blocs to maximize their power. Because Blacks and Latinos constitute significant minorities in the Texas legislature, it is not surprising that they have formed caucuses for this purpose. The Legislative Black Caucus concentrates on issues affecting Black Texans, such as hate crimes laws and the criminal justice system.

The House-based Mexican American Legislative Caucus focuses on such issues as voting rights and providing higher education opportunities in South Texas and along the Mexican border. Members of the caucus led efforts to establish the University of Texas–Rio Grande Valley, a merger of UT-Pan American and UT at Brownsville. In 2021, all members were Latinos except one Asian American.

legislative caucus
An organization of legislators who seek to maximize their influence over issues in which they have a special interest.

Ideological Caucuses House-based ideological caucuses have also emerged. With more than 70 members in 2021, the Texas Conservative Coalition attracts Republicans and conservative Democrats, whereas the liberal Legislative Study Group appeals to many Democrats (including several who are also members of the Legislative Black Caucus and the Mexican American Legislative Caucus). In 2021, the Texas Freedom Caucus with 9 members (all White Republican representatives) claimed to be "The Voice of Liberty-minded, Grassroots Texans." Conservative and liberal caucuses reflect opposing views on most issues.

Bipartisan Caucuses Some caucuses are framed around specific issues. Because an issue may be important to both Republicans and Democrats, caucus membership is bipartisan.

Co-chairs Joe Moody (D-El Paso) and Jeff Leach (R-Plano), along with five other Democrats and five Republicans, organized the Criminal Justice Reform Caucus. Among its objectives are changing Texas law on bail practices, arrests for nonjailable offenses, and seizing property without a criminal conviction.[23]

Other Caucuses Some caucuses are based on factors other than party identification, although the membership may include members of only one political party. For example, the Border Caucus is based on geography; but all of its members in 2021 were House Democrats representing districts on the Mexican border. Their principal objectives are to promote economic development along the border and to counter negative publicity about the area. Caucuses have also been formed around issues such as climate concerns (the Texas Caucus on Climate, Environment, and the Energy Industry) and LGBTQ rights (the House LGBTQ Caucus). Only Democratic legislators were members of these groups in 2021.

◆ Legislative Operations

LO 8.4   Outline the responsibilities of the Texas legislature.

As the chief agent in making public policy in Texas state government, the legislature must have powers to function. Legislators also need immunity from interference while performing their official duties. Thus, lawmaking is governed by detailed rules of procedure for each legislative chamber.

Powers and Immunities

Although bound by restrictions found in few state constitutions, the legislature is the dominant branch of Texas government and the chief agent in making public policy. Legislators control government spending, which makes state agencies and personnel—and, to some extent, units of local government—dependent upon them. Composed of one or more appropriation bills, the biennial state budget authorizes state spending. The budget is the most important legislation for regular (and sometimes special) sessions. To become law, an appropriation bill must pass in both legislative chambers, but it is subject to the governor's line-item veto power (see Chapter 9, The Executive Branch). Although appropriation bills may originate

✓ **8.3 Learning Check**

1. True or False: The speaker of the House of Representatives presides over that body but cannot vote on a bill or resolution.
2. In the Texas Senate, who determines the committee to which a bill will be sent after its introduction?

Answers at the end of this chapter.

in either the House or the Senate, all revenue-producing bills, such as a bill that imposes a state tax, must originate in the House. (For more on taxing and spending, see Chapter 11, Finance and Fiscal Policy.) Along with their powers, lawmakers have immunities from prosecution designed to allow them to function freely.

Making Public Policy The most typical exercise of legislative power involves making public policy by passing bills and adopting resolutions. All proposed legislation must be introduced by an elected senator or representative in the appropriate chamber; however, private citizens and interest groups often communicate their desire for new laws to elected officials. Commentators frequently criticize the legislative process, noting that campaign donors and their lobbyists are more likely to gain support for their proposals than the average citizen.

Each bill or resolution has a distinctive abbreviation that indicates the chamber of origin, and every legislative proposal is given a number indicating the order of introduction. For example, SB 75 would be the seventy-fifth bill introduced in the Senate during a session. An official website, *Texas Legislature Online*, maintains the history, text, analysis, and any fiscal note for each proposed bill or resolution. If requested, it alerts a legislator or any other person to any bill filed on a topic, Another website, *Legiscan*, also provides tracking for Texas legislation and that of other states, as well as the U.S. Congress.

A **simple resolution**, abbreviated HR (House Resolution) if introduced in the House and SR (Senate Resolution) if introduced in the Senate, involves action by one chamber only and is not sent to the governor. Adoption requires a simple majority vote (more than one-half) of members present. Matters dealt with by simple resolution affect only the chamber that is voting on the resolution and include rules of the House or Senate, procedures for House or Senate operations, and invitations extended to nonmembers to address a particular chamber.

After adoption by simple majority votes of members present in both the House and the Senate, a **concurrent resolution** (HCR or SCR) is sent to the governor, who has two options: sign it or veto it. Typical examples are resolutions that request action by the U.S. Congress; grant permission to sue the state; or name state icons, such as the state squash (pumpkin), state handgun (1847 Walker/Colt revolver), and state musical instrument (guitar). In addition, the chambers adopt a concurrent resolution to adjourn at the end of any legislative session—a measure that does not require approval by the governor.

Adoption of a **joint resolution** (HJR or SJR) requires approval by both houses but no action by the governor. The nature of a joint resolution determines whether a simple majority or a two-thirds vote is required. Proposed amendments to the Texas Constitution are examples of joint resolutions requiring a two-thirds majority vote of the membership of each house. (If you don't understand how joint resolutions affect the length of the Texas Constitution, remember this often-quoted comparison with Tolstoy's great novel: "Both the Texas Constitution and *War and Peace* are long, but *War and Peace* isn't getting any longer!") Ratification of proposed U.S. constitutional amendments that require a vote of state legislatures are approved with a joint resolution adopted by simple majority votes of members present in both houses. Likewise, the same simple majority vote is required to adopt a joint resolution requesting creation of a constitutional convention for proposing amendments to the U.S. Constitution.

simple resolution
A resolution that requires action by one legislative chamber only and is not acted on by the governor.

concurrent resolution
A resolution adopted by House and Senate majorities and then approved by the governor (for example, a request for action by Congress or authorization for someone to sue the state).

joint resolution
A resolution that must pass by a majority vote in each house when used to ratify an amendment to the U.S. Constitution or to request a constitutional convention to propose amendments to the U.S. Constitution. As a proposal for an amendment to the Texas Constitution, a joint resolution requires a two-thirds majority vote of the total membership for each house.

Before enactment, a proposed law is known as a **bill** (House bill [HB] or Senate bill [SB]). Each regular session brings forth an avalanche of bills, but only 19 percent became law in 2019. In that year's regular session of the 86th Legislature, 4,765 bills were introduced in the House and 2,559 in the Senate. Together, both chambers enacted 969 House bills and 460 Senate bills. The governor vetoed 41 House bills and 15 Senate bills.[24]

For purposes of classification, bills fall into three categories: special, general, and local. A special bill makes an exception to general laws for the benefit of a specific individual, class, or corporation. Of greater importance are general bills, which apply to all people or property in all parts of Texas. To become law, a bill must pass by a simple majority of votes of members present in both the House and the Senate, but a two-thirds majority vote of the membership in each chamber is required to pass an emergency measure that will take effect as soon as the governor signs it. A local bill creates or affects a single unit of local government (for example, a city, county, or special district). Such bills usually pass without opposition if sponsored by all legislators representing the affected area.

Administrative and Investigative Powers The legislature also defines responsibilities of state agencies and imposes restrictions on them through appropriation of money for operations and through **oversight** of activities. One form of oversight involves requiring state agencies to make periodic and special reports to the legislature.

Both the House and the Senate receive information from the state auditor concerning irregular or inefficient use of state funds by administrative agencies. The auditor is appointed by (and serves at the will of) the Legislative Audit Committee. This six-member committee is composed of the speaker, the chair of the House Appropriations Committee, the chair of the House Ways and Means Committee, the lieutenant governor, the chair of the Senate Finance Committee, and a senator appointed by the lieutenant governor.

Another control over state agencies is the legislature's Sunset Advisory Commission, which makes recommendations to the House and Senate concerning the continuation, merger, division, or abolition of nearly every state agency. Affected agencies are reviewed every 12 years (see Chapter 9, The Executive Branch).

Most of the governor's board and commission appointments to head state agencies must be submitted to the Senate and approved by at least two-thirds of senators present. Thus, the Senate influences the selection of many important officials. The unwritten rule of **senatorial courtesy** requires that the Senate "bust" (reject) an appointment if the appointee is declared "personally objectionable" by the senator representing the district in which the appointee resides. Consequently, a governor will privately seek prior approval by that senator before announcing a selection.

To support its power to exercise oversight of administrative agencies and to investigate problems that may require legislation, the legislature has authority to subpoena witnesses, administer oaths, and compel submission of records and documents. Such action may be taken jointly by the two houses as a body, by one house, or by a committee of either house. Refusal to obey a subpoena may result in prosecution for contempt of the legislature, which is punishable by a jail sentence of from 30 days to a year and a fine ranging from $100 to $1,000.[25]

bill
A proposed law or statute.

oversight
A legislative function that requires reports from state agencies concerning their operations; the state auditor provides information on agencies' use of state funds.

senatorial courtesy
Before making an appointment, the governor is expected to obtain approval from the state senator in whose district the prospective appointee resides; failure to obtain such approval will probably cause the Senate to "bust" the appointee.

Impeachment and Removal Powers The House of Representatives has power to **impeach** all elected state judges and justices in Texas, It may also impeach elected executive officers, such as the governor, and appointed state officials, such as members of boards of regents for public university systems. Governor James Ferguson was convicted and removed from office in 1917, as described in Chapter 9, The Executive Branch.

Impeachment involves bringing charges by a simple majority vote of House members present. It resembles the indictment process of a grand jury (see Chapter 10, The Judicial Branch) and the two congressional impeachments of President Donald Trump. After being impeached, an official is suspended from office until the Senate issues judgment. Following impeachment, the Senate conducts a proceeding with the Chief Justice of the Texas Supreme Court presiding, after which it renders judgment. Conviction requires a two-thirds majority vote of the Senate membership. The only punishment that the Senate may impose is removal from office and disqualification from holding any other public office under the Texas Constitution. If a crime has been committed, the deposed official may also be prosecuted before an appropriate court.

Immunities In addition to their constitutional powers, state senators and representatives enjoy legislative immunities conferred by the Texas Constitution. They may not be sued for slander or otherwise held accountable for any statements made in a speech or debate during a legislative proceeding. This protection does not extend to remarks made under other circumstances. They may not be arrested while attending a legislative session or while traveling to or from the legislature's meeting place for the purpose of attending, unless charged with "treason, felony, or breach of the peace."

Rules and Procedures

Enacting a law is not the only way to get things done in Austin. Passing bills and adopting resolutions, however, are the principal means whereby members of the Texas legislature participate in making public policy. The legislature conducts its work according to detailed rules of procedure.

To guide representatives in the 87th regular session, in January 2021, the House adopted HR 4, making several changes in the rules of the preceding session. For example, members, House officers and employees, and other people attending House sessions or committee meetings had to wear face masks that could be removed only for a few reasons, such as addressing the chamber or a committee. When taking testimony during public meetings, only two members had to be physically present to constitute a quorum. At the same time, the Senate adopted SR 2 that made a few changes in its rules. The apparent difference was that Lieutenant Governor Dan Patrick continued to serve as President of the Senate, but Dade Phalen was the newly elected as speaker.

Whether a bill is passed or defeated depends heavily on the skills of sponsors and opponents in using House rules and Senate rules. Experienced legislators are more likely to have bills approved because of their understanding of the rules and stronger relationships with the leadership.

impeach
Process in which the Texas House of Representatives, by a simple majority vote, initiates action (brings charges) leading to possible removal of certain judicial and executive officials (both elected and appointed) by the Senate.

The lieutenant governor and the speaker decide questions concerning interpretation of rules in their respective chambers. Because procedural questions may be complex and decisions must be made quickly, the Senate has one **parliamentarian** and an assistant parliamentarian, while the House has two parliamentarians. They are not legislators, but they assist presiding officers in interpreting rules. Positioned on the dais immediately to the left of the lieutenant governor or speaker, this expert on Senate or House rules provides answers to procedural questions.

How a Bill Becomes a Law

The Texas Constitution calls for regular legislative sessions divided into three periods for distinct purposes. The first 30 days are reserved for introduction of bills and resolutions, action on emergency appropriations, and confirmation or rejection of recess appointments (appointments made by the governor between sessions). Bills may be introduced during the second 30 days, but this period is generally devoted to committee consideration of bills and resolutions introduced earlier. The remainder of the session, which amounts to 80 days, is devoted to floor debate and voting on bills and resolutions. Throughout a session, action may be taken at any time on an emergency matter identified by the governor and incorporated into a bill that is introduced by a legislator.

In his biennial State of the State Address, delivered on February 1, 2021, Governor Greg Abbott designated five emergency items for the 87th Legislature:

- Expanding broadband Internet access
- Preventing cities from defunding police departments
- Fixing the bail system and keeping dangerous criminals off the streets
- Ensuring election integrity
- Providing civil liability for businesses, individuals, and healthcare providers that operated safely during the COVID-19 pandemic

On February 16, while millions of Texans suffered from unusually cold weather and loss of electricity, gas, and water, Abbott added a sixth emergency item: investigation of the Electric Reliability Council of Texas (ERCOT).

Released on February 23, Lieutenant Governor Dan Patrick's priority list of 31 items included Governor Abbott's emergency list and was headed by three conservative objectives (called "red-meat" items by critics):

- Limit abortion after detection of heartbeat
- Forbid transgender athletes from competing in women's sports
- Require playing the "Star Spangled Banner" before sporting events

Speaker Dade Phelan did not release a list but his priorities included:

- Balanced budget
- No cuts for public education
- Increased coverage by MEDICARE
- Expanding telemedicine

parliamentarian
An expert on rules of order who sits at the left of the presiding officer in the House or Senate and provides advice on procedural questions.

- Rural healthcare
- No more shutting down of businesses to cope with COVID-19

Drafting a bill and turning it into a law is complex. Many bills originate with a lobbyist or are based on models produced by the American Legislative Exchange Council (ALEC), a national nonprofit organization of private sector representatives and conservative legislators. Certain basic steps in making laws are clearly outlined in detail by House and Senate rules. Although most bills can originate in either chamber, the following paragraphs trace the path of a bill from introduction in the House to action by the governor.[26] Figure 8.4 illustrates this procedure.

1. Introduction in the House As a bill sponsor, any House member may introduce a bill by filing electronically with the chief clerk (or, as required by the Texas Constitution, filing 11 copies of a bill related to conservation and reclamation districts with that official). This staff person supervises legislative administration in the House. Prior to a regular session, members and members-elect (newly elected but not yet having taken the oath of office) may prefile bills as early as the first Monday after the November general election. Members may prefile bills 30 days before the start of a special session (so long as the bills relate to the topic for which the governor convened that session). It is common practice for an identical bill, known as a **companion bill**, to be introduced by a senator in the Senate at the same time the bill is introduced in the House. Likewise, a representative will introduce a companion bill for a bill introduced in the Senate. This action allows simultaneous committee action in the two chambers.

2. First Reading (House) and Referral to Committee The Texas Constitution requires three readings of each bill. After receiving a bill, the chief clerk assigns it a number in order of submission, although the first few numbers are reserved for the most important bills, such as the budget. Then the bill is given to the reading clerk for the first reading. The reading clerk reads aloud the caption (a brief summary of the bill's contents) and announces the committee to which the bill has been assigned by the Speaker.

3. House Committee Consideration and Report Before any committee action, the committee staff must distribute a bill analysis that summarizes important provisions of the bill to committee members.[27] The committee chair decides whether the bill needs a fiscal note (provided by the Legislative Budget Board) projecting the costs of implementing the proposed legislation for five years. The committee chair also decides whether a bill requires the Legislative Budget Board to prepare an impact statement. Among the types of bills requiring an impact statement are those that would alter punishment for a felony offense.

As a courtesy to sponsoring representatives, most bills receive a committee hearing at which lobbyists and other interested persons have an opportunity to express their views. Nevertheless, some bills are "pigeon-holed," which means they are put aside and get no further action. House rules require public notice of any formal meeting or public hearing. Witnesses may also submit online videos. Public hearings are livestreamed, and these hearings are archived on the *Texas*

companion bill
Filed in one house but identical or similar to a bill filed in the other chamber; this simultaneous filing speeds passage of a bill because committee consideration may take place at the same time in both chambers.

Figure 8.4 Route Followed by a House Bill from Texas Legislature to Governor

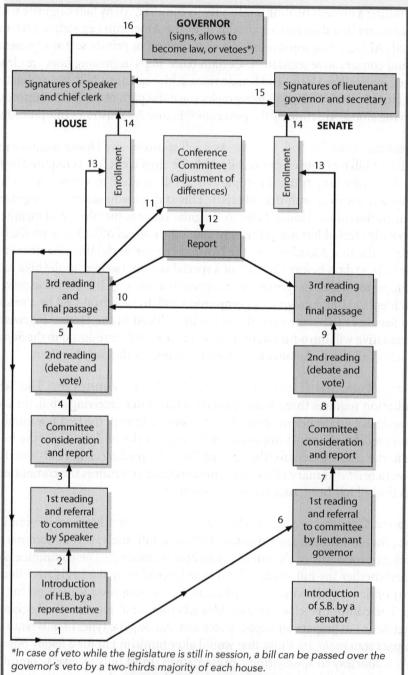

In case of veto while the legislature is still in session, a bill can be passed over the governor's veto by a two-thirds majority of each house.

Source: Prepared with the assistance of Dr. Beryl E. Pettus.

Competency Connection
☆ CRITICAL THINKING ☆

Should the process for a bill's becoming a law be simplified or made more complex?

Legislature Online site. The committee chair decides whether a bill will go to a subcommittee for a hearing. A subcommittee includes only some members of the full committee. After a hearing, the subcommittee submits a written report to the committee. Recommended changes to proposed bills may be made by amendments, in which event the legislature must vote on each proposed amendment, or by substituting a new bill for the proposed bill.

Two committees determine the order in which bills are cleared for floor action. The Local and Consent Calendars Committee and the Calendars Committee conduct sessions that are open to the public, the press, and all representatives. The Local and Consent Calendars Committee assigns three types of legislative proposals to the Local, Consent, and Resolutions Calendar:

- *Local bills* affecting a limited number of localities, districts, counties, or municipalities
- *Consent bills* that are uncontested and not likely to face opposition
- *Noncontroversial resolutions*, other than congratulatory and memorial resolutions

The Calendars Committee places other bills on four daily calendars:

- *Emergency Calendar*, for bills needing immediate action, as well as all taxing and spending bills
- *Major State Calendar*, for nonemergency bills that change policy in a major field of government activity and that have a major statewide impact
- *General State Calendar*, for nonemergency bills having statewide application but limited legal effect and policy impact
- *Constitutional Amendments Calendar*, for proposed amendments to the Texas Constitution

Within 30 days after receiving a bill, a calendars committee must decide by record vote whether to place the bill on a calendar for floor consideration. After this period expires, any representative may introduce a motion on the House floor to place the bill on an appropriate calendar. If the motion is seconded by five representatives and adopted by a simple majority vote, the House may schedule the bill for floor action without approval of a calendars committee. This procedure is seldom attempted. Because of the authority to decide if a bill will be placed on the calendar, the chair of the Calendars Committee is often identified as the fourth most powerful state government official, only less powerful than the lieutenant governor, the speaker, and the governor.

4. Second Reading, Debate, and Vote (House) Usually, the second reading is limited to caption only. The author of a bill, the committee member reporting on behalf of the committee, or another designated member has the privilege of beginning and ending floor debate with a speech of not more than 20 minutes. Other House members may speak for not more than 10 minutes each, unless extra time is granted. A computer on each representative's desk provides easy access to the text of amendments proposed during floor debate. After discussion ends and any amendments are added, a vote is taken on "passage

Image 8.4 Chamber of the Texas House of Representatives, 87th regular session, 2021.

Photo provided by the House Photography Department

Image 8.5 Chamber of the Texas Senate, 87th regular session, 2021.

Photo is provided by the Senate Photography Department.

Competency Connection
☼ **CRITICAL THINKING** ☼

Should the galleries be expanded to accommodate more visitors to each chamber?

to engrossment" (preparation of an officially inscribed copy). A quorum (the minimum number required to do business) is constituted when at least two-thirds of the House members (100 representatives) are present.

Approval of a bill on second reading requires a simple majority vote. A motion may be made to suspend the rules by a four-fifths majority vote of members present and to give the bill an immediate third reading. Thus, an exception can be made to the constitutional rule that all bills must be read on three separate days, though an exception for the third reading is seldom made in the House.

Provisions of the Texas Constitution, statutes, procedural rules, and practices within the respective chambers govern legislative voting. A record vote usually involves an electronic system. Votes are recorded and tallied as each representative presses the button on a desktop voting machine. This action turns on a light (green, yes; red, no; white, present but not voting) beside the representative's name on the two huge tote boards mounted on the wall behind the House speaker's podium. House and Senate journals list the record votes of members of the respective chambers. Action by three House members is required to call for a record vote. House rules prohibit **ghost voting** (pressing the voting button for another representative) unless a member has given permission for that vote to be cast. When a representative asks for "strict enforcement," the voting machine of an absent member is locked.

Occasionally (especially at the end of a session), representatives engage in lengthy debates on bills they do not oppose (called buffer bills) or on the actual bill they are opposing. Such action is intended to prevent the House from voting on a bill that would probably be approved if brought up for a vote. This delaying action is called **chubbing**. If 100 or more members vote to suspend House rules, chubbing can be ended.

ghost voting
A prohibited practice whereby one representative presses the voting button of another House member who is absent.

chubbing
A practice whereby representatives engage in lengthy debate for the purpose of using time and thus preventing a vote on a bill that they oppose.

To limit legislative logjams and discourage uninformed voting in the final days of a regular session, House rules contain prohibitions against second and third readings for the following bills:

- Nonlocal House bills during the last 17 days
- Local House bills during the last 10 days
- Senate bills during the last five days

Other detailed restrictions apply to House actions on the 126th to 139th days of a regular session. On the 140th, or final, day, House voting is limited to correcting bills that have passed. The Senate has similar end-of-session restrictions on considering legislation.

5. Third Reading and Final Passage (House) On the third reading, passage of a bill requires a simple majority vote of members present. Amendments may still be added at this stage, but such action requires a two-thirds majority vote. After the addition of an amendment, a copy of the amended bill is made, checked over by the chief clerk, and stamped "Engrossed."

6. First Reading and Referral to Committee (Senate) After a bill passes on the third reading in the House, the chief clerk adds a statement certifying passage and transmits the bill to the Senate (where the original House number is retained). In the Senate, the secretary of the Senate reads aloud the House bill's caption and announces the committee to which the bill has been assigned by the lieutenant governor. All House bills sent to the Senate must have a Senate sponsor; likewise, all Senate bills sent to the House must have a House sponsor.

7. Senate Committee Consideration and Report Senate procedure differs somewhat from House procedure. A senator may "tag" any bill by filing a request with either the Senate secretary or the committee chair to notify the tagging senator 48 hours before a hearing will be held on the bill. A tag usually kills the bill if done during the last days of a session.

If a majority of the committee members wants a bill to pass, it receives a favorable report. Bills are listed on the Senate's Regular Order of Business in the order in which the secretary of the Senate receives them. Unlike the House, the Senate has no calendar committees to control the flow of bills from standing committees to the Senate floor. At the beginning of each session, however, the Senate Administration Committee parks a "blocker" at the head of the line. For the 87th regular session in 2021, there were bill and joint resolution blocking measures by Sen. Charles Schwertner (R-Georgetown): SB 637 establishing a county park beautification program and SJR 37 authorizing the state to receive gifts of historic value. Bills and joint resolutions arriving later are designated "out of order," and a vote of five-ninths (18 senators) is required to suspend the regular order (that is, bypass the blocker) and bring the "out-of-order" bill or joint resolution to the Senate floor for debate. Since 2015, under Lieutenant Governor Dan Patrick's leadership, the supermajority required to bypass a blocker bill has been reduced (as Republican membership declined) from the two-thirds rule (21 senators) to the three-fifths rule (19 senators) and most recently to the **five-ninths rule** (18 senators) in 2021.

five-ninths rule
A procedural device to control bringing bills to the Senate floor for debate.

Image 8.6 Speaker Dade Phelan congratulates Baylor University's basketball coach, Scott Drew (left), basketball team members, and Baylor's president, Dr. Linda A. Livingstone (right), for winning the NCAA championship in 2021.

Photo provided by Senate Photography Department

— Competency Connection —
✿ **CRITICAL THINKING** ✿

Was it appropriate for Speaker Dade Phelan to take time in the House chamber to congratulate Baylor's team for winning the NCAA championship?

8. Second Reading, Debate, and Vote (Senate) As with second readings in the House, the Senate debates the bill and considers proposed amendments. A computer on the desk of each senator displays the texts of proposed amendments. During the debate, custom permits a senator to speak about a bill as long as physical endurance permits. This delaying tactic is known as **filibustering**. But a filibuster may be stopped if another senator is recognized for the privileged, nondebatable motion to "move the previous question," which means requiring an immediate vote. The motion must be seconded by at least five senators; and to pass, it requires a majority vote of senators who are present. Another privileged, nondebatable motion that can halt a filibuster is a motion to adjourn or recess. A filibuster is most effective if undertaken toward the end of a session when time is short.

In 2013, for example, Senator Wendy Davis killed an abortion bill (SB 5) during the 83rd Legislature's first special session. Through a series of procedural challenges from both Republicans and Democrats, Republican senators ended the filibuster with less than 15 minutes remaining. An outburst erupted from the crowd observing the Senate from the gallery located above the Senate chamber. This chaos continued so long that a timely vote did not occur.[28]

When debate ends, a roll call vote is called by the secretary of the Senate. Unless a senator holds up two fingers to indicate an intention to vote no, the presiding officer usually announces that the chamber unanimously approves the bill after only a few names are called. The vote is recorded only if requested by three senators. Each vote requires a quorum of 21 senators present. A simple majority of "yea" votes of members present is sufficient to pass a bill.

filibustering
A delaying tactic whereby a senator may speak, and thus hold the Senate floor, for as long as physical endurance permits, unless action is taken to end the filibuster.

9. Third Reading and Final Passage (Senate) If passed on the second reading, a bill can have its third reading immediately, assuming the rules have been suspended. This action is routinely taken in the Senate by the required four-fifths majority vote of members present. Amending a bill on the third reading requires a two-thirds majority vote of members present. A simple majority vote is required for passage.

10. Return to the House After passage by the Senate, a House bill returns to the chief clerk of the House, who supervises preparation of a perfect copy of the bill and delivers it to the Speaker. When an amendment has been added in the Senate (as usually happens), the change must be voted on in the House. If the House is not prepared to accept the amended bill, the ordinary procedure is to request a conference. Otherwise, the bill will die unless one of the chambers reverses its position.

11. Conference Committee When the two chambers agree to send the bill to conference, each presiding officer appoints five members to serve on the **conference committee**. Attempts are made to adjust differences and produce a compromise version acceptable to both the House and the Senate. At least three Senate members and three House members must agree before the committee can recommend a course of action in the two houses. The author of the bill usually serves as the conference committee chair.

12. Conference Committee Report The conference committee's recommended settlement of questions at issue must be fully accepted or rejected by a simple majority vote in each chamber. Most recommendations are accepted. Both chambers, however, may agree to return the report to the committee, or on request of the House, the Senate may accept a proposal for a new conference.

13. Enrollment After both chambers have accepted a conference report, the chief clerk of the House prepares a perfect copy of the bill and stamps it "Enrolled." The report is then presented to the House.

14. Signatures of the Chief Clerk and Speaker When the House receives the enrolled bill and the conference committee report, the bill is identified by chamber of origin and read by number only. Subsequently, it is signed by the chief clerk, who certifies the vote by which it passed. Then the House speaker signs the bill.

15. Signatures of the Secretary of the Senate and the Lieutenant Governor Next, the chief clerk of the House takes the bill to the Senate, where it is read by number only. After certifying a passing vote, the secretary of the Senate signs the bill. Then the lieutenant governor does likewise.

16. Action by the Governor While the legislature remains in session, the governor has three options:

- Sign the bill
- Allow the bill to remain unsigned for 10 days, not including Sundays, after which time it becomes law without the chief executive's signature, or
- Within the 10-day period, veto the bill by returning it to the House, unsigned, with a message giving a reason for the veto (or to the Senate if a bill originated there).

conference committee
A committee composed of representatives and senators appointed to reach agreement on a disputed bill and recommend changes acceptable to both chambers.

✓ **8.4 Learning Check**

1. What is the most typical way in which the legislature exercises its legislative power?
2. True or False: Members of the Texas House of Representatives have no way to delay a vote on a bill through debate.

Answers at the end of this chapter.

The Texas Constitution requires a vote of "two-thirds of the membership present" in the first chamber that considers a vetoed bill (in this case, the House of Representatives) and a vote of "two-thirds of the members" in the second chamber (in this case, the Senate) to override the governor's veto.[29]

Many important bills do not reach the governor's desk until the end of a legislative session. After a session ends, the governor has 20 days, counting Sundays, in which to veto pending legislation and file the rejected bills with the secretary of state. A bill not vetoed by the governor automatically becomes law at the end of the 20-day period. Because the legislature is no longer in session, the governor's post-adjournment veto is of special importance because it cannot be overridden. Govenor Abbott vetoed 20 bills after the end of the 87th regular session in 2021.

❂ Influences Within the Legislative Environment

LO 8.5 Explain the influences on legislators' voting decisions.

In theory, elected legislators are influenced primarily, if not exclusively, by their constituents (especially constituents who vote rather than those who make big campaign contributions). In practice, however, many legislators' actions bear little relation to the needs or interests of the "folks back home." Texas senators and representatives are not completely indifferent to voters, but many of them fall short of being genuinely representative.

Large numbers of citizens are uninterested in most governmental affairs and have no opinions about how the legislature should act in making public policy. Others may have opinions but are inarticulate or unable to communicate with their legislators. Therefore, lawmakers are likely to yield not only to the influence of the presiding officers in the House and Senate but also to pressure from the governor. A threatened gubernatorial veto can kill a bill, as occurred with proposed legislation to ban texting while driving during the 83rd legislative session. The chair of the Senate Transportation Committee allowed the bill to die in committee, remarking, "If it is not going to pass in the governor's mansion, why do we need to go through this?"[30] A similar bill was passed and signed by Governor Abbott in 2017. Other powerful political actors include the attorney general and judges who determine the constitutionality of laws; the state comptroller, who estimates state revenue for budgeting purposes; and lobbyists, who seek to win voluntary support or force cooperation for legislation that benefits the special interests they represent.

Events influence the introduction and passage of laws. Sources of information and influence include research organizations and the media.

Research Organizations

Policymakers need reliable information. Most Texas legislators depend heavily on information provided by staff personnel, by administrative agencies, and by

📋 Students in Action

An Internship in Texas Government

The Bob Bullock Scholars Program was established through an agreement involving the family of Bob Bullock, members of the Texas Senate, and Baylor University. Funding was provided to allow students to work on a full-time basis during sessions of the Texas Legislature. The first group of Bullock Scholars participated in the 2001 legislative session.

The Bob Bullock Scholars Program was named to honor the memory and numerous contributions to society by Bob Bullock. He graduated from Texas Tech University and Baylor Law School before beginning a career in public service in 1956, with election to the Texas House of Representatives. Following re-election in 1958 and return to private law practice, Bob Bullock served as an assistant attorney general and general counsel for Governor Preston Smith, and as secretary of state.

In 1975, Bob Bullock was elected Comptroller of Public Accounts and served until 1990, bringing Texas into national prominence as a leader in the areas of fiscal responsibility, financial research capabilities, and efficiency in tax collections. He was elected as lieutenant governor and president of the Texas Senate in 1991, a post to which he was re-elected in 1995. Bob Bullock demonstrated vast abilities in the formulation of public policy by empathizing hard work, nonpartisan legislation, and commitment to the people of Texas.

The Bob Bullock Scholars Program is a model for individuals who seek to serve others through a career in public service. Dr. Patrick Flavin, the Bob Bullock Professor of Public Policy and Administration

Legislative Internship Program

Student interns in the Texas Legislature are good examples of students in action. These Baylor interns are accompanied by Rep. Charles "Doc" Anderson (R-Waco), second from left, and Rep. Kyle Kacal (R-College Station), fifth from left.

at Baylor University, serves as the director of the Bob Bullock Scholars Program. Dr. Flavin arranges placements of interns in appropriate legislative offices of the Texas Legislature. Bullock Scholars live in Austin and work on a full-time basis for a member of the Texas Senate or the Texas House of Representatives. Interns are enrolled for a minimum of six semester hours at Baylor University. They receive a monthly stipend to cover living expenses in Austin during the legislative session. There are days of orientation prior to the legislative session.

Dr. Patrick J. Flavin, Bob Bullock Professor of Public Policy and Administration, One Bear Place # 97276, Baylor University, Waco, TX 76798; 254-710-7418; Patrick_J._Flavin@Baylor.edu

Competency Connection
⭐ PERSONAL RESPONSIBILITY ⭐

Would you recommend that a college student apply for a legislative internship? Why or why not?

lobbyists. In addition, legislators obtain information from official research bodies and independent providers of public policy research, sometimes called "think tanks."

The Texas Legislative Council Authorizing special research projects by its staff is one function of the Texas Legislative Council (TLC). This council is overseen by the lieutenant governor (joint chair), the speaker of the House (joint chair), six senators appointed by the lieutenant governor, the chair of the House Administration Committee, and five representatives appointed by the speaker. The council's employees provide bill drafting, advice for legislators, legislative research and writing, publishing and document distribution, interim study committee research support, demographic and statistical data compilation and analysis, computer mapping and analysis for redistricting, and other computer services.

The House Research Organization A bipartisan steering committee of 15 representatives, elected by the House membership for staggered four-year terms, governs the House Research Organization (HRO). Although the HRO is an administrative department of the House, it is independent of the House leadership. Its annual operating budget is set by the steering committee and the House Administration Committee.

In addition to producing reports on a variety of policy issues and House procedures, the HRO prepares the *Daily Floor Report* for each day the legislature is in session. In this publication, HRO personnel analyze important bills to be considered. They provide a summary of bill content and present arguments for and against each bill. After a regular session, HRO publishes *Major Issues*, a report on the session's important bills and resolutions, including some that were defeated.

The Senate Research Center Organized under the secretary of the Senate, the Senate Research Center analyzes bills under consideration by the Senate and conducts research on diverse issues. Primarily, it responds to requests from Senate members for research and information. The lieutenant governor, however, as president of the Senate, also calls on the center's information and expertise. Its periodic publications range from the semimonthly *Clearinghouse Update*, which presents brief accounts of issues facing Texas and the nation, to *Highlights of the [regular session number] . . . Legislature*, which summarizes hundreds of bills and joint resolutions for each regular session. Some other publications produced by the center include *Budget 101: A Guide to the Legislative Process; The Senate Guide to Ethics and Financial Disclosure*; and *Legislative Lexicon*, which defines words, terms, and phrases that form the "legislative lingo" used by legislators and staff.

Every Texan Founded in 1985 as an Austin office of the Benedictine Resource Center, Every Texan (previously known as the Center for Public Policy Priorities) began operating as an independent nonprofit organization in 1999. Its principal focus is on problems of low- and moderate-income families in Texas.[31] Some legislators and other public officials have used its policy analyses on issues ranging from state taxation and appropriations to public education and healthcare access, but critics contend that Every Texan is too liberal.

Texas Public Policy Foundation Established in 1989 in San Antonio, the Texas Public Policy Foundation (TPPF) is primarily funded by conservative activists. It is affiliated with the State Policy Network, which links conservative think tanks and advocacy organizations throughout the country. TPPF focuses its research on issues supporting limited government, free enterprise, private property rights, and individual responsibility. Using policy research and analysis, TPPF seeks to influence Texas government by recommending its findings to legislators and other policymakers, interest group leaders, media reporters, and the general public. An editorial in the liberal *Texas Observer* asserted, "the Texas Public Policy Foundation has become the in-house think tank of the state's current Republican leadership."[32] In fact, the activities and conservative influence of the foundation continue to increase as it operates from a headquarters building near the Capitol.[33]

The Media

Before the development of social media, measuring the influence of media on legislators' political decisions was difficult. (For details concerning social media, see Chapter 6, The Media and Politics.) Identifying the Twitter accounts most frequently followed by legislators now provides insight into the media sources on which officials rely for information. The most frequently followed is the online news site for the *Texas Tribune*. Other important media include the Texas Legislative Reference Library's *Legislative Clippings Service* that reproduces newspaper articles concerning the state's public affairs, *Quorum Report* (a daily online newsletter that focuses on Texas politics and state government), the *Austin American-Statesman* (the capital city's daily newspaper), *Texas Monthly* (a popular magazine), and *Texas Insider* (a website that redistributes press releases and articles from multiple sources). In addition, newsletters and other publications produced for subscribers or members of special interest groups highlight legislators' actions. On some policy issues, lawmakers may be influenced by newspaper editorials and articles, postings by bloggers, and editorial cartoons.[34]

> ### ✓ 8.5 Learning Check
>
> 1. True or False: The House Research Organization influences the House through the *Daily Floor Report*, which presents arguments for and against each bill.
>
> 2. How do social media provide insight on media sources that are important to legislators?
>
> *Answers at the end of this chapter.*

⊠ Keeping Current

Texas Legislature Online shows that 9,966 bills (7,053 House bills and 2,913 Senate bills) were filed for the 87th regular session. Among the 3,187 bills passed by both houses and signed by Governor Abbott were bills concerning

- Governance of the Public Utilities Commission, the Office of Public Utilities, and the Electric Reliability Council of Texas (SB 2)
- Preparing for, preventing, and responding to weather emergencies and power outages (SB 3)
- Abortion after detection of a heartbeat (SB 8)
- Paying college athletes for use of name, image, or likeness (SB 1385)
- Expanding Medicaid benefits for qualified mothers to six months after giving birth or experiencing miscarriage (HB 133)
- Creation of the Gulf Coast Protection District for controlling damage from storms (SB 1160)
- Unlicensed carrying of a gun by persons 21 years of age or older and not prohibited from possessing a firearm (HB 1927)

- Banning critical race theory in the social studies curriculum for public schools (HB 3979)

Most controversial among bills that failed to pass was SB 7. This bill was an election law package that Republicans claimed was needed for election integrity and security, including prevention of fraud. Governor Abbott became angry when Democrats broke a quorum by walking off the House floor and then meeting in the Fellowship Hall of Mount Zion Baptist Church shortly before a midnight deadline for voting on SB 7. A special session was called to begin July 8, 2021. Abbott used an item veto to strike the legislature from the budget for fiscal years 2022 and 2023. Not only would the governor's action prevent payment of salaries to state senators, representatives, and legislative staff, but it would defund the Legislative Council, the Legislative Reference Library, the State Auditor, and the Sunset Advisory Commission. Redistricting for the Texas House and Senate, and for the Texas delegation to the U.S. House of Representatives, were tasks for another special session in 2021.

Conclusion

The framework of the Texas legislature reflects public demand for representative government. Legislators are chosen in popular, partisan elections. Much of the work of both the House and the Senate is done in committees, but floor debate and votes on bills and resolutions attract more public attention. Through their control of state taxing and spending, legislators have an immediate impact on the state's economy and the well-being of all Texans.

Chapter Summary

LO 8.1 Describe the structure of the Texas legislature. The Texas legislature is a bicameral legislature composed of 31 senators elected for four-year terms and 150 representatives elected for two-year terms. Biennial regular sessions are limited to 140 days, and special sessions called by the governor are limited to 30 days. New legislative districts are drawn after each federal decennial census.

LO 8.2 Describe the membership of the Texas legislature. Legislators must be U.S. citizens, qualified Texas voters, and residents of their districts for one year. Minimum Texas residence is one year for representatives and two years for senators. Minimum age is 21 for representatives and 26 for senators. Legislators tend to be White, male, middle-aged Republicans. They are paid $7,200 per year in salary, but they also receive per diem payments and generous retirement benefits after several years of service.

LO 8.3 Compare the organization of the Texas House of Representatives and the Texas Senate. The lieutenant governor presides over the Senate, and the speaker presides over the House. Both appoint committee members and name committee chairs and vice chairs for their respective chambers. Senators and representatives form legislative caucuses, which are groups with common interests. There are party caucuses for Democrats and Republicans, racial/ethnic caucuses for Blacks and Latinos, ideological caucuses for conservatives and liberals, and some bipartisan caucuses organized around specific public policy issues.

LO 8.4 Outline the responsibilities of the Texas legislature. Legislators have primary responsibility for adopting public policy. In addition, they can check the power of the executive and judicial branches through use of their investigative and impeachment powers. Constitutional provisions and rules of the House and Senate control the detailed process whereby a bill is passed in both chambers. The governor may sign a bill, allow it to become law without signing, or veto it. A veto kills a bill unless the veto is overridden by a two-thirds vote in each chamber.

LO 8.5 Explain the influences on legislators' voting decisions. In theory, voters have the most influence over legislators because voters elect them to office. In practice, legislators are influenced by a number of third parties. Among the individuals and entities that influence legislators' policy decisions are the governor and other state officials, lobbyists, research organizations, and the media.

Key Terms

bicameral, p. 301
bill, p. 324
chubbing, p. 330
companion bill, p. 327
concurrent resolution, p. 323
conference committee, p. 333
descriptive representation, p. 309
filibustering, p. 332
five-ninths rule, p. 331
gerrymandering, p. 304
ghost voting, p. 320

impeach, p. 325
interim committee, p. 320
joint resolution, p. 323
legislative caucus, p. 321
multimember district, p. 305
oversight, p. 324
parliamentarian, p. 326
president of the Senate, p. 316
procedural committee, p. 320
reapportionment, p. 303
redistricting, p. 303

regular session, p. 302
select committee, p. 320
senatorial courtesy, p. 324
simple resolution, p. 323
single-member district, p. 304
Speaker of the House, p. 317
special session, p. 302
standing committee, p. 320
substantive committee, p. 320
substantive representation, p. 309
unicameral, p. 301

Learning Check Answers

8.1
1. A governor has more authority in a special session because he sets the legislative agenda and the time for meeting.
2. False. Gerrymandered districts are legal so long as they do not have unequal populations.

8.2
1. False. Although many legislators are practicing Christians, no religious requirements for elected office are included in state law.
2. The legislator's per diem allowance was $221 per day during the 87th legislative session. Legislators receive only $600 per month (or $7,200 per year) in salary.

8.3
1. False. The speaker of the House of Representatives cannot vote on bills.
2. The president of the Senate, who is the lieutenant governor, determines the Senate committee to which a bill will be sent after introduction.

8.4
1. The legislature most frequently exercises its power by passing bills and resolutions.
2. False. Members of the Texas House of Representatives can use chubbing to hasten a vote on a bill.

8.5
1. True. The House Research Organization influences the House through the *Daily Floor Report* that provides arguments for and against each bill.
2. Social media sites such as Twitter allow researchers to measure the number of times a legislator accesses a media outlet's account.

9 The Executive Branch

Learning Objectives

9.1 Explain the effect of checks and balances on the executive powers of the governor.

9.2 Analyze the shared power of the executive and legislative branches.

9.3 Illustrate powers the governor exercises over the judicial branch of state government.

9.4 Discuss the informal powers of the governor.

9.5 Summarize how the constitution and laws of Texas provide resources, as well as succession and removal procedures, for the governor.

9.6 Analyze gubernatorial elections and the impact of campaign funds on the politics of the governorship.

9.7 Describe the powers of elected department heads and the appointed secretary of state.

9.8 Describe the role of the bureaucracy in governing the state of Texas.

Image 9.1 Governor Greg Abbott, with Lieutenant Govenor Dan Patrick, provides an update on the state's COVID-19 response in June of 2020.

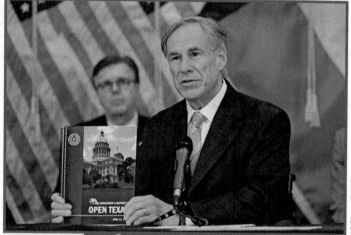

AP Photo/Eric Gay

Competency Connection
⊛ **SOCIAL RESPONSIBILITY** ⊛

How can Texas best balance the protection of human health and economic well-being?

On July 14, 2013, Texas Attorney General Greg Abbott announced that he would seek the Texas Republican Party's nomination for governor. He made the announcement on the 29th anniversary of the day that a falling oak tree changed his life forever, breaking his back, damaging his kidneys, and confining him permanently to a wheelchair. Abbott credits the accident with giving him a "spine of steel" and a focus not on the challenges life brings but on his response to challenges. When he met and overcame Democratic state Senator Wendy Davis's challenge in the 2014 gubernatorial election, Abbott's victory marked the end of an era in the Lone Star State. For most young Texans, Rick Perry was the only governor they had ever known, having served a record 14 years in the governor's office.

Perry's long tenure made him a nationally recognizable figure. He parlayed his name recognition into two campaigns for the U.S. presidency, an appearance on *Dancing with the Stars*, and eventually a position as U.S. Secretary of Energy in the Trump administration. Given the level of attention and media coverage the office receives, you might be surprised to learn that, unlike the president of the United States and the governors of most other states, the position of Texas governor is relatively weak with regard to formal powers.

Several of Texas's political traditions and institutions stem from the state's experiences after the Civil War (1861–1865). Even today, the state's executive structure shows the influence of anti-Reconstruction reactions against Governor E. J. Davis's administration (1870–1874). When Davis made aggressive use of state government power in an effort to enfranchise and protect freed slaves, a large majority of White Texans complained that numerous abuses of power occurred, committed by state officials reporting directly to Governor Davis.[1] This piece of Texas history helps explain why, after more than 140 years, many Texans still distrust the "strong" executive model of state government. The U.S. president (with Senate approval) appoints and can independently remove members of a cabinet. In Texas, however, Article IV of the Texas Constitution establishes a multiheaded executive branch, or plural executive, over which the governor has only limited formal powers (see Figure 9.1).

As you learn about the workings of the executive branch of Texas government, consider an observation by Dr. Brian McCall, a former member of the Texas House of Representatives and subsequently chancellor of the Texas State University System. In his book, *The Power of the Texas Governor: Connally to Bush*, McCall states: "It is widely reported that the governorship of Texas is by design a weak office. However, the strength of an individual governor's personality can overcome many of the limitations imposed on the office."[2] As you read this chapter, answer the following questions: Is the current head of Texas's executive branch a strong governor? How much power should other elected and appointed officials in this branch have?

Follow *Practicing Texas Politics* on Twitter
@PracTexPol

Figure 9.1 The Structure of Texas Government: Important Agencies and Offices (with number of governing body members)

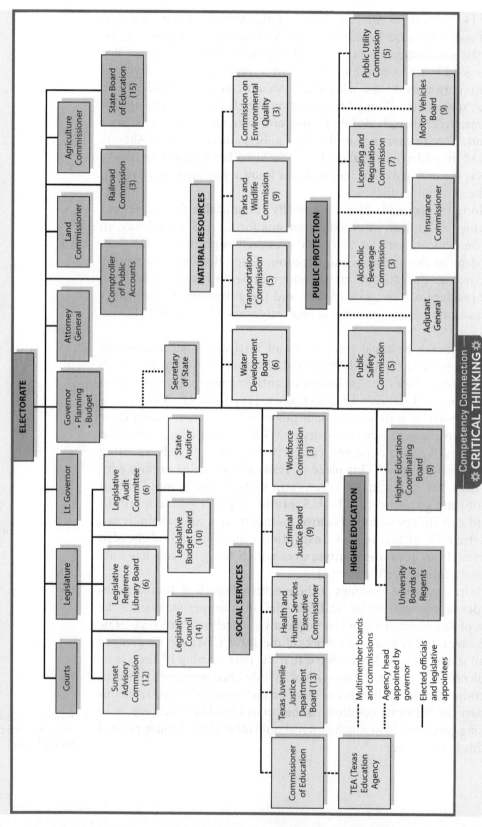

— Competency Connection —
❖ CRITICAL THINKING ❖

What are the advantages and disadvantages of having a plural executive?

⬓ Executive Powers of the Governor

LO 9.1 Explain the effect of checks and balances on the executive powers of the governor.

The governor of Texas is inaugurated on the third Tuesday in January of every fourth year, always in the odd-numbered year before a presidential election (e.g., January 21, 2019). In the inauguration ceremony, the governor swears to fulfill the role assigned to him or her by the Texas Constitution to "cause the laws to be faithfully executed." In other words, the governor is the state's **Chief Executive**.

Executive powers of the governor include nominating individuals to fill appointive offices (subject to approval of the Senate) and exercising limited control over state administration as authorized by the Texas Constitution and by statutes enacted by the Texas legislature. These powers are used to do the following:

- Nominate (and in some cases remove) state officials
- Deal with problems caused by civil disorder and natural disasters
- Participate in state budget making and budget management
- Announce policies by issuing executive orders
- Make public proclamations for ceremonial and other purposes
- Promote the economic development of Texas

In some respects, the governor exercises executive powers like those wielded by heads of other large organizations (for example, university presidents, business chief executive officers, union leaders, or the U.S. president), though with obvious differences. Of course, the executive powers of the governor of Texas resemble those of the country's other 49 state governors; however, different state laws and state constitutions give some governors more executive powers and other governors less.

Appointive Power

One of the most significant executive powers of the Texas governor is **appointive power**. Laws that create administrative agencies also allow a governor to nominate friends and political supporters to head them. The governor's ability to nominate citizens for these positions, subject to approval by the Texas Senate, remains both an important political tool and a fundamental management power.

Department heads appointed by the governor include the secretary of state; the adjutant general, who heads the Texas Military Forces; the executive director of the Office of State-Federal Relations; the executive commissioner of health and human services; commissioners of education, insurance, and firefighters' pensions; and the chief administrative law judge of the State Office of Administrative Hearings (SOAH). The governor has the power, "notwithstanding other law," to designate and change the chairs of most state boards and commissions, either by designating a current member or appointing a new member to serve as chair.

Chief Executive
The head of the executive branch of a government. The role of Chief Executive generally comes with the power to implement and enforce government policies, supervise the executive branch of government, and appoint and remove executive officials.

appointive power
The authority to name a person to a government office. Most gubernatorial appointments require Senate approval by two-thirds of the members present.

Not affected by this law are the presiding officers of governing bodies of higher education institutions and systems, along with those who advise or report to statewide elected officials other than the governor. Because he served for so long, Governor Perry managed to appoint allies and supporters to every appointed position available, making him more powerful than perhaps any governor in Texas history. As a result, Governor Abbott entered office with significantly less influence in the executive branch than his predecessor. Since then, he has significantly expanded the powers of his office.[3]

Gubernatorial appointive power is not without certain legal and political limitations. The Texas Constitution requires that all appointees (except personal staff) be confirmed by the Senate with a two-thirds vote of senators present. This practice is known as "advice and consent." To avoid rejection by the Senate, the governor respects the tradition of senatorial courtesy by obtaining approval of the state senator representing a prospective appointee's senatorial district before sending that person's name forward for Senate confirmation. Political prudence also demands that the appointments director in the **governor's office** conduct a background check on each appointee. This precaution is designed to avoid possible embarrassment—as occurred when, for example, Governor Dolph Briscoe appointed a dead man to a state board.

Governors may try to circumvent the Texas Senate by making appointments while the Senate is not in session. Texas's Constitution, however, requires that these **recess appointments** be submitted to the Senate for confirmation within 10 days after it convenes for a regular or special session. Confirmation hearings do not have to occur immediately. Failure of the Senate to confirm a recess appointment prevents the governor from reappointing that person to the same position.

One limitation on the governor's appointive power is that members of most state boards and commissions serve for six years, with overlapping terms of office. Thus, only one-third of the members finish a term every two years. A first-term governor must work with carryovers from previous administrations, even if such carryovers are not supportive of the new governor.

Appointive power of the governor extends to filling vacancies for elected heads of executive departments, members of the Railroad Commission, members of the State Board of Education, district attorneys, and judges (except those for county, municipal, and justice of the peace courts). These appointees serve until they are elected or replaced at the next general election. In addition, when a U.S. senator from Texas dies, resigns, or is removed from office before his or her term expires, the governor fills the vacancy with an interim appointee. That appointee serves until a successor is elected in a special election called by the governor. A vacancy in either chamber of the Texas legislature or in the Texas delegation to the U.S. House of Representatives does not result in an interim appointment. Instead, the governor calls a special election to fill the position. The winner of the special election serves until after the next regularly scheduled general election.

Removal Power

In creating numerous boards and commissions, the legislature gives the governor extensive appointive power but no independent **removal power** over heads of most state agencies. This limitation restricts gubernatorial control over the state

governor's office
The administrative organization through which the governor of Texas makes appointments, prepares a biennial budget recommendation, administers federal and state grants for crime prevention and law enforcement, and confers full and conditional pardons on recommendation of the Board of Pardons and Paroles.

recess appointment
An appointment made by the governor when the Texas legislature is not in session.

removal power
Authority to remove an official from office. In Texas, the governor's removal power is limited to staff members, some agency heads, and his or her appointees with the consent of the Senate.

bureaucracy. The legislature limits the governor's independent removal power to members of the governor's staff and three officials whose offices were created by the legislature. These statutory officials are the executive director of the Department of Housing and Community Affairs, the executive commissioner of health and human services, and the insurance commissioner.

Elected department heads and their subordinates are not subject to the governor's removal power. Moreover, the governor cannot directly remove most board and commission officials. The governor may informally pressure an appointee to resign or accept another appointment. Nevertheless, pressure is not as effective as the power of direct removal, and it requires expenditure of political capital. Except for the few positions described previously, governors may not remove someone appointed by a predecessor. They may remove their own appointees with the consent of two-thirds of state senators present; however, this authority still falls short of independent removal power.

Military Power

Article 4, Section 7, of the Texas Constitution states that the governor "shall be Commander-in-Chief of the military forces of the State, except when they are called into actual service of the United States." Appointed by the governor, the adjutant general commands the three branches of the Texas Military Forces (with approximate personnel numbers): Texas Army National Guard (19,000), Texas Air National Guard (3,000), and Texas State Guard (2,000).

Image 9.2 Governor Abbott appointed Major General Tracy Norris to be Adjutant General of Texas effective January 1, 2019. The first woman to hold the position, Norris commands the Texas Military Department.

AB Forces News Collection/Alamy Stock Photo

— Competency Connection —
☼ **CRITICAL THINKING** ☼

Should the Governor's appointment and removal power be expanded, kept the same, or reduced?

The president of the United States can order units of the Army National Guard and Air National Guard to federal service in time of war or national emergency. Pay for National Guard personnel while on active duty and for training periods (usually one weekend each month and an annual two-week period) is the same as that for regular military personnel of the same rank. Texas State Guard units serve within Texas and support the other two branches of the Texas Military Forces. For the most part, State Guard soldiers are not paid for training activities; but when activated by the governor and for a limited number of mandatory training days, they receive $151 daily, regardless of rank.

In June 1943, a Black man in Beaumont, Texas, was accused of raping a White woman, sparking a riot in which as many as 4,000 White citizens attacked Black neighborhoods and businesses with guns, axes, and hammers. Since all Texas National Guard personnel were in federal service because of World War II, acting governor A. M. Aiken used Texas State Guard units to impose **martial law** (temporary rule by state military forces and suspension of civil authority) on Beaumont.[4] In May 2020, Governor Greg Abbott activated 5,000 members of the Texas National Guard in response to protests following the murder of George Floyd. He also sent 1,000 members to Washington, D.C. for the January 20, 2021, inauguration of President Joe Biden due to threats of violence and insurrection. These actions were taken according to the constitutional provision that the governor "shall have power to call forth the militia to execute the laws of the State, to suppress insurrections, and to repel invasions." Until the constitution was amended in 1999, this power extended to "protecting the frontier from hostile incursions by Indians or other predatory bands."

As circumstances demand, the governor authorizes mobilization of Army and Air National Guard personnel to perform relief and rescue service in counties hit by hurricanes, floods, fires, and other natural disasters. In February 2021, Governor Abbott mobilized the Texas National Guard to assist local authorities in performing wellness checks and moving Texans to warming centers during severe winter weather. Mobilization of the state military for disaster relief is expected and common, but other uses are more controversial. In April 2015, Governor Abbott received much criticism when he responded to demands by conspiracy theorists by ordering the Texas State Guard to monitor U.S. military forces participating in Operation Jade Helm 15. This training exercise involved only about 1,200 federal personnel operating in Texas and other states in the Southwest. Nevertheless, some people claimed that they feared President Obama would send contingents of the Islamic State's foreign fighters or that Texans' firearms would be confiscated by the United Nations.[5]

Texas Army and Air National Guard personnel also fight alongside the U.S. Army, Navy, Air Force, and Marines in foreign combat. Since the invasion of Afghanistan in 2001, more than 33,200 Texas Guard personnel have served in Afghanistan, Iraq, and other countries. Despite this service, cuts to federal government spending meant that the Texas Guard lost many of their attack helicopters to active duty branches in 2014.[6]

martial law
Temporary rule by military authorities when civil authorities are unable to handle a riot or other civil disorder.

Law Enforcement Power

In Texas, law enforcement is primarily a responsibility of city police departments and county sheriffs' departments. Nevertheless, the Texas Department of Public Safety (DPS), headed by the Public Safety Commission, is an important law enforcement agency. The governor appoints the commission's five members, subject to Senate approval. The director of public safety is appointed by the commission and oversees more than 8,000 personnel in DPS. Included among the department's responsibilities are highway traffic supervision, driver licensing, and criminal law enforcement in cooperation with local and federal agencies.

If circumstances demand swift but limited police action, the governor is empowered to assume command of the Texas Rangers, a division of DPS composed of a small number of highly trained law enforcement personnel operating statewide. In June 2019 and November 2020, Abbott deployed DPS special agents, troopers, intelligence analysts, and Texas Rangers to Dallas to help fight violent crime.[7] As of October 2020, membership in the Texas Rangers totaled 180 men (131 White, 40 Latino, 8 Black, and 1 Native American) and 4 women (2 White and 2 Latina).

Budgetary Power

Gubernatorial **budgetary power** is subordinated in part to the legislature's prerogative of controlling the state's purse strings. By statutory requirement, the governor (assisted by personnel in the Governor's Office of Budget and Policy and the Legislative Budget Board) should prepare separate budgets for consideration by the legislature in regular session. Texas law requires distribution of the governor's budget to each legislator before delivery of the governor's State of the State message. Traditionally, both the House and the Senate have been inclined to give greater respect to the Legislative Budget Board's spending proposals. (For further discussion of the state's budget process, see Chapter 11 "Finance and Fiscal Policy.")

The Texas governor's principal control over state spending comes from constitutional power to veto an entire appropriations bill or to use the **line-item veto** to eliminate individual budget items. In June 2015, Governor Abbott claimed a 2016–2017 budget reduction of about $295 million from use of line-item vetoes, but $62 million were vetoes of **contingency riders** for bills that the legislature did not pass. Still, the Legislative Budget Board claimed that the governor had overstepped his authority in targeting riders. State Comptroller Glenn Hegar put the disputed funds on hold and requested an opinion from Attorney General Ken Paxton. The attorney general declared the vetoes to be valid, thus expanding the governor's power in budget negotiations. In June 2017, this decision allowed Abbott to cut approximately $95 million from environmental protection programs by using the line-item veto. Governor Abbott used his line-item veto power to cut about $120 million from the proposed budget that year. In 2019, he issued no line-item vetoes. In 2021, he issued a single line-item veto in which he rejected funding for the Texas Legislature in retribution for its failure to pass an election overhaul bill.[8]

The line-item veto is an important power even when not used, because legislators may avoid including items in the budget that the governor signals he will veto. Governor Perry's decision to oppose Medicaid expansion is an example.

budgetary power
The governor is supposed to submit a state budget to the legislature at the beginning of each regular session. When an appropriation bill is enacted by the legislature and certified by the comptroller of public accounts, the governor may veto the whole document or individual items.

line-item veto
Action by the governor to eliminate an individual budget item while permitting enactment of other parts of an appropriations bill.

contingency riders
Authorization for spending state money to finance provisions of a bill if the bill becomes law.

Under the Affordable Care Act, the federal government covered 100 percent of expanded access to the federal health-insurance program for low-income citizens until 2017, gradually declining to 90 percent by 2020. Texas has the largest uninsured population in the nation. In the first five years under the expanded program, Texas would have received $76 billion to provide healthcare coverage for poor citizens. Expansion was strongly supported by the Texas Medical Association, Texas Hospital Association, and many other groups. Yet opposition by Governor Perry and then by Governor Abbott was a clear signal to legislators that authorizing the funding would result in a gubernatorial veto. Therefore, expansion and funding were not proposed.[9]

Executive Orders and Proclamations

Although the Texas Constitution identifies the governor as the "Chief Executive Officer of the State," it does not empower him or her to tell other state officials what they must do unless such action is authorized by the legislature. Nevertheless, governors use **executive orders** to set policy within the executive branch and to create or abolish task forces, boards, commissions, and councils. Each executive order is identified by the governor's initials and is numbered chronologically.

Executive Orders are not used frequently in Texas. For example, Governor Abbott issued only one each year in 2016 and 2017, three in 2018, and two in 2019. Some are ceremonial, as when Abbott issued executive order GA-04 honoring the memory of George H. W. Bush after his passing. Others have a more substantive impact. In 2009, Perry's 73rd executive order (RP-73) affected college students and faculty when it directed the Texas Higher Education Coordinating Board, in cooperation with public colleges and universities, to look at "opportunities for achieving cost efficiencies." Subjects under review were state funding for higher education based on courses completed, faculty workload, distance learning, alternatives to new campuses, energy use, and cost of instructional materials. Executive Order RP-75, issued in August 2011, related to the establishment and support of WGU Texas (a partnership with the Western Governors University), a nonprofit independent university offering "online degrees based on demonstrated competence as opposed to degrees based on credit hours, clock hours or grades."

Executive orders took on a rare level of importance and frequency during the COVID-19 pandemic. From March to May of 2021, Abbott issued 29 executive orders, all related to the pandemic. Some sought to mitigate the spread of the virus, for example, by instituting restrictions on travel and visitation of prisons and nursing homes and by mandating the wearing of masks. Others sought to mitigate economic damage caused by the shutdown by ordering the reopening of businesses.[10]

Another instrument of executive authority is the **proclamation**, an official public announcement often used for ceremonial purposes (for example, naming April 2021 "Sexual Assault Awareness Month"). Some proclamations declare a state of emergency, as the March 2020 declaration of a state of emergency due to COVID-19. Other proclamations identify a county or other region to be a disaster area. For example, the governor regularly declares states of disaster for counties

executive orders
The governor issues executive orders to set policy within the executive branch and to create task forces, councils, and other bodies.

proclamation
A governor's official public announcement (such as calling a special election or declaring a disaster area).

damaged by hurricanes. Damage from Hurricane Harvey in 2017 was so extensive that Governor Abbott continued to issue proclamations renewing the state of disaster for 60 counties in Texas into 2021. In February 2021, he proclaimed a state of disaster due to Winter Storm Uri for all 254 counties in Texas. Additional uses of proclamations include calling special sessions of the legislature, calling special elections, declaring emergency items to be immediately considered by the legislature, and announcing the ratification of amendments to the U.S. Constitution. A month before the November 2020 election, Governor Abbott issued a proclamation limiting each county to one drop-off location for voters to hand-deliver their absentee ballots. Civil rights groups immediately sued in a federal court, but on October 27, 2020, the Texas Supreme Court upheld the governor's proclamation. Abbott's extensive use of executive orders and proclamations during the pandemic led the Legislature to seek to limit gubernatorial power during the 87th Legislative session in 2021 though the effort ultimately failed.[11]

Economic Development

The governor has direct control over efforts to attract investment and move businesses to Texas from other states and countries. Not only did Governor Abbott recruit specific corporations, such as moving the U.S. headquarters for Fortune 500 healthcare giant McKesson Corp. to Las Colinas near Dallas, he also oversaw media and public relations campaigns in other states. When the United Kingdom voted to exit the European Union in 2016, Governor Abbott launched a media campaign in England. He urged company executives who were uncertain about the stability of their country's economy to relocate to Texas.

Texas Enterprise Fund (TEF) was created in 2003 with $295 million from the state's "rainy day" fund (an account intended to pay for state operations in times of emergency). TEF is used to attract or retain industries. Additional multimillion-dollar appropriations for TEF were made in subsequent state budgets until 2013, when state funding was not requested. Instead the Office of the Governor asked to "retain the rider that allows for the reappropriation of unexpended balances and appropriation of revenue received in order to continue the program that is already in place."[12] To complement TEF money, Perry established TexasOne, a nonprofit, tax-exempt corporation that operated with directors appointed by the governor. Its primary mission was to attract businesses from other states and countries.

At Perry's urging, the Texas Legislature also established the Emerging Technology Fund (ETF) in 2005 to help small to midsize companies develop new technology for a wide range of high-tech industries. In 2014, the fund generated controversy even among Texas Republicans. Though ETF-funded businesses showed an overall positive return in terms of job creation and tax revenue during the life of the program, 16 recipients declared bankruptcy. Gubernatorial candidate Greg Abbott repeatedly declared that Texas should not be in the in the business of "picking winners and losers."[13] In 2015, Governor Abbott replaced the Emerging Technology Fund with the Governor's University Research Initiative. With the transfer of the $40 million remaining in the ETF, the new program is designed to bring nationally recognized researchers to universities in Texas. In June 2016,

Governor Abbott reintegrated TexasOne into the Texas Economic Development Corporation (TxEDC), which continued to rely on member organizations for funding. Abbott considers TxEDC and the Governor's Office of Economic Development and Tourism (EDT) to be the pillars of his economic development strategy. In 2017, the Governor's Office and TxEDC launched "GO BIG IN TEXAS®" to promote Texas as a premier destination for businesses. These efforts continued during the COVID-19 shutdown with some success. The governor's executive director of Economic Development and Tourism reported more prospects for corporate relocations or expansions to the state than before the pandemic.[14]

⬥ Legislative Powers of the Governor

LO 9.2   Analyze the shared power of the executive and legislative branches.

Perhaps the most stringent test of a Texas governor's capacity for leadership involves handling legislative matters. The governor has no direct lawmaking authority, but **legislative power** is exercised through four major functions authorized by the Texas Constitution:

- Delivering messages to the legislature
- Signing bills and concurrent resolutions
- Vetoing bills and concurrent resolutions
- Calling special sessions of the legislature

Success of a legislative program depends heavily on a governor's ability to bargain with influential lobbyists and legislative leaders (in particular, the Speaker of the House of Representatives and the lieutenant governor).[15]

Message Power

Article 4, Section 9, of the Texas Constitution requires the governor to deliver a State of the State address at the "commencement" (beginning) of each regular session of the legislature, but this directive is not interpreted to mean the first day of the session. On occasion, the governor may also present other messages, either in person or in writing, to the legislature. A governor's success in using **message power** to promote a harmonious relationship with the legislature depends on such variables as timing of messages concerning volatile issues, support of the governor's program by the chairs of legislative committees, and the governor's personal popularity with the public.

Bill Signing Power

While the legislature is in session, the governor indicates approval by signing bills and concurrent resolutions within 10 days (not counting Sundays) after receiving them. Bills and concurrent resolutions that are neither signed nor vetoed by the

legislative power
A power of the governor exercised through messages delivered to the Texas legislature, vetoes of bills and concurrent resolutions, and calls for special legislative sessions.

message power
The governor's effectiveness in communicating with legislators via the State of the State address at the commencement of a legislative session and other gubernatorial messages delivered in person or in writing.

governor during that period become law anyway. After the legislature adjourns, however, the governor has 20 days (counting Sundays) to veto pending bills and concurrent resolutions.

Most media coverage of signings is the result of photo ops staged in Austin or elsewhere weeks or even months after official signings. Defenders of these ceremonial re-signings contend that the events help inform Texans about new laws. Critics insist that the principal objective of the signings is to give favorable publicity to the governor, bill sponsors, and others who wish to be identified with the legislation.[16]

Veto Power

The governor's most direct legislative tool is the power to block legislation with a veto. During a legislative session, the governor vetoes a bill by returning it unsigned (with written reasons for not signing) to the chamber in which the bill originated. If the legislature is no longer in session, a vetoed bill is filed with the secretary of state. **Veto power** takes different forms. In addition to general veto authority, the governor has the line-item veto (described earlier in this chapter). This power can be used to eliminate one or more specific spending authorizations in an appropriation bill while permitting enactment of the remainder of the budget. Using the line-item veto power to refuse funding for a specific agency, the governor can effectively eliminate that agency. This line-item veto authority places the governor in a powerful bargaining position with individual legislators in the delicate game of **pork-barrel politics**. That is, the governor may strike a bargain with a senator or representative in which the chief executive promises not to deny funding for a lawmaker's pet project (the pork). In return, the legislator agrees to support a bill favored by the governor.

During a session, the governor's veto can be overridden by a two-thirds majority vote in both houses; but overriding a veto has occurred only once since the administration of Governor W. Lee O'Daniel (1939–1941). In 1979, the House and Senate overrode Governor Bill Clements's veto of a bill giving Comal County commissioners power to establish hunting and fishing regulations for the county. Strong constitutional veto power and the governor's informal power of threatening to veto a bill are formidable weapons for dealing with legislators.

The governor may also exercise a **postadjournment veto** by rejecting any pending legislation within 20 days after a session ends. Because most bills pass late in a legislative session, postadjournment veto allows the governor to veto measures without threat of any challenge. Throughout most of the 77th Legislature's regular session in 2001, Governor Perry vetoed only a few bills. But in what some critics termed the "Father's Day Massacre," he exercised 78 postadjournment vetoes at 9 P.M. on the last possible day to do so (June 17). Surpassing Governor Clements's 59 vetoes in 1989, Perry's total of 82 vetoes in 2001 set a record. For the following six regular legislative sessions, his veto totals varied between a low of 19 (79th session, 2005) and a high of 51 (80th session, 2007).

Governor Abbott's veto totals increased from 44 bills vetoed in 2015 to 50 bills in 2017 to 55 bills and 2 concurrent resolutions in 2019. He vetoed only 20 bills in 2021. He argued that most were well intended but either unnecessary or

veto power
Authority of the governor to reject a bill or concurrent resolution passed by the legislature.

pork-barrel politics
A legislator's tactic to obtain funding for a pet project, usually designed to be of special benefit for the legislator's district.

postadjournment veto
Rejection by the governor of a pending bill or concurrent resolution during the 20 days after a legislative session ends.

examples of government micromanagement. For example, Abbott vetoed a bill by Sen. Eddie Lucio (D - Brownsville) that would have made it a crime to chain up dogs and leave them without adequate shade, shelter or drinkable water. His veto statement argued that penalties for animal cruelty were already in place.[17]

Special Sessions Power

Included among the governor's powers is authority to call special sessions of the legislature. The Texas Constitution places no restrictions on the number of special sessions a governor may call, but the length of a special session is limited to 30 days. During a special session, the legislature may consider only those matters the governor specifies in the call or subsequently presents to it. Exceptions to this requirement of gubernatorial approval are confirmation of appointments and impeachment proceedings. Threatening to call a special session is another tool the governor wields to influence the legislature.

Rick Perry called 12 special sessions during his 15 years as governor, including three sessions in 2013. Satisfied with the legislature's support of his agenda, Governor Abbott did not call a special session after the 85th Legislature in 2015. Abbott did call a special session at the urging of Lieutenant Governor Dan Patrick in July 2017. Patrick wanted to pressure legislators to pass the controversial "bathroom bill" to require transgender individuals to use public bathrooms corresponding to their sex at birth (SB 6). Abbott agreed and added 19 items to the special session agenda, including antiabortion, education, property tax, and other proposals. By the last day of that special session, none of Abbott's 20 items had received an up or down vote. After Abbott threatened to call another special session, lawmakers passed nine items on his agenda and adjourned. Legislators urged the governor to declare a special session in 2019 to address gun violence and in 2020 to address the coronavirus pandemic and police reforms, but Abbott declined, giving the executive branch sole power to address these issues. In June 2021 Abbott signaled that he would call for two special sessions. He called one In July to deal with election and bail legislation and to restrict the teaching of critical race theory. Another was projected for September or October to address COVID-19 recovery and redistricting.[18]

9.2 Learning Check

1. True or False: During a session, the governor's veto can be overridden by a two-thirds majority vote in the House and in the Senate.
2. How can the legislature be convened for a special session?

Answers at the end of this chapter.

✪ Judicial Powers of the Governor

LO 9.3 Illustrate powers the governor exercises over the judicial branch of state government.

The governor exercises a few formal judicial powers, including the power to do the following:

- Fill vacancies on state (but not county or city) courts
- Play a limited but outdated role in removing judges and justices
- Perform acts of clemency to undo or reduce sentences for some convicted criminals

Appointment and Removal of Judges and Justices

More than half of state judges and justices first serve on district courts and higher appellate courts through gubernatorial appointment to fill vacancies. Such vacancies result from creation of a new state court or from a judge's death, resignation, or removal from office. Texas's judicial system has been heavily influenced by Governor Perry, whose long tenure allowed him to appoint almost 250 judges. Most of them share Perry's pro-business stance. As a result, winning cases against large corporations in Texas is difficult.[19] Like other governors, Perry used this power to diversify the state's judicial system. For example, Governor Perry twice made history with his appointments of Wallace B. Jefferson, initially as the first Black Texan to serve on the Texas Supreme Court and then, in 2004, as the first Black chief justice of that court. Chief Justice Jefferson returned to the private practice of law in 2013. In 2004, Perry appointed his former general counsel, David Medina, a Latino, to the Texas Supreme Court; and in 2009, he named Justice Eva Guzman as the first Latina to serve on that court. Nearly all Perry's appointees to the Texas Supreme Court won subsequent election.[20]

Governor Abbott was elected as a state district court judge in 1992. Three years later, Governor George W. Bush appointed him to the Supreme Court of Texas, where he served for seven years before being elected as the state's attorney general. During his first term as governor, Abbott appointed one Texas Supreme Court justice (Jimmy Blacklock), five courts of appeals justices, and 24 District Court judges. By the middle of his second term, he had appointed an additional three Supreme Court justices (Jane Bland, Brett Busby, and Rebecca Huddle), one Texas Court of Criminal Appeals justice (Jesse McClure), sixteen courts of appeals justices, and eleven district court judges.

According to Article XV, Section 8, of the Texas Constitution, the governor may remove any jurist "on address of two-thirds of each house of the Legislature for willful neglect of duty, incompetence, habitual drunkenness, oppression in office, or other reasonable cause which shall not be sufficient ground for impeachment." Governors and the legislature have not used this process for many years. Instead, they have left removal of state jurists to other proceedings and to voters. (See Chapter 10, "The Judicial Branch," for a discussion of the disciplining and removal of judges and justices.)

Acts of Executive Clemency

Until the mid-1930s, Texas governors had extensive powers to undo or lessen punishment for convicted criminals through acts of clemency that set aside or reduced court-imposed penalties. A constitutional amendment adopted in 1936 reduced the clemency powers of the governor and established the Board of Pardons and Paroles, which is now a division of the Texas Department of Criminal Justice.

Release of a prisoner before completion of a sentence on condition of good behavior is called **parole**. The seven-member Board of Pardons and Paroles, along with 14 commissioners appointed by the chair, grants parole without action by the governor. The governor, however, may perform various acts of executive clemency that set aside or reduce a court-imposed penalty through pardon,

parole
Supervised release from prison before completion of a sentence, on condition of good behavior.

reprieve, or commutation of sentence. Only if recommended by the Board of Pardons and Paroles can the governor grant a full pardon or a conditional pardon, but pardons are rare. Governor Abbott granted between four and eight pardons per year during his first five years in office. In fiscal year 2020, the board considered 93 requests for full pardon in noncapital cases and recommended clemency for 36 of these cases. It considered no requests for full pardon in capital cases but recommended clemency in the form of a 120-day reprieve in one case. Governor Abbott granted full pardons to seven people aged 41 years and younger for minor crimes such as driving with a suspended license, credit card abuse, and prostitution. He continued the tradition of announcing pardons around Christmas each year.[21] In February of 2020, Abbott launched an effort to help victims of human trafficking and domestic abuse apply "for a full pardon for crimes committed while under the grips of a trafficker or an abusive partner."[22]

A **full pardon** releases a person from all consequences of a criminal act and restores the same rights enjoyed by persons who have not been convicted of crimes. Pardons can be granted posthumously. In 2010, Governor Perry granted a full pardon to Timothy Cole after DNA evidence proved he had been wrongfully imprisoned for more than 13 years. Unfortunately, Cole died in prison nine years before the pardon. As attorney general, Abbott subsequently issued an opinion stating that pardons could be granted posthumously.[23]

Under a **conditional pardon**, the governor may withhold certain rights, such as being licensed to practice a selected occupation. A conditional pardon may be revoked by the governor if terms of that pardon are violated.

A governor may also independently grant one 30-day reprieve in a death sentence case or may grant a longer reprieve on the recommendation of the Board of Pardons and Paroles. **Reprieves** temporarily suspend execution of a condemned prisoner, but governors seldom grant them. In 2019, the Board of Pardons and Paroles recommended that Governor Abbott grant a 120-day reprieve for Rodney Reed, a prisoner sentenced to death for murder. Hours later, the Texas Court of Criminal Appeals took the decision out of Abbott's hands. Because there was substantial evidence of Reed's innocence, the Court halted execution and referred his case back to trial court for examination of new evidence and reconsideration. Because of the COVID-19 pandemic, the hearing was delayed until July 2021.[24]

If recommended by the Board of Pardons and Paroles, the governor may reduce a penalty through **commutation of sentence** and may remit (return) forfeitures of money or property surrendered as punishment. In 2005 Governor Perry commuted the sentences of 28 death row inmates convicted of crimes committed when they were younger than age 18. He took this action after the U.S. Supreme Court ruled in *Roper v. Simmons*, 543 U.S. 551 (2005), that the Eighth Amendment's ban on cruel and unusual punishment precludes execution of those who were minors at the time they committed their crimes. More than a decade and 140 executions later, Governor Abbott commuted his first sentence. He spared the life of Thomas Whitaker, who was convicted of paying a gunman to kill Whitaker's parents and brother. The father was wounded, and the brother was killed. Whitaker's death sentence was commuted less than an hour before his scheduled execution in February 2018, but he will remain in prison for life without possibility of parole.[25]

---

full pardon
An act of executive clemency, on recommendation of the Board of Pardons and Paroles, that releases a convicted person from all consequences of a criminal act and restores the same rights enjoyed by others who have not been convicted of a crime.

conditional pardon
An act of executive clemency, on recommendation of the Board of Pardons and Paroles, that releases a convicted person from the consequences of his or her crime but does not restore all rights, as in the case of a full pardon.

reprieve
An act of executive clemency that temporarily suspends execution of a sentence.

commutation of sentence
On the recommendation of the Board of Pardons and Paroles, the reduction of a sentence by the governor.

✓ **9.3 Learning Check**

1. True or False: A vacancy on a Texas district court or higher appellate court is filled by gubernatorial appointment.

2. Which Texas official has power to independently grant one 30-day reprieve in a death sentence case?

Answers at the end of this chapter.

⭐ Informal Powers of the Governor

LO 9.4 Discuss the informal powers of the governor.

In the United States, those who hold the formal role of chief executive (presidents and governors) also hold the informal role of **head of state**. In Texas, a governor's ability to sway public opinion and to direct or influence the actions of other government officials depends on more than constitutional powers or powers conferred by the legislature. Informal powers are not based on law; rather, they stem from a governor's popularity with the public and are based on traditions, symbols, and ceremonies.

The breadth and depth of this informal role cannot be fully measured, but its significance should not be underestimated in determining a governor's success. Effective governors must be able to make impressive speeches, to remain at ease while communicating in interviews with newspaper and television reporters, and to communicate directly with Texans by writing (usually with staff assistance) newspaper articles of their own.[26] Many of the governor's speeches and public appearances are political or even inspirational. For example, in 2020 Governor Abbott visited El Paso leaders after their city reported its highest number of

Image 9.3 Governor Greg Abbott greets Malik Jefferson after the Longhorns beat the Sooners on October 10, 2015.

Ronald Martinez/Getty Images

— Competency Connection —
✧ **CRITICAL THINKING** ✧

How does visiting events like the Texas-Oklahoma football game strengthen the governor's informal powers?

head of state
The person whose role is to represent and symbolize the unity and integrity of the state at home, in interaction with other state governments, the national government and abroad.

deaths due to COVID-19 and for dedication of the Grand Candela memorial to honor victims of the Cielo Vista Walmart shooting.[27] Of course, a governor cannot accept all invitations to deliver speeches or participate in dedications, banquets, and other public events. Within the limits of time and priorities, however, every governor does attempt to play the role of head of state.

Lacking sufficient constitutional powers, a Texas governor must rely on persuasion or resort to forceful arm-twisting. Although such pressure is usually without publicity, secrecy is not always the case. For example, Governor Abbott asked conservative pastors to pressure Texas lawmakers for support of SB 6, a bill that would have blocked transgender people from using public restrooms matching their gender identities. He then announced that he would create and publish a list of legislators who did not support this bill and 19 of his other positions, saying, "No one gets to hide. No one gets to play neutral. Everyone has to be all in."[28]

Yet arm-twisting has its legal limits. In April 2014, after complaints were filed by Texans for Public Justice, a special district judge impaneled a grand jury to determine whether Governor Perry abused his power in following through on a threat to veto $7.5 million in state funding for public corruption prosecutors. In August 2014, Perry became only the second Texas governor to be indicted. (The other was James E. "Pa" Ferguson in 1917.) This indictment charged Perry with "abuse of official capacity," a first-degree felony punishable by up to 99 years in prison. It also charged him with "coercion of a public servant," a third-degree felony that can result in up to 10 years in prison. For a discussion of this indictment, see Chapter 3, "Local Governments." In February 2016, the Texas Court of Criminal Appeals ruled in Perry's favor on the abuse of power charge and upheld a lower court's ruling with regard to the unconstitutionality of the coercion law.[29]

Governors also make use of social media to enhance their informal powers. In his 2010 campaign, Rick Perry recognized and made full use of the potential of social media as a campaign tool, and he continued to use it after the election to enhance his informal powers. He established direct links to his social media accounts through the official web page of the Office of the Governor, on which he also provided links for email updates, an RSS feed, and podcasts of his speeches. By the end of his time as governor, Perry's Facebook, Google, and Twitter pages were being regularly updated with highlights of his legislative victories, links to videos of his interviews and flattering news stories, photographs from his travels, holiday greetings to supporters, and more. He also posted to Flickr, YouTube, Instagram, and LinkedIn. Without filter of the media, direct communication with the public allowed Perry to rally support for his causes and campaigns quickly and effectively.

Even without the national celebrity status that Perry gained through his 2012 and 2016 presidential campaigns, Greg Abbott began his first term in 2015 with almost 400,000 likes on his Facebook page. By the midpoint of his second term, Abbott's Facebook politician page had almost 1.4 million likes, and his Office of the Governor Greg Abbott page had almost 208,500 likes. At the same time, Abbott's personal Twitter account had more than 576,900 followers and his official account more than 350,500. Although Abbott's YouTube channels attracted only 10,000 subscribers, he had posted 584 videos that reached more than 1.7 million viewers. Abbott also used Instagram, where his accounts had a combined 1974 posts and more than 128,200 followers; and he used LinkedIn, with over 500 followers. With less success, he has also attempted to build followings on Flickr, Pinterest, and Vimeo. As did Governor Perry, Governor Abbott uses social media accounts to enhance his informal powers by engaging the public directly and managing his image.[30]

Public involvement of family members may be a source of support for a governor. Laura Bush, for example, enhanced her husband's image as a governor committed to improving education, literacy, and reading. Anita Perry, with bachelor's and master's degrees in nursing and 17 years of experience in various fields of nursing, often spoke on such topics as Alzheimer's disease, breast cancer awareness, and prevention of family violence. In addition, she worked with her husband to host the annual Texas Conference for Women, which addresses such issues as women's health care, personal growth, and professional development. She made history by working as a consultant for the Texas Association Against Sexual Assault. No wife of any earlier governor was employed while her husband was in office.[31]

Cecilia Abbott, the first Latina first lady in Texas history, is a former teacher and principal in Catholic schools. She left her job as managing director of community relations for a healthcare provider to play a larger role in her husband's campaign but has maintained a lower profile than her predecessors. Though Cecilia Abbott prefers to avoid the media spotlight, in 2016 she launched an initiative called "Texanthropy" to promote voluntarism and service to others. In 2017 she also partnered with the Texas Department of Family and Protective Services to launch the "Network of Nurture" to increase support for children and families in the state's child welfare system. Texas's First Lady leads by example, volunteering for and visiting nonprofit organizations and charities, serving on the boards of several educational organizations, and maintaining memberships in numerous philanthropic groups. She also maintains a "First Lady Blog" on the website of the Office of the Texas Governor to promote events and discuss issues less political than those faced by the governor.[32]

Like Rick Perry, Governor Abbott has gained countrywide attention with statements concerning national affairs as well as state politics. On January 8, 2016, for example, he gave the keynote speech at the annual policy orientation event for the Texas Public Policy Foundation. In this address, Abbott unveiled a 92-page plan titled "Restoring the Rule of Law with States Leading the Way."[33]

Five months after gaining national attention with his Texas Plan, Abbott published a book that has been distributed throughout the country: *Broken but Unbowed: The Fight to Fix a Broken America*.[34] An autobiographical account of Abbott's struggle to survive the accident that put him in a wheelchair for the rest of his life, it is linked to a description of the conservative policy battles that led to his Texas Plan. This book was released to the public at the time of the Texas Republican Party's state convention in May 2016, two years before the next gubernatorial election. Abbott intends to campaign to retain the governorship in 2022, but has indicated that he may also be open to seeking the GOP nomination and election as U.S. president in 2024.

✓ **9.4 Learning Check**

1. True or False: The governor's informal powers are based on law.

2. True or False: Public involvement of family members may be a source of support for the governor.

Answers at the end of this chapter.

⬧ Resources and Limitations of the Governorship

LO 9.5   Summarize how the constitution and laws of Texas provide resources, as well as succession and removal procedures, for the governor.

The constitution and laws of Texas endow the governor with certain benefits and resources along with limits. Provided also are procedures for removing a governor from office and providing a successor if the governor does not finish an elected term.

Compensation and Benefits

The biennial state budget for fiscal years 2020–2021 set the governor's annual salary at $153,750, which is the same as salaries for the state's attorney general and comptroller of public accounts.[35] In 2011, Governor Perry stirred controversy when his federal campaign filings forced him to disclose that in addition to his salary, he also received retirement benefits from the state worth more than $92,000 per year. In a complex process that did not have to be disclosed under state law, Perry was able to retire as a state employee while continuing to receive pay as an elected official. Shortly after Perry left office, such "double-dipping" was banned (except for district attorneys) by House Bill 408 enacted by the 84th Legislature in 2015.[36]

State money pays the governor's expenses for official trips but not travel expenses for political campaigning or other nonofficial activities. Nevertheless, the Department of Public Safety provides security personnel to protect the governor at all times at state expense. Travel expenses and overtime for Perry's security detail during the 160 days he campaigned for the Republican Party's 2012 presidential nomination cost the state more than $3.6 million. This information caused some Texans to insist that such expenses should be covered by campaign funds. The Texas Supreme Court ruled that separating expenses between the governor's campaign and official functions would require the Department of Public Safety to provide a detailed breakdown of how money for the governor's security is spent. To do so, according to the court, compromises a governor's safety and is therefore confidential.[37]

With Greg Abbott in the governor's office, the cost of his security detail is likewise paid by Texas taxpayers. Abbott has traveled extensively throughout the United States and abroad during his terms as governor. He made trips to promote Texas businesses, publicize his book, speak at political events, take vacations, and campaign for himself and other Republican candidates. By May 2020, Abbott's travel and security detail had already cost taxpayers more than $2 million.

Other fringe benefits of the governor's office include staff and housing in the Governor's Mansion. This historic building near the Capitol is usually open for tours on a limited basis, although tours have been suspended during the COVID-19 pandemic. Whether taxpayers are responsible for a governor's legal expenses resulting from a criminal investigation is unresolved. Although taxpayers paid more than $132,000 for Governor Perry's legal defense lawyers prior to his indictment, after indictment he used campaign funds to cover such expenses. Political supporters may also cover the costs of luncheons, dinners, receptions, and other social activities at the governor's residence and elsewhere.[38]

The Texas Constitution forbids the governor and other executive officers (except the lieutenant governor) from holding any other civil or corporate office, and the governor may receive neither compensation nor the promise of pay for other employment after taking office. Nevertheless, governors do own property and make investments while serving. To avoid the appearance of conflict between their personal economic interests and the public's interest, both Governors Bush and Perry placed their assets in blind trusts. Under such legal arrangements, holdings are administered by others; and the elected official does not know which assets are in the trust. Governor Abbott did not do so.

Former governors also receive benefits. For the year after leaving office and moving to a new home in Round Top (population 90, Fayette County), Rick Perry reported state retirement income of $133,215 resulting from his government employment. As a well-connected politician, however, he found opportunities for other income. Prior to being nominated by President Trump to the position of Energy Secretary, Perry made hundreds of thousands of dollars in 2015 and 2016 by taking advantage of various opportunities. For example, he worked as a consultant for a heavy equipment company owned by one of his former campaign donors and appointees. In addition, he served on the board of Energy Transfer Partners, a Dallas pipeline company owned by another longtime donor, and he was a board member for Sunoco Logistics Partners. In addition, Perry worked as chief strategy officer for the Florida lobbying operations of dental insurance company MCNA Dental, which had contributed money to his presidential bid. He also received payment for speeches and media appearances, including a spot on *Dancing with the Stars*.

Staff

The Texas governor's hands are often tied when dealing with the state bureaucracy, but the chief executive's personal staff continues to function under direct gubernatorial supervision. A governor's success in dealing with lobbyists, legislators, reporters, and the general public depends largely on staff input and support. The governor's office staff directs programs mandated by the legislature, such as statewide planning (see Figure 9.2); but the governor can appoint and remove staff members.

As the state's population grew and governors embellished their roles in the 20th century, staff size burgeoned. Although fiscal belt-tightening has required recent governors to cut back, staff numbers are still substantially greater than in earlier years. From more than 300 on Governor Ann Richards's staff at the end of her term in January 1995, that number had dropped to 270 under Governor

Figure 9.2 The Office of the Governor.

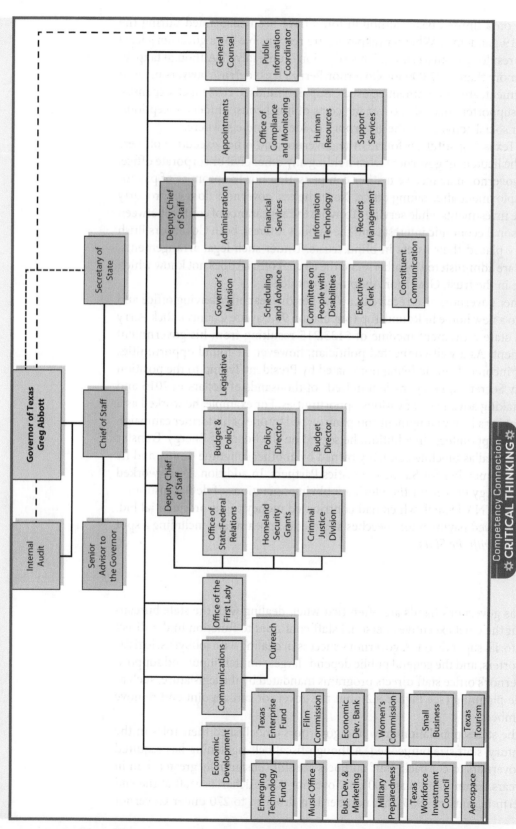

— Competency Connection —
☼ **CRITICAL THINKING** ☼

Does a larger staff make a governor more effective or less efficient?

Abbott 25 years later. Even the size of Abbott's staff dwarfs the 68 full-time staff employees who served under Governor John Connally in the 1960s. Over time, the governor's office has also become more diverse racially and with regard to gender.

The influence of a governor's appointed assistants and unofficial advisers on gubernatorial decisions is open to speculation. Protecting their chief is still a primary function of many staff assistants, particularly the press secretary (who tries to schedule interviews with friendly journalists) and the director of appointments (who evaluates potential appointees). All Texas governors have placed close friends and political associates in staff positions—persons who can be relied on for their loyalty to the chief executive.

Succession

Should a governor die, resign (as did George W. Bush after his 2000 election to the U.S. presidency), or be removed from office (as was James E. "Pa" Ferguson after his impeachment and conviction in 1917); or should a governor-elect refuse to take office or be permanently unable to fill the office, a successor serves for the remainder of the governor's four-year term. The lieutenant governor heads the constitutional order of succession. Next in line is the president pro tempore of the Senate. After these two officials, the legislature has designated the following line of succession: Speaker of the House, attorney general, and chief justices of the 14 courts of appeals in ascending numerical order, beginning with the chief justice of the First Court of Appeals and ending with the chief justice of the Fourteenth Court of Appeals, both of whom have their primary seats in Houston.

If the governor is temporarily unable to serve, is temporarily disqualified, or is impeached, the lieutenant governor exercises the powers of the governor until the governor becomes able or qualified to serve or is acquitted of impeachment charges. The lieutenant governor becomes acting governor while the governor is absent from the state. In the absence of both of these officials, the president pro tempore of the Texas Senate acts as governor. By custom, the Texas governor and lieutenant governor arrange their schedules so that, on at least one occasion during the tenure of a president pro tempore, both are conveniently out of state at the same time. In such circumstances, the president pro tempore of the Senate has the honor of becoming acting governor until the governor or lieutenant governor returns. If the president pro tempore is absent too, the Speaker of the House becomes acting governor.

Although the governor receives full pay when away from Texas, an acting governor receives an amount equal to the governor's daily pay (about $420) for each full day served. During Perry's run for the Republican Party's 2012 presidential nomination, the state paid Lieutenant Governor David Dewhurst a total of $29,589.[39] Even after Perry announced that he would not pursue another term as Texas governor in July 2013, Dewhurst was paid for more than 50 days as acting governor in less than a year. With an eye on another potential run for president, Perry used his final term as governor to travel around the country and to foreign destinations, such as Switzerland, Israel, the United Kingdom, and Palau. During his time in office, Governor Abbott has made trips to Mexico, Cuba, Israel, Australia, Japan, South Korea, India, and various European countries.

📊 How Do We Compare...

In Governor's Compensation and Staff Size?

Most Populous U.S. States	Governor's Annual Salary	Number of People Working in the Governor's Office	U.S. States Bordering Texas	Governor's Annual Salary	Number of People Working in the Governor's Office
California	$209,747	88	Arkansas	$151,838	50
Florida	$130,273	276	Louisiana	$130,000	93
New York	$225,000	180	New Mexico	$110,000	33
Texas	**$153,750**	**277**	Oklahoma	$147,000	34

Source: *The Book of the States:* 2020 (Lexington, KY: Council of State Governments, 2020), 110.

— Competency Connection —
✿ CRITICAL THINKING ✿

Is the Texas governor compensated too little, an appropriate amount, or excessively?

Removal from Office

Impeachment by the House of Representatives and conviction by the Senate form the only constitutionally prescribed method of forcing a Texas governor from office before the end of a term. Article XV, Section 1, of the Texas Constitution states, "The power of impeachment shall be vested in the House of Representatives." Each article of impeachment (similar to a grand jury's indictment) must be approved by a simple majority vote of the House. To remove the governor, one or more impeachment articles must be approved by a two-thirds majority vote of senators present. Once impeached, a governor is suspended from office and may not exercise any authority unless the senators decide against conviction at the end of the Senate trial.

The penalty for conviction on an impeachment charge is removal from office and disqualification from holding any other appointive or elective office at state or local levels in Texas. But conviction does not bar the person from holding a federal office, such as U.S. senator or representative. After removal, a former governor who has been ousted for violating a criminal law may be tried and convicted in a regular trial. Violation of a civil law may subject the individual to a money judgment. Grounds for removing governors or other officials in the executive branch are not stipulated in the Texas Constitution. Impeachment proceedings are highly charged political affairs with legal overtones.

Although all of Texas's state constitutions have provided for impeachment and removal of the governor, only Governor James E. "Pa" Ferguson has been impeached and removed. His troubles stemmed from misuse of state funds and a feud with faculty and administrators of the University of Texas. On September 25, 1917, the Senate convicted Ferguson on 10 articles of impeachment, one of which charged him with official misconduct. The other nine articles involved violations of the state's banking laws and use of state funds for private gain. Although indicted and subsequently removed from office, Ferguson did not stand trial in a criminal proceeding. Reporting the outrage of University of Texas students and powerful alumni when Ferguson used his veto power on the university's state appropriation, one historian noted, "Soon after Ferguson's 'war' with the University, the Ex-Students' Association voted to remain an independent organization, outside the sphere of state control, where it would be free to defend the University again if needed."[40]

This same group united in 2013 to protect University of Texas President William Powers from efforts by the University of Texas System Board of Regents to force his resignation. Powers resigned in 2014, but his resignation did not become effective until June 2015.

✓ 9.5 Learning Check

1. True or False: The Texas governor's staff is smaller today than ever before.
2. What is the constitutional procedure for removing a governor from office?

Answers at the end of this chapter.

✪ Gubernatorial Elections

LO 9.6 Analyze gubernatorial elections and the impact of campaign funds on the politics of the governorship.

The constitutionally limited executive power of the Texas governor does not discourage ambitious gubernatorial candidates who wage multimillion-dollar campaigns in their efforts to win this prestigious office.[41]

Successful gubernatorial candidates must meet constitutional prerequisites, including minimum age (30 years), U.S. citizenship, and Texas residency (for five years immediately preceding the gubernatorial election). According to Section 4 of the Texas Constitution's Bill of Rights, the governor and all other officeholders must also acknowledge the existence of a Supreme Being. In addition, there are numerous extralegal restraints facing those who would become governor. Historically, governors elected after the Reconstruction Era were Democrats with a conservative-moderate political ideology. This mold for successful gubernatorial candidates seemed unbreakable, but William P. ("Bill") Clements, Jr. (in 1978 and 1986) and George W. Bush (in 1994 and 1998) broke tradition by becoming Texas's first and second Republican governors, respectively, since E. J. Davis. (See *Texas Almanac, 2020–2021*, pp. 433–434, for a list of Texas governors.) As conservative businesspeople, Clements and Bush resembled most of their Democratic predecessors in the governor's office; however, their Republicanism, and the fact that they had not previously held elective public office, represented a dramatic departure from the past.[42]

Republican Rick Perry entered the governor's mansion at the end of 2000 without having won a gubernatorial election. He had served as a state legislator, agriculture commissioner, and for two years as lieutenant governor before Governor Bush was elected president of the United States. Although most states place term limits on governors, Texas does not. Therefore, in addition to serving the remainder of Governor Bush's term, Perry was elected three times after that (2002, 2006, and 2010), making him the longest serving governor in Texas history.[43] Greg Abbott has continued the new tradition of Republican dominance in statewide races by winning the gubernatorial elections of 2014 and 2018. He combined a career in the private sector as a lawyer with a career in public service, having served on the Texas Supreme Court and as attorney general before becoming governor.

Gubernatorial Politics: Money Matters

Regardless of a candidate's background and qualifications, to be a serious contender for the governor's office, he or she must raise a significant amount of campaign money. Campaign funds enable candidates to buy advertising time, hire consultants, travel the state, and stage rallies. In politics, money talks and is often, but not always, the deciding factor. South Texas Democrat Tony Sanchez Jr. spent more than double the amount raised by incumbent Rick Perry in 2002, but he lost by a wide margin. Since then, winners of all gubernatorial elections in Texas have raised and spent significantly more than their opponents. Governor Abbott continued raising funds through his first term, and by the beginning of 2017 (nearly two years before election day), he already had a war chest of $34.4 million. By election day, Abbott and groups supporting him had amassed more than $75 million to support his reelection. His opponent, Lupe Valdez, and her supporters raised less than $1.7 million.[44]

The practice of buying influence with campaign contributions permeates American politics. After pumping millions of dollars into a winning gubernatorial election campaign, donors of large amounts of money are often appointed to key policymaking positions. Texas politics is no exception; the governor often appoints major donors to positions on important boards and commissions. For example, in April 2020, Governor Abbott created a "Strike Force to Open Texas," a task force charged with leading the economy back to normal after the pandemic shutdowns. Of the 39 people on the task force's special advisory council, he appointed more than twenty who had contributed more than $6 million to his campaigns since 2015 and several others who had given between $500,000 and $1 million.[45]

Candidates also use their fundraising efforts to symbolize the support they hold among the people of Texas. Thus, they work hard to publicize large totals at filing deadlines or to put a positive spin on smaller totals. After a July 2018 filing deadline, Abbott announced a campaign war chest of $28.9 million, nearly 130 times more than the $222,000 held by opponent Lupe Valdez. Still, Valdez remained positive, releasing the statement, "These are hard-earned funds coming from everyday Texans who know that our vision of the future is the way forward. We may not have tens of millions, but we've gained ground in the polls over the last two months and our message continues to resonate with everyday Texans."[46]

Money can also serve as a tool to gain legislative support for a governor's agenda. In his 2018 campaign, Abbott spent more than $2 million targeting several GOP lawmakers considered not sufficiently supportive of his agenda and to help fellow conservatives whose election efforts faced credible threats by Democratic candidates. Such efforts aim to elect legislators friendly to a governor's policy goals and to send a warning signal to those who would oppose them.[47]

✔ **9.6 Learning Check**

1. What are the constitutional requirements for gubernatorial candidates?

2. True or False: Governors often reward campaign donors with appointments to government positions.

Answers at the end of this chapter.

⬡ Point/Counterpoint

Should the Texas Constitution Be Amended to Limit Terms Served by the State's Governor?

The Issue Rick Perry became governor of Texas for two years after Governor George W. Bush won the presidential election of 2000. Subsequently, Perry was elected to three four-year terms, making his total tenure as governor a record-breaking 14 years. Thirty-six states impose term limits on governors, but Texas and 13 other states do not have such restrictions. In 2015, Senator Don Huffines (R-Dallas) made an unsuccessful attempt to amend SJR 88, which would have imposed term limits.

For	Against
1. Limited terms produce new officeholders with fresh ideas.	1. Voters will not reelect someone who is incompetent or corrupt.
2. Election for a limited time causes an officeholder to place the interests of the public above that of a political party or special interests.	2. Representative democracies are based on the principle of popular election, which should not be restricted by reelection control.
3. Shorter tenure results in less corruption and fewer scandals.	3. Longer service provides more experience, which enhances governing skill.
4. Each term increases the age of an officeholder and the probability of death while in office.	4. A governor constrained by term limits will be disadvantaged when dealing with unelected lobbyists and bureaucrats, and with elected legislators and judges not subject to term limits.

Based on Einer Elhauge, "Are Term Limits Undemocratic?" *University of Chicago Law Review*, 64 (Winter, 1997), 83–201.

Competency Connection
COMMUNICATION SKILLS

Which elected leader might you contact to share your views on term limits, and how would you craft your message?

⬡ The Plural Executive

LO 9.7 Describe the powers of elected department heads and the secretary of state.

Politically, the governor is Texas's highest-ranking officer; but the governor and the lieutenant governor share executive power with four department heads elected for four-year terms. These department heads (with annual salaries budgeted by the legislature for the biennial period covering fiscal years 2021–2022) are the attorney general ($153,750), comptroller of public accounts ($153,750), commissioner of the General Land Office ($140,938), and commissioner of agriculture ($140,938). The secretary of state, with a salary of $197,415 in fiscal years 2020–2021, is appointed by, and serves at the pleasure of, the governor. Positions of governor, lieutenant governor, comptroller of public accounts, and commissioner of the General Land Office are created in Article IV of the Texas Constitution. The commissioner of agriculture holds an office created by statute, now located in the Texas Agriculture Code. These seven executive officials are referred to collectively as the state's **plural executive**. Also performing executive functions are the three elected members of the Railroad Commission of Texas (six-year term, $140,937 salary) and the 15 elected members of the State Board of Education (four-year term, nonpaying).

Elected department heads are largely independent of gubernatorial control. However, with the exception of the office of lieutenant governor, should one of these positions become vacant during an official's term of office, the governor, with Senate approval, appoints a successor who serves until the next general election.

State Representative Lyle Larson (R-San Antonio) points out that several states have a cabinet system wherein the governor appoints most agency heads. To increase efficiency and transparency in Texas, he and others suggest a series of constitutional amendments that would change the way the Lone Star State's top administrative officials are selected. Larson warns, "Though the status quo is comfortable and change rarely is, we must resist the temptation to avoid major overhauls that will ultimately improve our state." He insists, "If we want to change government, we need to change its architecture. Shaking the pillars of government can and often does lead to great outcomes."[48] Are Texans ready for a cabinet government rather than a plural executive?

The Lieutenant Governor

Constitutional qualifications for the office of lieutenant governor are the same as for the governor. Some observers consider the **lieutenant governor** to be the most powerful Texas official, yet this officer functions less in the executive branch than in the legislative branch, where he or she serves as president of the Senate. The Texas Constitution requires the Senate to convene within 30 days whenever a vacancy occurs in the lieutenant governor's office. Senators then elect one of their members to fill the office as acting lieutenant governor until the next general election. Thus, the Senate chose Senator Bill Ratliff (R-Mount Pleasant) to replace Lieutenant Governor Rick Perry when Perry succeeded Governor George W. Bush following the 2000 presidential election.

The annual state salary for the office of lieutenant governor is only $7,200, the same as that paid to members of the legislature. Like legislators, the lieutenant governor may also hold a paying job in private business or practice a profession. For example, from 1992 to 1998, Lieutenant Governor Bob Bullock was affiliated with the law firm of Scott, Douglass, & McConnico, LLP, in Austin, from which he received a six-figure annual salary.

With experience as a conservative talk-show host in Houston, Dan Patrick is a colorful campaigner. In the 2014 general election, with strong Tea Party support, he easily defeated Sen. Leticia Van de Putte (D-San Antonio). Four years later he won reelection by a narrower margin against Democratic challenger and accountant Mike Collier. Patrick chaired Donald Trump's 2016 presidential campaign in Texas. As president of the Senate for the 85th Legislature, Patrick took strong stands on hot-button social issues, such as the "bathroom bill" about

plural executive
The governor, elected department heads, and the secretary of state, as provided by the Texas Constitution and statutes.

lieutenant governor
Popularly elected constitutional official who serves as president of the Senate and is first in the line of succession if the office of governor becomes vacant before the end of a term.

transgender rights in public restrooms and restrictions on abortion. He continued his support for conservative social causes in the 86th and 87th legislatures; but pressure from voters and the business community led Patrick to increase focus on "meat and potatoes" issues such as property taxes, public education funding, pandemic recovery, and energy grid reform.

The Attorney General

One of Texas's most visible and powerful officeholders is the **attorney general**. Whether joining lawsuits to overturn federal healthcare reform, arguing affirmative action questions in court, or trying to resolve redistricting disputes, the state's chief lawyer is a major player in making many important public policy decisions. This officer represents the state in civil litigation and issues advisory opinions on legal questions if requested by state and local authorities. To qualify for the office of attorney general, one must have been a practicing attorney in Texas for at least five years before taking office.

In 2014, Sen. Ken Paxton (R-McKinney) was elected Attorney General to replace Greg Abbott, who was elected Governor. Paxton won the general election in November against Democratic challenger Sam Houston by more than 20 percentage points. Though he won reelection in 2018, it was by less than four percentage points.

Image 9.4 Attorney General Ken Paxton with wife Senator Angela Paxton (R-McKinney) at January 6, 2021 Washington, DC rally that led to Capitol riot.

Jacquelyn Martin/AP Photo

Competency Connection
✿ CRITICAL THINKING ✿

What are the benefits and drawbacks of directly electing members of the plural executive?

attorney general
The constitutional official elected to head the Office of the Attorney General, which represents the state government in lawsuits and provides legal advice to state and local officials.

With more than 4,200 employees, the Office of the Attorney General gives advice concerning the constitutionality of many pending bills. The governor, heads of state agencies, and local government officials also request opinions from the attorney general on the scope of an agency's or official's jurisdiction and the interpretation of vaguely worded laws. Although neither judges nor other officials are bound by these opinions, the attorney general's rulings are considered authoritative unless overruled by court decisions or new laws. As schools weighed their options for opening after COVID-19 infections continued to increase in many areas of the state in the summer of 2020, Paxton issued an advisory opinion in July that local health authorities would not be allowed to issue orders to close schools for the purpose of preventing future infections.[49]

Another power of the attorney general is to initiate, in a district court, quo warranto proceedings that challenge an official's right to hold public office. Such action may lead to removal of an officeholder who lacks a qualification set by law or who is judged guilty of official misconduct. Among its many functions, the Office of the Attorney General enforces child support orders issued by state courts and administers the Crime Victims' Compensation Fund.

As attorney general, Greg Abbott filed 34 lawsuits against the federal government between 2002 and 2014. Thirty-one of the cases were filed during the Obama administration. Most frequently, the attorney general sued the Environmental Protection Agency. He also brought lawsuits challenging the Affordable Care Act and asking federal courts to approve Texas's redistricting maps and voter identification law.[50] Attorney General Paxton continued the practice, suing to strike down Obama administration policies an additional 27 times. During the Trump administration, Paxton's focus shifted to using lawsuits to defend Trump's policy agenda and other socially conservative causes. For example, Texas initiated or joined lawsuits to allow businesses to refuse service to same-sex couples, to restrict the use of restrooms by transgender people, to place religious symbols in government buildings, to attack gun regulations, and to end DACA (a program allowing those brought as children to the United States illegally by their parents to remain in this country). With the advent of the Biden administration, Paxton began suing to protect Trump-era policies.

The attorney general may also sue other states, as Paxton did in a suit against four electoral battleground states in an attempt to overturn the results of the 2020 presidential election. Though dismissed by the U.S. Supreme Court, this suit garnered national attention. It secured Paxton a spot as a speaker at President Trump's January 6, 2021, rally in Washington, D.C., which resulted in a mob of rioters storming the U.S. Capitol. The suit also prompted the State Bar of Texas to investigate whether Paxton's efforts to overturn the election amounted to professional misconduct.[51]

The attorney general also submits *amicus curiae* briefs on behalf of the state's efforts to influence the outcome of court cases. In 2019, Paxton maintained his attack on the DACA program when his office led a multistate coalition in filing an *amicus curiae* brief with the U.S. Supreme Court in support of the Trump administration's decision to rescind the program.[52]

Although the attorney general is the state's chief legal officer, Paxton has had personal legal problems that have affected his service. Before he won the GOP nomination with strong Tea Party backing in 2014, Paxton was fined $1,000 by

Texas' State Securities Board for soliciting clients for an investment company without being licensed as an investment adviser. After the November 2014 election, Texans for Public Justice brought this matter to the attention of the Travis County district attorney. Subsequently, it was referred to the district attorney for Collin County, where Paxton had solicited clients for Mowery Capital Management. An investigation conducted by Texas Rangers uncovered additional evidence that indicated Paxton had also solicited investors, including some of his fellow legislators, for another company, Servergy, Inc. Paxton received 100,000 shares of stock for doing so and failed to disclose this information to potential investors. He had also failed to register as a dealer for this series of transactions. On July 28, 2015, a grand jury indicted Paxton on three state felony charges. While awaiting trial in state court, Paxton was hit with a civil complaint by the federal Securities and Exchange Commission in 2016 for misleading investors. The federal case against him was dismissed by jurors two years later. Battles over the venue for the state case and payments to special prosecutors have caused numerous delays in bringing that case to court. Five years after his indictment, it is still unclear when Paxton will face trial. He claims the cases are political witch hunts. In October 2020, seven of the most senior employees in the Attorney General's office sent a letter to its Human Resources Division expressing their belief that Paxton was violating a variety of federal and/or state laws related to "improper influence, abuse of office, bribery and other potential criminal offenses." They recommended, and the FBI began, a federal investigation. After the firing and resignation of numerous aides involved in filing the complaint, four of them filed a lawsuit alleging illegal retaliation by the Attorney General.[53]

The Comptroller of Public Accounts

One of the most powerful elected officers in Texas government is the **comptroller of public accounts**, the state's chief accounting officer and tax collector; but there are no formal qualifications for this office. After a biennial appropriation bill passes by a simple majority vote in the House and Senate, the Texas Constitution requires the comptroller's certification that expected revenue will be collected to cover all of the budgeted expenditures. Otherwise, an appropriation must be approved by a four-fifths majority vote in both houses. As explained in a newspaper editorial,

> The comptroller's estimate, always a touchy subject, has been more so since 2011, when then Comptroller Susan Combs issued what turned out to be a vastly underestimated estimate that showed a $27 billion dollar deficit. Legislators responded with a $5.4 billion cut in public education spending. To this day, some conspiracy theorists, including members of our editorial board, suspect that the extreme lowball was deliberate and that bringing the public education system to its knees was an endgame.[54]

comptroller of public accounts
An elected constitutional officer responsible for collecting taxes, keeping accounts, estimating revenue, and serving as treasurer for the state.

In 2014, Republican Glenn Hegar won election to the office of Comptroller of Public Accounts. He defeated Democratic challenger Joi Chevalier in a successful 2018 reelection bid. As the state's comptroller, Hegar supervises more than

2,900 employees. The comptroller's office promotes the cause of transparency in government by maintaining the Comptroller.Texas.Gov website. This site allows anyone to see how state tax money is being spent. For example, students and others can find the amount of money Hegar's department and other state agencies have paid to individual vendors for goods or services or to its employees for official travel expenses. One of the comptroller's duties is to designate hundreds of Texas financial institutions (mostly banks, but also a few savings associations and credit unions) to serve as depositories for state-collected funds. The comptroller's office also administers college savings plans, scholarships, and other financial aid.

As directed by the legislature, Hegar promotes consistency in accounting methods and standards for all state agencies. He does the same for Texas's counties, cities, and special districts. In a statement to the general public, Hegar describes his job as like that of a corporation's chief financial officer (CFO) and explains, "A CFO's duties usually include keeping the books, monitoring cash flows and maintaining a constant watch on the company's financial health. And that's my job—except I work for you."[55]

The Commissioner of the General Land Office

Although less visible than other elected executives, the **commissioner of the General Land Office** is an important figure in Texas politics; but there are no formal qualifications for this government position. Since the creation of the General Land Office under the Constitution of the Republic of Texas (1836), the commissioner's duties have expanded to include overseeing the state's public lands and thus awarding oil, gas, and sulfur leases for lands owned by the state (including wind rights, especially in the Texas tidelands); serving as chair of the Veterans Land Board; and sitting as an ex officio member of other boards responsible for managing state-owned lands. In addition to these responsibilities, the General Land Office maintains an archive of more than 35 million documents and historic maps relating to land titles in Texas. With more than 700 employees, the General Land Office also oversees growth of the Permanent School Fund. This fund is financed by oil and gas leases, rentals, and royalties that provide hundreds of millions of dollars annually to benefit the state's public schools.

In 2018, Land Commissioner George P. Bush sparked a battle with the State Board of Education over disbursement of education funds. Elected in 2014 and reelected in 2018, this Republican is a member of the third generation of the Bush family to hold office in Texas. George P. Bush is the grandson of former Texas congressman and president of the United States George H. W. Bush, and he is a nephew of former Texas governor and president of the United States George W. Bush. Under Commissioner Bush's leadership, the School Land Board declined in 2018 for the first time ever to allocate money from its fund to the State Board of Education (SBOE). In the past eight funding cycles, the School Land Board allocated part of its funding directly to school funding and part to the SBOE, which used it largely for textbooks. This time, Bush directed that all of its $600 million go to the Available School Fund, arguing that the Land Office's investment fund is more profitable and more directly beneficial to schools. After contentious

commissioner of the General Land Office
As head of Texas's General Land Office, this elected constitutional officer oversees the state's extensive landholdings and related mineral interests, especially oil and gas leasing, for the benefit of the Permanent School Fund.

hearings before the Texas Legislature, Bush agreed to release $55 million to the SBOE. Still, this was far less than the $490 million allocated in FY 2018–2019. The conflict led to a 2019 effort in the legislature to strip the School Land Board's investment authority, revoke its control of the funds, and send mineral revenues directly to the SBOE. Aggressive lobbying by Commissioner Bush kept such measures out of the reform bill sent to the governor for signature.[56]

Because the General Land Office administers vast landholdings for the state, the commissioner is involved in many legal disputes. In 2018, Commissioner Bush filed a federal lawsuit to lift habitat protections for the golden cheeked warbler, an endangered species of bird. Taking the warbler off the endangered species list would have opened a large area in Central Texas to increased development and road building. Environmental groups supported continued protections. In 2020, a U.S. court of appeals decided to return the issue to the U.S. Fish and Wildlife Service for an in-depth, 12-month review of the decision. This case is only the latest instance of the Texas government aligning with developers, industrial operators, and property rights advocates to target a wildlife species for delisting. The strategy was pioneered and used extensively by former comptroller Susan Combs, who assisted Bush in the warbler suit.[57]

The Commissioner of Agriculture

Under Section 5, Chapter 11 of the Texas Agriculture Code, for at least five of the 10 years before taking office as **commissioner of agriculture** a person must have had significant experience in the business of agriculture and owned or operated farm, ranch, or timber land. These criteria are important, but identification with the state's voters (most of whom live in suburbs or central cities) is the principal requirement for winning the office.

The commissioner of agriculture oversees about 700 employees in the Texas Department of Agriculture and is responsible for enforcing agricultural laws and for providing service programs to Texas farmers, ranchers, and consumers. Control over the use of often controversial pesticides and herbicides is exercised through the department's Pesticide Programs Division. This division restricts use of high-risk chemicals; and it licenses dealers, professional applicators, and private applicators who apply dangerous pesticides and herbicides on their own farms and ranches. Other enforcement actions of the department include inspections to determine the accuracy of commercial scales, pumps, and meters. Such inspections protect Texas consumers at grocery store scales, gasoline pumps, and other venues.

An endorsement by Governor Rick Perry and ties to rocker Ted Nugent helped Republican Sid Miller win election to the office of Agriculture Commissioner in 2014. He has generated controversy ever since. During his first year as commissioner of agriculture, Miller received criticism for some of his appointments and for bonuses paid to department employees, for dropping the ban on deep-fried food and soft drinks in school lunchrooms, and for making Facebook postings considered by many viewers to be anti-Muslim. When the legislature failed to appropriate money that he had requested for his agency, Miller alienated many farmers, business people, and legislators by increasing fees charged for its

commissioner of agriculture
The elected official, whose position is created by statute, who heads Texas's Department of Agriculture, which promotes the sale of agricultural commodities and regulates pesticides, aquaculture, egg quality, weights and measures, and grain warehouses.

services. In 2016, Texas Rangers investigated Miller's use of state funds and campaign money for 2015 trips to Oklahoma for medical treatment and to Mississippi to rope calves in a rodeo. Though he reimbursed travel costs to the state and prosecutors decided against pressing criminal charges, the Texas Ethics Commission fined Miller $500 for the Oklahoma trip four years later. Miller was an avid supporter of Donald Trump's 2016 presidential campaign, and Miller's Twitter account garnered national attention by identifying Hillary Clinton with a vulgar expletive. The commissioner's Facebook page receives much criticism because he regularly posts inflammatory attacks on people and groups with whom he disagrees and at times spreads false, misleading, or unsupported news stories.

In his 2018 reelection bid, numerous powerful statewide interest groups, including the Texas Farm Bureau, declined to endorse Miller despite endorsing every other Republican statewide candidate. In spite of the controversy, Miller survived a primary election challenge from two fellow Republicans and defeated Democratic challenger Kim Olson to win reelection in 2018. Miller maintained a high profile in his second term. In 2020 he launched a cable television show called *Texas Agriculture Matters*, which he uses to discuss agriculture policy, Texas products, western heritage, and rural lifestyle. Miller was also featured in the movie *Borat: Subsequent Moviefilm*. Politically, he took an active role in supporting President Trump's reelection efforts in 2020. He also stepped up challenges to the governor, participating in protests that accused "King Abbott" of tyranny in his executive orders regarding the COVID-19 pandemic and joining a lawsuit to block the governor's extension of the early voting period.[58]

📋 Students in Action

The Mickey Leland Environmental Internship Program

What it Is

The Mickey Leland Environmental Internship Program was founded in 1992 by the Texas Water Commission, which was a predecessor to the current Texas Commission on Environmental Quality. While representing Houston districts in the Texas House of Representatives (1973–1979) and the U.S. House of Representatives (1979–1989), Mickey Leland worked to promote a clean and healthy environment, proving to be an effective leader on environmental issues within Texas, as well as the entire nation. Congressman Leland was a member of the Subcommittee on Health and Environment, and he encouraged public awareness in the protection of public health, as well as environmental issues. In 1989, this Black Texan died in a plane crash while flying to visit a Sudanese refugee camp in Ethiopia. The internship in Leland's honor is designed to continue his work of increasing awareness of environmental issues, encouraging students to consider careers in the environmental field, and promoting participation of minorities and the disadvantaged in environmental policy development. Learn more at the internship's website, https://www.tceq.texas.gov/jobs/mickeyleland.

What You Can Do

Undergraduate students enrolled full-time are eligible to apply for the internship program. Depending on your area of study, this internship

(Continued)

involved
the leg
and d
as at
working
and assisting i
operations.

How it Helps

Any internship provides the ever-important real-world experience that businesses and professionals look for upon graduation. The Mickey Leland Internship is no exception and encourages careers in law, political science, communications, psychology, and education, among others.

The Mickey Leland Environmental Internship Program students, class of 2019.

offers the opportunity to fit a broad range of interests while providing a hands-on experience within the Texas legislature. Students are

---

Competency Connection
★ **PERSONAL RESPONSIBILITY** ★

How might an internship like this one empower you to develop your own skills and benefit your state?

The Secretary of State

The only constitutional executive officer appointed by the governor is the **secretary of state**. This appointment must be confirmed by a two-thirds vote of the Senate. The secretary of state has a four-year term concurrent with that of the governor but may be dismissed by the governor at any time. Most secretaries of state do not serve for a full term. The secretary of state oversees a staff of approximately 200 people and is the chief elections officer of Texas. Principal responsibilities of the office include the following:

- Administering state election laws in conjunction with county officials
- Tabulating election returns for state and district offices
- Granting charters (organizational documents) to Texas corporations
- Issuing permits to outside corporations to conduct business within Texas
- Processing requests for extradition of criminals to or from other states for trial and punishment

With these diverse duties, the secretary of state is obviously more than just a record keeper. How the office functions is determined largely by the occupant's relations with the governor. Greg Abbott appointed David Whitley, his former deputy chief of staff and appointments director, to be the 112th Texas Secretary of State in

secretary of state
The state's chief elections officer, with other administrative duties, who is appointed by the governor for a term concurrent with that of the governor.

December 2018. However, Whitley sparked national controversy by releasing a list of 98,000 registered voters who were at some point noncitizens and by referring the list to the Office of Attorney General for potential prosecution for voter fraud. Civil rights groups sued when an investigation uncovered that tens of thousands of those on the list had become citizens and were eligible to vote. A federal judge found no evidence of voter fraud and ended the state's investigation. Twelve Senate Democrats announced their opposition to Whitley's confirmation, enough to deny him the two-thirds majority he would need to be confirmed. In May 2019, Whitley resigned shortly before the vote that would have denied his confirmation. Governor Abbott immediately rehired him to a position in the governor's office and appointed attorney and small business owner Ruth Hughs as the 113th Secretary of State.[59]

In addition to her duties as the state's chief elections officer, Secretary Hughs served as the governor's advisor on border issues. She was the state's Border Commerce Coordinator, coordinating and facilitating initiatives with local officials, state agencies, and the federal governments of the United States, Mexico, and Canada. She also chaired the Border Trade Advisory Committee, which addresses border trade transportation challenges and served as one of 11 members of the Task Force on Infectious Disease Preparedness and Response, created in September 2020. Secretary Hughs resigned at the end of the 87th Legislative session amid speculation that her testimony to lawmakers describing the 2020 Texas election as "smooth and secure" led Senate Republicans to avoid confirming her.[60]

❖ The State Bureaucracy

LO 9.8 Describe the role of the bureaucracy in governing the state of Texas.

Texans' most direct connection to their state government is through the state's bureaucracy. Whether obtaining a driver's license, driving on the state's roads, or attending a public college or university, the state bureaucracy touches the lives of the state's residents. In addition to the plural executive positions, Texas has two popularly elected boards (the State Board of Education and the Railroad Commission) and more than 200 appointed boards, commissions, and departments that implement state laws and programs. Although the governor, with Senate approval, appoints nonelected officials, once they are in office the governor must rely on persuasion and personal or political loyalty to exercise influence. The almost 150,000 state employees who staff the agencies perform the day-to-day work of government and constitute what we frequently call the bureaucracy. In addition to delivering services to Texans, state agencies also regulate people, occupations, and businesses. Regulation commonly shifts costs and benefits from one group to another. For example, contaminated air hurts the quality of life and increases medical costs for children with respiratory problems such as asthma, as well as for the elderly; but regulations requiring special equipment to reduce emissions from smokestacks cost businesses money. Not surprisingly, regulatory policy is fraught with controversy. This section provides highlights of some of the more active agencies in the state.

The Institutional Context

The way in which the Texas executive branch is organized has a major effect on public policy. A key reason is that the fragmentation of authority strongly affects who has access to policy decisions, as well as how visible the decision process is to the public. The large number of agencies means they are covered less by the media and, therefore, are less visible to the public. The one state official to whom the public pays attention (the governor) has limited power. Special interest groups, on the other hand, have strong incentives (profits) to develop cozy relationships with agency personnel. Furthermore, most agencies do not have to defend their decisions before a higher authority (such as the governor), although an agency's regulatory decisions can be appealed to state courts.

Fragmentation of the state executive into so many largely independent agencies was an intentional move by the framers of the Texas Constitution and later legislatures to avoid centralized power. Administering state programs through boards was also thought to keep partisan politics out of public administration. Unfortunately, this fragmentation simply changes the nature of the politics, making it more difficult to coordinate efforts and hold agencies responsible to the public.

Boards governing state agencies are not typically full-time; instead, they commonly meet quarterly. In most cases, a full-time board-appointed executive director oversees day-to-day agency operations. Boards usually make general policy decisions and leave details to the executive director; however, some boards are much more active and involved (e.g., the Texas Commission on Environmental Quality). In recent years, the governor's influence has increased through the ability to name two powerful executive commissioners to run two major agencies—the Health and Human Services Commission and the Texas Education Agency. Two important boards—the Railroad Commission of Texas (RRC) that regulates the oil and gas industry and the State Board of Education (SBOE)—are elected. Members of both tend to be quite active; however, the State Board of Education is limited by its lack of authority over the commissioner of education, who heads the Texas Education Agency and reports to the governor.

Some agencies were created in the Texas Constitution. Others were created by the legislature, either as directed by the state constitution or independent of it. As problems emerge that elected officials believe government must address, they look to existing state agencies or create new ones to provide solutions. Sometimes, citizen complaints force an agency's creation. For example, citizen outrage at rising utility rates resulted in the creation in 1975 of the Public Utility Commission (PUC) to review and limit those rates. (Lobbying by special interest groups and the orientation of gubernatorial appointments over time, however, have changed the direction of the PUC's policies to again draw the ire of consumer advocates.) Lobbying is also important in the creation of agencies. The most famous Texas case was lobbying by oil and gas companies in the early 20th century to have the Railroad Commission create a system of regulation to reduce economic chaos in the fledgling petroleum industry.

The **sunset review process** is an attempt to keep state agencies efficient and responsive to current needs. Each biennium, a group of state agencies is examined

sunset review process
During a cycle of 12 years, each state agency is studied at least once to see if it is needed and efficient, and then the legislature decides whether to abolish, merge, reorganize, or retain that agency.

by the Sunset Advisory Commission, which recommends to the legislature whether an agency should be abolished, merged, reorganized, or retained. It is the legislature that makes the final decision. At least once every 12 years, each of about 140 state agencies and other government entities must be evaluated. (State universities and courts are not subject to the process.) The Sunset Advisory Commission is composed of 10 legislators (five from each chamber) and two public members. This commission has a staff of about 30 employees.

In 2019, Governor Abbott signed SB 68 into law. The law requires a strategic fiscal review and zero-based budgeting for all state agencies on a schedule tied to their sunset reviews. Instead of assuming current funding levels are justified, each agency must start with a budget of zero dollars and analyze each of its functions for needs and costs. For the 2020–2021 review cycle, the commission was scheduled to review 37 entities under the new rules. Included is the Texas Commission on Law Enforcement, which is tasked with creating and enforcing standards for highly trained and ethical law enforcement, corrections, and telecommunications personnel.

A major problem with the sunset review process, according to critics, is that the legislature has little taste for abolition or major restructuring of large agencies. For example, the Sunset Advisory Commission's staff found that the mission and byzantine regulations of the Alcoholic Beverage Commission are hopelessly outdated, yet the legislature continued the commission with only minor changes. From the Sunset Advisory Commission's authorization in 1977 through 2019, it conducted a total of 551 reviews of agencies (some agencies were reviewed multiple times). Approximately 83 percent of reviews resulted in the agency being retained, 7 percent abolished an agency, and 9 percent reorganized agencies in major ways (such as combining two or more agencies). Of those agencies retained, some had changes, such as adding public members (people not from the regulated industry) on governing boards, improving procedures, or changing policies. According to the commission, from 1977 through 2019, the sunset process saved the state $1 billion, generating a return of $19 for every $1 appropriated to it since 1985.[61]

State Employees

For most people, the face of state government is the governor, legislators, and other top officials. However, most of the work of Texas state government (called **public administration**) is done by people in agencies headed by elected officials and appointed boards. These **bureaucrats** (public employees), though often the subject of criticism or jokes about inefficiency and "red tape" (the rules and procedures that bureaucrats must follow), deliver governmental services to the state's residents. The public may see them in action as a clerk taking an application, a supervisor explaining why a request was turned down, or an inspector checking a nursing home.

The nature of bureaucracy is both its strength and its weakness. Large organizations, such as governments and corporations, need many employees doing specialized jobs with sufficient coordination to achieve the organization's goals. That means employees must follow set rules and procedures so they can provide

public administration
The implementation of public policy by government employees.

bureaucrats
Public employees.

relatively uniform results. When a bureaucracy works well, it harnesses individual efforts to achieve the organization's goals. Along the way, however, red tape slows the process and prevents employees from making decisions that go against the rules. State rules should mean the same in Dallas as in Muleshoe or Cut and Shoot, but making decisions may seem slow, and "street level" bureaucrats may not have the authority to make adjustments for differences in local conditions. Thus, bureaucracies are necessary but sometimes frustrating.

Number of State Employees Governments are Texas's biggest employers. In 2020, the equivalent of 333,072 Texans drew full-time state paychecks (including 187,024 employees of public colleges and universities). Although this number sounds like a lot, it represents only about 1 percent of the state population and places Texas among the bottom 10 states in number of state employees per capita. Texas is following a national pattern. The most heavily populated states tend to have fewer government employees relative to their population. As populations grow, most states, including Texas, hire proportionately fewer employees. From 1993 to 2020, the number of state employees declined relative to the population in both Texas and the nation because of economies of scale, meaning that as agencies grow, they may require more total employees but not as many relative to the population they serve. For example, as demand increases, many employees may be able to process more cases in the same amount of time. Another reason Texas ranks so low compared to other states is that Texas state government passes a great deal of responsibility to local governments. When local government workers are included in calculating the number of government employees, the total number of public employees increases from 105 per 10,000 residents to 600 per 10,000 residents.[62]

Competence, Pay, and Retention Although most public administrators do a good job, some are less effective than others. Observers tend to believe that bureaucratic competence improves with a civil service system along with good pay and benefits. In the first century of our nation, many people thought that any fool could do a government job. As a result, many fools worked in government. From local to national levels, government jobs were filled through the **patronage system**, also known as the spoils system. Government officials hired friends and supporters, with little regard for whether they were competent. The idea was that "to the victor belong the spoils." **Merit systems**, on the other hand, require officials to hire, promote, and fire government employees on the basis of objective criteria, such as tests, education, experience, and performance. If a merit system works well, it tends to produce a competent bureaucracy. A merit system that provides too much protection, however, makes it difficult to fire the incompetent and gives little incentive for the competent to excel.

Texas has never had a merit system covering all state employees, and the partial state merit system was abolished in 1985. What replaced it is a highly centralized compensation and classification system covering most of the executive branch but not the judicial and legislative branches or higher education. The legislature sets salaries, wage scales, and other benefits. Individual agencies are free to develop their own systems for hiring, promotion, and firing (so long as

patronage system
Hiring friends and supporters of elected officials as government employees without regard to their abilities.

merit systems
Hiring, promoting, and firing on the basis of objective criteria, such as tests, degrees, experience, and performance.

they comply with federal standards, where applicable). Critics worried that the result would be greater turnover and lower competence. A survey of state human resource directors, however, indicates that agencies have developed more flexible personnel policies that provide some protection for most employees. Moreover, patronage appointments have not become a major problem in state administration. In the words of one observer, "It's not uncommon for state agencies to become repositories for campaign staff or former officeholders…. But there are no wholesale purges" when new officials are elected.[63]

In Texas, most employees (public and private) are "at will"—that is, they can be fired or can quit for good, bad, or no reason unless they are under a contract or union agreement. The employment relationship is voluntary. Employers cannot fire workers for illegal reasons, such as race, retaliation for reporting illegal activity, or exercising civil liberties. For example, in a Virginia case, a federal appeals court held that a sheriff violated his employees' free speech rights by firing them for "liking" his opponent's campaign site on Facebook.

In recent years, Texas state government employee turnover has been consistently high: 17 to 19 percent in fiscal years 2012–2018. By comparison, in fiscal year 2014, turnover was slightly more than 6 percent for the federal government. In 2015, turnover cost the state government $361 million, according to the State Auditor's Office's most recent estimate. In fiscal year 2019, turnover reached 20.3 percent, its highest rate in 10 years. It then dropped to 18.6 percent in fiscal year 2020. Turnover was highest for workers in criminal justice, social services, custodial positions, and social services occupations. The highest turnover rate (59.4 percent) was among Juvenile Corrections Officers. Exit surveys (filled out by employees leaving state employment) reveal that the top reasons for leaving are retirement and desire for higher pay or better benefits.[64]

Other nonfinancial factors attract state employees. Studies consistently show that large numbers of government employees have a strong sense of service and thus find being a public servant rewarding. Three perks also increase the attractiveness of public employment: paid vacations, state holidays, and sick leave.

Another incentive for employment can be equitable treatment. For many years, Texas state government has advertised itself as an "equal opportunity employer;" however, a 2016 study conducted by the *Dallas Morning News* disclosed significant pay gaps between White men and all other gender, ethnic, and racial groups (except for Asian Americans). On average, female state government employees earned 92 cents for every dollar earned by their male counterparts in 2015. Pay disparities were even more pronounced for members of historical minority groups: Latinas earned 82 cents for every dollar earned by White men, and Black women earned 84 cents for every dollar earned by White men. The highest-paying positions were most frequently held by White men, and all high-level positions were more likely to be held by Whites than any other racial or ethnic group. White men outearned all other groups on a job-by-job comparison as well. For example, of the 14 Systems Analyst VI positions in the Office of the Attorney General (split equally between men and women), men's annual average earnings were $98,705, compared to women's average salaries of $84,831, a 16 percent pay gap. Earnings gaps are still smaller in government than in the

Table 9.1 Texas Minorities and Women in State Government Compared with the Total Civilian State Workforce (in percentage)*

Job Category	Black		Latino/a		Female	
	Govt.	Total Workforce	Govt.	Total Workforce	Govt.	Total Workforce
Official, administrator	11	8	15	22	54	40
Professional	11	11	16	20	56	55
Technical	18	14	26	29	61	55
Administrative support	18	14	34	36	82	72
Skilled craft	9	10	28	52	8	12
Service and maintenance	25	13	36	52	45	52
TOTALS	**18**	**12**	**22**	**37**	**57**	**45**

*State agencies' workforce includes executive agencies and higher education for fiscal year 2018; statewide civilian workforce includes both private and public workers and is for calendar year 2016.

Note on interpretation: The first cell indicates that 11 percent of Texas government officials and administrators are Black; the next cell to the right shows that 8 percent of the officials and administrators in the state's total economy are Black.

Source: Compiled from *"Equal Employment Opportunity and Minority Hiring Practices Report, Fiscal Years 2017–2018,"* Texas Workforce Commission, Civil Rights Division, January 2019, https://twc.texas.gov/files/twc/equal-employment-opportunity-minority-hiring-practices-report-2017-2018-twc.pdf.

─── Competency Connection ───
💬 COMMUNICATION SKILLS 💬

How would you describe the differences between the government workforce and the total workforce? Why do you think those differences exist?

private sector; but in Texas, that gap is widening in contrast to shrinking pay gaps in both the private sector and in other state governments.[65] Table 9.1 compares government employment patterns of women and historical minority groups to private sector employment patterns for the same groups.

Education

State Board of Education Oversight of Texas education is divided between the 15-member elected **State Board of Education (SBOE)** and the commissioner of education, who is appointed by the governor to run the Texas Education Agency. Over the years, the sometimes extreme ideological positions taken by many SBOE members prompted the legislature to whittle away the board's authority. For several years, the board was even made appointive rather than elective. Today, the greater power over state education is in the hands of the commissioner of education through control of the Texas Education Agency, but the SBOE remains important and highly controversial.

Among the board's most significant powers are curriculum approval for each subject and grade, textbook review for public schools, and investment management for the Permanent School Fund.[66] See Chapter 11, "Finance and Fiscal

State Board of Education (SBOE)
A popularly elected 15-member body with limited authority over Texas's K-12 education system.

Image 9.5 Texas SBOE member Marisa B. Pérez-Díaz, the youngest Latina in the nation ever elected to a state board of education, speaks outside a board meeting in 2018.

Competency Connection
★ **PERSONAL RESPONSIBILITY** ★

How should the state select those who set curriculum and textbook standards for its public schools?

Texas Education Agency (TEA)
Administers the state's public school system of more than 1,200 school districts and charter schools.

commissioner of education
The official who heads the TEA.

Policy," for a discussion of state revenue designated for public schools.

Despite these important responsibilities, there are no education or experience requirements for service on the board. Representing districts created by the legislature at the beginning of each decade, with approximately equal population (1.9 million), the 15 elected SBOE members serve without salary for overlapping terms of four years. The governor appoints, with Senate confirmation, a sitting SBOE member as chair for a two-year term. In September 2019 and again in March 2021, Governor Abbott appointed Republican Kevin Ellis to chair the board. Ellis is a chiropractor who had served as board president for Lufkin ISD.[67]

In the Lone Star State, the **Texas Education Agency (TEA),** headquartered in Austin, has about 1,000 employees. Created by the legislature in 1949, TEA today is headed by the **commissioner of education,** appointed by the governor to a four-year term with Senate confirmation. This official earns $220,375 per year. In December 2015, Governor Greg Abbott appointed Mike Morath, a Dallas Independent School District Board trustee and school choice proponent, to serve as commissioner. He was reappointed in 2019.

TEA has oversight authority over the state's public and charter schools, and it monitors statewide testing. Based on performance results, this agency issues school and district ratings and approves school accreditation. Prior to 2018, schools were rated as "met standards," "met alternative standard," or "improvement required." This rating was based on four indices combining test results, graduation rates, and other indicators. In 2017 the Texas Legislature passed HB 22, which established three categories for measuring performance: student achievement, school progress, and "closing the gaps," which measures progress among economically disadvantaged students. In 2018, school districts and individual campuses began receiving grades of "A" through "F" in each category and overall. The agency has power to revoke accreditation of school districts that consistently fail to meet performance or financial standards. Revocation can result in a school district's closure.[67]

Much of what the TEA does goes unnoticed by the general public, but some decisions receive considerable attention and have effects beyond education. Ratings of schools are advertised to draw home buyers into neighborhoods and subdivisions, and the decision to close a school or school district has profound effects on the community it serves. Thus, TEA has been cautious and often takes less drastic steps before closing schools or districts, including charter schools. In 2015, the Texas Legislature passed a law requiring TEA to take over a school board or close campuses in a district if a school receives "improvement required" ratings in five consecutive years. Marlin ISD reached its fifth year in 2016; and in 2017,

Lynda M. Gonzalez/American-Statesman

Commissioner Morath replaced its school board with a "board of managers." In 2018 and 2019, Marlin was one of five ISDs that had their accreditation revoked by the TEA, meaning the state of Texas no longer recognized them as public schools. Hoping they might improve, the agency granted abatements to the Marlin, Buckholts, Sierra Blanca, and Hearne ISDs, while Winfield ISD was absorbed into neighboring Mount Pleasant ISD. Because of school closures during the COVID-19 pandemic, TEA declared on April 3, 2020, that all districts across the state will receive a score of "Not Rated: Declared State of Disaster" for the year. As a result, ISDs with abatements will continue operations for at least another year.[69]

Boards of Regents Texas's public university systems, public universities outside the systems, and the Texas State Technical College System are governed by boards of regents. The governor appoints regents for six-year terms with Senate approval. A board makes general policy, selects each university's president, and provides general supervision of its universities. In the case of university systems (like the UT system), the board usually selects a chancellor to handle administration and to provide executive leadership. The president of one of the universities may simultaneously serve as chancellor. Day-to-day operation of each university is in the hands of the individual university's top officials (commonly the president and the academic vice president, though terminology varies). Governance of community colleges is by local boards, as discussed in Chapter 3, "Local Governments."

Texas Higher Education Coordinating Board The **Texas Higher Education Coordinating Board (THECB)** is not a superboard of regents, but it does provide some semblance of statewide direction for all public (not private) community colleges and universities. In the 2013 sunset review process, the legislature significantly changed the agency's focus from regulation of public higher education to coordination. The sunset bill removed significant parts of the agency's authority, including power to consolidate or eliminate low-producing academic programs and to approve capital projects.

The nine members of the board receive no pay and are appointed by the governor to six-year terms with Senate approval. A student representative is appointed also by the governor as a nonvoting member for a one-year term. In June 2021, Governor Abbott appointed Matthew B. Smith, a political science major at Texas State University, as a student representative on THECB.

Gubernatorial power also extends to designating two THECB members as chair and vice chair, with neither appointment requiring Senate confirmation. Governors have substantial influence over higher education because they generally maintain a close relationship with the board. The commissioner of higher education, who runs the agency on a day-to-day basis and plays a significant role in making higher education policy, is appointed (and can be removed) by the board. In October 2019, Governor Abbott appointed Harrison Keller to be the sixth Commissioner of Higher Education and chief executive officer for the THECB. Keller replaced Raymund Paredes, who had served as commissioner for 15 years.[70]

Texas Higher Education Coordinating Board (THECB)
An agency that provides some coordination for the state's public community colleges and universities.

Health and Human Services

The Texas Health and Human Services Commission (HHSC) coordinates social service policy. Sweeping changes were launched in 2003, when the 78th Legislature consolidated functions of 12 social service agencies under the **executive commissioner of the Health and Human Services Commission**. This legislation also began a process of privatizing service delivery, creating more administrative barriers to services, and slowing the growth of expenditures.

The executive commissioner of the HHSC is appointed by the governor for a two-year term and confirmed by the Senate. This official earns $290,258 per year and is not supervised by a board. Instead, the executive commissioner responds directly to the governor. As a result, governors maintain considerable influence over this area of policy. In July 2020, Governor Abbott appointed Cecile Young to be executive commissioner. Young has worked with the Department of Health and Human Services since its creation in 1991, most recently serving as acting executive commissioner from June 2018 to October 2018 and then as chief deputy executive commissioner. She is assisted by the nine-member Health and Human Services Council in making the agency's rules and policy. Members of the Council are nominated by the governor and approved by the Senate. (See Figure 9.3 for the commission's organization chart and tasks of the departments.) The HHSC itself handles centralized administrative support services, develops policies, and makes rules for its agencies. In addition, the commission determines eligibility for various programs, such as Temporary Assistance for Needy Families (TANF), the Supplemental Nutritional Assistance Program (SNAP), the Children's Health Insurance Program (CHIP), Medicaid, and long-term care services. COVID-19 put unexpected strain on all these programs, resulting in the agency taking unusual measures. For example, SNAP applications doubled in March 2020. HHSC automatically renewed benefits for recipients up for renewal and suspended the requirement that new and renewing SNAP applicants must be interviewed. Similar measures were implemented for other programs under the purview of HHSC.[71]

executive commissioner of the Health and Human Services Commission
Appointed by the governor with Senate approval, the executive commissioner administers the HHSC, develops policies, and makes rules.

Texas Workforce Commission (TWC)
A state agency headed by three salaried commissioners that oversees job training and unemployment compensation programs.

Employment

Texas's state employment services cut across three areas of policy: human services, education, and economic development. The **Texas Workforce Commission (TWC)** receives appropriations from the legislature in the category of business and economic development, which probably works to its advantage because of the legislature's friendly view of business and development. Both employers and workers are served by this agency. For employers, TWC offers recruiting, retention, training and retraining, outplacement services, and information on labor law and labor market statistics. For job seekers, TWC offers career development information, job search resources, training programs, and unemployment benefits. As part of this effort, the TWC matches unemployed workers with employers offering jobs.[72]

TWC also collects an employee payroll tax paid by employers. This revenue funds weekly benefit payments to unemployed workers covered by the Texas Unemployment Compensation Act. Unemployment benefits provides temporary income for workers who have lost their jobs through no fault of their own.

Figure 9.3 The Consolidated Texas Health and Human Services System.

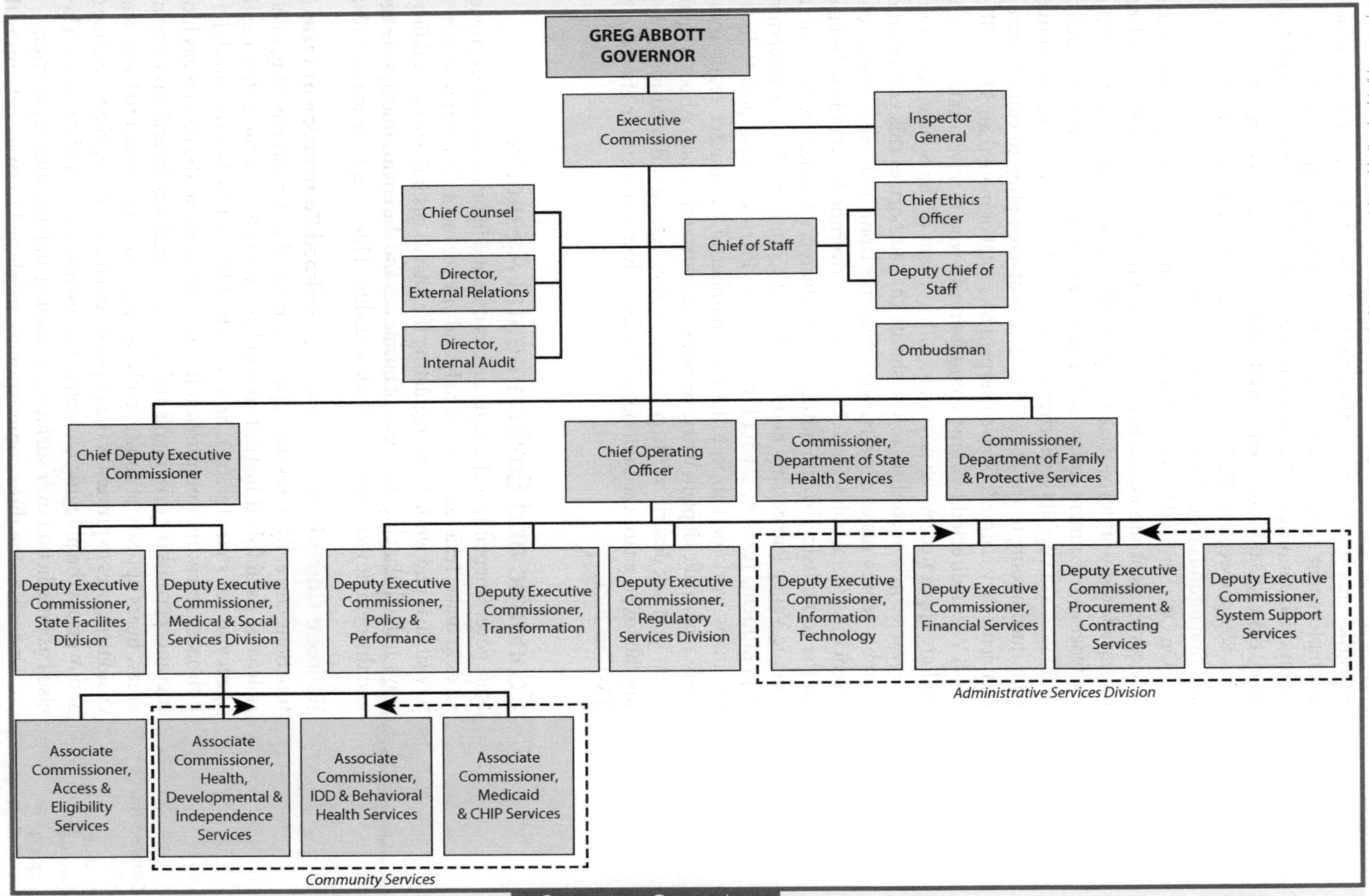

GREG ABBOTT GOVERNOR
Executive Commissioner
Inspector General
Chief Counsel
Director, External Relations
Director, Internal Audit
Chief of Staff
Chief Ethics Officer
Deputy Chief of Staff
Ombudsman
Chief Deputy Executive Commissioner
Chief Operating Officer
Commissioner, Department of State Health Services
Commissioner, Department of Family & Protective Services
Deputy Executive Commissioner, State Facilites Division
Deputy Executive Commissioner, Medical & Social Services Division
Deputy Executive Commissioner, Policy & Performance
Deputy Executive Commissioner, Transformation
Deputy Executive Commissioner, Regulatory Services Division
Deputy Executive Commissioner, Information Technology
Deputy Executive Commissioner, Financial Services
Deputy Executive Commissioner, Procurement & Contracting Services
Deputy Executive Commissioner, System Support Services
Administrative Services Division
Associate Commissioner, Access & Eligibility Services
Associate Commissioner, Health, Developmental & Independence Services
Associate Commissioner, IDD & Behavioral Health Services
Associate Commissioner, Medicaid & CHIP Services
Community Services

Source: Based on Texas Health and Human Services Commission, https://hhs.texas.gov/sites/hhs/files//documents/about-hhs/leadership/hhsc-org-chart.pdf

Competency Connection
CRITICAL THINKING

What is the most efficient and effective structure for the Texas Health and Human Services system?

Typically, the amount paid to a qualified claimant depends on wages earned in an earlier quarter (three months). COVID-19 put unprecedented strain on the unemployment system, causing difficulty in managing the agency's caseload. From the beginning of March to the end of 2020, TWC paid out $37.3 billion to more than 2.93 million unemployed Texans. Claimants received benefits ranging from $69 per week to $535 per week in state funds, with some Texans receiving additional funds from the federal government.

On October 5, 2020, with 1.8 million Texans still claiming unemployment, the U.S. government announced that it was awarding TWC a $27,685,179 federal grant to help address workforce-related impacts of COVID-19. In December of that year, the federal government authorized an extension of benefits through March of 2021 or 50 weeks of eligibility, whichever came first. At the same time, the commission continued adding to the 260,000 notices sent attempting to collect money from recipients they claimed to have overpaid by a total of more than $214 million.[73]

TWC is directed by three commissioners who receive a salary of $201,000 and are appointed by the governor, with consent of the Senate, for overlapping six-year terms. According to the statute that authorizes this commission, one member represents employers, one represents labor, and one is intended to represent the general public. In February 2016, Governor Abbott filled the labor seat on the commission by appointing Julian Alvarez, a former president of the Rio Grande Valley Partnership and Chamber of Commerce CEO. Concerning this appointment, Texas AFL-CIO President John Patrick complained, "I don't know too many workers who feel that the Chamber of Commerce really speaks for them. This makes it plain where working people stand in Gov. Abbott's agenda for Texas." Patrick described the governor's action as "a new dimension in appointing the fox to guard the henhouse."[73] Julian Alvarez was still in the labor seat at TWC in 2021.

Economic and Environmental Agencies

State governmental agencies regulate business and industry, as well as provide services to make Texas an economically and environmentally inviting area in which to visit, live, and work. From regulating the oil and gas industry to building highways and to balancing the needs of businesses and the environment, state agencies and their employees work to provide a quality of life acceptable to most Texans.

Railroad Commission of Texas The **Railroad Commission of Texas (RRC)** functions currently in several capacities, none of which has anything to do with railroads. Established in 1891 to regulate railroads, it is the oldest regulatory agency in the state. In 2005, however, the RRC lost its last responsibilities for railroads. Today, the commission focuses primarily on the oil and gas industry. It grants permits for drilling oil and gas wells, regulates natural gas rates in rural areas, hears appeals of municipally set gas rates for residential and business customers, tries to prevent waste of petroleum resources, regulates pipeline safety, and oversees the plugging of depleted or abandoned oil and gas wells. The RRC also has jurisdiction over surface coal mining and uranium exploration.

Under law, the three commissioners are elected to six-year terms with one commissioner seeking election every two years. However, the RRC is often

Railroad Commission of Texas (RRC)
A popularly elected three-member commission primarily engaged in regulating natural gas and petroleum production.

considered a way station in the career of rising politicians. Only a few commissioners stay six years, so many commissioners take office as a result of gubernatorial appointment. A high proportion of them come to office with much of their career in the oil and gas industry. They work full-time and earn $140,937 a year.

Public Utility Commission of Texas State regulation of Texas's utility companies did not begin until 1975 with creation of the **Public Utility Commission of Texas (PUC)**. Its five members are appointed by the governor, with Senate approval, to overlapping six-year terms. They work full-time and earn $201,000 a year.

PUC's regulatory authority is limited by both national and state policies. It does not regulate long distance calling, wireless, or cable TV (all regulated by the Federal Communications Commission [FCC]); natural gas utilities (Railroad Commission); water utilities (Texas Commission on Environmental Quality [TCEQ]); or municipal electric utilities (regulated by cities). Its two major responsibilities are local phone service and electric utilities, including regulating electric markets and overseeing the Electric Reliability Council of Texas (ERCOT). PUC and ERCOT came under fire by critics in the public, the press and both Executive and Legislative branches of state government when Texas's power grid failed during extreme winter weather in February 2021 and struggled to meet demand in June 2021.[75] The 87th Legislature passed, and Governor Abbott signed, two bills to address the failures of PUC and ERCOT. Among other provisions, SB 2 requires that power generation, natural gas, and transmission facilities weatherize to handle extreme conditions and improves communication from and between state agencies during weather emergencies and power outages. SB 3 includes ERCOT reforms such as requiring eight of the 11 board members to be fully independent and all board members to be residents of Texas.

Texas Department of Insurance The **commissioner of insurance** heads the Texas Department of Insurance (TDI) that regulates to some degree the insurance industry, which contributes some $38.5 billion to the state economy. This official is appointed by the governor for a two-year term and earns $177,498 a year. The Office of Public Insurance Counsel represents consumers in rate disputes. TDI deals with the wide range of insurance, including auto, health, home, life, wind, flood, and workers' compensation. It has a role in setting insurance rates, licenses agents and adjustors, and houses the office of the state fire marshal.

Texas Department of Transportation A wide range of transportation issues are managed by the **Texas Department of Transportation (TxDOT)**. Its major focus is planning, design, construction, and maintenance of the state's highways and bridges (more than 80,000 miles). However, TxDOT is also involved, though to a much lesser degree, with aviation, intracoastal waterways, rail, public transportation, safety, and toll roads. This agency is headed by a five-member commission appointed by the governor, with Senate concurrence, to six-year overlapping terms. Drawing no state salary, each commissioner must be a "public" member without financial ties to any company contracting with the state for highway-related business. The commission selects an executive director who administers the department and maintains relations with the legislature and other agencies. This executive director earns $344,000 a year.

Public Utility Commission of Texas (PUC)
A three-member appointed body with regulatory power over electric and telephone companies.

commissioner of insurance
Appointed by the governor, the commissioner heads the Texas Department of Insurance, which is responsible for ensuring the industry's financial soundness, protecting policyholders, and overseeing insurance rates.

Texas Department of Transportation (TxDOT)
Headed by a five-member appointed commission, the department maintains almost 80,000 miles of roads and highways and promotes highway safety.

Texas Parks and Wildlife Department
Texas agency that runs state parks and regulates hunting, fishing, and boating.

Texas Commission on Environmental Quality
The state agency that coordinates Texas's environmental regulation efforts.

Texas Parks and Wildlife Department Responsibility for preserving Texas's natural habitats and managing public recreational areas lies with the **Texas Parks and Wildlife Department.** Its nine unpaid commission members are appointed by the governor with Senate approval. The governor also designates the chair of the commission from among members. The commission members select an executive director who earns $200,643 a year for administering the department. Fees for fishing and hunting licenses and entrance to state parks are set by the commission. Game wardens employed by the department enforce state laws and departmental regulations that apply to hunting, fishing, trapping, and boating, as well as the Texas Penal Code and certain laws affecting clean air and water, hazardous materials, and human health.

Certification of Trades and Professions Citizens in more than 40 occupations—half of which are health related—are certified (licensed) to practice their profession by state boards. Each licensing board has at least one "public" member (not from the regulated occupation). All members are appointed to six-year terms by the governor with approval of the Senate. In addition to ensuring that practitioners qualify to enter a profession (giving them a license to practice), the boards are responsible for ensuring that licensees continue to meet professional standards.

Texas Commission on Environmental Quality (TCEQ) Commonly called "T-sec," the **Texas Commission on Environmental Quality** coordinates the Lone Star State's environmental policies. Three full-time commission members earning $201,000 per year, an executive director earning $223,277 a year, and almost 2,830 employees oversee environmental regulation in Texas. Commissioners are named by the governor, with consent of the Senate, for six-year staggered terms. One commissioner is designated as chair by the governor, but the commissioners choose the executive director.

✓ 9.8 Learning Check

1. True or False: The Sunset Advisory Commission has authority to recommend the abolition of state agencies.
2. Who has more control over public education in Texas: the commissioner of education or members of the State Board of Education?

Answers at the end of this chapter.

Conclusion

Texas's constitutionally weak governor has grown stronger in recent years; however, the term *chief executive* still does not accurately describe the head of the state's executive branch. The state constitution created a plural executive that diffuses power among a variety of independently elected officials. Governor Perry's power was enhanced by his long tenure and subsequent ability to appoint thousands of supporters to government posts. This advantage has begun to accrue to Governor Abbott because his ability to raise campaign money and to appeal to voters enabled him to win reelection. Use of executive, legislative, and judicial powers vested in the Texas governor by statutes and the state constitution—when combined with political leadership and informal powers not based on law—enhance the importance of this office. The executive branch also includes more than 200 appointed and elected boards, commissions, and departments that do the work of state government by implementing state laws and programs in the Lone Star State.

Chapter Summary

LO 9.1 Explain the effect of checks and balances on the executive powers of the governor. Some department heads and the members of multiple boards and commissions are appointed by the governor with approval of the Texas Senate. The legislature and the plural executive limit the governor's removal power, but the governor checks the budgetary power of the legislature with strong veto powers, including a line-item veto. The governor may also use proclamations to call the legislature into special sessions.

LO 9.2 Analyze the shared power of the executive and legislative branches. To be successful in promoting their favored legislation, governors must bargain with lobbyists and legislators. To do so, they need to make skillful use of their formal legislative powers, which include delivering messages to the legislature, signing or vetoing bills and concurrent resolutions, and calling special sessions of the legislature.

LO 9.3 Illustrate powers the governor exercises over the judicial branch of state government. The governor fills vacancies on state courts caused by creation of a new court or by a judge's death, resignation, or removal from office. Governors may remove judges, but only with direction by two-thirds of each house of the legislature, making it a rare occurrence. The governor may also grant clemency to undo or reduce sentences for some convicted criminals.

LO 9.4 Discuss the informal powers of the governor. Since 1876, Texas governors have held a weak constitutional office. They must rely heavily on their informal powers, which derive from their popularity with the public and are based on traditions, symbols, and ceremonies. Modern governors may enhance their informal powers by public appearances, use of traditional and electronic media, and support of family members.

LO 9.5 Summarize how the constitution and laws of Texas provide resources, as well as succession and removal procedures, for the governor. The constitution and laws of Texas provide governors with financial compensation of $153,750 per year, along with travel and security funds, fringe benefits, and a sizable staff. Succession procedures are in place for those who do not finish their terms because they resign, die, or are removed from office. Governors may be removed by House impeachment and Senate conviction, though this has only happened once.

LO 9.6 Analyze gubernatorial elections and the impact of campaign funds on the politics of the governorship. Successful gubernatorial candidates must meet constitutional requirements for the office, including a minimum age of 30, U.S. citizenship, Texas residency, and acknowledgment of a Supreme Being. Historically, conservative-moderate Democrats dominated races for the office, though the trend in recent decades is for conservative Republicans to win decisive victories. Serious gubernatorial candidates must procure substantial campaign funds. After election, governors often reward large campaign donors by appointing them to important government positions.

LO 9.7 Describe the powers of elected department heads and the secretary of state. All governors must share executive power with the lieutenant governor and four elected department heads: the attorney general (who acts as the state's chief lawyer), state comptroller (who acts as the state's chief accounting officer and tax collector), land commissioner (who manages the state's land and the revenue it produces), and agriculture commissioner (who both regulates and promotes Texas agriculture). The only appointed executive department head provided for in the Texas Constitution is the secretary of state, whose responsibilities include administering elections, granting charters and permits to corporations, and processing requests for extradition of criminals.

LO 9.8 Describe the role of the bureaucracy in governing the state of Texas. Boards, commissions, and departments are agencies that implement state laws and programs in Texas. Day-to-day work of governing the state is done by more than 325,000 state employees. Every 12 years (and sometimes more frequently) agencies are reviewed by the Sunset Advisory Commission. This commission provides recommendations to the legislature on continuation and any needed modifications for reviewed agencies. Important state services like education, health, and human services are overseen by state agencies. In addition, insurance, business, and the environment are regulated by the state through boards, commissions, and departments.

Key Terms

Learning Check Answers

9.1
1. False. Most gubernatorial appointments must be approved by a two-thirds vote of the Senate.
2. The governor may veto an entire appropriation bill or use the line-item veto to eliminate individual budget items.

9.2
1. True. During a session, the governor's veto can be overridden by a two-thirds majority vote in the House and in the Senate.
2. The governor can call a special session.

9.3
1. True. A vacancy on a Texas district court or higher appellate court is filled by gubernatorial appointment.
2. The governor can independently grant one 30-day reprieve in a death sentence case.

9.4
1. False. Informal powers of the governor are not based on law.
2. True. Public involvement of family members may be a source of support for the governor.

9.5
1. False. Although the size of the governor's staff has shrunk in recent years, it is much larger now than earlier in Texas history.
2. The Texas Constitution provides for impeachment by a simple majority vote of the House and conviction by a two-thirds majority vote of the Senate.

9.6
1. Governors of Texas are constitutionally required to be U.S. citizens, to be Texas residents for five years immediately preceding the gubernatorial election, and to acknowledge the existence of a Supreme Being.
2. True. Major donors to gubernatorial campaigns are frequently appointed to government posts.

9.7
1. False. The heads of state agencies, along with the governor and even local government officials, may request opinions from the attorney general on the scope of their jurisdiction.
2. The secretary of state grants charters to Texas corporations.

9.8

1. True. The Sunset Advisory Commission can recommend the abolition of an agency, but only the legislature can eliminate a state agency.

2. The commissioner of education has significantly more authority over public and charter schools than the State Board of Education, because the commissioner heads the Texas Education Agency. Among its powers, this agency oversees statewide testing, determines if schools are meeting performance and financial standards, and has authority to close chronically noncompliant schools and school districts.

10 The Judicial Branch

Learning Objectives

10.1 Identify the sources of Texas law.

10.2 Compare the functions of all participants in the justice system.

10.3 Describe the judicial procedure for the adjudication of civil lawsuits.

10.4 Describe the judicial procedure for the adjudication of criminal cases.

Image 10.1 Reactions to the Black Lives Matter movement highlighted divergent views on race. Judges and attorneys dealt with how to address the issues of race relations and implicit bias training.

Carmen K. Sisson/Cloudybright/Alamy Stock Photo

— Competency Connection —
⚙ **SOCIAL RESPONSIBILITY** ⚙

To assure people have confidence in the justice system, judges should be perceived as impartial and attorneys should fully protect their clients' interests. How could a judge's implicit bias affect his or her judicial decisions? How could an attorney's implicit bias affect his or her representation of a client?

Some commentators suggest that without our judicial system, society would descend into anarchy.[1] Our courts have additional burdens, however. To be effective, the public must view them as having **judicial legitimacy**—having moral authority to enforce laws and decisions. People who accept judicial institutions as being legitimate are more likely to believe everyone has an obligation to follow laws and court decisions.[2] Studies suggest that "the roots of legitimacy lie in people's assessment of the fairness of the decision-making procedures used by authorities and institutions."[3] Texans, like all Americans, recognize the legitimacy of their courts if decisions are fair, just, and predictable.[4] Researchers define this perception of fairness as procedural justice.

A complicating factor in achieving procedural justice, and thus legitimacy, is implicit bias. Unconscious attitudes or stereotypes are the basis of implicit bias. These attitudes and stereotypes can affect a person's actions and decisions. One result of implicit bias is that people are more likely to view those who are unlike them unfavorably. As a result, research shows that criminal punishment is different for Whites and Blacks. These findings reveal that Blacks receive harsher punishment than Whites, especially when authorities are White. Unlike a conscious bias, people are not aware they hold these beliefs. Implicit attitudes may even conflict with an individual's conscious beliefs.[5] Nonetheless, these unconscious attitudes affect a person's decisions. Researchers have discovered that, with training, people can identify their implicit biases and diminish them.

In 2020, the need for implicit bias training was recognized by the State Bar of Texas (SBOT), an organization that oversees all attorneys in the state, and the Texas Judicial Council, an advisory body that monitors the effectiveness of the state's court system. State Bar President Larry McDougal's tweet suggesting a poll worker wearing a Black Lives Matter shirt should be charged with a Class C misdemeanor for electioneering prompted this awareness. Further examination revealed Facebook posts and tweets calling the Black Lives Matter movement "a terrorist group" and another demeaning a female attorney.[6] Many lawyers and private citizens called for McDougal's ouster. Meetings with members of the African American Law Section and SBOT directors and a series of public apologies followed. McDougal was allowed to retain his position. Both McDougal and SBOT Board members were required to take implicit bias training. After extensive consideration and debate, the SBOT recommended, but did not require, similar training for all attorneys. Although voluntary, implicit bias courses can be applied to meet an attorney's ethics training requirements. In this same period, the Texas Judicial Council recommended that judges be required to complete implicit bias training.

Lawyers and judges are not the only participants in the judicial system. Disputing parties, juries, and court personnel are also involved. When disagreements end up in the courts, procedural rules apply to assure a fair, just, and predictable result. As you read this chapter, consider whether the Texas judicial system has met the ideal of being fair, just, and predictable and whether the corrective actions suggested by the SBOT and Texas Judicial Council are helpful in achieving these goals.

judicial legitimacy
The belief that courts have the right or authority to make and enforce decisions because judges are fair and impartial.

Follow *Practicing Texas Politics* on Twitter @ **PracTexPol**

★ State Law in Texas

LO 10.1 Identify the sources of Texas law.

Texans have given substantial power to their justice system. Both the Texas Constitution and state statutes grant government authority, under appropriate circumstances, to take a person's life, liberty, or property. In addition to resolving disputes, the judicial branch interprets and applies state constitutional provisions, statutory laws, agency regulations, and the common law (traditions, customs, and practices dating back to medieval England that the court recognizes). Through their interpretations, judges are involved in the policymaking process. Yet judges attract less public attention than state legislative and executive officials, even though their decisions affect Texans every day. In addition, Texas voters select almost all judges through popular, partisan elections. It is, therefore, important that the state's residents understand the purpose and workings of the judicial branch.

With approximately 3,300 justices and judges, and almost that many courts, Texas has one of the largest judicial systems in the country. Including traffic violations, millions of cases are processed each year. Texas courts deal with cases involving **civil law** (for example, disputes concerning business contracts, divorces, and personal injury claims). They also hear cases involving **criminal law** (proceedings against persons charged with committing a **misdemeanor**, such as using false identification to purchase liquor, which is punishable by a fine and jail sentence; or a **felony**, such as armed robbery, which is punishable by a prison sentence and a fine). A court's authority to hear and decide a particular case is its **jurisdiction**.

Sources of Law

Regardless of their jurisdiction, Texas courts interpret and apply state law.[7] These laws include provisions of the Texas Constitution; statutes enacted by the legislature; regulations adopted by state agencies; and judge-made common law. A court may apply a constitutional provision, statute, regulation, or common law, or any combination of these laws, in the same case. Procedures for filing a case, conducting a trial, and appealing a judgment depend on whether the case is civil or criminal.

The Texas Constitution and statutes are available at Texas Legislature Online. Thomson Reuters Westlaw publishes the same information in *Vernon's Annotated Statutes and Codes*. Newly enacted laws are compiled and made available through the Office of the Secretary of State's website. Regulations of state agencies (for example, the Railroad Commission) are codified in the *Texas Administrative Code*. Common law is found in individual court decisions. Although all levels of courts render decisions that affect the common law, only appellate court decisions are reported in the *South Western Reporter* series, published by Thomson Reuters Westlaw, and reported online through LexisNexis.

Code Revision

In 1963, the legislature charged the Texas Legislative Council with the responsibility of reorganizing Texas laws related to specific topics (such as

civil law
The body of law concerning disputes between individuals and other noncriminal matters, such as business contracts and personal injury.

criminal law
The body of law concerning felony and misdemeanor offenses by individuals against other persons and property, or in violation of laws or ordinances.

misdemeanor
Classified as A, B, or C, a misdemeanor may be punished by fine and/or jail sentence.

felony
A serious crime punished by fine and prison confinement.

jurisdiction
A court's authority to hear and decide a particular case.

✓ 10.1 Learning Check

1. True or False: Civil law cases involve misdemeanors and felonies.

2. True or False: Texas state law includes judge-made common law based on custom and tradition.

Answers at the end of this chapter.

education) into a systematic and comprehensive arrangement of legal codes. Almost 60 years later, the council continues to work on this project. In addition to piecemeal changes resulting from routine legislation, the legislature also sometimes undertakes extensive revision of an entire legal code. In 2003, the 78th Legislature authorized the council to compile all statutes related to local governments into the Special District Local Laws Code, a project that is ongoing.

★ Courts, Judges, Lawyers, and Juries

LO 10.2 Compare the functions of all participants in the justice system.

Since the early 1700s, the structure of Texas's judicial system has been shaped by Western European influences. Under Spanish law three municipalities were established: Bexar (1716), Nacogdoches (1716), and Laredo (1787). Mexico continued the traditions of Spanish law, and White settlers brought the influence of English judicial practices to the Republic of Texas. As the Lone Star State's population grew, its court system became more complex. Today's Texas judicial system has many participants, including almost 3,300 judges (excluding senior, retired, and associate judges) who preside over the state's courts, more than 100,000 attorneys who represent clients in legal proceedings, and thousands of jurors who decide the facts in both civil and criminal trials each year.

Article V of the Texas Constitution, "Judicial Department," vests all state judicial power "in one Supreme Court, in one Court of Criminal Appeals, in Courts of Appeals, in District Courts, in County Courts, in Commissioners Courts [which now have no judicial authority, as discussed in Chapter 3, 'Local Governments'], in Courts of Justice of the Peace and in such other courts as may be provided by law." Exercising its constitutional power to create other courts, the Texas legislature has established municipal (city) courts, county courts-at-law, and **probate** courts.[8] Probate matters relate specifically to decedents' estates, primarily establishing the validity of wills. Courts with probate jurisdiction also handle guardianship proceedings and mental competency determinations. In guardianship proceedings, a court appoints someone to care for the person and/or the property of individuals unable to do so for themselves because of age, physical disability, or mental incapacity. Probate courts and county courts-at-law are referred to as statutory courts. The legislature has also authorized the creation of a number of specialty courts to meet specific needs of particular groups of the state's residents, such as veterans, children, and those with mental health issues.

probate
Proceedings that involve the estates of decedents. Courts with probate jurisdiction (county courts, county courts-at-law, and probate courts) also handle guardianship and mental competency matters.

original jurisdiction
The power of a court to hear and decide a case first.

Trial and Appellate Courts

Texas's judicial system is complex. (See the structure of the current judicial system presented in Figure 10.1.) A law that creates a particular court fixes the court's subject matter jurisdiction (civil, criminal, or both). Further, constitutional provisions or statutes determine whether a court has **original jurisdiction**, which

Figure 10.1 Court Structure of Texas

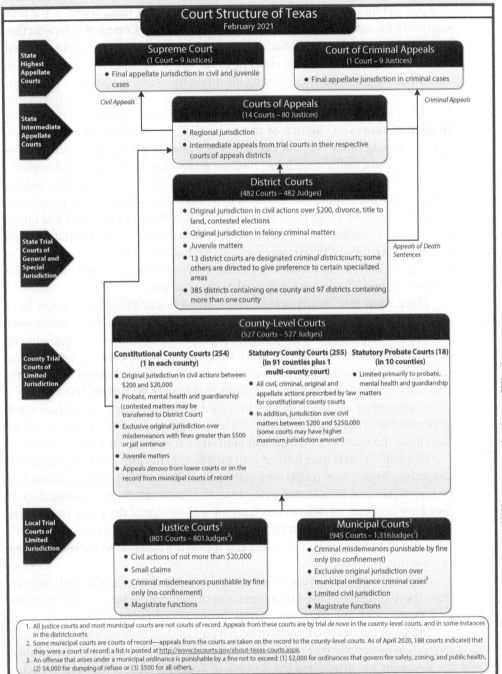

Court Structure of Texas
February 2021

State Highest Appellate Courts

Supreme Court
(1 Court – 9 Justices)
- Final appellate jurisdiction in civil and juvenile cases

Court of Criminal Appeals
(1 Court – 9 Justices)
- Final appellate jurisdiction in criminal cases

Civil Appeals   *Criminal Appeals*

State Intermediate Appellate Courts

Courts of Appeals
(14 Courts – 80 Justices)
- Regional jurisdiction
- Intermediate appeals from trial courts in their respective courts of appeals districts

State Trial Courts of General and Special Jurisdiction

District Courts
(482 Courts – 482 Judges)
- Original jurisdiction in civil actions over $200, divorce, title to land, contested elections
- Original jurisdiction in felony criminal matters
- Juvenile matters
- 13 district courts are designated *criminal district courts*; some others are directed to give preference to certain specialized areas
- 385 districts containing one county and 97 districts containing more than one county

Appeals of Death Sentences

County Trial Courts of Limited Jurisdiction

County-Level Courts
(527 Courts – 527 Judges)

Constitutional County Courts (254)
(1 in each county)
- Original jurisdiction in civil actions between $200 and $20,000
- Probate, mental health and guardianship (contested matters may be transferred to District Court)
- Exclusive original jurisdiction over misdemeanors with fines greater than $500 or jail sentence
- Juvenile matters
- Appeals *de novo* from lower courts or on the record from municipal courts of record

Statutory County Courts (255)
(in 91 counties plus 1 multi-county court)
- All civil, criminal, original and appellate actions prescribed by law for constitutional county courts
- In addition, jurisdiction over civil matters between $200 and $250,000 (some courts may have higher maximum jurisdiction amount)

Statutory Probate Courts (18)
(in 10 counties)
- Limited primarily to probate, mental health and guardianship matters

Local Trial Courts of Limited Jurisdiction

Justice Courts[1]
(801 Courts – 801 Judges[2])
- Civil actions of not more than $20,000
- Small claims
- Criminal misdemeanors punishable by fine only (no confinement)
- Magistrate functions

Municipal Courts[1]
(945 Courts – 1,316 Judges[2])
- Criminal misdemeanors punishable by fine only (no confinement)
- Exclusive original jurisdiction over municipal ordinance criminal cases[3]
- Limited civil jurisdiction
- Magistrate functions

1. All justice courts and most municipal courts are not courts of record. Appeals from these courts are by trial *de novo* in the county-level courts, and in some instances in the district courts.
2. Some municipal courts are courts of record—appeals from the courts are taken on the record to the county-level courts. As of April 2020, 188 courts indicated that they were a court of record; a list is posted at http://www.txcourts.gov/about-texas-courts.aspx.
3. An offense that arises under a municipal ordinance is punishable by a fine not to exceed: (1) $2,000 for ordinances that govern fire safety, zoning, and public health, (2) $4,000 for dumping of refuse or (3) $500 for all others.

Source: https://www.txcourts.gov/media/1452084/court-structure-chart-february-2021.pdf

Competency Connection
◉ **SOCIAL RESPONSIBILITY** ◉

How would simplifying the state's court system improve or harm the judicial system in Texas?

is authority to try cases being heard for the first time; **appellate jurisdiction**, authority to rule on lower court decisions; or both. A court may have both exclusive and concurrent jurisdiction. A court that has **exclusive jurisdiction** is the only court with the authority to decide a particular type of case. **Concurrent jurisdiction** means that more than one court has authority to try a specific dispute. In that instance, a plaintiff selects the court in which to file the case. Qualifications and compensation for judges vary among the different courts, as shown in Table 10.1.

Local Trial Courts The courts with which Texans are most familiar are **municipal courts** and **justice of the peace** (JP) courts. These local trial courts handle, among other types of cases, charges involving Class C misdemeanors (including most traffic violations), the least serious category of criminal offenses. Municipal judges and justices of the peace, like other Texas justices and judges, may, but are not required to, perform marriages. If a judge or justice performs weddings, then the judge must be willing to marry both heterosexual and same-sex couples. Local trial court judges also serve as magistrates of the state. In this latter capacity, these officials issue warrants for the arrest of suspects and conduct hearings to determine whether a person charged with a criminal act will be released on bail or jailed pending further court action.

More than 900 incorporated cities, towns, and villages in Texas have municipal courts. Mayors of general law cities have authority to preside over municipal courts (unless the city council provides for the election or appointment of someone to perform this function). Usually, municipal court judges of home rule cities are named by city councils for two-year terms. Under state law, only municipal judges who preside over municipal **courts of record** (courts with a court reporter or electronic device to record testimony and proceedings) must be licensed attorneys. City councils also set professional qualifications, as well as determine the number of judges and judicial salaries for their municipalities.

Municipal courts have limited civil jurisdiction in cases involving owners of dangerous dogs. These courts have no appellate jurisdiction. Their original and exclusive criminal jurisdiction extends to all violations of city ordinances, and they have criminal jurisdiction concurrent with justice of the peace courts over Class C misdemeanors committed within city limits. Individuals dissatisfied with the result of a municipal court ruling can appeal the decision to the county court or a county court-at-law.

Approximately 20 percent of municipal courts are courts of record. Appeals from those courts are based on a transcript of trial proceedings. If a court is not a court of record, appeals receive a trial de novo (a completely new trial).

Justice of the peace courts have been a part of the Texas judicial system since ratification by popular vote of the Constitution of 1836. That document established the governmental structure of the Republic of Texas. A justice of the peace is elected by voters residing in a precinct with boundaries created by the county commissioners court. The Texas Constitution mandates the minimum number of precincts per county (one to four) according to population. County commissioners may exceed this minimum by creating up to eight precincts (also based on population) and establish the number of JPs (one or two) per precinct. Since 1997, commissioners courts have abolished more than 40 justice courts to save money for their counties.

appellate jurisdiction
The power of a court to review and decide cases after they have been tried elsewhere.

exclusive jurisdiction
The authority of only one court to try a particular type of case.

concurrent jurisdiction
The authority of more than one court to try a case. For example, a civil dispute involving more than $200 but less than $20,000 may be heard in either a justice of the peace court, a county court (or county court-at-law), or a district court.

municipal court
City-run court with jurisdiction primarily over Class C misdemeanors committed within a city's boundaries.

justice of the peace
A judge elected from a justice of the peace precinct who handles minor civil and criminal cases, including small claims.

court of record
A court that has a court reporter or electronic device to record testimony and proceedings.

Table 10.1 Texas Judges and Justices

Court	Judicial Qualifications	Term of Office	Annual Salary	Method of Selection	Method of Replacement
Local Courts Municipal Courts	Varies; set by each city	Varies; set by each city	Paid by the city; highly variable	Appointment or election, as determined by city charter	Method determined by city charter
Justice of the Peace Courts	None	Four years	Paid by the county; highly variable, ranging from a few thousand dollars to more than $140,000	Partisan precinctwide elections	Commissioners Court
County Courts Constitutional County Courts	Must be "well informed" in Texas law; law degree not required	Four years	Paid by the county; highly variable, ranging from a few thousand dollars to almost $200,000	Partisan countywide elections	Commissioners Court
Statutory County Courts (courts-at-law and probate courts)	Age 25 or older; licensed attorney with at least four to five years' experience, depending on statutory requirements; two years' county residence	Four years	Paid by the state and county; somewhat variable ranging from $139,000 to $193,400, depending on county salary supplements and longevity; must be not less than $1,000 less than district judge's salary in same county with same longevity	Partisan countywide elections	Commissioners Court
State Courts District Courts	Ages 25–74; licensed attorney with at least four years' experience; two years' county residence	Four years	$140,000 to $194,400, depending on county salary supplements and longevity; must be $5,000 less than court of appeals justices' salaries with same longevity	Partisan districtwide elections	Governor, with advice and consent of Senate
Courts of Appeals	Ages 35–74; licensed attorney with at least 10 years' experience	Six years	$154,000 to $203,040, depending on county salary supplements and longevity; chief justice receives a $2,500 supplement; must be $5,000 less than Texas Supreme Court justices' salaries with same longevity	Partisan districtwide elections	Governor, with advice and consent of Senate
Court of Criminal Appeals	Ages 35–74; licensed attorney with at least 10 years' experience	Six years	$168,000 to $211,680 depending on longevity; presiding judge receives a $2,500 supplement	Partisan statewide elections	Governor, with advice and consent of Senate
Supreme Court	Ages 35–74; licensed attorney with at least 10 years' experience	Six years	$168,000 to $211,680 depending on longevity; chief justice receives a $2,500 supplement	Partisan statewide elections	Governor, with advice and consent of Senate

Sources: Compiled from Texas Association of Counties, "Salary Survey, 2020," https://www.county.org/TAC/media/TACMedia/Resources%20for%20County%20Officials/2020/Salary-Survey.pdf; and Office of Court Administration, "Judicial Salaries Effective September 1, 2019," https://www.txcourts.gov/media/1446571/judicial-salaries-september-2019.pdf.

Competency Connection
☼ **CRITICAL THINKING** ☼

State judges' compensation is based in part on years of service or longevity. Should judges be paid more based on the number of elections they have won?

As in seven other states, the position of JP requires neither previous legal training nor experience.[9] Justice John Payton, the subject of Students in Action below, ran for and was first elected to office while still in high school. Fewer than 10 percent of Texas's JPs (usually in large cities) are lawyers who may engage in private legal practice while serving as a justice of the peace. Within a year after election, a justice of the peace who is not a lawyer must complete an 80-hour course in performing the duties of that office. Thereafter, the JP is supposed to receive 20 hours of instruction annually, of which 10 hours must include topics related to civil trial procedure. Failure to complete annual training violates a JP's duties under the law.

In urban areas, being a justice of the peace is a full-time job, whereas justices in many rural precincts hear few cases. In addition to presiding over the justice court, a justice of the peace serves as an ex officio notary public (someone

📋 Students in Action

In 1990, high school senior John Payton decided to begin his political career by running for the position of Justice of the Peace in Collin County (Plano). His opponent in the Republican Primary was 50-year old incumbent Jim Murrell, who had held the position for six years.

With his mother as his campaign manager and driver, Payton went door-to-door campaigning for the position. Not taking his young opponent seriously, Murrell did little campaigning. After his primary loss, Murrell launched an unsuccessful write-in campaign and sought an investigation of Payton's high school records and his having been fired from a part-time job at a local golf course. The school refused to release his records and the manager of the golf club confirmed that Payton had left his job voluntarily so he would have time to campaign.

Payton had no Democratic opponent in the general election and won the position with 83 percent of the vote. He took office just prior to his 19th birthday. He was named by the *Guinness Book of World Records* as Texas's youngest judge in history and appeared on national television shows.

For the next 28 years, Payton continued to serve the residents of Collin County as Justice of the Peace Precinct 3. He became known in the county for the creative and effective ways in which he handled school truancy cases. Frequently sentencing truant students to community service with nonprofits such as Habitat for Humanity, he often worked beside the young offenders to lead by example. He was also instrumental in establishing a Teen Court in Collin County. During this time, he also earned an Associate's degree in communication from Collin College.

In 2018, Payton retired from his Justice of the Peace position to seek the Republican nomination for Texas House of Representatives in District 89. He was unsuccessful in that election.

Sources: Robert G. Wieland, "Texas-Size Ambition: 18-Year-Old Running for Justice of the Peace," *AP News*, October 17, 1990, https://apnews.com/article/06716cf2ed07a97ee23c0dd8b8fb28f6; "After 20 Years on Collin County Court, World's Youngest Judge as Committed as Ever," *Dallas Morning News*, December 9, 2010, https://www.dallasnews.com/news/2010/12/09/after-20-years-on-collin-county-court-world-s-youngest-judge-as-committed-as-ever/.

— Competency Connection —
⚙ SOCIAL RESPONSIBILITY ⚙

John Payton's opponent argued that the 18-year-old was too young and inexperienced to handle a position as responsible as justice of the peace, yet he won a decisive victory. What benefits does having someone so young on the bench bring to the judicial system?

who verifies signatures on legal documents). A JP also functions as a coroner, determining cause of death, when the county commissioners court has not named a county medical examiner. Lack of medical expertise caused some to question whether justices of the peace accurately identified COVID-related deaths during the pandemic.

Justice of the peace courts have both criminal and civil jurisdiction. In all cases, their jurisdiction is original. In criminal matters, these local courts try Class C misdemeanors; however, any conviction may be appealed to the county court or a county court-at-law for a new trial. Because these courts are not courts of record, all appeals are de novo.

Justices of the peace have jurisdiction over four types of civil cases: debt claims, repair and remedies (a law that requires landlords to maintain rental property in a safe condition), small claims (civil disputes with less than $20,000 in controversy), and evictions. Due to the COVID-19 pandemic, eviction cases for non-payment of rent were limited beginning in March 2020 and continuing through June 2021. Rules of evidence and procedure, though uniform for all justice courts, are not as formal for most cases as in other court proceedings. As a result, ordinary people can represent themselves more easily without hiring a lawyer, thus earning these courts the nickname "the people's court."[10] A justice may question witnesses directly to develop the facts in a case and limit the types and amount of potential evidence each party must provide the other party prior to trial (a process called discovery). In most debt collection cases, rules of evidence and procedure that are more formal still apply.

Exclusive civil jurisdiction of JP courts is limited to cases in which the amount in controversy is $200 or less, not including interest. Concurrent civil jurisdiction is shared with county and district courts (for amounts in controversy in excess of $200), as long as the disputed amount does not exceed $20,000. Appeals from JP courts, in which more than $250 is in controversy, are taken to the county level. A justice of the peace court is the court of last resort if the amount in controversy does not exceed $250, thus making its decisions final in these cases.

County Trial Courts Each of Texas's 254 counties has a **constitutional county court** and a county judge, as prescribed by the state constitution. In the more than 90 counties that have one or more county-level courts created by statute, county judges generally do not hear cases. As the presiding officer over the county's commissioners court, their time is devoted to administrative matters like budget preparation that does not involve court cases. Judges of constitutional county courts need not be attorneys. Statutory county court judges must be experienced attorneys. Like district court and appellate court judges and justices, all county-level judges who preside over courts must take Texas Supreme Court–approved courses in court administration, procedure, and evidence.

Most constitutional county courts have original and appellate jurisdiction, as well as probate, civil, and criminal jurisdiction. Original civil jurisdiction is limited to cases involving between $200 and $20,000. Original criminal jurisdiction includes all Class A and Class B misdemeanors.

constitutional county courts
Trial courts created in the Texas Constitution for each of Texas's 254 counties. If a county has one or more county courts-at-law, constitutional county courts do not usually hear and decide cases.

Appellate criminal jurisdiction extends to cases originating in JP courts and municipal courts. A constitutional county court's appellate jurisdiction is final with regard to criminal cases involving fines of $100 or less. For cases in which greater fines are imposed, the plaintiff may appeal to a court of appeals. Civil cases are heard on appeal from JP courts.

In counties with large populations, the legislature has authorized more than 250 statutory courts (most commonly called **county courts-at-law**) to relieve constitutional county court judges of some or all courtroom duties. With few exceptions, the criminal jurisdiction of county courts-at-law is limited to misdemeanors. Civil jurisdiction of most county courts-at-law is restricted to controversies involving amounts of $200 to $250,000. District court rules for juries apply for cases involving disputes in excess of $250,000. In 10 urban counties, the legislature has created statutory county **probate courts**.

State Trial Courts Texas's principal trial courts are district-level courts of general and special jurisdiction. Most state trial courts are designated simply as **district courts**. Some are criminal or civil district courts. Each district-level court has jurisdiction over one or more counties. Heavily populated counties may have several district courts with countywide jurisdiction. The 87th Legislature considered the creation of business courts to deal with disputes involving $10 million or more against businesses. Although strongly favored by business groups, this proposal failed to pass.

Most district court judges are authorized to try both criminal and civil cases, though a statute creating a court may specify that the court give preference to one or the other. All felony criminal cases are matters of original jurisdiction. Misdemeanor jurisdiction is limited to cases transferred from constitutional county courts, cases specifically authorized by the state legislature, and offenses involving misconduct by government officials while acting in an official capacity. Appeal after a death penalty sentence or a decision about DNA-forensic testing for someone sentenced to death is taken directly to the Court of Criminal Appeals. Other criminal convictions are appealed to an intermediate appellate court.

District courts have exclusive original jurisdiction over civil cases involving divorce, land titles, contested elections, contested wills, slander, and defamation of character, unless the legislature has granted concurrent jurisdiction to a county court-at-law. District courts have concurrent original jurisdiction with lower courts in controversies involving $200 or more; above the maximum dollar amount jurisdiction of those courts, district courts exercise exclusive civil jurisdiction. Appeal of a civil case goes to a court of appeals.

Intermediate Appellate Courts The legislature has divided Texas into 14 state **courts of appeals** districts and has established a court of appeals in every district. Each of these courts has three or more judges or justices (a chief justice and from 2 to 12 justices). Their six-year terms are staggered so that one-third of the members are elected or reelected every two years. This arrangement ensures that at any given time—barring death, resignation, or removal from office—each appellate court has two or more judges with experience. Decisions are reached by majority vote of the assigned judges after they examine the written record of the

county courts-at-law
Trial courts created by statute to assume the responsibilities of constitutional county courts in counties with larger populations.

probate courts
Statutory courts that only handle administration of decedent's estates, mental competency proceedings, and guardianship proceedings.

district courts
State trial courts that hear and decide both civil and criminal cases.

courts of appeals
Intermediate-level appellate courts that hear and decide appeals from trial court decisions.

case, review briefs (written arguments) prepared by the parties' attorneys, and hear oral arguments by the attorneys. At least three judges must hear and decide each case, unless the court's chief justice orders that the entire court hear and decide a case (an en banc proceeding). These courts hear appeals of civil and criminal cases from district courts and county courts. A dedicated business appeals court with appointed justices dedicated to hearing appeals of complex business litigation failed to pass in the 87th Legislature.

Final jurisdiction includes cases involving divorce, slander, boundary disputes, and elections held for purposes other than choosing government officials (for example, bond elections). A decision requires a majority vote of a panel of justices.

Highest Appellate Courts Texas and Oklahoma are the only states in the Union that have **bifurcated** (divided) court systems for dealing with criminal and civil appeals. Texans continue to resist creation of a unified judicial system, which would have a single appellate court of last resort for both criminal felony cases and complex civil cases.[11] Both of Texas's highest courts have nine justices (Supreme Court) or judges (Court of Criminal Appeals) who serve six-year terms. One-third of the positions on each court are open for election or reelection in each general election. Members of the courts are elected on a statewide basis. The Supreme Court of Texas and the Court of Criminal Appeals are authorized to answer questions about Texas law if asked by federal appellate courts (for example, the U.S. Fifth Circuit Court of Appeals or the U.S. Supreme Court).

bifurcated
A divided court system in which different courts handle civil and criminal cases. In Texas, the highest-level appeals courts are bifurcated.

📊 How Do We Compare...

In salaries of highest court justices and judges?

Annual Salaries of Highest Court Justices and Judges (in dollars as of 2020)

Most Populous U.S. States	Amount*	U.S. States Bordering Texas	Amount*
California	$261,949	Arkansas	$181,860
Florida	$220,600	Louisiana	$168,583
New York	$233,400	New Mexico	$148,207
Texas	**$211,680****	Oklahoma	$161,112

*In most states (including Texas), the chief presiding judge or justice receives a supplement due to the additional workload. In Texas the amount is $2,500.

**Texas has a tiered system of compensation based on longevity on the court. The reported salary reflects 12+ years of service.

Source: National Center for State Courts, "Survey of Judicial Salaries," July 2020, https://www.ncsc.org/__data/assets/pdf_file/0017/51164/JSS-Handout-July-2020.pdf.

Competency Connection
💬 COMMUNICATION SKILLS 💬

Share with a classmate, whether you believe Texas compensates its highest court justices and judges fairly.

In Texas, the highest tribunal with criminal jurisdiction is the **Court of Criminal Appeals**. This court hears criminal appeals exclusively. Most appeals come to the court from courts of appeals. Death penalty defendants in capital felonies or DNA-forensic testing cases have an automatic right of appeal from a district court to the Court of Criminal Appeals. Of the almost 5,500 matters considered in 2019, only nine were direct appeals of death penalty verdicts.

Voters elect one member of the Court of Criminal Appeals as presiding judge. Sharon Keller, the first woman to head the Texas Court of Criminal Appeals, was elected in 2000. As of 2021, three of the other eight judges were women. One judge on the court was Black, one judge was Latina, and the remainder were White. All members of the court since 1996 have been elected as Republicans. In 2013, however, former Judge Lawrence Meyers' decision to become a Democrat temporarily made the court bipartisan. His change in political parties also meant that for the first time since 1998, statewide officeholders included a Democrat. When Meyers did not win reelection in 2016, Democrats again had no elected statewide official.

Officially titled the **Supreme Court of Texas**, the state's highest court with civil jurisdiction has nine members: one chief justice and eight justices. No Democrats have served on the Texas Supreme Court since 1998. When Wallace Jefferson was appointed

Court of Criminal Appeals
The state's highest court with criminal jurisdiction.

Supreme Court of Texas
State's highest court with civil jurisdiction.

Image 10.2 Courts of appeals and the Texas Supreme Court frequently convene on college and university campuses. Here the 10th Court of Appeals (Waco) conducts appellate hearings at Sam Houston State University (Huntsville).

The Center for Law, Engagement, and Politics

Competency Connection
☼ **CRITICAL THINKING** ☼

What are some advantages and disadvantages of having appellate courts travel to college campuses to conduct hearings?

to the Texas Supreme Court in 2001, he became the first Black justice to serve on that court. From 2004–2013, Jefferson served as chief justice. In 2021, the court was less diverse than it had been earlier in the 21st century. After Justice Eva Guzman resigned in June 2021 to seek the office of Attorney General, the court included four women (two Latinas and two Whites). All men on the court were White.

This high court is supreme only in cases involving civil law. Because it has severely limited original jurisdiction (for example, cases involving denial of a place on an election ballot), nearly all of the court's docket involves appeals of cases that it determines must be heard. Much of the supreme court's work involves handling petitions for review, which can be requested by a party who argues that a court of appeals made a mistake on a question of law. If as many as four justices favor granting an initial review, the case is scheduled for argument in open court. In 2019, the Texas Supreme Court granted an initial review for approximately 9 percent of the more than 1,000 petitions that were filed, a significant decline over previous years. Justices do not make public their votes on petitions for review.

Other functions of the Texas Supreme Court include establishing rules of civil procedure for the state's lower courts and transferring cases to equalize workloads among the courts of appeals. Early in each regular session of the Texas legislature, the chief justice is required by law to deliver to the legislature a State of the Judiciary message, either orally or in written form.

The Supreme Court is required to take a leadership role in responding to the effects of natural disasters on the judicial system. Texas's erratic weather resulted in the state's being well-prepared to address the COVID-19 pandemic. Responding to the effects of Hurricane Harvey, the 86th Legislature amended the *Texas Government Code* to allow trial and appellate courts to conduct proceedings in alternate locations and extended this provision to include the entire state, not just coastal counties.[12] The same law authorizes the Texas Supreme Court to issue emergency orders to suspend and otherwise modify court proceedings for up to 90 days and gives the chief justice unilateral power to extend the orders as needed.

Within four hours of Governor Greg Abbott's issuance of his first emergency declaration responding to the COVID-19 pandemic in March 2020, the Supreme Court, joined by the judges on the Court of Criminal Appeals, issued the First Emergency Order to allow courts to suspend deadlines and mandate remote participation by all parties (except jurors) in court proceedings. Over the next 12 months, in a series of additional emergency orders, the Supreme Court suspended all jury trials and ultimately allowed remote jury trials. In February 2021, Chief Justice Nathan Hecht testified that these measures had resulted in a severe case backlog that would likely take more than three years to resolve. In an effort to continue its work despite the pandemic, the Texas Supreme Court assumed a national leadership role when it became the first nine-member court in the nation to hold virtual oral arguments in April 2020.[13]

Specialty Courts Texas established its first specialty drug court almost 30 years ago. Over the following decades, municipalities and counties in the Lone Star State have developed more than 250 **specialty courts** to deal with particular types of problems or specific populations. These courts can be divided between (1) those designed to assist children and supported by state and

specialty courts
Courts designed to deal with particular types of problems, such as drug-related offenses or specific populations, such as veterans or foster children.

federal funds and (2) those designated to assist other special categories of defendants and often initially funded by the Criminal Justice Division of the Office of the Governor and the federal government. All specialty courts are required to meet reporting requirements of the state's Office of Court Administration. For a description of each court's jurisdiction and other information about specialty courts, see Table 10.2.

The courts have a dual rationale: efficiency and therapy. Courts with a nontherapeutic purpose, such as Children's Protective Services courts, are intended to increase the court system's efficiency by placing foster children into permanent homes more quickly. Others, such as drug courts, are designed with a therapeutic rationale to improve outcomes for participants. Attorneys, judges,

Table 10.2 Specialty Courts

Type of Court	Goal	Population Served	Number
Child Protection Courts	Designed to assist rural areas in handling child neglect and abuse cases.	Children	31
Child Support Courts	Established to meet the federal mandate to expedite the handling of child support cases.	Children	36
Drug Court	Integration of drug treatment and rehabilitation programs for defendants.	Adults	95
Family Drug Court	Integration of substance abuse treatment to reunite families.	Families	14
Veterans' Treatment Court	Incorporating drug treatment and rehabilitation programs, along with family support, for defendants.	Military veterans	30
Juvenile Drug Treatment Court	Integration of drug treatment and rehabilitation programs for juvenile offenders.	Juveniles	20
Mental Health Court	Integration of mental health services and mental retardation services for defendants.	Adults	18
Commercially Sexually Exploited Persons Court	Integration of treatment and support to reduce the demand for the commercial sex trade and trafficking.	Adults (4)/Juveniles (1)	5
DWI Court	Integration of substance abuse treatment programs into cases involving individuals charged with a DWI.	Adults	1
Public Safety Employees Treatment Court	Integration of substance abuse and mental health treatment and rehabilitation options for public safety (law enforcement) employees.	Public Safety Employees	1
TOTAL			251

Sources: Compiled from Office of Court Administration, Child Protection Courts, September 4, 2020, https://www.txcourts.gov/media/1444268/child-protection-courts-run-09_04_20.pdf; *Child Support Courts*, September 4, 2020, https://www.txcourts.gov/media/1446644/child-support-courts-09_04_20.pdf; *Texas Specialty Courts*, September 17, 2019, https://www.txcourts.gov/media/1444764/specialty-courts-by-county-sept-2019.pdf; and *Texas Government Code*, Chapters 121–129 (2019).

— Competency Connection —
⭑ **PERSONAL RESPONSIBILITY** ⭑

Why do you believe the Texas legislature and federal government have authorized the creation of specialty courts? Is it fair to allow special treatment for some populations?

and mental health personnel develop and monitor individualized treatment plans. If treatment is successful, the presiding judge can enter an order of nondisclosure for most offenders, thus keeping the public from learning about an offense. Some reviews of these courts suggest many are meeting their dual mission of efficiency and therapy; other studies offer less conclusive results.[14]

Alternative Dispute Resolution The state has adopted several methods to encourage litigants to resolve their disputes without going to trial. To reduce workloads, speed the handling of civil disputes, and cut legal costs, each county is authorized to set up a system for **alternative dispute resolution (ADR)**. This procedure allows an impartial third party with training as a mediator or arbiter to negotiate disputes between and among litigants. ADR is frequently cited as a significant factor in the "vanishing jury trial."[15] Many lawsuits are now settled prior to trial. A settlement occurs when the parties resolve their disputes without going to trial.

Collaborative divorce is another nonadversarial method for resolving disputes outside the courtroom. If either spouse elects to litigate (go to court) after the process begins, attorneys for both spouses must resign. If family violence is involved, however, the abuse victim must expressly request using a collaborative process. Furthermore, the victim's lawyer must work with the client to devise procedures to limit the possibility of further violence.

Selecting Judges and Justices

Texas, along with Alabama, Louisiana, and North Carolina, chooses all judges (except municipal judges) in partisan elections. For 75 years, judges, legislators, and special commissions have sought to change the Lone Star State's judicial selection process. Most recently, the legislatively created Texas Commission on Judicial Selection, discussed in the Point/Counterpoint feature below, could not reach consensus on an alternative system to partisan elections.

Harvard Law professor Jed Handelsman Shugerman observed that foreign countries that follow the American legal system seldom adopt "the peculiar [American] institution" of electing judges.[16] One complaint is the appearance that "justice is for sale" to the highest campaign donor.[17] Another is that elections unfairly favor White judicial candidates. After the election of 17 Black women to judgeships in Harris County in 2018, Gary Bledsoe, representing the NAACP, testified before the Commission on Judicial Selection and argued for continuation of partisan, popular elections. He explained that changing voter demographics were achieving more diverse election results.[18]

Judicial selection methods are far from uniform, with at least 15 different variations in use across the country.[19] Many opponents of the popular election of judges favor some version of the merit selection process initiated by the state of Missouri in 1940 and identified as a "governor and assisted appointments" system by the Judicial Selection Commission. The **Missouri Plan** features a nominating commission that recommends a panel of names to the governor when a judicial vacancy is to be filled. If the governor fails to appoint someone from the list, the nominating commission makes the appointment. After a period

alternative dispute resolution (ADR)
Use of mediation, conciliation, or arbitration to resolve disputes among individuals without resorting to a regular court trial.

Missouri Plan
A judicial selection process in which a commission recommends a panel of names to the governor, who appoints a judge for one year or so before voters determine whether the appointee will be retained for a full term.

▣ Point/Counterpoint

Should Texas Change Its Judicial Selection Process?

The Issue The 15-member Texas Commission on Judicial Selection, created by the 86th Legislature (2019), was comprised of attorneys, legislators, and retired judges. The commission identified three basic types of judicial selection processes:

- partisan election
- nonpartisan election
- gubernatorial and assisted appointment. Assisted appointment schemes require an external commission or other external entity to review and approve nominee qualifications.

The commission offered no definitive plan for a more effective judicial selection process than that already in place. As attorney Lynne Liberato noted, "The research and hearings in which we have engaged show that other methods are no less flawed; they merely have different flaws." Review the advantages and disadvantages of each of the selection processes to determine if you agree or disagree with the commission's failure to make a recommendation.

Partisan election disadvantages	Nonpartisan election disadvantages	Gubernatorial and assisted appointments disadvantages
Voters tend to select judges based on political party and no other qualifications	Voters are uninformed, and without the guidance of a candidate's political party affiliation may select candidates who do not represent their opinions	Judges may be selected because of their ideology, not their qualifications
Can result in partisan sweeps in which most or all experienced and capable judges lose elections because of their political party affiliation	In many instances, political party is revealed indirectly	Voters are removed from the process
Running in partisan elections is expensive and forces candidates to solicit funding from attorneys and special interest groups	Possibility of electing unqualified judges	Vests power in an unelected body (the commission)
People perceive judges as making decisions based on political considerations and not the rule of law		Commissions can be co-opted by interest groups
Greater likelihood of electing unqualified judges		

appointment-retention system
A plan for judicial selection in which the governor makes an appointment to fill a court vacancy for an interim period, after which the judge must win a full term in an uncontested popular election.

of service, voters decide whether to give the new judge a full term. In subsequent elections, the judge runs unopposed. If voters do not approve a judge, then the selection process is repeated. More than 99 percent of appointees retain their positions.[20]

Others favor an **appointment-retention system** for all courts of record. In this system, the governor appoints a judge and voters determine whether to retain the appointee. Although no reform proposals have succeeded, many Texans share the concerns of former Chief Justice Wallace Jefferson, who observed, "a justice system built on some notion of Democratic judging or Republican judging is a system that cannot be trusted."[21]

Partisan election advantages	Nonpartisan election advantages	Gubernatorial and assisted appointments advantages
Party affiliation provides important information to voters	Because party affiliation is not disclosed reduces political considerations	Allows greater judicial independence
Judges are directly accountable to voters	Judges are directly accountable to voters	Judges do not need to raise campaign donations
Voters have a direct say in who can hold office	Voters have a direct say in who can hold office	Includes qualified nominees who do not want to become politicians
	Reduces campaign costs	Avoids partisan sweeps
	Distinguishes the judicial branch from the policymaking branches of government	Judges are perceived as different from other officeholders

Source: Public Policy Research Institute-Texas A&M University, "Texas Commission on Judicial Selection Final Report," December 2020, https://www.txcourts.gov/media/1450219/201230_tcjs-final-report_compressed.pdf.

Competency Connection
★ PERSONAL RESPONSIBILITY ★

If voters are responsible for the selection of judges, how should you, as a voter, evaluate judicial candidates?

Disciplining and Removing Judges and Justices

Each year, a few of Texas's judges and justices commit acts that warrant discipline or removal. These judges can be removed by voters at the next election; by trial by jury; or if they are state court judges, by legislative address or impeachment. The State Commission on Judicial Conduct, however, plays the most important role in disciplining the state's judiciary. This 13-member commission is composed of six judges, each from a different level court; two attorneys; and five private citizens who are neither attorneys nor judges.

Although most investigations are based on written complaints by someone outside the agency, commission staff sometimes undertake investigations on their own. A racially charged interview and letter to the editor in the *Houston Chronicle* from former Harris County District Court Judge Michael McSpadden caused the commission to take action. McSpadden's claims that the Black Lives Matter movement was a "rag-tag organization" and that Black men were receiving bad advice from their parents on responding to police and respecting the law "cast public discredit upon the judiciary and administration of justice" according to commission findings. A Democratic opponent defeated McSpadden in the 2018 election.[22]

Social media can be problematic for judicial officials. Several judges have received public reprimands for misuse of their social media accounts, especially to endorse political candidates.[23] Court decisions have been challenged because judges followed parties' attorneys on Twitter.

Just as attorneys must do, judges must follow the same rules of communication for social media as for all other media. Former Supreme Court Justice Don Willett observed, "Whether they're crafting a 140-page opinion or a 140-character tweet, judges must always be judicious."[24]

The State Commission on Judicial Conduct has been criticized for being too lenient with judges. In 2019, the commission resolved almost 1,700 complaints. Of the 80 cases that were not dismissed, the commission issued sanctions or suspensions to 76 judges. Four judges resigned to avoid disciplinary action. Unsuccessful litigants in civil lawsuits and criminal defendants file the most complaints.

Since the inception of electronic filing in 2016, complaints have almost doubled. Legislators and others have charged the commission with both a lack of expediency and transparency in disposing of cases.[25] While serving as a commissioner, attorney Steve Fischer created a Facebook page and regularly sent tweets criticizing the commission's lack of transparency and some of its decisions that were unrelated to judicial complaints. These actions resulted in the commission chair's filing a formal complaint and Fischer's being replaced.[26]

The commission's jurisdiction extends to judges and justices at all levels of the court system. Both the presiding judge of the Court of Criminal Appeals, Sharon Keller, and the chief justice of the Texas Supreme Court, Nathan Hecht, have been disciplined by the commission. These disciplinary actions were reversed in appellate proceedings.[27]

In addition to a public reprimand, any judge can receive a private reprimand or be ordered to take additional training. All punitive rulings can be appealed to the chief justice of the Texas Supreme Court, who appoints a Special Court of Review (a three-judge panel of appellate judges) to hear the appeal. The commission has authority to recommend removal of a judge. Such a recommendation is considered by a seven-member tribunal appointed by the Texas Supreme Court. If the tribunal votes to remove the judge, the decision may be appealed to the Texas Supreme Court.

Judges who may be suffering from substance abuse or mental health issues have access to assistance through the State Bar of Texas's Texas Lawyers Assistance Program (TLAP). This service provides volunteer judges to counsel and mentor their peers. Pursuant to state law, information about program participants is confidential.

Lawyers

Both the Texas Supreme Court and the State Bar of Texas play roles in regulating the 105,000 practicing attorneys licensed by the state of Texas. The Supreme Court of Texas supervises the licensing of lawyers. The State Bar of Texas oversees and disciplines the state's lawyers. Accreditation of law schools is largely a responsibility of the American Bar Association. Nine Texas law schools are fully accredited. The University of North Texas at Dallas College of Law, the state's newest law school, has received provisional accreditation and must meet all ABA standards by June 2022 to achieve full accreditation. Attempts to establish additional public law schools have been unsuccessful in recent legislatures.

Over the past decade, attorneys in the state have become increasingly diverse in terms of gender, race, and ethnicity. In 2019, more than 50 percent of the Lone Star State's law students were women. Members of historical minority groups made up almost 45 percent of students in Texas's law schools. In that same year, women constituted 37 percent of practicing attorneys in Texas; and only 22 percent of active attorneys were members of historical minority groups. The trend of increasing diversity seems likely to continue.[28]

State Bar of Texas To practice, a licensed attorney must be a member of the State Bar of Texas (SBOT) and pay dues for its support. Mandatory dues and some of the activities of the SBOT, such as diversity initiatives and financial support of no-cost legal services for the poor, have been challenged in the lawsuit of *McDonald v. Sorrells*. As of mid-2021, this case was not resolved.

The SBOT also enforces ethical standards for Texas lawyers. An administrative agency of the state, the organization disciplines, suspends, and disbars attorneys. In 2021, the SBOT investigated Attorney General Ken Paxton for professional misconduct for having filed a lawsuit to set aside presidential election results in 2020. The use of social media has presented special challenges. In 2020, the Committee on Disciplinary Rules and Referenda, including both attorneys and non-attorneys, proposed amendments to the disciplinary rules governing lawyers in response to changes in social media usage. Distinguishing between media posts intended to educate the public versus those designed to advertise a lawyers' services was critical. For example, LinkedIn accounts generally do not constitute advertising that requires regulation; however, Facebook pages intended to tout a lawyer's courtroom accomplishments do.[29] Information about an attorney's professional disciplinary record is available from the Find-A-Lawyer link on the state bar's website. In addition, the entity oversees an extensive continuing legal education program.

Legal Services for the Poor Many attorneys and judges agree with former U.S. Supreme Court Justice Lewis Powell that "[e]qual justice under law is … one of the ends for which our entire legal system exists… [I]t is fundamental that justice should be the same, in substance and availability, without regard to economic status."[30] Under the Bill of Rights in the Texas Constitution and the Sixth Amendment to the U.S. Constitution, indigent individuals accused of felonies are entitled to legal representation at the state's expense. A person whose claim arises from a physical injury may hire an attorney on a **contingency fee** basis, in which the lawyer is paid from any money recovered in a lawsuit or settlement. Representation in such legal matters as divorce, child custody, or contract disputes, however, requires the client to make direct payment to the attorney for legal services. Free legal help for civil cases is often provided by an

contingency fee
A lawyer's compensation paid from money recovered in a lawsuit or settlement.

attorney with the Legal Services Corporation, more commonly referred to as Legal Aid. Limited funding in recent years has reduced the assistance available through this program.

The Texas Access to Justice Foundation estimates that more than 90 percent of qualified applicants are denied services due to limited resources.[31] Many middle-income individuals earn too much to qualify for legal aid but still cannot afford to hire an attorney. Lack of access to legal representation creates a "justice gap." To aid in addressing this issue, the Texas Access to Justice Commission was created by the Texas Supreme Court to coordinate and increase delivery of legal services to the state's poor. This 15-member commission includes judges, lawyers, and private citizens. The State Bar of Texas and the Texas Access to Justice Foundation support and collaborate with these efforts. The foundation maintains a website that provides information, forms, and links to low- and no-cost legal services providers. One source of funding is interest earned on trust accounts maintained by lawyers on behalf of their clients. Working with approximately 50 partner banks, the foundation has negotiated payment of higher interest rates on these accounts to provide support to the approximately 5.6 million Texans who qualify for legal aid assistance.

Attorney volunteers fill some of the legal representation gap. Special programs, such as Texas Lawyers for Texas Veterans, target particular populations for legal services. Retired, inactive, and out-of-state attorneys can volunteer through the New Opportunities Volunteer Attorney (NOVA) program specifically designed to engage some of the more than 18,000 inactive attorneys in the state.[32] State bar officials recommend that lawyers donate 50 hours per year assisting needy clients. SBOT also supports recognition of attorneys and law firms that make exceptional contributions of their time.

Juries

A jury system lets citizens participate directly in the administration of justice. Texas has two types of juries: grand juries and trial juries (also called petit juries). The state's Bill of Rights guarantees that individuals may be charged with a felony only by grand jury indictment. It also provides that anyone charged with either a felony or a misdemeanor has the right to trial by jury. If requested by either party, jury trials are required in civil cases. In recent years, the number of civil jury trials in Texas has steadily declined.

The COVID-19 pandemic all but eliminated jury trials. Beginning in May 2020, in-person jury trials were prohibited by Emergency Orders issued by the Texas Supreme Court, except for a few trials authorized by the Office of Court Administration. Limitations on in-person jury trials remained in place until March 2021. Some counties, like Bexar County, were even more restrictive.[33]

Texas courts were the first in the country to conduct remote trials, for both civil cases (May 2020 in Collin County [near Dallas]) and criminal cases (August 2020 in Travis County [Austin]). With support from the Office of Court Administration, Zoom became available to all courts in Texas by mid-March 2020 and judges and court personnel began training the following week. Although many litigants and their attorneys were resistant to remote jury trials, judges could force the use of video conferencing for civil trials and make it available for criminal trials. Problems for jurors in the use of remote platforms are the same as those faced by students—poor internet service, limited access to technology, poor technology skills, and an inability to remain attentive in a remote environment. By Emergency Orders beginning in mid-March 2020, the Texas Supreme Court suspended all non-essential court proceedings. Throughout 2021, these proceedings slowly resumed, though many were conducted remotely.

Grand Jury Composed of 12 citizens, a **grand jury** is chosen at random from a list of 20 to 125 prospective grand jurors selected and summoned in the same way that civil jury panels are identified. The grand jury process is then explained to the panel. Some judges attempt to elicit volunteers; others select the first 12 qualified jurors. In addition, four alternate jurors are chosen.

Members of a Texas grand jury must have the qualifications of trial jurors and not be a complainant (the accused) in a grand jury proceeding. County commissioners determine the pay for grand jurors, and thus pay varies across the state, although it is similar to pay for service on a trial jury. The district judge appoints one juror to serve as presiding juror or foreman of the jury panel. A grand jury's life is three months in length, though a district judge may extend a grand jury's term up to 90 days. During this period, grand juries have authority to inquire into all criminal actions but devote most of their time to felony matters. Although grand juries usually consider indictments for cases presented by the district attorney, they can act independently.[34]

If, after investigation and deliberation (often lasting only a few minutes), at least nine grand jurors decide there is sufficient evidence to warrant a trial, an indictment is prepared with the aid of the prosecuting attorney. The indictment is a written statement accusing some person or persons of a particular felony (for example, burglary of a home). An indictment is referred to as a true bill; failure to indict constitutes a no bill. In a misdemeanor case, a grand jury information (with the same effect as an indictment in a felony case) may be prepared, but, unlike in felony cases, is not constitutionally required, for prosecution. Jurors and witnesses are sworn to keep secret all they hear in grand jury sessions.

Many counties used virtual grand jury proceedings during the pandemic. The constitutionality of these proceedings remained unsettled after defense attorneys challenged indictments issued by a McLennan County [Waco] grand jury, in which half the grand jurors attended a session in person and the remainder attended via Zoom. Defense attorneys argued that all grand jurors must be "present" in the same place to issue an indictment. Ultimately, the grand jury was reconvened for an in-person session.[35]

Petit Jury Although relatively few Texans ever serve on a grand jury, many can expect to be summoned for duty on a trial jury (**petit jury**). Official qualifications for jurors are not high. To ensure that jurors are properly informed concerning their work, the court gives them brief printed instructions (in English and Spanish) that describe their duties and explain basic legal terms and trial procedures. In urban counties, these instructions are often shown as a video in English and other languages common to segments of the county's population, such as Spanish or Vietnamese.

grand jury
Composed of 12 persons (and four alternates) with the qualifications of trial jurors, a grand jury serves three months while it determines whether sufficient evidence exists to indict persons accused of committing crimes.

petit jury
A trial jury of 6 or 12 members.

Qualifications, Selection, and Compensation of Jurors A qualified Texas juror must be

- a citizen of the United States and of the state of Texas;
- eighteen years of age or older;
- of sound mind;
- able to read and write (with no restriction on language), unless literate jurors are unavailable; and
- neither convicted of a felony nor under indictment or other legal accusation of theft or any felony.

Qualified persons have a legal responsibility to serve when called, unless exempted or excused. Exemptions include

- being age 70 or older;
- having legal custody of a child or children younger than age 10;
- being enrolled in and attending a university, college, or secondary school;
- being the primary caregiver for an invalid;
- being employed by the legislative branch of state government;
- having served as a petit juror within the preceding two years in counties with populations of at least 200,000 or the preceding three years in counties with populations of more than 250,000; or
- being on active military duty outside the county.

Judges may excuse others from jury duty in special circumstances. A person who is legally exempt from jury duty may file a signed statement with the court clerk at any time before the scheduled date of appearance. In most counties, prospective jurors complete necessary exemption forms online. Anyone summoned for jury duty can reschedule the reporting date once (at least twice in urban counties), as long as the new date is within six months of the original. Subsequent rescheduling requires an emergency that could not have been previously anticipated, such as illness. During the COVID-19 pandemic, potential jurors could also be excused if they were vulnerable to the virus or lived with someone who was. For remote trials, having poor Internet service or inadequate technology also became a valid excuse from jury service. Failure to report for jury duty or falsely claiming an exemption is punishable as contempt of court, and a guilty individual can be fined up to $1,000.

A **venire** (panel of prospective jurors) is chosen by random selection from a list provided by either the secretary of state, another governmental agency, or a private contractor selected by the county commissioners court. The list includes the county's registered voters, licensed drivers, and persons with identification cards issued by the Department of Public Safety. A trial jury is composed of six or twelve citizens, one of whom serves as foreman or presiding juror: six serve in a justice of the peace court, municipal court, or county court, whereas 12 serve in a district court or for some statutory county court cases. A jury panel generally includes more than the minimum number of jurors.

Attorneys question jurors through a procedure called **voir dire** (which means "to speak the truth") to identify any potential jurors who cannot be fair

venire
A panel of prospective jurors drawn by random selection. These prospective jurors are called veniremen.

voir dire
Courtroom procedure in which attorneys question prospective jurors to identify any who cannot be fair and impartial.

and impartial. Prospective jurors can expect to be asked about their social media habits, such as whom they follow on Twitter. An attorney may challenge for cause any venire member suspected of bias. If the judge agrees with the attorney, the prospective juror is excused from serving.

An attorney challenges prospective jurors either by peremptory challenge (up to 15 per side, depending on the type of case, without having to give a reason for excluding the venire members) or by challenge for cause (an unlimited number). Jurors may not be eliminated on the basis of race or ethnicity. For a district court and in some county court-at-law cases, a trial jury is made up of the first 12 venire members who are neither excused by the judge nor challenged peremptorily by a party in the case. For lower courts, the first six venire members accepted form a jury. A judge may direct the selection of alternate jurors to replace any seated juror who can no longer serve. Once impaneled, jurors are sworn in and receive further instructions from the court. They will be instructed to avoid communication with others about the trial during the proceedings. Not only is direct communication disallowed, but jurors are also prohibited from sending information about the trial through social media. Attempts to communicate with parties to the trial, such as "friending" them, is also prohibited.

The COVID-19 pandemic and related health requirements for social distancing and wearing masks for in-person events forced courts to become creative at all points in jury selection and service. Counties contracted with hotels and sports venues for use of ballrooms and similar large facilities such as NRG Stadium in Harris County (Houston) for jury selection. Jury deliberations occurred in courtrooms, rather than the smaller jury deliberation rooms. Jurors were seated in the gallery rather than the juror box in many courts. Remote trials required the use of Zoom's breakout rooms and other features.

Although daily pay for venire members and jurors varies from county to county, minimum pay for juror service is $6 for all or part of the first day of jury duty and may be as high as $50 for each subsequent day. Under state law, counties fund the first $6 per juror each day, and the state reimburses the counties up to $34 per juror for each subsequent day of service. Employers are not required to pay wages to an employee summoned or selected for jury duty; however, they cannot fire, intimidate, or punish in any way permanent employees for such service.

> ### ✔ 10.2 Learning Check
>
> 1. A court must have jurisdiction to hear a case. What does this mean?
> 2. True or False: It is the responsibility of the grand jury to determine whether a defendant is guilty.
>
> *Answers at the end of this chapter.*

⬛ Judicial Procedures in Civil Cases

LO 10.3 Describe the judicial procedure for the adjudication of civil lawsuits.

The term "civil law" generally refers to matters not covered by criminal law. The following are important subjects of civil law: **torts** (for example, unintended injury to another person in a traffic accident); contracts (for example, agreements to deliver property of a specified quality at a certain price); and domestic relations or family law (such as divorce). Civil law disputes usually involve individuals or corporations in lawsuits that seek money damages or injunctive relief (requiring someone to do or cease doing something). In criminal cases, a person is prosecuted by the state.

tort
An injury to a person or an individual's property resulting from the wrongful act of another.

State legislatures frequently change both criminal and civil law. In recent years, the Texas legislature (through statutes and proposed constitutional amendments) and the people of Texas (by ratification of constitutional amendments) have greatly limited money damage recoveries in tort cases. Originally, juries determined the maximum amount of money judgments. Now, most of these recovery amounts are restricted by law.[36]

A major justification for limiting recoveries in tort cases is that individuals and businesses must pay high liability insurance premiums for protection against the risk of lawsuit judgments. After limitations were placed on recoveries in medical malpractice cases, many insurers reduced their malpractice insurance rates, and the number of physicians relocating to Texas increased. In 2017, the state issued twice as many new medical licenses as it did in 2003, the year the law was enacted. In that same period, the number of filed medical malpractice lawsuits dropped by 90 percent.[37] Physicians maintain they deliver better patient care because they no longer have to practice defensive medicine by over-prescribing medication or ordering unnecessary tests. As one doctor observed, "We understand that it's our job to practice good medicine. We don't need a lawyer to tell us that, or the threat or intimidation … of a lawsuit for that."[38] Skeptics noted that the cost of healthcare and health insurance premiums for consumers continued to rise.[39] Trial lawyers argue that the law has eroded "the rights and remedies" of injured parties.[40]

Recoveries for other types of torts, such as those arising from product liability, have not been so restricted. In 2018, a Dallas County jury awarded more than $240 million (reduced to $194 million by an appeals court) to the parents and their two young children for injuries the children sustained in an auto accident. Both children were in child-safety seats in the back of their parents' Lexus when the car was hit from behind. The car's front seats were designed to collapse backward in a rear-end collision. Plaintiffs alleged this design was defective, because when the seats collapsed, both children sustained traumatic brain injuries.[41]

Civil Trial Procedure

The Supreme Court of Texas makes rules of civil procedure for all courts with civil jurisdiction. These rules, however, cannot conflict with any general law of the state. Rules of civil procedure are enacted unless they are rejected by the legislature.

Civil cases normally begin when the **plaintiff** (injured party) files a petition, a document that includes the plaintiff's complaints against the **defendant** and the remedy sought—usually money damages. This petition is filed in the county in which the lawsuit is contemplated through efiletexas.gov and the court clerk issues a citation. In a process called service of citation, the citation is delivered to the defendant in person or via certified mail, directing that person to answer the charges. If neither method is successful, a judge can authorize service in any other way that is likely to notify the defendant, including through her or his email or social media accounts.[42] To contest the suit, the defendant must file an answer to the plaintiff's charges. The answer explains why the plaintiff is not entitled to the remedy sought and asks that the plaintiff be required to prove every charge made in the petition.

Some individuals represent themselves pro se (without a lawyer) and file multiple frivolous lawsuits. If a defendant prevails in having the plaintiff declared a

plaintiff
The injured party who initiates a civil suit or the government in a criminal proceeding.

defendant
The person sued in a civil proceeding or prosecuted in a criminal proceeding.

vexatious litigant by a court, the person's name is placed on a list maintained online by the Office of Court Administration. Vexatious litigants must either file a bond with the court or, in some instances, obtain prior permission before proceeding with a lawsuit. Through 2020, trial courts had identified approximately 330 lawsuits as being filed by vexatious litigants. Many such individuals had filed multiple lawsuits.[43]

Before the judge sets a trial date (which may be many months or even years after the petition is filed), all interested parties should have had an opportunity to file their petitions, answers, or other pleas with the court. These instruments constitute the pleadings in the case and form the basis of the trial. Prior to the trial, the parties also have an opportunity to gather from each other information related to the pending case. This process, known as **discovery**, includes examining documents, obtaining written and oral answers to questions, inspecting property under the control of the other party, and similar activities. Information obtained during discovery may become evidence in the case. Among the items that attorneys research are any electronic communications, such as email, a party might have created or received, as well as postings on social media sites. Some unethical practitioners attempt to friend a party to get into the more private areas of these sites.

Either party has the option to have a jury determine the facts. Over the past 25 years, the number of cases decided by a jury has decreased by more than 60 percent.[44] Less than 0.4 percent of civil lawsuits are tried by a jury. After the jury determines the facts, the judge applies the law to that version of the facts. If no one demands a jury, the trial judge decides all facts and applies the law. Fewer than one-third of all filed lawsuits are tried by the judge in a proceeding known as a bench trial. In recent years, the number of bench trials has also been in rapid decline while the number of cases settled by agreement between the plaintiff and defendant has increased (approximately 12 percent of civil law disputes and almost one-third of family law cases). The remaining cases are dismissed.

Trial and Appeal of a Civil Case

As a trial begins, lawyers for each party make brief opening statements. The plaintiff's case is presented first. The defendant has an opportunity to contest all evidence introduced and may cross-examine the plaintiff's witnesses. After the plaintiff's case has been presented, it is the defendant's turn to offer evidence and the testimony of witnesses. The plaintiff may challenge this evidence and testimony. The judge is the final authority as to what evidence and testimony may be introduced by all parties, although objections to the judge's rulings can be used as grounds for appeal.

In a jury trial, after all parties have concluded, the judge writes a charge to the jury, submits it to the parties for their approval, makes any necessary changes they suggest, and reads the charge to the jury. In the charge, the judge instructs the jury on the rules governing their deliberations and defines various terms. After the charge is read, attorneys make their closing arguments to the jurors. Then, the jury retires to elect one of its members to serve as the presiding juror (commonly referred to as foreman) and to deliberate.

The jury will not be asked directly whether the plaintiff or the defendant should win. Instead, the jury must answer a series of questions that will establish the facts of the case. These questions are called **special issues**. Judgment is based

discovery
Gathering information from the opposing party and witnesses in a lawsuit, including examination of relevant documents, obtaining written and oral answers to questions, inspecting property under the control of the other party, and similar activities.

special issues
Questions a judge gives a trial jury to answer to establish the facts in a civil case.

on jurors' answers. To decide a case in a district court or some county court-at-law cases, at least the same 10 of the 12 jurors must agree on answers to all of the special issues; in a county court or JP court, the same five of six must agree. If the required number of jurors cannot reach agreement, the foreman reports a hung jury. If the judge agrees, the jury is discharged. Any party may then request a new trial, which will be scheduled unless the case is dismissed. If the judge disagrees with the foreman's report, jurors continue to deliberate.

A jury's decision is a **verdict**. When there is no jury, the judge arrives at a verdict. In either case, the judge prepares a written decision, or the **judgment** or decree of the court. Any party may then file a motion for a new trial based on the reasons the party believes the trial was unfair. If the judge agrees, a new trial is ordered; if not, the case may be appealed to a higher court. A complete written record of the trial is sent to the appellate court. The usual route of appeals is from a county or district court to a court of appeals and then, in some instances, to the Texas Supreme Court.

✓ 10.3 Learning Check

1. What are the parties to a civil lawsuit called?
2. True or False: In a civil jury trial, jurors will be asked to decide which party should win.

Answers at the end of this chapter.

✪ Judicial Procedures in Criminal Cases

LO 10.4 Describe the judicial procedure for the adjudication of criminal cases.

Criminal cases occur when someone violates the rules of society by committing an offense for which the government can seek the offender's life, liberty, or property. The rules and procedures in criminal cases include many more checks on the system than in civil cases. From the moment a person is taken into custody until all appeals have been exhausted, the law is designed to assure the highest level of protection for the defendant's rights.

Criminal Justice System

Rules of criminal procedure are made by the legislature. The Texas Code of Criminal Procedure is written to comply with U.S. Supreme Court rulings regarding confessions, arrests, searches, and seizures. Additional rules of procedure have been adopted to promote fairness and efficiency in handling criminal cases.

Thousands of illegal acts (including traffic violations) are committed daily in Texas. After an arrest and before questioning, police must advise suspects of their constitutional rights to remain silent and to have an attorney present. When a prosecuting attorney (either the district attorney or the county attorney) files charges, a suspect must appear before a judicial officer (usually a justice of the peace), who names the offense or offenses charged and provides information concerning the suspect's legal rights. A person charged with a noncapital offense may be released on personal recognizance (promising to report for trial at a later date), released on bail by posting personal money or money provided for a charge by a bail bond service, or denied bail and jailed.

verdict
A judge's or jury's decision about a court case.

judgment
A judge's written opinion based on a verdict.

People who cannot afford to hire a lawyer must be provided with the services of an attorney in any felony or misdemeanor case in which conviction may result in a prison or jail sentence. The state's counties pay most of the cost for indigent defense. In 2019, counties paid more than 90 percent of the $300 million spent on indigent defense.[45] The 13-member Texas Indigent Defense Commission (comprised of judges, attorneys, and legislators) oversees development of statewide policies and procedures for representation of the poorest defendants. In addition, the commission monitors county compliance and coordinates state monetary assistance for these programs.

Private attorneys, appointed by judges, provide most of the defense for indigent defendants; but an increasing number of counties maintain public defenders' offices to meet some of the representation needs of the poor. A study of the results achieved by the public defenders' office in Harris County found that although per case cost was higher for public defender representation, fewer defendants received guilty verdicts.[46] Public defenders in Harris County also attempt to be seen as a resource for all criminal defense attorneys, offering access to their law library and clothing appropriate for court appearances for criminal defendants. The Texas Fair Defense Act requires counties to devise standards for appointed counsel and establishes minimum attorney qualifications for the appointment of counsel for indigent defendants charged with capital crimes.

Private criminal defense attorneys often oppose the creation of public defenders' offices, in part because they fear a loss of income. An alternative that assures private attorney representation of indigent defendants and increases the efficiency of court appointments is the establishment of a managed assigned counsel office. This option allows a nonprofit organization or local bar association to oversee appointment of private attorneys. Some judges oppose this system because they no longer have authority over which attorneys receive court appointments.[47]

Under Texas law, the right to trial by jury is guaranteed in all criminal cases. Except in death penalty cases, defendants may waive a jury trial (if the prosecuting attorney agrees), regardless of the plea—guilty, not guilty, or nolo contendere (no contest). To expedite procedures, prosecuting and defense attorneys may engage in plea bargaining, in which the accused pleads guilty in return for a promise that the prosecutor will seek a lighter sentence or will recommend community supervision. Usually, a judge will accept a plea bargain. If the defendant waives a trial by jury and is found guilty by a judge, that judge also determines punishment.

Criminal Trial and Appeal

After the trial jury has been selected, the prosecuting attorney reads an information (for a misdemeanor) or an indictment (for a felony) to inform the jury of the basic allegations of the state's case. The defendant then enters a plea.

As plaintiff, the state (prosecuting attorney) begins by calling its witnesses and introducing any evidence supporting the information or the indictment. The defense may then challenge evidence and cross-examine witnesses. Next, the defense presents its case, calling witnesses and submitting evidence that, in turn, the prosecution attacks. After all evidence and testimony have been presented, the judge charges the jury by instructing jurors on rules governing their deliberations and explaining the applicable law. Both prosecuting and defense attorneys then address final arguments to the jury before it retires to reach a verdict.

The jury must reach a unanimous decision to return a verdict of guilty or not guilty. If jurors are hopelessly split, the result is a hung jury. In that event, the judge declares a mistrial and discharges the jurors. When requested by the prosecuting attorney, the judge orders a new trial with another jury.

If a jury brings a verdict before a court, the judge may choose to disregard it and order a new trial on the grounds that the jury failed to arrive at a verdict that achieves substantial justice. In a jury trial, the jury may determine the sentence if the convicted person so requests; otherwise, the judge assesses the sentence. In a capital felony case in which the death penalty is being sought, the jury must determine punishment. A separate hearing on the penalty is held, at which time the person's prior criminal or juvenile record, general reputation, and other relevant factors may be introduced, such as facts concerning the convicted person's background and lifestyle as determined by a presentence investigation.

A convicted defendant has the right to appeal on grounds that an error in trial procedure occurred. All appeals (except for death penalty cases) are heard first by the court of appeals in the district in which the trial was held. A few of these appeals are ultimately reviewed by the Texas Court of Criminal Appeals. Death penalty appeals are made directly from a district court to the Texas Court of Criminal Appeals.

✓ 10.4 Learning Check

1. True or False: In criminal cases, a majority of jurors must return a verdict of guilty or not guilty.
2. A capital felony for which the defendant received the death penalty is appealed to which court?

Answers at the end of this chapter.

✖ Keeping Current

The Impact on Texas

The popular, partisan election of judges affected judicial selection in both statewide and local elections in 2018 and 2020. At the state level, voters elected only Republican candidates in both elections. The national split between urban and rural voters is also present in Texas. In urban areas like Dallas and Harris Counties, Democratic Party judicial candidates have won all district court judgeships since 2016. One of the defeated Republican Harris County district judges, Jesse McClure, was appointed to the Court of Criminal Appeals in December 2020.

In 2018, Democrats also won all county and courts of appeals judgeships in these urban counties. Democrats won all but two courts of appeals judgeships in these same counties in 2020.

At the court of appeals level, Democrats now hold a majority on seven of the state's 14 courts of appeals. As with previous elections, the party affiliation, not the record or incumbency of a candidate, appeared to be the most important factor in the likelihood of a judicial candidate's winning election to office. Two of the Republican court of appeals justices who were defeated in 2018, Brett Busby and Jane Bland, were subsequently appointed to the Supreme Court of Texas.

The 86th Legislature addressed salary concerns for state judges and justices, creating a tiered system that awarded longevity pay to officials with more seniority. Of ongoing importance was whether the state should continue to select all judicial officials through popular, partisan elections. Generally, Republicans favored appointive processes and Democrats supported continuing to choose judges through popular elections. Texas's changing demographics and increasing alignment with the Democratic Party have influenced the selection of judges.

Conclusion

Texas's legal system is indeed confusing. From sorting out overlapping court jurisdictions to identifying elected judges and justices—the system appears to be shrouded in mystery and anonymity. Often understood only by those who use the system daily—Texas lawyers—decisions of criminal and civil court judges affect every Texan. For the justice system to work effectively, Texans must understand these complex proceedings. Technology has affected all aspects of the judicial branch. The ability of computers to process and organize large volumes of data has made judicial processes more efficient and allowed the judicial system to continue to operate despite disruptions caused by the COVID-19 pandemic. Ease of communication through social media has sometimes confused its users, whether judges, lawyers, or jurors. Yet, videoconferencing platforms, such as Zoom, allowed court hearings and trials to proceed even when parties and jurors were required to limit face-to-face interactions. The move into the 21st century has included problems not contemplated by those who designed the judicial branch.

Chapter Summary

LO 10.1 Identify the sources of Texas law. The role of courts is to settle disputes by interpreting and applying the law. Texas state law includes both civil law and criminal law. Sources of law include the state's constitution, its statutes, regulations, and the common law (judge-made law). In an attempt to organize its laws, the legislature has instructed the Texas Legislative Council to place laws that cover specific topics into codes.

LO 10.2 Compare the functions of all participants in the justice system. Both constitutional and statutory laws have been used to create the state's court system. Courts may have original or appellate jurisdiction, or both. Texas has local, county, trial, and appellate courts. Some trial courts are now specialty courts that provide more direct oversight of particular types of cases or those involving specific populations. The state's emphasis on parties' resolving their disputes outside the courtroom has resulted in fewer trials. Almost all Texas judges are elected through popular, partisan elections, a system followed in only three other states. Once in office, judges, as well as the lawyers who appear before them, are subject to regulation and discipline. There are two types of juries both of which are chosen from a panel of randomly selected veniremen: grand juries (which determine if adequate cause exists to bring a defendant to trial in a criminal case) and petit juries (which determine the facts in civil cases, whether a defendant is guilty or not guilty in a criminal case, and may determine punishment in criminal cases).

LO 10.3 Describe the judicial procedure for the adjudication of civil lawsuits. The civil justice system includes contract cases, tort cases, family law matters, and juvenile justice cases. The Texas legislature has limited the amount of damages in some tort cases. In jury trials for civil cases, the jury determines the facts of the case by answering special issues, and the judge applies the law. In Texas's bifurcated court system, the highest appellate court for civil cases is the Texas Supreme Court.

LO 10.4 Describe the judicial procedure for adjudication of criminal cases. Criminal law regulates many types of behavior. Protections that are built into the law, for accused felons in particular, include a defendant's being advised of his or her constitutional rights, the right to appointed counsel if someone is indigent, and the right to trial by jury. Felony defendants have the right to a grand jury indictment. Except in capital murder cases, a defendant can waive the right to a jury trial. Jury verdicts in criminal cases must be unanimous. In Texas's bifurcated court system, the highest appellate court for criminal cases is the Texas Court of Criminal Appeals.

Key Terms

alternative dispute resolution (ADR), p. 405
appellate jurisdiction, p. 396
appointment-retention system, p. 406
bifurcated, p. 401
civil law, p. 393
concurrent jurisdiction, p. 396
constitutional county courts, p. 399
contingency fee, p. 409
county courts-at-law, p. 400
Court of Criminal Appeals, p. 402
court of record, p. 396
courts of appeals, p. 400

criminal law, p. 393
defendant, p. 414
discovery, p. 415
district courts, p. 400
exclusive jurisdiction, p. 396
felony, p. 393
grand jury, p. 411
judgment, p. 416
judicial legitimacy, p. 392
jurisdiction, p. 393
justice of the peace, p. 396
misdemeanor, p. 393
Missouri Plan, p. 405
municipal court, p. 396

original jurisdiction, p. 394
petit jury, p. 411
plaintiff, p. 414
probate, p. 394
probate courts, p. 400
special issues, p. 415
specialty courts, p. 403
Supreme Court of Texas, p. 402
tort, p. 413
venire, p. 412
verdict, p. 416
voir dire, p. 412

Learning Check Answers

10.1 **1.** False. Misdemeanors and felonies are considered criminal law cases.

2. True. Texas courts interpret and apply judge-made common law based on custom and tradition in addition to state laws that include the provisions of the Texas Constitution, statutes enacted by the legislature, and regulations adopted by state agencies.

10.2 **1.** Jurisdiction means that the court has the authority to hear a particular kind of case. Jurisdiction may be granted in the Texas Constitution or in the statute creating a court.

2. False. A grand jury only determines if there is enough evidence to go to trial in a criminal case. A petit jury determines if a defendant is guilty.

10.3 **1.** The parties to a civil lawsuit are the plaintiff, who is the injured party bringing the lawsuit, and the defendant, who is the person being sued.

2. False. In a civil jury trial, jurors answer special issues, or a series of questions about the facts in the case. The judge then applies the law to the answers to the special issues and renders a judgment establishing who won the case.

10.4 **1.** False. A jury verdict in a criminal case, whether guilty or not guilty, requires a unanimous decision by the jury. If jurors are split, the result is a hung jury.

2. A capital felony for which the defendant received the death penalty is appealed directly to the Court of Criminal Appeals.

11

Finance and Fiscal Policy

Learning Objectives

11.1 Assess the fairness of Texas's budgeting and taxing policies.

11.2 Identify the sources of Texas's state revenue.

11.3 Describe the procedure for developing and approving a state budget.

11.4 Evaluate the effectiveness of the state's financing of public services.

Image 11.1 The Texas Lottery Commission maintains a Twitter account

Texas Lottery ✔
@TexasLottery

👤+ Follow

RT to say "THANK YOU" to #TexasTeachers! #TeacherAppreciationDay

Thank You!

RETWEETS 3   LIKES 2

10:00 AM - 3 May 2016

Source: Twitter

--- Competency Connection ---
⋆ PERSONAL RESPONSIBILITY ⋆

Should ethical concerns about gambling influence whether a government-sponsored lottery is an appropriate revenue source for public education?

In January 2019, as required by the Texas Constitution, State Comptroller Glenn Hegar submitted his *Biennial Revenue Estimate* to the 86th Texas Legislature. Based on this information, the legislature passed a balanced budget for the 2020–2021 biennium. Hegar's forecast was optimistic but cautious. He identified "heightened uncertain[ies]" in the oil and gas industry, the investment markets, and U.S. trade policies as the reason for his caution. The comptroller anticipated "continued but slowing expansion of the Texas economy."[1]

Hegar predicted that by the end of fiscal year (FY) 2020 (August 31, 2020), businesses would create 245,500 new jobs; unemployment would remain below 4 percent; and state tax collections would increase by more than 8 percent. His upbeat forecast included an additional cautionary note: "[This forecast] does not incorporate the possible impacts of unanticipated one-time or unusual events that could impact economic performance and revenue collections."[2] In other words, the comptroller's predictions did not account for the economic devastation of a pandemic and a severely depressed oil and gas market.

In March 2020, Governor Greg Abbott declared a statewide emergency brought about by the COVID-19 pandemic. By April, in part because of COVID and in part due to a dispute over oil between Russia and Saudi Arabia, oil and gas prices plummeted. Almost all revenue sources for the state rapidly declined. An exception was the state lottery featured in the opening image.

At the end of FY2020, the state had collected $2.1 billion less in taxes than it had in the previous fiscal (budget) year. Due to an additional $16.2 billion in funding from the federal government, including $8 billion in special funding to assist with COVID-19 relief in the state, Texas finished FY2020 with $2.6 billion more in revenue than it received in FY2019. By November 2020, the Texas economy had lost almost 475,000 jobs and the state's unemployment rate was in excess of 8 percent. In July 2020, Comptroller Hegar had revised his predictions to reflect the grim reality of the state's economy. Four months later (November 2020), he amended his forecast saying the damage was not as severe as he had originally thought.

In January 2021, the comptroller issued *Biennial Revenue Estimate 2022–2023* for the 87th legislative session. He cautioned that although he was predicting a steady recovery for the Lone Star State, his estimates were far from certain due to an ongoing pandemic and vagaries of consumer behavior in such an environment. Winter Storm Uri, in February 2021, had a negative effect on consumer spending, thus further reducing state tax collections. Hegar's long-term predictions were further upended in April 2021, when the U.S. government rescinded an agreement to fund emergency care for uninsured Texans. Failure of the Trump administration to follow regulatory requirements in approving the agreement was the reason given for the cancellation. The annual loss to the state of Texas was approximately $11 billion beginning in 2023. Nonetheless, by May 2021, Hegar determined that the state would have a budget surplus for FY2021 and that conditions were normalizing. He increased his revenue estimate for the 2022-2023 budget by $3.12 billion.

This chapter examines the balance between costs and services and also provides an overview of the Lone Star State's fiscal policies, budgeting processes, and most costly public policy areas. Taxing, public spending, and governmental policy priorities will continue to have significant impacts on 21st-century Texans.

★ Fiscal Policies

LO 11.1   Assess the fairness of Texas's budgeting and taxing policies.

During the 86th legislative session in 2019, legislators were able to extend Texas's traditional low-tax approach to **fiscal policy** (public policy that concerns taxes, government spending, public debt, and management of government money). Because of a robust economy, the state's tax collections exceeded projections and unemployment was at a record low. The oil industry and other economic sectors were experiencing high levels of productivity. As a result, the 86th Legislature had sufficient funds to address several long-term concerns faced by the Lone Star State, most especially public school financing. A major impact of this reform was the state's subsidizing school districts to lower local property taxes. (For a discussion of property taxes, see Chapter 3 "Local Governments.") Increased state funding for public education was accomplished without raising state taxes.

Tax revenue includes a general state sales tax, as well as taxes on specific items, such as cigarettes, motor vehicles, and gross receipts from businesses. Revenue sources other than taxes include oil and gas royalties, land sales, and federal grants-in-aid. When economic conditions are poor, the legislature achieves a balanced budget by using a number of accounting maneuvers, like deferring some mandatory payments beyond the end of the biennial budget period, encouraging early payment of taxes to speed up revenue collection, and intentionally underfunding high-cost items such as Medicaid.[3] In difficult economic times, the legislature also looks for ways to reduce spending, especially for high-cost items such as education and healthcare. When the economic outlook is more favorable, the legislature restores funding and reduces taxes. Once taxes have been reduced, legislators are reluctant to increase them to raise revenue during subsequent economic downturns.

Texans remain committed to pay-as-you-go spending and low taxes, no matter the strength of the economy. The Lone Star State's fiscal policy has not deviated from its 19th-century origins. Today, the notion of a balanced budget, achieved by low tax rates and low-to-moderate government spending levels, continues to dominate state fiscal policy. Consequently, state government, its employees, and its taxpayers face the daily challenge of meeting higher demands for services with fewer resources.

The state's elected officials appear to adopt the view expressed by economist and Nobel Prize winner Milton Friedman (1912–2006) that "the preservation of freedom requires limiting narrowly the role of government and placing primary reliance on private property, free markets, and voluntary arrangements."[4] Texas legislators and other state leaders have repeatedly demonstrated a willingness to reduce services, outsource governmental work to decrease the number of employees on the state's payroll, and maintain or lower tax rates as solutions to the state's fiscal problems.

Taxing Policy

Texans have traditionally opposed mandatory assessments for public purposes, or **taxes**. Residents have pressured their state government to maintain low taxes. When the state experiences budget surpluses, pressure increases to eliminate or

fiscal policy
Public policy that concerns taxing, government spending, public debt, and management of government money.

tax
A mandatory assessment exacted by a government for a public purpose.

lower taxes. For example, the 84th Legislature (2015) had the benefit of a significant budget surplus. An effect of this surplus was the legislature's ability to repeal eight different taxes, including, among others, the fireworks tax, the oil regulation tax, and the controlled substances tax. That same legislature reduced the franchise tax, a tax paid by most businesses in Texas, by 25 percent. Savings to state taxpayers were estimated at more than $6.5 billion in the five years after passage.[5]

When additional revenues have been needed, Texans have indicated in poll after poll their preference for **regressive taxes** that favor the rich and fall most heavily on the poor ("the less you make, the more government takes"). Under such taxes, the burden decreases as personal income increases. Figure 11.1 illustrates the impact of regressive taxes on different levels of income. An attempt to increase the sales tax rate in exchange for a reduction in property taxes failed in the 86th Legislature, however. The Legislative Budget Board's report and media accounts that under this plan taxes would increase for anyone with an annual income of less than $100,000 were likely instrumental in the defeat. No such attempt was made by the 87th Legislature.

Texas lawmakers have developed one of the most regressive tax structures in the nation. A general sales tax and selective sales taxes have been especially popular. **Progressive taxes** (taxes in which the impact increases as income rises—"the more you make, the more government takes") have been unpopular. Texas officials and citizens so oppose state income taxes that the state constitution requires a popular referendum before an income tax can be levied. Deeming this requirement inadequate, the constitution was further amended in 2019 to prohibit any tax on personal income.

regressive tax
A tax in which the effective tax rate decreases as the tax base (such as individual income or corporate profits) increases.

progressive tax
A tax in which the effective tax rate increases as the tax base (such as individual income or corporate profits) increases.

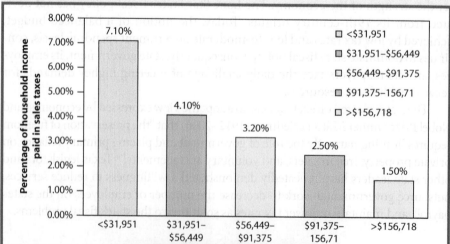

Figure 11.1 Percent of Average Annual Family Income Paid in Sales Tax in Texas (FY2020)

Source: Glenn Hegar, Tax Exemptions and Tax Incidence: A Report to the Governor and the 86th Texas Legislature (Austin: Texas Comptroller of Public Accounts, December 2020), https://comptroller.texas.gov/transparency/reports/tax-exemptions-and-incidence/.

— Competency Connection —
◉ SOCIAL RESPONSIBILITY ◉

What arguments support the fairness of poorer people paying a higher percentage of their income in taxes than the wealthy do?

To finance services, Texas government depends heavily on sales taxes, which rank among the highest in the nation. In addition, the Lone Star State has a dizzying array of other taxes. The Texas state comptroller's office collects almost 30 separate taxes, fees, and assessments on behalf of the state and local governments.[6] Yet the sales tax remains the most important source of state revenue.

Many observers have criticized the regressive characteristics of Texas's tax system as being unfair. An additional concern is that the state primarily operates with a 19th-century land- and product-based tax system that is no longer appropriate to the knowledge- and service-based economy of the 21st century. Local governments rely heavily on real estate taxes for their revenue. More than half of the state's general revenue tax collections are sales and use taxes. Until 2006, business activities of **service sector** employers (including those in trade, finance, and the professions) remained tax-free. In that year, however, the state altered the **franchise tax** law (a tax imposed by a state for the privilege of conducting business activities with limited or no personal liability). This change required most Texas businesses to pay taxes calculated on their profit margins. Extension of the franchise tax subjected many service sector entities to taxation. Service sector functions (especially professional services) remain exempt from the sales tax, an exemption that the comptroller argues costs the state more than $10 billion in revenue each year.[7]

Texas's tax structure ranks as the 18th most volatile in revenue fluctuation among the states.[8] Contributing to this volatility is the state's reliance on **severance taxes** (those assessed when oil, gas, and other minerals are mined or pumped from the earth). In addition, a comparison of sales and use tax collections ($34.1 billion) and franchise tax collections ($4.4 billion) for fiscal year 2020 reflects the extent to which the Lone Star State persists in relying on sales tax revenue. Changes in Texas's economy, without corresponding changes in its tax system, are projected to continue to erode the tax base. Under the current structure, the part of the economy generating the greatest amount of revenue frequently pays the least amount in taxes.

The state also charges special fees and assessments that are not called taxes but involve payments to the government. Texas legislators, reluctant to raise taxes, have often assessed these fees and surcharges. Is a **fee**, defined as a charge "imposed by an agency upon those subject to its regulation,"[9] different from a tax? Some argue that such assessments represent an artful use of words, not a refusal to raise taxes, and that these charges meet the definition of a tax if the proceeds benefit the general public. For example, the state requires attorneys to pay an annual legal services fee to fund legal assistance for the poor. Attorneys who fail to pay this fee lose their right to practice law in Texas. No matter the designation, this mandatory fee is money that an attorney must pay to finance government services for the general public.

Budget Policy

Hostility to public debt is demonstrated in constitutional and statutory provisions that are designed to force the state to operate with a pay-as-you-go **balanced budget**. The Texas Constitution prohibits the state from spending more than

service sector
Businesses that provide services, such as finance, healthcare, food service, data processing, or consulting.

franchise tax
A tax levied on the annual receipts of businesses that are organized to limit the personal liability of owners for the privilege of conducting business in the state.

severance tax
An excise tax levied on a natural resource (such as oil or natural gas) when it is severed (removed) from the earth.

fee
A charge imposed by an agency upon those subject to its regulation.

balanced budget
A budget in which total revenues and expenditures are equal, producing no deficit.

its anticipated revenue "[e]xcept in the case of emergency and imperative public necessity and with a four-fifths vote of the total membership of each House."[10] In addition, the cost of debt service limits the state's borrowing power. This cost cannot exceed 5 percent of the average balance of general revenue funds for the preceding three years.

To ensure a balanced budget, the comptroller of public accounts must submit to the legislature, in advance of each regular session, a sworn statement of cash on hand and revenue anticipated for the succeeding two years. The amount certified includes revenue available in both the General Revenue Fund and the General Revenue–Dedicated Fund. Appropriation bills enacted at that particular session, and at any subsequent special session, are limited to not more than the amount certified, unless a four-fifths majority in both houses votes to ignore the comptroller's predictions or the legislature provides new revenue sources. Initial budgets proposed by the two chambers of the 87th Legislature exceeded the comptroller's January 2021 estimates. After adjustments to the comptroller's estimates in May 2021, and budget negotiations between the House and Senate, the legislature submitted a $248.6 billion balanced budget for 2022-2023. The approved budget did not include $16 billion in federal pandemic-relief funding.

Texas accounts for the state's revenue and spending in several different budgets. The All Funds Budget includes all sources of revenue and all spending. In addition, reference is often made to the General Revenue Funds Budget. This budget includes the nondedicated portion of the **General Revenue Fund** (money that can be appropriated for any legal purpose by the legislature) plus some of the funds used to finance public education (the Available School Fund, the State Instructional Materials Fund, and the Foundation School Fund). Casual deficits (unplanned shortages) sometimes arise in the General Revenue Fund. Like a thermometer, this fund measures the state's fiscal health. If the fund shows a surplus (as Comptroller Hegar predicted for fiscal years 2020–2021), fiscal health is good; but, if a deficit occurs (as would have been the situation without COVID relief funds for fiscal years 2020–2021), then fiscal health is poor. Less than one-half of the state's expenditures come from the General Revenue Fund; the remainder comes from other funds that state law designates for use for specific purposes.

The General Revenue–Dedicated Funds Budget includes more than 200 separate funds. Because of restrictions on use, these accounts are defined as **dedicated funds**. In most cases, the funds can only be used for their designated purposes, although in some instances money can be diverted to the state's general fund. Even amounts that can only be spent for a designated purpose may be manipulated to satisfy the mandate for a balanced budget. The legislature can incorporate any unspent balances into its budget calculations. In the 82nd legislative session (2011), for example, the legislature refused to appropriate more than $5 billion in General Revenue–Dedicated Funds in order to give the appearance of a balanced budget. State lawmakers justify these actions by noting that the high costs of programs such as Medicaid force them to freeze these balances. Former State Representative Sylvester Turner (D-Houston, and subsequently mayor of Houston) characterized this practice somewhat differently, calling it "dishonest governing,"[11] because it is an accounting trick that makes money appear available on paper that in fact is not available. Subsequent legislative sessions varied in

General Revenue Fund
An unrestricted state fund that is available for general appropriations.

dedicated fund
A restricted state fund that has been identified to be spent for a designated purpose. If the fund is consolidated within the General Revenue Fund, it usually must be spent for its intended purpose. Some unappropriated amounts of dedicated funds, even those required to be used for a specific purpose, can be included in the calculations to balance the state budget.

their reliance on unappropriated, dedicated funds to balance the budget. An attempt by the House of Representatives to restrict the number of dedicated funds that could be used to balance the budget failed in the 86th Legislature.

The Federal Funds Budget includes all funding from the U.S. government. These amounts must be spent for their designated purposes. Likewise, the Other Funds Budget includes an additional 200-plus dedicated funds, each of which must be spent for its stated purpose, such as the Property Tax Relief Fund that must be used to fund public education.

Spending Policy

Historically, Texans have shown little enthusiasm for state spending. In addition to requiring a balanced budget, the Texas Constitution restricts increases in spending that exceed the rate of growth of the state's economy and limits welfare spending in any fiscal year to no more than 1 percent of total state expenditures. By statute, spending cannot exceed the rate of population growth adjusted for inflation. Public expenditures have remained low. Texas consistently ranks in the bottom 20 percent of states in spending per capita. Although Texas voters are willing to spend for highways, roads, and other public improvements, they have not supported welfare programs, recreational facilities, and other social services.

> ✔ **11.1 Learning Check**
>
> 1. What are three characteristics of Texas's fiscal policy?
> 2. The state of Texas has one of the highest sales tax rates in the nation. It does not have a state income tax. Is Texas's tax structure an example of a regressive or a progressive tax system?
>
> *Answers at the end of this chapter.*

⬧ Revenue Sources

LO 11.2   Identify the sources of Texas's state revenue.

Funding for government services primarily comes from those who pay taxes. In addition, the state derives revenue from fees for licenses, sales of assets, investment income, gambling, borrowing, and federal grants. When revenue to the state declines, elected officials have only two choices: (1) increase taxes or other sources of revenue or (2) decrease services. In times of projected budget shortfalls, as occurred prior to the 2022–2023 biennium, the legislature's favored responses have been to decrease services and manipulate accounts within the budget. An improved economy and federal funding allowed the 87th Legislature to avoid anticipated reductions. When revenue is plentiful, pressure builds to reduce taxes.

The Politics of Taxation

Taxes are but one source of state revenue.[12] According to generally accepted standards, each tax levied and the total tax structure should be just and equitable. Opinions vary widely about what kinds of taxes and what types of structures meet these standards. Conflicts are most apparent in the struggle to finance the state's public schools as elected officials strive to lower real estate taxes for the state's property owners and replace local funding with additional state-level taxes. Texas has a constitutional mandate to provide "an efficient system of public free schools," and the state's courts have defined adequate funding as a key element of this requirement. Determining who should pay taxes to finance public education is a challenge.

The legislature has engaged in a long-running attempt to alter the way the state finances public schools, especially by lowering local property taxes. To decrease local taxes, state legislators increased or expanded some state-level taxes. Beginning in 2006, the number of businesses required to pay franchise taxes increased. Over the years, exemptions for smaller businesses (those making $1,000,000 or less per year in annual income) and lower tax rates have depressed the amount of tax revenue available. These modifications reflect the political strength of business owners. The 86th Legislature substantially increased state funding for public schools and reduced and limited increases of local property taxes. Increased state funding and reduction of local property taxes remained priorities for the 87th Legislature, including an unsuccessful bill to eliminate property taxes.

Sales Taxes By far the most important single source of state tax revenue in Texas is sales taxation. (See Figure 11.2 for the sources of state revenue.) Altogether, sales taxes accounted for 60 percent of state tax revenue and approximately 25 percent of all revenue in fiscal year 2020. These sales taxes function as a regressive tax, and the burden imposed on individual taxpayers varies with spending patterns and income levels.

For more than 60 years, the state has levied and collected two kinds of sales taxes: a **general sales tax** and several selective sales taxes. First imposed in 1961, the limited sales, excise, and use tax (commonly referred to as the general sales tax) has become the foundation of the Texas tax system. The current (2021) statewide rate of 6.25 percent is one of the nation's highest (ranking as the 14th-highest rate among the 45 states that imposed a sales tax as of 2020).[13] Local governments have the option of levying additional sales taxes for a combined total of state and local taxes at 8.25 percent (see Chapter 3, "Local Governments"). The base of the tax is the sale price of "tangible personal property" and "the storage, use, or other consumption of tangible personal property purchased, leased, or rented." Among exempted tangible property are the following: receipts from water, telephone, and telegraph services; sales of goods otherwise taxed (for example, automobiles and motor fuels); food and food products (but not restaurant meals); medical supplies sold by prescription; nonprescription drugs; animals and supplies used in agricultural production; sales by university and college clubs and organizations (as long as the group has no more than one fundraising activity per month); and equipment used in the manufacture, processing, or fabrication of tangible personal property.

Because the general sales tax primarily applies to tangible personal property, many services are untaxed. Sales taxes are charged for dry cleaning, football tickets, and parking; however, accountants, architects, and consultants provide their services tax-free. Because professional service providers and businesses represent some of the most powerful and well-organized interests in the Lone Star State, proposals that would require these groups to collect a sales tax have faced strong resistance. (See Chapter 7, "The Politics of Interest Groups.") Although the comptroller estimates that eliminating sales tax exclusions for professional and other service providers would generate more than $10 billion in additional annual revenue, even in difficult economic times, legislators have made no effort to change the law.[14]

general sales tax
Texas's largest source of tax revenue, applied at the rate of 6.25 percent to the sale price of tangible personal property and "the storage, use, or other consumption of tangible personal property purchased, leased, or rented."

Figure 11.2 Sources of State Revenue, Fiscal Year 2020

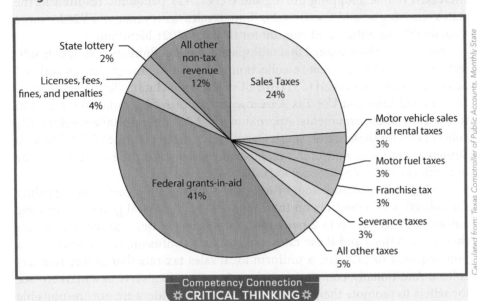

Calculated from: Texas Comptroller of Public Accounts, Monthly State Revenue Watch: All Funds Monthly Collections (Historical Data), Fiscal 2020, https://comptroller.texas.gov/transparency/revenue/watch/all-funds/.

— Competency Connection —
☼ **CRITICAL THINKING** ☼

What are some risks and benefits of relying so heavily on the national government for financial support?

Through 2018, decisions of the U.S. Supreme Court, interpreting the Commerce Clause of the U.S. Constitution, prohibited states from forcing online retailers to charge sales tax on sales transactions, unless the seller had a facility or employee in the state. The physical presence of the facility or person created an affiliate nexus or connection to the state. Court decisions provided that only Congress could authorize states to tax sales if the seller did not have an affiliate nexus. Then, the court reversed its previous decisions. In *South Dakota v. Wayfair*, 585 U.S. ___ (2018), the court held that merchants who have no affiliate nexus in a state, but conduct considerable business in the state, establish an economic nexus. That economic nexus is sufficient to allow states to tax the sales of remote online retailers. South Dakota's standard of applying the tax to online merchants whose annual sales exceeded $100,000 or 200 separate transactions annually met the court's definition of a business having conducted "considerable business" in the state. In Texas, any company that has $500,000 in sales must collect sales tax on purchases.

Noting the pervasiveness of Internet sales, the court determined that remote online retailers, who could avoid collecting sales taxes on their transactions, had an unfair advantage over in-state merchants who were required to charge these taxes. The court further recognized that requiring an affiliate nexus before a state legislature could levy taxes against a merchant created an artificial barrier to taxation in a world in which so many transactions occur virtually. In his written opinion, Justice Anthony Kennedy observed: "A virtual showroom can show far more inventory, in far more detail, and with greater opportunities for consumer and seller interaction than might be possible for local stores." Increased online shopping during the COVID-19 pandemic resulted in the state's receiving an additional $1.3 billion in sales tax revenue in FY2020, more than double the anticipated amount for the 2020-2021 biennium.[15]

Some sellers have argued that multiple rates and definitions of products subject to state sales taxes create a collection nightmare. Through the Streamlined Sales Tax Governing Board (SSTGB), 24 states, not including Texas, have signed Streamlined Sales and Use Tax Agreements that provide a uniform tax system to overcome these arguments. Approximately 2,000 online retailers voluntarily collect taxes for these states. South Dakota is a member of the SSTGB. The U.S. Supreme Court took note of this membership in upholding the constitutionality of South Dakota's sales tax on goods sold online.

The 86th Legislature sought to address some of the concerns regarding the collection of a sales tax on Internet sales. Because local governments have authority to collect up to 2 percent in sales taxes on items purchased within their jurisdictions and these rates vary, to limit confusion, the comptroller is now required to calculate a uniform local sales tax rate that online retailers collect. Additionally, companies such as Amazon often serve as a marketplace for sellers to promote their goods. Marketplace providers are now responsible for collecting and remitting sales taxes on goods sold through their sites. As a result of this change, the Legislative Budget Board estimated an additional $700 million in state and local taxes would be collected in the 2020–2021 biennium for state and local governments. All state proceeds are deposited in the Tax Reduction and Excellence in Education Fund to assist in lowering local property taxes. During the 2022–2023 biennium, revenue to this Fund is projected to be $1.8 billion.

The Lone Star State has used its sales tax laws to negotiate jobs and an improved economy for Texans. For example, as part of a settlement agreement entered in 2012 for payment of disputed sales taxes, Amazon agreed to invest more than $200 million in the state and create an additional 2,500 jobs. As of 2020, the company had 15 fully operating fulfillment centers where items are stored; two additional fulfillment centers under construction, one in Waco and the other in San Antonio; and four sortation centers where shipments are sorted by zip code. Corporate officials stated they had created almost 45,000 well-paying jobs with healthcare and retirement benefits for Texans and invested more than $16.9 billion in facilities and staff.[16]

selective sales tax
A tax charged on specific products and services.

sin tax
A selective sales tax on items such as cigarettes, other forms of tobacco, alcoholic beverages, and admission to sex-oriented businesses.

Since 1931, when the legislature first imposed a sales tax on cigarettes, many items have been singled out for **selective sales taxes**. These items may be grouped into three categories: highway user taxes, **sin taxes**, and miscellaneous sales taxes. Highway user taxes include taxes on fuels for motor vehicles that use public roads. (Registration fees for the privilege of operating those vehicles also support transportation costs.) Sin taxes have a dual purpose: to raise tax revenue and to curtail behaviors that are viewed as unhealthy or immoral. The principal sin taxes are those on cigarettes and other tobacco products, alcoholic beverages, and mixed drinks. Other selective sales taxes include hotel and motel room rentals ("bed tax") and taxes on retail sales of boats and boat motors.

Business Taxes As with sales taxes, Texas imposes both general and selective business taxes. A general business tax is assessed against a wide range of business operations. Selective business taxes are those levied on businesses engaged in specific or selected types of commercial activities.

Commercial enterprises operating in Texas have historically paid three general business taxes:

- Sales taxes, because businesses are consumers
- Franchise taxes, because many businesses operate in a form that attempts to limit personal liability of owners (that is, corporations, limited liability partnerships, and similar structures)
- Unemployment compensation payroll taxes, because most businesses are also employers

The franchise tax, which has existed for more than 100 years, is imposed on businesses for the privilege of doing business in Texas with legal protections against an individual's personal liability. As a part of the restructuring of the state's school finance system in 2006, the legislature expanded the franchise tax to include all businesses operating in a format that limited the personal liability of owners. Sole proprietorships; general partnerships wholly owned by natural persons; passive investment entities (such as real estate investment trusts or REITs); and small businesses, those that make $1 million or less in annual income or that owe less than $1,000 in franchise taxes, are exempt. The tax is levied on a business's taxable margin, which is the amount of money earned in Texas that is equal to the least of (1) total revenue minus the cost of goods sold, (2) total revenue minus compensation and benefits paid to employees, (3) 70 percent of total revenue, or (4) total revenue minus $1 million. For many businesses, being able to deduct the cost of goods sold provides the most favorable tax treatment.

Although proponents estimated that the restructured franchise (margins) tax would produce about $6 billion in state revenue each fiscal year, actual collections have been far less. In the fiscal year of 2020, franchise tax collections were $4.44 billion. For the two-year period covering the 2022–2023 biennium, the comptroller projected total collections of $9 billion (or approximately $4.5 billion per fiscal year). Several reasons have been cited for this shortfall, including a weak economy, the increase in the small business exemption to eliminate taxes on businesses earning less than $1 million a year, a definition of "cost of goods sold" that includes deductions not available under federal law, and decreases in the tax rate. The tax is highly unpopular among small business owners, who continue to seek its repeal, both in the legislature and in the courts.[17]

All states have unemployment insurance systems supported by **payroll taxes**. Paid by employers to insure employees against unemployment, these taxes are levied against a portion of the compensation paid to workers. Although collected by the state, the proceeds are deposited into the Unemployment Trust Fund in the U.S. Treasury. Benefits are distributed to qualified workers who lose their jobs.

payroll tax
An employer-paid tax levied against a portion of the wages and salaries of workers to provide funds for payment of unemployment insurance benefits in the event employees lose their jobs.

The most significant of the state's selective business taxes are levied on the following:

- Oil and gas production
- Insurance company gross premiums
- Public utilities gross receipts

Selective business taxes accounted for approximately 15 percent of the state's tax revenue in the 2018–2019 biennium, when the economy was strong and oil and gas prices and production were high. By fiscal year 2020, these taxes accounted for less than 13 percent of the state's tax revenue. Improving economic conditions in 2019 caused the comptroller to project an increase in collections for all business taxes, except natural gas production. The COVID-19 pandemic demolished these predictions, reducing anticipated collections by more than $1 billion for FY2020. Based on assumptions of increased demand and improving prices in the 2022–2023 biennium, the comptroller estimated an increase of 10 percent in oil production tax collections and a 67 percent increase in natural gas production tax collections over actual collections in the 2020–2021 biennium.

One of the more important selective business taxes is the severance tax. Texas has depended on severance taxes, which are levied on a natural resource, such as oil or natural gas, when it is removed from the earth. The underlying principle is that a non-renewable resource is being removed and most likely will be sold to out-of-state consumers. Therefore, the state must be compensated for loss of a resource that cannot be replaced. Texas severance taxes are based on the quantity of minerals produced or on the value of the resource when removed. The Texas crude oil production tax and the gas-gathering tax were designed with two objectives in mind: to raise substantial revenue and to regulate the amount of natural resources mined or otherwise recovered. Each of these taxes is highly volatile, reflecting dramatic increases and decreases as the price and demand for natural resources fluctuate. The downturn in the oil and gas market that occurred in FY2020 had a devastating effect on this source of tax revenue.[18] Although oil and gas prices were expected to generate an estimated $10.7 billion in revenue in the 2020–2021 biennium, by January 2021 the comptroller adjusted his prediction downward to $8 billion. For the 2022–2023 biennium collections were expected to increase to $10 billion.

Oil and gas production in Texas relies heavily on hydraulic fracture stimulation (fracking). Controversies about the environmental impact of this recovery method on groundwater and on underground stability and water supply, together with opposition from President Joe Biden's administration, could reduce production and, therefore, decrease severance tax revenue to the Lone Star State.[19]

Inheritance Tax The 84th Legislature (2015) repealed all of Texas's inheritance tax laws, noting that no significant taxes were collected under existing law ($12,000 in 2014) and that the comptroller did not need to invest resources in enforcing such an insignificant tax.[20]

Tax Burden Texas places well below the national average for the state tax burden imposed on its residents. In 2018, the Lone Star State's tax burden was 47th among the 50 states.[21] The Tax Foundation ranks Texas as having the 11th most business-favorable tax system in the nation. A candidate's "no new taxes" pledge remains important to many Texas voters and results in state officials' choosing fewer state-funded services over higher taxes to balance the budget. Because local governments then have a higher service burden and therefore higher taxes, businesses pay much more in total taxes than in most other states.[22]

Tax Collection As Texas's chief tax collector, the comptroller of public accounts collects more than 90 percent of state taxes, including those on motor fuel sales, oil and gas production, cigarette and tobacco sales, and businesses. Amounts assessed by the comptroller's office can be challenged through an administrative proceeding conducted by that office. Taxpayers dissatisfied with the results of their hearings can appeal the decision to a state district court.

Some taxpayers commit tax fraud by not paying their full tax liability. Electronic sales suppression devices and software, like zappers and phantom-ware, are used to report fewer sales than retailers actually have. These devices allow users to maintain an electronic set of books for tax purposes that erases some credit card and cash transactions from the register's memory. The devices and software are difficult to detect. Their use reduces the payment of any taxes based on a business's receipts, such as sales taxes, mixed drink taxes, and the gross margins or franchise tax. Possession, sale, purchase, or use of this type of device is a state jail felony, punishable by up to two years in a state jail.[23] (For a discussion of different categories of felonies and the related punishment, see Chapter 13, "The Criminal Justice System.")

Revenue from Gambling

The Lone Star State receives revenue from three types of gambling operations (called "gaming" by supporters): horse racing and dog racing (both live and simulcast), a state-managed lottery, and bingo. The state has an uncomfortable relationship with the concept of raising revenue through games of chance and other forms of wagering. Opposition from social conservatives and religious groups is strong. Some out-of-state casino operators, particularly from neighboring states, demonstrate their opposition through campaign donations to candidates who oppose additional gambling operations in Texas.[24]

Two of the state's most influential elected officials (Governor Greg Abbott and Lieutenant Governor Dan Patrick) have historically disapproved any expansion of gambling activities in the state,[25] yet proceeds from gambling activities provide revenue for needed services like public education. House Speaker Dade Phelan (87th Legislature) did not prioritize expansion of gambling, although in previous sessions he sponsored unsuccessful bills to allow fantasy sports contests, arguing that results from these games rely on skill not luck.[26]

In 2013, the Texas House of Representatives voted to abolish the Texas Lottery Commission. When proponents argued the legislature would have to replace $2.2 billion in biennial funding for public schools if the lottery were eliminated, some opponents changed their votes.[27] As a result, the Texas Lottery Commission will continue in existence through 2025, although the same bill created the Legislative Committee to Review the Texas Lottery and Texas Lottery Commission. When this committee investigated the viability of phasing out the lottery, it determined that funding provided for public education, veterans' benefits, and healthcare facilities was valuable and that the lottery should be continued.[28]

Pressure favoring expansion of gambling opportunities increased in 2020, when international gambling magnate, Sheldon Adelson, launched an effort to legalize casino gambling in the state. Adelson, and his wife Miriam, donated $4.5 million to an account for 2020 Republican legislative candidates through the Republican State Leadership Committee. Adelson's company, Las Vegas Sands, hired multiple lobbyists to lobby elected officials during the 87th Legislature.[29] Adelson's death in 2021 and a stronger than anticipated economy stifled this attempt to liberalize gaming laws in Texas.

In addition, owners and operators of gambling facilities, as well as the Texas Lottery Commission, continue to urge expansion of gambling opportunities. The state's three Native American tribes (the Kickapoo nation near Eagle Pass, the Alabama-Coushatta in East Texas, and the Tigua near El Paso) argue for the right to operate Las Vegas–style casinos. The Kickapoo, who obtained tribal recognition from the United States prior to 1987, operate the Lucky Eagle Casino in Eagle Pass, without fear of closure. Gambling activities are restricted to games such as bingo and a slot-like machine based on bingo. Gaming activities of the Alabama-Coushatta and the Tigua have, however, remained the subject of ongoing litigation by the state. Both tribes obtained tribal recognition from the U.S. government under a 1987 treaty that prohibits them from engaging in any gaming activities not otherwise legal in Texas. Intermittent closures of both tribes' casinos have been ordered by courts over the past three decades. Both state and federal courts have consistently ruled against the tribes in any litigation, holding that they remained subject to state gambling prohibitions. In 2021, the U.S. House of Representatives passed a bill to override state law and allow gaming activities by the two tribes. Whether the bill would succeed in the U.S. Senate remained questionable due to the opposition of U.S. Senator John Cornyn (R-Texas).

Both the Texas Racing Commission and the Texas Lottery Commission have tested the resolve of the state's leadership to limit gambling activities. In these instances, state officials have responded negatively. When the Texas Racing Commission voted to expand gambling at the state's dog and horse racing tracks to include historical racing terminals, in which players bet on unidentified, previously run races, the Legislative Budget Board froze funding to the agency. After a year-long battle, the commission rescinded its ruling and funding was restored.

The Texas Lottery Commission's executive director explored creating games tied to the results of fantasy sports teams in 2016. Governor Abbott ordered agency employees to abandon these plans. The Commission was forced to follow his order after Attorney General Ken Paxton issued an Attorney General Opinion that fantasy sports betting through online providers, such as DraftKings and FanDuel, is illegal in Texas.[30] This strong opposition to expanding gambling operations did not yield to Speaker Phelan's support of fantasy sports contests as another attempt to legalize fantasy sports wagers failed in the 87th Legislature.

Racing Pari-mutuel wagers on horse races and dog races are taxed. This levy has never brought Texas significant revenue, and betting has consistently declined since 2000. Proceeds from uncashed mutuel tickets, minus the cost of drug testing animals at the racing facility, revert to the state. In most years, the Racing Commission collects far less revenue than its operating expenses. Texas has four types of horse racing permits, ranging from Class 1 (with no limit on the number of race days per year) to Class 4 (limited to five race days annually). As of 2021, the Lone Star State had seven permitted horse racing tracks (four that were active and three that were inactive), no training facilities, and three dog tracks providing live and simulcast racing events on which people could wager legal bets.

Lottery Texas operates one of 44 state-run lotteries, and participates in two multistate lotteries: Mega Millions and Powerball. Through June 2021, Texans had won approximately $70 billion in prizes since the first lottery tickets were sold in 1992. Chances of winning the state lottery jackpot, however, are 1 in 26 million. Texans have won 14 Mega Millions jackpots and only two Powerball jackpots since the state began participating in these lotteries in 2003. Chances of winning Mega Millions' jackpot are 1 in 302 million. Powerball odds are less daunting: 1 in 292 million.

The Texas Lottery Commission administers the state's lottery. Appointed by the governor, the five members of this commission serve six-year terms. Because the commission also oversees bingo operations, one member must have experience in the bingo industry. Among the commission's functions are determining the amounts of prizes, overseeing the printing of tickets, advertising ticket sales, and awarding prizes. The commission maintains a Twitter account through which the public receives regular updates on winning lottery numbers, upcoming jackpot amounts, and previous winners. This account, shown in the opening image for this chapter, is a public relations tool to remind Texans of the lottery's benefits, such as providing funds for public education and veterans' services.

Most profits from the lottery are dedicated to public education spending. In 2020, almost $1.7 billion went to the Texas Foundation School Fund. This amount constituted only a small portion (4.8 percent) of the state's budgeted expenditure of approximately $35.2 billion on public education in that same year. Proceeds from a Veteran's Cash scratch-off game benefit the Veterans' Assistance Fund, which received $22 million from ticket sales in 2020. Unclaimed prizes from the Texas lottery revert to the state 180 days after a drawing. These funds are transferred to the Foundation School Fund. Five percent of ticket sale revenue is used to pay commissions to retailers who sell the tickets.

Bingo State law allows bingo operations to benefit charities (for example, churches, veterans' organizations, and service clubs). Each person who wins more than $5 is required to pay 5 percent of the proceeds as a prize fee. One-half of the fee is remitted to the Texas Lottery Commission and the balance is paid to local governments, if a city or county has opted to receive payments, or is used for charitable purposes by the sponsoring nonprofit organization. State revenue from bingo taxes collected from more than 300 bingo halls remains low. Local charities benefit somewhat from the portion of the proceeds that is distributed to them. In 2018, the last year for which information is available, these donations were approximately $33.6 million. In that same year, the Texas Lottery Commission reported gross receipts from charitable bingo games of $812 million, of which $622 million was used to pay winners' prizes.

Often conducted in large meeting halls, bingo games required social distancing, masks, and capacity limits during the COVID-19 pandemic. Stay-at-home requests proved even more disruptive. In response, some bingo halls began offering drive-in bingo. Players tuned their radios to a designated frequency to hear the caller call out the bingo numbers. Winners honked their horns or flashed their lights.[31]

Other Nontax Revenues

Less than 50 percent of all Texas state revenue comes from taxes and gambling operations; therefore, other nontax revenues are important sources of funds. The largest portion of these revenues comes from federal grants. State business operations (such as sales of goods by one government agency to another government agency) and borrowing also are significant sources of revenue. In addition, the state has billions of dollars invested in interest-bearing accounts and securities. In 2021, Governor Abbott led an effort to crowdfund construction of a border wall.

Federal Grants-in-Aid Gifts of money, goods, or services from one government to another are defined as **grants-in-aid**. Federal grants-in-aid contribute more revenue to Texas than any single tax levied by the state. More than 95 percent of federal funds are directed to three programs: health and human services, business and economic development (especially highway construction), and education. In the 2020–2021 biennium, funding from the federal government was expected to be approximately one-third of state revenue or $88 billion (approximately $44 billion per fiscal year). This projection was consistent with federal funding levels for recent years. Due in part to more than $8 billion in economic relief in response to the COVID-19 pandemic, the Lone Star State actually received more than $58 billion in aid for FY2020, an amount equivalent to more than 40 percent of the state budget in that year. Of the $38 billion in federal pandemic relief funds authorized for Texas in 2021, approximately $16 billion was available for state government operations.

State participation in federal grant programs is voluntary. Participating states must (1) contribute a portion of program costs (varying from as little as 10 percent to as much as 90 percent) and (2) meet performance specifications established by federal mandate. Funds are usually allocated to states on the basis of a formula. These formulae often include (1) lump sums (made up of identical amounts to all states receiving funds) and (2) uniform sums (based on items that vary from state to state, such as population, area, highway mileage, need and fiscal ability, cost of service, administrative discretion, and special state needs).

Land Revenues Texas state government receives nontax revenue from public land sales, rentals, and royalties. Sales of land, sand, shell, and gravel, combined with rentals on grazing lands and prospecting permits, accounted for approximately 1 percent of the state's budget in the 2020–2021 biennium. A substantial portion of revenue from state lands is received from oil and natural gas leases and from royalties derived from mineral production. The instability of oil and natural gas prices causes wide fluctuations in the amount the state receives from these mineral leases. For example, collections for the budget year of 2020 represented a $450 million decrease from the prior year's land revenues.

grant-in-aid
Money, goods, or services given by one government to another (for example, federal grants-in-aid to states for financing public assistance programs for poor Texans).

Oil and gas is not the only energy-related resource that provides revenue for the state. In addition, the General Land Office, the agency responsible for managing the more than 13 million acres of land surface and mineral rights that the state owns, leases onshore and offshore sites for energy production from wind, solar, and geothermal sources. Hard minerals, such as sand, gravel, caliche, and sulfur, are also mined from state-owned land, and producers pay a royalty to the state. Because the General Land Office can take payment from oil and gas producers in cash or in kind, Texas also maintains an energy marketing program through which the state sells natural gas and electricity to local governments, public colleges and universities, and state agencies. One of the principal beneficiaries of monies received from these programs is the Permanent School Fund. The General Land Office proclaims on its website that its business activities "turn oil into textbooks for Texas children."[32]

The Tobacco Suit Windfall Early in 1998, the American tobacco industry settled a lawsuit filed by the state of Texas. During a period of 25 years, cigarette makers were required to pay the Lone Star State $18 billion in damages for public health costs incurred by the state as a result of residents' tobacco-related illnesses. These funds support a variety of healthcare programs, including the Children's Health Insurance Program (CHIP), Medicaid, tobacco education projects, and endowments for health-related institutions of higher education. Payments averaged approximately $500 million per year through 2015. Because of increases in taxes that have reduced consumption in Texas and other states, revenue from the sale of tobacco products has decreased in recent years. As a result, the settlement payments from the tobacco lawsuit declined to approximately $438 million for FY2020 and was projected to be $440 million per year in the 2022–2023 biennium. An additional $2.3 billion is administered as a trust by the state comptroller to reimburse local governments (cities, counties, and hospital districts) for unreimbursed healthcare costs.

Miscellaneous Sources Fees, permits, and income from investments are major miscellaneous nontax sources of revenue. Fee sources include those for motor vehicle inspections, college tuition, student services, state hospital care, and certificates of title for motor vehicles. The most significant sources of revenue from permits are those for trucks and automobiles; sale of liquor, wine, and beer; and cigarette tax stamps. These fees are collected by a variety of agencies at both the state and local levels of government. For example, the Department of Motor Vehicles collects motor vehicle registration and certificate-of-title fees through county tax collectors' offices; the State Board of Insurance collects insurance fees; and the Department of Public Safety collects driver's license, motor vehicle inspection, and similar fees. Relying on forecasts of a strong economy, the comptroller predicted an increase in income from these sources for the 2020–2021 biennium, but this income source also experienced a decline due to the economic chaos caused by the COVID-19 pandemic.

At any given moment, Texas has billions of dollars on hand, invested in securities or on deposit in interest-bearing accounts. Trust funds constitute the bulk of money invested by the state (for example, the Texas Teacher Retirement Fund, the State Employee Retirement Fund, the Permanent School Fund, and the Permanent University Fund). Investment returns closely track fluctuations in the stock market. Continued strengthening of the stock market from 2008 through 2020 benefited these funds, in some instances resulting in a 450 percent increase in value over that period of time.

The Texas state comptroller is responsible for overseeing the investment of most of the state's surplus funds. Restrictive money management laws limit investments to interest-bearing negotiable order withdrawal (NOW) accounts, U.S. Treasury bills (promissory notes in denominations of $1,000 to $1 million), and repurchase agreements (arrangements that allow the state to buy back assets such as state bonds) from banks. Interest and investment income was expected to provide 1.1 percent of state revenue in the 2020–2021 biennium. Because of strong financial markets, in FY2020, investment income accounted for 1.7 percent of revenue to the state. The comptroller projected a 25 percent increase in investment earnings for the 2022-2023 biennium over earnings for the 2020-2021 biennium.

The University of Texas Investment Management Company (UTIMCO) invests the Permanent University Fund and other endowments for the University of Texas and Texas A&M University systems. Its investment authority extends to participating in venture capital partnerships that fund new businesses. Board members for UTIMCO include the chancellor and three regents from the University of Texas System, two individuals selected by the Board of Regents of the Texas A&M University System, and three outside investment professionals. This nonprofit corporation was the first such investment company in the nation affiliated with a public university.

The Public Debt

When expenditures exceed income, governments finance shortfalls through public borrowing. Such deficit financing is essential to meet short- and long-term crises and to pay for costly projects, such as prison construction. Most state constitutions, including the Texas Constitution, severely limit the authority of state governments to incur indebtedness.

Bonded Indebtedness For 75 years, Texans have sought, through constitutional provisions and public pressure, to force state government to operate on a pay-as-you-go basis. Despite those efforts, the state is allowed to borrow money by issuing **general obligation bonds** (borrowed amounts repaid from the General Revenue Fund) and **revenue bonds** (borrowed amounts repaid from a specific revenue source, such as college student loan bonds repaid by students who received the funds). Commercial paper (unsecured short-term business loans) and promissory notes also cover the state's cash flow shortages. Whereas general obligation bonds and commercial paper borrowings require voter approval, other forms of borrowing generally do not. Outstanding bonded debt, including bonds issued by the state's universities, was approximately $62.44 billion as of the end of fiscal year 2020, of which $55.44 billion was issued as revenue bonds, described as "self-supporting debt." Seven billion dollars was issued as "not self-supporting debt," including $6.5 billion in general obligation

general obligation bond
Amount borrowed by the state that is repaid from the General Revenue Fund.

revenue bond
Amount borrowed by the state that is repaid from a specific revenue source.

bonds and $500 million required to be repaid from the state's general revenue fund, even though classified as non-general obligation bonds.[33]

Bond Review Specific projects to be financed with bond money require legislative approval. Bond issues also must be approved by the Texas Bond Review Board. The four members of this board are the governor, lieutenant governor, speaker of the house, and comptroller of public accounts. This board approves all borrowings by the state or its public universities with a term in excess of five years or an amount in excess of $250,000.

Economic Stabilization Fund The state's Economic Stabilization Fund (popularly called the **Rainy Day Fund**) operates like a savings account. It is intended for use when the state faces an economic crisis and was originally created to prevent or eliminate temporary cash deficiencies in the General Revenue Fund. By legislative mandate, the balance cannot be reduced below $7.5 billion. The Rainy Day Fund is financed with one-half of any excess money remaining in the General Revenue Fund at the end of a biennium (an event that has only happened twice) and with one-half of 75 percent of oil and natural gas taxes that exceed 1987 collections (approximately $1.3 billion in that year). A constitutional amendment allocates the remaining one-half of excess oil and natural gas taxes to the State Highway Fund. If necessary, the legislature can direct the money intended for the State Highway Fund to the Rainy Day Fund.

Like a savings account, the Rainy Day Fund has provided temporary support for programs like public education, Medicaid, and the criminal justice system. Withdrawals require legislative approval by supermajorities. Three-fifths of members present must approve a withdrawal to cover deficits and two-thirds of members present must approve withdrawals for any other purpose. The largest transfer in the Rainy Day Fund's history ($6.2 billion) occurred in 2019. Most funds were used to cover costs of Hurricane Harvey damage. Only $531 million was used to fund the FY2022-2023 budget. Another $800 million was loaned to the Energy Reliability Council of Texas (ERCOT) to reduce losses to power wholesalers.

Weakness or strength of the Texas economy is revealed in collections by the Rainy Day Fund. Although a budget surplus transfer was made from the 2006–2007 budget, no transfers have been made since. When the 87th Legislature convened in January 2021, legislators had $10.7 billion available in the Economic Stabilization Fund. The comptroller predicted no budget surplus would be available from the 2020–2021 biennium. The Rainy Day Fund remained well below the maximum amount of $18.8 billion that could be held in the account. Deposits to the Rainy Day Fund are limited to an amount equal to 10 percent of revenue collections from the previous biennium. Should the maximum be reached, the state suspends transfers and deposits all earned interest in the General Revenue Fund. The 86th Legislature extended the comptroller's authority to invest more of the Rainy Day Fund in higher-yield investments to protect against economic declines beginning in FY2022. Arguing that Texas's previous investment strategy was like "burying the [state's] money in a hole on the Capitol lawn,"[34] Comptroller Hegar predicted his enhanced investment authority would yield substantial additional revenue to the state.

Rainy Day Fund
A fund used like a savings account for stabilizing state finance and helping the state meet economic emergencies when revenue is insufficient to cover state-supported programs.

✓ 11.2 Learning Check

1. What is the largest source of tax revenue for the state of Texas?

2. What is the stated purpose of the Rainy Day Fund?

Answers at the end of this chapter.

⬛ Budgeting and Fiscal Management

LO 11.3 Describe the procedure for developing and approving a state budget.

The state's fiscal management process begins with a statewide vision for Texas government and ends with an audit.[35] Other phases of this four-year process include development of agency strategic plans, legislative approval of an appropriations bill, and implementation of the budget. Each activity is important if the state is to derive maximum benefit from the billions of dollars it handles each year.

Budgeting Procedure

budget
A plan of financial operation indicating how much revenue a government expects to collect during a period (usually one or two fiscal years) and how much spending is authorized for agencies and programs.

fiscal year
A one-year budget period. For Texas's state government, each fiscal year begins on September 1 and ends on August 31 of the following year.

Legislative Budget Board (LBB)
A 10-member body co-chaired by the lieutenant governor and the Speaker of the House. This board and its staff prepare a biennial current services budget. In addition, they assist with the preparation of a general appropriation bill at the beginning of a regular legislative session. If requested, staff members prepare fiscal notes that assess the economic impact of a proposed bill or resolution.

A plan of financial operation is usually referred to as a **budget**. In modern state government, budgets serve a variety of functions, each important in its own right. A budget includes an estimate of anticipated revenue and outlines a plan for spending that shows a government's financial condition at the close of one budget period and the anticipated condition at the end of the next budget cycle. Based on estimated revenue, the budget also makes spending recommendations for the coming budget period. In Texas, the budget period covers two fiscal years. A **fiscal year** is a one-year budget period. Each fiscal year begins on September 1 and ends on August 31 of the following year. The fiscal year is identified by the initials FY (for "fiscal year") preceding the number for the ending year. For example, FY2021 began on September 1, 2020, and ended on August 31, 2021.

Texas is one of 19 states that have some form of a biennial (every two years) budget period. Many political observers argue that today's economy fluctuates too rapidly for this system to be efficient. The Lone Star State's voters, however, have consistently rejected proposed constitutional amendments requiring annual state appropriations.

Legislative Budget Board By statute, the **Legislative Budget Board (LBB)** is a 10-member joint body of the Texas House of Representatives and the Texas Senate. Its membership includes as joint chairs the lieutenant governor and the Speaker of the House of Representatives. Assisted by its director and staff, the LBB prepares a biennial (two fiscal years) current services–based budget. This type of budget projects the cost of meeting anticipated service needs of Texans over the next biennium.

Constitutional limits are in place to control how much the state can spend. The legislature has no discretion in how dedicated funds can be spent (although the funds are not required to be spent). The comptroller of public accounts furnishes the board with an estimate of the growth of the Texas economy covering the period from the current biennium to the next biennium. Legislative appropriations from undedicated tax revenue cannot exceed that rate of growth. Based on several projections, the LBB capped the growth of appropriations from undedicated tax revenue at 7.06 percent for the 2022–2023 biennium.

The board's staff also helps draft the general appropriations bill for introduction at each regular session of the legislature. If requested by a legislative committee chair, staff personnel prepare fiscal notes that estimate the potential economic impact of a bill or resolution. Employees of the LBB also assist agencies in developing performance evaluation measures and audits, and they conduct performance reviews and **strategic fiscal reviews** to determine how effectively and efficiently state agencies are functioning.

Governor's Office of Budget and Policy Headed by an executive budget officer who works under supervision of the governor, the Governor's Office of Budget and Policy (GOBP) is required by statute to prepare and present a biennial budget to the legislature. Traditionally, the governor's plan is policy based. It presents objectives to be attained and a plan for achieving them. As a result of this dual arrangement, two budgets, one legislative in origin and the other executive, should be prepared every two years. Governor Greg Abbott used a policy-based model in his proposed biennium budgets (for the biennia 2018–2023). These proposed budgets identified his priorities. For example, his requests for the 2022–2023 biennium included improvements to the foster care system, expanded access to high-speed Internet throughout the state, and increased limitations on taxes. Policy-based budgets do not incorporate specific line-item requests; rather they provide general requests for "full funding" or increased funding in excess of prior years' budgets.[36]

Budget Preparation Compilation of each budget begins with development of a policy statement for Texas by the governor in cooperation with the LBB. That vision for the 2022–2023 biennium was one that recognized "an unprecedented amount of [economic] uncertainty."[37] Every even-numbered year, each operating agency requesting appropriated funds must submit a five-year strategic operating plan to the GOBP and to the LBB. These plans must incorporate the state's mission and philosophy of government, along with quantifiable and measurable performance goals. Texas uses performance-based budgeting; thus, strategic plans provide a way for legislators to determine how well an agency is meeting its objectives. For example, in 2021, the Commission on the Arts submitted a strategic plan in which the agency set a goal of providing and supporting arts and cultural grants for arts education programs. One performance measure was to assure that 25 percent of agency grants were awarded to organizations to supplement arts instruction for public school students. This goal met the agency purpose of advancing the state culturally and economically by investing in a "creative Texas."[38]

Legislative Appropriation Request forms and instructions are prepared by the LBB. (See Figure 11.3 for a diagram of the budgeting process.) These materials are sent to each spending agency in late spring in every even-numbered year. For several months thereafter, representatives of the budgeting agencies work to complete their proposed departmental requests. An agency's appropriations request must be organized according to strategies that the agency intends to use in implementing its strategic plan over the next two years. Each strategy, in turn, must be listed in order of priority and tied to a single statewide functional goal.

strategic fiscal review
A review conducted by the Legislative Budget Board of every program administered by an agency in the sunset review process. The report includes a review of a program's purpose, cost, funding sources, and the impact of program elimination.

Figure 11.3 Texas Biennial Budget Cycle

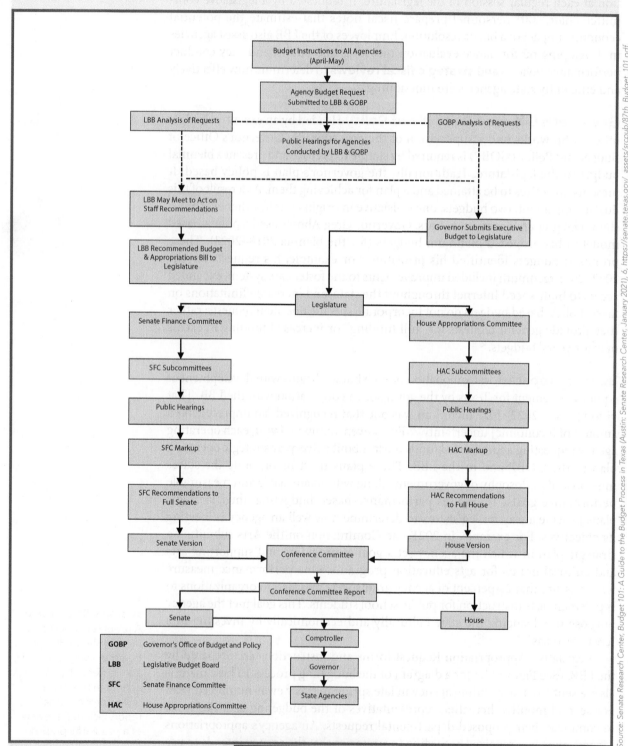

Source: Senate Research Center, Budget 101: A Guide to the Budget Process in Texas (Austin: Senate Research Center, January 2021), 6, https://senate.texas.gov/_assets/srcpub/87th_Budget_101.pdf.

Competency Connection
☼ CRITICAL THINKING ☼

How could Texas's budgeting process be made more efficient?

By early fall in even-numbered years, state agencies submit their departmental estimates to the LBB and GOBP. These budgeting agencies then carefully analyze all requests and hold hearings with representatives of spending departments to clarify details and glean any additional information needed. At the close of the hearings, budget agencies traditionally compile their estimates of expenditures into two separately proposed budgets, which are then delivered to the legislature.

Thus, in each regular session, legislators normally face two sets of recommendations for all state expenditures to be made during the succeeding biennium. Since the inception of the **dual budgeting system**, the legislature has shown a marked preference for the recommendations of its own budget-making agency, the LBB, over those of the GOBP and the governor. Therefore, as noted earlier, the governor's proposed budget frequently varies little, if at all, from the LBB's proposed budget and often focuses on policy, not line-item expenditures.

By custom, the legislative chambers rotate responsibility for introducing the state budget between the chair of the Senate Finance Committee and the chair of the House Appropriations Committee. At the beginning of each legislative session, the comptroller provides the legislature with a biennial revenue estimate. The legislature can only spend in excess of this amount upon the approval of four-fifths of each chamber. In subsequent months, the legislature debates issues surrounding the budget, and members of the Senate Finance Committee and the House Appropriations Committee conduct hearings with state agencies, including public universities and colleges, regarding their budget requests. During the hearings, agency officials are called upon to defend their budget requests and the previous performance of their agencies or departments.

The committees then make changes to the appropriations bill (a practice known as "markup") and submit the bill to each chamber for a vote. (For a discussion of how a bill becomes a law, see Chapter 8, "The Legislative Branch.") After both chambers approve the appropriations bill, the comptroller must certify that the state of Texas will collect sufficient revenue to cover the budgetary appropriations. Only upon certification is the governor authorized to sign the budget. The governor can veto any specific spending provision in the budget through the line-item veto as occurred when Governor Abbott vetoed spending on the legislature in 2021.

Historically, the state has relied on incremental budgeting, in which requestors only had to justify requests for budget increases. In May 2020, Senate Finance Chair Jane Nelson announced that she would rely on zero-based budgeting, by which she would require requesting agencies to justify all expenditures, whether new or ongoing.[39] This procedure was an extension of a law she had proposed, and the legislature had adopted, in the 86th Legislature to require strategic fiscal reviews of agencies. A strategic fiscal review is conducted by the LBB to report on every program administered by any agency in the sunset review process. (For a discussion of the sunset review process, see Chapter 9 "The Executive Branch.") The review includes, among other items, each program's purpose, cost, funding sources, and the impact of eliminating the program. For example, a review of the Texas Racing Commission noted that one program the agency administered was to inspect and provide emergency care to race animals. This program costs approximately $600,000 in dedicated funds each biennium. Without the program, the LBB stated that animals would be at risk of physical and drug abuse, trainers and others who worked with the animals would likewise be endangered, and the

dual budgeting system
The compilation of separate budgets by the legislative branch and the executive branch.

general public would lose confidence in the racing industry. The Sunset Review Commission asks the question: Is this agency necessary? The LBB provides input on whether an agency's programs are worth the cost.

Budget Expenditures

Analysts of a government's fiscal policy classify expenditures in two ways: functional and objective. Services being provided by government represent the state's functional budget. When the money spent is categorized by the object of expenditures, such as employees' salaries, the budget report is described as objective. Figure 11.4 illustrates Texas's proposed functional expenditures for fiscal years 2020 and 2021. For more than five decades, functional expenditures have centered on three principal functions: public education, health and human services, and highway construction and maintenance (included under business and economic development). Subsequent biennial budgets reflected the same priorities.

Budget Execution

In most state governments, the governor's office or an executive agency responsible to the governor supervises **budget execution** (the process by which a central authority in government oversees implementation of a spending plan approved

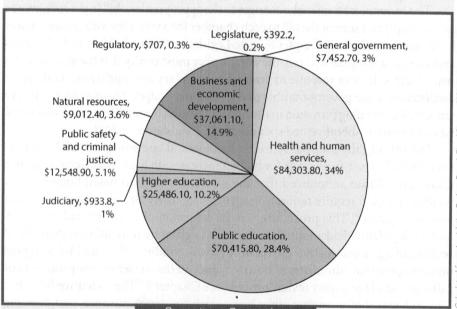

Figure 11.4 All Texas State Funds Appropriations ($248.3 billion) by Function for Fiscal Years 2020–2021 (in millions)

- Legislature, $392.2, 0.2%
- Regulatory, $707, 0.3%
- General government, $7,452.70, 3%
- Business and economic development, $37,061.10, 14.9%
- Natural resources, $9,012.40, 3.6%
- Public safety and criminal justice, $12,548.90, 5.1%
- Health and human services, $84,303.80, 34%
- Judiciary, $933.8, 1%
- Higher education, $25,486.10, 10.2%
- Public education, $70,415.80, 28.4%

Calculated from: Legislative Budget Board, Fiscal Size-up 2020-21 Biennium, May 2020, p. 2, https://www.lbb.state.tx.us/FSU.aspx.

Competency Connection
◉ **SOCIAL RESPONSIBILITY** ◉

As a result of the COVID-19 pandemic, the State of Texas was forced to reduce spending for FY2022–2023. From which functions do you believe the state should have reduced spending?

budget execution
The process whereby the governor and the Legislative Budget Board oversee (and, in some instances, modify) implementation of the spending plan authorized by the Texas legislature.

---

by the legislative body). The governor and the LBB have limited power to prevent an agency from spending part of its appropriations, to transfer money from one agency to another, or to change the purpose for which an appropriation was made. Proposed gubernatorial modifications must be made public, after which the LBB may ratify it, reject it, or recommend changes. If the board recommends changes in the governor's proposals, the chief executive may accept or reject the board's suggestions.

The governor can transfer funds in the event of a disaster. In 2021, after issuing a Disaster Proclamation for 34 counties along the state's southern border, he ordered the transfer of $250 million from the Texas Department of Criminal Justice to his office as a down payment for border wall construction.

Purchasing

Agencies of state government must make purchases through or under the supervision of the Statewide Procurement Division within the Office of the Comptroller of Public Accounts. Depending on the cost of an item, agency personnel may be required to obtain competitive bids. This division places greater emphasis on serving state agencies for which it purchases goods than on controlling what they purchase. It also provides agencies with administrative support services, such as mail distribution and management of vehicle fleets. In addition, the division negotiates contracts with airlines, rental car agencies, and hotels to obtain lower prices for personnel traveling on state business. These services are also available to participating local governments.

Facilities

A seven-member appointed board oversees the Texas Facilities Commission. This agency provides property management services for state facilities. In addition, agency personnel, in collaboration with the Longhorn Foundation, manage football parking and tailgating on state property in Austin. The agency begins taking online reservations in June of each year. Due to the COVID-19 pandemic, the agency suspended tailgating on state property during the 2020 football season.

Accounting

The comptroller of public accounts oversees management of the state's money. Texas law holds this elected official responsible for maintaining a double-entry system, in which a debit account and a credit account are maintained for each transaction. Major accounting tasks of the comptroller's office include processing warrants (checks) used to pay state obligations, acknowledging receipts from various state revenue sources, and recording information concerning receipts and expenditures in ledgers. Contrary to usual business practice, state accounts are set up on a cash basis rather than an accrual basis. In cash accounting, expenditures are entered when the money is actually paid rather than when the obligation is incurred. In times of fiscal crisis, the practice of creating obligations in one fiscal year and paying them in the next allows a budget to appear balanced. Unfortunately, it complicates the task of fiscal planning by failing to reflect an accurate picture of current finances at any given moment. The comptroller issues monthly and annual reports that include general statements of revenues and expenditures. These reports allocate spending based on the object of expenditures that are the goods, supplies, and services used to provide government programs. Salaries, wages, and employment benefits for state employees consistently lead all objective expenditures.

Auditing

State accounts are audited (examined) under direct supervision of the state auditor. This official is appointed by, and serves at the will of, the Legislative Audit Committee, a six-member committee composed of the lieutenant governor; the Speaker of the House of Representatives; one appointed member from the Senate; and the chairs of the Senate Finance Committee, the House Appropriations Committee, and the House Ways and Means Committee. The auditor may be removed by the committee at any time without a hearing.

The office of state auditor has remained vacant since 2016. Some have speculated that political animosity among members of the Legislative Audit Committee may have resulted in this stalemate.[40] Approximately 180 staff members have continued to provide reports and conduct random reviews of government agency financial records and transactions after expenditures. Auditing involves reviewing the records and accounts of disbursing officers and custodians of all state funds to assure compliance with the law. Another important duty of the State Auditor's Office is to examine the activities of each state agency to evaluate the quality of its services, determine whether duplication of effort exists, and recommend changes. Managing the state's compensation and job classification system and reporting on employment and compensation needs to the legislature are other responsibilities. The agency conducts audits in order of priority by reviewing activities most subject to potential or perceived abuse first. Its stated mission is to provide elected officials with information to improve accountability in state government.

✓ 11.3 Learning Check

1. What is a fiscal year?
2. Texas has a dual budgeting system. How does this process work?

Answers at the end of this chapter.

✪ Future Demands

LO 11.4 Evaluate the effectiveness of the state's financing of public services.

Elected officials have worked to keep taxing levels low. As a result, Texas has also kept its per capita spending levels among the lowest in the nation. Some observers believe that this limited funding is merely deferring the state's problems in the areas of education, social services, and infrastructure to the coming years. Problems that continue to compete for public money include increasing enrollment in our public schools, colleges, and universities; additional public assistance needs; and outdated roadway, water, electrical, and broadband systems.

Public Education

The state, together with local school districts, is responsible for providing a basic education for all Texas school-age children. Every week the local, state, and national governments spend $1.2 billion to operate public schools in the Lone Star State. Even so, state and local spending on public education remains below the national average ($9,606 per student in Texas versus $12,612 nationally for FY2018).[41] Public education accounted for 28 percent of the state's projected expenditures ($35.2 billion per year) for the 2020–2021 biennium. Because of substantial reforms to the school finance system by the 86th Legislature, state funding for school operations increased. Annual state funding reached approximately 50 percent of the actual cost of public education. All remaining costs for public education must be covered with local taxes and federal grants.

This hybrid arrangement may explain some of the difficulties in operating and financing Texas's schools. Is public education a national issue deserving of federal funding, attention, and standards, similar to the interstate highway system, in which the federal government pays for roads that connect all parts of the nation? Or should education be a state function, similar to the state's role in building and maintaining state highways so that all Texans are entitled to drive on the same quality of paved roads? Or should we treat public education as a local responsibility, more akin to city streets so that towns with more money have better-quality streets than their poorer neighbors? Although education appears to integrate all three levels of government—national, state, and local—into one system, confusion and conflict surround the fiscal responsibility and role of each in the state's educational system. When the Texas legislature created the Property Tax Relief Fund in 2006, state leaders predicted that by 2008 the state would provide at least 50 percent of public school funding. Erosion of the gross receipts tax, in particular, reduced receipts for the Property Tax Relief Fund. Public school finance reforms by the 86th Legislature increased state support for public schools, decreased local property taxes, and created the Tax Reduction and Excellence in Education Fund (TREE) financed primarily with sales and use tax revenue from online market providers, such as Amazon. These changes achieved a 50 percent funding level by the state.

Sources of Public School Funding Texas state government has struggled with financing public education for more than half a century.[42] Table 11.1 provides a history of relevant court decisions, state constitutional provisions, and legislative responses that have established funding sources and shaped the ways in which those sources are administered. In promoting public education, Texas state government has usually confined its activity to establishing minimum standards and providing basic levels of financial support. School districts and state government share the cost of three elements—salaries, transportation, and operating expenses. Local funding of school systems relies primarily on the market value of taxable real estate within each school district, because local schools raise their share primarily through property taxes. Average daily attendance of pupils in the district, types of students (for example, elementary, secondary, or disabled), and local

Table 11.1 History of Texas Public School Finance in the Courts

Case	Year	Question	Decision	Legislative Response
Rodriguez v. San Antonio (U.S. Supreme Court)	1971	Does Texas's school funding system violate the Equal Protection Clause?	No, because education is not a federally protected right.	None
Edgewood v. Kirby (Texas Supreme Court)	1989	Is Texas's school funding system "efficient" as required by the Texas Constitution?	No, a 9-to-1 difference in per-student funding is inefficient. An efficient system must produce "similar revenue for similar effort."	Decided to study the issue.
Edgewood v. Kirby (Texas Supreme Court)	1991	Is Texas's school funding system "efficient"?	No	Authorized county education districts.
Carrollton-Farmers Branch v. Edgewood (Texas Supreme Court)	1992	Do countywide education districts create a statewide property tax, a practice prohibited by the Texas Constitution?	Yes	Established a program to recapture wealth from property-rich districts to redistribute to property-poor districts (also known as the "Robin Hood" plan).
Edgewood v. Meno (Texas Supreme Court)	1995	Is a recapture program constitutional?	Yes, because it provides funding for a "general diffusion of knowledge."	None
West Orange-Cove v. Neeley (Texas Supreme Court)	2005	Does the need for most districts to tax at the maximum allowable tax rate create a statewide property tax?	Yes	Lowered the property tax by establishing the Property Tax Relief Fund at the state level.
Morath v. Texas Taxpayer and Student Fairness Coalition, et al. Multiple cases involving more than 600 school districts, parents, the Texas Association of Business, and the Texas Charter School Association (Texas Supreme Court)	2016	Is Texas's school funding system "efficient"?	Yes, the current school funding system meets "minimal constitutional requirements."	Legislature urged to revise the school funding system and "upend an ossified regime ill-suited for 21st century Texas," but not required to do so. The 86th Legislature made extensive modifications to public school finance, lowering property taxes and increasing state support.

Sources: Compiled from Albert H. Kauffman, "The Texas School Finance Litigation Saga: Great Progress, Then Near Death by a Thousand Cuts," *St. Mary's Law Journal* 40, no. 2 (2008): 511–579; Morgan Smith, "A Guide to the Texas School Finance Lawsuits," *Texas Tribune*, February 29, 2012, http://www.texastribune.org/texas-education/public-education/how-navigate-texas-school-finance-lawsuits/; and Morgan Smith, "Texas School Finance Trial Enters Phase Two," *Texas Tribune*, January 21, 2014, http://www.texastribune.org/tribpedia/school-finance/; and *Morath v. Texas Taxpayer and Student Fairness Coalition*, 490 S.W 3d 826 (2016).

Competency Connection
✿ **CRITICAL THINKING** ✿

What amount of financial support should the state provide for funding public schools?

economic conditions determine the state's share. The COVID-19 pandemic ravaged schools' average daily attendance, as schools turned to online instruction for which many students, their families, and the state's broadband infrastructure were woefully unprepared. In response, the state suspended on-campus average daily attendance as the basis for state funding from the 2020 spring semester through the 2020–2021 academic year.

In 1949, the Texas legislature passed the Gilmer-Aiken Law, intended to provide a minimum level of state support for every public school student in Texas. This law established the Minimum Foundation Program (now called the Foundation School Program). Local property taxes fund programs beyond the minimum level of services financed by the Foundation School Program. (For a discussion of school district taxing procedures, see Chapter 3, "Local Governments.")

Money to finance the Foundation School Program is allocated to each school system from the Foundation School Fund. This fund accounts for more than 70 percent of state funding for public schools. Other sources of state revenue are used to support public schools and include the following:

- Available School Fund (revenue received from a variety of state taxes and income from the Permanent School Fund, primarily funded by public land proceeds)
- School Taxing Ability Protection Fund (money appropriated by the legislature to offset revenue reduction incurred by rural school districts)
- Texas Lottery
- Property Tax Relief Fund (money appropriated to offset loss of revenue from local property taxes)
- Tax Reduction and Education Excellence Fund (sales and use taxes paid by online marketplace providers to subsidize local property taxes)
- General Revenue Fund

Funding Equalization As Table 11.1 indicates, a continuing controversy surrounding public school finance in Texas has been court-mandated funding equalization. The legislatively enacted wealth equalization plan, labeled the **"Robin Hood" plan** by its critics, requires a wealthier district to choose among a series of options to reduce its local revenue level in excess of the amount to which it is entitled. This process is called recapture. A school district's entitlement is determined by using a number of factors, such as the number of economically disadvantaged students enrolled in district schools, to calculate the cost of meeting the basic education needs of its students. These funds are transferred to the state for redistribution to property-poor school districts. Despite court challenges, the "Robin Hood" plan has been found to be constitutional. One-third of the state-administered Property Tax Relief Fund may be used to equalize funding among districts. Despite continuing disparities in per-student funding among school districts, both the 86th and 87th Legislatures restricted the amount of funding required of

"Robin Hood" plan
A plan for equalizing financial support for school districts by transferring tax money from rich districts to poor districts.

wealthier districts. As a result, these districts saved approximately $3.7 billion in the 2020–2021 and 2022-2023 biennia.[43]

At the heart of the dispute regarding how to achieve equalized funding is whether all students in the state are entitled to receive the same quality of education. Although court decisions have granted Texas students the right to equal educational opportunities, these determinations do not address the reality that not all students enter school equally prepared to succeed. Frequently, parents of economically disadvantaged students are unable to offer their children the same learning opportunities as those provided by more affluent parents. To make up for this difference in preparation, both the state and federal governments provide additional funding to help school districts equalize learning outcomes for low-income students. The 86th Legislature also addressed this issue through school finance reform (HB 3) with a number of specific requirements and funding preferences to meet the needs of economically disadvantaged students.

After decades of minimal funding, the 86th Legislature increased spending on public education by more than $11.6 billion for the 2020–2021 biennium. Teachers received raises; districts were rewarded for successful student outcomes; the legislature funded specific evidence-based teaching and learning strategies, such as dual language instruction for bilingual students; and property owners' tax bills were reduced. A framework was in place for continued state support for these many initiatives. The COVID-19 pandemic introduced new concerns, as the state faced declining revenues, districts dealt with extremely low daily attendance, and provisions in HB 3 had greatly restricted the ability of local school districts to increase taxes.[44] Although school officials were especially concerned that reducing spending for public education was the way the state would seek to deal with any revenue shortfall, the governor and state legislators actually increased funding. Without adequate financial support, school districts will continue to struggle in their attempts to provide students with an adequate education to compete in the 21st-century workplace.

Public Higher Education

Like public schools, the public higher education system endures the dual pressures of increasing enrollment of students with greater educational needs and declining state support. In 2015, the Texas Higher Education Coordinating Board (THECB) announced its 60x30TX initiative. The primary goal of 60x30TX is to assure that at least 60 percent of 25- to 34-year-old Texans have a postsecondary credential (either a certificate or degree) by 2030. As of 2018 (the last year for which data are available), only 43.5 percent of 25- to 34-year-old Texans met this standard. To increase both completion rates and the number of students enrolling in colleges and universities, public institutions of higher education will have to increase faculty, staff, and facilities. Additional provisions of 60x30TX seek to increase annual graduates, assure that all degree and certificate programs incorporate identifiable marketable skills, and lower student debt load. To achieve the cost-savings goals, colleges and universities will have to reduce costs. Despite ongoing THECB calls for increased state funding, the legislature has failed to respond. The 87th Legislature did not decrease funding. Even so, lower enrollment at some institutions, especially community colleges, reduced their state support.[45]

Furthermore, the success of 60X30TX depends on more low-income, underprepared students enrolling in institutions of higher education. These students are much less likely to complete a postsecondary degree or certificate within six years of high school graduation. Of all students who started eighth grade in 2008, only 23 percent had received a postsecondary credential by 2020 (six years after their high school graduation). For students identified as economically disadvantaged, success was even more elusive with only 14 percent having completed a postsecondary program by 2020.[46] Students graduating from Texas high schools frequently are not career-ready or college-ready. This lack of preparation occurred in two-thirds of the state's top-ranked high schools in 2018. Results for lower-ranked schools were even worse.[47] To lower the cost of developmental education for these students, Texas now requires colleges to integrate developmental course work into credit-bearing courses. The Texas Higher Education Coordinating Board (THECB) directs programs to strengthen remediation in writing, reading, and math for students who are underprepared for college. Through OnCourse, a program coordinated by the University of Texas at Austin, these efforts continued throughout the pandemic. In an effort to reduce the number of students who need developmental courses, public school districts receive financial incentives for increases in the number of students who are career, military, or college ready upon graduation. In addition, THECB staff collaborate with public schools to assure high school graduates are better prepared to succeed in college. Results of these efforts are not yet available because accountability ratings and evaluations for public school districts were waived for academic year 2019–2020 due to the COVID pandemic.

State financial aid for college and university students is insufficient to meet demand. Because the number of eligible students who receive assistance is far lower than the number who qualify for aid, higher education institutions have reduced the amount of some awards.[48] At the same time, colleges and universities are increasing tuition to cover their operating costs. Low levels of state funding have forced students to bear more of the costs of their education by paying higher tuition and taking out more and larger loans.

At the core of this dilemma is a philosophical conflict about the nature of higher education and the role of government. Is higher education a public good that benefits society in which government should invest? Or, is higher education a commodity that benefits the individual who should, therefore, bear the cost of that personal benefit? The Point/Counterpoint feature addresses arguments for and against reducing state funding for higher education.

⬛ Point/Counterpoint

Should states reduce funding for higher education?

Over the past decades, state funding for public colleges and universities has declined. Some argue that reduced funding is a natural and desirable outcome of smaller government and lower taxes. Others maintain that this approach is a short-term solution that will result in harmful long-term consequences. Consider the arguments for and against reduced government spending for higher education institutions.

For	Against
1. States have more urgent and immediate needs than higher education, including items such as health care and K-12 public education.	1. Higher education is an economically sound investment that benefits society as a whole. Increased funding, especially in community colleges, results in higher college completion rates and a more affluent and physically healthier population.
2. College graduates will earn more money than those who are nongraduates. These students should therefore pay for this privilege.	2. Reduced state funding for higher education institutions reduces the overall quality of a student's education.
3. Because of tuition increases, colleges have more revenue today than they did previously.	3. Making up budget shortfalls through tuition increases limits access to higher education for lower income students, many of whom are Black and Latino. Limited access has a negative effect on equality of opportunity for all.
4. If college administrators were more fiscally responsible and reduced expenditures, they would have adequate funding.	4. Any decrease in funding has a negative effect on student outcomes.
5. State funding decreases have been small and had an insignificant effect on college budgets.	

Sources: Karen Fischer and Jack Stripling, "An Era of Neglect," *Chronicle of Higher Education,* March 2, 2014, https://www.chronicle.com/article/an-era-of-neglect/; Scott Carlson, "When College Was a Public Good," *Chronicle of Higher Education,* November 27, 2016, https://www.chronicle.com/article/when-college-was-a-public-good/; Andrew Gillen, "The Myth of State Disinvestment in Higher Education," *Texas Public Policy Foundation Center for Innovation in Education,* September 2019, https://files.texaspolicy.com/uploads/2019/09/11141549/Gillen-The-Myth-of-State-Disinvestment-in-Higher-Education.pdf; Rajashri Chakrabarti, Nicole Gorton, and Michael F. Lovenheim, "State Investment in Higher Education: Effects on Human Capital Formation, Student Debt, and Long-term Financial Outcomes of Students (Working Paper 27885)," *National Bureau of Economic Research,* October 2020, http://www.nber.org/papers/w27885.

Competency Connection
✿ **CRITICAL THINKING** ✿

Is a college education a privilege that benefits each person who receives a degree for which that individual should bear all or most of the cost? Or is it a public good that benefits society as a whole for which government should bear all or most of the cost?

Public colleges and universities receive most of their state income through formula funding, a method that uses specific factors, such as number of enrolled students, to calculate how much money each institution receives. In recent years, the governor, the legislature, and the Texas Higher Education Coordinating Board have argued for a change in the factors used to determine the state's portion of funding. Each favors an outcomes-based funding formula that links the amount of state funding for a college or university to the number of students who successfully complete courses and the number of students who graduate (and, if a community college, transfer to a university). Former Governor Rick Perry expressed his support for outcomes-based funding in 2011: "Texans deserve college graduation for their hard-earned tax dollars, not just college enrollment."[49] Proponents maintain that the emphasis on successful outcomes improves higher education. Opponents argue that such a funding structure reduces the amount of financial support institutions receive and therefore has a negative effect on students who need the most assistance.[50]

A portion of state funding for community colleges is now outcomes based. The state awards success points for desired outcomes, such as graduation, transfer, and successful completion of 15 and 30 credit hours. A formula that varies with each legislative session is then used to calculate the amount of money a college will receive based on the number of success points awarded. Although THECB has requested supplements (or bonuses) for universities equal to their number of graduates, the legislature has remained unwilling to support such a measure.

Community College Funding Public community colleges receive their funding from the following sources: student tuition and fees, the state of Texas, local taxpayers, the federal government, and private (individual, foundation, and corporate) donations. The General Revenue Fund is used to provide state financing of public community or junior colleges. Funding calculations were restructured by the 83rd Legislature (2013) to include three components: core operations funding, contact hour funding, and success points funding (the outcomes-based measure). Each community college district in the state receives a minimum amount to cover core operations, $1.4 million per district for the 2020–2021 biennium. The legislature appropriates an additional amount ($1.53 billion in 2020–2021) based on a "contact hour of instruction" rate for vocational-technical and academic courses. This rate is determined by calculating the hours of contact between an instructor and students and, when combined with core operations funding, represents almost 90 percent of state financial support. Payment for achieving student success points provides the balance of state funding. Funding for community colleges remains significantly below 1998 formula funding levels. Costs continue to increase, while state financial support declines. This gap in funding is financed by students and local taxpayers. With the support of community college interest groups, the 87th Legislature established the 12-member Texas Commission on Community College Finance to study ways to improve funding for community colleges.

Over the years, the legislature has reduced funding to community colleges by a greater percentage than university funding. One report by the *Texas Public Higher Education Almanac* suggests that 51 percent of undergraduates attend community colleges. The majority of these students (almost 60 percent) are Black or Latino. For some observers, this reduction in funding constitutes inequality between universities and community colleges[51] and, arguably because of student population demographics, unequal treatment based on race.

University Funding Texas's state universities and the Texas State Technical College System obtain basic financing through tuition and legislated biennial appropriations from the General Revenue Fund. They also obtain money from fees other than tuition, such as student service and computer use fees (which are deposited in the General Revenue Fund), auxiliary services income (for example, rent for campus housing and food service fees), grants, gifts, and special building funds. The University of Texas and the Texas A&M University systems share revenue from the Permanent University Fund (PUF) investments and surface income from 2.1 million acres of public lands. Royalty income from oil and gas production from these public lands cannot be distributed. This revenue must be invested. An annual distribution is made through the Available University Fund (AUF). The University of Texas System receives two-thirds of this distribution and Texas A&M University and some of its system schools receive one-third. Total distributions from the AUF were approximately $1.6 billion in FY2020, including a one-time distribution to the University of Texas System to endow a tuition-free scholarship fund at the University of Texas at Austin for students whose families earn $65,000 or less in annual income.[52]

Controversy has surrounded limited state funding for universities in South Texas and border regions, most especially in the Rio Grande Valley. In 1987, unequal allocation of state funding for universities was challenged in the case of *Richards v. LULAC*, 868 SW2d 306 (1993). Although the plaintiffs failed to establish racial bias in the funding of higher education to the satisfaction of the Texas Supreme Court, in 1989 the legislature created the South Texas/Border Initiative with a focus on funding parity for higher education in these areas of the state.[53] The 83rd Legislature (2013) authorized the creation of a regional comprehensive university in the Rio Grande Valley that included a new medical school located in Harlingen. Combining the campuses of UT-Pan American (in Edinburg), UT-Brownsville (in Brownsville), and the Regional Academic Health Center (in Harlingen), the University of Texas Rio Grande Valley (UTRGV) was given direct access to PUF money. The university enrolled its first class in September 2015. Because UTRGV represented a combination of existing universities, the school also graduated its first class in December 2015. The medical school opened in 2016 and graduated its first class in 2020 in a virtual commencement ceremony.

Tuition Deregulation In late 2002, the University of Texas System led an effort to eliminate legislative caps on tuition and fees. According to university officials, funding limitations threatened the University of Texas at Austin's ability to remain a premier research institution. Despite fears that escalating tuition and fees would limit access to higher education for Texas's lower income students, the proposal became law in 2003.

📋 Students in Action

The Texas Higher Education Coordinating Board (THECB) includes nine Board members who are appointed by the governor and serve six-year staggered terms. Additionally, the Board includes a non-voting student representative who is appointed by the governor and serves for a one-year term. Student representatives are expected to participate in meetings and share a student perspective.

To be appointed to the Board, a student must be recommended by the college's or university's student government and nominated by the president or chancellor. The governor appoints the student representative no later than June 1st each year. Student representatives must maintain a 2.5 GPA and be enrolled at a public college or university throughout their entire term of office.

In June 2020, Governor Greg Abbott appointed Levi McClenny as the student representative to the THECB for 2020–2021. McClenny was a doctoral student in the Department of Electrical and Computer

(Continued)

Engineering at Texas A&M University. Previously, he had served as a Student Regent on the Texas A&M University System Board of Regents. An officer in the United States Army Reserve, he was also a pilot and conducted research with the Army Research Lab.

Source: "Texas Higher Education Coordinating Board: Non-voting Student Representative," Texas Higher Education Coordinating Board, http://reportcenter.highered.texas.gov/agency-publication/miscellaneous/non-voting-student-representative-on-board-background-qualifications-deadlines-submissions/.

Competency Connection
⊛ SOCIAL RESPONSIBILITY ⊛

What role should students have in determining policies of the Texas Higher Education Coordinating Board?

Public universities, as well as public community colleges, quickly moved to raise tuition. Both the dollar increase in tuition and the rate of increase have been dramatic. Since 2003, universities have raised tuition rates and fees approximately 185 percent above their 2002 levels (from an annual average of $3,801 in academic year 2002–2003 to $10,810 in academic year 2020–2021). At the same time, state support of universities and community colleges declined. A comparison of tuition and fees for colleges and universities in multiple states, including Texas, is highlighted in the "How Do We Compare" feature.

Elected officials have expressed concern about the rapid increase in tuition and fees. Public universities are now required to establish programs that lock in tuition rates for four years for entering freshmen who choose to participate. Another effort, the Texas Affordable Baccalaureate (TAB) Program, begun in 2014, is designed to lower the cost of and shorten the time to a baccalaureate degree. Texas A&M-Commerce and South Texas College were the first schools to offer applied sciences baccalaureate degrees through this program. By 2020, eight institutions across the state were participating in TAB and offered degrees in 13 different subject areas. TAB schools accept competency-based credits for past work experience and offer their programs fully online in an effort to lower costs. Four community colleges (Brazosport, Midland, South Texas, and Tyler) now offer applied sciences and applied technology baccalaureate degrees at much lower tuition costs than their university counterparts. Despite these efforts, many legislators believe that tuition rates will remain affordable only if the Texas legislature reclaims control of setting them.[54]

Texas Tomorrow Funds The Texas Guaranteed Tuition Plan and the Texas Tuition Promise Fund comprise the Texas Tomorrow Funds. The Tuition Plan provides a way for parents to save for their children's education and to lock in the cost of tuition and fees at the state's public colleges and universities. Tuition increases have also affected these programs. The Texas Guaranteed Tuition Plan (Plan) is backed by the full faith and credit of the state of Texas. Because of rapid tuition increases, the state closed the Plan to new participants in 2003. As of the end of FY2020, the Plan had an unfunded liability of approximately $483 million, an amount the state will be required to finance from general revenue. More than $271 million was allocated from the General Revenue Fund to pay these obligations for the 2022–2023 biennium. Beginning in 2022, the state will

TEXAS Grants Program
"Toward Excellence, Access, and Success" is a college financial assistance program that provides funding for qualifying students.

pay all outstanding tuition payments because the Plan will have fully depleted its assets. In 2008, the fund reopened as the Texas Tuition Promise Fund, although at much higher rates. Most important, the Texas Tuition Promise Fund is not guaranteed by the full faith and credit of the state of Texas, so participants bear the risk of increased tuition costs, not the state. College living costs can be covered by investment in Tomorrow's College Investment Plan.

State Grant and Loan Programs Rather than give money to colleges and universities, legislators across the country have preferred to give students direct funding and allow them to select the institution at which the funds will be spent. The Texas Tuition Equalization Grants program, created in 1971, subsidizes tuition expenses for eligible students who demonstrate financial need and attend private, nonprofit colleges and universities in Texas. These students must maintain a 2.5 GPA to continue receiving aid. A second type of grant is the **TEXAS Grants Program** (Toward Excellence, Access, and Success), the state's largest financial aid program. Fewer than 60 percent of qualified students receive grant funding to pay all tuition and fees at any public university in the state. They must be Texas residents, enroll in college within 16 months of high school graduation, show financial need, and have no convictions for a crime involving a controlled substance. Participating students must maintain a 2.5 GPA and complete at least 24 semester hours each academic year. The Texas Educational Opportunity Grant Program (TEOG) provides financial aid to financially needy community college students who maintain a 2.5 cumulative GPA and complete 75 percent of attempted hours. Students are only eligible for four years after initial enrollment, for the first 75 hours of attempted credit hours, or until receiving an associate degree, whichever first occurs.

🎞 How Do We Compare...

In Tuition and Fees?

Average Tuition and Fees for Academic Year 2020–2021

Most Populous U.S. States	Public University	Public Community College	U.S. States Bordering Texas	Public University	Public Community College
California	$9,940	$1,430	Arkansas	$9,070	$3,810
Florida	$6,370	$3,240	Louisiana	$9,920	$4,190
New York	$8,500	$5,700	New Mexico	$8,120	$1,940
Texas	**$10,810**	**$2,940**	Oklahoma	$8,970	$4,580

Note: Tuition rates are for in-state students at public universities and community colleges.

Source: The College Board, "Tuition and Fees by Sector and State over Time," *Trends in College Pricing* (2020), https://trends.collegeboard.org/college-pricing/figures-tables/tuition-fees-sector-state-over-time.

Competency Connection
⭐ PERSONAL RESPONSIBILITY ⭐

Who should pay the costs of your college education: you or taxpayers?

Other programs are available to reward students who obtain their degrees quickly or to assist those who are aging out of the foster care system. Students who attempt no more than three credit hours beyond the hours required for their degree and graduate within four years of initial enrollment in college are eligible for a $1,000 rebate upon graduation from a public university. Youth who have aged out of the foster care system may be eligible for tuition and fee waivers from public universities and colleges. Current information about financial aid programs is available on the THECB's website. Utilizing social media, the THECB maintains Twitter, YouTube, and Facebook accounts and an interactive web tool, entitled College for All Texans, to help users learn about various aspects of higher education at Texas's public universities and colleges, including costs.

Public Assistance

Enrolling more students in high-quality public schools and institutions of higher education are ways in which Texas's political leaders hope to combat poverty. Income disparity between the wealthiest 20 percent of Texans and the poorest 20 percent continues to widen. Even after implementation of the federal Patient Protection and Affordable Care Act (Obamacare), a higher percentage and number of Texans continue to lack health insurance than residents of any other state. The COVID-19 pandemic exacerbated the problem. More than 650,000 Texas adults under the age of 65 lost their jobs and their insurance coverage in the first months of the pandemic. As a result, almost five million working adults in Texas (29 percent of the population) were without insurance by May 2020.[55] The number of children without coverage also ranks highest in the nation, in both percentage and sheer numbers. Poverty levels remain above the national average. Notable differences in levels of poverty also exist among racial and ethnic groups, and especially among children: Black children (27 percent) and Latino children (29 percent), compared to Asian children (10 percent) and White children (9 percent).[56]

Increasing healthcare costs for the poor present significant challenges to state government. The percentage of the total state budget dedicated to health and human services is second only to spending on all levels of education ($96.0 billion for education versus $84.3 billion for health and human services in the 2020–2021 biennium). The cost of Medicaid and the **Children's Health Insurance Program (CHIP)** (an insurance program with minimal premiums for children from low-income families) frequently exceeds budget allocations, even though many eligible individuals do not receive benefits from these programs.

Coverage for children remains an issue for lawmakers. In 2019, the state had the largest number of uninsured children in the nation: almost 1,000,000. The problem of uninsured children worsened dramatically in the period between 2016 and 2019, with Texas accounting for more than one-third of all children (250,000) who became uninsured during that time.[57] Some observers suggest that up to one-half of uninsured children qualify for Medicaid or CHIP and yet do not receive any health insurance benefits.

Limiting access to Medicaid lowers the state's obligation to pay for benefits, but at what cost? The federal government funds 60 cents of every dollar paid for Medicaid services. In addition, the federal portion of CHIP expenditures is

Children's Health Insurance Program (CHIP)
A program that provides medical insurance for minimal premiums to children from low-income families.

approximately 84 cents of every dollar paid for medical services. The 83rd Legislature increased state funding for Medicaid to accommodate an additional 450,000 recipients by FY2015, because many children previously on CHIP became eligible for Medicaid under the Affordable Care Act. Although the state refused to extend Medicaid benefits to adults who were not primary caregivers for a minor, it was not allowed to limit extending coverage to more children. According to some observers, state officials' refusal to expand Medicaid coverage to adults likely cost the state almost $100 billion in federal funding over the period from 2014 to 2021. Under the expanded program, the federal government is responsible for 90 percent of costs. Elected officials argued that the federal government provided no guarantee that such high levels of support would continue. Thus, any expansion could devastate the state's budget if these extraordinary levels of federal support were reduced. As of 2021, Texas remained one of 12 states that refused to expand Medicaid to all those eligible for coverage under federal guidelines.

The Lone Star State received substantial federal funding through waivers that allowed the state to continue receiving federal funds without complying with full Medicaid expansion. Under the waiver Texas was able to provide reimbursement for uncompensated care to hospitals and health care providers. Most uncompensated care is for medical treatment of those who are uninsured. Originally intended as a short-term solution to assist states until they expanded Medicaid, Texas officials manipulated the program to receive funding from 2011 through September 2021. In the final days of the Trump administration, the state received a 10-year extension of these waivers until September 2030. In April 2021, the Biden administration rescinded the 10-year extension. As noted in the opening of this chapter, estimated cost of the rescission was $11 billion annually. Legislators faced the challenge of increasing state support to pay these costs, having providers bear the burden of uncompensated care likely bankrupting many rural hospitals, or expanding Medicaid. As further incentive for expansion, the American Rescue Plan Act of 2021 included provisions to pay a 5 percent bonus on federal Medicaid reimbursements to any non-expansion state that opted into the full Medicaid program.[58] None of these incentives was sufficient to induce the 87th Legislature to expand coverage. Instead, the state's attorney general sued the federal government to reinstate the waiver.

Much of the cost and care burden for uninsured residents, both children and adults, has shifted to local governments, hospitals, and the insured. Counties and hospitals must subsidize unreimbursed costs for treating the uninsured by charging higher rates to the insured, which translates into higher insurance premiums, as well as higher county property taxes. Analysts project a continuing increase in indigent healthcare costs in the years to come. Ability of local entities to meet social service needs of Texas's low-income residents is one of the key challenges of the 21st century.

Infrastructure Needs

In addition to demands for education, health, and human services, Texans look to state government to meet other needs. The state of Texas has a responsibility to provide an infrastructure for its residents, including highway, water, electrical, and broadband systems. Limited resources and growing demands are evident in the provision of these services as well.

Transportation Consistent with Texas's pay-as-you-go budget system is its pay-as-you-ride system of financing construction and maintenance of roads and highways. Texas roads have been financed through the State Highway Fund that includes a combination of motor fuel taxes, motor vehicle registration fees, and the Federal Highway Trust Fund (to which certain federal highway user taxes are allocated). In response to concerns about severe underfunding of the state's transportation system,[59] the legislature proposed, and Texas voters adopted, constitutional amendments to provide alternative revenue sources for transportation needs. Proposition 1 and Proposition 7 (as identified in Table 11.2) significantly increased funding for construction and maintenance of public roadways. Even so, the Texas Department of Transportation's *Texas Transportation Plan 2050* reported that additional alternative funding sources would be required to meet expenses for a growing population and aging infrastructure in the coming decades. Of special concern is the reliance on motor fuels and oil and gas revenues for funding in a time when vehicles are becoming more energy efficient and less dependent on fossil fuels.[60] Increasing costs also require borrowing concessions, as allowed by Texas voters through constitutional amendment. Authorized in 2001, the Texas Mobility Fund permits the state to issue bonds and use the proceeds for road construction. See Table 11.2 for a listing of funding sources for transportation and estimated revenue in FY2020–2021.

Historically, as increases in roadway construction costs have exceeded funding, much of this expense has been transferred to users in the form of tolls. The reality of financing new highway construction with tolls was perhaps best

Table 11.2 Estimated Transportation Funding (in billions) for FY2020–2021

Fund	Source	Usage	Amount (FY 2020–2021)
State Highway Fund	State Motor Vehicle Fuels Tax Vehicle Registration Fees Other taxes and fees	Roadways only	$9.3
	Federal Highway Fund	Roadways only	$11.31
	Proposition 1 Funds (oil and gas severance taxes)	Roadways only (no toll roads)	$3.89
	Proposition 7 Funds (sales and use taxes)	Roadways only (no toll roads)	$5.0
General Revenue	Undedicated funds	Roadways and any other form of transportation	$.02
Texas Mobility Fund	Certificate of Title Fees; Driver Record Info Fees; Driver's License Fees; Vehicle Inspection Fees Other special subsidies and investment interest	Repay bonds issued for road construction	$.95
Tolls and other concessions	Toll road fees and other local fees	Must be remitted to local government for use in local region for roadways and any other form of transportation	$.31
		Total	$30.78

Source: Compiled from "Texas Transportation Funding for Fiscal Years 2020–2021," *Texas Department of Transportation*, https://ftp.txdot.gov/pub/txdot-info/fin/funding-brochure2020.pdf.

expressed by former Texas Transportation Commission chair Ric Williamson, who described the policy as, "It's the no road, the toll road, or the slow road."[61] Texans' willingness to provide alternative funding for road construction is coupled with a resistance to toll roads. Neither Proposition 1 funds nor Proposition 7 funds may be used for toll road construction or maintenance.

Water An ongoing Texas drought began in 2007, abated briefly in 2008, and finally ended in 2015. It highlighted the state's water needs. In 2012, the Texas Water Development Board issued its state water plan. Six years in development, the plan had dire predictions for Texans if efforts were not made to increase the state's water supply in the coming years.[62] A constitutional amendment, ratified by voters in 2013, led to the creation of two special funds to finance, through low-interest loans, certain water projects under the State Water Plan to ensure the availability of adequate water resources in the future. In 2014, the comptroller of public accounts focused attention on the continuing need for additional state funding and more reliance on technology, noting that "conservation's not enough."[63]

A new state water plan was developed in 2021. Looking ahead to 2070, the Water Development Board had alarming observations and predictions. In the period between 2012 and 2021, both surface water reserves (rivers and streams) and groundwater resources (aquifers) declined more rapidly than originally predicted. Projected cost to provide adequate water supplies for anticipated population growth was $80 billion. If the state took no action, in the event of a significant drought in 2070, the report estimated annual losses of $153 billion in income.[64]

The state's droughts are as dramatic as their endings. In 2017, Hurricane Harvey dumped as much as 60-plus inches of rain on large portions of Southeast Texas causing $125 billion in property damage and killing at least 68 people. Climatologists predict continued cycles of extreme droughts and floods. Texas's surging population will only worsen conditions as dwindling water supplies will be used to meet increased demand.[65] The Texas Demographic Center predicts the state's population will increase from 29.7 million residents in 2020 to 47.3 million by 2050.[66] Concern continues over how the state will accommodate these new Texans, including how the state will provide adequate water supplies.[67]

Broadband Among issues highlighted by the COVID-19 pandemic were inadequacies of the state's broadband system. Although the governor and comptroller worked to build awareness,[68] not until schools and businesses were forced to rely on the Internet for delivering education and business services did the severity of the issue become apparent. In response, the 87th Legislature established the 17-member Broadband Development Council to evaluate and coordinate the state's broadband infrastructure needs. Although the Broadband Development Office was created in the Office of the Comptroller to serve as a distribution site for information and funding, no state money was appropriated for that purpose. Instead, legislators looked to the federal government for assistance.

Utilities When Winter Storm Uri plunged millions of Texans into darkness with no heat or water, the state's lack of preparedness for delivering electricity and other utilities during extreme weather conditions was spotlighted. A similar incident in

11.4 Learning Check

1. True or False: Tuition deregulation resulted in lower tuition at the state's public colleges and universities.

2. On which public service does Texas spend the most money?
   a. Education
   b. Welfare
   c. Highways
   d. Water

Answers at the end of this chapter.

2011[69] had been largely ignored. The 87th Legislature attempted a more effective response, including adopting requirements for natural gas facilities to prepare for extreme weather conditions. If predictions of increased health and weather emergencies prove accurate, Texans will need to take decisive action to limit the negative consequences of these events.

Conclusion

Although Texas experienced a remarkable economic turnaround after the global economic crisis that erupted in 2008, predictions were less optimistic for a full and robust economic recovery after the COVID-19 pandemic subsided. The 86th Legislature focused on lowering property taxes and finding alternative revenue sources to finance the state's public school system. In part because of substantial funding of COVID relief efforts by the federal government, the 87th Legislature was able to sustain these efforts. A well-educated and well-trained population remains a critical goal to assure a successful future.

Chapter Summary

LO 11.1 Assess the fairness of Texas's budgeting and taxing policies. Texas remains a low-cost, low-services state. The Lone Star State has one of the most regressive tax systems in the United States because of its heavy reliance on the sales tax and its having no state income tax. Texans require that the state operate with a balanced budget, limit borrowing, and limit spending on social services.

LO 11.2 Identify the sources of Texas's state revenue. The state relies on taxes, fees, gambling revenue, sales of assets, oil and gas royalties, investments, and the federal government to fund state services. Rather than raise taxes, Texas's elected officials often increase fees, fines, and other assessments. Voters have restricted the amount of money the state can borrow. Additionally, the state has a Rainy Day Fund that operates like a savings account and is intended to provide one-time funding for emergencies.

LO 11.3 Describe the procedure for developing and approving a state budget. Each biennium, the Legislative Budget Board and the Governor's Office of Budget and Policy are required to prepare proposed budgets. Before a budget can be approved, the comptroller of public accounts must provide an estimate of available revenue for the upcoming biennium and certify that spending will not exceed revenue. Tax collection, investment of the state's surplus funds, and overseeing management of the state's money are responsibilities of the comptroller of public accounts. The governor and the Legislative Budget Board oversee implementation of the budget and have limited authority to redirect agency spending. The State Auditor's Office is responsible for examining all state accounts to ensure honesty and efficiency in agency spending of state funds.

LO 11.4 Evaluate the effectiveness of the state's financing of public services. State revenue pays for services to Texas's residents. Most state money pays for public education (including higher education) and public assistance, especially Medicaid. Higher numbers of low-income students enrolled in the state's public schools will likely increase the cost of public education. In 2019, the 86th Legislature reformed public school finance by increasing the amount of money the state would provide to school districts and forcing school districts to lower property taxes. The burden for the cost of higher education is shifting to students, consistent with a philosophy that treats higher education as a commodity for which the individual is responsible. Providing access to medical care remains an important state issue, despite the Affordable Care Act. Access to quality healthcare was exacerbated by the COVID-19 pandemic. The state also has infrastructure needs. To repair the state's decaying roads and bridges, construct adequate roadways to meet the needs of a growing population, overcome severe water shortages, develop an efficient broadband system, and assure utilities are available even during weather emergencies will be costly to the state's taxpayers in the years ahead.

Key Terms

balanced budget, p. 425
budget, p. 440
budget execution, p. 444
Children's Health Insurance Program
(CHIP), p. 457
dedicated fund, p. 426
dual budgeting system, p. 443
fee, p. 425
fiscal policy, p. 423
fiscal year, p. 440

franchise tax, p. 425
general obligation bond, p. 438
General Revenue Fund, p. 426
general sales tax, p. 428
grants-in-aid, p. 436
Legislative Budget Board (LBB),
    p. 440
payroll tax, p. 431
progressive tax, p. 424
Rainy Day Fund, p. 439

regressive tax, p. 424
revenue bond, p. 438
"Robin Hood" plan, p. 449
selective sales tax, p. 430
service sector, p. 425
severance tax, p. 425
sin tax, p. 430
strategic fiscal review, p. 441
tax, p. 423
TEXAS Grants Program, p. 456

Learning Check Answers

11.1
1. Texas requires a balanced budget, favors low taxes, and spends at low to moderate levels.

2. Texas has a regressive tax system, which means that poor people pay a higher percentage of their incomes in taxes than do wealthier residents.

11.2
1. The general sales tax is the state's largest source of tax revenue.

2. The Rainy Day Fund is to be used when the state faces an economic crisis.

11.3
1. A fiscal year is a budget year. The fiscal year for the State of Texas begins on September 1 and ends on August 31 of the following calendar year.

2. A state with a dual budgeting system requires both the executive branch and the legislative branch to prepare and submit proposed budgets to the legislature. In Texas, both the governor and the Legislative Budget Board submit proposed budgets.

11.4
1. False. Since tuition deregulation, student tuition has risen 185 percent over 2002 levels at public colleges and universities.

2. The state spends more money on education than any other service.

12 Public Policy and Administration

Learning Objectives

12.1 Describe how public policy is made in Texas.

12.2 Analyze major challenges faced by the Texas education system.

12.3 Describe the major health and human services programs in Texas, and discuss how efforts to address the needs of its citizens have been approached.

12.4 Compare the roles of government in generating economic development while maintaining a safe, clean, and prosperous environment for the state's residents.

12.5 Describe the various aspects and complexities in Texas's immigration policy.

Image 12.1 Texans, particularly students, have a long tradition of protesting government actions and demanding changes in policy. After the election of President Trump, women's marches were organized throughout the country. Here's a picture of the "Woman's March" in Austin.

Michael Silver Editorial/Alamy Stock Photo

— Competency Connection —
⚙ **CRITICAL THINKING** ⚙

Are marches an effective way for students to be heard? What are other ways for students to impact public policy?

O ne good way to see what is important in public policy is to follow the money. For many years in Texas, the state government has spent most of each year's budget on four areas. For example, in the 2022–2023 biennium (two-year budget cycle), the legislature appropriated roughly $248 billion as follows:

- Education: 35 percent
- Health and human services: 38 percent
- Business and economic development: 15 percent
- Public safety and criminal justice: 5 percent
- Everything else: 7 percent[1]

In one other important policy area, the money trail leads to the private sector. Although regulation costs the state government little (0.3 percent of the total), it has profound cost effects on individuals, companies, and local governments. Regulation commonly shifts costs and benefits from one group to another. For example, contaminated air hurts the quality of life and increases medical costs for children with respiratory problems, such as asthma, as well as for the elderly, but regulations requiring special equipment to reduce emissions from smokestacks cost businesses money. Deciding who should pay the bill is controversial and is largely answered in the battles over government regulations.

State government policies profoundly affect the lives of all of us. Services, subsidies, taxes, and regulations affect students from kindergarten through graduate school, poor people, the middle class, rich people, and all businesses. State policies affect our safety and health as well as the profitability of businesses. The impact of a given policy varies by group. (Who gets a tax cut? Who doesn't?) Thus, public policy is a source of great conflict because groups compete to gain benefits and reduce costs to themselves. As we will see, some groups are better positioned than others to win this battle.

This chapter examines two aspects of public policy in Texas: (1) circumstances of the situation and behavior of people and agencies implementing policies, and (2) the nature and impact of these policies. Covered are the major policy areas of education, health and human services, business and economic development, the environment, and immigration. The other big-ticket item in Texas state government—public safety and criminal justice—is covered in Chapter 13, "The Criminal Justice System," and details on state spending are provided in Chapter 11, "Finance and Fiscal Policy." State regulatory agencies are discussed in Chapter 9, "The Executive Branch."

Follow *Practicing Texas Politics* on Twitter **@PracTexPol**

public policy
What government does to or for its citizens to meet a public need or goal as determined by a legislative body or other authorized officials.

✚ Making Public Policy in Texas

LO 12.1 Describe how public policy is made in Texas.

Surprisingly, scholars who study public policy have not agreed on a single definition of the term "public policy." One simple and useful definition for **public policy** is what government does to or for its citizens to meet a public need or goal as determined by a legislative body or other authorized officials.[2] Policy is both action, such as state or local governments raising or lowering speed limits, and inaction, such as Texas state government not accepting federal funds for expansion of Medicaid under the Affordable Care Act (Obamacare).

Models of Policymaking

Scholars who study public policy have made use of several models (conceptual maps) of how the process works. Models simplify and clarify our thinking and focus attention on important aspects of how systems work. No one model is sufficient by itself, but together, different models can give us a more complete picture. The following models are useful in explaining how public policy works:

- Institutional model, which focuses attention on the structure and processes of government in order to understand why some proposed policies are adopted and others are not.

- Group model, which focuses attention on the groups involved and their interests. It sees group interaction as the central element of politics and policy as the outcome of group struggles.

- Elite model, which holds that public policy reflects the preferences of social and economic elites. The public is seen as apathetic, with opinions that tend to be shaped by the elite.

- Rational model, which suggests that public policy should be determined by weighing costs and benefits before adopting policies. It is frequently invoked as the "way things should be" but seldom are the way policy development really works.

- Incremental model, which sees "new" public policy as only a slightly modified continuation of past policy. Policymakers do not review all policy regularly. They lack time, resources, and incentive to do so. Rather, they take existing policies as a starting point, perhaps modify them slightly, and then focus on new policies. (Clearly, the incremental model is a rejection of the rational model.)

All of these models are helpful in understanding policymaking in Texas. The organization of Texas government and its rules and practices, as we will see, give elites and some groups more access to policymakers than others. Chapter 7, "The Politics of Interest Groups," describes the numerous and powerful economic interest groups in the state. Throughout this textbook, the strong role of economic elites should be apparent.

For studying all state governments, the rational model is useful in seeing how policy could be improved; nevertheless, this model casts little light on actual processes. In Texas, legislators work part-time, because the legislature meets only part of every other year to consider literally thousands of proposals. Lawmakers have neither the time nor resources to gather all the information they would need to choose the best policy in each area. Similarly, the agencies that implement the laws passed by the legislature lack resources, and often lack incentives, to compile all the information they would need to weigh all costs and benefits.

With respect to the incremental model, some important breaks in Texas public policy have occurred; but once established, policies tend to change only incrementally. For example, testing was first mandated in Texas schools in 1980 and became a major policy tool in 1990. Through several changes in form, testing has remained a major tool of educational assessment ever since. Similarly, privatization of social services was first mandated by the legislature in 2003 and, through several ups and downs, has continued. (Privatization involves governments contracting with private companies to provide certain government services, in this case handling citizens' applications for social services such as Medicaid.) As we saw in Chapter 9, "The Executive Branch," the sunset process requires a substantial review of most state agencies every 12 years. Through the sunset process, the legislature has generally enacted only incremental changes for most agencies and has abolished only a few smaller, weaker ones.

Not included among previously listed models is the participatory democratic model in which the public shows high levels of interest, knowledge, and participation in civic life. (These levels tend to be low in Texas.) In this model, citizens would understand their needs; and through elections, they would demand that their representatives enact policies reflecting the voters' wishes. In practice, clear messages from the electoral process that produce policy are quite rare. Most policy decisions made by the legislative and executive branches are unknown or poorly understood by the general public. Citizens who are part of the economic elite, belong to an interest group, or feel very strongly about an issue are more likely to be heard. For example, polling in 2018 conducted by the University of Texas at Austin in concert with the *Texas Tribune* indicated that 59 percent of registered voters approved continuation of the Deferred Action for Childhood Arrivals (DACA) policy, while 30 percent wanted to see it end. However, when looking at the issue of immigration, Texans seem split on whether to immediately deport undocumented immigrants or not—51 percent against and 44 percent in favor of immediate deportation.[3]

Individual citizens are not completely ignored in policymaking, but the process is complex; and citizen impact tends to be filtered through groups and the political process. Elections generally don't send clear, specific policy preferences to our elected representatives. Nevertheless, interest groups that represent us, along with the desire of elected representatives to avoid being defeated, push policymakers to make policies that a majority of the voting public support.

Studies comparing opinion and policy outcomes in the 50 states indicate that public policy is influenced by public opinion. There are similar findings at the national level. However, studies also indicate that public influence happens primarily for issues that are relevant and important to the public, and, therefore, issues to which the public pays attention.[4] Most Texas policy issues don't fit this description. One national study found that the strongest influence on public policy was the opinion of the affluent, followed in descending order by business interest groups, mass-based interest groups, and average citizens.[5] This is a pattern that may well fit Texas.

In addition to the models, the environment of Texas influences public policy. Included are such factors as wealth and income level, political ideology, and political culture. Wealth and income affect the resources that different groups can use to influence the political process. It is also the case that wealthier states tend to spend more on government and poorer states less. Wealthier, urban, industrialized states such as California and New York tend to spend more money per capita on public services such as education. Poorer states such as Louisiana and Mississippi spend less. Texas has a large economy and is highly urban, which push it toward greater government spending. However, Texas is slightly below the national average for median household income; and Texans have a tradition of conservatism and an individualistic/traditionalistic political culture that values small government. The tension between the two forces has caused Texas to spend more per capita on government over time but to keep government much smaller than is the case in other large, urban states.

Another way of understanding how public policy is made is to look at the steps commonly involved. Generally, one or more interest groups begins the process by bringing problems to the attention of government officials and then lobbying for solutions that benefit members of the group. Second, political parties and chief executives (such as the Texas governor) often select and combine proposals of interest groups into a manageable number and include them as part of their program or agenda. In Texas, the weakness of the governor and the large number of agencies mean that agency heads play this role for most of the issues affecting their area of responsibility. (The agriculture commissioner, for example, tries to aggregate demands made by various agricultural interest groups and then proposes his/her agenda to the legislature.)

Third, the legislature then accepts some proposals through passage of laws, creation or modification of agencies, and appropriation of money to carry out policies. Fourth, the executive branch implements policies. At the national level, the president provides instructions for the agencies that actually carry out policies. In Texas, more than 200 agencies have substantial independence from the governor. Therefore, state agencies have more latitude and independence than federal agencies in determining legislative intent and in applying the law to unforeseen circumstances. Finally, when disputes arise about the interpretation of the law itself or its implementation by the executive branch, the Texas attorney general may be asked for an opinion, court suits may be filed, or the legislature may be lobbied for changes (or all of the above).

These steps are commonly followed in the order just discussed, but in many cases, steps are skipped or reversed. For example, in an emergency such as a major hurricane, the governor may take actions and issue directives (some with the force of law, others as suggestions) with little or no input from interest groups or the legislature. Making public policy is a dynamic and varied process.

Public policy is the product of a series of formal and, probably more important, informal interactions among a variety of groups and individuals. These participants include wealthy, powerful, and well-placed individuals; interest groups; the governor, agency heads, and other political leaders; legislative leaders and committees; judges and the Texas attorney general; and officials of the federal government. Which actors are more important at which stages varies. Interest groups try to influence every step of the process. They initiate proposals; lobby the parties, other interest groups, the governor and relevant agencies, and the legislature; and they file lawsuits or amicus curiae (friend of the court) briefs. (Amicus curiae briefs are filed by someone interested in the outcome of a case but who is not a party to the lawsuit.)

The Institutional Context

How the Texas executive branch is organized has a major effect on public policy. A key reason is that fragmentation of authority strongly affects who has access to policy decisions, as well as how visible the decision process is to the public. The large number of agencies means they are individually covered less by the media and, therefore, are less visible to the public. Even the power of Texas's governor is quite limited in comparison with the powers of governors of many other states. Special interest groups and the economic elite, on the other hand, have strong incentives (profits) to develop cozy relationships with agency personnel. Furthermore, most Texas agencies do not have to defend their decisions before a higher authority (such as the governor). Thus, it is not surprising that comparative studies of the states find a strong role for interest groups and the elite in Texas policymaking.

Bureaucracy and Public Policy We often think of public administrators as simply implementing laws passed by the legislature, but the truth is that they must make many decisions about situations not clearly foreseen in the law. Not surprisingly, their own views, their bosses' preferences, their agency's culture, and the lobbying they receive make a difference in how they apply laws passed by the legislature. Agencies also want to protect or expand their turf. Lobbyists understand the role of the bureaucracy in making public policy, so they work as hard to influence agency decisions as they work to influence legislation.

Public agencies also must build good relations with state leaders (such as the governor), key legislators, and executive and legislative staff members. These people determine how much money and authority an agency receives. Dealing with the legislature often involves close cooperation between state agencies and lobbyists for groups that the agencies serve or regulate. For example, the Texas Good Roads/Transportation Association (mostly trucking companies and road contractors) and the Texas Department of Transportation have long worked closely, and relatively successfully, to lobby the legislature for more highway construction money.

In Texas, three factors are particularly important in determining agencies' success in achieving their policy goals: the vigor and vision of their leadership, their resources, and the extent to which elites influence implementation (called **elite access**).

Many Texas agencies define their jobs narrowly and make decisions on limited, technical grounds without considering the broader consequences of their actions. Other leaders of agencies, however, take a proactive approach. The Texas Comptroller's Office, for example, became a major player in the Texas government, a more aggressive collector of state taxes, a problem solver for other agencies,

elite access
The ability of the business elite to deal directly with high-ranking government administrators in order to avoid full compliance with regulations.

and under Carole Keeton Rylander Strayhorn (1999-2007), a focus of controversy. In 2006, Strayhorn issued a report on undocumented immigration in Texas. She declared that deporting undocumented immigrants would be too costly to the state at nearly $18 billion.[6] A Rice University study in 2020 traced the study of the Comptroller using the same methodology used in 2006 to look at updated numbers. The study showed if undocumented immigrants were deported the state would have lost roughly $420.9 million in revenue for fiscal year 2018. According to the study, ". . . for every dollar spent on public services for undocumented immigrants, they provide $1.21 in fiscal revenue for the state of Texas."[7] Strayhorn's report in 2006 countered the tough immigration stance of her party, but according to the recent study done by Rice University, it seems she was correct.

The second factor important in determining agencies' success is their resources. Historically, Texas government agencies have had minimal funds to implement policy. Consider the example of nursing homes, which are big business today and are primarily for-profit enterprises. Almost two-thirds of Texas nursing home residents depend on Medicaid to pay for their care. However, Medicaid rates, set by the state, have not increased as fast as costs. According to the *Skilled Nursing News,* in 2019 a bill that would have boosted Medicaid rates for Texas nursing homes died before a vote was taken by legislators. "With a $945 million shortfall for all nursing homes in Texas, the failure to pass the bills means that SNFs will have to find new ways to cope—and quickly", this according to Kevin Warren, president and CEO of the Texas Health Care Association.[8] As of 2019, Texas was ranked the worst among the 50 states and the District of Columbia in nursing home care quality. Low rates depress nursing home profitability. Less scrupulous companies maintain profits by cutting staff and services.[9]

The third relevant factor is elite access. Nursing home company executives' access, for instance, to top-level agency administrators demonstrates this process. Nursing home residents are generally weak and unable to leave if service is bad or threatens their well-being. Therefore, residents depend heavily on government inspectors to ensure that they are treated well. Unfortunately, the number of nursing home inspectors in Texas has been like a roller coaster—sometimes up, sometimes down. When the number of inspectors relative to the number of residents decreases, the number of inspections decreases, and abuse tends to increase. Even when there are enough inspectors, nursing home company executives' connections to top-level agency administrators often ensure that infractions result in a slap on the wrist and a promise to do better.

A growing problem in 2020 further adding to the concerns of nursing homes in Texas is COVID-19. Prior to COVID-19, facilities were given the most severe citations for infection-control deficiencies, which means that the nursing home was putting their residents in "immediate jeopardy," but they received no federal financial penalties. This light regulation has put nursing homes in even greater risk of contracting COVID-19.[10] As of September 27, 2020, Texas was ranked 2nd in the nation (behind California) in the total number of COVID-19 cases among nursing home residents, and 4th in the total number of resident deaths from COVID-19.[11] As of May 2021 Texas has reported nearly 81,000 COVID-19 cases among nursing home residents, and nearly 9,000 residents have died from COVID-19. The state has had 1,222 nursing facilities that have reported outbreaks as of May 2021.[12] Governor Abbott and the Health and Human Services Commission announced that they will allocate $3.6 million to nursing home facilities for technology to help keep residents in touch with family, another $9 million to help monitor, prevent, and stop the spread of COVID-19, and $3.5 million for resources to promote safe visitations. Over the years, the Health and Human Services Commission, the governor, and the state attorney general have been criticized for their lack of fervor in pursuing nursing home violations and assistance.

As these criticisms indicate, weak leadership, lack of resources, as well as elite access make state policy less effective and abuse more common in Texas nursing homes. Four other factors also contribute to lower quality care in Texas:

- Shortage of nurses, in part because of too few nursing programs
- High proportion of lower income patients (who are less able to make effective demands)
- Large nursing facilities (where patients are more anonymous and thus easier to neglect)
- Prevalence of for-profit facilities (which tend to reduce staff and services to lower expenses)

At least since the 1990s (when reliable data became available), Texas has had more severe and repeated violations of federal patient care standards than most other states. A study in 2019 by Families for Better Care, a nursing home advocacy group based in Austin, ranked Texas the worst nursing home state, failing on five of eight statistical measures. Families for Better Care found that 1 in 5 Texas nursing homes have been cited for severe deficiencies—which is reported as the highest rate for the state of Texas.[13] Severe deficiencies include harm to residents through neglect, physical and verbal abuse, injury, and death. For-profit nursing homes tend to do more serious and repeated harm to residents than do government and nonprofit homes.[14] Clearly, government administrators greatly affect policy, and their decisions have an impact on people's lives.

✪ Education

LO 12.2 Analyze major challenges faced by the Texas education system.

Texas's commitment to education began with its 1836 constitution, which required government-owned land to be set aside for establishing public schools and "a University of the first class." Later, framers of the 1876 constitution mandated an "efficient system of public free schools." This chapter examines attempts of Texas public schools and universities to meet the needs of a changing student body and to improve the quality of education in a rapidly changing world. Chapter 11, "Finance and Fiscal Policy," discusses how and how much we pay to meet those challenges.

Public Schools

In the 21st century, public school students have increasingly come from families that are ethnic minorities or economically disadvantaged. According to Texas Education Agency data, in the 2019–2020 academic year, 53 percent of Texas students were Latino, 27 percent White, 13 percent Black, 4 percent Asian, and 3 percent other (multiracial, Native American, and Pacific Islander). In addition, 60 percent of Texas students were economically disadvantaged (defined as those eligible for free or reduced-price lunches), and 19 percent had limited English language proficiency.

Historically, Texas has not served minority and less affluent students as well as it has served White and middle-class students. If this pattern continues, studies project that Texans' average income will decline, while the costs of welfare, prisons, and lost tax revenues will increase.[15] Table 12.1 provides data on how Texas's educational efforts and outcomes compare to those of other states.

One indication that the state can do better comes from the *U.S. News and World Report*'s 2020 ranking of the nation's best high schools (based on criteria

Table 12.1 Effort and Outcomes in Texas Education (Rank Among the 50 States)

Texas Public Schools	
State and local expenditure per pupil	36th
Average teacher salary	39th
High school graduation rate	1st
Comparison of average scores in math on NAEP* for 8th graders	38 states higher than Texas, 9 similar, 2 lower
Comparison of average scores in reading on NAEP* for 8th graders	35 states higher than Texas, 11 similar, 3 lower
Texas Public Higher Education	
Expenditure per full-time student	8th
Average university faculty salary	22nd
Average community college faculty salary	22nd
Average tuition and fees at public universities	23rd**
Average tuition and fees at community colleges	4th**
University graduation rate	31st
Percent of population with a bachelor's degree or higher	32nd

*National Assessment of Educational Progress, called the Nation's Report Card.

**23rd and 4th cheapest.

Source: Alex Samuels, "Texas Ranks 36th Nationally in Per Student Education Spending. Here's How Much It Spends," *The Texas Tribune*, May 15, 2018; "Per Pupil by State 2020," *World Population Review*, https://worldpopulationreview.com/state-rankings/per-pupil-spending-by-state. "2020 Texas Public Higher Education Almanac," *Texas Higher Education Coordinating Board*, https://reportcenter.highered.texas.gov/agency-publication/almanac/2020-texas-public-higher-education-almanac/.

— Competency Connection —
☼ **CRITICAL THINKING** ☼

Education is often said to be important to individuals, the state, and the nation. What do the numbers suggest about Texans' commitment to excellence in education?

such as college readiness, math and reading scores, and graduation rates). About 17,000 high schools across the United States achieved a Best High School Ranking. Of 2,075 Texas high schools, 1,485 made the list. Eleven Texas high schools were ranked among the top 100 in the nation, including one of the nation's highest-ranked schools, Dallas's School for the Talented and Gifted, which was ranked 6th in the nation and #1 in Texas. In 2020, there were two schools making the top 100 located in South Texas—in Castle Hills and Laredo. However, it's important to note that five of the national top 100 Texas schools were in North Texas and Texas' top three high schools were in Dallas. Of the 20 highest-achieving high schools in Texas, 18 had a non-White majority, and 11 had a majority of economically disadvantaged students.[16]

Today, more than 1,580 independent school districts and about 171 charter operators shoulder primary responsibility for delivery of educational services to roughly 5.5 million students. (Chapter 3, "Local Governments," discusses the organization and politics of local school districts.) Although local school districts have somewhat more independence than in the past, they are part of a relatively centralized system. State authorities substantially affect local decisions, from what is taught to how it is financed. As was discussed in Chapter 9, "The Executive Branch," Texas public schools are heavily regulated by the Texas Education Agency (TEA), headed by the state commissioner of education and, to a lesser extent, the State Board of Education (SBOE). Less regulated than the independent school districts and sometimes more controversial are charter schools.

Alternatives to Traditional Public Schools For many years, there has been controversy over where Texas schoolchildren should go to school. Today there are alternatives to traditional public schools: private schools, homeschools, and charter schools. Other options include online learning programs and the High School Equivalency Program.

Over the years, some critics have called for vouchers as an option to public schools, labeling the issue as "school choice." Vouchers would use government funds to pay tuition for students attending private schools. In 2017, Governor Abbott and Lieutenant Governor Dan Patrick attended a rally on the steps of the Texas Capitol urging lawmakers to vote to give parents state money for private school attendance by their children. However, in the 2019 legislative session, support for school vouchers waned after Speaker Dennis Bonnen stated that the House would not pass legislation approving vouchers. Because vouchers have not been passed in Texas there have been organizations, such as the National School Choice Week, a nonpartisan organization, that helps provide information for "school choices" for families. Governor Abbott officially proclaimed January 26–February 1, 2020 as the Texas School Choice Week. During that time nearly 5,000 events and activities were held across Texas that equally looked at traditional public, charter, magnet, online, private, and home education options for families. Due to COVID-19, over 2800 state schools and organizations independently planned virtual events to celebrate School Choice Week 2021.

Supporters of vouchers argue that parents should have the choice to take their children out of low-performing public schools and place them in better-performing private schools. In addition, competition should encourage public schools to perform better. Opponents argue that vouchers would take talented students, particularly middle-class children, out of the public schools. Loss of these students would likely lower their parents' political support to fund and improve public schools. They argue that the poor, who are the focal point of voucher arguments, would be unlikely to move their children in significant numbers.

Others have called for homeschooling, in which parents are responsible for their children's education. In 1994, the Texas Supreme Court ruled that homeschooling was a legal alternative to public schools. In Texas, the state has three requirements in order for homeschooling to be legal: the instruction must be real (not a sham), visual (such as a book or video screen), and cover at least five subjects (reading, spelling, grammar, mathematics, and good citizenship). There is no hard data on homeschooling in Texas. According to the Texas Homeschool Coalition (THSC), in 2018–2019 it was estimated that 350,000 students were homeschooled in Texas supported by 317 local homeschool groups.[17] THSC reported homeschooling tripled during spring 2020 and fall 2020. Further, the number of homeschool students may have increased because homeschool students and parents are not legally required to register with any agency or department.

Supporters of homeschooling argue that parents will take more responsibility for their own children's education and teach them the family's values. Opponents argue that wide variation exists in educational outcomes. Many homeschooled students are well educated and go on to be successful in college and work; others get little education and are unable to compete effectively with their peers.

Charter schools are another option for Texas children. In 1995, the legislature authorized charters for schools that would be less limited by TEA rules. Charter schools are open-enrollment, draw students from across district lines, use a variety of teaching strategies, and are exempt from many rules, such as state teacher certification requirements. State law requires fiscal and academic accountability for these schools, together with monitoring and accreditation by TEA. With greater flexibility, legislators hoped charter schools could deal more effectively with at-risk students. Compared with students at traditional schools, charter school students are more economically disadvantaged, more are Black, slightly more are Latino, and fewer are White.

Charter schools are public schools responsible to the state but not to the local school district. Charters are granted to nonprofit corporations that, in turn, create a board to govern the school. Organizational structures vary from school to school. Charter schools commonly have multiple campuses. In 2020-2021, according to the TEA, there were 931 charter schools and campuses in Texas serving 336,745 students (or 6.3 percent of all public school students).

In 2013, the Texas legislature passed a major revision of charter school regulations, including raising the cap on the number of charters granted from 215 in 2013 to 305 in 2019. This legislation also toughened standards and moved responsibility for initial charter approval from the SBOE to the commissioner of education. There has been some volatility in charter schools in the state. In 2016, TEA announced closure of seven charter schools for failing to meet higher accountability standards; and 11 charter schools closed voluntarily. As of October 2020, the total number of charters that had been granted was 338, of which 157 schools had been closed (56 of those by TEA), leaving 181 active[18]

Two major policy controversies have arisen over charter schools. Whether the state has adequately financed these schools has been the subject of lobbying efforts and court decisions. Effectiveness of their programs in improving student performance has also been disputed.

Charter schools receive most of their funding from the state based on attendance, with the rest coming from federal and private sources. Generally, open-enrollment charter schools may not charge tuition for students eligible through their admissions process, but there are a few exceptions.[19] Charter schools are entitled to per-pupil facilities aid from the state education fund for capital construction and they may receive funding through issue bonds (borrow) for new construction. Charter schools argue that under state funding formulas they have less revenue per pupil (by $1,000) than do traditional schools.[20] The calculations are complex, and opponents argue that the difference is actually small. After failing to convince the legislature to provide additional funding, the Texas Charter Schools Association filed suit over the issues of facilities funding and the state cap on the number of charters. In May 2016, the Texas Supreme Court ruled on this and other suits involving over half of the state's school districts. In its 100-page opinion, the court described Texas's school finance system as Byzantine but satisfying minimum constitutional requirements.[21] This opinion urged the legislature to fix the system but did not order it to do so. Thus, charter schools will have to convince the legislature that they need and deserve more money.

Charter school officials believe they have an ally in education commissioner Michael Morath. He appointed three charter school experts to high-level positions in the TEA within months of taking office in 2016 and maintained cordial relations with the Texas Charter School Association.

Effectiveness of charter schools in meeting needs of at-risk students is sharply debated. Some Texas charter schools have "compiled terrific records of propelling minority and low-income kids into college."[22] Others have given misinformation as they claim a 100 percent college acceptance rate. Not known by the public is the fact that some charter schools require students to be accepted to a four-year university in order to graduate. In the 2021 *U.S. News and World Report* listing of the nation's best high schools, 5 of the 20 best high schools in Texas were charter schools located in Westlake, Brownsville, McAllen and San Antonio. Some other charter schools have been marked by corruption and academic failure.

A six-year study (2007–2013) by Stanford University researchers found that charter school results varied by state. In 2017, however, another Stanford report found that students who attend Texas charter schools show more growth in reading compared to those attending Texas public schools. There was no significant difference found in math. Charter school students from low socioeconomic backgrounds and English language learners gained more than their counterparts in traditional public schools.[23] Other studies suggest a continuing variability in the quality of charter schools. These schools are still a work in progress. On average they are comparable to traditional schools in effectiveness but vary widely in quality.

Two alternatives to public schools are online schools and the High School Equivalency Programs (HSEPs). Starting in 2009, the Texas Virtual School Network (TxVSN) began providing students and schools with online courses taught by state-certified and credentialed teachers. Third through twelfth grade students may be eligible through their schools.

On March 19, 2020 an executive order was issued by the governor to close all Texas schools due to COVID-19. Soon thereafter, in April 2020, an executive order was issued closing schools to in-person learning for the remainder of the 2019–2020 school year. In July 2020, the governor, lieutenant governor, and Speaker of the House Bonnen, along with the Senate and House Education Committee Chairs released a statement on school openings for fall 2020–2021 school year. Schools would be granted a transitional period where they could offer solely remote instructional learning, if needed and approved by the school board. Then four weeks later they could extend the transition period if approved by the school board. If the school district felt it needed more time than the eight weeks they were given, due to COVID-19 related issues, then the TEA would review each request on a case-by-case basis.[24]

According to the *Texas Tribune*, the number of students testing positive for coronavirus has substantially increased since the start of classes, as more districts started reopening. The article estimated a cumulative total of roughly 53,000 Texas students along with nearly 7,000 staff members have tested positive as of May 11, 2021 (this does not include private schools). Dr. Escott also found that Travis County children and teens ages 10–19 are testing positive for the virus at a rate three times higher than the general public.[25]

Testing One of the sharpest debates in Texas education is over the role of state-mandated standardized tests (sometimes called accountability testing). The state's top policymakers agree that the educational system needs objective *assessment* of success or failure and *accountability* for that success or failure. Educators and political leaders are sharply divided, however, about how to assess student progress and whether student test scores should affect such matters as student graduation, along with teacher and administrator pay. Nevertheless, testing as a major assessment and accountability tool is now federal and state policy. Texas first mandated a standardized test in 1980 and began to rely heavily on testing in 1990. Five tests have been used over the years, each more rigorous than its predecessors.

An essential component of the state testing program is the **Texas Essential Knowledge and Skills (TEKS)**, a core curriculum adopted in 1998. It sets out for every subject matter and grade level the knowledge students are expected to gain and use. This curriculum is required by the legislature and is approved by the State Board of Education.

The TEKS is similar to the Common Core, a curriculum used by 44 other states. Because Texas had invested time and money in developing TEKS and some experts found it marginally better in some areas than the Common Core, state authorities were inclined to keep their own system. When the federal government required states to switch to the Common Core to be eligible for a pool of

Texas Essential Knowledge and Skills (TEKS)
A core curriculum (a set of courses and knowledge) setting out what students should learn.

funds to encourage innovation, the issue became primarily ideological and about state versus federal authority. The 2013 legislature prohibited use of the Common Core by both state education agencies and local school districts. Because Texas is such a large textbook market, publishers adapted textbooks to reflect the TEKS. Some districts, however, use instructional materials in keeping with the Common Core.

The current testing program is the **State of Texas Assessment of Academic Readiness (STAAR)**. Mandated by the legislature in 2007 and 2009, STAAR went into effect in the spring of 2012. It included a number of key mandates:

- End-of-course examinations in the four high school core subject areas (math, science, English, and social studies).
- A requirement to pass both end-of-course tests and courses in order to graduate.
- For grades 3 through 8, new tests to assess reading and math for each level, as well as writing, science, and social studies for certain grade levels.
- The new tests and curriculum to be more closely tied to college readiness and preparation for the workplace.
- The new tests would become more rigorous and standards would be gradually raised through 2016.

In the first round of STAAR tests, statewide passing rates for freshmen varied from 55 percent for writing to 87 percent for biology. However, if the 2016 standards had been applied, a majority of students would have failed in each subject. Not surprisingly, the results were met with controversy.

Increasing the number of tests, how much they count, and their level of difficulty caused a strong backlash. In 2013, the legislature decreased the number of end-of-course tests from 15 to five and cut testing for high-performing students in grades 3 through 8. In 2015, the legislature allowed students to graduate if they passed three of five state end-of-course exams and if a school committee approved. This was set to expire in 2017 but was extended to 2019. Overall, 92 percent of the Class of 2015 passed all five exams. Another 6 percent failed one or two tests, but most were able to graduate. Similarly, most grade school students failing an exam were promoted by a campus committee. In 2016, administration of the STAAR test was plagued with problems, and a group of parents filed suit to have its results for that year blocked. In 2018, a Texas Appeals Court found that the parents did have the right to sue. However, in 2020, Education Commissioner, Morath, filed a plea with the Texas Supreme Court. The Respondents, the parents in the case, decided to stop pursuing their claim, so the Supreme Court dismissed the appeal, holding that the case was moot.

One of the most controversial aspects of the testing programs is that test results are used to evaluate teachers, administrators, and schools. This practice, continued under STAAR, is intended to increase "accountability"—that is, to hold teachers and administrators responsible for increasing student learning. Many educators object to having their pay—and perhaps their jobs—depend on student performance as measured by a test, because student success is highly affected by

State of Texas Assessment of Academic Readiness (STAAR)
A state program of end-of-course and other examinations begun in 2012.

students' backgrounds and home environments. The dilemma is that although research shows quality teaching makes a major contribution to student learning, it is not clear whether tests adequately measure each teacher's contribution.

In January 2012, then-Texas education commissioner Robert Scott, who led much of the development of use of tests as a policy tool, complained that testing had become a "perversion." Over the previous decade, he argued, too much reliance had been placed on tests. Scott wanted test results to be "just one piece of the bottom line, and everything else that happens in a school year [to be] factored into that equation."[26]

Since the 1980s, when standardized tests were first used, there have been cries of protest from parents, educators, school districts, and students themselves. Social conservatives argue that the program tramples on local control of schools, whereas Black and Latino critics charge that the tests are discriminatory. Educational critics complain that "teaching to the test" raises scores on the test but causes neglect of other subjects and skills. Questions were also raised when the federal No Child Left Behind program (now the Elementary and Secondary Education Act) produced substantially different evaluations of some schools than the Texas system (because the two assessment systems use different criteria). Supporters of testing argue that the policy holds schools responsible for increasing student learning. As proof, they point to improved test scores of most groups of students since the program began.

Because test results are so important to both students and their schools, there has been controversy over how high standards should be. Some parents and advocates for disadvantaged students argue that minimum passing scores are too high. STAAR's higher standards have created pushback. In August 2018, the Texas Education Agency replaced the pass/fail system for schools and now uses the A–F grading system to bolster accountability and transparency. However, in this new system, 40 percent of a school's rating will be based on STAAR test results. While school boards and others have argued against this new system, Lieutenant Governor Dan Patrick says the system is "here to stay."[27]

Some critics believe that national tests, such as the National Assessment of Educational Progress (NAEP), are better measures because they are not "taught to" and do provide a basis of comparison with changes in other states. In broad terms, Texas student performance (as measured on state and national tests) improved from at least 1980 to around 2011. In varying degrees, gaps among White, Black, and Latino students diminished. However, scores on the NAEP have tended to be flat or dropping. STAAR scores have shown little improvement. Table 12.1 compares NAEP scores in Texas to those of other states.

Both supporters and critics of testing tend to agree that STAAR is not working well but disagree as to why. Supporters of testing argue that the test should be more rigorous and that teachers and administrators must stop fomenting fear and test anxiety. Opponents say students are over-tested, and they contend that the testing model has grown stale. On July 2020, Governor Abbott announced that grade promotion requirements related to the STAAR test for students in 5th and 8th grade would be waived for the 2020–2021 school year due to COVID-19. "The traditional A–F rating system will remain in place, albeit with certain adjustments due to COVID-19."[28] Controversies over testing will continue.

Colleges and Universities

Texas has many colleges and universities—100 public and 53 private institutions of higher education serving nearly 1.5 million students annually. A growing number of for-profit and nonprofit online institutions also offer degrees and certificates. Most potential Texas students live within commuting distance of a campus. Public institutions include 37 universities, 10 health-related institutions, 50 community college districts (many with multiple campuses), three two-year state colleges, and six colleges (with 10 campuses) of the Texas State Technical College System. All receive some state funding and, of course, state oversight and regulation.

The Struggle for Tier-One Status Texas has three universities widely recognized as being among the prestigious tier-one national research universities: Rice University (private), the University of Texas at Austin (public), and Texas A&M University in College Station (public). All three are ranked by *U.S. News and World Report* among the top 100 national universities, along with three private schools, Southern Methodist University, Baylor University, and Texas Christian University. Two other Texas universities made the second 100 for 2021: University of Texas-Dallas (143rd) and University of Houston (176th).[29]

Among public universities, the University of Texas at Austin and Texas A&M University in College Station are commonly referred to as the state's "flagship" universities. They have traditionally been the most prestigious academically and the most powerful politically. Most observers believe that Texas needs more flagship universities to serve the increasing number of highly qualified students and to conduct the research necessary to attract new businesses and grow the economy. In 2009, a state constitutional amendment sought to increase the number of tier-one schools by giving access to funding to seven public universities through the Texas Research Incentive Program. These schools include the Universities of Texas at Arlington, Dallas, El Paso, and San Antonio; Texas Tech University; University of Houston; and University of North Texas (UNT). In 2016, these four institutions received the "Carnegie Tier One" status. In 2012, Texas State University, San Marcos, was added to the list of emerging research institutions by the Texas Higher Education Coordinating Board (THECB).

There are no universally accepted criteria for tier-one status. However, schools are expected to receive at least $100 million a year in research grants and belong to the prestigious, invitation-only Association of American Universities (AAU). In Texas, only the University of Texas at Austin, Texas A&M University in College Station, and Rice University are members. Another important step toward tier-one status is listing by the Carnegie Classification of Institutions of Higher Education as one of the 115 schools highest in research activity.

Access to Higher Education Two sets of issues have challenged Texas higher education in recent years: funding and providing access to Texas's highly diverse population. Low state funding and the sharp increase in tuition rates are discussed in Chapter 11, "Finance and Fiscal Policy."

📋 Students in Action

Show Me Your Papers State

In May 2017, SB 4 (referred to by many as the "Show Me Your Papers" law) was signed by Governor Greg Abbott. This law allows law enforcement and certain government entities to ask anyone an officer lawfully detains (even during a traffic stop) or arrests about their immigration status, including witnesses or victims of a crime. Further, the law bans "sanctuary cities." It requires sheriffs and police chiefs to detain undocumented immigrants for U.S. Immigration and Customs Enforcement (ICE) or face possible penalties.

Diana Vecchio, a student at Austin Community College, joined activists from ACLU, MALDEF, and LULAC, along with fellow students at the Austin Capitol, to protest SB 4 on May 29, 2017. She felt a need to join the protest in place of undocumented people who had no voice and were too afraid to come forward. Diana joined this protest as a way to speak out on the injustice she saw.

Diana felt there are several flaws with SB 4. One of the perceived flaws is that it is an attempt to punish law enforcement for not complying with a political agenda. Diana found that withholding funding from "sanctuary cities" was being used to punish city officials who disagreed with the law. Another major flaw, according to Diana, is that undocumented immigrants would be less likely to speak up if they saw a crime, or less inclined to seek help if a crime was committed against them. Diana believes this law makes us all less safe.

The protest was a way for Diana to get her voice heard. She believes it's a way that any student or citizen can make a difference. Diana remembers the day of the protest and making her way up to the capitol—the feeling of togetherness—as a group of people marched with signs while chanting and

Sam Houston State University Alumni Association

others would join in. As she entered the capitol rotunda waiting to hear results of the vote, Diana felt a sense of solidarity with others and a sense of empowerment.

In 2018, a federal appeals court upheld most of SB 4. As of 2020, law enforcement officers in Texas have the right to decide whether to assist ICE in investigations and enforcing immigration laws. If they decline to assist ICE, there will not be hefty penalties as originally stated in the bill.

What's the Advice to Students?

"Students can make a difference by showing up. Showing up at protests and demonstrations is important, as is showing up to vote. Politicians will be forced to listen and cooperate if enough people speak out and get involved."

Source: Interview with Diana Vecchio, November 14, 2020.

— Competency Connection —
☼ CRITICAL THINKING ☼

What issues mobilize students to action?

Improving the educational opportunities of Texas's ethnic minorities and the economically disadvantaged is an important but controversial issue and one with a long history in the state. A 1946 denial of admission to the University of Texas law school on the grounds of race led to the "landmark [U.S. Supreme Court] case, *Sweatt v. Painter*, that helped break the back of racism in college admissions" throughout the country.[30] Texas's long history of official and private discrimination still has consequences today. Although many Latinos and African Americans have become middle class since the civil rights movement of the 1960s and 1970s, both groups remain overrepresented in the working class and the ranks of the poor. Poverty rates for Latinos and African Americans are twice the rate of Whites in Texas. In 2021, Hispanics made up roughly 39 percent of the population, but more than half, 51 percent, of those living below the poverty level.

To deal with these inequalities, in 2000 the Texas Higher Education Coordinating Board adopted an ambitious program called Closing the Gaps. Its goal was to increase college enrollment and graduation rates for all groups by 2015. The program was highly successful. By 2019, enrollment and graduation had increased. African Americans receiving degrees or certificates rose slightly from 41,027 in 2017 to 41,077 in 2019; Latino graduates went from 111,344 in 2017 to 121,589 in 2019. As of 2019, 127,986 undergraduates categorized as "economically disadvantaged" had received their degree or certificate. This was more than halfway to the goal of 246,000 slated for 2030. The proportion of both men and women attending postsecondary programs has also increased. Building on the success of Closing the Gaps, the Coordinating Board developed a new plan, 60x30TX, to expand student achievement and build a "globally competitive Texas workforce by 2030." The goal is to assure that 60 percent of young Texans (ages 25–34) have a post-secondary credential (either a degree or certificate) by 2030. In 2016, 42 percent of young Texans had a degree or certificate. Based on the 2018 data and since the program was implemented, the annual number of certificates and bachelors and masters degrees awarded in Texas have increased 7.25 percent.[31] Texas public institutions of higher education are to serve all students well, regardless of ethnicity or economic background.

equal opportunity
Ensures that policies and actions do not discriminate on factors, such as race, gender, ethnicity, religion, or national origin.

affirmative action
Takes positive steps to attract women and members of racial and ethnic minority groups; may include using race in admission or hiring decisions.

A study financed by the Bill and Melinda Gates Foundation concluded that if the goals of Closing the Gaps were achieved, "When all public [state and local] and private costs are considered, the annual economic returns per $1 of expenditures by 2030 are estimated to be $24.15 in total spending, $9.60 in gross state product, and $6.01 in personal income."[32]

Texas colleges and universities commonly describe themselves as equal opportunity/affirmative action institutions. **Equal opportunity** simply means that the school takes care that its policies and actions do not produce prohibited discrimination, such as denying admission on the basis of race or sex. **Affirmative action** means that the institution takes positive steps to attract women and members of historical minority groups. For institutions of higher education, affirmative action means taking such noncontroversial steps as making sure that the school catalog has pictures of all groups—Whites and minorities, men and women—and recruits in predominantly minority high schools, not just schools with majority White student populations. Some selective universities have actively considered race along with other factors in admissions and aid, and other schools have offered scholarships for minority students. This side of affirmative action has created conflict.

Affirmative action issues have been largely addressed in the courts. Some White applicants denied admission or scholarship benefits challenged the second form of affirmative action programs in the courts. In the case of *University of California v. Bakke* (1978), the U.S. Supreme Court ruled that race could be considered as one factor, along with other criteria, to achieve diversity in higher education enrollment; however, setting aside a specific number of slots for one race was not acceptable.[33] (Remember that U.S. Supreme Court decisions establish precedents that must be followed throughout the country.) Relying on the *Bakke* decision, the University of Texas Law School created separate admission pools based on race and ethnicity, a practice the U.S. Fifth Circuit Court of Appeals declared unconstitutional in *Hopwood v. Texas* (1996).[34]

After the *Hopwood* ruling, Texas schools looked for ways to maintain minority enrollment. In 1997, Texas legislators mandated the **top 10 percent rule**, which provided that the top 10 percent of the graduating class of every accredited public or private Texas high school could be admitted to tax-supported colleges and universities of their choosing, regardless of admission test scores. Thus, students with the best grades at Texas's high schools (including those that are heavily minority, economically disadvantaged, or in small towns) can gain automatic admission to a flagship institution or other public college or university of their choosing. The top 10 percent rule has helped all three groups.

For students not admitted on the basis of class standing, the University of Texas at Austin used a "holistic review" of all academic and personal achievements, which may take into consideration family income, race, and ethnicity (with no specific weight and no quotas). Use of race in the holistic review produced another court challenge (*Fisher v. University of Texas*), which was heard before the U.S. Supreme Court during the fall of 2012.[35] (This case is often identified as *Fisher I* to distinguish it from a 2016 case with the same title.) The Supreme Court held that a university's use of race must meet a test known as "strict scrutiny," meaning that affirmative action will be constitutional only if it is "narrowly tailored." Courts can no longer simply accept a university's determination that it needs to consider race in order to have a diverse student body. Instead, courts themselves will need to confirm that the use of race is "necessary." The Fifth Circuit Court found that the University of Texas met this standard, and the admissions program was upheld by the U.S. Supreme Court in the 2016 case (*Fisher II*).[36]

The University of Texas at Austin has been sued three times over its affirmative action program by a group called Students for Fair Admissions. The most recent lawsuit was in July 2020. This same group was behind the *Fisher II* case, but its lawsuits have been unsuccessful in overturning UT Austin's affirmative action policy. According to the Students for Fair Admission's president, Edward Blum, the 2020 lawsuit was filed because UT had not followed instructions from *Fisher II* "to continue to evaluate use of race in its admissions policy."[37]

top 10 percent rule
Texas law gives automatic admission into any Texas public college or university to those graduating in the top 10 percent of their Texas high school class, with limitations for the University of Texas at Austin.

Have student bodies at the two flagship schools changed in response to changes in the law? From fall 2010 to fall 2020, Whites were a minority of incoming freshman to the University of Texas at Austin—nearly 39 percent in 2020–2021—although they remained a majority of the total student body until 2012. In 2003–2004, Texas A&M University in College Station announced that it would not use race in admissions decisions. Instead, minority recruiting would be increased and more scholarships would be provided for first-generation, low-income students. (First-generation students are the first in their immediate family to attend college.) Texas A&M also dropped preferences for "legacies" (relatives of alumni), who were predominantly White. In fall 2020, Whites made up roughly 60 percent of undergraduates, while the transfer acceptance rate was 53 percent.

The top 10 percent rule is controversial, especially among applicants from competitive high schools denied admission to the state's flagship institutions. In fall 2009, the rule qualified 86 percent of students offered admission to the University of Texas at Austin. This situation left little room for students to be admitted on the basis of high scores or talents such as music and leadership. According to the university's president, even football might have to be abolished. (No one believed him.) In response, the legislature modified the rule so that UT-Austin would not have to admit more than 75 percent of its students on the basis of class standing. Class standing has varied by year: top 8 percent for fall 2016; 7 percent for 2015, 2017, and 2018; and 6 percent from 2019 through fall 2022. Initially, the 75 percent cap was in effect only through the 2015–2016 school year; however, the 84th Legislature repealed the expiration date. In 2017, Texas Senator Kel Seliger (R-Amarillo) authored a bill to repeal the top 10 percent rule, stating that doing so would lead to greater diversity in the long run. However, even with Governor Abbott's support for repeal or substantial modification, the bill did not make it to a vote.

Research by economists at Texas A&M University, College Station, over a 20-year period, indicates that the top 10 percent policy has not increased access for African Americans and Latinos as much as proponents would have hoped. Enrollment of Latinos has slightly increased, making up roughly 28 percent of UT Austin's student population in fall 2020. In large part, this is due to an increase in the Latino population overall in Texas. Black enrollment increased slightly to roughly 6 percent of UT Austin's student population in fall 2020. Overall, the study found that students who attended high schools that sent large numbers of students to flagship universities were likely to do this with or without the top 10 percent policy. Public high schools that never sent students to UT Austin or Texas A&M, College Station, before adoption of the top 10 percent rule were still unlikely to send students to these flagship universities after adoption. This study shows that these universities need to do more outreach and recruitment at remote and less familiar high schools. On its own, the top 10 percent rule will not increase diversity in the state's colleges and universities.[38]

✓ 12.2 Learning Check

1. Why is standardized testing so controversial in Texas?
2. What is the "top 10 percent rule" in Texas higher education?

Answers at the end of this chapter.

▣ Point/Counterpoint

Should Texas Continue to Use the "Top 10 Percent Rule"?

The Issue To promote diversity in Texas colleges and universities without using race as an admission criterion, the state legislature in 1997 passed a law guaranteeing admission to any public college or university in the state to Texas students who graduate in the top 10 percent of their high school class. This law sought to promote greater geographic, socioeconomic, and racial/ethnic diversity. The law applies to all public colleges and universities in the state, but it has had its greatest effect on the two flagship universities: the University of Texas at Austin and Texas A&M University in College Station. Both are prestigious schools with more qualified applicants than they can admit. The 10 percent rule has increased minority representation at both schools but more so at the University of Texas. In 2009, the legislature capped automatic admission to the University of Texas at Austin at 75 percent.

For	Against
1. The top 10 percent rule is doing what it was designed to do—increase diversity among highly qualified students.	1. The top 10 percent rule unfairly puts students who attend high schools with rigorous standards at a disadvantage. Thus, they are tempted to take lighter loads or attend less demanding high schools.
2. Virtually all top 10 percent students from competitive high schools who choose UT-Austin or TAMU-College Station gain admission there.	2. So many students are admitted under this one criterion that the universities have too little discretion, and students with other talents (such as music and the arts) are left out.
3. The problem is not that Texas has too many students entering schools under automatic admission. Rather, the issue is that Texas has too few flagship universities to accommodate the number of qualified students.	3. The rule is creating a brain drain. Many top students are leaving Texas to attend college in other states, where they often remain after graduation.

— Competency Connection —
✿ CRITICAL THINKING ✿

Underlying the argument about the top 10 percent rule is concern for opportunity and for diversity on campus. Should Texas look for an alternative to the top 10 percent rule? If so, what?

❑ Health and Human Services

LO 12.3 Describe the major health and human services programs in Texas, and discuss how efforts to address the needs of its citizens have been approached.

Most people think of Texas as a wealthy state. Indeed, the Lone Star State has many wealthy residents and a substantial middle class. Texas, however, also has long been among the states with the largest proportion of its population in poverty. From 2000 to 2019, Texas's poverty rate varied between 14 to 18.5 percent of the population. This rate has declined in recent years, albeit irregularly. Poverty is particularly high for children and members of historical minority groups, as can be seen in Table 12.2. Poverty is highest in South Texas and about half of the metropolitan areas. It is lowest in suburban counties surrounding major cities. Poverty is defined in terms of family size and income. In 2021, according to federal poverty levels, poverty was an annual family income of less than $21,960 for a family of three. For a family of four, it was $26,500.

Even more Texans are classified as low income, meaning they earn an income above the poverty line but insufficient for many "extras," such as health insurance. A common measure of low income is an income up to twice the poverty level. In 2019, Texas led the nation in child poverty, with 1.5 million children below the poverty line.

Access to health care is a national issue that is even more acute in Texas. Although the state's major cities have outstanding medical centers, their facilities are of little use to those who lack resources to pay for care.[39] For at least the last decade, studies comparing health care in the various states consistently rank Texas near the bottom. The Commonwealth Fund is a well respected foundation that ranked Texas's health system performance in the bottom quarter in 2019—an overall ranking of 49th.[40]

A key factor in access to health care is health insurance. In Texas, the percent of people without health insurance dropped from 26 in 2010, when the Affordable Care Act became law, to 18.4 in 2020. With nearly 5 million people uninsured, the state led the nation in percent of uninsured, as it had since at least 1988. Uninsured rates are particularly high for Latino Texans, as the "How Do We Compare " table in this chapter shows. Texas also leads in the percent of uninsured children.

Table 12.2 Families in Poverty in Texas and the United States (2019)

	Texas (Percent)	United States (Percent)
Families	13*	11
Whites	8	9
Latinos	19	17
African Americans	18	21
Children 0–18	19	17
Adults 19–64	12	12
Age 65 and older	11	10

*Family income is used by many specialists in poverty as a better indicator. Among individual Texans, the percentage was 13.6.

Source: "Demographics and the Economy," Kaiser Family Foundation, 2020, https://www .kff.org/state-category/demographics-and-the-economy/people-in-poverty/.

— Competency Connection —
☼ CRITICAL THINKING ☼

How does poverty in Texas impact all Texans?

The Patient Protection and Affordable Care Act (popularly known as ACA or Obamacare), was passed by Congress in 2010. Its aim is to improve this situation. Some provisions of the act are widely supported: for example, young adults up to age 26 can be on their parents' insurance; preexisting conditions are covered in many cases; and caps on lifetime benefits have been lifted.

The heart of ACA is an attempt to provide health insurance to almost all Americans. People who can afford it, purchase their health insurance. Medicaid covers those who cannot afford to buy insurance on their own. Both provisions have met with controversy. Analysts attribute a significant part of the drop in the number of uninsured Texans to the ACA. For people who do not already have a health insurance plan that meets ACA requirements, states can provide insurance "exchanges" or "marketplaces" to assist them. For states such as Texas that opt not to have an exchange, the federal government's exchange provides assistance. Republicans in the U.S. Congress, along with former President Donald Trump, have tried to "repeal and replace" ACA; but as of mid-2021, it remained in force. However, changes over the past few years have significantly impacted ACA. There have been estimates that half a million fewer people enrolled for ACA because of cuts to outreach and advertisement alone.

Another major effort of the ACA was to expand coverage of **Medicaid**, the joint federal–state program providing medical care for the poor. In June 2012, the U.S. Supreme Court upheld most of the Affordable Care Act in a suit brought by Texas and 25 other states (*National Federation of Independent Business v. Sebelius*, 132 S. Ct. 2566 [2012]). However, the court held that the national government could not use the threat to withhold existing Medicaid funds to coerce states into expanding Medicaid coverage. This holding allowed Texas and other states to opt out of Medicaid expansion.

Evolution of Social Services Since the Great Depression of the 1930s, state and national governments have gradually increased efforts to address the needs of the poor, the elderly, and others who cannot afford adequate medical care. In the 20th century, social welfare became an important part of the federal relationship (see Chapter 2, "Federalism and the Texas Constitution," and Chapter 3, "Local Governments"). Over time, the national government has taken responsibility for relatively popular social welfare programs, such as Social Security, Medicare, and aid to the blind and disabled. States, on the other hand, have responsibility for less popular welfare programs that have less effective lobbying behind them, such as Medicaid, Supplemental Nutrition Assistance Program (SNAP, formerly food stamps), and Temporary Assistance for Needy Families (TANF). The federal government pays a significant part of the cost of state social welfare programs; but within federal guidelines the states administer these programs, make eligibility rules, and pay part of the cost.

Health and human services programs are at a disadvantage in Texas for two reasons. First, the state's political culture values individualism, self-reliance, and business interests. Thus, anything suggesting welfare is difficult to fund at more

Medicaid
Funded in large part by federal grants and in part by state appropriations, Medicaid is administered by the state. It provides medical care for poor persons.

than a minimal level. In addition, the neediest Texans lack organization and resources to compete with special interest groups representing the business elite and the middle class. Thus, the Lone Star State provides assistance for millions of needy Texans, but at relatively low benefit levels. Many people are left out.

Privatization When the legislature consolidated Texas agencies under the Health and Human Services Commissioner in 2003, it also mandated a major change in the state's approach to social services—**privatization**. A majority of legislators were convinced that private contractors can provide public services more cheaply and efficiently than can government. Under a legislative mandate, local social services offices and caseworkers were replaced with call centers operated by private contractors. Applicants for social services were encouraged to use the telephone and internet to establish eligibility for most social services. A similar but much smaller privatized system had worked reasonably well in 2000. However, this new, larger system performed poorly. After 2003, the number of children covered by insurance dropped sharply, and eligible people faced long waits and lost paperwork. In response to these problems, the private contractor was replaced, many former state employees were rehired, and attempts were made to bring children back into the social welfare system. In 2010, however, a federal official complained about Texas's "five-year slide" to last place among states in the speed and accuracy of handling food stamp applications after privatization.[41] Promised savings and better service have yet to appear.

State officials say the problem is that privatization is still a work in progress and that there is no turning back. Critics argue that profit incentives for contractors and social services for the public are inherently in conflict. Officials have continued to promote privatization, but more gradually, with the result that some Texas social services are a mixture of public and private administration. Private contractors are both for-profit and nonprofit. An example is foster care administered by Texas Department of Family and Protective Services (DFPS), which had responsibility for about 16,000 children as of August 2020. With too little money, too few caseworkers, and inadequate accountability, foster care in Texas has performed poorly under both public and privatized management. Child welfare advocates view the current privatized plan as stretching limited resources even thinner and adding a layer of private bureaucracy.[42] In 2015, a federal judge in Corpus Christi ruled in a class-action lawsuit brought by a New York-based advocacy group that the Texas foster care system violated children's constitutional rights. The judge ordered reforms (including more caseworkers) and appointed two special masters, both experts in the area of foster care, to make recommendations to the state. In April 2016, Governor Abbott appointed the retired chief of the Texas Rangers, Hank Whitman, to lead the agency. Texas appealed the 56 recommendations from the experts appointed by the federal judge. In October 2018, the 5th U.S. Circuit Court of Appeals reviewed the case. A majority of this court's members agreed with the federal district court judge's call for major reform. Nevertheless, the majority scrapped a key recommendation to limit the number of cases per caseworker. Other recommendations were pulled also, but the dissenting judge stated, "In place of the discipline imposed by the district court's order, the majority inexplicably affords what it terms a "prudent"

privatization
Transfer of government services or assets to the private sector. Commonly, assets are sold and services contracted out.

and "creative" bureaucracy the flexibility to set its own course and to proceed at its own pace—ignoring that this is what DFPS (Texas Department of Family and Protective Services) has been doing for twenty years."[43]

Human Services

The Health and Human Services Commission (HHSC) administers a variety of programs, three of which have long received a great deal of attention and prompted debate: TANF, SNAP, and Medicaid. All three are administered by the executive commissioner of HHSC within federal guidelines. These programs are funded by the federal government and to a lesser extent by the state. In the words of budget analyst Eva DeLuna Castro, eligibility for these and other "public assistance programs in Texas is very restrictive compared to other states, the benefits are lower, and health benefits for poor adults are more limited. As a result, a smaller share of the poor in Texas receives any public assistance."[44] In addition, all three programs suffered financially from the budget cutbacks carried out by the 2011 legislature and only partially recovered in 2013 and 2015. In 2020, the state has still done little to increase assistance for those most in need.

Most Texas social welfare programs provide specific services or assistance for a specific need. SNAP, for example, provides a mechanism to buy food, and Medicaid provides access to medical care. **Temporary Assistance for Needy Families (TANF)**, on the other hand, provides very limited cash assistance that can be spent for various needs. In Texas, this program is aimed at extremely poor families. For a family of three in 2021, the poverty level was $21,960 in annual income (or $1,810 per month). To receive TANF that year, a family of one parent and two children could earn no more than $2,256 a year (12 percent of the poverty level). The family would receive $308 a month. Texas increased the amount by $5 in 2021, with a lifetime limit of 60 months if one of the recipients was an adult. Children who qualify for TANF benefits can receive benefits on their own until age 18. Along with other requirements, caretakers must be U.S. citizens or legal residents and agree to work or to enroll in a job training program. As of July 2020, Texas had one of the lowest average benefits for families that need TANF. TANF benefits in all states, including Texas, "are at or below 60 percent of the poverty line and fail to cover rent for a modest two-bedroom apartment. TANF does a poor job of providing assistance to Latino and especially Black children, whose parents and communities in which they live are more likely to feel the devastating effects of COVID-19 and the resulting economic crisis."[45]

According to HHSC, the "most common" TANF caretaker is a woman about 30 years old with one or two children younger than age 11. She is unemployed, has no other income, and receives a TANF grant of $303 or less per month for fewer than 12 months. In addition to the small amount of cash provided by TANF, recipients may receive benefits from other programs, such as SNAP and Medicaid. To reduce abuse, benefits for both TANF and SNAP are provided through a plastic Lone Star Card that functions like a debit card.

A second federal–state program administered by the commission is the **Supplemental Nutritional Assistance Program (SNAP)**, formerly called food stamps. It makes food available to elderly or disabled people, families, and single

Temporary Assistance for Needy Families (TANF) Provides financial assistance to the very poor in an attempt to help them move from welfare to the workforce.

Supplemental Nutritional Assistance Program (SNAP) Joint federal–state program administered by the state to provide food to low-income people.

adults who qualify because of low income, defined as no more than 130 percent of the poverty level. Approximately 80 percent of those who benefit from SNAP receive no TANF support. Benefits vary, depending on income and the number of people in a household. In 2020, for example, a qualified Texas household composed of three people could earn up to $2,987 a month and obtain groceries costing up to $535 each month. Adults between the ages of 16 and 59 must look for work or be in a work program. If they are employed, they cannot quit without a good reason.[46]

To assist in connecting eligible Texans to service providers, several private groups use social media sites, such as Twitter and Facebook, as well as blogs. *Less Than* is a documentary that shares stories about how Amarillo families have survived economic hardships. COVID-19 created new hardships for Texans. Government and private organizations are working to use different media outlets to inform and assist those in need.

Health and Mental Health Services

The third major federal–state program administered by HHS is Medicaid. Part of President Lyndon B. Johnson's Great Society initiatives in the 1960s, Medicaid is designed to provide medical care for the poor people. Four categories are eligible: (1) the aged, blind, and disabled; (2) parents with dependent children and with household incomes up to 15 percent of the poverty level; (3) children with household incomes up to 201 percent of the poverty level (adults would not be eligible); and (4) pregnant women with household incomes up to 198 percent of the poverty level. Resources not counted against the poverty level limit are a home, personal possessions, and a low-value motor vehicle. As of August 2020, Medicaid and CHIP, the related children's program, covered roughly 4.7 million Texans.

Not to be confused with Medicaid is **Medicare**, another Great Society initiative. A federal program providing medical assistance to qualifying applicants age 65 and older, Medicare is administered by the U.S. Department of Health and Human Services without use of state funds. Because Medicaid is considered to be welfare and serves the poor, it has much less political clout than Medicare, which serves a more middle-class clientele. Medicaid has much more difficulty gaining funding. Furthermore, benefits for clients and reimbursements for service providers tend to be lower. Benefits are so low that many Texas doctors now refuse new Medicaid patients, and nursing homes have trouble covering their costs. Medicare reimbursement amounts are set by the federal government. Payments are higher than those for Medicaid but are also low, thus reducing physician access for some patients.

Under the 2010 national Affordable Care Act, states were required to expand Medicaid coverage to virtually all nonelderly adults and children earning up to 133 percent of the poverty level. States that did not provide expanded coverage risked losing their existing federal Medicaid funds. However, as mentioned earlier, the U.S. Supreme Court held that the federal government could not use threats of withholding funding to coerce expansion of Medicaid for adults. Thus, states have the option of participating in the

Medicare
Funded entirely by the federal government and administered by the U.S. Department of Health and Human Services, Medicare primarily provides medical assistance to qualified applicants age 65 and older.

expansion or keeping their existing adult programs. Editorials in most of Texas's major newspapers supported the expansion; however, in July 2012, then-Governor Rick Perry informed federal authorities that Texas would not participate in the expansion of Medicaid. As of October 2020, some 39 states (including the District of Columbia) had expanded Medicaid coverage, and 12 states (including Texas) have not done so. (The "How Do We Compare" table shows the decision of other large states and Texas's neighbors.) As of 2019, public support for Medicaid expansion remained strong, with 56 percent in support of expansion.

For those states participating, the federal government pays the entire cost of expansion for the first three years and at least 90 percent beyond that. Payments for primary care physicians are also raised to Medicare levels. Estimates are that opting out of Medicaid expansion cost Texas more than $100 billion that would have been paid by the federal government.

📊 How Do We Compare...

In (1) Proportion of Uninsured by Race/Ethnicity and (2) Expansion of Medicaid Under the Affordable Care Act (ACA)?

Most Populous States	(Percent)				(Yes/No) Expanded Medicaid
	White	Latino	Black	Total Population	
California	5	14	6	9	Yes
Florida	13	21	17	16	No
New York	4	11	7	6	Yes
Texas	**13**	**31**	**16**	**21**	**No**
States Bordering Texas					
Arkansas	9	26	9	11	Yes*
Louisiana	9	29	10	10	Yes
New Mexico	8	12	NA	12	Yes
Oklahoma	14	28	17	18	No

*Expanded using an alternative method.
NA = Not available.

Source: "Status of State Medicaid Expansion Decisions: Interactive Map," *Kaiser Family Foundation*, November 2, 2020, https://www.kff.org/medicaid/issue-brief/status-of-state-medicaid-expansion-decisions-interactive-map/.

Competency Connection
⚙ CRITICAL THINKING ⚙

What patterns do you see in the data? Do the patterns appear to have any relation to whether states expanded Medicaid under the ACA?

Without the expansion of Medicaid, Texas remains a national leader in the number of uninsured. Nearly 1.4 million Texans (of the state's 5 million uninsured) are left uncovered by the decision as of mid-2021. One study from Families USA reported that an additional 659,000 more Texans lost their jobs due to COVID-19 and therefore became uninsured between February 2020 and May 2020.[47] Several studies have examined the consequences of not expanding Medicaid and concluded that it will lead to preventable deaths. In Texas, one conservative projection is that 1,800 to 3,000 lives a year could be lost and large numbers of illnesses will not be detected early or will go untreated.[48] Nearly 640,000 Texans have no realistic access to insurance without Medicaid expansion. According to the *New York Times*, a report by the Georgetown Center for Children and Families found, "One-third of the total increase in the number of uninsured children from 2016 to 2019 live in Texas."[49]

The Department of State Health Services (DSHS), a part of HHSC, performs a wide variety of functions that include public health planning and enforcement of state health laws. As with public assistance, state health policies are closely tied to several federal programs. One example is the Special Supplemental Nutrition Program for Women, Infants, and Children (WIC), a delivery system for healthy foods, nutritional counseling, and healthcare screening.

A more visible role of the DSHS is providing information and resources on public health concerns. A few examples in the past decade have been Ebola, the Zika virus, the HIV/AIDS epidemic, and most recently COVID-19. In September 2014, Texas's first Ebola case received substantial publicity and posed a challenge to the DSHS, which educates Texans on infectious diseases. In 2016, attention focused on the Zika virus, a serious mosquito-borne disease. A long-term problem in Texas is acquired immunodeficiency syndrome (AIDS) caused by the human immunodeficiency virus (HIV). It is commonly transmitted by sexual contact (both homosexual and heterosexual) and contaminated needles used by drug addicts. AIDS is an international epidemic but has been more stable in Texas.

COVID-19, a world-wide pandemic, has taken its toll on Texas. DSHS has been working closely with the federal Centers for Disease Control and Prevention (CDC) in coming up with a response to this contagious disease. As of June 8, 2021, DSHS reported over 2.5 million confirmed cases and nearly 50,700 fatalities in Texas—the first state to surpass over a million COVID-19 cases in the U.S. Texas has been experiencing nearly 4,000 new cases a day. As of November 1, 2020 Texas administered over 9 million coronavirus tests. DSHS has found that coronavirus remains highly active in predominantly Latino counties of South Texas. According to analysis by the *New York Times*, Brownsville-Harlingen, Eagle Pass, Rio Grande City, Corpus Christi, and Laredo have had the highest "rate of new coronavirus cases per capita in the country."[50] One of the hardest hit cities in Texas and the United States is El Paso, where 10 mobile morgues had to be used to handle the overflow of bodies. El Paso County Judge Curtis Parrish ordered a curfew and issued a stay-at-home order to help stop the spread, but Texas Attorney General Ken Paxton challenged this action through the courts. The state's Eighth District Court of Appeals on November 13, 2020, ruled in favor of the state. It held that local directives cannot supersede Governor Abbott's statewide orders.

COVID-19 has impacted Texans in different ways. Texas has experienced a health crisis that has driven our healthcare workers and hospitals to the brink as they deal with COVID-19 cases, mental health issues, an increase in addiction, and more. Our economy has been impacted as monthly sales tax revenue plunged. Unemployment has been another significant issue related to COVID-19.

Texas's Department of State Health Services and its Department of Aging and Disability Services provide public mental health programs for persons unable to afford private therapy. However, looking at access for Texans to mental health care programs, Texas ranked 51st nationwide (including the District of Columbia) in 2020 according to the non-profit organization, Mental Health America.[51] Texas's per capita funding for mental health programs ranked between 48th and 51st between 2013 and 2020. With per capita spending at $45.23 in 2020, only 3 other states spent less than Texas.[52] According to the *Texas Tribune*, in the 2017 legislative session, legislators launched "a community grant program for mental health services, [which] addressed how health insurance companies offer mental health benefits, and funding to renovate state mental health hospitals." But Texas still falls below most other states' efforts. As a result, the state serves only a fraction of those needing assistance. From at least 1995 to 2020 the number of psychiatric hospital beds per 100,000 population has declined, creating long waiting lists.[53]

State hospitals have other problems:

- Large residential facilities are appropriate for a limited number of patients at best.
- State hospitals are deteriorating.
- Inadequate training and rapid turnover of staff are rampant.

Reports of abuse in living centers brought an agreement in 2009 between the U.S. Department of Justice and Texas to increase the number of health workers. Since then, the number of workers has increased, but failure to increase wages for direct care workers has contributed to continuing high rates of neglect.

Like most states, Texas relies heavily on community outpatient services for mental health treatment, which is the cheaper and medically preferred option for most patients. Because of the shortage of programs, the number of patients receiving community mental health services has been relatively flat, fluctuating from 62,000 to 70,000 annually during the 2007 to 2016 period. As of April 2021, 206 out of 254 counties in Texas were designated as Mental Health Professional Shortage Areas. As population growth in Texas has doubled the national average, so has an increased demand for HHSC-funded services. Houston has roughly seven public mental health beds per 100,000 residents, whereas national standards call for the number of beds to be increased ten times. An unknown number of Texas's mentally ill are detained in jails and prisons or are living on the streets. Reportedly, there are roughly 18,000 inmates in the Harris County Jail, and some 3,000 of them receive psychiatric treatment every day, "more than any other mental health hospital in Texas."[54] For a discussion of mental health issues among inmates, see Chapter 13 "The Criminal Justice System."

Employment

The Texas Unemployment Compensation Act is funded by an employer-paid payroll tax and is administered by the Texas Workforce Commission (TWC). This law authorizes payments to workers who lose their jobs through no fault of their own (such as being laid off). Amounts paid to the unemployed workers depend on wages earned in an earlier quarter (three months). In 2020 the maximum weekly compensation was $521, and the minimum was $69. That same year, the average tax rate paid by employers was .93 percent of the first $9,000 of each employee's earnings. The Great Recession (2007–2009) increased unemployment and claims, although Texas unemployment remained below the national average. After a fall in petroleum prices devastated the oil and gas sector, unemployment in Texas exceeded the national average.

The coronavirus outbreak sent Texas's economy into a recession, with nearly 3.8 million Texans filing for unemployment relief from mid-March 2020 to November 2020. Texas' unemployment rate has more than doubled since the start of the year. Our state's outdated and understaffed unemployment insurance agency (TWC) has left many Texans confused, frustrated, and without unemployment benefits. Economists predict that "weakened oil prices, high unemployment, and the ongoing public health crisis will slow Texas' economic recovery."[55]

Since 1913, Texas has had a **workers' compensation** program to help workers injured on the job receive medical care and recover some lost wages. Employers purchase insurance from private companies to cover expenses of those injured or made ill by work conditions. By the mid-1980s, the program had become highly controversial, with complaints of low benefits for injured workers and high insurance premiums for employers. A two-year lobbying and legislative struggle produced a major modification of the program in 1989, when lobbying by a coalition of employers and insurance companies defeated a coalition of plaintiffs' lawyers and labor unions. As a result of this legislative contest, the process for injured workers became more administrative and less judicial. Workers were less likely to win and more likely to receive lower benefits. The major source of the problem, Texas's dangerous workplaces (particularly transportation, construction, and oil and gas) and lax safety standards, received scant improvement. Since 2000, Texas has generally led the nation in workplace deaths.

The state "workers" compensation system is governed by the Division of Workers' Compensation (DWC) of the Texas Department of Insurance. Since creation of the DWC in 2005, lawyers who represent injured workers have complained that the agency is too close to the insurance companies; and the commissioner testified in 2014 that workers were losing an increasing proportion of disputes in the agency's court-like system that resolves disputes. Both the number of claims by workers and insurance rates charged employers have declined.

Texas is the only state in the union that does not require employers to provide workers' compensation insurance. Failure to provide this insurance puts the employer at risk for expensive court suits, which are generally forbidden

workers' compensation
A system of insurance that pays benefits to workers injured or made ill by their work.

by law if the employer provides workers' compensation insurance. About two-thirds of Texas's employers provide this insurance. A recent trend has been the development of opt-out insurance plans in which the employer provides a private plan that generally covers fewer injuries, cuts off benefits sooner, and gives employers more control of the process.

⬛ Economic and Environmental Policies

LO 12.4 Compare the roles of government in generating economic development while maintaining a safe, clean, and prosperous environment for the state's residents.

Education, health, and human services account for three-fourths of Texas state government expenditures. Business promotion, economic development, and regulation together amount to 13 percent of the budget, but they have a substantial and often direct effect on the lives of Texans. The state tries to generate economic development that, when successful, produces jobs and profits. Regulations affect the prices for electricity and insurance, as well as the quality of the air.

Historically, regulation was supported as a means to protect the individual, the weak, and the general public against the economically powerful and special interests. In practice, this protection has been difficult to achieve because the benefits of regulation tend to be diffuse and the costs specific. For example, cleaner air benefits a broad range of the public, but few can put a dollar amount on their own personal benefit. On the other hand, companies that must pay to clean up their air emissions see a specific (and sometimes large) cost. Thus, companies are more apt to spend money to fight regulation than are people who benefit from it.

Moreover, businesses are better organized, have more connections to policymakers, and employ more lobbyists than the public does. For most of Texas's history, including the long period of conservative Democratic domination, economic and regulatory policies have tilted toward business. Republican ascendancy in recent years has enhanced this tendency, although consumer, environmental, and labor advocates are being heard.

Business, however, is not monolithic. Battles over taxes, subsidies, and regulation produce conflicts between different kinds of businesses. Established businesses, for example, often try to limit competition by seeking regulation of newcomers. When cable television emerged, broadcast television successfully sought burdensome requirements and limitations that slowed development of the new industry. Similarly, when the Texas legislature began to regulate smokestack emissions, established companies sought successfully to be "grandfathered" (that is, existing smokestacks were exempted from the new regulations, which gave old companies a cost advantage). In recent years, coal producers and users, natural gas companies, and wind energy farm operators and carriers have been at odds over issues such as environmental regulations, pipeline and powerline rights of way, and tax and subsidy policy. As a consequence of the divisions, some policy issues are fought by coalitions with business, labor, consumer, and environmental interests on both sides.

Business Promotion

Some cynical observers contend that the business of Texas government is business. Others argue that boosting business strengthens the economy and creates jobs that benefit the lives of all Texans. Certainly, the state's political culture and the strength of business lobbyists make government responsive to business. Free-market advocates who compare policies in the states have consistently identified Texas as a business-friendly state in the last decade. In 2018 the Small Business and Entrepreneurship Council ranked Texas second among the 50 states in "policy environment" for entrepreneurship, behind Nevada but far ahead of Texas's neighboring states. The same group ranked Texas second in its small business tax index in 2018, and one researcher found Texas to have the third least burdensome regulatory structure.[56]

There are costs to these rankings. In 2018, the Institute on Taxation and Economic Policy ranked Texas's tax system as the second most unfair state and local tax system in the country, which is putting a greater burden on those of lower income and less burden on those with more wealth. The Social Science Research Council's human development index is a composite of health, education, and income levels. It ranks Texas 34th.[57]

Economic Regulatory Policy

Have you ever complained about a high telephone bill, a big automobile insurance premium, or the cost of a license to practice a trade or profession for which you have been trained? Welcome to the Lone Star State's regulatory politics. For businesses seeking to boost profits or professional groups trying to strengthen their licensing requirements, obtaining or avoiding changes in regulations can be costly but rewarding. Less-organized consumers and workers often believe they are left to pick up the tab for higher bills and fees and, on occasion, inferior service.

Traditionally, government regulation focused on prohibitions or requiring certain procedures to be followed. However, in the last decade, Texas regulators have increasingly sought to use economic competition to reduce costs to consumers and prevent harmful practices. This policy has produced great controversy. Although Texans tend to believe strongly in the merits of competition in much of the economy, there is not as much agreement that competition works for utilities and in protection of the environment. The reader will see this conflict played out across most of the areas of this section.

Business Regulation The Railroad Commission (RRC) and the Public Utility Commission (PUC) are among Texas's most publicized agencies. RRC regulates the oil and gas industry, which experienced a spectacular resurgence in its influence during the recent oil boom; and PUC affects the telephone and electric power bills paid by millions of Texans.

Textbooks often cite the Railroad Commission as the classic case of "agency capture," a situation in which a regulated industry exerts excessive influence over the agency intended to regulate it. Despite legislation requiring protection of consumers and the environment, RRC has long seen its major function as maintaining profitability of Texas's oil and gas industry. This industry's earlier decline and the state's greater economic diversity reduced industry dominance somewhat. However, resurgence of the oil and gas industry enhanced its political power and influence. The more recent decline that began in 2014 is once again reducing the industry's influence over state policies.

A controversy facing RRC is hydraulic fracturing (generally called fracking). This process involves injecting large amounts of water, sand, and chemicals underground at high pressure to break up shale formations, allowing oil or gas to flow up the wellbore. Fracking and horizontal drilling have been key to the rebirth of the oil and gas industry in Texas and other states. However, major questions have been raised about fracking's effect on the environment, including the safety of our underground water supply and disposal of contaminated water that returns to the surface.

Given Texas's growing water shortage, this additional use for water is causing concern. Another problem arising from exploration and production is damage to roads in the area of the Eagle Ford Shale (in South Texas). Given the tendency of state agencies to define their role narrowly, neither problem may be readily addressed. Decline in oil and gas production may provide a more effective solution by reducing both water usage and road damage. Fracking has had an immediate consequence: an oversupply of oil and gas that has resulted in lower prices. Additionally, this new technology has had two longer-term effects. First, it has extended the use of fossil fuels for decades. Second, availability of relatively cheap and clean natural gas has reduced carbon emissions created by much dirtier coal but also made it more difficult for clean, renewable sources of energy such as wind and solar to compete.[58]

Regulation of Public Utilities Through Competition The major responsibility of the Public Utility Commission of Texas (PUC) is regulation of local phone service (not long distance or wireless) and electric utilities. Since 2002, PUC has followed a national trend in state regulatory policy to rely on competition to protect consumer interests. Traditionally, rates charged by utility companies, such as those providing electricity and telephone service, were set or approved by government regulators. (Prices were said to be *regulated.*) Texas regulators, responding to legislative direction, have embraced **deregulation**, under which business practices (such as setting rates) are governed more by market conditions. The belief is that competition will produce fair prices and protect the public interest. Critics say they were half right.

Allowing consumers to choose their telephone service supplier was expected to result in reasonable telephone bills and reliable service from companies that must compete for customers. With the growth of competition from cell phones, this system seems to work. According to critics, however, deregulation of most Texas electricity suppliers has raised rates in comparison to those of other states— a reversal of two decades of lower-than-average rates under state regulation. A

deregulation
The elimination of government restrictions to allow free market competition to determine or limit the actions of individuals and corporations.

review of the average retail cost of a unit of power from 2011 to 2020 shows that the average price in the United States as of November 2020 was 13.6 cents per kilowatt hour (kWh). The state fluctuates in our ranking, but as of January 2020, Texas ranked as the 8th highest state all 50 states in terms of the highest average electric rate.[59] Over the last four years of regulation and the first 10 years of deregulation, electricity was relatively expensive but then saw an improvement. Both sides of the issue can claim support for their position.

Complicating this assessment is the significant drop in wholesale cost of electricity (the price utilities pay power producers) from 2002 to 2020. This development was brought about by cheaper natural gas replacing coal as the leading fuel for power plants and by Texas's national lead in cheap wind power, adequate power supply, and slower than expected growth in demand for electricity. The U.S. Energy Information Administration, a think-tank, has forecasted "2.2% less electricity consumption in the United States in 2020 in comparison to 2019."[60] It also has forecasted that residential retail sales would increase in 2020 by roughly 3 percent due to a hot summer and because more people have been working and studying from home. In addition, consumers can shop among electricity providers and significantly reduce their rates, although most people do not do so.

Another comparison is between the 85 percent of Texans in the deregulated sector and the 15 percent served by regulated entities (such as municipal power companies in Austin and San Antonio). Regulated rates have been consistently lower.[61]

Insurance Regulation At the beginning of 2003, Texans who owned homes and automobiles paid the highest insurance rates in the country. Rates were unregulated and rising rapidly. In response to public outcry, the 2003 legislature gave the commissioner of insurance authority to regulate all home insurers doing business in Texas. The following year, Texas began a largely deregulated "file and use" system for auto and homeowners insurance. Insurers set their own rates, but the commissioner of insurance is authorized to order reductions and refunds if rates are determined to be excessive. Advocates of this system expected it to produce reasonable rates by promoting competition among insurance companies. However, by 2018, Texas homeowner insurance rates were consistently high (seventh highest in the nation that year and $717 above the national average). In the more competitive car insurance industry, during the period 2010 to 2018, Texas fluctuated between the middle of the 50 states in average cost and being significantly higher. Cost of car insurance in Texas is nearly 27 percent more than the national average. As of October 2020, Texas had the 15th highest car insurance rates in the nation.[62]

Because of the frequent occurrence of natural disasters (such as hurricanes, hail, and fire), insurance in Texas tends to be expensive. But are Texas rates more costly than necessary, as consumer groups argue? The "loss ratio," which is considered the best measure of insurance company profitability, is what a company pays in benefits as a percentage of the premium money it receives. The insurance industry prefers a loss ratio of 60 percent or less, but consumer advocates prefer a higher percent. From 1995 to 2004, the average loss ratio for Texas insurance companies was 69 percent; and from 2005 to 2014, it was 59 percent.[63] This was good for insurers, thanks to rate increases and only one year of losses. In the 84th Legislature, however, insurers supported legislation intended to limit homeowner lawsuits against them. Sponsored by Sen. Larry Taylor (R-Friendswood), an insurance agent, the bill passed the Senate but was not voted on by the House of Representatives. In 2017, however, HB 1774 was passed and signed into law by Governor Abbott. It limits "the ability of policyholders to sue insurance companies over property claims following extreme weather events…".[64] Originally, this legislation only addressed lawsuits related to hailstorms, but it was amended to include severe natural events, such as earthquakes, wildfires, floods, tornados, lightning, hurricanes, wind, snowstorms, or rainstorms. Insurance companies believe this legislation will protect against frivolous lawsuits. In contrast, critics insist that this legislation will limit "the ability of property owners to hold insurers accountable for underpaid claims or poorly handled claims investigations."[65]

Regulating Highways Texans' love affair with their cars and pickups has led to traffic congestion and accidents. In recent years, Texans spent an average of 25 minutes commuting to work (one way), which is the national average. However, this number conceals huge differences—from a few minutes in small towns to much more than the average in densely populated areas and some suburbs. On the other hand, since 2000, the percentage of workers commuting by private vehicle has declined slightly in Texas's major cities.

With an increasing number of motor vehicles on the road, total accidents tend to increase. However, from 2010 to 2017, traffic deaths per 100 million miles driven remained relatively steady in the nation and Texas (for the state, from 1.27 to 1.38 deaths). The reasons, according to research, are safer roads, vehicles, and behavior by drivers (such as use of seatbelts and designated drivers). In 2018, impaired drivers were involved in 40 percent of Texas traffic deaths compared to 29 percent for the nation. Speeding and, more recently, distracted driving are the other major causes of fatal accidents. In September 2017, a state law was passed that made it illegal to read, write, or send a text message while driving. In the same year, of more than 530,000 car accidents, 100,687 or 19 percent were caused by distracted drivers. One in every five car accidents in Texas was caused by a distracted driver.

While the state's traffic record has improved over time, it does not compare well to that of most other states. In 2020, Texas was ranked 6th in the nation with the worst drivers and 1st for speeding. Texas's average highway speed limit is 80 miles per hour, compared to the national average of roughly 68 miles per hour. The state ranks 17th in deaths per 100 million miles driven. As of February 2020, not one day had passed in 20 years without a traffic related fatality in Texas.

The Texas Department of Transportation (TxDOT) is widely viewed as one of the most successful state agencies in lobbying the legislature for appropriations. However, it too follows the state pattern of scarce resources for government agencies. Highway mileage and public transportation have not kept up with population growth, and road and bridge maintenance has lagged seriously. TxDOT's Texas Transportation Plan 2040 recommends that Texas invest nearly $400 billion in state and federal monies to maintain, repair, and expand roads, or about $15 billion each year through 2040.[66]

Faced with strong legislative opposition to new taxes, how should highway improvements be financed? Texas has relied on government borrowing through sale of bonds, but this resource is approaching its limits. Historically, Texas officials showed a marked preference for toll roads built by private companies. However, strong public opposition to toll roads, particularly to privately run toll roads, resulted in their being limited by the 84th Legislature. For a discussion of toll roads and other issues related to infrastructure financing, see Chapter 11, "Finance and Fiscal Policy."

In keeping with state officials' encouragement of private transportation efforts, Texas Central Partners, a private developer, is planning construction of a high-speed passenger rail for a 90-minute trip between Dallas and Houston. It will run through 11 counties with nearly 250 miles of track. Supporters hope this $20 billion plan for the nation's first bullet train will be complete by 2024. The biggest issues involve eminent domain concerns and public funding; but with nearly a third of the land acquired through purchase, the plan is moving forward. This train is projected to bring in $2.5 billion in taxes and provide more than 1,000 permanent jobs. As of September 2020, the train had been approved by the Federal Railroad Administration. It was expected that construction would begin in the first half of 2021, after approval by the federal Surface Transportation Board.

Compared with highways, public transportation has less governmental and user support. Only a few Texas cities have light rail (such as Austin's Capital MetroRail) for public transportation. In Texas, 95 percent of public transportation is by bus. Statewide, the proportion of commuters using public transit has increased slightly since 2000, but cities have varied in usage (El Paso and Austin up but Dallas and Houston down).[67]

In 2020, Texas had eight urban transit agencies serving areas with 200,000 or more residents. These agencies provide approximately 90 percent of Texans' public transit trips. The most common organizational form (seven of eight) is a metropolitan transit authority (MTA), which is a regional government that can impose taxes and service the central city and surrounding suburbs. The Texas Department of Transportation (TxDOT) has little role in the planning, finance, or operation of MTAs. In addition, 30 urban transit agencies and 39 rural transit systems served smaller communities. More than 135 operators provided transportation services to the elderly and to individuals with disabilities under varying arrangements with local governments.

Regulating Tourism, Parks, and Recreation Tourism is the third largest industry in the Lone Star State. The state park system attracts 7 to 10 million visitors a year (both Texans and out-of-state tourists) and usually generates over $1 billion a year for the economy. With Texas ranked 49th in state money spent on parks in the first years of this century, however, state parks were suffering deterioration in quality and services. Fewer parks and park amenities hurt business and were a loss to middle- and working-class Texans, many of whom depend on public parks for recreation. Since 2007, appropriations for the Texas Department of Parks and Wildlife have fluctuated. The 2009 legislature kept the increased level of funding, but the revenue-strapped 2011 legislative session reduced the budget. The 2013 session increased appropriations but to less than the 2007 level. This amount was reduced by the 2015 legislature.

In 1993, the legislature passed a law that granted all money generated by taxes on sporting goods to be spent on state parks and historic sites. However, only about 40 percent of the collected taxes have been given to state parks. A constitutional amendment proposed in the 86th legislative session requires 100 percent of all taxes from sporting goods to go to parks and historic sites. In November 2019, this amendment was adopted by Texas voters. A poll conducted by the Texas Parks and Wildlife Foundation found that 84 percent of Texans surveyed supported protection of natural areas, and it found parks to be "necessary for a healthy and active lifestyle."[68]

Environmental Regulation

Among Texas's many public policy concerns, none draws sharper disagreements than how to maintain a clean and safe environment while advancing business development that will provide jobs and profits. Because of the nature of its industries and Texans' love for driving, the Lone Star State has been among the most polluted states for years. Texas industries, for example, produce more toxic contaminants (chemical waste) than do those of any other state. This grim reality confronts local, state, and national policymakers; and decisions of all three affect quality of air and water.

Since the early 1970s, federal policies have driven state and local environmental efforts, with Texas officials generally resisting or slowing the impact of federal policies. Mandates from the national level have been issued by the U.S. Environmental Protection Agency (EPA) and by the U.S. Congress through the Clean Air and Clean Water Acts. Under the Obama administration, the EPA became more active, and the number of conflicts with Texas officials increased. Their responses have included public complaints, legislation introduced by the state's representatives in Congress, requests for waivers, and state-filed lawsuits. Under former Attorney General Greg Abbott and his successor, Ken Paxton, suits against the federal government became much more common, particularly in the environmental area. (From January 2009, when President Obama took office, through mid-May 2021, there were 62 suits, including 31 against the EPA.) Concern about climate change and Texas's substantial greenhouse gas emissions have also increased federal–state conflict.

Texas businesspeople usually support state policies designed to forestall federal regulations. Tracking corporate Texas's every step, however, is a growing array of public watchdogs (such as the Sierra Club) that inform the public concerning environmental problems. Environmental groups have embraced technology to aid their cause. Cell phone cameras and GPS help document pollution, and social media are major tools for organizing and informing the public.

Air and Water The Texas Commission on Environmental Quality (TCEQ) coordinates environmental policy in the state. Unfortunately, it has come under so much influence from the businesses it regulates that TCEQ is accused of being another example of agency capture. For example, TCEQ's top leadership often overrules recommendations from the agency's technical staff and specialists if they conflict with the business goals of those with political connections. Permitting of a West Texas nuclear waste site provides an example. In 2009, after several years of controversy and against the unanimous recommendation of staff specialists, TCEQ's executive director ordered a license issued to Waste Control Specialists, LLC for construction of a low-level radioactive waste site. Within six months, the executive director left TCEQ and went to work for this operator. One observer has noted that from 1993 to 2010, "former TCEQ higher-ups—including commissioners, general counsels, and a deputy director … earned as much as $32 million lobbying for the industries they once policed."[69]

Air quality has been a source of pride in San Antonio. Through 2018, it was the only major U.S. city never to have been in nonattainment status (though it had come close). San Antonio's success in attracting the Toyota plant came in part because of its clean air record. With a growing population and contaminants blowing in from oil and gas production in nearby Eagle Ford Shale, air quality has declined since 2008. By 2015, local leaders were worried about receiving nonattainment status if the EPA toughened standards.

Texas's growing population and economy have increased demand for electric power. Many recent environmental conflicts between the EPA and Texas have involved pollution produced by coal-burning power plants. Significantly cleaner natural gas is becoming the preferred fuel for generating plants in Texas and elsewhere because of its lower cost. Wind and solar power are making small but growing inroads.

Water is another important issue in a state that is largely arid. Texas's growing population, industry, and irrigation-based agriculture face serious water shortages. In addition, drought and flooding are regular problems for many areas.[70] TCEQ, working with local prosecutors, deals with contamination of waterways. Major sources of water pollution include industry (through both air emissions and improper

Image 12.2 Cracks in the dry bed of Lake Lavon, northeast of Dallas. Texas's alternating periods of drought and flooding, together with the highly unequal distribution of rainfall from one region to another, make water policy a critical element of the state's development.

MATT SLOCUM/AP Photo

— Competency Connection —
☼ **CRITICAL THINKING** ☼

With limited control over the weather, what can we do to better deal with alternating drought and flooding?

disposal of toxic waste), agriculture (particularly from chemical fertilizer, manure, and pesticide runoff), and poorly treated sewage. Three sets of interconnected issues frame the water supply debate:

- Conflicts over who controls the water: Under Texas law, surface water (in lakes and rivers) belongs to the state, but citizens and companies may be granted rights to it. Water is over appropriated—that is, if every entity actually received the amount it has been allocated by the state, then lakes and rivers would be dry. Underground water (called groundwater) has almost no regulation. Under a legal concept known as the **rule of capture**, landowners own the water below the surface of their property. Problems arise when upstream landowners pump so much water that downstream landowners' wells and springs dry up.

- Desire of metropolitan areas and parts of Central and Western Texas to build lakes and lay pipelines to capture and move water from wetter areas, such as East Texas: Many communities want to keep their water. Others object to the loss of land to lakes and damage to rivers and wetlands. Closely related are conflicts among the users of water—agriculture, cities, and industry—and with environmentalists over who gets priority over water.

- Maintenance of the quality and quantity of underground water: Underground reservoirs of water, such as the Ogallala aquifer (in part, located in the Texas Panhandle) and the Edwards aquifer (located in South Central Texas) supply water for many cities, farms, and rivers. Depleting these underground water sources threatens industries and people that rely on them.

Most Texans agree that their state needs an effective water plan. Texas has had a series of water plans, but they have had little impact. In 2013, the legislature agreed to a two-pronged approach. With approval of voters, $2 billion from the state's Rainy Day Fund would be (1) to encourage conservation and (2) to build new water projects, such as reservoirs. No one believes that the plan will fully solve the water shortage problem, but people are encouraged that some action is being taken. Rainy Day money is being used more for projects than conservation. With continued growth of population and the needs of agriculture and industry, conflicts over water continue to grow in importance.

The issue of water supply is made more critical by Texas's periodic droughts, which are often followed by flooding. Between 1980 and 2020, Texas experienced more than 260 weather and climate disasters costing an excess of $1 billion each, including 17 droughts, 70 severe storms, 8 flood events, 7 wildfires, and 1 freeze.[71] A Senate bill passed during the 86th legislative session authorized taking $1.7 billion from the Rainy Day Fund to be used to pay for flood control projects and repairs from flooding throughout the state. (The 2010–2011 drought, for example, cost $8–13 billion; and associated fires destroyed more than 4 million acres of timber, pasture, and residences.) In a majority of years, there are lesser droughts or floods in one or more regions of the state. Water problems are also discussed

rule of capture
A rule of law that a landowner can capture and own the natural resources extracted from the land. Thus, groundwater belongs to the landowner.

in Chapter 1, "The Environment of Texas Politics," and financial implications are covered in Chapter 11, "Finance and Fiscal Policy."

Hazardous Waste Hazardous waste is a fact of modern life. From use of low-level radioactive materials for disease diagnosis in hospitals to industrial production of plastics and chemicals, we generate large quantities of dangerous waste. This waste ranges in danger from high-level radioactive material with potential toxicity for thousands of years to nonradioactive hazardous waste. Producers of hazardous materials want to get rid of waste as cheaply as possible, and they have the money and incentive to succeed in keeping costs of disposal low. Although environmental groups in Texas have increased in power and political skill, they generally can only delay and modify actions favored by pollution producers. For its part, much of the public simply says "Not in my backyard" (NIMBY).

Concerning low-level radioactive waste, there has been a series of political skirmishes stretching back to the 1970s, lack of a coordinated plan, and a growing amount of waste. By 2009, a private radioactive waste dumpsite had been established in sparsely populated Andrews County near the border with New Mexico and a permit issued by TCEQ. In 2012, the first loads of waste arrived. Initially, under terms of an interstate compact, the waste was only to be from Texas and Vermont. From 2012 into 2016, however, 82 percent of the waste was from outside the two compact states.[72]

Substantial campaign contributions and lobbying by the site's developer, Waste Control Specialists, and its owner led to charges of crony capitalism (government officials favoring and subsidizing their friends in the private sector who have helped them). In 2018 the Texas site was the only one in the nation serving the estimated $30 billion a year demand for disposal,[73] and there were proposals to expand the dump's size and to allow storage of higher-level radioactive waste.

Generated largely by Texas's petrochemical industry, nonradioactive hazardous waste stored in landfills presents another environmental dilemma. Poorly stored materials may leak into the water table or nearby waterways, or this pollution may contaminate the soil above them. Some housing and commercial land developers covet landfill sites for their building projects because of costs and location. TCEQ has tended to approve less restrictive guidelines for these sites. As the state's population increases in the years ahead, even greater demands will be placed on the quality of its air, water, and land.

✓ **12.4 Learning Check**

1. True or False: Business regulation in Texas tends to be tough on businesses.
2. What are some demands that state environmental policymakers must balance?

Answers at the end of this chapter.

🔲 Immigration

LO 12.5 Describe the various aspects and complexities in Texas's immigration policy.

Immigration policy is often thought of as a federal responsibility. In practice, however, states also are involved. A policy issue that has received attention from federal and state governments, including Texas, is how to treat immigrants without lawful immigration status (undocumented immigrants).

Chapter 1, "The Environment of Texas Politics," provides context regarding immigration to Texas. It notes the failure of several attempts to end pro-immigration policies during the 84th session of the Texas Legislature in 2015. Attempts to eliminate a policy allowing noncitizens, including some immigrants without lawful immigration status, to pay in-state tuition at public universities and colleges failed. In 2017, the Texas legislature passed a bill banning "sanctuary cities." It allows local law enforcement officers to question the citizenship of anyone they detain or arrest, including persons stopped for a routine traffic violation.

The 84th Legislature did pass House Bill 11, a law that attempts to boost border security and fight crime linked to unlawful immigration.[74] Among other provisions, HB 11 increased penalties for human smuggling, authorized hiring more state troopers, and created an intelligence center to analyze crime data.[75] For his part, Governor Abbott continued Governor Perry's use of the Texas National Guard to patrol the state's border with Mexico.[76]

Other states, such as Arizona and Alabama, have passed legislation that has been described as harsh toward immigrants.[77] Texas, however, grants in-state college tuition to some immigrants without lawful immigration status. A potential explanation for why Texas has different policies than those of other states is the role of business groups, in particular the influential Texas Association of Business. These groups argue that repeal of the in-state tuition law

Image 12.3 Texans protest the expansion of immigration detention centers during the COVID-19 pandemic; they are concerned with the alleged abuse and mistreatment of those detained in these centers.

https://grassrootsleadership.org/

Competency Connection
✿ **CRITICAL THINKING** ✿

Are detention centers the best response to illegal immigrants coming into Texas?

would be bad for the economy because Texas businesses need a highly educated workforce.[78] Moreover, Mexican Americans are a major and growing part of the Texas electorate; and there has been a long and close, if sometimes testy, relationship with Mexico.

Business groups in Texas argue that the nation requires comprehensive immigration policy reform.[79] In 2012, President Barack Obama signed an executive order, the Deferred Action for Childhood Arrivals (DACA). This order allowed children brought to the United States illegally to apply for deferred action for deportation and to apply for a work permit with specific requirements. In 2018, in a U.S. district court, Texas Attorney General Ken Paxton sought an injunction against the federal government to end DACA. He requested that the federal government stop issuing or renewing additional permits under this law. The court agreed with the legal arguments made by Paxton, but it declined to issue an injunction. Finally, on June 18, 2020, the U.S. Supreme Court temporarily blocked the Trump administration from dismantling a program that has protected nearly 700,000 undocumented children (roughly 107,000 in Texas) who were brought illegally to the United States. This matter was remanded back to the Department of Homeland Security (DHS), which could provide a more thorough reasoning to end the program. On January 20, 2021, President Joe Biden's first day in office, he issued a memo calling on the Secretary of Homeland Security, along with the Attorney General, to preserve and fortify DACA in concert with applicable laws. On May 15, 2021 President Biden met with DACA recipients in the Oval Office to bring attention to the issue of overhauling immigration laws.

In December 2014, President Obama issued an executive order on immigration known as Deferred Action for Parental Accountability (DAPA). This order allowed as many as four million immigrants without lawful immigration status to remain in the United States. (See Chapter 1, "The Environment of Texas Politics," for more information on DAPA.) Texas, joined by 25 other states, sued the Obama administration on the legality of DAPA. In February 2015, federal district court Judge Andrew Hanan, located in Brownsville and an appointee of George W. Bush, issued a stay prohibiting implementation of DAPA. This case was appealed to the U.S. Supreme Court, which reached a 4–4 tie and thus let the district court's ruling stand.[80] Constitutionality of the president's executive order has not yet been determined.

Immigration policy is contradictory. The United States is a nation of immigrants, yet it struggles to develop immigration policy. Some people say that they do not want immigrants, yet immigrants (whether with or without lawful immigration status) work (oftentimes in undesirable jobs), pay taxes, and are a reason why Texas continues to grow both economically and in population.[81]

✓ 12.5 Learning Check

1. True or False: Texas business groups took an equally hard line on both border policy and treatment of undocumented immigrants.

2. Has Texas policy been harsher on border security or undocumented immigrants?

Answers at the end of this chapter.

Conclusion

A variety of actors beyond the legislators and the governor shape Texas public policy, including the bureaucrats who implement it. The state's public policies affect many aspects of Texans' lives. The education system faces challenges created by serving large numbers of disadvantaged students, coupled with a reluctance to devote sufficient state resources to education. Texas has a large proportion of poor and working-class citizens needing help for health and human services; but this segment of the population has little political power to effectively satisfy their needs. In the areas of economic development and regulation, public policy has often tended to serve the interests of business over those of consumers. Immigration remains a controversial and unsettled issue for both the nation and the State of Texas.

Chapter Summary

LO 12.1 Describe how public policy is made in Texas. Public policymaking is a dynamic process in which a variety of actors, including the bureaucracy, play a vital role in shaping the nature of policy. Models and the policymaking process are useful tools for understanding policy. Texas's political culture and political process produce public policies that are responsive to business and government elites but that provide a weaker social safety net than the majority of other states. Success of state agencies in Texas is influenced by vigor of their leaders, lack of resources for most agencies, and elite access.

LO 12.2 Analyze major challenges faced by the Texas education system. Whether in public school districts, institutions of higher education, or the legislature, policymakers face the challenge of achieving educational excellence at a price that Texas taxpayers can afford and that voters will support. Texas schools face the challenge of a changing student body—more ethnically diverse and from less affluent families. Failure to respond to the challenge is likely to damage the state's economy. Testing remains a major tool for trying to improve education in the state. It is also a source of great controversy. Better serving the needs of Texas's rapidly diversifying population and the top 10 percent rule have been major issues in college admissions.

LO 12.3 Describe the major health and human services programs in Texas, and discuss how efforts to address the needs of its citizens have been approached. State responsibility for many public assistance programs and the state's high poverty rate continue to place demands on Texas's social service agencies to assist needy families and those physically or mentally ill, aged, or disabled. Health and human services programs in Texas are politically weak and poorly funded.

LO 12.4 Compare the roles of government in generating economic development while maintaining a safe, clean, and prosperous environment for the state's residents. Privatization of service delivery has a mixed record in Texas, with some major failures. Whether deregulation (the current direction of regulators) will be more effective than regulation in protecting the public interest remains unresolved. Meanwhile, Texas consumers demand low-cost utilities, safe and plentiful drinking water, and cleaner air. State regulators tend to be protective of the industries they are charged to regulate. Deterioration of state parks because of funding shortages may cause Texas to lose tourist dollars. Texas has long had major pollution problems and public policies that have done little to improve the environment. Challenges to polluters are increasing, but change is slow. Ownership, protection, use, and availability of water have become major public policy issues.

LO 12.5 Describe the various aspects and complexities in Texas's immigration policy.
Texas immigration policy has contradictions that reflect the state's reality. State leaders express concern about the security of the border. Legislators passed a bill to assist in strengthening the border. On the other hand, Texas has not passed the kinds of strong anti-immigrant policies adopted in some other states. Business leaders have urged adoption of legislation to encourage education of young, undocumented immigrants. Texas business people also recognize that they need workers and the purchasing power of immigrants, whatever their legal status.

Key Terms

affirmative action, p. 480
deregulation, p. 495
elite access, p. 468
equal opportunity, p. 480
Medicaid, p. 485
Medicare, p. 488
privatization, p. 486

public policy, p. 464
rule of capture, p. 501
State of Texas Assessment of
 Academic Readiness (STAAR),
 p. 476
Supplemental Nutritional Assistance
 Program (SNAP), p. 487

Temporary Assistance for Needy
 Families (TANF), p. 487
Texas Essential Knowledge and
 Skills (TEKS), p. 475
top 10 percent rule, p. 481
workers' compensation, p. 492

Learning Check Answers

✓ 12.1 **1.** False. Public administrators must make many decisions not clearly specified in the law. Their own views, their bosses' preferences, and their agency culture all make a difference in how they apply laws passed by the legislature.

2. The vigor of agency leaders, resources, and elite access are particularly important in determining how successful agencies are in achieving their policy goals.

✓ 12.2 **1.** Major criticisms include whether the test used measures real learning, that tests overshadow or distort other learning (teaching to the test), whether tests should be used to evaluate teachers and administrators, that a particular test is too hard or too easy, that tests discriminate against some students, and that standardized testing weakens local control.

2. According to the top 10 percent rule, Texas students graduating in the top 10 percent of their high school class must be admitted to the public college or university of their choice.

12.3 **1.** Health and human services programs are at a disadvantage in Texas because of the state's political culture and the lack of resources and organization of those needing the services.

2. Medicare is better funded than Medicaid.

12.4 **1.** False. Regulation of business in Texas tends not to be tough on businesses (consider the Railroad Commission, for example).

2. State environmental policymakers must balance federal directives, business pressures, and demands from environmental groups.

12.5 **1.** False. Business groups played a major role in convincing political leaders to support education for potential workers, whatever their status.

2. Texas policy has been harshest toward border security.

13 The Criminal Justice System

Learning Objectives

13.1 Describe the different classifications of criminal offenses.

13.2 Analyze issues of the death penalty in Texas.

13.3 Explain the role of Texas's jail and prison system in handling corrections and rehabilitations.

13.4 Compare the juvenile justice system to the adult correctional system.

13.5 Evaluate the fairness of Texas's justice system.

Image 13.1 Despite reform laws in Texas that have helped decrease recidivism, incarceration rates remain high.

Mayra Beltran/©Houston Chronicle

— Competency Connection —
☼ CRITICAL THINKING ☼

Texas has been rated one of the top states in terms of percentage of people incarcerated. What factors are contributing to high rates of incarceration in Texas?

Crime and punishment affect the lives of all Texans, especially those who commit crimes, victims of criminals, law enforcement officers, judges, lawyers, probation and parole officers, jailors, prison personnel, and many others. Taxpayers bear the economic burden of paying for our justice system's institutions, personnel, and programs. As the following murder case reveals, however, administering criminal justice can be a slow and imperfect process.

In 1996, a young, White, 19-year-old woman, Stacey Stites, was abducted, raped, and murdered in Bastrop, Texas. Rodney Reed, a Black man, was found guilty of this crime and given the death penalty by an all-White jury in 1998. Reed initially claimed he didn't know Stites; however, DNA evidence collected from Stites's body matched Reed's DNA. Then Reed changed his story, claiming that he and Stacey were having an affair and that they had consensual sex the day before she was murdered.

Stites had been living with her fiancé, Jimmy Fennell, a Bastrop police officer. She was scheduled to go to work on April 22 at 3:30 a.m.; but when she didn't show up, her co-worker called the police. Nearly six months after Stites's murder, Reed was arrested and charged with kidnapping, beating, attempted rape, and murder of another woman. Similarities in the two cases led police to further investigation.

During this investigation, a hair was found on Stites' body that couldn't be traced to Reed, so Fennell became a person of interest. The case against Reed was heavily dependent on DNA evidence, because there was neither additional physical evidence nor eyewitness testimony. Nevertheless, the jury found Reed guilty; and the prosecutor called for the death penalty due in large part to allegations of his previous attacks on six other women. Reed had been charged but acquitted in one of these cases. The allegations of past attacks could have swayed the jury toward the death penalty.

Bryce Benjet, Reed's attorney, has been working on the case for over 18 years. Benjet claims he has evidence and witness statements that may clear Reed; and he asserts, "I don't think you can ignore the role that racism plays in our criminal justice system. In a rural part of Texas the accusation of a black man raping a white woman is essentially a charge."[1]

The Innocence Project, an organization that works to exonerate wrongfully convicted felons, has repeatedly requested that a belt used to strangle Stites should be tested for DNA; but the Texas Court of Criminal Appeals has denied this request. Reed's legal team of forensic scientists also disputes the timeline for the murder as laid out by the prosecution. The team argues that it's possible that Stites was killed before she should have left for work. Forensic experts admitted that the prosecution's estimated time of Stites's death was not necessarily accurate.

Stites's fiancé, Fennell, was accused in 2007 of detaining and raping a woman while he worked as a police officer in Georgetown. Fennell pled guilty to a lesser charge and was sentenced to 10 years in prison. He was released in March 2018. While Fennell was incarcerated, he allegedly confessed to Arthur Snow, a member of the Aryan Brotherhood, that he had killed Stites. Snow gave a sworn affidavit that Fennell confessed to killing Stites because of her affair with Reed. Another affidavit came from Charles Fletcher, a Bastrop County police officer and friend of Fennell and Stites. Fletcher said that Fennell told him, before Stites was murdered, that he believed she was having an affair with a Black man. Another affidavit, given by a former Bastrop sheriff's deputy, Richard Derleth, states that employees who worked with Stites would warn her when Fennell came to the store where she was employed, so that she could "run and hide from Jimmy."[2] In addition, a man who lived in the apartment below Fennell and Stites stated that he often heard verbal and potentially physical abuse taking place in the apartment upstairs; but Bastrop police did nothing about his report.

On November 15, 2019, the Texas Board of Pardons and Paroles unanimously recommended a 120-day reprieve of Reed's execution to Governor Abbott. Hours after the Board's recommendation, the Texas Court of Criminal Appeals issued an indefinite stay of execution for Reed. His legal team filed an application for appeal based on four claims: (1) the state suppressed exculpatory evidence, (2) false testimony was presented by the state, (3) Reed's trial counsel was ineffective, and (4) Reed is innocent.[3]

In *Brady v. Maryland,* 373 U.S. 83 (1963), the U.S. Supreme Court ruled that any evidence that might exonerate an accused person is **exculpatory evidence**. The Texas Court of Criminal Appeals determined that in Reed's case the first three claims, given above, satisfy requirements of Habeas Corpus, which is "used to bring a prisoner before the court to determine if the person's imprisonment or detention is lawful."[4] Reed was granted an evidentiary hearing, which has been rescheduled for a third time, to be conducted in July 2021. Meanwhile, he remains on death row without an execution date.

Follow *Practicing Texas Politics* on Twitter @PracTexPol

★ Elements of the Criminal Justice System

LO 13.1 Describe the different classifications of criminal offenses.

The Texas **criminal justice system** classifies different types of crimes as either felonies or misdemeanors (discussed in Chapter 10, "The Judicial Branch"). The **Texas Penal Code** is a codified body of laws that covers crime and its punishment. After each legislative session, the State of Texas updates its penal code to include new laws while keeping the core chapters and titles the same. Punishment of crimes in Texas varies from a fine to imprisonment based on the severity and category of a crime. Arguments have been made for continuing to strengthen criminal justice laws and policies while at the same time examining concerns about how Texas carries out justice. Laws may be applied differently based on the resources of local law enforcement and the prevailing attitudes of one's community.

exculpatory evidence Evidence that helps a defendant and may exonerate the defendant in a criminal trial.

criminal justice system The system that involves prosecution, defense, sentencing, and punishment of those suspected or convicted of committing a crime.

Texas Penal Code The body of Texas law covering crimes, penalties, and correctional measures.

Criminal Justice Law

Felonies in Texas are classified according to the seriousness of the offense by five categories: (1) capital felonies, (2) first degree felonies, (3) second degree felonies, (4) third degree felonies, and (5) state jail or "fourth degree" felonies. Less serious offenses are classified as misdemeanors. Features of the Texas Penal Code include **graded penalties** for noncapital offenses and harsher penalties for repeat offenders. First-, second-, and third-degree felonies may involve imprisonment and fines in cases involving the most serious noncapital crimes. Some lesser offenses (especially those involving alcohol and drug abuse) are defined as state-jail felonies (so-called fourth-degree felonies) and are punishable by fines and confinement in jails operated by the state. The three classes of misdemeanors (A, B, and C) may involve county jail sentences and/or fines. (See Table 13.1 for categories of noncapital offenses and ranges of penalties.) People who engage in organized criminal activity, repeat offenders, and those who commit hate crimes (crimes motivated by bias against a person's race, ethnicity, religion, age, gender, disability, or sexual preference) are punished as though the offender had committed the next higher degree of felony. This practice is called **enhanced punishment**.

Under the Texas Penal Code, a person commits murder if there is evidence of intent to kill or cause serious bodily harm to the victim. Presence of additional circumstances, such as the victim's age or role as a law enforcement official, can make the crime a **capital felony**, for which the death penalty may be applied.

Criminal Justice Policy

Policymaking in Texas takes into account public opinion, the state's budget, and federal court rulings. The Lone Star State's political culture requires elected officials to be seen as "tough on crime." Lengthy imprisonment is expensive, however, and Texas has one of the highest incarceration rates in the nation. Detention practices that do not result in cruel and unusual punishment (including provision of adequate facilities, healthcare, and prisoner safety) add to the cost of confinement. Increasing racial and ethnic diversity in Texas also creates tension among all its residents. These factors influence the state's policies with regard to criminal law. Criminal law in Texas has not been balanced, particularly when it comes to race and ethnicity. Two areas where criminal justice reform is needed are in drug and hate crimes.

Drug Crimes and Drug Courts Since the 1980s, arrests for drug possession have ballooned in Texas. Most arrests are for possession of a controlled substance. Many people who are prosecuted for low-level drug crimes are dealing with a range of other issues, including mental illness, homelessness, and poverty. Prisons and jails are not equipped to treat these problems. Untreated inmates

graded penalties
Depending on the nature of the crime, noncapital felonies are graded as first degree, second degree, third degree, and state jail; misdemeanors are graded as A, B, and C.

enhanced punishment
Additional penalties or prison time for those who engage in organized crime or hate crimes, and for repeat offenders.

capital felony
A crime punishable by death or life imprisonment without parole.

Table 13.1 Selected Texas Noncapital Offenses, Penalties for First Offenders, and Courts Having Original Jurisdiction

Selected Offense	Offense Category	Punishment	Court
Murder Theft of property valued at $300,000 or more	First-degree felony	Confinement for 5–99 years or life Maximum fine of $10,000	District court
Theft of property valued at $150,000 or more but less than $300,000 Marijuana drug possession (50 to 2,000 pounds)	Second-degree felony	Confinement for 2–20 years Maximum fine of $10,000	District court
Theft of property valued at $30,000 or more but less than $150,000 DWI (third offense)	Third-degree felony	Confinement for 2–10 years Maximum fine of $10,000	District court
Theft of property valued at $2,500 or more but less than $30,000 Possession or fraudulently using someone's identifying information	State-jail felony	Confinement for 180 days to 2 years Maximum fine of $10,000	District court
Theft of property valued at $750 or more but less than $2,500 Resisting arrest	Class A misdemeanor	Confinement for 1 year Maximum fine of $4,000	Constitutional county court and county court-at-law
Theft of property valued at $100 or more but less than $750 Presenting a fraudulent degree	Class B misdemeanor	Confinement for 180 days Maximum fine of $2,000	Constitutional county court and county court-at-law
Theft of property valued at less than $100 Possession of drug paraphernalia	Class C misdemeanor	No confinement Maximum fine of $500	Justice of the peace court and municipal court (if offense committed within city limits)

— Competency Connection —
✿ **CRITICAL THINKING** ✿

In analyzing Table 13.1, do the punishments fit the crimes?

are more likely to continue using drugs and commit other crimes when released. Texas has relied heavily on incarceration as a primary response to drug offenses. However, state officials have slowly evolved in the methods used to handle drug crimes.

In the current century, state legislators have searched for less costly and more effective ways to address high incarceration rates for drug offenses. Solutions include easing parole criteria for nonviolent offenders, establishing in-prison treatment options, and creating specialty drug courts (see Chapter 10, "The Judicial Branch"). The 84th Legislature opted out of a 19-year-old federal policy that denied food stamps to felony drug offenders for life. Texas now allows those who are first-time felony drug offenders to receive food stamp benefits (although they are still ineligible for cash help through welfare). Offenders who commit second drug offenses lose these benefits. Forty-nine states, with the one exception being South Carolina, have either ended the food stamp ban or have modified it. Research from Harvard University's Olin Center for Law, Economics, and Businesses showed that recently released felons provided full access to public benefits were less likely to return to prison within a year.[5] States with a modified ban have imposed stipulations on receiving aid, such as drug tests. In addition to denying social service benefits to drug offenders, criminal laws have included harsh penalties. As a result, state jail and prison populations have increased dramatically over the last 40 years. When Texas legislators shifted their focus to rehabilitation and reintegration of offenders into society, they achieved positive outcomes. After reforming its criminal justice policies, the Lone Star State experienced a reduction in crime.

Criminal justice reformers report racial disparities in arrests and incarceration rates involving people in possession of a gram or less of controlled substances in Travis County. A study found that 29.4 percent of possession cases involved African Americans, yet only 9 percent of the population of that county is African American. Travis County stands out among counties as having 2.5 times more drug possession cases than other Texas counties. Its courts have seen a 67 percent increase in felony-related drug possession cases. The study also found that 5 percent of possession arrests were made when police were responding to a medical or mental health crisis.[6]

All Texas counties with populations over 550,000 must establish drug courts. These courts provide more extensive supervision than other programs. An example of a successful drug court is in McLennan County, where the DWI-Drug Court was created in 2008. This county court-at-law was recognized in 2019 as having the state's most outstanding program. It has probation officers, a defense attorney, a prosecutor, a chaplain, and substance abuse counselors. The program is set apart from others because of it's unique affiliation with Baylor University's psychology department and doctoral students who are an invaluable resource. Although drug court programs have been successful, they are not available to all defendants in Texas.

Access to successful drug court programs by minorities and the poor can also be a problem. An *Austin American-Statesman* investigation found that the structure of the Travis County Drug Diversion Court's program limited access by disadvantaged groups. Between 2010 and 2018, participation in the drug court program by Blacks and Latinos dropped by more than half. Judges observed that low minority participation rates were due in part to lawyers not referring their clients to the program. Defense attorneys argued that the program structure was time intensive and too inflexible. They complained that it required extensive therapy sessions, random drug tests, and additional community service for missed court appointments or failed drug tests. Lower recidivism rates and individual rehabilitation successes confirm that drug courts work. Travis County's drug court offers defendants an opportunity to keep their records clean if they complete the yearlong treatment plan.[7] When Texans who suffer from addiction are incarcerated, the county and state limit the addicted person's ability to become a healthy, productive member of the community. Studies show that people who have been previously incarcerated were 10 times more likely to become homeless than the general population.[8] The cost is much lower for drug treatment programs than for incarceration: under $4,000 per inmate per year for treatment compared to almost $19,000 per inmate per year for incarceration.[9] Equal access to successful programs for all groups, regardless of race, ethnicity, or economic status, should have a positive effect in the criminal justice system; conversely, limited access may well have a negative effect.

Hate Crimes Since 1993, Texas law has provided enhanced punishment for hate crimes, which are criminal acts against another person motivated by bias or prejudice against a group of which the victim is a member. In 1998, one of Texas's most horrific hate crimes occurred in Jasper, located in East Texas. James Byrd, Jr., Black man, was chained by his ankles to the back of a pickup truck and dragged for miles to his death by three White men. Authorities believe that he was conscious throughout the incident until his head hit the side of the road and he was decapitated. In response, the legislature passed the James Byrd, Jr. Hate Crimes Act in 2001. This act strengthened Texas law by identifying specific targeted groups who were the most likely victims of hate crimes.

According to an FBI report released in November 2020, hate crimes are at the highest level in over a decade. In 2019, there were 51 hate crime murders. This number includes 22 people killed in an El Paso Walmart in August of that year. The suspected shooter wanted to scare Latinos into leaving the United States.[10] According to data from the FBI, the number of hate crimes in Texas increased by almost 240 percent from 2017 to 2018.[11]

Violent acts that are perpetrated on specific groups of Texans are a threat to all Texans. In 2019 (the most recent year for which data are available), the Federal Bureau of Investigation identified 407 criminal incidents as hate crimes in the state. This number increased from 192 cases reported in 2017.[12] Race was identified as the primary motivation for Texas hate crimes, followed by hate crimes based on sexual orientation. According to the FBI, Austin leads the state in hate crimes.[13] Policymakers use the collected data to determine if laws and policies are effective.

While Texas's James Byrd, Jr. Hate Crimes Act protects against hate crimes based on race, religion, color, sex, disability, age, national origin, or sexual orientation, it does not protect against offenses based on the victim's gender identity. Since 2007, State Representative Garnet Coleman (D-Houston) and others have worked to get five words added to the Texas hate crimes law—"or gender identity or expression." According to State Representative Coleman, transgender people are 28 times more likely to experience physical violence than others.[14] The former head of the LGBTQ group, Equality Texas, said, "Texas, sadly, leads the country in the number of transgender people who have been murdered. The majority of those people have been transgender women of color."[15] Some Texas cities (including Austin, Dallas, Fort Worth, and El Paso) have ordinances to help protect transgender Texans.

It is noteworthy that district attorneys determine which cases are prosecuted as hate crimes. Their reluctance to use this law is reflected in the fact that there has been roughly only one conviction per year in which the statute has been officially invoked. Often prosecutors have used the law as leverage for a **plea bargain**, in which defendants plead guilty to a lesser charge or receive a shorter

plea bargain
An agreement between the prosecutor and the defendant in a criminal case in which the defendant agrees to plead guilty to a specific charge and in return gets certain concessions from the prosecutor, such as a reduction in charges, a shortened prison term, or probation.

sentence. In response, civil rights groups have called for a law that would require the Texas attorney general's office to conduct a study analyzing the effectiveness of the Hate Crimes Act. To date, no such law has been enacted.

✪ The Death Penalty

LO 13.2 Analyze issues of the death penalty in Texas.

Texas is one of 27 states, along with the federal government, that imposes the death penalty as punishment for the most serious crimes. The death penalty has taken many forms in Texas. Before 1923, counties carried out executions by hanging. After 1923, the legislature required the state to execute offenders by electrocution. Due to a series of court challenges, no executions occurred in Texas between 1964 and 1982. In 1972, in the case of *Furman v. Georgia*, 408 U.S. 238 (1972), the U.S. Supreme Court ruled that the state's use of the death penalty was unconstitutional because its use was arbitrary and racially biased.

Reinstitution of the Death Penalty

Following the *Furman* decision, Texas rewrote its death penalty laws in 1973 to meet the U.S. Supreme Court's demands for standardization and fairness. The first execution under the new law occurred in 1982, when Texas became the first state in the nation to use lethal injection. During the past three decades, no state has executed more capital felons than Texas (565 men and six women executed from January 1982 through May 2021). Texas has performed roughly 39 percent of the nation's executions even though only 8.1 percent of the nation's population lives in the Lone Star State.[16]

A capital murderer can receive the death penalty in a variety of circumstances. Murder becomes a capital felony if the victim was younger than 10 or if the victim was a police officer, firefighter, or prison employee acting in his or her official capacity. In addition, murders become capital felonies when they occur during the commission of another felony, such as robbery or rape.

Murder for hire, serial murders (includes killing a pregnant woman or her unborn child), and inmate-on-inmate murder are also capital felonies. Although state law allows the death penalty after a second conviction for rape of a child under the age of 14 or in cases involving human trafficking in children for sexual purposes, legal commentators argue this law is unconstitutional. The U.S. Supreme Court has ruled that the death penalty can only be imposed for murder. Through June 2021, the Texas law had not been challenged.

After a jury has found a defendant guilty of a capital offense, jurors must unanimously determine whether the accused represents a continuing threat to society and whether circumstances in the defendant's life warrant life imprisonment rather than death. The minimum sentence for a capital felony is life imprisonment without parole. If the state seeks the death penalty, all jurors must agree to the sentence. The death certificate of someone who has been executed lists the cause of death as "judicially ordered execution." Capital punishment remains controversial, particularly when one considers the issue of racial bias.[17]

The issue of racial bias in use of capital punishment has never been fully resolved. Trial courts have allowed testimony that a person's race may make the accused a continuing threat to society. In the case of Duane Buck, an African American, who was sentenced to death for a 1995 murder in Houston, a psychologist testified, "race [was] a factor associated with future dangerousness." The psychologist provided similar testimony in five other cases involving Black or Latino defendants. All were sentenced to death. In 2000, then-Texas Attorney General John Cornyn agreed to new trials for these five defendants because of possible racial bias in the psychologist's testimony. Buck, however, was not granted a new trial because his attorney, not the prosecutor, had hired the psychologist to testify about race. In 2011, Buck appealed to the U.S. Supreme Court, but his appeal was denied, even though the justices described the psychologist's testimony as "bizarre and objectionable." Buck filed a subsequent appeal claiming ineffective counsel because his lawyer had solicited the racially biased testimony that resulted in his conviction. On October 5, 2016, the U.S. Supreme Court heard oral arguments in Buck's case. His lawyers argued that the death sentence he was given was racially biased. On February 22, 2017, the U.S. Supreme Court ruled in favor of Buck. The Court stated, "law punishes people for what they do, not who they are."[18] Duane Buck's sentence was commuted from death to life in prison.

Another issue that is controversial is whether there is racial bias by prosecutors seeking the death penalty. In Harris County, where Duane Buck was tried, prosecutors are three times more likely to seek the death penalty for Black defendants than for Whites. Twenty of the last twenty-one defendants that received the death penalty in Harris County were people of color. In October 2019, the first White person since 2004 was sentenced to death in Harris County.[19] African Americans are overrepresented on Texas's death row. They make up approximately 12 percent of the state's population but almost 44 percent of its death row inmates. The *Texas Tribune* has created an app called "Faces of Death Row" that shows photos of death row inmates, gives a summary of their crimes, identifies the age and race of each inmate and the location of each crime, and includes the amount of time each prisoner has spent on death row. Users can scan through over 200 inmate photos and use filters to find specific inmates based on age, gender, race, or time spent on death row.[20]

In addition to issues regarding racial bias, questions have arisen about the possible innocence of some of the people who have been executed. Moreover, concerns remain about the method used to execute capital felons and the callousness of some officials. For nearly 30 years (December 1982 through July 2012), Texas used a three-drug process that first rendered a prisoner unconscious, then induced paralysis, and finally stopped the heart. In 2011, prison administrators became concerned about a shortage of the execution drug used to render prisoners unconscious, sodium thiopental. Texas officials contacted Oklahoma officials for advice on dealing with the scarcity of this drug. Records show that the Oklahoma assistant attorney general wrote colleagues that the state might help Texas in exchange for football tickets to the Red River Rivalry, a football game between the University of Oklahoma and the University of Texas.[21] Although the lawyer was criticized for being so callous about the death penalty, no drugs were exchanged.

Because of the unavailability of some of the drugs in the three-drug mix, Texas prison officials now give a lethal injection of pentobarbital, the same drug used to euthanize animals. State officials stockpiled pentobarbital (sold under the trade name Nembutal) after European pharmaceutical manufacturers announced in 2011 they would no longer produce the drug for use in human executions.[22] When Texas ran out of the drug in September 2013, the state turned to compounding pharmacies for custom-made pentobarbital. Compounding pharmacies are unregulated by the U.S. Food and Drug Administration (FDA). In October 2013, several death row inmates in Texas filed a federal civil complaint against the Texas Department of Criminal Justice (TDCJ). This complaint alleged that TDCJ had falsified a prescription for pentobarbital, purchased from a Houston compounding pharmacy, for an inmate and facility that did not exist. Attorneys for the inmates argued unsuccessfully that using untested drugs from unregulated pharmacies was against the Eighth Amendment's ban on cruel and unusual punishment. TDCJ did not have a physician's prescription for the compounded drugs, required by state law in most cases. When the pharmacy requested return of the pentobarbitol, TDCJ refused to do so.

In addition to altering the drug protocol for lethal injections and using compounding pharmacies to obtain necessary drugs, states have responded to shortages of drug supplies in other ways. One approach is the sharing of drugs between states. When Texas officials needed an additional vial of pentobarbital for a 2013 execution, Virginia's Department of Corrections supplied the drug. In September 2015, Texas reciprocated by furnishing Virginia officials with three vials of pentobarbital for an upcoming execution.[23] In April 2016, the Virginia legislature authorized the state to contract with compounding pharmacies to supply drugs for executions. Further, the legislation allowed prison officials to keep confidential the names of the state's drug suppliers. Texas passed a similar law in 2015. Ability of the Lone Star State to maintain the confidentiality of its suppliers' names was challenged. In April 2019, the Texas Supreme Court ruled that TDCJ can withhold the name of the compounding pharmacy that provided execution drugs in 2014. As of June 2021, Texas had 16 doses of pentobarbital stockpiled, according to the *Texas Tribune*. Further complicating this issue is the lack of uniformity and oversight of death penalty practices.

Revisiting the Death Penalty

Imposition of the death penalty has declined across the United States and in Texas in recent years. Concerns about possible executions of innocent people have had some effect. (From 1973 through June 2021, Texas released 13 wrongfully convicted death row inmates.) As of 2005, juries have had a choice in the punishment phase of a death penalty case: They may choose to give life without parole or the death penalty. This choice has provided an alternative punishment for capital felons.

Some states have placed a moratorium on the death penalty.[24] A **moratorium** is a delay or suspension of an activity or law. In March 2020, Colorado became the 22nd state to abolish capital punishment; and the Colorado governor commuted all existing death sentences to life without parole. Although the American Bar Association has encouraged all states with death penalty to at least consider a moratorium, Texas legislators have consistently rejected the idea. The Texas Moratorium Network (TMN) argues that if Texans were better educated on the death penalty, capital punishment would be temporarily, or perhaps even permanently, suspended.

One factor that supports continued use of the death penalty is deterrence. Nevertheless, according to the Death Penalty Information Center, from 1990 to 2016, states with the death penalty had higher rates of homicide than states without the death penalty.[25] A survey of the nation's top academic criminologists indicates that 88 percent of these experts do not believe the death penalty deters homicides.[26] These findings have been challenged, however, as not establishing a causal relationship between executions and deterrence.

According to the Death Penalty Information Center, five counties have been responsible for one in five executions since the death penalty was reinstated in 1976. These counties are Harris, Dallas, Bexar, and Tarrant Counties in Texas, and Oklahoma County in Oklahoma. From 1976 to 2019, the same counties were responsible for 315 out of 1,493 executions. Professor Evan Mandery of John Jay College for Criminal Justice states, "It doesn't really make sense to talk about the death penalty in the United States. The death penalty is exclusively a Southern phenomenon."[27] The South accounts for the majority (80 percent) of the nation's executions. Death Penalty Information Center's data show that "murder rates in non-death penalty states have remained consistently lower in comparison with death penalty states" and the gap has grown since the 1990s.[28]

A problem in determining whether the death penalty deters crime is that the time between sentencing and execution is quite lengthy. According to the TDCJ, the average time spent on death row prior to execution is nearly 11 years.[29] Some argue that the punishment loses its deterrent effect because people do not see the immediate impact of the death penalty. Former Texas Attorney General Jim Mattox interviewed several condemned inmates who were ultimately executed. Based on the inmates' responses, Mattox concluded, "It is my own experience that those executed in Texas were not deterred by the existence of the death penalty. I think in most cases you'll find that the murder was committed under severe drug and alcohol abuse."[30]

Some capital defendants are exempt from the death penalty. As the result of U.S. Supreme Court decisions and state law, for example, the death penalty cannot be used as punishment for anyone who was younger than 18 when committing a capital crime (*Roper v. Simmons*, 543 U.S. 551 [2005]) or anyone who is "mentally retarded" (now classified as intellectually disabled) (*Atkins v. Virginia*, 536 U.S. 304 [2002]). This penalty cannot be imposed if a defendant is found to have been mentally incompetent at the time of committing a capital crime.

Another factor affecting who receives the death penalty is whether the convicted person is mentally ill. Texas law requires that defendants must understand the connection between execution and acts that led to their conviction.[31] Establishing mental illness in Texas, however, requires significant

moratorium
The delay or suspension of an activity or law. A moratorium may be imposed when something is seen as needing improvement.

evidence. For example, the state has continued to seek the execution of some individuals who may have suffered from mental illness in one form or another. This includes the cases of Bobby Moore, in which the U.S. Supreme Court tossed out a lower court's ruling that he wasn't intellectually disabled based on nonmedical standards; John Battaglia, who (according to several forensic psychologists) suffered from bi-polar disorder; and Andre Thomas, who (while incarcerated for the murder of his ex-girlfriend and two small children) plucked out both his eyes with his bare hands and ate one of them. Thomas was described by Texas Court of Criminal Appeals Judge Cathy Cochran as "clearly 'crazy,' but . . . also 'sane' under Texas law."[32]

The U.S. Supreme Court, under *Atkins v. Virginia*, allows each state to determine a procedure for determining intellectual disability. In April 2019, the Texas House passed a bill that would have created a pretrial hearing to determine intellectual disability that could exempt a defendant from the death penalty. However, the Texas Senate's Criminal Justice Committee removed the pretrial requirement from the bill. Ultimately, the bill went to a conference committee to reconcile the two versions, but a compromise could not be reached and it died. Currently, the state allows courts to determine how to decide a defendant's intellectual ability. In 1990, Bobby Moore, as mentioned earlier, fatally shot a store clerk during a robbery in Houston. He was sentenced to death. In 2017, the U.S. Supreme Court tossed out the Texas Court of Criminal Appeals ruling that Moore was not intellectually disabled and thereby not exempt from the death penalty. The Court determined that Texas's methodology for diagnosing intellectual disabilities was inadequate. Further, the Court found that Texas relied too heavily on I.Q. scores and other factors not rooted in medicine. A Texas appeals court resentenced Moore to life in prison in November 2019, making him eligible for parole. On August 6, 2020, after serving 40 years on death row, Moore was paroled because he was deemed by the U.S. Supreme Court to be intellectually disabled.

▧ Point/Counterpoint

Should Solitary Confinement Be Used as an In-Prison Punishment?

The Issue Death row inmates are placed in solitary confinement, also known in the United States as administrative segregation, throughout their entire time on death row. Other inmates in state and federal prisons across the United States receive the same punishment. As of June 2021, an estimated 300,000 inmates are held in solitary confinement or administrative segregation in the country, an increase due to the pandemic. Texas is one of the top-ranking states in the nation that uses solitary confinement as an in-prison punishment.

Administrative segregation occurs when an inmate is separated and isolated from other inmates. The incarcerated person is placed in a room without any human contact except with prison guards. On weekdays prisoners may be in their cells up to 23 hours, emerging only to shower and spend time outdoors ("in the yard") under strict supervision. Weekend conditions are even more restrictive, with some prisoners remaining in isolation for up to 48 continuous hours. Inmates are placed in solitary confinement for a variety of reasons in addition to having received the death penalty, including: committing violent acts against correctional officers or other inmates, membership in a gang, or for their own safety.

(Continued)

Many proponents of solitary confinement believe it is an effective form of punishment. No court has ruled the practice to be a violation of the U.S. Constitution's ban on "cruel and unusual punishment." Yet others criticize the practice as being cruel, inhumane, and a violation of human rights. President Barack Obama was the first U.S. president to denounce the use of solitary confinement in prisons. In 2019, New Jersey passed a law limiting the length of solitary confinement to 20 consecutive days for all prisoners and detainees, making it one of the strongest laws in the nation. Other states (but not Texas) are discussing reforms.

For	Against
1. Solitary confinement can protect inmates from the general population. Inmates who are pedophiles, murderers, or ex–gang members may face threats from other prisoners. Solitary confinement provides security and protection, making it difficult for high-risk inmates to be harmed.	1. Solitary confinement may cause mental illness in inmates or exacerbate existing mental health conditions. Many inmates suffer from mental illness. Isolating an inmate may intensify a mental illness, causing hallucinations, delusions, paranoia, and disorientation. Inmates in isolation lose a sense of control of their environment, which leads to anxiety, claustrophobia, and violence toward prison officials or themselves. Prisoners such as death row inmates, with no hope of release and limited human contact, present a significant risk to themselves and correctional officers.
2. Solitary confinement provides correctional officers with the ability to maintain order. Guards may use solitary confinement as a form of punishment and also as a means of deterrence. Inmates do not want to face weeks or longer in isolation. Further, solitary confinement can be used when prisoners are a threat to staff or other inmates.	2. A primary goal of prisons should be to offer inmates a chance at rehabilitation. Solitary confinement is used as a punishment, in some cases for minor infractions. Rehabilitation of inmates requires human interaction and access to services and programs. Inmates in solitary confinement have no human contact other than with correctional personnel and no access to services or programs. Yet each year, about 1,200 Texas inmates are released directly from solitary confinement into society. Prisoners who go directly back into society may have difficulty reintegrating because of their previous lack of social interaction or emotional or mental problems.
3. In some cases, solitary confinement can be used to keep prisoners safe from themselves. Inmates in solitary confinement are less likely to commit suicide because they are carefully monitored. In addition, suicidal prisoners often use objects in their cells, such as bedsheets, towels, phone cords, or personal items like socks to harm themselves. However, in solitary confinement they do not have access to these items. Therefore, solitary confinement can be used to keep inmates safe.	3. Some deem solitary confinement a form of torture. The United Nations Convention against Torture states that "torture is an act through which severe pain and suffering, whether physical or mental, is inflicted intentionally on someone for punishment, intimidation, information, or other reasons, such as discrimination." Opponents say this description is applicable to solitary confinement.

— Competency Connection —
✿ **CRITICAL THINKING** ✿
What punishments do you believe are appropriate to lessen violence in prisons?

Another case concerning the question of mental illness involved John Battaglia. In May 2001, he called his ex-wife on the phone so she could hear him murder their nine-year-old daughter, Faith, and their six-year-old daughter, Liberty. After the shooting, Battaglia went with his girlfriend to a bar and a tattoo parlor, where he had two roses with the girls' names tattooed on his arm. Battaglia then left a voice message to his daughters, "I love you and wish you had nothing to do with your mother. She was evil and vicious and stupid."[33] Battaglia's attorney argued that his client was delusional and incapable of communicating effectively with his lawyers. In arguments before the U.S. Fifth Circuit Court of Appeals, the attorney noted that Battaglia believed others were to blame for the murder of his daughters. Included among them were the Ku Klux Klan, his ex-wife, and even the Dallas County district attorney. In 2016, the Fifth Circuit Court of Appeals granted a stay of execution to allow lower courts to determine Battaglia's mental competency. However, Battaglia was found to be malingering, and his execution was reinstated. On February 1, 2018, he taunted his ex-wife, saying "hello" to her before he was injected with a lethal dose of phenobarbital.

✓ 13.2 Learning Check

1. Which Supreme Court case deemed the death penalty unconstitutional in 1972 and why?
2. According to the Texas Department of Criminal Justice, what is the average time spent on death row before an execution?

Answers at the end of this chapter.

✚ Correction and Rehabilitation

LO 13.3 Explain the role of Texas's jail and prison system in handling corrections and rehabilitations.

Confinement in a prison (either a penitentiary or a state jail) or in a county or municipal jail is designed to punish lawbreakers, deter others from committing similar crimes, and isolate offenders from society, thus protecting the lives and property of citizens who might otherwise become victims of criminals. Ideally, while serving a sentence behind bars, a lawbreaker will be rehabilitated and, after release, will obey all laws, find employment, and make positive contributions to society. According to a *Houston Chronicle* article in 2019, the recidivism rate was nearly 23 percent in Texas.[34] This article conerns inmates in state prisons or jails who violated conditions of their release or who committed other crimes after being released and were therefore resentenced to prison.[35] Juvenile justice systems, which actually conduct their proceedings as civil cases and are, therefore, outside the criminal justice system, have a similar design but with a greater emphasis on rehabilitation than punishment. Descriptions of the criminal justice system in this section relate to adults; references to the juvenile justice system include individuals between the ages of 10 and 16.

Texas's rate of incarceration has declined in recent years, although it remains high. As of 2021, Texas ranked sixth in the nation with the highest rate of incarceration. In response to high crime rates at the end of the 20th century, the Texas legislature and the Texas Board of Pardons and Paroles concentrated resources on incarceration and punishment. A few years later, the legislature shifted its emphasis to rehabilitation. This shift in policy reduced the rate of incarceration, as evidenced by a modest decrease in the inmate population between 2013 and 2014. In that period the prison population decreased by about 1 percent or approximately 2,200 inmates.[36] After 2014, changes in criminal justice policies and resulting practices continued to improve the integration and rehabilitation of inmates. This new focus has been instrumental in reducing both the number of people incarcerated and the crime rate.

The Texas Department of Criminal Justice

The principal criminal justice agencies of the state are organized within the Texas Department of Criminal Justice (TDCJ). This department has a four-part mission:

- To provide public safety
- To promote positive behavioral changes
- To reintegrate offenders into the general society
- To assist crime victims

The organizational structure of TDCJ includes governance by the nine-member, non-salaried Texas Board of Criminal Justice; a full-time executive director hired by the board; and directors of the department's divisions, who are selected by the executive director. Each division director is responsible for hiring division personnel. Nearly 35,000 Texans worked for TDCJ in 2021. These employees are responsible for a prison population in 2020 of approximately 122,000 inmates. According to TDCJ spokesperson Jeremy Desel, ". . . that's the lowest prison population for TDCJ since 1995."[37] The Community Justice Assistance Division monitors local community supervision programs that oversee an additional half a million offenders on probation.

Providing Public Safety For many years, the primary focus of the Texas legislature, and therefore the TDCJ, was on providing public safety. Legislators classified an increasing number of actions as felonies, lengthened sentences for all types of crimes, funded construction of additional prison units, and helped to balance the state's budget by reducing drug treatment programs and other interventions intended to change behavior. Because a large prison population and high recidivism rates proved costly, a bipartisan legislative effort redirected funding efforts to expand treatment and counseling services.

The current focus on rehabilitation and re-entry has reduced the escalating imprisonment rates that Texas experienced in the 20th century. Reversing a decades-long trend, Texas's adult prison and juvenile detention populations began to decline in 2010. Officials predicted that the number of inmates in the state's prisons would remain steady and is expected to fall 1.6 percent below the TDCJ's operating capacity for fiscal years 2019–2024.[38] In a longer period (2012–2020), Texas's general population is expected to increase by 5 percent;[39] therefore, the incarceration rate remains in decline, even though the actual number of inmates may increase. Since 2011, Texas has closed eleven state prisons, and in 2020 it temporarily shut down three others. These actions suggest that increasing the use of probation and job training is a smart fiscal choice. Between 2005 and 2015, lower numbers of prisoners and fewer prison facilities saved taxpayers more than $3 billion.[40] Additionally, the three prisons permanently shut down in 2020 are saving Texans over $20 million, according to the TDCJ spokesman.

The TDCJ division responsible for ensuring public safety is the Correctional Institutions Division. Staff members in this division supervise the operation and management of state prisons, state jails, and other specialized facilities. Private contractors operate seven prisons, four state jails, and various prerelease, work, substance abuse, and intermediate sanctions facilities. Figure 13.1 shows the location of prison and state jail units in Texas.

Maintaining a trained workforce to provide security has been an ongoing problem for the Correctional Institutions Division. Historically, difficult working conditions (including low pay and lack of air conditioning in prison facilities) has produced annual turnover rates for correctional officers (nearly 30 percent). High turnover rates create a number of problems. Chronic understaffing causes a dangerous struggle in TDCJ. Demand for corrections officers sometimes results in the state's hiring personnel who have not been properly screened, who fail to meet physical requirements for the job, or who have not been adequately trained to deal with the challenging inmate population.[41] Salary increases, signing bonuses, and job cuts in the oil and gas industry may improve staff retention. As of 2021, the average salary of full-time corrections officers was slightly more than $42,600 a year.

An additional problem faced by TDCJ is lack of air conditioning in its facilities. Out of the 104 state prisons in Texas, only 30 have air conditioning in their inmate housing areas. A 2014 study conducted by the University of Texas

📊 How Do We Compare...

In Prison Incarceration Rates?

Number of Prisoners per 100,000 Adult State Residents (as of December 2019) (includes both federal and state prisoners)

Most Populous U.S. States	Number of Prisoners per 100,000 Residents	U.S. States Bordering Texas	Number of Prisoners per 100,000 Residents
California	399	Arkansas	762
Florida	552	Louisiana	887
New York	282	New Mexico	408
Texas	709	Oklahoma	840

Source: E. Ann Carson, *Bureau of Justice Statistics Bulletin: Prisoners in 2019*, (Washington, D.C.: U.S. Department of Justice, October 2020), https://www.bjs.gov/content/pub/pdf/p19.pdf.

Competency Connection
⚙ CRITICAL THINKING ⚙

Analyze the chart. Does the rate of incarceration in neighboring states have an impact on Texas? If so, how?

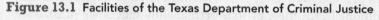

Figure 13.1 Facilities of the Texas Department of Criminal Justice

Source: Texas Department of Criminal Justice, https://www.tdcj.state.tx.us/unit_directory/unit_map.html.

— Competency Connection —
☼ CRITICAL THINKING ☼

How does having a state jail or prison facility in or near a community affect the community?

Law School's Human Rights Clinic described prison conditions as "violating both international human rights standards and the Constitution." Since 2007, fourteen inmates have died because of extreme heat exposure inside Texas prisons. In 2013, more than 90 correctional officers reported heat-related illnesses. This is a serious problem for inmates and correctional officers who are taking high blood pressure medications, psychotropic medications, have asthma, are older than 55, or have diabetes. Inmates who suffer heat exhaustion or a heat stroke often avoid getting medical treatment because the cost for doctor's visits has risen from a $3 copay to a $100 annual fee that is collected on the inmate's first physician's visit.[42]

In 2014, prisoners in the Wallace Pack Unit (Navasota) filed a lawsuit alleging lack of air conditioning was cruel and unusual punishment. This lawsuit was in response to the deaths of 11 Texas inmates in the heatwave of 2011. In other units, the heatwave was over 100 degrees for 74 days in that year. TDCJ has no maximum temperature standards for its facilities. In some Texas prisons, the heat index on a unit has been measured at nearly 150 degrees. TDCJ has claimed the primary reason for not installing air conditioning in Texas state prisons was the cost; yet in 2013, TDCJ spent $750,000 to install climate control units for hogs living in the large barns on prison grounds. Although inmates can purchase personal electric fans in the commissary, the $20 cost is prohibitive for many indigent prisoners. Clothing such as shorts, which could keep inmates cooler, is not provided but is available for purchase in the commissary. Cost again, is an issue for indigent prisoners. Seventeen wrongful death lawsuits have been filed against TDCJ for heat-related inmate deaths. The union that represents correctional officers has expressed support for the plaintiffs' complaints. Since 2006, TDCJ has paid over half a million dollars in workers' compensation claims for heat-related illnesses. In June 2014, some state prisons had large fans installed to reduce heat. Even so, the Centers for Disease Control (CDC) stated that fans sold to inmates and the fans installed by TDCJ were ineffective in Texas's extreme heat conditions.[43] In February 2018, TDCJ settled the Pack Unit class action lawsuit and agreed to install air conditioning in housing areas. TDCJ has also implemented revised heat protocols and has discussed other ways to combat hot conditions. However, TDCJ has ignored this problem and recommendations made by several organizations for many years, so it remains to be seen if or when all state prisons in Texas will have air conditioning.

Lack of air conditioning in most prisons is further exacerbating the growing number of prisoners and correctional officers with COVID-19. Prison conditions act as an incubator for COVID-19. There's no way to social distance, and basic methods to protect against this contagious disease are nearly impossible behind bars. A report from the University of Texas at Austin has shown that Texas inmates are "testing positive at a rate 40% higher than the national prison population average."[44] Texas is second to Florida for infection rates in prison, per 10,000 people. According to TDCJ data, more than 34,000 inmates and nearly 12,000 staff had tested positive for the disease by June 2021, and at least 260 inmates and 48 employees had died.[45]

There have been concerns about how TDCJ has handled COVID-19. For example, initially employees were not allowed to wear protective masks inside a prison, but in April 2020, TDCJ reversed its decision and allowed correctional officers to wear masks issued by the agency. At the beginning of the pandemic, Texas, along with Michigan, New Jersey, and Ohio had the highest count of prison COVID-19 deaths in the nation. All four states were reporting 30 to 40 deaths each month. The other three states were able to quickly reduce the number of their inmates dying to about five a month. However, at the end of the summer, Texas continued to report more than 30 inmates dying monthly. The University of Texas at Austin study also found that "several incarcerated Texans who had died from the virus had already been approved for parole, while more than half were eligible for parole. A large majority of those who died in jails were not yet convicted of a crime."[46] TDCJ says they have taken precautions since the beginning—stopping visitations, requiring daily temperature checks, and making more than 1.5 million cloth masks for their employees and offenders.

Image 13.2 Texas state prisons deployed tens of thousands of COVID-19 tests that will be administered at TDCJ prison units throughout Texas.

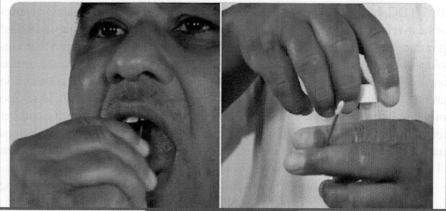

Thanks to Texas Governor Greg Abbott (@GovAbbott), along with the help of the Texas Department of Emergency Management (@TDEM), TDCJ this week is beginning a new expanded testing program to help prevent the spread of COVID-19.

For more info, please visit the TDCJ Facebook page.

Marjorie Kamys Cotera/Bob Daemmrich Photography/Alamy Stock Photo

— Competency Connection —
✪ **CRITICAL THINKING** ✪
Why should the state help inmates combat COVID-19 in Texas prisons?

administrative segregation
Commonly referred to as solitary confinement, this practice isolates an inmate in a separate cell as punishment, typically for violent or disruptive behavior.

The Lone Star State's prisons face other problems. Several gangs exist within the prison system. In 2020, more than 4,400 violent inmates and gang members (identified by prison officials as "security threat groups") were held in **administrative segregation**, often referred to as solitary confinement. (See the Point/Counterpoint feature in this chapter.) Commentators argue that prisoners without hope of release and with limited human contact present a significant risk to correctional officers. According to the *Texas Observer*, inmates in "restrictive housing" (another word for solitary) are kept isolated for at least 22 hours a day in a small cell. A study done by the Association of State Correctional Administrators and the Arthur Liman Center for Public Interest Law at Yale University found that Texas has more prisoners in long-term solitary confinement than any other state and the federal prison system combined. According to TDCJ, there are nearly 1,300 inmates that have been in isolation for six years or longer, more than 680 inmates who have been isolated for six to ten years, and 129 inmates in isolation for between 20 and 30 years. Roughly 18 Texas inmates have been in solitary for more than 30 years.[47] Black and Latino inmates account for roughly two-thirds of the prison population, but they make up three-fourths of inmates in solitary. "Ten of the 12 prison gangs that TDCJ identifies as 'security threat groups' are Black or Latinx," according to the *Texas Observer*.[48]

TDCJ has tried focusing on treatment and rehabilitation programs rather than solitary confinement. One such program, Gang Renouncement and Disassociation Process (GRAD), allows gang members to break ties with their gangs and go through a nine-month intensive program. This rehabilitation effort includes behavioral therapy, anger management courses, and substance abuse programs. Inmates who successfully complete the GRAD program can be released from administrative segregation and returned to the general prison population.

Oversight of solitary confinement is an issue that has been brought before the Texas legislature many times, but it has not received serious consideration. Other states have made changes to curtail the practice. Georgia has agreed to limit solitary confinement to two years. In 2019, New Jersey's campaign of prison reform led to a law that has nearly eliminated long-term isolation. Colorado, in 2017, became the first state to adopt United Nations standards for prisoner treatment, defining solitary over 15 days as a form of torture. Will reform of solitary confinement be prioritized by the Texas legislature and TDCJ?

The Texas inmate population's general characteristics highlight some common issues, including poor education levels and substance abuse. Approximately 45 percent of Texas prisoners have less than a high school education, and one-third are functionally illiterate. Nationally and in Texas, the number of inmates with a serious mental illness is also high. Studies of jail and prison populations report that roughly 56 percent of state prisoners, 45 percent of federal prisoners, and 64 percent of jailed inmates suffer from a mental illness. The profile of Texas prisoners in Table 13.2 identifies some characteristics of the state's incarcerated population.

Promoting Positive Behavioral Changes Several departments and divisions of TDCJ are responsible for programs to correct or modify the behavior of incarcerated felons. Training and instructional programs are used to rehabilitate inmates and equip them with a means of self-support after release. Self-discipline and education are the primary means of combating **recidivism** (criminal behavior resulting in reimprisonment after release). Every prisoner must be given a job but may elect not to work. Prisoners' labor saves money for state and local governments, and, in some instances, it generates revenue for the state. Prisoners repair engines; manufacture furniture, including dorm room furnishings for several state universities; and even make the wooden gavels used by the presiding officers of the Texas legislature.

Southwestern Baptist Theological Seminary operates an extension program at the Darrington Unit, a maximum-security prison near Houston. Inmates can complete a four-year program for a bachelor of science degree in biblical studies that prepares them to assist chaplains and help counsel inmates. In 2018, the Heart of Texas Foundation provided a newly renovated $2.1 million building at the Darrington Unit for this program. From May 2015 to May 2019, each year 33 to 35 inmates were awarded degrees. Program graduates were among the most

recidivism
Criminal behavior that results in reincarceration after a person has been released from confinement for a prior offense.

Table 13.2 Some Characteristics of Texas's Prison Population (2019)

Characteristic	Measurement (Percent)
Gender	
Male	92
Female	8
Race	
African American	33
White	34
Hispanic	33
Type of Offense Leading to Incarceration	
Violent	58
Property	12
Drugs	17
Other	14
IQ	
Average	90.3 points

Source: "Fiscal Year 2019 Statistical Report," *Texas Department of Criminal Justice*, https://www.tdcj.texas.gov/documents/Statistical_Report_FY2019.pdf.

Competency Connection
☼ **CRITICAL THINKING** ☼

How might studying the characteristics of the prison population influence lawmakers' criminal justice policies?

violent criminals; but after graduation, they have traveled to prisons throughout the state to convince other inmates to change their ways. Prison officials report a reduction in prison violence since the program began. Unlike most inmate education programs that are designed to prepare prisoners for parole, Darrington Unit Seminary targets inmates who will likely never be released.

More than one-half of Texas prisoners are enrolled in vocational and academic classes offered through the prison system's Windham School District. In addition, some prisoners take community college and university courses. Thousands of prisoners complete vocational training each year. Other inmates graduate with college degrees ranging from associate's to master's. The state pays tuition costs for vocational training, but once released, the former inmate must reimburse the state. Tuition for college academic courses must be paid by the prisoner.

Reintegrating Offenders A major goal of treatment and education programs is to equip prisoners with the skills needed to succeed upon release. TDCJ's Reentry and Integration Division provides extensive support to released offenders. This division has more than 60 reentry counselors located throughout the state to assist released inmates.

Two divisions are responsible for convicted criminals who serve all or a part of their sentences outside of prison walls: the Community Justice Assistance Division and the Parole Division. The Community Justice Assistance Division establishes minimum standards for county programs involving community supervision and community corrections facilities (such as a boot camp or a restitution center). In cases involving adult first-time offenders convicted of misdemeanors and lesser felonies, jail and prison sentences are commonly commuted to community supervision (formally called adult probation). These convicted persons are not confined if they fulfill certain court-imposed conditions. Through specialty courts, judges have also become directly involved in community supervision (see Chapter 10, "The Judicial Branch").

The Parole Division manages Texas's statewide parole and mandatory supervision system for convicted felons. The seven-member Board of Pardons and Paroles recommends acts of clemency (such as pardons) to the governor and grants or revokes paroles. The board's presiding officer employs and supervises 12 commissioners, who assist the board with parole and revocation decisions. A three-member panel, comprised of at least one parole board member along with one or more commissioners, reviews inmate applications and decides whether to grant or deny parole. The board may impose restrictions deemed necessary to protect the community. If a parolee violates any conditions of release, a board panel determines whether to revoke parole.

Prisoners who have served some portion of their sentences may be eligible for parole. Felons who commit serious, violent crimes, such as rape or murder, must serve 30 to 40 years of "flat time" (without the possibility of having prison time reduced for "good-time" credit for good behavior). Other offenders may apply for parole after serving one-fourth of a sentence or 15 years, whichever is less (minus good-time credit).

Successful reintegration of offenders is complicated by a number of barriers to re-entry. Not only do those convicted of felonies lose many civil rights, such as the right to serve on juries and administer estates, but, along with those convicted of misdemeanors, they also encounter lifetime impediments to employment, housing, and student loans. According to the Equal Employment Opportunity Commission (EEOC), use of blanket exclusions against applicants with arrest or conviction records could violate civil rights laws. Employers can protect themselves from a discrimination claim if they can show "its selection criteria is job-related and consistent with business necessity." Disqualification from employment and housing makes an offender's reintegration difficult. The jobless rate for ex-felons is roughly 27 percent. Many are calling for a new approach to support offenders' reintegration.

One new approach came in 2019 with the passing of House Bill 918, which went into effect in January 2020. This law requires the prison system to help qualified released inmates obtain their birth certificates or Social Security cards, because without these documents it's impossible to find employment. HB 918 also allows released inmates to have certificates showing any training or job skill courses they completed while incarcerated. In order to further assist them

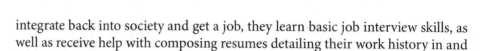

integrate back into society and get a job, they learn basic job interview skills, as well as receive help with composing resumes detailing their work history in and outside of prison.

Further support for ex-convicts has come from community programs, such as that offered by Goodwill of Central Texas. Goodwill focuses on offender assessment and case management while providing training and job placement assistance. Goodwill officials realized that former prisoners need services and guidance as they transition out of the criminal justice system. Staff establish close relationships with ex-offenders and their families; and they provide support through different services, such as education and career help. Goodwill invites others to share their experiences and opinions through its Twitter site, #WorkIsTheAnswer. Programs such as Goodwill's help both the former inmate and the greater community, because successful reentry lowers the likelihood of recidivism.

At the end of 2007, TDCJ prison units housed almost 154,000 adult inmates. By December 2020, that number was reduced to approximately 122,000 prisoners. From 2007 to July 2020, Texas's incarceration rate dropped 34 percent.[49] The state's elected and appointed officials have adopted the view that the better solution is to have inmates on probation working toward integration into society rather than remaining behind bars. Further, this approach is helpful to taxpayers because of lowered costs—probation costs less than $2 a day per probationer compared to incarceration at a cost of more than $50 a day per inmate.[50]

The Texas legislature has passed several pieces of legislation aimed at reintegrating offenders back into society. The 84th Legislature sought to assist first-time offenders who receive deferred adjudication. Many who agreed to deferred adjudication assumed they had no criminal record, which was not true. Although charges were dismissed upon successful completion of deferred adjudication, the offender still had a criminal record. Now, first-time offenders who successfully complete deferred adjudication after committing low-level, nonsexual, nonviolent crimes can petition a court to have their criminal records sealed to the general public. If the request is granted, the offender can check "no" on college, job, housing, and loan applications in response to questions about whether he or she has ever been convicted of a felony or misdemeanor.

The City of Austin has also taken steps to aid those who have served their jail or prison sentences. In 2015, Austin became the first city in the state to "ban the box," a movement that refers to eliminating the criminal-record box on employment applications. Only after a conditional offer of employment has been given can the employer initiate a background check. Austin, along with 36 states and over 150 cities and counties, including Washington, D.C., applies such fair-chance hiring policies to private employers.[51] These types of laws lessen the lifetime effect of a criminal conviction. Roughly three-fourths of people live in an area where "ban the box" or another fair-chance policy has been implemented.

Assisting Victims The fourth prong of TDCJ's mission directs attention to crime victims and their close relatives. The Victim Services Division provides information to crime victims about any change in an offender's status within the TDCJ system, as well as notification of pending parole hearings. Upon a finding of guilt, and before sentencing, victims may deliver victim impact statements in open court. They may also complete written statements that remain available to prison and parole officials. When an inmate is executed, up to five family members and close friends of the victim may witness the execution, as well as up to five family members or close friends of the offender. Procedures are in place to make sure that the victim's and the offender's witnesses remain separated during the entire execution process.

The State of Texas maintains a Crime Victims' Compensation Fund through the Office of the Attorney General. This program provides up to $50,000 to victims and their families for expenses related to a crime ($125,000 in the event of total disability). Covered costs include medical treatment, counseling, and burial expenses that are not covered by insurance or another government program, such as Medicaid. In June 2016, the attorney general's office opened an updated online system to allow advocacy agencies, law enforcement, prosecutors, and victim service providers access to the application form and other information for crime victims. The general public can only view historical information. Those seeking assistance can still contact the attorney general's office by phone. This program is funded by court costs, fees, and fines collected from convicted offenders, as well as juror donations of their compensation for serving as jurors.

Local Government Jails

In addition to prisons and state jails operated by the Texas Department of Criminal Justice, counties and cities across the state operate jails. These facilities are financed largely by county and municipal governments, respectively. Like penal institutions of the TDCJ, local government jails are used to control lawbreakers by placing them behind bars.

All but 19 Texas counties maintain a jail. Some counties have contracted with commercial firms to provide "privatized" jails, but most counties maintain public jails operated under the direction of the county sheriff. Originally established to detain persons awaiting trial and to hold those serving sentences for misdemeanor offenses, county jail facilities vary in quality and, except in some urban areas, do not offer rehabilitation programs. The Texas Commission on Jail Standards has oversight responsibility for county jails. These facilities have not been without problems.

Harris County has one of the largest detention facilities in the nation, housing an average of 9,000 inmates at any point in time. This county also has the highest pretrial lock-up rate in the state and is less likely to release those arrested on personal recognizance bonds than other Texas counties. A personal recognizance bond authorizes a defendant's release based solely on his or her promise to appear at trial. Approximately 70 percent of Harris County jail inmates have not been convicted of any crime, but instead are awaiting trial because they cannot afford to post bond. Being held in county jail prior to trial is not only disruptive to people's lives, but jail conditions place them at risk of serious harm or even death. Fifty-five inmates died while in pretrial custody in Harris County from 2009 through 2015. Some died from untreated medical conditions, others from suicide, and still others as the result of beatings from fellow inmates. In 2017, U.S. District

Judge Lee H. Rosenthal agreed that the bail system of Harris County was unfair to the indigent. The county commissioners court, misdemeanor judges, plaintiffs, and the sheriff have all agreed on a new bail system that would allow roughly 85 percent of defendants to be released on a personal recognizance bond.[52]

A disproportionate percentage of persons being detained are poor or members of historical minority groups. For example, African Americans make up 19 percent of Harris County's population, yet the jail inmate population is 45 percent African American. In April 2016, the district attorney for Harris County unveiled a criminal justice reform plan to reduce overcrowding in the county's jails and to address the disparate treatment of minorities and the poor. The overall three-year goal is to reduce the number of prisoners by approximately 1,800 inmates or 21 percent of the jail population. In 2017, District Attorney Kim Ogg helped begin a diversion program that would allow those caught with four ounces or less of marijuana to take a four-hour drug education program and thus avoid charges.[53] This program is estimated to help 10,000 people a year avoid spending time at the Harris County jail. In January 2019, District Attorney Ogg requested $21 million for hiring additional prosecutors, but the commissioner's court rejected her request. In a statement, the district attorney said her office needs more resources and staff to ensure cases are processed quickly and fairly. However, the Texas ACLU and other civil rights organizations criticized her request because it could increase incarceration rates in Harris County.

Texas has approximately 350 municipal jails, most of which are not regulated by the state. In large cities, these facilities often house hundreds of inmates who have been arrested for a variety of offenses ranging from Class C misdemeanors to capital murder. Those charged with more serious crimes are usually held temporarily until they can be transferred to a more secure county jail.

Private Prisons and Jails

In the 1980s, Texas had some of the nation's worst overcrowding due to the state's tough sentencing guidelines and a rise in illegal immigration apprehensions. Both state and local governments contracted with private companies to construct and operate incarceration facilities and direct prerelease programs. Texas has more privately operated incarceration facilities than any other state. Approximately 10 percent of Texas's inmates are housed in private prisons. These facilities are under the supervision of the Private Facility Contract Monitoring/Oversight Division of TDCJ. The Texas Juvenile Justice Department oversees community-based private contract juvenile facilities. In addition to prisons and jails, private contractors also provide substance abuse treatment programs and halfway houses, where state and county prisoners are confined in privately operated units.

In the past two decades, the state's elected officials realized that incarceration was too costly; thus, they began a move to reduce the length of prison sentences and to limit the number of inmates incarcerated for minor offenses. While good for taxpayers, the smaller prison population had a devastating effect on private prisons. In 2013, two private prisons were closed, one in Mineral Wells and the other in downtown Dallas, because they were no longer needed. In February 2015, prisoners rioted over alleged poor conditions that included lack of medical care and contaminated food at the Willacy County Correctional Center, a privately operated facility in Raymondville (South Texas). The facility was closed because of the extensive damage caused by the riot. From 2011 to 2017, Texas closed eight prisons due to tight budgets and a shrinking prison population. The Legislative Budget Board estimated the state saved nearly $50 million because of the closures.[54]

Critics have expressed growing concern over a justice system that makes money on crime. High recidivism rates produce return "customers" and benefit private prisons. These "for profit" facilities provide little to no job training, and they make inmate–family interactions more difficult. For example, one private prison required prisoners to pay $1 per minute for video conference calls with family members instead of allowing face-to-face visits. Both job training and family interaction are known to reduce recidivism, but private prisons have no incentive to provide either.[55]

✓ **13.3 Learning Check**

1. What are the two primary means of combating recidivism?
2. How has the change in the state's prison population affected private prisons?

Answers at the end of this chapter.

✪ Juvenile Justice

LO 13.4 Compare the juvenile justice system to the adult correctional system.

Texas's juvenile justice system distinguishes between youthful pranks and violent, predatory behavior. In general, young Texans at least 10 years of age but younger than 17 are treated as "delinquent children" when they commit acts that would be classified as felonies or misdemeanors if committed by adults. Children are designated as "status offenders" if they commit noncriminal acts, such as running away from home, failing to attend school, or violating a curfew established by a city or county. From 1957 to 2011, the Texas Youth Commission (TYC) was responsible for the rehabilitation and training of delinquent youth. After several years of scandal highlighting deficiencies in the agency, the 82nd Legislature (2011) abolished the TYC. The Texas Juvenile Probation Commission, the agency that oversaw county juvenile probation departments, was abolished at the same time. As a part of the sunset review process (see Chapter 9, "The Executive Branch"), the legislature created the Texas Juvenile Justice Department (TJJD) to assume the responsibilities of the abolished agencies. The 11-member board of TJJD, appointed by the governor with consent of the Senate, is charged with unifying juvenile justice services from an offender's entry into the system through departure.

State and Local Agencies

Each county has a juvenile probation board that designates one or more juvenile judges, appoints a chief juvenile probation officer, and makes policies carried out by a juvenile probation department. When youth must be incarcerated, the responsibility rests with the TJJD. In fiscal year 2020, approximately 31,000 cases were referred to juvenile probation departments for disposition. A juvenile probation department has discretion to impose a variety of punishments ranging from nonjudicial dispositions (such as referral to social service providers), to probation, to commitment to a TJJD secure facility. The primary goal of TJJD has shifted from sending juveniles to facilities far from their families to keeping them within their local area. If children must be removed from family settings, the law reflects a preference for group homes over correctional facilities.

For over a decade, the Texas Juvenile Justice Department has been rocked by physical and sexual abuse allegations involving staff and other offenders. In 2018, after a massive shakeup over the TJJD leadership, the director, Camille Cain, and others proposed short-term and long-term plans to Governor Abbott. Cain's ideas include some measures that will need legislative action.[56]

In October 2020, Texas Appleseed and Disability Rights Texas, two legal interest groups, registered a complaint with the Department of Justice's Civil Rights Division. This complaint alleged "grievous violations of children's constitutional rights" from the TJJD. Widespread sexual abuse and other scandals have been a long-time problem with youth offenders under TJJD. The complaint reported that youth lockups throughout the nation accounted for roughly 7 percent of reported sexual abuse incidents in 2018, but in Texas the rate of reports was much higher. In four of Texas's juvenile facilities, at least 1 in 8 youths reported sexual victimization. Some of the problems cited in the complaint "include a large number of incidents of physical abuse from staff, staffing shortages, and a lack of mental health workers, a third of whom are not licensed."[57] In the wake of decade-long scandals, the new director of the TJJD began implementing a strategy to address these problems. Director Cain noted in 2018 that the state-run youth lockups have been processing more reviews in order to release qualified youth. The cost to house juveniles is over $400 daily per youth. As costs have increased over the years, there has been an effort to reduce the population in TJJD facilities. As a result. the number of juvenile offenders that were housed dropped from roughly 5,000 in 2005 to around 900 in 2018.[58] Recommendations have called for more community-based programs for youth offenders. Studies show that juvenile offenders kept closer to home in community-based supervised programs are less likely to reoffend than those in state facilities.[59] According to a study by the nonprofit Council of State Governments Justice Center, juveniles in state facilities are 21 percent more likely to be rearrested and three times more likely to commit a felony when they reoffend, as compared to those in community-based programs close to home.[60] There has been a call by many to close state-run youth lockups and replace them with community-based rehabilitation and treatment centers.

Procedures

Although juvenile offenders are arrested by the same law enforcement officers who deal with adult criminals, they are detained in separate facilities. Counseling and probation are the most widely used options for dealing with juvenile offenders, but residential treatment and TJJD facilities remain as alternatives. An arresting officer has the discretion to release a child or refer the case to a local juvenile probation department. Other referrals come from public school officials, victims, and parents. Approximately 130,000 Texas youths enter the state's juvenile justice system annually.

Trials in juvenile courts are termed **adjudication hearings**. Juvenile courts are civil rather than criminal courts; therefore, any appeal of a court's ruling will be made to a higher court with civil jurisdiction. A few cases are ultimately appealed to the Texas Supreme Court. Juvenile court proceedings may be closed to the public by the presiding judge.

A juvenile determinate sentencing law covers more than 20 serious offenses. Under this sentencing provision, juveniles who commit offenses such as capital murder or aggravated sexual assault can be transferred to adult prisons when they reach the age of 19 and can be held there for as long as 40 years. In addition, approximately 1 percent of juveniles charged with serious crimes stand trial and are punished as adults. Prior to a determination of guilt, these young offenders remain in juvenile facilities "separated by sight and sound" from adult offenders detained in the same facility; but once found guilty, convicted youth are transferred to the adult prison system.

An issue Texas legislators are trying to resolve is whether to raise the age of adulthood to 18 for criminal matters. Researchers and lawmakers find that steering 17-year-olds to juvenile courts and lockups instead of adult jails would save money, reduce arrest rates, and eliminate the inconsistent treatment of youth—they can be considered adults in the criminal justice system but still be regarded as children with regard to voting or buying lottery tickets and cigarettes. Federal law requires that 17-year-olds be separated from others when housed in adult prisons or jails, which may be costly to the state and counties. Most studies find that trying youths as adults results in these young people being more likely to reoffend than those held in the juvenile system under similar circumstances.[61] As of 2021, Texas was one of three states that excluded 17-year-olds from the juvenile system. These youthful offenders are handled entirely in the adult criminal justice system.[62] Advocates of reform, such as the Campaign for Youth Justice, argue that adulthood should start at age 18 for criminal justice purposes.[63] In June 2018, Missouri passed a bill that will move the age for juvenile jurisdiction from 17 to 18 by 2021, wherein they will no longer be placed in the adult system. In 2020, Vermont became the first state to expand it's juvenile status to 18 and will raise it up to 19 years old by 2022, with some exceptions for violent offenses.

✔ **13.4 Learning Check**

1. What agency oversees Texas's juvenile justice system?

2. True or False: Young Texans at least 6 years of age but younger than 19 are treated as "delinquent children" when they commit offenses that would be classified as felonies or misdemeanors if committed by adults.

Answers at the end of this chapter.

⬥ Problems and Reforms: Implications for Public Policy

LO 13.5 Evaluate the fairness of Texas's justice system.

Legislators must deal with the 21st-century issues of overcrowding and mental illness in prisons, electronic and scientific technology, changing demographics, and misconduct by district attorneys. It is important for our policymakers to respond to issues within the criminal justice system that will assure fairness for all.

adjudication hearing
A trial in a juvenile court.

Overcrowding and Mental Illness in Prison

Decades of increasing problems with overcrowding in Texas prisons have begun to ease, with the state's overall prison population dropping from a high of 156,500 in 2011 to 122,000 in 2020. This decline comes as a result of aggressive work by the state government to create alternative sentencing options through special courts for drugs, veterans, prostitution, and drunk driving. In addition, expanded rehabilitation, probation, and parole options, together with a general drop in the crime rate, have resulted in a decrease in the state's prison population.[64] Still, many problems exist in the system, especially in municipal and county jails.

Overcrowded facilities and chronic understaffing have caused an increase in inmate-on-inmate violence resulting in serious injury or death. Telford Unit, a maximum security prison that holds more than 2,500 men, is located in Northeast Texas near Texarkana. Problems at this prison have a lot to do with the shortage of guards. In 2018, the prison was short 200 guards and operated with only 65 percent of full-time guards. It has the highest rate of vacancies in the state and the highest rate of serious assaults on staff.[65] The persistent problem of staff shortages, high turnover of staff, and lack of training have also been connected to the increase in the use-of-force by correctional officers on inmates. Since 2015, 19 correctional officers were convicted of misdemeanors involving use-of-force on an inmate. It is difficult to get correctional officers charged for assault or even for homicide, because state law allows more discretion to officers to use force to maintain prison security.[66]

An additional problem is that many inmates have complicating conditions such as mental illness. In Texas, depending on availability of psychiatric facilities, a person with a serious mental illness is 10 times as likely to be incarcerated as to receive treatment. Results can be fatal. The high-profile 2015 death of Sandra Bland in the Waller County jail brought attention to the increasing problem of suicide among the incarcerated. In 2018, prison reports showed that an average of 167 inmates tried committing suicide each month. However, in 2019, TDCJ reported the number of recorded suicide attempts fell from 23 in September to 12 in October. The drastic change comes after TDCJ more narrowly defined what it deemed as a suicide attempt. According to TDCJ's spokesman, Jeremy Desel, "We recognized that we were over-counting."[67] Now TDCJ records a suicide attempt if it's based on a mental-health evaluation of what happened, not the type of incident to which the correctional officer responded. The Commission on Jail Standards has regulations on how to deal with inmates at risk of committing suicide, including face-to-face monitoring of the inmates while in custody.

Inmates at risk of suicide are often dealing with mental health issues. Former Harris County Judge Ed Emmett estimates that approximately one-third of inmates housed in county facilities are mentally ill. Harris County spends about $54 million a year to incarcerate those with mental illness. Many offenders have undiagnosed or untreated mental illnesses that may lead them to commit crimes. The State Commission on Jail Standards has established screening procedures to determine whether someone taken into custody has mental health issues. Although many inmates receive treatment during their incarceration, after they are out of the system, they are left with little assistance. In the 86th (2019)

Legislative session, TDCJ requested $281 million in the two-year budget for medical services for inmates. This would help with dental and other health-care costs, an aging population, and mental health issues. The legislature allocated close to 150 million to TDCJ for 2022–2023.[68]

Technology

Technology now touches many areas of the criminal justice system. Websites and social media provide different avenues for inmates to communicate with each other and the outside world. Forensic science, especially DNA testing, has been a resource that aids both defendants and prosecutors.

Since March 1980, Houston's KPFT has aired *The Prison Show* on Friday nights. This show can be heard live online and downloaded as a podcast. Additionally, the hosts maintain a Facebook page. Families and inmates have an opportunity to communicate through an on-air format. Friends and family members call in to the show while inmates listen. Sometimes the messages are words of encouragement and support; at other times, callers use the time to update an inmate about family matters such as a child's doctor visit.

Image 13.3 Solitary confinement's overuse has had a devastating impact on the mental health of inmates. Mental health issues need to be addressed by the criminal justice system of Texas in order to reduce recidivism, particularly among the mentally ill inmates.

Andrew Lichtenstein/Corbis/Getty Images

— Competency Connection —
❖ CRITICAL THINKING ❖

What type of assistance should mentally ill inmates receive upon release?

Communication technology has raised new issues regarding prisoner contact with the outside world. Cell phones are now the most common contraband item, but their possession is the least-prosecuted offense.[69] Although prisoners do not have direct access to the Internet, until 2016 many inmates had social media accounts, like Facebook pages, that were created and maintained by their families or friends. Some prison officials even advocated for Internet-enabled tablets to provide a distraction and deter inmates from inappropriate activities. In 2016, concerns over prisoners using the Internet to profit from their crimes or to continue criminal activity, along with social media policies that bar running an account in another person's name, led TDCJ to take a harder line. The department announced a rule that bars inmates from having social media accounts, even if maintained by friends or family outside prison walls. Civil liberties advocates question whether the rule violates first amendment free speech rights.[70]

DNA testing, developed by geneticist Alec Jeffreys, transformed the criminal justice system. Biological evidence is used to identify suspects, as well as to exonerate the innocent. The state maintains a DNA database. Both TDCJ and TJJD collect DNA samples from all inmates convicted of felony-level offenses. Convicted felons who receive community supervision must provide DNA samples. Juveniles released on probation who have committed the most serious offenses (for example, murder, rape, or aggravated robbery) or who used a weapon to commit their offenses, must also furnish DNA samples. Crime scene evidence can then be tested against the state's database samples. DNA evidence not only aids in identifying the guilty, it may also establish innocence, which is what occurred in the Michael Morton case. Morton was found guilty of murdering his wife in 1986 and spent 25 years in prison for a crime he did not commit. After meeting resistance from the Williamson County district attorney's office for seven years, Morton's attorneys were able to have a bloody bandana found at the crime scene tested for DNA evidence. The results set him free.[71] Delays that Morton experienced in having evidence submitted for testing are no longer possible due to laws passed by the 82nd Legislature (2011).

Laws, agencies, and commissions have been established by the state to prevent the miscarriage of justice. For example, state law requires all public crime labs to be accredited and DNA evidence to be held for retesting. An 11-member Texas Forensic Science Commission, appointed by the governor, investigates charges of negligence and misconduct.

Exoneration Issues

The Fourteenth Amendment to the U.S. Constitution guarantees that no state may "deprive any person of life, liberty, or property without due process of law." Rules and procedures that must be followed in criminal cases are specifically designed to protect people from losing life, liberty, or property as a result of arbitrary acts by the government. Even so, people are sometimes wrongfully convicted and incarcerated. A few of these inmates may subsequently be found innocent and released. When the state admits a person is innocent of the crime for which he or she was incarcerated, the prisoner is **exonerated**. According to the National Registry of Exonerations, a project of the University of Michigan Law School, 2,468 inmates across the nation were exonerated between 1989 and 2019. Of this total, Texas had 363 exonerations, the most of any state in the nation.[72] Roughly 15 percent of exonerations in the United States were at least partly based on DNA evidence.

Although DNA test results have contributed to the release of innocent prisoners, this evidence is not the panacea that will eliminate all wrongful imprisonment. In fact, only 17 out of 143 people who were released from prison in 2019 (nationally) had DNA evidence to exonerate them.[73] One of the least reliable forms of evidence, and perversely one of the most trusted forms, is eyewitness testimony. Although scientists have long suspected the accuracy of eyewitnesses, law enforcement officials and jurors have presumed its validity. As incarceration rates have risen, so too have wrongful incarcerations. According to the Innocence Project, a group that uses DNA evidence to obtain the exoneration and release of those wrongly convicted, "Nationally, 69 percent of DNA exonerations—252 out of 367 cases—have involved eyewitness misidentification, making it the leading contributing cause of these wrongful convictions".[74] Research indicates several flaws in this type of evidence, including overlooking facial features of people of different races, transference to an individual encountered in a different setting, and poor recall due to the stress of being a crime victim or witness.[75] In response to these concerns, the 82nd Legislature revised state law in 2011 to require police departments and other agencies to develop written procedures for conducting photo and live lineups.

Although most people convicted of a crime are guilty, the probability of exoneration is remote, even for the innocent. The political reality is that to obtain a pardon and be fully exonerated requires the agreement of district attorneys, judges, the Board of Pardons and Paroles, and the governor. Posthumous pardons can be granted, should someone be exonerated after his or her death. The State of Texas compensates individuals wrongfully incarcerated. Someone found innocent after being imprisoned is entitled to $80,000 for each year he or she was wrongly incarcerated, $25,000 for each year on parole or required registration on a sex offender registry, tuition for training or college, a lifetime annuity, and assistance in accessing social service providers. Over the past 25 years, the state has paid over $109 million to more than 100 men and women who were wrongfully sent to prison. In 2019, Texas exonerated 15 people, which was the third highest rate of exonerations in the country.[76] Lump sum payments can be made to the heirs of those exonerated after death. The 84th Legislature established the Timothy Cole Exoneration Review Commission to identify patterns in wrongful convictions and make recommendations on how to limit the number of wrongful convictions in the state. (Timothy Cole was wrongfully convicted of sexual assault and died in prison in 1999. He was exonerated and fully pardoned in 2010.) The commission submitted its report in December 2016. In the report, the commission made broad recommendations to the legislature in such areas as recording interrogations, eyewitness identification, new practices for forensic science, false accusations, and jail house informants.

exonerated
The definition of a person convicted of a crime who has received the state's official declaration of his or her innocence.

Racial Bias in the Criminal Justice System

Changes in the state's demography have affected its justice system. Underrepresentation of Blacks and Latinos in elected and appointed leadership positions is matched by their overrepresentation in the criminal justice system.[77] If the race or ethnicity of those enforcing the law is consistently different from those against whom the law is enforced, the system has less credibility and may be viewed as unfair. Events in Texas and other states illustrate this point.

Protestors across the country have demonstrated to confront the deaths of people of color at the hands of police officers. The Black Lives Matter movement began in 2013 after the killer of Trayvon Martin was acquitted. Then on May 25, 2020, Houston-native George Floyd, an African American, was killed in Minneapolis, Minnesota, while being arrested. A White police officer knelt on Floyd's neck as he was handcuffed, lying face down, and crying out, "I can't breathe," for over nine minutes. The next day, the world watched a video of Floyd's death. This triggered a worldwide protest against police brutality and lack of police accountability. The U.S. Department of Justice, in the wake of Floyd's death, authorized $3 million in grants and established a National Response Center. The Center's focus is to strengthen police reform as well as reduce the use of excessive force by police.[78] Should more be done?

In 2019, according to a report by the attorney general's office, police shot and killed 117 people in Texas. One incident involved African American, Javier Ambler, who died when sheriff deputies in Williamson County pulled him over for failing to dim his SUV headlights. He was held down and stunned with a Taser. Reportedly he told the police officers he wasn't resisting arrest and that he couldn't breathe. Another incident that occurred in Austin involved the death of Mike Ramos, an African American and Latino man. A 911 call said Ramos and his girlfriend were doing drugs in a parking lot. A neighbor recorded a video showing Ramos standing by his car with his hands up, shouting he was unarmed, right before an officer shot a bean bag round, hitting him on his side. Ramos gets back into the car and pulls away as another officer fires bullets killing him. Police confirmed that he didn't have a gun. These are just a few incidents that have occurred in Texas where it seems police used excessive force.

The Texas Commission on Law Enforcement Standards and Education requires law enforcement agencies to provide annual racial profiling reports. Racial profiling is the practice of targeting members of historical minority groups for stops and searches. These racial profiling reports make public the number of traffic stops by race, gender, and age of the person stopped, as well as subsequent action, such as searches and arrests, that resulted from the stops. However, according to a *Houston Chronicle* article, the 2017 Sandra Bland Act was the most recent update to the effort to monitor traffic stops and racial profiling. But researchers found that the Texas Commission on Law Enforcement left out the driver's race in their reports. "After two decades and three separate laws, efforts to identify which of the state's nearly 2,000 law enforcement agencies have glaring racial disparities in their policing have largely failed, yielding only a patchwork of numbers with widely varying degrees of usefulness," according to the *Houston Chronicle*.[79] Instances of racial and ethnic bias are the subject of growing concern as Texas has evolved into a state in which two historical minority groups, African Americans and Latinos, make up the majority population.

The perception of racial bias in the criminal justice system can have deadly results for law enforcement personnel as well. According to a report by the National Law Enforcement Officers Memorial Fund, Texas led the nation in 2019 in the number of officer fatalities. Marcia Ferranto, CEO of the Fund, said the main circumstances under which officers are likely to be killed with firearms involve serving high risk warrants, conducting investigations, and responding to domestic violence calls. Also, many officers are killed in traffic-related incidents.[80] What can be done to stop the divisiveness between police and citizens?

Questions remain about the targeting of members of historical minority groups by the police in the use of lethal force. According to a study by Texas A&M University researchers in 2020, White police officers are more likely to use force than their nonwhite counterparts, particularly in minority neighborhoods. The study found that White officers were 60 percent more likely, on average, than Black officers to use force and twice as likely to fire guns. White officers are "five times as likely to fire a gun in predominately Black neighborhoods," according to the study.[81] The long history of police mistreatment of people of color is a widespread concern. Law enforcement will have a hard time combating crime and protecting civilians if they don't have the trust of the people.

Misconduct by District Attorneys and Prosecutors

The main responsibility of a district attorney (DA) is to represent the State of Texas in criminal cases. A DA works with law enforcement officials to put together a criminal case that may be brought before criminal courts. Although most district attorneys are fair and effective, some unfortunately misuse their power. According to the National Registry of Exonerations, "only 4 percent of prosecutors in the United States who were involved in wrongful conviction cases tainted by prosecutorial misconduct have faced any kind of personal or professional discipline."[82] In June 2018, Stacey Soule, a state prosecutor sat before the House Criminal Jurisprudence Committee and stated that the Texas Court of Criminal Appeals had granted relief in only four cases of prosecutorial misconduct over the past year. The rate of official misconduct by law enforcement officials or prosecutors is highest in murder cases and child sexual assault cases. When misconduct occurs, prosecutors are rarely disciplined.[83] Only a handful of prosecutors face any serious disciplinary action like disbarment from practicing law. Instead, many are simply given a brief suspension or reprimanded by the State Bar of Texas.

The Code of Criminal Procedure requires that DAs not focus on convictions, but instead must see that justice is done. At times, prosecutors are guilty of prosecutorial aggressiveness. In these instances, either law enforcement officials, including the DA, are blind to the possibility that the accused is innocent or they use tactics that increase the likelihood of conviction. Ignoring the primary focus of achieving justice can have serious consequences for both the accused and the prosecutor.

In 1994, Anthony Graves was convicted of capital murder. Charles Sebesta, the district attorney in Burleson and Washington counties, withheld exculpatory evidence and obtained false statements from witnesses in his efforts to send Graves to death row, according to the U.S. Fifth Circuit Court of Appeals. Sebesta was disbarred for his conduct in February 2016.[84] Graves spent 12 years on death row for a crime he did not commit.

Another example of injustice by a DA can be observed in the case of Michael Morton, mentioned earlier. As a result of his failure to disclose exculpatory evidence to both the trial judge and Morton's attorneys, former Williamson County DA Ken Anderson was found in contempt of court. Further, the State

📋 Students in Action

Getting Involved in the Black Lives Matter Movement

Annaleesah Pina, a student at Austin Community College, grew up in a poor part of Houston. She saw the way people of color, including her own family, were treated. Regularly she would hear news about another person of color killed by law enforcement. She was upset about the injustice. She wanted to be a part of the human rights protests in Dallas, where she lived. After hearing about George Floyd's death, she felt a call to action. Pina, along with her boyfriend, decided to make posters and protest outside of Houston's City Hall and Dallas's City Hall for the Black Lives Matter (BLM) movement.

Travis County Justice Complex

Annaleesah is proud of her generation and others stepping forward to give a voice to the voiceless. While at the protest rallies, she saw artistic people sharing their thoughts and ideas about the injustices for minorities through music, art, and

literature. She felt a profound connection to those who wanted to rise up and fight the injustice of police brutality and lack of accountability.

Annaleesah feels the central theme of the Black Lives Matter Movement is justice—for everyone. Protesters chanted and demonstrated with the hope of bringing people of all backgrounds together. In speaking with others in the movement, she found that people were tired of law enforcement officers shooting innocent people because they have the power to do so, with little to no consequences. Annaleesah's boyfriend is a young Black man. She's seen him get nervous or scared when he sees police officers, not because of anything he's done, but because of the color of his skin.

Annaleesah's advice to students is to peacefully get involved—through protests, demonstrations, petitions, voting, and so on. She believes it's our duty as Americans, students, and human beings to speak up and speak out. She advises students to

educate themselves about what's going on. The Black Lives Matter movement is a movement to make people aware of the brutality that people of color have faced and the systemic racism that exists in the United States. The BLM movement has taught Annaleesah how to organize and get involved. She feels it's a good way for students to be active and expand on what they read or see on television. Annaleesah believes that we need activism from all people to help gain attention and make change.

Source: Interview conducted with Annaleesah Pina on January 17, 2021.

Competency Connection
☼ CRITICAL THINKING ☼

Have you been involved in political activism? Why or why not?

of Texas brought a civil lawsuit accusing Anderson of official misconduct in the case. In 2013, Anderson spent 10 days in the Williamson County jail—the same jail where he had served as district attorney. Anderson was also required to serve 500 community service hours, and pay a $500 fine to resolve the contempt case. In addition, his law license was revoked. Morton served 25 years for a crime he did not commit. Anderson, as of 2020, has been the only prosecutor who has spent time in jail for misconduct that led to a wrongful conviction.

One case pending is that of Paul Storey. In 2006, during the robbery of a miniature golf course near Fort Worth, Storey murdered the assistant manager. In 2008, he was sentenced to death. However, in 2017, the Texas Court of Criminal Appeals halted the execution because of a claim that the prosecutor had lied to jurors during the original trial. The prosecutor told the jury that the victim's family was for the death penalty, but the parents vigorously denied this statement; they strongly opposed the death penalty. In October 2019, the Court of Criminal Appeals rejected a lower court's decision to reduce Storey's sentence to life without parole. However, Storey's lawyers have requested that the appeals court reconsider their opinion. As of June 2021, Storey remains on death row without a set execution date. Should Storey's sentence be reduced to life without the possibility of parole?

A district attorney is a powerful figure in the criminal justice system. He or she has the authority to ask the courts, on behalf of the state, to take someone's life, liberty, or property; but the opportunity to misuse that power was limited by the 83rd Legislature. The Michael Morton Law requires prosecutors to disclose almost all relevant information they have on a case to the defendant upon request. Any exculpatory information that might establish a defendant's innocence must be shared with the defendant as soon as the prosecutor obtains it, even if the information becomes available after the defendant is convicted.[85]

✓ 13.5 Learning Check

1. True or False: DNA evidence is a panacea for exonerations.
2. What does the Code of Criminal Procedure require district attorneys to focus on?

Answers at the end of this chapter.

Conclusion

The Texas criminal justice system is complex. Issues of fairness and efficiency remain paramount in ensuring that residents accept the legitimacy, or authority, of the criminal justice system. In recent years, the shift of emphasis in Texas from punishment to rehabilitation has made the state a leader in reducing the number of prisoners and lowering the cost of the criminal justice system. The legal system, however, is not error-free. Issues of concern with criminal justice policies, the death penalty, rehabilitation, and fairness of the process need to be addressed. Only by understanding the system can citizens and lawmakers develop effective solutions.

Chapter Summary

LO 13.1 Describe the different classifications of criminal offenses. Criminal law regulates many types of behavior. Less severe crimes are classified as Class A, B, or C misdemeanors and result in fines or detention in a county jail. More severe crimes include state-jail felonies; first-, second-, and third-degree felonies; and capital felonies. Policies have been adopted to deal with different criminal justice issues, such as substance abuse and hate crimes.

LO 13.2 Analyze issues of the death penalty in Texas. Texas is one of 27 states in the United States that use the death penalty, but there are problems and concerns with the method and usage of this penalty. The number of death penalty cases has declined, but concerns remain about whether innocent people may be executed and whether there is proper handling of the mentally ill on death row.

LO 13.3 Explain the role of Texas's jail and prison system in handling corrections and rehabilitations. Approximately 620,000 Texans were under the supervision of state and local judicial or correctional officers in 2019. Recent changes in state laws have emphasized the rehabilitative role of incarceration. The Texas Department of Criminal Justice has a four-pronged mission to handle issues of correction and rehabilitation: providing public safety, promoting positive behavioral changes, reintegrating offenders, and assisting crime victims.

LO 13.4 Compare the juvenile justice system to the adult correctional system. The juvenile justice system deals with correction and rehabilitation for juveniles (those between ages 10 and 16) and is administered through the Texas Family Code. Years of scandal at Texas Youth Commission (TYC) facilities resulted in abolition of the TYC and the Texas Juvenile Probation Commission. The Texas Juvenile Justice Department replaced those agencies in 2011.

LO 13.5 Evaluate the fairness of Texas's justice system. A number of issues remain problematic for the Texas justice system. These problems include overcrowding in county jails and mental illness in jails and prisons, effects of technological and scientific advances, probable innocence of some inmates, possible racial and ethnic bias in the justice system, and misconduct by district attorneys.

Key Terms

adjudication hearing, p. 535
administrative segregation, p. 526
capital felony, p. 511
criminal justice system, p. 510

enhanced punishment, p. 511
exculpatory evidence, p. 510
exonerated, p. 539
graded penalties, p. 511

moratorium, p. 518
plea bargain, p. 514
recidivism, p. 527
Texas Penal Code, p. 510

Learning Check Answers

 13.1
1. People who engage in organized criminal activity, repeat offenders, and those who commit hate crimes may receive enhanced punishment. This means the offender will be punished as though he or she had committed the next higher degree of felony.

2. True. Most low-level drug offenders are dealing with other issues like homelessness and poverty.

13.2
1. The Supreme Court ruled in *Furman v. Georgia* that the death penalty was unconstitutional because there was racial bias in its application.

2. According to the TDCJ, the average time spent on death row is nearly 11 years.

 13.3
1. Self-discipline and education are the primary means of combating recidivism.

2. Private prisons are closing as the prison population decreases.

13.4
1. The legislature created the Texas Juvenile Justice Department (TJJD) to oversee Texas's juvenile system. TJJD replaced the abolished Texas Youth Commission (TYC) and the Texas Juvenile Probation Commission.

2. False. In general, young Texans at least 10 years of age but younger than 17 are treated as "delinquent children" when they commit crimes labeled felonies or misdemeanors if committed by adults.

13.5
1. False. Although DNA evidence has been used to obtain exonerations, fewer than 20 percent of the wrongfully imprisoned were released because of DNA evidence in 2015.

2. According to the Code of Criminal Procedure, a district attorney's primary responsibility is to seek justice, not convictions.

Glossary

Numbers in parentheses indicate the chapter in which the term is found.

A

adjudication hearing A trial in a juvenile court. (13)

administrative segregation Commonly referred to as solitary confinement, this practice isolates an inmate in a separate cell as punishment, typically for violent or disruptive behavior. (13)

adversarial Reporting featuring opposition and a combative style. Also called attack journalism. (6)

affirmative action Takes positive steps to attract women and members of racial and ethnic minority groups; may include using race in admission or hiring decisions. (12)

affirmative racial gerrymandering Drawing the boundaries of a district designed to favor representation by a member of a historical minority group (for example, Black Americans) in a legislative chamber, city council, commissioners court, or other representative body. (5)

agenda setting Affecting the importance given issues by government and public leaders. (6)

alternative dispute resolution (ADR) Use of mediation, conciliation, or arbitration to resolve disputes among individuals without resorting to a regular court trial. (10)

annex To make an outlying area part of a city. Now, this must be done by vote or petition of those to be annexed. (3)

appellate jurisdiction The power of a court to review and decide cases after they have been tried elsewhere. (10)

appointive power The authority to name a person to a government office. Most gubernatorial appointments require Senate approval by two-thirds of the members present. (9)

appointment-retention system A plan for judicial selection in which the governor makes an appointment to fill a court vacancy for an interim period, after which the judge must win a full term in an uncontested popular election. (10)

at-large district An area in which representatives are elected from an entire entity, and not a single-member district. (5)

at-large election Members of a policymaking body, such as a city council, are elected on a citywide basis rather than from single-member districts. (3)

attack ads Advertisements meant as a personal attack on an opposing candidate or organization. (6)

attorney general The constitutional official elected to head the Office of the Attorney General, which represents the state government in lawsuits and provides legal advice to state and local officials. (9)

automatic delegate An unpledged party official or elected official who serves as a delegate to a party's national convention. (4)

B

balanced budget A budget in which total revenues and expenditures are equal, producing no deficit. (11)

bicameral A legislature with two houses or chambers, such as Texas's House of Representatives and Senate. (8)

bifurcated A divided court system in which different courts handle civil and criminal cases. In Texas, the highest-level appeals courts are bifurcated. (10)

bill A proposed law or statute. (8)

biotechnology Also known as "biotech," this is the use and/or manipulation of biological processes and microorganisms to perform industrial or manufacturing processes or create consumer goods. (1)

Black Lives Matter A decentralized social movement advocating non-violent protest and civil disobedience in reaction to police brutality and racially motivated violence against Black people. (1)

block grant Congressional grant of money that allows the state considerable flexibility in spending for a program, such as providing welfare services. (2)

blogs Websites or web pages on which a writer or group of writers record opinions, information, and links to other sites on a regular basis. (6)

bond A mechanism by which governments borrow money. (3)

budget A plan of financial operation indicating how much revenue a government expects to collect during a period (usually one or two fiscal years) and how much spending is authorized for agencies and programs. (11)

budgetary power The governor is supposed to submit a state budget to the legislature at the beginning of each regular session. When an appropriation bill is enacted by the legislature and certified by the comptroller of public accounts, the governor may veto the whole document or individual items. (9)

budget execution The process whereby the governor and the Legislative Budget Board oversee (and, in some instances, modify) implementation of the spending plan authorized by the Texas legislature. (11)

bureaucrats Public employees. (9)

business organizations An economic interest group, such as a trade association (for example, Texas Gaming Association), that lobbies for policies favoring business. (7)

C

Campaign Reform Act Enacted by the U.S. Congress and signed by President George W. Bush in 2002, this law restricts donations of soft money and hard money for election campaigns, but its effect has been limited by federal court decisions. (5)

canvass To scrutinize the results of an election and then confirm and certify the vote tally for each candidate. (5)

capital felony A crime punishable by death or life imprisonment without parole. (13)

Capitol press corps Reporters assigned to cover state-level news, commonly working in Austin. (6)

caucus A meeting at which members of a political party assemble to select delegates and to make policy recommendations at the precinct, county, or state senatorial district, and state levels. (4)

Chief Executive The head of the executive branch of a government. The role of Chief Executive generally comes with the power to implement and enforce government policies, supervise the executive branch of government, and appoint and remove executive officials. (9)

Children's Health Insurance Program (CHIP) A program that provides medical insurance for minimal premiums to children from low-income families. (11)

chubbing A practice whereby representatives engage in lengthy debate for the purpose of using time and thus preventing a vote on a bill that they oppose. (8)

civic engagement Actions by citizens to address issues of public concern. (6)

civil law The body of law concerning disputes between individuals and other noncriminal matters, such as business contracts and personal injury. (10)

civil society Organizations, groups, and networks outside of government that better lives independently of government but also provide tools for influencing government and the private sector. (3)

closed primary A primary in which voters must declare their support for a party before they are permitted to participate in the selection of its candidates. (5)

colonia A low-income community, typically located in South Texas and especially in counties bordering Mexico, that lacks running water, sewer lines, and other essential services. (3)

commissioner of agriculture The elected official, whose position is created by statute, who heads Texas's Department of Agriculture, which promotes the sale of agricultural commodities and regulates pesticides, aquaculture, egg quality, weights and measures, and grain warehouses. (9)

commissioner of education The official who heads the TEA. (9)

commissioner of insurance Appointed by the governor, the commissioner heads the Texas Department of Insurance, which is responsible for ensuring the industry's financial soundness, protecting policyholders, and overseeing insurance rates. (9)

commissioner of the General Land Office As head of Texas's General Land Office, this elected constitutional officer oversees the state's extensive landholdings and related mineral interests, especially oil and gas leasing, for the benefit of the Permanent School Fund. (9)

commissioners court A Texas county's policymaking body, with five members: the county judge, who presides, and four commissioners representing single-member precincts. (3)

commission form A type of municipal government in which each elected commissioner is a member of the city's policymaking body and heads an administrative department (e.g., public safety with police and fire divisions). (3)

commutation of sentence On the recommendation of the Board of Pardons and Paroles, the reduction of a sentence by the governor. (9)

companion bill Filed in one house but identical or similar to a bill filed in the other chamber; this simultaneous filing speeds passage of a bill because committee consideration may take place at the same time in both chambers. (8)

comptroller of public accounts An elected constitutional officer responsible for collecting taxes, keeping accounts, estimating revenue, and serving as treasurer for the state. (9)

concurrent jurisdiction The authority of more than one court to try a case. For example, a civil dispute involving more than $200 but less than $20,000 may be heard in either a justice of the peace court, a county court (or county court-at-law), or a district court. (10)

concurrent resolution A resolution adopted by House and Senate majorities and then approved by the governor (for example, a request for action by Congress or authorization for someone to sue the state). (8)

conditional pardon An act of executive clemency, on recommendation of the Board of Pardons and Paroles, that releases a convicted person from the consequences of his or her crime but does not restore all rights, as in the case of a full pardon. (9)

conference committee A committee composed of representatives and senators appointed to reach agreement on a disputed bill and recommend changes acceptable to both chambers. (8)

conservative A person who advocates minimal intervention by government in economic matters and who gives a high priority to reducing taxes and curbing public spending, while supporting a more active role for government in traditional social issues. (4)

constable An official elected to assist the justice of the peace by serving papers and in some cases carrying out security and investigative responsibilities. (3)

constitutional amendment election Election, typically in November of an odd-numbered year, in which voters are asked to approve one or more proposed constitutional amendments. An amendment must receive a majority of the popular vote to be approved. (2)

constitutional amendment process Process for changing the Texas Constitution in which an amendment is proposed by a two-thirds vote of each chamber of the legislature and approved by a simple majority of voters in a general or special election. (2)

constitutional county courts Trial courts created in the Texas Constitution for each of Texas's 254 counties. If a county has one or more county courts-at-law, constitutional county courts do not usually hear and decide cases. (10)

constitutional guarantees Rights and protections assured under the U.S. Constitution. For example, among the guarantees to members of the Union include protection against invasion and domestic uprisings, territorial integrity, a republican form of government, and representation by two senators and at least one representative for each state. (2)

constitutional revision convention A body of delegates who meet to make extensive changes in a constitution or to draft a new constitution. (2)

constitutional revision Extensive or complete rewriting of a constitution. (2)

contingency fee A lawyer's compensation paid from money recovered in a lawsuit or settlement. (10)

contingency riders Authorization for spending state money to finance provisions of a bill if the bill becomes law. (9)

council-manager form A system of municipal government in which an elected city council hires a manager to coordinate budgetary matters and supervise administrative departments. (3)

council of governments (COGs) A voluntary association of local governments to assist in regional planning, development, and cooperation. Provides expert assistance on federal and state grants. (3)

county attorney An official elected to represent the county in civil and criminal cases, unless a resident district attorney performs these functions. (3)

county auditor A person appointed by the district judge or judges to check the financial books and records of other officials who handle county money. (3)

county chair Elected by county party members in the primaries, this key party official heads the county executive committee. (4)

county clerk An official elected to perform clerical chores for the county courts and commissioners court, keep public records, maintain vital statistics, and administer public elections, if the county does not have an administrator of elections. (3)

county convention A party meeting of delegates held in even-numbered years on a date and at a time and place prescribed by the party's state executive committee to adopt resolutions and to select delegates to the party's state convention. (4)

county courts-at-law Trial courts created by statute to assume the responsibilities of constitutional county courts in counties with larger populations. (10)

county executive committee Composed of a party's precinct chairs and the elected county chair. (4)

county judge An official popularly elected to preside over the county commissioners court, perform some administrative duties, and in smaller counties, hear civil and criminal cases. (3)

county sheriff A citizen popularly elected as the county's chief law enforcement officer; the sheriff is also responsible for maintaining the county jail. (3)

county tax assessor-collector This elected official no longer assesses property for taxation but does collect taxes and fees and commonly handles voter registration. (3)

county Texas is divided into 254 counties that serve as an administrative arm of the state and provide important services at the local level, especially in rural areas. (3)

county treasurer An elected official who receives and pays out county money as directed by the commissioners court. (3)

Court of Criminal Appeals The state's highest court with criminal jurisdiction. (10)

court of record A court that has a court reporter or electronic device to record testimony and proceedings. (10)

courts of appeals Intermediate-level appellate courts that hear and decide appeals from trial court decisions. (10)

criminal justice system The system that involves prosecution, defense, sentencing, and punishment of those suspected or convicted of committing a crime. (13)

criminal law The body of law concerning felony and misdemeanor offenses by individuals against other persons and property, or in violation of laws or ordinances. (10)

crossover voting A practice whereby a person participates in the primary of one party, then votes for one or more candidates of another party in the general election. (5)

cumulative voting When multiple seats are contested in an at-large election, voters cast one or more of the specified number of votes for one or more candidates in any combination. It is designed to increase representation of historically underrepresented ethnic minority groups. (3)

D

dark money Political spending by nonprofit groups, with the money coming from anonymous sources because the nonprofits do not need to disclose the sources of their contributions. (5)

dealignment Occurs when citizens have no allegiance to a political party and become independent voters. (4)

decentralized government Decentralization is achieved by dividing power between national and state governments and separating legislative, executive, and judicial branches at both levels. (7)

dedicated fund A restricted state fund that has been identified to be spent for a designated purpose. If the fund is consolidated within the General Revenue Fund, it usually must be spent for its intended purpose. Some unappropriated amounts of dedicated funds, even those required to be used for a specific purpose, can be included in the calculations to balance the state budget. (11)

defamation, libel, and slander Communicating something untrue that damages a person's reputation (defamation) may be subject to a civil lawsuit. If the comment is written, it is called libel; if spoken, it is slander. (6)

defendant The person sued in a civil proceeding or prosecuted in a criminal proceeding. (10)

delegated powers Specific powers entrusted to the national government by Article I, Section 8 of the U.S. Constitution (for example, regulate interstate commerce, borrow money, and declare war). (2)

deregulation The elimination of government restrictions to allow free market competition to determine or limit the actions of individuals and corporations. (12)

descriptive representation Constituents' ethnic and social characteristics represented by an elected representative. (8)

Dillon's Rule A legal principle, still followed in the majority of states including Texas, that local governments have only those powers granted by their state government. (3)

direct primary A nominating system that allows voters to participate directly in the selection of candidates for public office. (5)

discovery Gathering information from the opposing party and witnesses in a lawsuit, including examination of relevant documents, obtaining written and oral answers to questions, inspecting property under the control of the other party, and similar activities. (10)

district attorney An official elected to serve one or more counties who prosecutes criminal cases, gives advisory opinions, and represents the county in civil cases. (3)

district clerk A citizen elected to maintain records for the district courts. (3)

district courts State trial courts that hear and decide both civil and criminal cases. (10)

dual budgeting system The compilation of separate budgets by the legislative branch and the executive branch. (11)

Duverger's Law Plurality single member district systems favor a 2-party system, and proportional electoral (PR) systems favor multiparty systems. (4)

E

early voting Conducted at the county courthouse and selected polling places before the designated primary, special, or general election day. (5)

economic interest group An interest group that exists primarily to promote their members' economic self-interest. Trade associations and labor unions are classified as economic interest groups because they are organized to promote policies that will maximize profits and wages. (7)

electioneering Active campaigning by an interest group in support of, or in opposition to, a candidate; actions urging the public to act on an issue. (7)

election judge Official appointed by the county commissioners court to administer an election in a voting precinct. (5)

elections administrator Person appointed to supervise voter registration and voting for a county. (5)

elite access The ability of the business elite to deal directly with high-ranking government administrators in order to avoid full compliance with regulations. (12)

enhanced punishment Additional penalties or prison time for those who engage in organized crime or hate crimes, and for repeat offenders. (13)

equal opportunity Ensures that policies and actions do not discriminate on factors, such as race, gender, ethnicity, religion, or national origin. (12)

exclusionary zoning The use of local government zoning ordinances to exclude certain groups of people from a given community. (1)

exclusive jurisdiction The authority of only one court to try a particular type of case. (10)

exculpatory evidence Evidence that helps a defendant and may exonerate the defendant in a criminal trial. (13)

executive commissioner of the Health and Human Services Commission Appointed by the governor with Senate approval, the executive commissioner administers the HHSC, develops policies, and makes rules. (9)

executive orders The governor issues executive orders to set policy within the executive branch and to create task forces, councils, and other bodies. (9)

exonerated The definition of a person convicted of a crime who has received the state's official declaration of his or her innocence. (13)

extraterritorial jurisdiction (ETJ) The limited authority a city has outside its boundaries. The larger the city's population size, the larger the reach of its ETJ. (3)

F

federal grants-in-aid Money appropriated by the U.S. Congress to help states and local governments provide needed facilities and services. (2)

fee A charge imposed by an agency upon those subject to its regulation. (11)

felony A serious crime punished by fine and prison confinement. (10)

filibustering A delaying tactic whereby a senator may speak, and thus hold the Senate floor, for as long as physical endurance permits, unless action is taken to end the filibuster. (8)

fiscal policy Public policy that concerns taxing, government spending, public debt, and management of government money. (11)

fiscal year A one-year budget period. For Texas's state government, each fiscal year begins on September 1 and ends on August 31 of the following year. (11)

five-ninths rule A procedural device to control bringing bills to the Senate floor for debate. (8)

framing Identifies which aspects of a problem are relevant and important. (6)

franchise tax A tax levied on the annual receipts of businesses that are organized to limit the personal liability of owners for the privilege of conducting business in the state. (11)

full faith and credit clause Most government actions of another state must be officially recognized by public officials in Texas. (2)

full pardon An act of executive clemency, on recommendation of the Board of Pardons and Paroles, that releases a convicted person from all consequences of a criminal act and restores the same rights enjoyed by others who have not been convicted of a crime. (9)

G

general-law city A municipality with a charter prescribed by the legislature. (3)

general election Held in November of even-numbered years to elect county, state, and federal officials from among candidates nominated in primaries or (for minor parties) in nominating conventions. (5)

general obligation bond Amount borrowed by the state that is repaid from the General Revenue Fund. (11)

General Revenue Fund An unrestricted state fund that is available for general appropriations. (11)

general sales tax Texas's largest source of tax revenue, applied at the rate of 6.25 percent to the sale price of tangible personal property and "the storage, use, or other consumption of tangible personal property purchased, leased, or rented." (11)

gentrification A relocation of middle class or affluent people into deteriorating urban areas, often displacing low-income residents. (1)

gerrymandering Drawing the boundaries of a district, such as a state senatorial or representative district, to include or exclude certain groups of voters and thus affect election outcomes. (5, 8)

ghost voting A prohibited practice whereby one representative presses the voting button of another House member who is absent. (8)

government A public institution with authority to formulate, adopt, implement, and enforce public policies for a society. (1)

governor's office The administrative organization through which the governor of Texas makes appointments, prepares a biennial budget recommendation, administers federal and state grants for crime prevention and law enforcement, and confers full and conditional pardons on recommendation of the Board of Pardons and Paroles. (9)

graded penalties Depending on the nature of the crime, noncapital felonies are graded as first degree, second degree, third degree, and state jail; misdemeanors are graded as A, B, and C. (13)

grandfather clause Although not used in Texas, the law exempted people from educational, property, or tax requirements for voting if they were qualified to vote before 1867 or were descendants of such persons. (5)

grand jury Composed of 12 persons (and four alternates) with the qualifications of trial jurors, a grand jury serves three months while it determines whether sufficient evidence exists to indict persons accused of committing crimes. (10)

grants-in-aid Money, goods, or services given by one government to another (for example, federal grants-in-aid to states for financing public assistance programs for poor Texans). (11)

grassroots Local (as in grassroots government or grassroots politics). (3)

group leadership Individuals who guide the decisions of interest groups. Leaders of groups tend to have financial resources that permit them to contribute money and devote time to group affairs. (7)

H

hard money Campaign money donated directly to candidates or political parties and restricted in amount by federal law. (5)

hard news News that focuses on the facts, provides more depth, and commonly has implications for public policy. (6)

head of state The person whose role is to represent and symbolize the unity and integrity of the state at home, in interaction with other state governments, the national government and abroad. (9)

home-rule city A municipality with a locally drafted charter. (3)

homogenization of news Making news uniform regardless of differing locations and cultures. (6)

horserace journalism News that focuses on who is ahead in the race (poll results and public perceptions) rather than policy differences. (6)

hydraulic fracturing Also known as "fracking," this method of extracting oil and natural gas involves forcing open fissures in subterranean rocks by introducing liquid at high pressure. (1)

I

impeach Process in which the Texas House of Representatives, by a simple majority vote, initiates action (brings charges) leading to possible removal of certain judicial and executive officials (both elected and appointed) by the Senate. (8)

implied powers Powers inferred by the constitutional authority of the U.S. Congress "to make all laws which shall be necessary and proper for carrying into execution the foregoing [delegated] powers, and all other powers vested by this Constitution in the government of the United States, or in any department or officer thereof." (2)

independent candidate A candidate who runs in a general election without party endorsement or selection. (4, 5)

independent expenditures Expenditures that pay for political campaign communications and expressly advocate the nomination, election, or defeat of a clearly identified candidate but are not given to, or made at the request of, the candidate's campaign. (5)

independent school district (ISD) Created by the legislature, an independent school district raises tax revenue to support its public schools. Voters within the district elect a board that hires a superintendent, determines salary schedules, selects textbooks, and sets the district's property tax rate. (3)

initiative A citizen-drafted measure proposed by a specific number or percentage of qualified voters, which becomes law if approved by popular vote. In Texas, this process occurs only in home-rule cities. (2, 3)

interest group An organization that seeks to influence government officials and their policies on behalf of members sharing common views and objectives (for example, labor unions or trade associations). (7)

interest group technique An action (such as lobbying, personal communication, giving favors and gifts, grassroots activities, electioneering, campaign financing by political action committees, and, in extreme instances, bribery and other unethical practices) intended to influence government decisions. (7)

intergovernmental relations Relationships between and among different governments that are on the same or different levels. (3)

interim committee A House or Senate committee appointed by the speaker or lieutenant governor to study an important policy issue between regular sessions. (8)

J

Jim Crow laws Discriminatory laws that segregated Blacks and denied them access to public services for many decades after the Civil War. (1)

joint resolution A resolution that must pass by a majority vote in each house when used to ratify an amendment to the U.S. Constitution or to request a constitutional convention to propose amendments to the U.S. Constitution. As a proposal for an amendment to the Texas Constitution, a joint resolution requires a two-thirds majority vote of the total membership for each house. (8)

judgment A judge's written opinion based on a verdict. (10)

judicial legitimacy The belief that courts have the right or authority to make and enforce decisions because judges are fair and impartial. (10)

junior college or community college district Establishes one or more two-year colleges that offer both academic and vocational programs. (3)

jurisdiction A court's authority to hear and decide a particular case. (10)

justice of the peace A judge elected from a justice of the peace precinct who handles minor civil and criminal cases, including small claims. (3, 10)

L

labor organizations A union that supports public policies designed to increase wages, obtain adequate health insurance coverage, provide unemployment insurance, promote safe working conditions, and otherwise protect the interests of workers. (7)

Latin America Countries in the western hemisphere south of the United States where Spanish, Portuguese and French are the official languages. (1)

Legislative Budget Board (LBB) A 10-member body co-chaired by the lieutenant governor and the Speaker of the House. This board and its staff prepare a biennial current services budget. In addition, they assist with the preparation of a general appropriation bill at the beginning of a regular legislative session. If requested, staff members prepare fiscal notes that assess the economic impact of a proposed bill or resolution. (11)

legislative caucus An organization of legislators who seek to maximize their influence over issues in which they have a special interest. (8)

legislative power A power of the governor exercised through messages delivered to the Texas legislature, vetoes of bills and concurrent resolutions, and calls for special legislative sessions. (9)

liberal A person who advocates government support in social and economic matters and who favors political reforms that extend democracy, achieve a more equitable *distribution* of wealth, and protect individual freedoms and rights. Liberals tend to favor less government regulation in the private lives of individuals. (4)

libertarianism The concept of advocating minimal government intervention in both economic and social issues. (4)

lieutenant governor Popularly elected constitutional official who serves as president of the Senate and is first in the line of succession if the office of governor becomes vacant before the end of a term. (9)

line-item veto Action by the governor to eliminate an individual budget item while permitting enactment of other parts of an appropriations bill. (9)

literacy tests Although not used in Texas as a prerequisite for voter registration, the test was designed and administered in ways intended to prevent Black Americans from voting. (5)

lobbying Communicating with legislators or other government officials for the purpose of influencing decision-makers. (7)

local government Counties, municipalities, school districts, and other special districts that provide a range of services, including rural roads, city streets, public education, and protection of persons and property. (2)

M

maquiladoras Industrial plants on the Mexican side of the border which are partnered with American companies. Such plants typically use low-cost labor to assemble imported parts for a wide range of consumer goods and then export these goods back to the United States or to other countries. (1)

martial law Temporary rule by military authorities when civil authorities are unable to handle a riot or other civil disorder. (9)

media Major means of mass communication. (6)

media market Area in which people receive the same traditional media—television and radio stations and newspapers. (6)

Medicaid Funded in large part by federal grants and in part by state appropriations, Medicaid is administered by the state. It provides medical care for poor persons. (12)

Medicare Funded entirely by the federal government and administered by the U.S. Department of Health and Human Services, Medicare primarily provides medical assistance to qualified applicants age 65 and older. (12)

merit systems Hiring, promoting, and firing on the basis of objective criteria, such as tests, degrees, experience, and performance. (9)

message power The governor's effectiveness in communicating with legislators via the State of the State address at the commencement of a legislative session and other gubernatorial messages delivered in person or in writing. (9)

metro government Consolidation of units of local government within an urban area under a single authority. (3)

middle class Social scientists identify the middle class as those people with white-collar occupations (such as professionals and small business owners). (3)

misdemeanor Classified as A, B, or C, a misdemeanor may be punished by fine and/or jail sentence. (10)

Missouri Plan A judicial selection process in which a commission recommends a panel of names to the governor, who appoints a judge for one year or so before voters determine whether the appointee will be retained for a full term. (10)

mobilization Actions such as voter registration drives, making phone calls, using social media, knocking on doors, and holding campaign rallies that political organizations, political parties, and candidates take to get individuals to turn out and vote. (5)

moratorium The delay or suspension of an activity or law. A moratorium may be imposed when something is seen as needing improvement. (13)

motor-voter law Federal legislation requiring certain government offices (for example, motor vehicle licensing agencies) to offer voter registration applications to clients. (5)

multimember district A district in which all voters participate in the election of two or more representatives to a policymaking body. (8)

municipal (city) government A local government for an incorporated community established by law as a city. (3)

municipal court City-run court with jurisdiction primarily over Class C misdemeanors committed within a city's boundaries. (10)

N

national supremacy clause Article VI of the U.S. Constitution states, "This Constitution, and the laws of the United States which shall be made in pursuance thereof; and all treaties made, or which shall be made, under the authority of the United States, shall be the supreme law of the land." (2)

neoliberal A political ideology that advocates less government regulation of business and supports governmental involvement in social programs. (4)

net neutrality A legal principle that Internet service providers and government officials should treat all data on the Internet equally, not discriminating or charging differentially and not blocking content they do not like. (6)

news websites Internet sites that provide news. These sites are often affiliated with a newspaper or television station, but increasingly, many are independent. (6)

niche journalism (narrowcasting) A news medium focusing on a narrow audience defined by concern about a particular topic or area. (6)

noneducation special districts Special districts, other than school districts or community college districts, such as fire prevention or municipal utility districts, that are units of local government and may cover part of a county, a whole county, or areas in two or more counties. (3)

nonpartisan election An election in which candidates are not identified on the ballot by party label. (3)

O

off-year or midterm election A general election held in the even-numbered year following a presidential election. (5)

open meetings Meetings of public entities that are required by law to be open to the public. (6)

open primary A primary in which voters are not required to declare party affiliation. (5)

open records Government documents and records that are required by law to be available to the public. (6)

ordinance A local law enacted by a city council or approved by popular vote in a referendum or initiative election. (3)

organizational patterns The structure of a special interest group. Some interest groups have a decentralized pattern of organization. Others are centralized. (7)

original jurisdiction The power of a court to hear and decide a case first. (10)

oversight A legislative function that requires reports from state agencies concerning their operations; the state auditor provides information on agencies' use of state funds. (8)

P

parliamentarian An expert on rules of order who sits at the left of the presiding officer in the House or Senate and provides advice on procedural questions. (8)

parole Supervised release from prison before completion of a sentence, on condition of good behavior. (9)

party identification A psychological identification individuals have with a political party. It is an important concept in understanding political preferences. (4)

patronage system Hiring friends and supporters of elected officials as government employees without regard to their abilities. (9)

payroll tax An employer-paid tax levied against a portion of the wages and salaries of workers to provide funds for payment of unemployment insurance benefits in the event employees lose their jobs. (11)

permanent party organization In Texas, the precinct chairs, county and senatorial district executive committees, and the state executive committee form the permanent organization of a political party. (4)

petit jury A trial jury of 6 or 12 members. (10)

plaintiff The injured party who initiates a civil suit or the government in a criminal proceeding. (10)

platform A document that sets forth a political party's position on public policy issues, such as income tax, school vouchers, or the environment. (4)

plea bargain An agreement between the prosecutor and the defendant in a criminal case in which the defendant agrees to plead guilty to a specific charge and in return gets certain concessions from the prosecutor, such as a reduction in charges, a shortened prison term, or probation. (13)

plural executive The governor, elected department heads, and the secretary of state, as provided by the Texas Constitution and statutes. (9)

political action committee (PAC) An organization created to collect and distribute contributions to political campaigns. (5)

political culture Widely shared attitudes, habits, and general behavior patterns that develop over time and affect the political life of a state or region. (1)

political ideology A collection of beliefs about the appropriate order of society and how to achieve it. (4)

political party An organization with the purpose of controlling government by recruiting, nominating, and electing candidates to public office. Those who share the same beliefs and values often identify with a specific political party. (4)

politics The process of policymaking that involves conflict and cooperation between political parties and other groups that seek to elect government officials or to influence those officials when they make public policy. (1)

poll tax A tax levied in Texas from 1902 until voters amended the Texas Constitution in 1966 to eliminate it; failure to pay the annual tax made a citizen ineligible to vote in party primaries or in special and general elections. (5)

pork-barrel politics A legislator's tactic to obtain funding for a pet project, usually designed to be of special benefit for the legislator's district. (9)

postadjournment veto Rejection by the governor of a pending bill or concurrent resolution during the 20 days after a legislative session ends. (9)

power group An effective interest group strongly linked with legislators and bureaucrats for the purpose of influencing decision-making and having a continuing presence in Austin as a repeat player from session to session. (7)

precinct chair The party official responsible for the interests and activities of a political party in a voting district. (4)

precinct convention A convention, held at the voting precinct level, to adopt resolutions and to select delegates to the party's county or senatorial district convention. (4)

presidential preference primary A primary in which the voters indicate their preference for a person seeking nomination as the party's presidential candidate. (4)

president of the Senate Title of the lieutenant governor in his or her role as presiding officer for the Texas Senate. (8)

primary An election conducted within the party to nominate candidates who will run for public office in a subsequent general election. (5)

priming Issues emphasized by the media frequently become the issues the public uses to evaluate leaders and policy. (6)

prior restraint Suppression of material before it is published, commonly called censorship. (6)

privatization Transfer of government services or assets to the private sector. Commonly, assets are sold and services contracted out. (12)

privileges and immunities Article IV of the U.S. Constitution guarantees that "citizens of each state shall be entitled to the privileges and immunities of citizens of the several states." According to the U.S. Supreme Court, this provision means that citizens are guaranteed protection by government, enjoyment of life and liberty, the right to acquire and possess property, the right to leave and enter any state, and the right to use state courts. (2)

probate Proceedings that involve the estates of decedents. Courts with probate jurisdiction (county courts, county courts-at-law, and probate courts) also handle guardianship and mental competency matters. (10)

probate courts Statutory courts that only handle administration of decedent's estates, mental competency proceedings, and guardianship proceedings. (10)

procedural committee These permanent House committees (such as the Calendars Committee and House Administration Committee) consider bills and resolutions relating primarily to procedural legislative matters. (8)

proclamation A governor's official public announcement (such as calling a special election or declaring a disaster area). (9)

professional group An organization of physicians, lawyers, accountants, or other professional people that lobbies for policies beneficial to members. (7)

professionalism Reporting that is objective, neutral, and accurate. (6)

progressive Favoring and working for progress in conditions facing the majority of society or in government. (1)

progressive tax A tax in which the effective tax rate increases as the tax base (such as individual income or corporate profits) increases. (11)

property tax A tax that property owners pay according to the value of real estate and other tangible property. At the local level, property owners pay this tax to the city, the county, the school district, and often other special districts. (3)

public administration The implementation of public policy by government employees. (9)

public interest group An organization claiming to represent a broad public interest (such as environmental, consumer, political participation, or public morality) rather than a narrow private interest. (7)

public officer and employee group An organization of city managers, county judges, law enforcement, or other public employees or officials that lobbies for public policies that protect group interests. (7)

public policy What government does to or for its citizens to meet a public need or goal as determined by a legislative body or other authorized officials. (1, 12)

Public Utility Commission of Texas (PUC) A three-member appointed body with regulatory power over electric and telephone companies. (9)

R

racial and ethnic groups Organizations that seek to influence government decisions that affect a particular racial or ethnic group, such as the National Association for the Advancement of Colored People (NAACP) and the League of United Latin American Citizens (LULAC), which seek to influence government decisions affecting African Americans and Latinos, respectively. (7)

racial covenants Agreements written into real estate documents by property owners, subdivision developers, or real estate operators in a given neighborhood, binding property owners not to sell, lease, or rent property to specified groups because of race, creed, or color. (1)

Railroad Commission of Texas (RRC) A popularly elected three-member commission primarily engaged in regulating natural gas and petroleum production. (9)

Rainy Day Fund A fund used like a savings account for stabilizing state finance and helping the state meet economic emergencies when revenue is insufficient to cover state-supported programs. (11)

realignment Occurs when there is a major change in the support of political parties. (4)

reapportionment Allotment of legislative seats according to population. (8)

recall A process for removing elected officials through a popular vote. In Texas, this power is available only for home-rule cities. (3)

recess appointment An appointment made by the governor when the Texas legislature is not in session. (9)

recidivism Criminal behavior that results in reincarceration after a person has been released from confinement for a prior offense. (13)

redistricting Redrawing of boundaries after the federal decennial census to create single-member districts with approximately equal population (e.g., legislative, congressional, commissioners court, and city council districts in Texas). (3, 8)

redlining A discriminatory rating system used by federal agencies to evaluate the risks associated with loans made to borrowers in specific urban neighborhoods. Today, the term also refers to the same practice among private businesses like banks and real estate companies. (1)

referendum A process by which issues are referred to the voters to accept or reject. Voters may also petition for a vote to repeal an existing ordinance. In Texas, this process occurs at the local level in home-rule cities. At the state level, state constitutional amendments and bonds secured by taxes must be approved by the voters. (3)

regressive tax A tax in which the effective tax rate decreases as the tax base (such as individual income or corporate profits) increases. (11)

regular session A session of the Texas legislature that is constitutionally mandated and begins on the second Tuesday in January of odd-numbered years and lasts for a maximum of 140 days. (8)

religion-based group An interest group, such as the Texas Freedom Network, that lobbies for policies to promote its religious interests. (7)

removal power Authority to remove an official from office. In Texas, the governor's removal power is limited to staff members, some agency heads, and his or her appointees with the consent of the Senate. (9)

reprieve An act of executive clemency that temporarily suspends execution of a sentence. (9)

reserved powers Reserved powers are derived from the Tenth Amendment of the U.S. Constitution. Although not spelled out in the U.S. Constitution, these reserved powers to the states include police power, taxing power, proprietary power, and power of eminent domain. (2)

revenue bond Amount borrowed by the state that is repaid from a specific revenue source. (11)

right-to-work laws Laws that limit the power of workers to bargain collectively and form and operate unions, increasing the power of employers relative to their employees. (1)

right of association The U.S. Supreme Court has ruled that this right is part of the right of assembly guaranteed by the First Amendment to the U.S. Constitution and that it protects the right of people to organize into groups for political purposes. (7)

"Robin Hood" plan A plan for equalizing financial support for school districts by transferring tax money from rich districts to poor districts. (11)

rule of capture A rule of law that a landowner can capture and own the natural resources extracted from the land. Thus, groundwater belongs to the landowner. (12)

runoff primary Held after the first primary to allow party members to choose a candidate from the first primary's top two vote-getters if no candidate received a majority vote. (5)

S

secretary of state The state's chief elections officer, with other administrative duties, who is appointed by the governor for a term concurrent with that of the governor. (9)

select committee This committee, created independently by the House speaker or the lieutenant governor, may consider legislation that crosses committee jurisdictional lines or may conduct special studies. (8)

selective sales tax A tax charged on specific products and services. (11)

senatorial courtesy Before making an appointment, the governor is expected to obtain approval from the state senator in whose district the prospective appointee resides; failure to obtain such approval will probably cause the Senate to "bust" the appointee. (8)

senatorial district convention Held in even-numbered years on a date and at a time and place prescribed by the party's state executive committee in counties that have more than one state senatorial district. Participants select delegates to the party's state convention. (4)

senatorial district executive committee Composed of a party's precinct chairs who reside within a senatorial district. (4)

separation of powers The assignment of lawmaking, law-enforcing, and law-interpreting functions to separate branches of government. (2)

service sector Businesses that provide services, such as finance, healthcare, food service, data processing, or consulting. (11)

severance tax An excise tax levied on a natural resource (such as oil or natural gas) when it is severed (removed) from the earth. (11)

shield law A law protecting journalists from having to reveal confidential sources to police or in court. (6)

simple resolution A resolution that requires action by one legislative chamber only and is not acted on by the governor. (8)

single-member district An area that elects only one representative to a policymaking body, such as a state House, a state Senate, or the U.S. Congress. (8)

single-member district election Voters in an area (commonly called a district, ward, or precinct) elect one representative to serve on a policymaking body (e.g., city council, county commissioners court, state House and Senate). (3)

sin tax A selective sales tax on items such as cigarettes, other forms of tobacco, alcoholic beverages, and admission to sex-oriented businesses. (11)

SLAPP Strategic lawsuits against public participation are suits filed primarily to silence criticism and negative public discussion. (6)

social construct concept or belief developed and maintained by the collective views of a society rather than existing inherently or naturally. (1)

social interest group A group concerned primarily with social issues, including organizations devoted to civil rights, racial and ethnic matters, religion, and public interest protection. (7)

social media Websites and computer applications that allow users to engage in social networking and create online communities. Social media provide platforms for sharing information and ideas through discussion forums, videos, photos, documents, audio clips, and the like. (6)

soft money Unregulated political donations made to national political parties or independent expenditures on behalf of a candidate that are used to fund election activities but are not directly donated to a political campaign. (5)

soft news News that is more entertaining, sensationalized, covers only the surface, and has little connection to public policy. (6)

sound bite A brief statement intended to be easily quotable by the news media that is designed to convey a specific message that a campaign wishes to make. (5)

Speaker of the House The state representative elected by House members to serve as the presiding officer for that chamber. (8)

special district A unit of local government that performs a particular service, such as providing schools, hospitals, or housing, for a particular geographic area. (3)

special election An election called by the governor to fill a vacancy (for example, U.S. congressional or state legislative office) or to vote on a proposed state constitutional amendment. (5)

special issues Questions a judge gives a trial jury to answer to establish the facts in a civil case. (10)

special session A legislative session called by the governor and limited to no more than 30 days. (8)

specialty courts Courts designed to deal with particular types of problems, such as drug-related offenses or specific populations, such as veterans or foster children. (10)

standing committee A permanent Senate or House committee whose members are appointed by the president of the Senate or the speaker for the purpose of considering proposed bills and resolutions before possible floor debate and voting. (8)

State Board of Education (SBOE) A popularly elected 15-member body with limited authority over Texas's K-12 education system. (9)

state convention Convenes every even-numbered year to make rules for a political party, adopt a party platform and resolutions, and select members of the state executive committee; in a presidential election year, it elects delegates to the national convention, names members to serve on the national committee, and elects potential electors to vote if the party's presidential candidate receives a plurality of the popular vote in the general election. (4)

state executive committee Composed of a chair, vice chair, and two members from each senatorial district, this body is part of a party's permanent organization. (4)

State of Texas Assessment of Academic Readiness (STAAR) A state program of end-of-course and other examinations begun in 2012. (12)

statutory county court Court created by the legislature at the request of a county; may have civil or criminal jurisdiction or both, depending on the legislation creating it. (3)

straight-ticket voting Voting for all the candidates of one party. (4)

stratarchy A political system in which power is diffused among and within levels of party organization. (4)

strategic fiscal review A review conducted by the Legislative Budget Board of every program administered by an agency in the sunset review process. The report includes a review of a program's purpose, cost, funding sources, and the impact of program elimination. (11)

strong mayor-council form A type of municipal government with a separately elected legislative body (council) and an executive head (mayor) elected in a citywide election with veto, appointment, and removal powers. (3)

substantive committee With members appointed by the House speaker, this permanent committee considers bills and resolutions related to the subject identified by its name (such as the House Agriculture and Livestock Committee) and may recommend passage of proposed legislation to the appropriate calendars committee. (8)

substantive representation Lawmakers work on behalf of constituents without regard for their ethnic and social characteristics. (8)

suffrage The right to vote. (2)

sunset review process During a cycle of 12 years, each state agency is studied at least once to see if it is needed and efficient, and then the legislature decides whether to abolish, merge, reorganize, or retain that agency. (9)

super PAC Independent expenditure-only committees that may raise unlimited sums of money from corporations, unions, nonprofit organizations, and individuals. (5)

Supplemental Nutritional Assistance Program (SNAP) Joint federal–state program administered by the state to provide food to low-income people. (12)

Supreme Court of Texas State's highest court with civil jurisdiction. (10)

systemic racism Systems, structures, procedures, or processes that disadvantage people of color. Also known as "institutional racism" or "structural racism." (1)

T

tax A mandatory assessment exacted by a government for a public purpose. (11)

tax appraisal district The district appraises all real estate and commercial property for taxation by units of local government within a county. (3)

tax increment reinvestment zone (TIRZ) Also called a Tax Increment Finance District (TIF). An area in which municipal tax incentives are offered to encourage businesses to locate in and contribute to the development of a blighted urban area. Commercial and residential property taxes may be frozen. (3)

Tejano A term referring to early Mexican settlers of Mexican Texas and the Republic of Texas. All residents of Texas today are referred to as Texans. (1)

Temporary Assistance for Needy Families (TANF) Provides financial assistance to the very poor in an attempt to help them move from welfare to the workforce. (12)

temporary party organization Primaries and conventions that function briefly to nominate candidates, adopt resolutions, adopt a party platform, and select delegates to party conventions at higher levels. (4)

Tenth Amendment The Tenth Amendment to the U.S. Constitution declares that "the powers not delegated by the Constitution, nor prohibited by it to the States, are reserved to the States, respectively, or to the people." (2)

term limit A restriction on the number of terms officials can serve in a public office. (3)

Texas Bill of Rights Article I of the Texas Constitution guarantees protections for people and their property against arbitrary actions by state and local governments. Protected rights include freedom of speech, press, religion, assembly, and petition. (2)

Texas Commission on Environmental Quality The state agency that coordinates Texas's environmental regulation efforts. (9)

Texas Constitution of 1876 The lengthy, much-amended state constitution, a product of the post-Reconstruction era that remains in effect today. (2)

Texas Department of Transportation (TxDOT) Headed by a five-member appointed commission, the department maintains almost 80,000 miles of roads and highways and promotes highway safety. (9)

Texas Education Agency (TEA) Administers the state's public school system of more than 1,200 school districts and charter schools. (9)

Texas Election Code The body of state law concerning parties, primaries, and elections. (5)

Texas Equal Legal Rights Amendment (ELRA) Added to Article I, Section 3, of the Texas Constitution, it guarantees that "equality under the law shall not be denied or abridged because of sex, race, color, creed, or national origin." (2)

Texas Essential Knowledge and Skills (TEKS) A core curriculum (a set of courses and knowledge) setting out what students should learn. (12)

Texas Ethics Commission A state agency that enforces state standards for lobbyists and public officials, including registration of lobbyists and reporting of political campaign contributions. (5)

Texas Ethics Commission A state agency that enforces state standards for lobbyists and public officials, including registration of lobbyists and reporting of political campaign contributions. (7)

Texas Grange A farmers' organization, also known as the Patrons of Husbandry, committed to low levels of government spending and limited governmental powers; a major influence on the Constitution of 1876. (2)

TEXAS Grants Program "Toward Excellence, Access, and Success" is a college financial assistance program that provides funding for qualifying students. (11)

Texas Higher Education Coordinating Board (THECB) An agency that provides some coordination for the state's public community colleges and universities. (9)

Texas Parks and Wildlife Department Texas agency that runs state parks and regulates hunting, fishing, and boating. (9)

Texas Penal Code The body of Texas law covering crimes, penalties, and correctional measures. (13)

Texas Workforce Commission (TWC) A state agency headed by three salaried commissioners that oversees job training and unemployment compensation programs. (9)

Texian A term referring to early White settlers of Mexican Texas and the Republic of Texas, especially those who supported the Texas Revolution. All residents of Texas today are referred to as Texans. (1)

third party A party other than the Democratic Party or the Republican Party. Sometimes called a "minor party" because of limited membership and voter support. (4)

top-two primary A nominating process in which voters indicate their preferences by using a single ballot on which are printed the names and respective party labels of all persons seeking nomination. A candidate who receives more than 50 percent of the vote is elected; otherwise, a runoff between the top two candidates must be held. (5)

top 10 percent rule Texas law gives automatic admission into any Texas public college or university to those graduating in the top 10 percent of their Texas high school class, with limitations for the University of Texas at Austin. (12)

tort An injury to a person or an individual's property resulting from the wrongful act of another. (10)

U

undocumented immigrant A person who enters the United States in violation of federal immigration law or overstays a legal visa and thus lacks proper documentation and identification. (1)

unicameral A one-house legislature, such as the Nebraska legislature. (8)

United States–Mexico–Canada Agreement (USMCA) A trade agreement between the United States, Canada, and Mexico which revised and replaced the North American Free Trade Agreement (NAFTA). Major changes to NAFTA focus on the auto industry, new labor and environmental standards, intellectual property law, and some digital trade provisions. (1)

universal suffrage Voting is open for virtually all persons 18 years of age or older. (5)

urban renewal The relocation of businesses and people, the demolition of structures, and the use of eminent domain to take private property for development projects. (1)

V

venire A panel of prospective jurors drawn by random selection. These prospective jurors are called veniremen. (10)

verdict A judge's or jury's decision about a court case. (10)

veto power Authority of the governor to reject a bill or concurrent resolution passed by the legislature. (9)

voir dire Courtroom procedure in which attorneys question prospective jurors to identify any who cannot be fair and impartial. (10)

voter turnout The percentage of voters (either voting age population, voting eligible population, or registered voters) casting a ballot in an election. (5)

voting center A countywide voting system that allows voters to vote, after being electronically verified, at any voting center in a county. (5)

voting precinct The basic geographic area for conducting primaries and elections; Texas is divided into more than 8,500 voting precincts. (5)

W

weak mayor-council form A type of municipal government with a separately elected mayor and council, but the mayor shares appointive and removal powers with the council, which can override the mayor's veto. (3)

white primary A nominating system designed to prevent Black Americans and some Latinos from participating in Democratic primaries from 1923 to 1944. (5)

women's organization A women's group, such as the League of Women Voters, that engages in lobbying and educational activities to promote greater political participation by women and others. (7)

workers' compensation A system of insurance that pays benefits to workers injured or made ill by their work. (12)

working class Social scientists identify the working class as those people with blue-collar (manual) occupations. (3)

Y

yellow journalism Journalism that is based on sensationalism and exaggeration. (6)

Endnotes

Chapter 1

1. For the text of the declarations, see "Governor Abbott Declares State of Disaster In Texas Due To COVID-19," *Office of the Texas Governor*, March 13, 2020, https://gov.texas.gov/news/post/governor-abbott-declares-state-of-disaster-in-texas-due-to-covid-19; and "Dr. John Hellerstedt Issues Public Health Disaster Declaration In Texas," *Texas Department of State Health Services*, March 19, 2020, https://www.dshs.state.tx.us/news/releases/2020/20200319.aspx

2. For an investigation of Texas's influence nationwide, see Kenneth P. Miller, *Texas vs. California: A History of Their Struggle for the Future of America*, (New York: Oxford University Press, 2020).

3. For census information, see "State and County QuickFacts," *U.S. Department of Commerce, Census Bureau*, July 1, 2019, https://www.census.gov/quickfacts/tx

4. Elizabeth Kolbert, "There's No Scientific Basis for Race—It's a Made-Up Label," *National Geographic*, March 12, 2018, https://www.nationalgeographic.com/magazine/2018/04/race-genetics-science-africa/. For further discussion of race and ethnicity, see Erin Blakemore, "Race and Ethnicity: How Are They Different?" *National Geographic*, February 22, 2019, https://www.nationalgeographic.com/culture/topics/reference/race-ethnicity/#close

5. For a historical timeline of the U.S. Census Bureau's treatment of race and ethnicity, see "Measuring Race and Ethnicity Across the Decades: 1790–2010," *U.S. Department of Commerce, Census Bureau*, https://www.census.gov/data-tools/demo/race/MREAD_1790_2010.html

6. In the past, the term "Anglo" was used in Texas to indicate a white, English-speaking American as distinct from a white Hispanic American. We have used "Anglo" in previous versions of PTP but will use "White" in this edition as it is the most common way to refer to non-Hispanic Whites. Since "Latino" and "Latina" are gendered terms, there is a growing movement to adopt the term "Latinx" as a non-gendered or non-binary alternative. Because Latinx is controversial and not widely used within the Latino/a community in Texas, we will continue to use Latino/a.

7. Cal Jillson, *Lone Star Tarnished: A Critical Look at Texas Politics and Public Policy* (New York: Routledge, 2012), 154.

8. For an in-depth look at the Comanches and their role in Texas history, see S. C. Gwynne, *Empire of the Summer Moon: Quanah Parker and the Rise and Fall of the Comanches, the Most Powerful Indian Tribe in American History* (New York: Scribner, 2010).

9. James L. Haley, *Passionate Nation: The Epic History of Texas* (New York: Free Press, 2006), 6, 19, and 230–231.

10. For alternative views of the Texas revolution, see Josefina Zoraida Vásquez, "The Colonization and Loss of Texas: A Mexican Perspective," in Jaime E. Rodríguez O. and Kathryn Vincent eds., *Myths, Misdeeds, and Misunderstandings: The Roots of Conflict in U.S.–Mexican Relations* (Wilmington, DE: Scholarly Resources Inc., 1997), 47–77; and Bryan Burrough and Chris Tomlinson, *Forget the Alamo: The Rise and Fall of an American Myth*, (New York: Penguin Press, 2021).

11. Frederick Law Olmsted, *A Journey Through Texas* (New York: Dix, Edwards, 1857; New York: Burt Franklin, 1969), 296. For more information on Texas Indian tribes, see David LaVere, *The Texas Indians* (College Station: Texas A&M University Press, 2004).

12. Jillson, *Lone Star Tarnished*, 60.

13. Three weeks before adoption of Texas' Ordinance of Secession, the convention adopted Texas's Declaration of Causes on February 2, 1861. The importance of the slavery issue is emphasized with several references to African slavery, which is described as "a beneficent and patriarchal system." For the full text, see "Declaration of Causes," *Texas State Library and Archives Commission*, https://www.tsl.texas.gov/ref/abouttx/secession/2feb1861.html

14. For more on lynching in Texas, see John R. Ross, "Lynching," in *Handbook of Texas Online*, http://www.tshaonline.org/handbook/online/articles/jgl01 and "Lynching in Texas," Sam Houston State University, https://www.lynchingintexas.org/

15. Jillson, *Lone Star Tarnished*, 61.

16. For information on Texas Latinos, a history of the civil rights movement in Texas, and more, see *Handbook of Texas Online*, https://tshaonline.org/handbook/online

17. Relations between police and protestors varied widely. For an account of a high-conflict incident in Austin, see Andrew Weber, "'They Shot All Of Us': An Austin Medic Recalls a Weekend of Police Violence Amid Peaceful Protests," *KUT*, June 4, 2020, https://www.kut.org/post/they-shot-all-us-austin-medic-recalls-weekend-police-violence-amid-peaceful-protests; and for a low-conflict incident, see Chris Blake and Scott Gordon, "Fort Worth Police Take Knee to Dissolve Tense Confrontation," *NBCDFW*, June 1, 2020, https://www.nbcdfw.com/news/local/hundreds-march-peacefully-in-downtown-fort-worth/2380387/. For the Governor's declaration, see "Governor Abbott Declares State of Disaster Following Violent Protests," *Office of the Texas Governor*, May 31, 2020, https://gov.texas.gov/news/post/governor-abbott-declares-state-of-disaster-following-violent-protests2

18. For an in-depth discussion about policing and police reform in Texas following the death of George Floyd, see Todd Wiseman, Jeremiah Rhodes, and Jolie McCullough, "Watch: Texas' Police Use-of-Force Tactics Scrutinized after George Floyd protests," *Texas Tribune*, July 20, 2020 https://www.texastribune.org/2020/07/02/texas-police-george-floyd/. For the impact of the protests on Confederate Monuments, see "Confederate Monuments Continue to Come Down in Racial Justice Protests," *Texas Public Radio*, June 19, 2020, https://www.tpr.org/post/confederate-monuments-continue-come-down-racial-justice-protests

19. Valerie D'Orazio, "Black Entrepreneurship 2020: A Special Report and Definitive 50-State Ranking," *Fit Small Business*, February 18, 2020, https://fitsmallbusiness.com/black-entrepreneurship-2020/. See also Ross Ramsey, "Texas Voters Split on Police Violence Protests, Open to Moving Confederate Statues, Poll Finds," *Texas Tribune*, July 6, 2020, https://www.texastribune.org/2020/07/06/texas-protests-confederate-statues/

20. For more on the conflict over tribal gambling facilities in Texas, see Emily Foxhall, "Alabama-Coushatta Tribe Fights for Right to a Gaming Center—Again," *Houston Chronicle*, February 27, 2018, https://www.houstonchronicle.com/news/houston-texas/houston/article/Alabama-Coushatta-fight-for-the-right-to-a-gaming-12707848.php. See also Erin Wides, "Congressman's Bill to Save Alabama-Coushatta Gaming facility Held Up in the Senate," *KTRE.com*, September 16, 2020, https://www.ktre.com/2020/09/16/congressmans-bill-save-alabama-coushatta-gaming-facility-held-up-senate/

21. For more about recent trends in immigration to the United States, see Jynnah Radford, "Key Findings about U.S. Immigrants," *Pew Research Center*, June 17, 2019, https://www.pewresearch.org/fact-tank/2019/06/17/key-findings-about-u-s-immigrants/

22. "American Community Survey Data Release," *U.S. Department of Commerce, Census Bureau*, December 10, 2019, https://www.census.gov/newsroom/press-kits/2019/acs-5-year.html

23. Jens Manuel Krogstad, "Hispanics Have Accounted for More Than Half of Total U.S. Population Growth Since 2010," *Pew Research Center*, July 10, 2020, https://www.pewresearch.org/fact-tank/2020/07/10/hispanics-have-accounted-for-more-than-half-of-total-u-s-population-growth-since-2010/. See also Alexa Ura and Connie Hanzhang Jin, "Texas Gained Almost Nine Hispanic Residents for Every Additional White Resident Last Year," *Texas Tribune*, June 20, 2019, https://www.texastribune.org/2019/06/20/texas-hispanic-population-pace-surpass-white-residents/. Note that the economic downturn caused by the COVID-19 pandemic will have changed poverty rates across Texas and the United States, but specific data will not be available for some time. For this reason, we report on the most recent poverty data available prior to the pandemic.

24. For a comprehensive national list, see the NALEO Educational Fund's National Directory of Latino Elected Officials at https://naleo.org/wp-content/uploads/2019/12/2019_National_Directory_of_Latino_Elected_Offcials.pdf

25. For a comprehensive list of Texas cities by percentage White residents, see "Cities with the Highest Percentage of Whites in Texas," *ZipAtlas*, http://zipatlas.com/us/tx/city-comparison/percentage-white-population.htm

26. For the most recent statistics, which predate the COVID-19 pandemic, see "Poverty Rate by Race/Ethnicity," *Henry J. Kaiser Family Foundation*, http://kff.org/other/state-indicator/poverty-rate-by-raceethnicity; and Kids Count Data Center, *Annie E. Casey Foundation*, https://datacenter.kidscount.org/data#TX/2/16/17,18,19,20,22,21,2720/char/0. See also "State Offices for Minority and Women Business Enterprises," *U.S. Department of Commerce, Minority Business Development Agency*, https://www.mbda.gov/media/3100

27. Daniel Elazar, *American Federalism: A View from the States,* 3rd ed. (New York: Harper & Row, 1984), 109–149. For a different view of political culture, see Dante Chinni and James Gimpel, *Our Patchwork Nation: The Surprising Truth about the "Real" America* (New York: Penguin Group, 2010) and its website at https://www.jeffersoninst.org/projects/patchwork-nation. This view identifies 12 political cultures nationally, of which nine are present in Texas.

28. David Cullen and Kyle G. Wilkison, *The Texas Left: The Radical Roots of Lone Star Liberalism* (College Station: Texas A&M University Press, 2010), 53–91.

29. See Mike Kingston, "A Brief Sketch of Texas History," in *Texas Almanac 2018–2019,* ed. Robert Plocheck (Austin, TX: Texas State Historical Association, 2019), 28–41. For a description of events that led to Texas's war for independence from Mexico, see James Donovan, *The Blood of Heroes: The 13-Day Struggle for the Alamo—and the Sacrifice that Forged a Nation* (New York: Little Brown, 2012).

30. For more polls about Texans' views on politics and government, see "The Texas Politics Project," University of Texas at Austin, https://texaspolitics.utexas.edu/polling/search/topic/government-operations-94/topic/federal-government-334?page=1. For information about Texans' resistance to COVID-19 restrictions, see Jim Henson and Joshua Blank, "Analysis: A Governor Balancing Noisy Resistance to Staying at Home with the Rest of His Political Base," *Texas Tribune,* April 27, 2020, https://www.texastribune.org/2020/04/27/texas-abbott-coronavirus-stay-home-politics/; and Valeria Olivares, "Nearly 80 Texas Counties Have Opted Out of Gov. Greg Abbott's Mask Order. Others Refuse to Enforce It," *Texas Tribune,* July 9, 2020, https://www.texastribune.org/2020/07/09/texas-mask-order-enforcement/

31. Kingston, "A Brief Sketch of Texas History," 43; and Rupert N. Richardson, Adrian Anderson, Cary D. Wintz, and Ernest Wallace, *Texas: The Lone Star State, 10th ed.* (Upper Saddle River, NJ: Prentice Hall, 2010), 151–154.

32. For an interactive map of Confederate symbols around the nation, see "Whose Heritage? Public Symbols of the Confederacy," *Southern Poverty Law Center,* https://www.splcenter.org/20190201/whose-heritage-public-symbols-confederacy

33. For more information on the Texas transportation system, see "Roadway Inventory Annual Reports," *Texas Department of Transportation,* https://ftp.txdot.gov/pub/txdot-info/tpp/roadway-inventory/2019.pdf; and Kevin McPherson, Jessica Donald, and Bruce Wright, "Transportation Infrastructure," *Texas Comptroller of Public Accounts: Fiscal Notes,* https://comptroller.texas.gov/economy/fiscal-notes/2018/may/transportation.php

34. "The 15 Fastest-Growing Large Cities - By Percent Change: 2010-2019," *U.S. Department of Commerce, Census Bureau,* May 21, 2020, https://www.census.gov/library/visualizations/2020/demo/fastest-growing-cities-2010-2019.html

35. Steve White, Lloyd B. Potter, Helen You, Lila Valencia, Jeffrey A. Jordan, Beverly Pecotte, and Sara Robinson, "Urban Texas," *Texas Demographic Center,* August 2017, http://demographics.texas.gov/Resources/publications/2017/2017_08_21_UrbanTexas.pdf

36. Marc Seitles, "The Perpetuation of Residential Racial Segregation in America: Historical Discrimination, Modern Forms of Exclusion, and Inclusionary Remedies," *Journal of Land Use & Environmental Law* 14 (Fall 1998): 89–124, https://ir.law.fsu.edu/cgi/viewcontent.cgi?article=1191&context=jluel

37. For examples in Austin, see "Austin Gentrification Maps and Data," *Governing the States and Localities,* http://www.governing.com/gov-data/austin-gentrification-maps-demographic-data.html

38. Kiah Collier, "As Oil and Gas Exports Surge, West Texas Becomes the World's 'Extraction Colony,'" *Texas Tribune,* October 11, 2018, https://www.texastribune.org/2018/10/11/west-texas-becomes-worlds-extraction-colony-oil-gas-exports-surge. See also Behany McLean, "Coronavirus May Kill Our Fracking Fever Dream," *New York Times,* April 10, 2020, https://www.nytimes.com/2020/04/10/opinion/sunday/coronavirus-texas-fracking-layoffs.html

39. For a map coronavirus infections rates by Texas county that is updated weekly, see "Texas coronavirus map: What do the trends mean for you?" *Mayo Clinic,* https://www.mayoclinic.org/coronavirus-covid-19/map/texas

40. For more on Dallas County leadership during the COVID crisis, see Rachel Williams, "Clay Jenkins Is Leading the COVID-19 Response While Governor Abbott Stalls," *Texas Monthly,* March 25, 2020, https://www.texasmonthly.com/politics/clay-jenkins-dallas-coronavirus/. For more on GOP fundraising in North Texas, see Patrick Svitek, "New Super PAC Raises Nearly $10 Million to Register New Republican Voters in Texas," *KERA News,* July 31, 2019; and Maria Recio, "Big Texas Donors Still Prefer GOP," *Austin American-Statesman,* November 5, 2018.

41. Shelby Webb, "'A positive thing for Houston': Oil closes above $70 a barrel for first time since 2018," *Houston Chronicle,* June 8, 2021, https://www.houstonchronicle.com/business/energy/article/A-positive-thing-for-Houston-Oil-closes-16234262.php

42. Kristian Hernandez, "Many Texas Ranchers Won't Survive Multibillion-Dollar Financial Hit from Coronavirus," *Fort Worth Star-Telegram,* May 10, 2020. https://www.star-telegram.com/article242512221.html

43. Jessie Higgins, "U.S. Cotton Industry Quietly Faces Crisis from China Trade War," *United Press International,* August 28, 2019, https://www.upi.com/Top_News/US/2019/08/28/US-cotton-industry-quietly-faces-crisis-from-China-trade-war/2021566927276/. See also "Prices good, drought bad for Texas cotton," *Cotton Farming,* May 1, 2021, https://www.cottonfarming.com/web-exclusive/prices-good-drought-bad-for-texas-cotton/

44. James Cozine, *Saving the Big Thicket: From Exploration to Preservation, 1685–2003* (Denton: University of North Texas Press, 2004). See also Robert S. Maxwell, "Lumber Industry," and Ronald H. Hufford, "Tree Farming," *Handbook of Texas Online*, https://www.tshaonline.org/handbook/online/articles

45. For information on the impact of the trade war and the coronavirus pandemic on the timber industry, see Diana Olick, "China Trade War Triggers Closings, Layoffs at US Hardwood Lumber Mills," *CNBC*, October 4, 2019, https://www.cnbc.com/2019/10/04/china-trade-war-triggers-closings-layoffs-at-us-hardwood-lumber-mills.html and Shrabana Mukherjee, "Wood Industry's Near-Term Prospects Dimmed by Coronavirus," *Yahoo! Finance*, May 7, 2020 https://www.yahoo.com/entertainment/wood-industrys-near-term-prospects-151603448.html. To track timber price trends over time, see "Landownder Assistance: Timber Price Trends," *Texas A&M Forest Service*, https://tfsweb.tamu.edu/TimberPriceTrends/

46. For an account of the history of the early years of the oil industry in Texas, see Roger M. Olien and Diana Davids Olien, *Oil in Texas: The Gusher Age, 1895–1945* (Austin: University of Texas Press, 2002).

47. To track the price of oil over time, see "Crude Oil Price History Chart," *Macrotrends*, http://www.macrotrends.net/1369/crude-oil-price-history-chart; and for more detail on those prices, see "Petroleum and Other Liquids," *U.S. Energy Information Administration*, https://www.eia.gov/dnav/pet/pet_pri_spt_s1_m.htm

48. See Mitchell Ferman, "Texas Oil Price Plummets into the Negatives as the Coronavirus Pandemic's Economic Woes Continue Battering the State," *Texas Tribune*, April 20, 2020, https://www.texastribune.org/2020/04/20/texas-oil-price-twi-coronavirus/. To track state revenue from oil production and from all other sources over time, see "Monthly State Revenue Watch," *Texas Comptroller of Public Accounts: Transparency*, https://comptroller.texas.gov/transparency/revenue/watch/all-funds/

49. For statistics and continuous updates on the Texas economy, see "Texas Economy," *Federal Reserve Bank of Dallas*, https://www.dallasfed.org/research/texas

50. To explore the Fortune 500 list, see https://fortune.com/fortune500/

51. "Texas Unemployment Rate at 3.5 Percent," *Texas Workforce Commission*, January 24, 2020, https://www.twc.texas.gov/news/texas-unemployment-rate-35-percent. For monthly updates on the Texas Labor Market, see "Texas Labor Market Review," *Texas Work-force Commission*, https://texaslmi.com/api/GetHomeLinks/TLMR. For continuously updated in-formation about the Texas Labor Market, see "Texas Labor Market Information," *Texas Workforce Commission*, https://texaslmi.com/

52. For a broad review of the many studies linking air pollution from the burning of fossil fuels to respiratory and cardiovascular disease, premature birth, infant and adult mortality, and more, see Bert Brunekreef and Stephen Holgate, "Air Pollution and Health," *The Lancet* 360 (2002): 1233–1242. For the American Academy of Pediatrics official statement about the impact on children, see "Ambient Air Pollution: Health Hazards to Children," *Pediatrics* 114, no. 6 (2004), http://intl-pediatrics.aappublications.org/content/114/6/1699.full

53. Meredith Lawrence, "Texas Produced More Energy from Renewable Sources Than Coal Last Year," *Dallas Observer*, January 10, 2020. For an interactive map that illustrates energy production facilities by state, see "U.S. Energy Mapping Systems," *U.S. Energy Information Administration*, https://www.eia.gov/state/maps.php

54. For an overview of energy in Texas, see "Texas State Profile and Energy Estimates," *U.S. Energy Information Administration*, http://www.eia.gov/state/?sid=TX#tabs-1. For an interactive map with projections of state wind capacity until 2050, see "Wind Vision," *U.S. Department of Energy*, https://www.energy.gov/maps/map-projected-growth-wind-industry-now-until-2050

55. Patrick Graves and Bruce Wright, "Solar Power in Texas: The Next Big Renewable?," *Texas Comptroller of Public Accounts: Fiscal Notes*, April 2018, https://comptroller.texas.gov/economy/fiscal-notes/2018/april/solar.php. See also Joanna H. Slusarewicz and Daniel S. Cohan, "Assessing Solar and Wind Complementarity in Texas," *Renewables: Wind, Water, and Solar*, 5 (2018): 7, https://jrenewables.springeropen.com/articles/10.1186/s40807-018-0054-3

56. Erin Douglas, Kate McGee and Jolie McCullough, "Texas leaders failed to heed warnings that left the state's power grid vulnerable to winter extremes, experts say," *The Texas Tribune*, February 17, 2021, https://www.texastribune.org/2021/02/17/texas-power-grid-failures/

57. For a brief history of the venture that served as a driving force to bring high tech to Texas, see "Sematech," in *Handbook of Texas Online*, https://tshaonline.org/handbook/online/articles/dns03. For key findings and an interactive map about the high-tech sector today, see "Cyberstates," *CompTIA*, https://www.cyberstates.org/#interactiveMap?geoid=48

58. Dom DiFurio, "Texas Ranks No. 2 for Tech Jobs, Even as Openings Decline During Pandemic," *Dallas Morning News*, June 9, 2020, https://www.dallasnews.com/business/technology/2020/06/09/texas-ranks-no-2-for-tech-jobs-even-as-openings-decline-during-pandemic/

59. For the state government's efforts to promote biotech, see "Texas Biotechnology and Life Sciences," *Office of the Texas Governor*, March 2020, https://gov.texas.gov/uploads/files/business/BioTech-March2020.pdf and "Biotechnology and Life Sciences," *Go Big in Texas, Texas Economic Development Corporation*, https://businessintexas.com/industries/biotechnology-life-sciences

60. Lori Hawkins, "Texas Service Sector Contracts, Retail Sales Plunge as Outbreak Lingers," *Austin American-Statesman*, July 28, 2020, https://www.statesman.com/business/20200728/texas-service-sector-contracts-retail-sales-plunge-as-outbreak-lingers

61. For more on hemp in Texas, see Morgan O'Hanlon, "Struggling Texas Farmers Thought Hemp Might Save Them. The Crop Hasn't Yet Delivered," *Texas Monthly*, August 10, 2020, https://www.texasmonthly.com/news/hemp-farming-texas-cbd/. For more on employment in agriculture, see "Texas Workforce Report: 2018–2019," *Texas Workforce Commission*, https://lmci.state.tx.us/shared/PDFs/Workforce_Report.pdf. For more detail on Texas agricultural production, see "Texas Ag Stats," *Texas Department of Agriculture*, https://texasagriculture.gov/About/TexasAgStats.aspx

62. For more information on challenges facing Texas agriculture, see April Simpson, "Pandemic, China Trade Deal Fuel Farmer Doubts," *Pew Stateline*, July 10, 2020, https://www.pewtrusts.org/fr/research-and-analysis/blogs/stateline/2020/07/10/pandemic-china-trade-deal-fuel-farmer-doubts and Madlin Mekelburg, "Texas facing more than $600M in agricultural losses after February winter freeze," *Austin American-Statesman*, March 12, 2021, https://www.statesman.com/story/news/environment/2021/03/11/texas-winter-storm-farmers-face-600-million-losses-february-freeze/4645220001/

63. M. Angeles Villarreal and Ian F. Fergusson, *U.S.-Mexico-Canada (USMCA) Trade Agreement*, (Washington, D.C.: Congressional Research Service, July 1, 2020), https://crsreports.congress.gov/product/pdf/IF/IF10997. See also Imelda García, "Five Ways Texas Benefits from the New USMCA Trade Deal Taking Effect Today," *Dallas Morning News*, July 1, 2020, https://www.dallasnews.com/business/economy/2020/07/01/five-ways-texas-benefits-from-the-new-usmca-trade-deal-taking-effect-today/

64. For an in-depth look at the difficulties facing *maquiladora* workers, see Stephanie Navarro, "Inside Mexico's Maquiladoras: Manufacturing Health Disparities," *Stanford Medicine,* https://med.stanford.edu/content/dam/sm/schoolhealtheval/documents/StephanieNavarro_HumBio122MFinal.pdf

65. For more on AMLO and his relationship with the United States, see Earl Anthony Wayne, "Harris signals a potential breakthrough in US-Mexico cooperation," *The Hill*, June 18, 2021, https://thehill.com/opinion/international/558753-harris-signals-a-potential-breakthrough-in-us-mexico-cooperation?rl=1; For more on economic relations with Mexico, see M. Angeles Villarreal, *U.S.-Mexico Economic Relations: Trends, Issues, and Implications* (Washington, D.C.: Congressional Research Service, June 25, 2020), https://fas.org/sgp/crs/row/RL32934.pdf

66. For more on childhood poverty, see "Child Poverty in America 2018: State Analysis," *Children's Defense Fund*, September 26, 2019, https://www.childrensdefense.org/wp-content/uploads/2019/09/Child-Poverty-in-America-2018-State-Factsheet.pdf, and "Kids Count National Indicators," *KIDS COUNT Data Center, Annie E. Casey Foundation*, https://datacenter.kidscount.org/data#USA/2/16/17,18,19,20,22,21,2720/char/0. For more on homelessness, see "The 2020 Annual Homeless Assessment Report (AHAR) to Congress," *U.S. Department of Housing and Urban Development, Office of Community Planning and Development*, https://www.huduser.gov/portal/sites/default/files/pdf/2020-AHAR-Part-1.pdf

67. For more on the broader impacts of a large uninsured population, see David Mills, "Why You Should Care If Your Neighbor Doesn't Have Health Insurance," *Healthline*, May 21, 2018, https://www.healthline.com/health-news/why-you-should-care-if-your-neighbor-doesnt-have-health-insurance; and Joey Berlin, "Far-Reaching Implications: The Ripple Effects of Texas' Uninsured Rate," *Texas Medical Association*, December 2019, https://www.texmed.org/TexasMedicineDetail.aspx?id=52056

68. Note that studies of the uninsured often exclude the elderly because they are covered by Medicare. For more on the impact of COVID-19 on health insurance, see Stan Dorn, "The COVID-19 Pandemic and Resulting Economic Crash have Caused the Greatest Health Insurance Losses in American history," *Families U.S.A.*, July 13, 2020, https://www.familiesusa.org/resources/the-covid-19-pandemic-and-resulting-economic-crash-have-caused-the-greatest-health-insurance-losses-in-american-history/. For more on the uninsured in Texas, see "The Uninsured in Texas," *Texas Medical Association*, https://www.texmed.org/Uninsured/

69. "Map: A-F Grades, Rankings for States on School Quality," *Education Week*, September 1, 2020, https://www.edweek.org/policy-politics/map-a-f-grades-rankings-for-states-on-school-quality/2020/09

70. For a variety of statistics regarding Texas students, see "Student Data," *Texas Education Agency*, https://tea.texas.gov/Reports_and_Data/Student_Data

71. Interview with Jacob Peña, August 12, 2020.

72. Scott E. Page, *The Diversity Bonus: How Great Teams Pay Off in the Knowledge Economy* (Princeton, NJ: Princeton University Press, 2017).

73. Avery Ruxer Franklin, "Economic Benefits of Illegal Immigration Outweigh the Costs, Baker Institute Study Shows," *Rice University, News and Media Relations Office of Public Affairs,* May 18, 2020, https://news.rice.edu/2020/05/18/economic-benefits-of-illegal-immigration-outweigh-the-costs-baker-institute-study-shows/. See also Angelos Angelou, William Mellor, and Anthony Michael, "Texans for All: Economic Impact of Senate Bill 4," *AngelouEconomics,* November 2017, https://assets.documentcloud.org/documents/4177307/TexansForAll.pdf

74. For a discussion of immigration reform from the business perspective, see Stan Marek and Leon Steffy, *Deconstructed: An Insider's View of Illegal Immigration and the Building Trades* (College Station: Texas A&M University Press, 2020).

75. Jacob Beltran, "San Antonio Sues Feds for Testimony in Sanctuary City Lawsuit Defense," *San Antonio Express-News,* April 29, 2020, https://www.expressnews.com/news/local/article/San-Antonio-sues-feds-for-testimony-in-sanctuary-15234000.php

76. Nina Totenberg, "Supreme Court Rules for DREAMers, Against Trump," *NPR,* June 18, 2020, https://www.npr.org/2020/06/18/829858289/supreme-court-upholds-daca-in-blow-to-trump-administration

77. For updates on the construction of the wall, see "Border Wall System," *U.S. Customs and Border Protection,* https://www.cbp.gov/border-security/along-us-borders/border-wall-system. For the Supreme Court's opinion, see *Donald Trump, President of the United States et al. v. Sierra Club et al.* 588 U.S. 2019, https://www.supremecourt.gov/opinions/18pdf/19a60_o75p.pdf

78. Marice Richter and Lisa Maria Garza, "Texas Governor Extends National Guard to Monitor Border," *Reuters,* December 15, 2015, http://www.reuters.com/article/us-texas-immigration-idUSKBN0TZ01B20151216

79. R. G. Ratcliffe, "Menéndez: Does Texas Still Need to Spend $800 Million on Border Security?" *Texas Monthly,* April 10, 2018, https://www.texasmonthly.com/politics/menendez-texas-senate-hispanic-caucus

80. For a timeline of family separation at the border, see "Family Separation under the Trump Administration – a Timeline," *Southern Poverty Law Center (SPLC),* June 17, 2020. https://www.splcenter.org/news/2020/06/17/family-separation-under-trump-administration-timeline. For more on COVID-19 in detention centers, see Parsa Erfani, Nishant Uppal, Caroline H. Lee et al, "COVID-19 Testing and Cases in Immigration Detention Centers, April–August 2020," *Journal of the American Medical Association Research Letter* (October 29, 2020), https://jamanetwork.com/journals/jama/fullarticle/2772627#:~:text=From%20April%20to%20August%202020%2C%20the%20mean%20monthly%20case%20rate,2.0%20to%206.9%20per%20month/. For changes initiated by the Biden Administration, see John Hudak and Christine Stenglein, "Biden's immigration reset," *Brookings,* February 19, 2021, https://www.brookings.edu/blog/fixgov/2021/02/19/bidens-immigration-reset/

81. "Best States 2019: Texas," *U.S. News and World Report,* https://www.usnews.com/news/best-states/texas

82. Priceonomics, "The Most (And Least) Toxic Places in America," *Forbes,* November 7, 2017, https://www.forbes.com/sites/priceonomics/2017/11/07/the-most-and-least-toxic-places-in-america/#2474aabd4ac1

83. Andrew J. Kondash, Nancy E. Lauer, and Avner Vengosh, "The Intensification of the Water Footprint of Hydraulic Fracturing," *Science Advances* 4: 8 (August 15, 2018), http://advances.sciencemag.org/content/4/8/eaar5982

84. For information about loan and grant programs, see "Financial Assistance," *Texas Water Development Board,* accessed August 7, 2020, http://www.twdb.texas.gov/financial/index.asp

85. Scot Schraufnagel, Michael J. Pomante II, and Quan Li, "Cost of Voting in the American States: 2020," *Election Law Journal: Rules, Politics, and Policy,* 19 (December 15, 2020): 503–509, https://www.liebertpub.com/doi/10.1089/elj.2020.0666

Chapter 2

1. David B. Walker, *The Rebirth of Federalism: Slouching toward Washington,* 2nd ed. (New York: Chatham House, 2000), 260.

2. Rick Perry, *Fed Up! Our Fight to Save America from Washington* (New York: Little, Brown and Co., 2010), 32.

3. For a discussion of the history and meaning of this clause, see Gary Lawson, Geoffrey P. Miller, Robert G. Natelson, and Guy I. Seidman, *The Origins of the Necessary and Proper Clause* (New York: Cambridge University Press, 2013).

4. *Garcia v. San Antonio Metropolitan Transit Authority,* 469 U.S. 528 (1985).

5. For a description of the procedure, see "The Solution," *Convention of States,* https://conventionofstates.com/. See also, Greg Abbott, *Broken Not Unbowed: The Fight to Fix a Broken America* (New York: Threshold Editions, 2016).

6. *U.S. Term Limits v. Thornton,* 514 U.S. 115 (1995).

7. *Sweatt v. Painter*, 339 U.S. 629 (1950).

8. Paul Burka, "The M Word," *Texas Monthly*, January 2006, 14–16.

9. *U.S. v. Windsor*, 570 U.S. 744 (2013).

10. *Obergefell v. Hodges*, 576 U.S. 644 (2015). See also Lauren McGaughy, "High Court Calls Same-Sex Marriage a Fundamental Right," *Houston Chronicle*, June 27, 2015.

11. *Kimel v. Florida Board of Regents*, 528 U.S. 62 (2000); *Alden v. Maine*, 527 U.S. 706 (1999); and *Seminole Tribe v. Florida*, 517 U.S. 44 (1996).

12. *Frew v. Hawkins*, 540 U.S. 431 (2004). See also Carlos Guerra, "High Court Orders Texas to Honor Its Word and Pay Up," *San Antonio Express-News*, January 15, 2004.

13. *Kelo v. New London*, 545 U.S. 469 (2005).

14. For a description of a common carrier, see "How Eminent Domain Works in Texas," *State Impact*, https://stateimpact.npr.org/texas/tag/eminent-domain. See also Morgan Smith and Jim Malewitz, "In Big Bend, Trans-Pecos Pipeline Clears Last Hurdle," *Texas Tribune*, May 6, 2016, https://www.texastribune.org/2016/05/06/big-bend-trans-pecos-pipeline-clears-last-hurdle/. Timothy Gardner, "Montana Judge Upholds Ruling that Canceled Keystone XL Pipeline Permit," *REUTERS*, https://www.reuters.com/article/us-usa-pipelines-court/montanta-judge-upholds-ruling-that-canceled-keystone-xl-pipeline-permit-idUSKBN22O07T

15. *United States v. Lopez*, 514 U.S. 549 (1995).

16. *Gonzales v. Raich*, 545 U.S. 1 (2005).

17. "State Medical Marijuana Laws," National Conference of State Legislatures, https://www.ncsl.org/research/health/state-medical-marijuana-laws.aspx

18. Neena Satija, "Interactive: Texas vs. the Federal Government," *Texas Tribune*, January 17, 2017, https://www.texastribune.org/2017/01/17/texas-federal-government-lawsuits/. See also Lauren McGaughy, "Texas vs. the Feds—A Look at the Lawsuits," *Houston Chronicle*, November 20, 2015, http://www.houstonchronicle.com/news/politics/texas/article/Texas-taxpayer-tab-for-suing-feds-tops-5-million-6647726.php

19. Lauren McGaughy, "With Trump in Charge, Why is Texas still Suing the Federal Government? Because Now it Can Win," *The Dallas Morning News*, February 8, 2018, https://www.dallasnews.com/news/politics/2018/02/08/with-trump-in-charge-why-is-texas-still-suing-the-federal-government-because-now-it-can-win/

20. *National Federation of Independent Business v. Sebelius*, 567 U.S. 519 (2012).

21. *King v. Burwell*, 576 U.S. 473 (2015). See also Tim Eaton, "U.S. Supreme Court Rules in Favor of Obama, Affordable Care Act," *Austin American Statesman*, June 26, 2015.

22. *California v. Texas*, Oyez, Oral Argument, November 10, 2020, https://www.oyez.org/cases/2020/19-840

23. See Jess Bravin and Byron Tau, "Supreme Court to Rule on Obama's Bid to Block Deportations," *Wall Street Journal*, January 20, 2016. Also see *United States v. Texas*, 579 U.S. ___ (2016).

24. Nina Totenberg, "Supreme Court Rules for DREAMers, Against Trump," National Public Radio, https://www.npr.org/2020/06/18/829858289/supreme-court-upholds-daca-in-blow-to-trump-administration

25. Sanford F. Schram, "Welfare Reform: A Race to the Bottom?" *Publius: The Journal of Federalism* 28 (Summer 1998): 1–8. (Special issue: "Welfare Reform in the United States: A Race to the Bottom?" edited by Sanford F. Schram and Samuel H. Beer.)

26. "CARES Act, How the CARES Act Helps Texans," John Cornyn, United States Senator for Texas, https://www.cornyn.senate.gov/node/5431?tab=cares-act

27. Perry, *Fed Up!* 187–188.

28. To review his proposal, see Greg Abbott, "Restoring the Rule of Law with States Leading the Way," *Office of the Governor*, https://gov.texas.gov/uploads/files/press/Restoring_The_Rule_Of_Law_01082016.pdf

29. For a more detailed account of early Texas constitutions, see John Cornyn, "The Roots of the Texas Constitution: Settlement to Statehood," *Texas Tech Law Review* 26, 4 (1995): 1089–1218. (Note: The author served as a member of the Texas Supreme Court and as the state's attorney general before being elected to the U.S. Senate in 2002.)

30. Leobardo F. Estrada, F. Chris Garcia, Reynaldo Flores Macias, and Lionel Maldonado, "Chicanos in the United States: A History of Exploitation and Resistance," in *Latinos and the Political System*, ed. F. Chris Garcia (Notre Dame, IN: University of Notre Dame Press, 1988), 28–64. See also, Roberto Juarez, "The American Tradition of Language Rights: The Forgotten Right to Government in a 'Known Tongue,'" *Law & Inequality: A Journal of Theory and Practice* 13, 2 (1995): 495–518.

31. Charles William Ramsdell, *Reconstruction in Texas* (New York: Columbia University Press, 1910); and T. R. Fehrenbach, *Lone Star: A History of Texas and the Texans* (New York: Macmillan, 1968), especially chap. 22, "The Carpetbaggers."

32. Patrick G. Williams, *Beyond Redemption: Texas Democrats after Reconstruction* (Austin: University of Texas Press, 2007); Carl H. Moneyhon, *Edmund J. Davis of Texas: Civil War General, Republican Leader, Reconstruction Governor* (Fort Worth: TCU Press, 2010); and Barry A. Crouch, *The Dance of Freedom: Texas African Americans during Reconstruction*, ed. Larry Madaras (Austin: University of Texas Press, 2007).

33. An alternative view on writing Texas's seventh constitution is presented in Patrick G. Williams, "Of Rutabagas and Redeemers: Rethinking the Texas Constitution of 1876," *Southwestern Historical Quarterly* 106, 2 (2002): 230–253.

34. Roy Walthall, "Celebrate Texas's Anniversary with a Reorganized Constitution," *Waco Tribune-Herald*, March 5, 2011.

35. Jane Elliott, "Gay Marriage Ban Put in Texas Constitution," *Houston Chronicle*, November 9, 2005. See also "Summary Report of the 2005 Constitutional Election Results," *Secretary of State*, http://www.sos.texas.gov/elections/forms/enrrpts/2005con.pdf

36. Samuels, Alex, "Texas Voters Approve State Income Tax Ban, Most Other Constitutional Amendments," *The Texas Tribune*, November 6, 2019. https://www.texastribune.org/2019/11/05/texas-constitutional-amendments-uniform-election-results-2019/

37. Ralph Haurwitz, "From College to Beach, All Amendments Pass," *Austin American-Statesman*, November 4, 2009; Holly Hacker, "Prop. 4 Would Let Colleges Tap Fund," *Dallas Morning News*, October 4, 2009; and "Constitutional Amendments Proposed for November 2009 Ballot," Focus Report No. 81-8 (Austin: House Research Organization, Texas House of Representatives, August 20, 2009), http://www.hro.house.state.tx.us/pdf/focus/amend81.pdf

38. See Greg Abbott, "Governor Urges Vote for Prop. 6," *McAllen Monitor*, October 20, 2015.

39. See "Amendments Proposed for November 2015 Ballot: Focus Report," *House Research Organization*, http://www.hro.house.state.tx.us/pdf/focus/amend84.pdf

40. See "Amendments Proposed for November 2017 Ballot: Focus Report," *House Research Organization*, http://www.hro.house.state.tx.us/pdf/focus/amend85.pdf

41. See "Condensed Analyses of Proposed Constitutional Amendments," *Texas Legislative Council*, August 2919, https://tlc.texas.gov/docs/amendments/analyses19-condensed.pdf. See also, "Texas Proposition 4, Prohibit State Income Tax on Individuals Amendment (2019), *Ballotpedia*, https://ballotpedia.org/Texas_Proposition_4,_Prohibit_State_Income_Tax_on_Individuals_Amendment_(2019)#Election_results

42. *Book of the States,* 2017, "Constitutional Amendment Procedure: By Initiative," http://knowledgecenter.csg.org/kc/system/files/1.3%202016.pdf

43. Texas's right-to-work law was enacted in 1947 by the 50th Legislature. The law bans the union shop arrangement whereby newly hired workers must join a union after employment.

44. Jim Lewis, "Getting Around to a New Constitution," *County* (January/February 1999): 11–13. For a profile of Representative Rob Junell and his collaboration with Senator Bill Ratliff, see Janet Elliott, "Maverick in the Middle," *Texas Lawyer* (January 1999): 19–20.

45. For the text of the Ratliff-Junell draft constitution, refer to Texas Legislature Online, https://capitol.texas.gov/BillLookup/Text.aspx?LegSess=76R&Bill=HJR1

46. See Roy Walthall, "Waco Group Reorganizes Texas Constitution," *Waco Tribune-Herald*, November 15, 2010; Roy Walthall, "Texas Constitution Needs Makeover," *Amarillo Globe-News*, October 23, 2011; and "Waco Group Hoping to Reorganize Texas Constitution," accessed October 31, 2013, www.WacoTrib.com. See also a legislative history of the concurrent resolution. Refer to the Texas Legislature Online, https://capitol.texas.gov/BillLookup/History.aspx?LegSess=84R&Bill=HCR37

47. For an analysis of amendments proposed between 1976 and 1989, see James G. Dickson, "Erratic Continuity: Some Patterns of Constitutional Change in Texas Since 1975," *Texas Journal of Political Studies* 14 (Fall–Winter 1991–1992): 41–56.

48. For the text of Junell's constitutional proposal, refer to Texas Legislature Online, http://www.capitol.state.tx.us/BillLookup/Text.aspx?LegSess=77R&Bill=HJR69

49. For detailed analyses of the contents of the Texas Constitution, see Janice C. May, *The Texas State Constitution: A Reference Guide* (Westport, CT: Greenwood Press, 1996); The Texas Constitution can be found at the Texas Legislature's website, https://statutes.capitol.texas.gov/

50. *Santa Fe v. Doe*, 530 U.S. 290 (2000).

51. *Van Orden v. Perry*, 545 U.S. 677 (2005).

52. For details concerning the struggle for equal legal rights, see Rob Fink, "Hermine Tobolowsky, the Texas ELRA, and the Political Struggle for Women's Equal Rights," *Journal of the West* 42 (Summer 2003): 52–57; and Tai Kreidler, "Hermine Tobolowsky: Mother of Texas Equal Rights Amendment," in *The Human Tradition in Texas*, ed. Ty Cashion and Jesus de la Teja (Wilmington, DE: SR Books, 2001), 209–220.

53. Jason Embry, "School Tax System Unconstitutional: State Supreme Court Wants a Fix by June 1," *Austin American-Statesman*, November 23, 2005. See also Gary Scharrer, "Justices Warn that Changes Will Have to Be Significant," *San Antonio Express-News,* November 23, 2005.

54. See Kiahh Collier, "Experts: Expect Early 2016 School Finance Ruling," *Texas Tribune*, September 17, 2015, https://www.texastribune.org/2015/09/17/experts-expect-early-2016-school-finance-ruling/. See also, Kiahh Collier, "Texas Supreme Court Upholds School Funding System," *Texas Tribune*, May 13, 2016, https://www.texastribune.org/2016/05/13/texas-supreme-court-issues-school-finance-ruling/

55. *Shelby County v. Holder*, 570 U.S. 529 (2013).

56. See Manny Fernandez, "Texas' Voter ID Law Does Not Discriminate and Can Stand, Appeals Panel Rules, April 27, 2018, https://www.nytimes.com/2018/04/27/us/texas-voter-id.html

Chapter 3

1. *Clinton v. Cedar Rapids and the Missouri River Railroad*, 24 Iowa 455 (1868).

2. *People v. Hurlbut*, 24 Mich. 44, 95 (1871).

3. Jesse J. Richardson Jr., Meghan Zimmerman Gough, and Robert Puentes, "Is Home Rule the Answer? Clarifying the Influence of Dillon's Rule on Growth Management," *Brookings Institution*, January 2013, http://www.brookings.edu/research/reports/2003/01/01metropolitanpolicy-richardson

4. FEMA, "Declared Disasters," accessed September 6, 2020, https://www.fema.gov/disasters/disaster-declarations?field_dv2_state_territory_tribal_value=TX&field_year_value=All&field_dv2_declaration_type_value=All&field_dv2_incident_type_target_id=All&page=0

5. FEMA, "State Profiles," accessed September 6, 2020, https://recovery.fema.gov/state-profiles

6. Claudia Rivas, "Boundary Dispute Ends in San Patricio County's Favor," *The News of San Patricio*, October 21, 2018, https://www.mysoutex.com/san_patricio_county/news/features/boundary-dispute-ends-in-san-patricio-county-s-favor/article_0e25f9ce-d30f-11e8-8ca6-3b6e9468eca0.html

7. See *Texas Local Govt. Code Ann. Chapter* 5 (1987).

8. Russell Gold, "Texas Prohibits Local Fracking Bans," *Wall Street Journal*, May 15, 2015.

9. Matt Zapotosky, "This Might Be the Most Corrupt Little Town in America," *Washington Post,* March 5, 2016, https://www.washingtonpost.com/world/national-security/this-might-be-the-most-corrupt-little-town-in-america/2016/03/05/341c21d2-dcac-11e5-81ae-7491b9b9e7df_story.html; and Garrett Brnger, "Crystal City Will Hold Recall Election," *KSAT,* March 8, 2016, http://www.ksat.com/news/crystal-city-will-hold-recall-election

10. Alexa Ura, "Bathroom Fears Flush Houston Discrimination Ordinance," *Texas Tribune*, November 3, 2015, https://www.texastribune.org/2015/11/03/houston-anti-discrimination-ordinance-early-voting

11. Adrienne Lafrance and Rose Eveleth, "Are Taxis Safer Than Uber?" *Atlantic*, March 3, 2015, http://www.theatlantic.com/technology/archive/2015/03/are-taxis-safer-than-uber/386207

12. The seminal work is Robert Lineberry and Edmund Fowler, "Reformism and Public Policies in American Cities," *American Political Science Review* 61 (September 1967): 701–717. But see Chris Tausanovitchy and Christopher Warshawz, "Representation in Municipal Government," *American Political Science Review*, 108 (March 2014): 605–641.

13. *Tex. Elec. Code Ann.* §143.003

14. Christopher S. Elmendorf, Kevin M. Quinn, and Marisa J. Abrajano, "Racially Polarized Voting," *University of Chicago Law Review*: Vol. 83, 2016, https://chicagounbound.uchicago.edu/uclrev/vol83/iss2/2

15. See Robert Bezdek, David Billeaux, and Juan Carlos Huerta, "Latinos, At-Large Elections, and Political Change: Evidence from the Transition Zone," *Social Science Quarterly* 81 (March 2000): 207–225. Data collected from city websites by author, 2012 and 2020.

16. The definition of a minority opportunity district varies by source and situation. It is particularly affected by the degree of ethnic polarization in voting. Commonly, it would require that a group be 50 percent of the citizens of voting age; but for Latinos, the percentage may be as high as 65 percent. Rudolph Bush, "Justice Department Approves Dallas Redistricting Plan," *Dallas Morning News*, December 21, 2011.

17. National Association of Latino Elected and Appointed Officials (NALEO) Educational Fund, *2019 National Directory of Latino Elected Officials,* 2019, https://naleo.org/; Reflective Democracy Campaign, "2018-19 Demographics of Power," 2019, https://wholeads.us/resources/for-researchers/ Sonia R. García, Valerie Martinez-Ebers, Irasema Coronado, Sharon Navarro, and Patricia Jaramillo, *Politicas: Latina Trailblazers in the Texas Political Arena* (Austin: University of Texas Press, 2008) provides biographical essays on the first Latina elected public officials in Texas.

18. Throughout, local government finance data are analyzed by the author, drawing primarily from U.S. Census Bureau, "Census of Governments 2017," https://www.census.gov/programs-surveys/cog.html;

Urban Institute, "State and Local Finance Data," 2020, https://state-local-finance-data.taxpolicycenter.org/pages.cfm; www.USGovernmentSpending.Com; Texas Comptroller, https://comptroller.texas.gov/; and local government websites.

19. Ryan Holeywell, "Forget What You've Heard, Houston Really Does Have Zoning (Sort Of)," Rice Kinder Institute, September 8, 2015, https://kinder.rice.edu/2015/09/08/forget-what-youve-heard-houston-really-does-have-zoning-sort-of

20. www.USGovernmentSpending.Com

21. "Crude Oil Prices," *Macrotrends*, 2020, https://www.macrotrends.net/1369/crude-oil-price-history-chart

22. Eduardo Porter, "When Public Outperforms Private in Services," *New York Times*, January 15, 2013, https://www.nytimes.com/2013/01/16/business/when-privatization-works-and-why-it-doesnt-always.html; Allegra Hill, "Competitive Contracting—Dull but Effective," *Austin American-Statesman*, December 8, 2015.

23. Texas Comptroller of Public Accounts, *Tax Rates and Levies*, https://comptroller.texas.gov/taxes/property-tax/rates/index.php

24. John S. Kiernan, *WalletHub*, February 25, 2020, https://wallethub.com/edu/states-with-the-highest-and-lowest-property-taxes/11585/#real-estate

25. Tony Plohetski, "Grand Jury Investigating Gov. Rick Perry Convenes," *Austin American-Statesman*, May 16, 2014.

26. Jolie McCullough, "Report: Harris County's Bail Reforms…," *The Texas Tribune*, September 3, 2020, https://www.texastribune.org/2020/09/03/harris-county-bail-reform/

27. J. Mac McCullough, and Jonathon P. Leider, "The Importance of Health and Social Services Spending to Health Outcomes in Texas, 2010–2016," *Southern Medical Journal*, February 2019, https://www.ncbi.nlm.nih.gov/pmc/articles/PMC6530967/

28. Sean Collins Walsh, "Travis County Oks $951 Million Budget, In-person Jail Visits," *Austin American-Statesman*, September 29, 2015.

29. Gyusuck Geon and Geoffrey K. Turnbull, "The Effect of Home Rule on Local Government Behavior: Is There No Rule Like Home Rule?" Georgia State University, September 2004, https://www.researchgate.net/publication/228426796_The_Effect_of_Home_Rule_on_Local_Government_Behavior_Is_There_No_Rule_Like_Home_Rule

30. Good introductions to the problems of colonia residents are Sophie Novack, "Under Water," *Texas Observer*, April 27, 2020, https://www.texasobserver.org/underwater/; and Gaby Galvin, "On the Border, Out of the Shadows," *US News*, May 16, 2018, https://www.usnews.com/news/healthiest-communities/articles/2018-05-16/americas-third-world-border-colonias-in-texas-struggle-to-attain-services

31. Dennis Foley, "Are Texas Border Cities Actually Safer Than Other Cities?" *KTSA News*, January 9, 2019, https://www.ktsa.com/are-texas-border-cities-actually-safer-than-other-cities/; and FBI, *Crime in the United States, 2019*, https://ucr.fbi.gov/crime-in-the-u.s/2019/crime-in-the-u.s.-2019/topic-pages/violent-crime

32. Alexandra Hutzler, "New Poll Shows Residents Closest to Trump's Border Wall Oppose President's Immigration Policies, Distrust Border Agents," *Newsweek*, November 7, 2019, https://www.newsweek.com/poll-southwestern-border-residents-disagree-trump-immigration-policies-1470418; Alfredo Corchado, "Poll Finds U.S.-Mexico Border Residents Overwhelmingly Value Mobility, Oppose Wall," *Dallas Morning News*, July 18, 2016, http://interactives.dallasnews.com/2016/border-poll/; Madlin Mekelburg, "Polls Show People in Texas Are Divided on the Border Wall," *Politifact*, February 26, 2019, https://www.politifact.com/factchecks/2019/feb/26/joaquin-castro/polls-show-people-texas-are-divided-border-wall/

33. Texas Education Agency, "Snapshot 2019: State Totals," 2020, https://rptsvr1.tea.texas.gov/perfreport/snapshot/2019/state.html

34. Texas Comptroller, "Texas Community Colleges," 2020, https://comptroller.texas.gov/economy/economic-data/colleges/

35. Taylor Goldenstein, "Abbott Signs Bill Limiting Annexation," *Austin American Statesman*, updated September 22, 2018, https://www.statesman.com/NEWS/20170816/Abbott-signs-bill-limiting-annexation-powers-of-cities

Chapter 4

1. Michael S. Lewis-Beck, *The American Voter Revisited* (Ann Arbor: University of Michigan Press, 2008), 112.

2. Keith Smith, "Why Just Two Parties? A Voting Game to Illustrate Duverger's Law." *PS: Political Science & Politics* 45 (2012): 759–764.

3. Alex Briseno, "Third-party candidates in Texas elections endured long journeys to get on the Nov. 3 ballot," *Dallas Morning News*, October 19, 2020.

4. Robert S. Erikson and Kent L. Tedin, *American Public Opinion.* 10th ed. (New York, Routledge, 2019), 68.

5. Robert S. Erikson and Kent L. Tedin, *American Public Opinion.* 10th ed. (New York, Routledge, 2019), 74.

6. Scott Clement and John C. Green, "The Tea Party and Religion," *Pew Research Center*, February 23, 2011, http://www.pewforum.org/2011/02/23/tea-party-and-religion

7. For discussions of contemporary Texas conservatism, see Karl Rove, *Courage and Consequence: My Life as a Conservative in the Fight* (New York: Threshold, 2010); Gail Collins, *As Texas Goes ... How the Lone Star State Hijacked the American Agenda* (New York: Liveright, 2012); and Wayne Thorburn, *The Republican Part of Texas: a Political History* (Austin: University of Texas Press, 2021).

8. Jim Henson, "GOP Candidates, Voters and Creationism," *The Texas Politics Project*, December 17, 2013.

9. David R. Brockman, "'We Got Nothing:' Few Wins for the Christian Right in the 86th Texas Legislature." *The Texas Observer*, June 12, 2019, https://www.texasobserver.org/we-got-nothing-few-wins-for-the-christian-right-in-the-86th-texas-legislature/

10. For a discussion of contemporary Texas liberalism, see Mary Beth Rogers, *Turning Texas Blue: What It Will Take to Break the GOP Grip on America's Reddest State* (New York: St. Martin's Press, 2016).

11. Angel Saavedra Cisneros, *Latino Identity and Political Attitudes: Why Are Latinos Not Republican?* (New York: Palgrave Macmillan, 2017).

12. "5 Facts About Black Democrats," *Pew Research Center*, February 27, 2020, https://www.pewresearch.org/fact-tank/2020/02/27/5-facts-about-black-democrats/

13. David Kirby and Emily Ekins, "Libertarian Roots of the Tea Party," *Policy Analysis*, August 6, 2012, http://object.cato.org/sites/cato.org/files/pubs/pdf/PA705.pdf

14. Matt Obrien, "Republicans Couldn't Possibly Be More Hypocritical About the Economy," May 15, 2019, https://www.washingtonpost.com/us-policy/2019/05/15/republicans-couldnt-possibly-be-more-hypocritical-about-economy/

15. Edward G. Carmines, and James A. Stimson, *Issue Evolution: Race and the Transformation of American Politics.* (Princeton: Princeton University Press, 1989).

16. Charles S. Bullock, Donna R. Hoffman, and Ronald Keith Gaddie, "Regional Variations in the Realignment of American Politics, 1944–2004," *Social Science Quarterly*, 87 (September 2006): 494–518; and Robert S. Erikson and Kent L. Tedin, *American Public Opinion,* 9th ed. (Boston: Pearson, 2015).

17. For more information on the Populist Party in Texas, see Alwyn Barr, *Reconstruction to Reform Texas Politics, 1876–1906* (Dallas: Southern Methodist University Press, 2000).

18. Teresa Palomo Acosta, "Raza Unida Party," *The Handbook of Texas Online*, http://www.tshaonline.org/handbook/online/articles/war01

19. Tex. Elec. Code Ann. §142.007 (2010).

20. "Ballot access requirements for political candidates in Texas," *Ballotpedia*, https://ballotpedia.org/Ballot_access_requirements_for_political_candidates_in_Texas

21. For an alternate view, see Carl Moneyhon, *Edmund J. Davis of Texas: Civil War General, Republican Leader, Reconstruction Governor* (Fort Worth: TCU Press, 2010).

22. Dick Smith, "Department of Banking," *The Handbook of Texas Online*, http://www.tshaonline.org/handbook/online/articles/mcdcg

23. See Gregg Cantrell, "A Host of Sturdy Patriots: The Texas Populists," in *The Texas Left: The Radical Roots of Lone Star Liberalism*, ed. David O'Donald Cullen and Kyle G. Wilkison (College Station: Texas A&M University Press, 2010), 53–73.

24. Nancy Beck Young, "Democratic Party," *The Handbook of Texas Online*, http://www.tshaonline.org/handbook/online/articles/wad01

25. Edward G. Carmines, and James A. Stimson, *Issue Evolution: Race and the Transformation of American Politics.* (Princeton: Princeton University Press, 1989).

26. Jessica Montoya Coggins, "Fifty Years after 'Viva Kennedy' and Its Political Impact on Latinos," *NBC Latino*, November 15, 2013, http://nbclatino.com/2013/11/15/fifty-years-after-viva-kennedy-and-its-impact-on-latinos

27. Teresa Palomo Acosta, "Raza Unida Party," *The Handbook of Texas Online*, http://www.tshaonline.org/handbook/online/articles/war01

28. John Nichols, "When the Republicans Really Were the Party of Lincoln," *Moyers on Democracy*, July 2, 2014, https://billmoyers.com/2014/07/02/when-the-republicans-really-were-the-party-of-lincoln/

29. Mark Odintz, and Mary Beth Rogers, "Jordan, Barbara Charline," *Handbook of Texas Online*, https://tshaonline.org/handbook/online/articles/fjoas

30. Nancy Beck Young, "Democratic Party," *The Handbook of Texas Online*, http://www.tshaonline.org/handbook/online/articles/wad01

31. Patrick Svitek and Alex Samuels, "Texas Republicans Embraced Donald Trump For Four Years. Now They Face a Reckoning." *Texas Tribune*, January 19, 2021, https://www.texastribune.org/2021/01/19/donald-trump-texas-republicans-reckoning/

32. Danny Osborne, David O. Sears, and Nicholas A. Valentino, "The End of the Solidly Democratic South: The Impressionable-Years Hypothesis." *Political Psychology* 32 (2011): 81–107.

33. Danny Osborne, David O. Sears, and Nicholas A. Valentino, "The End of the Solidly Democratic South: The Impressionable-Years Hypothesis." *Political Psychology* 32 (2011): 81–107.

34. "Texas Report," *Latino Decisions*, February 2014, http://www.latinodecisions.com/files/5413/9488/2480/Texas_AV_Report.pdf

35. Mary Beth Rogers, "How to Turn Texas Blue," *Texas Observer*, January 19, 2016, http://www.texasobserver.org/how-to-turn-texas-blue; "2018 voter poll results: Texas," *Washington Post*, November 30, 2018, https://www.washingtonpost.com/graphics/2018/politics/voter-polls/texas.html?noredirect=on&utm_term=.ff71037d0226

36. University of Texas/Texas Tribune Polls (TX Poll) from 2009, 2011, 2013, 2015, 2017, and 2019 are used for the analyses. Three TX Polls are done per year (spring, summer, and fall) and are merged. The 2009 and 2011 Texas Polls had 800 respondents for each poll, except for June 2009 that had 924 respondents. Hence, merging the three 2009 polls results in 2524 respondents and 2011 has 2400 combined respondents. The 2013, 2015, 2017, and 2019 polls all include 1200 respondents per survey, yielding 3600 per year. The complete merging of polls yields 19,324 respondents. The surveys are available at https://texaspolitics.utexas.edu/polling-data-archive/. For a more complete analysis of these surveys, see Juan Carlos Huerta and Beatriz Cuartas, "Red to Purple? Changing Demographics and Party Change in Texas," *Social Science Quarterly*, https://doi.org/10.1111/ssqu.12991/

37. Party identification is measured as follows: strong Republican, weak Republican, lean Republican, independent = does not identify as a Democrat; lean Democrat, weak Democrat, strong Democrat = identify as a Democrat.

38. Samuel J. Eldersveld and Hanes Walton Jr., *Political Parties in American Society*, 2nd ed. (New York: Palgrave Macmillan, 2000), 125–126.

39. "General Rules for All Conventions and Meetings," *Republican Party of Texas,* https://www.texasgop.org/rules/

40. *The Rules of the Texas Democratic Party, 2020-2021*, Texas Democratic Party, https://www.texasdemocrats.org/wp-content/uploads/2020/04/TDP-Rules-4_15_2020.pdf

41. For example, in April 2016, delegates to the Green Party of Texas State Convention met to nominate statewide candidates and select delegates for the Green Party National Convention. Green Party presidential candidate Jill Stein was awarded 15 of the 23 delegates. "Stein Wins Majority of Texas Convention Delegates," *Green Party Watch*, April 10, 2016, http://www.greenpartywatch.org/2016/04/10/stein-wins-majority-of-texas-convention-delegates

42. Ken Herman, "The Texas GOPs Most Unconventional Convention," July 21, 2020, *Austin American Statesman.*

43. See "Party Primaries" at https://www.uh.edu/hobby/texasprimary101/parties/ for additional information about presidential preference primaries in Texas.

44. Eleanor Dearman, "Veronica Escobar Discusses Mass Shooting, Announces Texas Votes at Democratic Convention," *El Paso Times*, August 19, 2020, https://www.elpasotimes.com/story/news/politics/elections/2020/08/18/democratic-national-convention-us-rep-veronica-escobar-announces-texas-votes-urges-end-gun-violence/3398046001/

45. Scott Detrow, "DNC Officials Vote to Scale Back Role of 'Superdelegates' in Presidential Nomination," June 27, 2018, *NPR*, https://www.npr.org/2018/06/27/623913044/dnc-officials-vote-to-scale-back-role-of-superdelegates-in-presidential-nominati

46. "General Rules for All Conventions and Meetings," *Republican Party of Texas,* https://www.texasgop.org/rules/ Andrews, Bennett, and Parlapiano, "2016 Primary Results and Calendar."

47. Carla Astudillo, "Texas Primary 2020 Results: Watch Live Updates Here," *The Texas Tribune*, March 6, 2020, https://apps.texastribune.org/features/2020/primary-election-results/?_ga=2.165749118.1545481707.1598126450-1654320273.1570396260

48. Eleanor Dearman, "Abbott Calls for Nueces Co. GOP Party Chair to Resign over George Floyd Conspiracy Theory," *Corpus Christi Caller-Times*, June 4, 2020, https://www.caller.com/story/news/local/2020/06/04/texas-governor-greg-abbott-calls-for-nueces-county-republican-party-chair-jim-kaelin-resignation/3148809001/

49. Jonathan Tilove, "Allen West Ousts James Dickey as Texas GOP Chair," *Austin American-Statesman*, July 21, 2020.

50. Julie Moreno, "Here's How Texans Voted on the Propositions on the Primary Election Ballots," *KSAT*, March 4, 2020, https://www.ksat.com/vote-2020/2020/03/04/heres-how-texans-voted-on-the-propositions-on-the-primary-election-ballots

51. Julie Moreno, "Here's How Texans Voted on the Propositions on the Primary Election Ballots," *KSAT*, March 4, 2020, https://www.ksat.com/vote-2020/2020/03/04/heres-how-texans-voted-on-the-propositions-on-the-primary-election-ballots

Chapter 5

1. United States Election Project, "2020 November General Election Turnout Rates," electproject.org, accessed December 8, 2020, http://www.electproject.org/2020g

2. *Yick Wo v. Hopkins*, 118 U.S. 356, 370 (1886).

3. Jeremy Wallace, "Texas Voter Turnout Was Best in Almost 30 Years," *Houston Chronicle,* November 7, 2020.

4. United States Election Project, "2020 November General Election Turnout Rates," electproject.org, accessed December 8, 2020 http://www.electproject.org/2020g

5. For voting eligible and voting age turnout results see United States Election Project, "2020 November General Election Turnout Rates," electproject.org, accessed December 9, 2020, http://www.electproject.org/2020g. For registered voter turnout see "Texas Election Results," Texas Secretary of State, accessed December 9, 2020, https://results.texas-election.com/contestdetails?officeID=1001&officeName=PRESIDENT%2FVICE-PRESIDENT&officeType=FEDERAL%20OFFICES&from=race

6. "2018 November General Election Turnout Rates," *United States Election Project*, December 14, 2018, http://www.electproject.org/2018g

7. *Canvassing Report: City of San Antonio Run-Off Election, Saturday, June 8, 2019*, https://www.sanantonio.gov/Portals/0/Files/Clerk/Election%20Results/June%208%202019%20Canvassing%20Report%20OFFICIAL.pdf?ver=2019-06-20-113554-770

8. "2011 General Election Summary," City of Corpus Christi, https://www-cdn.cctexas.com/sites/default/files/CTYSEC-2012-general-election-summary.pdf; "City of Corpus Christi, November 3, 2020 General Election," Nueces County, https://www.nuecesco.com/Home/ShowDocument?id=27613

9. See John H. Aldrich, Jamie L. Carson, Brad T. Gomez, and David W. Rohde, *Change and Continuity in the 2016 & 2018 Elections* (Los Angeles: Sage/CQ Press, 2020).

10. Texas Politics Project, "October 2020 University of Texas/Texas Tribune Poll," accessed December 11, 2020, https://texaspolitics.utexas.edu/polling-data-archive

11. United States Election Project, "Turnout Rates: Age," electproject.org, accessed December 14, 2020, http://www.electproject.org/home/voter-turnout/demographics

12. Erica Grieder, "Younger Voters Help Power Historic Early Voting Turnout in Texas," *Houston Chronicle*, November 4, 2020.

13. John H. Aldrich, Jamie L. Carson, Brad T. Gomez, and David W. Rohde, *Change and Continuity in the 2016 & 2018 Elections* (Los Angeles: Sage/CQ Press, 2020).

14. Bernard L. Fraga, *The Turnout Gap* (Cambridge, United Kingdom: Cambridge University Press, 2018).

15. U.S. Census Bureau, "Table 4b. Reported Voting and Registration by Sex, Race and Hispanic Origin, for States: November 2018," accessed December 17, 2020, https://www.census.gov/data/tables/time-series/demo/voting-and-registration/p20-583.html

16. Bryon Allen and Chris Wilson, "Just How Big Was Turnout in Texas, and What Does It Mean?" *TribTalk*, January 7, 2019, https://www.tribtalk.org/2019/01/07/just-how-big-was-turnout-in-texas-and-what-does-it-mean/

17. Anna Bauman, "Record Turnout Seen Among Asian American Voters," *Houston Chronicle,* November 20, 2020.

18. The League of Women Voters of Texas, https://my.lwv.org/texas; MOVE Texas, https://movetexas.org; and Voto Latino, https://votolatino.org

19. Christopher Long, "Ku Klux Klan," *Handbook of Texas Online, August* 20, 2013, https://www.tshaonline.org/handbook/online/articles/vek02

20. Chandler Davidson, "African Americans and Politics," *Handbook of Texas Online, March* 5, 2016, http://www.tshaonline.org/handbook/online/articles/wmafr

21. David Montejano, *Anglos and Mexicans in the Making of Texas, 1836–1886* (Austin: University of Texas Press, 1987), 143.

22. Sanford N. Greenberg, "White Primary," *Handbook of Texas Online*, March 5, 2016, http://www.tshaonline.org/handbook/online/articles/wdw01; and Charles L. Zelden, *The Battle for the Black*

Ballot: *Smith v. Allwright and the Defeat of the All-White Primary* (Lawrence, KS: University of Kansas Press, 2004).

23. Janie Boschma, "What It's Like to Be a Nonwhite Lawmaker Representing a White-Majority District (and Vice Versa)," *Atlantic,* January 30, 2015, http://www.theatlantic.com/politics/archive/2015/01/what-its-like-to-be-a-nonwhite-lawmaker-representing-a-white-majority-district-and-vice-versa/431829

24. Bernard L. Fraga, *The Turnout Gap* (Cambridge, United Kingdom: Cambridge University Press, 2018).

25. For more information on racial gerrymandering and the use of at-large districts to disenfranchise minorities, see Christopher M. Burke, *The Appearance of Equality: Racial Gerrymandering, Redistricting, and the Supreme Court* (Westport, CT: Greenwood Press, 1999).

26. Charles L. Cotrell and R. Michael Stevens, "The 1975 Voting Rights Act and San Antonio, Texas: Toward a Federal Guarantee of a Republican Form of Local Government," *Publius,* 8 (1978): 79–99.

27. Sahil Kapur, "Justice Ginsburg Slams Supreme Court's 'Hubris' in Fiery Dissent on Voting Rights Act," *Talking Points Memo,* June 25, 2013, http://talkingpointsmemo.com/dc/justice-ginsburg-slams-supreme-court-s-hubris-in-fiery-dissent-on-voting-rights-act

28. 42 U.S.C. Sec. 1973 (1982).

29. Sean Richey, "Voting by Mail: Turnout and Institutional Reform in Oregon," *Social Science Quarterly* 89 (2008): 902–915.

30. National Conference of State Legislatures, "Online Voter Registration," ncsl.org, accessed December 22, 2020, https://www.ncsl.org/research/elections-and-campaigns/electronic-or-online-voter-registration.aspx

31. Jinhai Yu, "Does State Online Voter Registration Increase Voter Turnout?" *Social Science Quarterly* 100 (2019): 620–634; and John B. Holbein and D. Sunshine Hillygus, "Making Young Voters: The Impact of Preregistration on Youth Turnout," *American Journal of Political Science* 60 (2016): 364–382.

32. National Conference of State Legislatures, "Preregistration for Young Voters," ncsl.org, accessed February 4, 2021, https://www.ncsl.org/research/elections-and-campaigns/preregistration-for-young-voters.aspx

33. Chuck Lindell, "Texas Complies with Court-Ordered 'Motor Voter' Change," *Austin American Statesman,* September 25, 2020.

34. Texas Politics Project, "Turnout as a Percentage of Voting-Age Population in Five Types of Texas Elections and Presidential Elections Nationwide, 1970–2019," accessed December 18, 2020, https://texaspolitics.utexas.edu/educational-resources/comparing-turnout-constitutional-elections

35. Gary Bledsoe and Jennifer L. Clark, "Texas Lawmakers Are Busy Making It Harder to Vote," *Dallas Morning News,* May 19, 2015.

36. Tim Eaton, "Federal Appeals Court: Texas' Voter ID Law Violates Voting Rights Act," *Austin American Statesman,* August 6, 2015; Jim Malewitz, "After Appeals Court Ruling Against Texas Voter ID Law, Now What?," *Austin American Statesman,* July 23, 2016; Krista M. Torralva, "Texas Voters without Photo ID Can Cast Ballots, Judge Rules," *Corpus Christi Caller-Times,* August 10, 2016, http://www.caller.com/news/local/-texas-voters-without-photo-id-can-cast-ballots-judge-rules-39ba448d-10ec-2d5b-e053-0100007fea06-389778781.html; and Jeremy Wallace, "Revised Texas Voter ID Law Upheld by Appeals Court," *San Antonio Express-News,* April 28, 2018.

37. Christian Belanger, "PolitiFact: Texas Voter ID Fraud Cases about as Rare as Lightning Hits," *Austin American Statesman,* August 24, 2015.

38. Alexandra Villarreal, "Texas Is a 'Voter Suppression' State and One of the Hardest Places to Vote. Will it Help Trump Win?" *Guardian,* September 18, 2020, https://www.theguardian.com/us-news/2020/sep/18/texas-voting-restrictions-rights-coronavirus

39. Ross Ramsey, "Analysis: It's Harder to Vote in Texas Than in Any Other State," October 19, 2020, https://www.texastribune.org/2020/10/19/texas-voting-elections/

40. For an overview of group differences in voting, see John H. Aldrich, Jamie L. Carson, Brad T. Gomez, and David W. Rohde, *Change and Continuity in the 2016 & 2018 Elections* (Los Angeles: Sage/CQ Press, 2020).

41. Jackie Coe, "Map Shows How Texas Counties Voted in 2020 Presidential Election," *El Paso Times,* November 11, 2020 https://www.elpasotimes.com/story/news/politics/2020/11/11/map-shows-how-texas-counties-voted-biden-trump-2020-election/6241745002/

42. George N. Green, "O'Daniel, Wilbert Lee [Pappy]," *Handbook of Texas Online,* February 22, 2016, http://www.tshaonline.org/handbook/online/articles/fod11

43. Issie Lapowsky, "The Dot-Vote Crusade to Defend Politicians from Cybersquatters," *Wired,* January 24, 2016, http://www.wired.com/2016/01/the-dotvote-crusade-to-defend-politicians-from-cybersquatters

44. Stephen Paulsen, "Local Candidate Blames "Sabotage" in Controversy over Racist Tweets," *Big Bend Sentinel*, June 3, 2020, https://bigbendsentinel.com/2020/06/03/local-candidate-blames-sabotage-in-controversy-over-racist-tweets/; and Stephen Paulsen, "Portillo Exits Brewster County Sheriff's Race," *Big Bend Sentinel*, August 12, 2020, https://bigbendsentinel.com/2020/08/12/portillo-exits-brewster-county-sheriffs-race/

45. Shirin Ghaffary, "Civil Rights Leaders Are Still Fed up with Facebook over Hate Speech." *Vox*, July 7, 2020, https://www.vox.com/recode/2020/7/7/21316681/facebook-mark-zuckerberg-civil-rights-hate-speech-stop-hate-for-profit

46. Robert T. Garrett, "Cornyn-Hegar Senate Race Takes a Nasty Turn with Negative Ads by the Candidates, Outside Groups," *Dallas Morning News*, October 31, 2020.

47. Kim L. Fridkin and Patrick J. Kenney, "Variability in Citizens' Reactions to Different Types of Negative Campaigns," *American Journal of Political Science* 55 (2011): 307–325.

48. "Most Expensive Races," *OpenSecrets.org*, https://www.opensecrets.org/overview/topraces.php?cycle=2018&display=currcandsout; "Texas Senate Race," *OpenSecrets.org*, https://www.opensecrets.org/races/summary?id=TXS2&cycle=2018

49. Jasper Scherer, "Turner Gets Fundraising Surge but Still Outspent by Buzbee, while Council Runoffs See Lopsided Money Totals," *Houston Chronicle: Web Edition Articles*, December 6, 2019, https://infoweb-newsbank-com.manowar.tamucc.edu/apps/news/document-view?p=WORLDNEWS&docref=news/177B93F790CB5CB8

50. "Payday Loans," *Federal Trade Commission*, https://www.consumer.ftc.gov/articles/0097-payday-loans

51. Mitchell Schnurman, "Payday-Loan Industry Spreads the Money in Texas," *Dallas Morning News*, April 7, 2015.

52. "TRIBPEDIA: Texas Ethics Commission," *Texas Tribune*, http://www.texastribune.org/tribpedia/texas-ethics-commission/about; and Steve Wolens, "The Texas Ethics Commission Is Surprisingly Nonpartisan. What Can this Group Teach the Rest of Us?" *Dallas Morning News*, February 26, 2019, https://www.dallasnews.com/opinion/commentary/2019/02/26/the-texas-ethics-commission-is-surprisingly-nonpartisan-what-can-this-group-teach-the-rest-of-us/

53. Bipartisan Campaign Reform Act of 2002, 2 U.S.C. § 431 (2002).

54. "Super PACs," *OpenSecrets.org*, https://www.opensecrets.org/pacs/superpacs.php

55. Texas Ethics Commission, "Campaign Finance Guide for Judicial Candidates and Officeholders," October 1, 2019, https://www.ethics.state.tx.us/resources/judicial/JCOH_guide.php#CONTR_LIMITS

56. Texas Ethics Commission, "Personal Financial Statement Form PFS - Instruction Guide," January 31, 2020, https://www.ethics.state.tx.us/data/forms/pfs/PFS_ins.pdf

57. "What Is 'Dark Money,' and How Are States Responding to It," *San Antonio Express-News*, December 20, 2015.

58. David Saleh Rauf, "Texas Set to Require Disclosure of Some 'Dark Money' Ads," *San Antonio Express-News*, October 6, 2015.

59. Taylor Goldenstein, "Court Case Could Reveal Unprecedented Insight into Dark Money Group Empower Texans," *Houston Chronicle*, August 3, 2020.

60. David Saleh Rauf, "Texas 'Dark Money' Rule Set for Court Fight Ahead of Primaries," *San Antonio Express-News*, November 23, 2015; and "Federal Judge Tosses Lawsuit Against Texas Dark Money Regulation," *San Antonio Express-News*, March 15, 2016, http://www.expressnews.com/news/politics/texas_legislature/article/Federal-judge-tosses-lawsuit-against-Texas-dark-6891323.php; Campaign Legal Center, "Empower Texans, Inc. & Michael Quinn Sullivan v. Texas Ethics Commission," campaignlegal.org, January 29, 2021, https://campaignlegal.org/cases-actions/empower-texans-inc-michael-quinn-sullivan-v-texas-ethics-commission

61. Texas Demographic Center, "Texas Demographic Trends and Projections and the 2020 Census," demographics.texas.gov, accessed 2/8/2021, https://demographics.texas.gov/Resources/Presentations/OSD/2021/2021_01_29_MexicanAmericanLegislativeLeadershipFellowship.pdf. Language is constantly evolving, as an author team we have decided on Latino for consistency throughout the book.

62. Rodrigo Domínguez-Villegas, Nick Gonzalez, Angela Gutierrez, Kassandra Hernández, Michael Herndon, Ana Oaxaca, Michael Rios, Marcel Roman, Tye Rush, and Daisy Vera, "Vote Choice of Latino Voters in the 2020 Presidential Election," UCLA Latino Policy and Politics Initiative, January 19, 2021, accessed February 8, 2021, https://latino.ucla.edu/wp-content/uploads/2021/01/Election-2020-Report-1.19.pdf

63. John C. Moritz, "Texas Democrats in the 2020 Presidential Race Doesn't Automatically Mean Texas Is in Play," *Corpus Christi Caller-Times*, March 18, 2019.

64. Texas Supreme Court Justice Rebeca Aizpuru Huddle was appointed to the Supreme Court of Texas by Governor Greg Abbott in October 2020 to fill a vacancy, and the term ends December 31, 2022.

While she holds a position that is elected statewide, she has not yet been elected to the position. Supreme Court Justice Eva Guzman resigned in June 2021.

65. The National Association of Latino Elected and Appointed Officials (NALEO) Educational Fund publishes the "National Directory of Latino Elected Officials" that contains information about the number of Latino elected officials in each state. The most recent report was published in 2019, https://naleo.org/wp-content/uploads/2019/12/2019_National_Directory_of_Latino_Elected_Offcials.pdf

66. Latino Decisions, "Texas and the Latino Vote," November 3, 2020, https://latinodecisions.com/blog/texas-and-the-latino-vote/

67. Francisco Pedraza and Bryan Wilcox-Archuleta, "Donald Trump Did Not Win 34% of Latino Vote in Texas. He Won Much Less," *Washington Post*, December 2, 2016, https://www.washingtonpost.com/news/monkey-cage/wp/2016/12/02/donald-trump-did-not-win-34-of-latino-vote-in-texas-he-won-much-less/?noredirect=on&utm_term=.87354c83dccf

68. Latino Decisions, "American Election Eve Poll 2018 - Texas - Latino, African American, and AAPI Voters," http://www.latinodecisions.com/files/3515/4155/5782/TX_2018_groups.pdf

69. Angel Saavedra Cisneros, *Latino Identity and Political Attitudes: Why Are Latinos Not Republican?* (New York: Palgrave Macmillan, 2017).

70. For an overview of Texas Latinos in the 2020 general election see Arelis R. Hernandez and Brittney Martin, "Why Texas's Overwhelmingly Latino Rio Grande Valley Turned Toward Trump," *Washington Post*, November 9, 2020; https://www.washingtonpost.com/national/texas-latino-republicans/2020/11/09/17a15422-1f92-11eb-ba21-f2f001f0554b_story.html; Stephania Taladrid, "Deconstructing the 2020 Latino Vote," *New Yorker*, December 31, 2020, https://www.newyorker.com/news/news-desk/deconstructing-the-2020-latino-vote; Jack Herrera, "Trump Didn't Win the Latino Vote in Texas. He Won the Tejano Vote," *Politico*, November 17, 2020, https://www.politico.com/news/magazine/2020/11/17/trump-latinos-south-texas-tejanos-437027; Amelia Thomson-DeVeaux, Geoffrey Skelley and Laura Bronner, "What We Know About How White and Latino Americans Voted In 2020," *FiveThirtyEight*, November 23, 2020, https://fivethirtyeight.com/features/what-we-know-about-how-white-and-latino-americans-voted-in-2020/; and Rodrigo Domínguez-Villegas, Nick Gonzalez, Angela Gutierrez, Kassandra Hernández, Michael Herndon, Ana Oaxaca, Michael Rios, Marcel Roman, Tye Rush, and Daisy Vera, "Vote Choice of Latino Voters in the 2020 Presidential Election," UCLA Latino Policy and Politics Initiative, January 19, 2021, accessed February 8, 2021, https://latino.ucla.edu/wp-content/uploads/2021/01/Election-2020-Report-1.19.pdf

71. Olivia P. Tallet, "Parties Misjudge Latino Vote Power," *Houston Chronicle*, October 14, 2018; Arelis R. Hernandez and Brittney Martin, "Why Texas's Overwhelmingly Latino Rio Grande Valley Turned Toward Trump," *Washington Post*, November 9, 2020.

72. Liz McKenna, "To Learn about the Democratic Party's Future, Look at what Latino Organizers Did in Arizona," *Washington Post*, February 9, 2021, https://www.washingtonpost.com/politics/2021/02/09/learn-about-democratic-partys-future-look-what-latino-organizers-did-arizona/

73. Catherine Rampell, "Trump Has Done the Opposite of Everything the GOP Said It Needs to Do to Survive," *Washington Post*, March 31, 2016, https://www.washingtonpost.com/opinions/opposite-day-at-the-trump-campaign/2016/03/31/92032d00-f77c-11e5-8b23-538270a1ca31_story.html

74. "Latino Republican Voters in Texas," *NPR*, November 4, 2018, https://www.npr.org/2018/11/04/664103241/latino-republican-voters-in-texas

75. Texas Demographic Center, "Texas Demographic Trends and Projections and the 2020 Census," demographics.texas.gov, accessed 2/8/2021, https://demographics.texas.gov/Resources/Presentations/OSD/2021/2021_01_29_MexicanAmericanLegislativeLeadershipFellowship.pdf

76. Juan Carlos Huerta and Beatriz Cuartas, "Is Texas Finally Turning Blue? We Looked at the Electorate to Find Out," December 18, 2018, *Washington Post*, https://www.washingtonpost.com/news/monkey-cage/wp/2018/12/18/are-texass-demographics-finally-turning-the-state-blue-we-looked-at-the-electorate-to-find-out/?noredirect=on&utm_term=.c9d1d22f97a1

77. Latino Decisions, "The American Election Eve Poll," accessed February 11, 2021, https://electioneve2020.com/poll/#/en/demographics/black/tx

78. Latino Decisions, "American Election Eve Poll 2018 - Texas - Latino, African American, and AAPI Voters," accessed February 11, 2021, https://latinodecisions.com/wp-content/uploads/2019/06/TX_2018_groups.pdf

79. Mark Dent, "Tarrant County Trending Blue for Biden, Data Show," *Fort Worth Star-Telegram*, November 10, 2020.

80. Brooke A. Lewis and Nick Powell, "Fort Bend Makes History, Elects Eric Fagan as First Black Sheriff Since Reconstruction," *Houston Chronicle*, November 5, 2020.

81. Alex Samuels, "Why Asian American Voters in Texas May Hold Outsized Importance in Key Races this Year," *Texas Tribune*, October 22, 2020, https://www.texastribune.org/2020/10/22/texas-asian-american-voters/

82. For more information about the diversity of the Asian American and Pacific Islander populations in Texas, see Hojun Choi, "Harris Stirs Asian American Voters," *Austin American-Statesman*, October 7, 2020.

83. Alex Samuels, "Why Asian American Voters in Texas May Hold Outsized Importance in Key Races this Year," *Texas Tribune*, October 22, 2020, https://www.texastribune.org/2020/10/22/texas-asian-american-voters/

84. Erin Donaghue, "2,120 Hate Incidents Against Asian Americans Reported During Coronavirus Pandemic," *CBS News*, July 2, 2020, https://www.cbsnews.com/news/anti-asian-american-hate-incidents-up-racism/

85. Alex Samuels, "Why Asian American Voters in Texas May Hold Outsized Importance in Key Races this Year," *Texas Tribune*, October 22, 2020, https://www.texastribune.org/2020/10/22/texas-asian-american-voters/

86. Brooke A. Lewis and Nick Powell, "Fort Bend Makes History, Elects Eric Fagan as First Black sheriff since Reconstruction," *Houston Chronicle*, November 5, 2020.

87. Academics use the concept "intersectionality" when referring to the importance of taking race, ethnicity, and socioeconomic status into consideration when studying women so the focus is not on the views of White women. For a summary of intersectionality, see Anne Sisson Runyan, "What Is Intersectionality and Why Is It Important?" American Association of University Professors, November–December, 2018, https://www.aaup.org/article/what-intersectionality-and-why-it-important#.YCau_HdKg6g

88. Mattie Parker succeeded Betsy Price as mayor of Fort Worth.

89. Lori Cox Han and Caroline Heldman, *Women, Power, and Politics* (New York: Oxford University Press, 2018).

90. Jay Root, "Davis' Daughters Fire Back at Critics of Their Mother," *Texas Tribune,* January 28, 2014, http://www.texastribune.org/2014/01/28/davis-daughters-fire-back-critics

91. Lori Cox Han and Caroline Heldman, *Women, Power, and Politics* (New York: Oxford University Press, 2018).

92. Christopher Adams, "Suburban Women Have Role to Play in November Election, but It's Complicated," *Reform Austin*, July 31, 2020, https://www.reformaustin.org/elections/suburban-women-have-role-to-play-in-november-election/

93. Latino Decisions, "The American Election Eve Poll," accessed February 13, 2021, https://electioneve2020.com/poll/#/en/demographics/black/tx

94. Hannah Wiley, "In Texas, the 'Rainbow Wave' Outpaces the Blue One," *Texas Tribune*, November 7, 2018, https://www.texastribune.org/2018/11/07/texas-midterm-election-rainbow-wave-lgbtq-candidates/

95. Taylor Pettaway, "Some Big Things Happened for Texas LGBTQ this Election. Here"s a Round-up," MySA.com, November 13, 2020, https://www.mysanantonio.com/news/local/article/Some-big-things-happened-for-Texas-LGBTQ-this-15722094.php

96. Bandon Lingle, "Texas Lawmakers to Seek LGBTQ Nondiscrimination Laws—and Economic Boost," *San Antonio Express-News*, October 31, 2020.

97. Julie Moreau, "Anti-LGBTQ Attack Ads Ramp Up Ahead of Election Day," *NBC News*, November 2, 2020, https://www.nbcnews.com/feature/nbc-out/anti-lgbtq-attack-ads-ramp-ahead-election-day-n1245774

98. Sami Sparber, "Texas Democrats Are Trying to Draw LGBT Republicans Snubbed by State GOP Leaders," *Texas Tribune*, March 9, 2020, https://www.texastribune.org/2020/03/09/democrats-want-recruit-lgbt-republicans-snubbed-state-gop-leaders/

99. The *Texas Election Code* is a compilation of state laws that govern voter qualifications, procedures for nominating and electing party and government officials, and other matters related to suffrage and elections.

100. Tex. Elec. Code Ann. §11.001 (2010) and §11.002 (2013).

101. John C. Moritz, "Texas Elections: Voting During Pandemic Will Have Challenges, but Robust Turnout Expected," *Abilene Reporter-News*, October 11, 2020; and Chuck Lindell, "Appeals Court Allows Abbott to Close Multiple Ballot Drop-off Sites," *Austin American-Statesman*, October 14, 2020.

102. Tex. Elec. Code Ann. Sec. 82.001-Sec. 82.007 (2010).

103. John C. Moritz, "Texas Elections: Voting During Pandemic Will Have Challenges, but Robust Turnout Expected," *Abilene Reporter-News*, October 11, 2020.

104. Analeslie Muncy, "Texas Municipal Election Law Manual," 4th ed. (Denton, TX: Texas Municipal Clerks Association, 2015); Anastasiya Boltony, "Nearly 80 Texas Counties Allowing Voters to Cast Their Ballots at Any County Polling Place," *KHOU*, September 28, 2020, https://www.khou.com/article/news/politics/elections/more-than-80-texas-counties-allowing-voters-to-cast-their-ballots-at-any-county-polling-place/285-511502d0-c8c1-48a8-a1bf-dbf7aa232536

105. "Primary Election Showed the Voting Problems Texas Must Solve before Nov. 3," *Corpus Christi Caller-Times*, March 6, 2020, https://www.caller.com/story/opinion/2020/03/06/primary-election-showed-voting-problems-texas-must-solve/4963083002/

106. Tex. Elec. Code Sec. 61.014 (2007).

107. Jolie Mccullough, "Voters in Harris County May Continue Using Drive-thru Voting, Texas Supreme Court rules," *Texas Tribune*, October 22, 2020, https://www.texastribune.org/2020/10/22/drive-thru-voting-texas-harris-county/; and "Nearly 127,000 Harris County Drive-thru Votes Appear Safe after Federal Judge Rejects GOP-led Texas Lawsuit," *Texas Tribune*, November 2, 2020, https://www.texastribune.org/2020/11/02/texas-drive-thru-votes-harris-county/

108. "Starting a Party and Nominating Candidates," *Texas Secretary of State*, http://www.sos.state.tx.us/elections/candidates/guide/minor.shtml

109. Alex Ura, "Texas Delaying May Primary Runoff Elections in Response to Coronavirus," *Texas Tribune*, March 20, 2020, https://www.texastribune.org/2020/03/20/texas-delaying-primary-runoff-election-response-coronavirus-outbreak/

110. Tex. Elec. Code Ann. §172.024 (2013).

111. National Conference of State Legislatures, "Ranked-Choice Voting," NCSL.org, February 2, 2021, https://www.ncsl.org/research/elections-and-campaigns/ranked-choice-voting636934215.aspx; "Ranked Choice Voting 101" FairVote.org, accessed on February 20, 2021, https://www.fairvote.org/rcv#where_is_ranked_choice_voting_used

Chapter 6

1. Annette Strauss Institute for Civic Life, University of Texas at Austin, *2018 Texas Media & Society Survey: Topline Results*, https://moody.utexas.edu/centers/strauss/texas-media-society-survey; *Dallas Morning News*/University of Texas at Tyler, *Texas Registered Voter Sample*, July 2020, https://www.uttyler.edu/politicalscience/pollingcenter/; and Amy Mitchell, "Key Findings on the Traits and Habits of the Modern News Consumer," *Pew Research Center*, July 7, 2016, http://www.pewresearch.org/fact-tank/2016/07/07/modern-news-consumer

2. The Texas Politics Project at the University of Texas at Austin, *April* 2020 *University of Texas/Texas Tribune Poll*, https://texaspolitics.utexas.edu/polling

3. Strauss Institute, *2018 Texas Media & Society Survey*.

4. Katerina Eva Matsa and Nami Sumida, "Explore Local News Habits in Your City with Our Interactive," Pew Research Center, March 26, 2019, https://www.pewresearch.org/fact-tank/2019/03/26/explore-local-news-habits-in-your-city-with-our-interactive/

5. Margaret Spellings and Wynn Rosser, "Commentary: Many Texans Lack Access to High-Speed Internet," *San Antonio Express-News,* February 28, 2020, https://www.expressnews.com/opinion/commentary/article/Commentary-Many-Texans-lack-access-to-high-speed-15093514.php

6. Mark Jurkowitz, "The Growth in Digital Reporting: What It Means for Journalism and News Consumers," *Pew Research Center: Journalism and Media*, March 26, 2014, http://www.journalism.org/2014/03/26/the-growth-in-digital-reporting

7. International Media & Newspapers, "2019 Newspaper Web Rankings | North America," 2019, https://www.4imn.com/topNorth-America/

8. Julissa Treviño, "A Texas Republican's Unbiased News Site Skews to the Right," *Columbia Journalism Review*, July 16, 2019, https://www.cjr.org/united_states_project/the-texan-konni-burton.php; and Media Bias/Fact/Check, "The Texan," May 30, 2020, https://mediabiasfactcheck.com/?s=the+texan

9. Sean O'Neal, "The Six Texas Politicians Addicted to Twitter–For Better or Worse," *Texas Monthly*, September 13, 2019, https://www.texasmonthly.com/politics/texas-politicians-addicted-twitter/

10. Texas Politics Project, *April 2020 Poll;* and *Dallas Morning News*/University of Texas at Tyler, *Texas Registered Voter Sample*, June 2020.

11. "2016 National Election Study Time Series," *Survey Documentation and Analysis*, University of California, Berkeley, http://sda.berkeley.edu, analyzed by author, January 15, 2019.

12. Texas Politics Project, *April 2020 Poll*; and Amy Mitchell, Mark Jurkowitz, J. Baxter Oliphant and Elisa Shearer, "Americans Who Mainly Get Their News on Social Media Are Less Engaged, Less Knowledgeable," Pew Research Center, July 30, 2020," https://www.journalism.org/2020/07/30/americans-who-mainly-get-their-news-on-social-media-are-less-engaged-less-knowledgeable/

13. Strauss Institute, *2018 Texas Media & Society Survey*. There are mixed findings at the national level.

14. Bud Kennedy, "Activists Staged Shelley Luther's Stunt Against Greg Abbott, to the Tune of $500,000," *Fort Worth Star-Telegram*, May 17, 2020, https://www.star-telegram.com/news/politics-government/article242594286.html; and Dan Solomon, "Arrested Dallas Hairdresser's GoFundMe Launched Before She Even Reopened," *Texas Monthly*, May 8, 2020, https://www.texasmonthly.com/news/dallas-salon-arrest-gofundme/

15. Federal Communications Commission, "Broadcast Radio Links," March 18, 2021, https://www.fcc.gov/media/radio/broadcast-radio-links#FAM

16. Robert S. Erikson and Kent L. Tedin, *American Public Opinion*, 8th ed. (Boston: Pearson Longman, 2011), 248–249.

17. "Texas Observer," *Media Bias/Fact Check*, November 2, 2018, https://mediabiasfactcheck.com/the-texas-observer

18. Shown by six Texas surveys 2011–2019 found in Texas Politics Project, https://texaspolitics.utexas.edu/polling/search/topic/abortion-9. For national patterns, see Erikson and Tedin, *American Public Opinion*, 111–112; and Carroll J. Glynn et al., *Public Opinion*, 3rd ed. (Boulder: Westview, 2016), 278–279.

19. Jeremy Blackman, "Abbott Eluding Media Scrutiny," *Houston Chronicle*, July 19, 2020, p. A1.

20. Daniel Diana, "Evaluating State Open Records Request Compliance: The Best, the Worst, and Texas," *Logikcull,* August 14, 2019, https://www.logikcull.com/blog/evaluating-state-open-records-request-compliance-the-best-the-worst-and-texas; Ross Ramsey, "Analysis: A Cloudy Day for Sunshine Laws in Texas," *Texas Tribune*, February 7, 2018, https://www.texastribune.org/2018/02/07/analysis-cloudy-day-sunshine-laws-texas; "Texas Public Information Act," *Freedom of Information Foundation of Texas*, 2016, http://foift.org/resources/texas-public-information-act; and David Montgomery, "Texas Gets D- Grade in 2015 State Integrity Investigation," *Center for Public Integrity,* November 9, 2015, https://www.publicintegrity.org/2015/11/09/18532/texas-gets-d-grade-2015-state-integrity-investigation

21. Cory Schouten, "Who Files the Most FOIA Requests? It's Not Who You Think," *Columbia Journalism Review*, March 17, 2017, https://www.cjr.org/analysis/foia-report-media-journalists-business-mapper.php

22. "Public Information in North Texas," *Dallas Morning News*, January 23, 2015, http://res.dallasnews.com/interactives/records

23. Doris A. Graber and Johanna Dunaway, *Mass Media and American Politics*, 9th ed. (Los Angeles: CQ Press, 2015), 349.

24. "The 5 Types of Attack Ads Defining the 2020 Congressional Elections," *Seeing 2020*, October 17, 2020, http://seeing2020.us/the-5-types-of-attack-ads-defining-the-2020-congressional-elections/

25. Texas Politics Project, "Polling Graphics Search," https://texaspolitics.utexas.edu/polling/search/topic/coronavirus-716/group/party-id

26. *Dallas Morning News*/University of Texas at Tyler, *Texas Registered Voter Sample*, June 2020.

27. Rosalee A. Clawson and Zoe M. Oxley, *Public Opinion: Democratic Ideals, Democratic Practice*, 3rd ed. (Washington, D.C.: CQ Press, 2017), 105.

28. Kasey S. Pipes, "Inside Rick Perry's Campaign Strategy," *FoxNews.com*, August 11, 2011, http://www.foxnews.com/opinion/2011/08/11/inside-rick-perrys-campaign-strategy-how-it-worked-in-his-race-for-governor-and.html

29. Strauss Institute, *2018 Texas Media & Society Survey*, https://moody.utexas.edu/centers/strauss/texas-media-society-survey

30. SPLC, "In 2020, We Tracked 54 Hate Groups in Texas," Southern Poverty Law Center, 2021, https://www.splcenter.org/hate-map?state=TX; and ADL, "Patriot Front," Anti-Defamation League, 2020, https://www.adl.org/resources/backgrounders/patriot-front

31. *Dallas Morning News*/University of Texas at Tyler, *Texas Registered Voter Sample*, 2020.

32. SPLC, "Whose Heritage? Public Symbols of the Confederacy," Southern Poverty Law Center, February 01, 2019, https://www.splcenter.org/20190201/whose-heritage-public-symbols-confederacy

33. Mike Wendling. "The (Almost) Complete History of 'Fake News,'" *BBC Trending*, January 22, 2018, https://www.bbc.com/news/blogs-trending-42724320

34. Texas Politics Project, *April 2020 University of Texas/Texas Tribune Poll*, https://texaspolitics.utexas.edu/polling; and *2018 Texas Lyceum Statewide Poll Crosstabs,* August 1, 2018, https://www.texaslyceum.org/2018-lyceum-poll

35. David H. Weaver, Randal A. Beam, Bonnie J. Brownlee, Paul S. Voakes, and G. Cleveland Wilhout, *The American Journalist in the 21st Century* (Mahwah, NJ: Lawrence Erlbaum Associates, 2007).

36. "CNN," Fox News," and "MSNBC," MediaBias/FactCheck.com, March 16, 2021, https://mediabiasfactcheck.com/

37. Charles S. Taber and Milton Lodge, "Motivated Skepticism in the Evaluation of Political Beliefs," *American Journal of Political Science*, 50 (July 2006): 755–769.

38. Graber and Dunaway, *Mass Media and American Politics*, 344; Dave D'Alessio and Mike Allen, "Media Bias in Presidential Elections: A Meta-Analysis," *Journal of Communication*, 50 (Autumn 2000), 133–156; and W. Lance Bennett, *News: The Politics of Illusion*, 9th ed. (New York: Longman, 2012).

The problems of objective reporting are discussed by long-time Texas reporter Bill Minutaglio in two of his columns on the "State of the Media" published in the *Texas Observer*: "Jim Moore Calls for *The Texas Tribune* to Distance Itself from Funders," May 10, 2014, and "To Each According to Greed: Rick Perry, Toyota and the Texas Enterprise Fund," June 12, 2014, http://www.texasobserver.org/blog/stateofmedia

39. Timothy E. Cook, *Governing with the News: The News Media as a Political Institution*, 2nd ed. (Chicago: University of Chicago Press, 2005), 71.

40. "Digital-only Platforms Drive Race and Gender Inclusion Among Newsrooms in 2019 ASNE Newsroom Diversity Survey," September 10, 2019, https://www.newsleaders.org/2019-diversity-survey-results; and Michael Barthel, "In the News Industry, Diversity Is Lowest at Smaller Outlets," *Pew Research Center*, August 4, 2015, http://www.pewresearch.org/fact-tank/2015/08/04/in-the-news-industry-diversity-is-lowest-at-smaller-outlets

41. Progress Texas Institute, "REPORT: Texas Media Coverage Lacks Diverse Sources of Political Analysis in 2020 Election Coverage," *Progress Texas*, July 28, 2020, https://progresstexas.org/blog/report-texas-media-coverage-lacks-diverse-sources-political-analysis-2020-election-coverage; Staff, "Seven Men Dominate Political Analysis in Texas," *Texas Research Institute*, March 26, 2015, http://texasresearch.org/blog/seven-men-dominate-political-analysis-texas; and Andrea Grimes, "State of the Media: Building a Better Punditocracy," *Texas Observer*, May 4, 2015, https://www.texasobserver.org/state-of-the-media-texas-political-media

42. Mingxiao Sui and Newly Paul, "Latino Portrayals in Local News Media: Underrepresentation, Negative Stereotypes, and Institutional Predictors of Coverage," *Journal of Intercultural Communication Research*, Vol. 46, 2017, Issue 3, https://www.tandfonline.com/doi/abs/10.1080/17475759.2017.1322124?scroll=top&needAccess=true&journalCode=rjic20; but see Erik Bleich et al., "The Good, the Bad, and the Ugly: A Corpus Linguistics Analysis of US Newspaper Coverage of Latinx, 1996–2016, *Journalism*, 2018, https://journalistsresource.org/studies/society/news-media/news-media-portray-latinos/

43. Merdies Hayes, "Mass Murders Expose Bias, Stereotypes in Media Coverage," *Our Weekly*, October 8, 2015, http://ourweekly.com/news/2015/oct/08/mass-murders-expose-bias-stereotypes-media-coverag/

44. *Polling Results on the Coverage of Race in the News Media 50 Years Post-Kerner Commission*, Ford Foundation, 2018, https://www.fordfoundation.org/the-latest/news/50th-anniversary-of-the-kerner-commission-report-poll-results-on-the-coverage-of-race-in-the-news-media/

45. Elisa Shearer, "Hispanic Media: Fact Sheet," *Pew Journalism*, June 2016, http://www.journalism.org/files/2016/06/State-of-the-News-Media-Report-2016-FINAL.pdf

46. Erik Bleich et al., "The Good, the Bad, and the Ugly: A Corpus Linguistics Analysis of US Newspaper Coverage of Latinx, 1996–2016," *Journalism*, 2018, https://journalistsresource.org/studies/society/news-media/news-media-portray-latinos/

47. Sara Atske, Michael Barthel, Galen Stocking and Christine Tamir, "7 Facts about Black Americans and the News Media," Pew Research Center, August 7, 2019, https://www.pewresearch.org/fact-tank/2019/08/07/facts-about-black-americans-and-the-news-media/

48. The Texas Politics Project at the University of Texas at Austin, *April 2020 University of Texas/Texas Tribune Poll*, https://texaspolitics.utexas.edu/polling/search/topic/media-78/group/race/year/2020

49. Atske, Barthel, Stocking, and Tamir, "7 Facts."

50. *Lesher v. Coyel*, June 16, 2014 No. 05-12-01357-CV.

51. Nickie Louise, "These 6 Corporations Control 90% of the Media Outlets in America. The Illusion of Choice and Objectivity 2020," *Tech Startups*, September 18, 2020, https://techstartups.com/2020/09/18/6-corporations-control-90-media-america-illusion-choice-objectivity-2020/; and Ben H. Bagdikian, *The Media Monopoly*, 6th ed. (Boston: Beacon Press, 1997), xxii, 30.

52. "The State of the News Media, 2006," *Pew Project for Excellence in Journalism*, http://stateofthemedia.org/2006/a-day-in-the-life-of-the-media-intro/local-tv

53. Erica Grieder, "National State of Mind," *Texas Monthly*, March 2016, 16.

54. Crosswind Media & Public Relations, "Crosswind Texas Pulse Poll Shows 1 in 3 Texans Believe the Economy Is the Most Important Issue Facing the Lone Star State," 2020, https://crosswindpr.com/crosswind-texas-pulse-poll-1-in-3-texans-believe-economy-most-important-issue-facing-lone-star-state/; Texas Politics Project at the University of Texas at Austin, October 2020, https://texaspolitics.utexas.edu/polling/search/year/2020?fulltext_search=OR&fulltext=issue

55. Paul Burka, "The Capitol Press Corpse," *Texas Monthly*, January 2008, http://www.texasmonthly.com/story/capitol-press-corpse; and Elise Hu, "A Lively Political Press in a State Where Everything's Bigger," *NPR*, July 5, 2013, http://www.npr.org/blogs/itsallpolitics/2013/07/05/197987945/a-lively-political-press-in-a-state-where-everything-s-bigger. An oft-cited pessimistic assessment is Mark Lisheron, "Reloading at the Statehouse," *American Journalism Review*, September 2010, no longer online.

56. Carol Guensburg, "When the Story Is about the Owner," *American Journalism Review*, 20 (December 1998), no longer online; and Gabriel Rossman, "Elites, Masses, and Media Blacklists: The Dixie Chicks Controversy," *Social Forces*, 83 (2004): 61–78.

57. "Local TV News Project 2001," *Pew Research Journalism Project*, November 1, 2001, http://www.journalism.org/2001/11/01/local-tv-news-project-2001; and Bagdikian, *The Media Monopoly*, 6th ed., 30.

58. Bill Minutaglio, "Jim Moore Calls for *The Texas Tribune* to Distance Itself from Funders," *Texas Observer*, May 10, 2014, https://www.texasobserver.org/close-comfort; and Andrea Grimes, "The Trouble with Trib Talk," *Texas Observer*, July 14, 2014, https://www.texasobserver.org/trouble-tribtalk

Chapter 7

1. Burdett A. Loomis and Allan J. Cigler, "Introduction: The Changing Nature of Interest Group Politics," in *Interest Group Politics* 9th ed., ed. Allan J. Cigler and Burdett A. Loomis (Washington, D.C.: CQ Press, 2015), 2.

2. Joseph M. Bessette, John J. Pitney Jr., Lyle C. Brown, Joyce A. Langenegger, Sonia R. García, Ted A. Lewis, and Robert E. Biles, *American Government and Politics: Deliberation, Democracy and Citizenship* (Boston: Wadsworth, 2012), 273.

3. Christy Hoppe, "Business Lobby Flexes Muscle in Legislature," *Dallas Morning News*, April 12, 2003.

4. Peggy Fikac, "Perry Signs Hate Crimes Legislation," *San Antonio Express-News*, May 12, 2001.

5. Gary Scharrer, "Board Rejects Rebel Plate," *San Antonio Express-News*, November 11, 2011. See *Walker v. Sons of the Confederate Veterans*, 576 U.S. ___ (2015). See also, Aman Batheja, "Supreme Court: Texas Can Ban Confederate License Plates," *Texas Tribune*, June 18, 2015, http://www.texastribune.org/2015/06/18/supreme-court-rules-texas-confederate-license-plat/

6. For an examination of the origins of LULAC and its founders, Alonso S. Perales and Adela Sloss-Vento, see Cynthia Orozco, *No Mexicans, Women, or Dogs Allowed: The Rise of the Mexican American Civil Rights Movement* (Austin: University of Texas Press, 2009).

7. See Sonia R. García, Valerie Martinez-Ebers, Irasema Coronado, Sharon A. Navarro, and Patricia A. Jaramillo, *Politicas: Latina Public Officials in Texas* (Austin: University of Texas Press, 2008). Chapter 3 concerns Representative Irma Rangel.

8. For information on the role of the Christian Coalition, see James Lamare, Jerry L. Polinard, and Robert D. Wrinkle, "Texas: Religion and Politics in God's Country," in *The Christian Right in American Politics: Marching Toward the Millennium*, ed. John C. Green, Mark J. Rozell, and Clyde Wilcox (Washington, D.C.: Georgetown University Press, 2003), 59–78.

9. Peggy Fikac, "Alliance Formed to Monitor Radical Right," *Houston Chronicle*, October 1, 1995.

10. See Dennis Shirley, *Valley Interfaith and School Reform: Organizing for Power in South Texas* (Austin: University of Texas Press, 2002).

11. For a history of COPS, see Mark R. Warren, *Dry Bones Rattling: Community Building to Revitalize an American Democracy* (Princeton, NJ: Princeton University Press, 2001).

12. Richard Kearney, "Political Parties, Interest Groups and Campaigns," in Ann O'M. Bowman and Richard Kearney, *State and Local Government*, 9th ed. (Boston: Wadsworth Cengage Learning, 2014), 117–127.

13. H. C. Pittman, *Inside the Third House: A Veteran Lobbyist Takes a 50-Year Frolic Through Texas Politics* (Austin: Eakin Press, 1992), 219. See also John Spong, "State Bar," *Texas Monthly*, July 2003, 110–113, 148–149.

14. "Doctors' Orders: Medical Lobby Becomes a Powerhouse in Austin," *Wall Street Journal*, May 19, 1999.

15. "Austin's Oldest Profession: Texas' Top Lobby Clients & Those Who Service Them," *Texans for Public Justice*, 2013/2014, http://info.tpj.org/reports/pdf/Oldest2013WithCover.pdf

16. Search Lobby Registrations and Lobby Activity Reports, "Lobby Registration Lists, 20 Lists," *Texas Ethics Commission*, https://www.ethics.state.tx.us/search/lobby/loblistsREG2016-2020.php

17. Keith E. Hamm and Charles W. Wiggins, "Texas: The Transformation from Personal to Informational Lobbying," in *Interest Group Politics in the Southern States*, ed. Ronald J. Hrebenar and Olive S. Thomas (Tuscaloosa: University of Alabama Press, 1992), 80.

18. "Testimony by Thomas J. Kim, MD, MPH, Committee on Public Health on Telemedicine in Texas," *Texas Medical Society*, February 10, 2016, https://www.texmed.org/Template.aspx?id=35277

19. Revolving Door Prohibition, "National Conference of State Legislatures," https://www.ncsl.org/research/ethics/50-state-table-revolving-door-prohibitions.aspx

20. "Major Issues of the 84th Legislature," *House Research Organization*, September 22, 2015, http://www.hro.house.state.tx.us/pdf/focus/major84.pdf, 66. See also, Jay Root, "Ethics Reform Not Swept Under Rug, But Not Sweeping Either," *Texas Tribune,* June 1, 2017, https://www.texastribune.org/2017/06/01/ethics-reform-not-swept-under-rug-not-sweeping-either/

21. Texas Ethics Commission, "Recommendations for Statutory Changes," December 20201, https://www.ethics.state.tx.us/legislation/. See also, "Ethics and Elections: Legislation Passed by the 2019 Texas Legislature", Bolder Advocacy, https://www.bolderadvocacy.org/2019/06/18/ethics-elections-legislation-passed-by-the-2019-texas-legislature/

22. Jay Root, "Legislature Approves Bill Requiring Disclosure of Government Contracts," *Texas Tribune*, May 28, 2017, https://www.texastribune.org/2017/05/28/bill-requiring-disclosure-government-contracts-approved/

23. Matt Stiles, "Are Gifts Used as Calling Cards or as Keys to Legislators' Offices?" *San Antonio Express-News*, February 5, 2009. See also David Saleh Rauf, "Free Tickets Just Part of Game for Legislators," *San Antonio Express-News*, September 8, 2013.

24. Tom Benning, "Gun Bills Dominated Social Media Chatter on the Legislature," *Dallas Morning News*, July 6, 2015, http://trailblazersblog.dallasnews.com/2015/07/gun-bills-dominated-social-media-chatter-on-the-legislature/

25. Ryan McCrimmon, "Panel of #txlege Members "likes" Texas Hashtag Proposal," *Texas Tribune*, April 28, 2015, https://www.texastribune.org/2015/04/28/members-txlege-approve-state-hashtags/

26. Texas Ethics Commission, "Recommendations for Statutory Changes," December 2020, https://www.ethics.state.tx.us/legislation/

27. Campaign Finance Reports Search & Lists. "Political Committee Lists," *Texas Ethics Commission*, https://www.ethics.state.tx.us/search/cf/cANDelists2020-2016.php#2020

28. For an examination of the total expenditures by PACS during the 2018 election cycle, see Campaign Finance Reports Search & Lists, "Political Committee Lists, Total Contributions and Expenditures Each Year by PAC by Year, 2018," https://www.ethics.state.tx.us/search/cf/. See also "Top 10 PACS of the 2018 Texas Election Cycle," at https://www.transparencytexas.org/top-ten-pacs-of-the-2018-texas-election-cycle

29. Ross Ramsey, "Analyzing 2019: The Fall of a House Speaker," *Texas Tribune*, December 29, 2019, https://www.texastribune.org/2019/12/23/2019-fall-texas-house-speaker-dennis-bonnen/

30. Ralph Blumenthal and Carl Hulse, "Judge Lets Stand 2 of 3 Charges Faced by Delay," *New York Times*, December 6, 2005; and Gary Martin, "Texas Jury Indicts Delay," *San Antonio Express-News*, September 29, 2005.

31. "A Brief Overview of the Texas Ethics Commission and Its Duties," *Texas Ethics Commission*, September 22, 2009, https://www.ethics.state.tx.us/about/. See also on the same website, "Campaign Finance Guide for Political Committees," *Texas Ethics Commission*, June 16, 2016, https://www.ethics.state.tx.us/data/forms/coh/COH_ins.pdf

32. "Sworn Complaint Open Orders," *Texas Ethics Commission*, https://www.ethics.state.tx.us/enforcement/sworn_complaints/orders/search/

33. "Vetoes of Legislation, 83rd Legislature," *House Research Organization*, August 21, 2013, http://www.hro.house.state.tx.us/pdf/focus/veto83.pdf

34. David Saleh Rauf, "Dark Money Disclosure Fight Heading Back to the Texas Legislature," *San Antonio Express-News*, March 18, 2016.

35. Dave Lieber, "Texas Ethics Laws Are Tightened, but Not as Much as They Could Have Been," *Fort Worth Star-Telegram*, June 26, 2009. See also "2011 Legislation," *Texas Ethics Commission*, https://www.ethics.state.tx.us/rules/commission/ch12.php

36. "Lobby Watch: Ethics Commission's Teeth in Perry's Hands," *Texans for Public Justice*, June 16, 2011, http://www.tpj.org/search/label/Lobby%20Watch

37. "Adopted Rules," *Texas Ethics Commission*, https://www.ethics.state.tx.us/resources/rulings/US_Supreme_Court_Ruling.php

38. Sam Kinch Jr. with Anne Marie Kilday, *Too Much Money Is Not Enough: Big Money and Political Power in Texas* (Austin: Campaigns for People, 2000).

39. Molly Ivins, "Who Let the PACs Out? Woof, Woof!" *Fort Worth Star-Telegram*, February 18, 2001.

40. "With Perry's Signature, Texas Campaign Laws Will Get Boost They Need," *Austin American-Statesman*, June 9, 2003; Ginger Richardson, "Stronger Ethics Rules Hang on House Vote," *Fort Worth Star-Telegram*, June 2, 2003.

41. Clive S. Thomas and Ronald J. Hrebenar, "Political Parties, Interest Groups and Campaigns," in *State and Local Government*, 8th ed., ed. Ann O'M. Bowman and Richard Kearney (Boston: Wadsworth, 2010), 157.

42. Nicholas Kusnetz, "Only Three States Score Higher than D+ in State Integrity Investigation; 11 Flunk," *Center for Public Integrity*, updated November 23, 2015, https://publicintegrity.org/accountability/how-does-your-state-rank-for-integrity/

Chapter 8

1. "'Gay Hitler' Texas Lawmaker Kyle Biederman[n] Introduces Bill Aimed at Seceding from the Union," *Daily Beast*, February 2, 2021, https://www.thedailybeast.com/gay-hitler-texas-lawmaker-kyle-biederman-introduces-bill-aimed-at-seceding-from-the-united-states?ref=scroll. Concerning Biedermann at the Washington riot on January 6, 2021, see Dillon Collier "Video Shows Texas Lawmaker Near Steps of U.S. Capitol as Rioters Clashed with Officers," https://www.ksat.com/news/local/2021/03/22/video-shows-texas-lawmaker-near-steps-of-capitol-as-rioters-clashed-with-officers/; and "What We Know About the 'Unprecedented Capitol Riot Arrests," https://www.cbsnews.com.news/capitol-riot-arrests-2021-03-25/

2. See Ken Herman, "Texas Secession Bill Filed in House," *Austin American-Statesman*, January 28, 2021; Andrea Zelinski, "What the Newest Lone Star Secessionists Really Want," *Texas Monthly*, February 11, 2021, https://www.texasmonthly.com/politics/texas-secession-kyle-biedermann/; and Rep. Bierdeman's explantion of what his proposed referendum will do, https://www.msn.com/en-us/news/us/representative-who-filed-texit-bill-clears-up-what-it-means/ar-BB1dkKf5

3. Alan Rosenthal, *Heavy Lifting: The Job of the American Legislature* (Washington, DC: CQ Press, 2004), 246–247. See also Alan Rosenthal, *Engines of Democracy: Politics and Policymaking in State Legislatures* (Washington, DC: CQ Press, 2009), 8–11.

4. For the experiences of Melissa and Rick Noriega (D-Houston), see Paul Burka, "Duty Calls," *Texas Monthly*, March 2006, 12, 14, 16.

5. "How the Pandemic Is Affecting the First Weeks of the Texas Leg Session," *Texas Monthly*, https://www.texasmonthly.com/politics/texas-lege-covid-delays/?utm_source=Texas+Monthly&utm_campaign=b260f73271-News+%26+Politics+2-2-21&utm_medium=email&utm_term=0_92f99d7313-b260f73271-53417275

6. Patrick Svitek, "Gov. Abbott Calls Special Session on Bathrooms, Abortion, School Finance," *Texas Tribune*, June 6, 2017, https://www.texastribune.org/2017/06/06/abbott-special-session-announcement/

7. For chapters by Gary Keith and six other authorities on redistricting in the Lone Star State, see Gary Keith, ed., *Rotten Boroughs, Political Thickets, and Legislative Donnybrooks: Redistricting in Texas* (Austin: University of Texas Press, 2013).

8. Kevin Stewart, *Texas Legislative Law Handbook*, 3rd ed. (Coppell, TX: Law Offices of Kevin C. Stewart, 2021), 242 -244; and Roland Graves, "Redistricting 101: How Census Data Affects Elections," *Fiscal Notes* (January 2020), https://comptroller.texas.gov/economy/fiscal-notes/2020/jan/redistricting.php

9. Quoted by AP journalist Mike Sherman in "High Court Upholds '1 person, 1 vote,'" *Waco Tribune-Herald*, April 5, 2016. See also Michael S. Kang, "Gerrymandering and the Constitutional Norm Against Government Partisanship," *Michigan Law Review* 116 (December 2017), 351–420; and Lyle Denniston's opinion analysis, "Leaving a Constitutional Ideal Still Undefined," *SCOTUS blog* (April 4, 2016).

10. For a comprehensive study of gerrymandering in the Lone Star State, see Steve Bickerstaff, *Gerrymandering in Texas*, edited by C. Robert Heath (Lubbock: Texas Tech University Press, 2020). See also, Steve Bickerstaff, *Lines in the Sand: Congressional Redistricting in Texas and the Downfall of Tom Delay* (Austin: University of Texas Press, 2007); and Steve Bickerstaff, *Election Systems and Gerrymandering Worldwide* (Cham: Springer Nature, Switzerland, 2017), 39–40 and 222–224.

11. Kenneth Lowande, Melinda Richie, and Erin Lauterbach, "Descriptive and Substantive Representation in Congress: Evidence from 80,000 Congressional Inquiries," *American Journal of Political Science*, 63 (2019), 644–659.

12. For a detailed report on characteristics of the 87th Legislature, with impressive graphs, see Alexa Ura and Carla Astudillo, "In 2021, White Men Are Still Overrepresented in the Texas Legislature," *Texas Tribune*, January 11, 2021, https://texastribune.org/features/2020/2021-texas-legislature-representation/. At the time this report was published, one House seat was vacant; and the racial identity of one legislator could not be confirmed.

13. See Lloyd W. Criss, *Rough & Tumble Texas Political Combat* (La Marque, TX: Diane Criss Publishing, 2009).

14. Seth Musket, "Why Political Science Doesn't Like Term Limits," https://www.mischiefsoffaction.com/post/political-science-term-limits

15. Jay Root, "Bill Stripping Pensions from Felon Politicians Advances," *Texas Tribune, May* 8, 2017, http://www.texastribune.org/2017/05/08/bill-stripping-pensions-from-corrupt-politicians-advances

16. Some former lieutenant governors have been the subjects of books that give insight into this role. Ben Barnes served as Speaker of the House from 1965 to 1969 and as lieutenant governor from 1969 to 1973. For information on his service as presiding officer in each chamber, see Ben Barnes with Lisa Dickey, *Barn Burning, Barn Building: Tales of a Political Life, From LBJ to George W. Bush and Beyond* (Albany, TX: Bright Sky Press, 2006). Bob Bullock's years as lieutenant governor (1991–1999) are covered in Dave McNeely and Jim Henderson, *Bob Bullock: God Bless Texas* (Austin: University of Texas Press, 2008). Bill Hobby's experiences and observations from 18 years as lieutenant governor (1973–1991) are related in Bill Hobby with Saralee Tiede, *How Things Really Work: Lessons from a Life in Politics* (Austin: Center for American History, University of Texas at Austin, 2010). For information on Lieutenant Governor David Dewhurst's 12 years in office (2003–2015), see his interview with Erica Grieder, "The David Dewhurst Exit Interview," *Texas Monthly*, December 2014, 126–127, 178, 180, 182, and 184. Erica Grieder provides a profile of Dan Patrick shortly after his 2014 election as lieutenant governor in her "Master of the Senate," *Texas Monthly*, December 2014, 122–125, 186, 188, 190, 192, 194, 200, and 205–206.

17. Quoted by Tim Eaton and Chuck Lindell, "Sine Die: The Gavel Falls, the Session Ends," *Austin American-Statesman*, June 2, 2015.

18. The changing role of the Speaker since 1876 is described by authors Patrick L. Cox and Michael Phillips in *The House Will Come to Order: How the Texas Speaker Became a Power in State and National Politics* (Austin: University of Texas Press, 2010).

19. For one speaker pro tempore's responses to questions about his role in the 78th and 79th Texas legislatures, see Monica Gutierrez, "Turner on a Tightrope: A Few Questions with Speaker Pro Tempore Sylvester Turner," *Texas Observer*, June 24, 2005, 10–11, 18.

20. Laylan Copelin, "Judge Tosses Out Spending Restrictions for Speaker Elections," *Austin American-Statesman*, August 26, 2008. See also *Free Market Foundation v. Reisman*, 573 F Supp 2nd 997 (W.D. Tex. 2008).

21. Cassandra Pollock, "Texas House Speaker Dennis Bonnen Won't Seek Reelection after Recording Scandal," *Texas Tribune*, October 22, 2019, https://www.texastribune.org/2019/10/22/Dennis-Bonnen-to-not-seek-reelection-to-Texas-House/; and Christopher Hooks, "The Speaker and Creeper: Everything You Need to Know About the Craziest Texas Political Scandal in Years," *Texas Monthly*, https://www.texasmonthly.com/politics/texas-house-speaker-dennis-bonnen-michael-quinn-sullivan/

22. Taylor Goldenstein, "Judge Orders Empower Texans CEO Micheael Quinn Sullivan to Pay Ethics Fines," *Houston Chronicle*, January 24, 2021, https://www.houstonchronicle.com/politics/texas/article/Judge-orders-Empower-Texans-CEO-Michael-Quinn-15885153.php

23. Jolie McCullough, "After Defeats in 2019, a Group of Texas Lawmakers Is Teaming Up to Push Criminal Justice Reform," *Texas Tribune*, July 18, 2019, https://www.texastribune.org/2019/07/18/texas-house-criminal-justice-reform-caucus/

24. *Major Issues of the 86th Legislature*, Focus Report No. 86-5 (Austin: House Research Organization, Texas House of Representatives), December 18, 2019, 4, http://hro.house.texas.gov/pdf/focus/major86.pdf

25. Concerning the Texas Rangers and violence in South Texas, one of the most famous investigations in Texas history responded to a complaint by Representative J. T. Canales. See "Canales Investigation," https://www.tsl.texas.gov/arc/onlinecollections

26. For a more detailed description of the lawmaking process, see *How a Bill Becomes a Law: 86th Legislature*, Focus Report No. 86-2 (Austin: House Research Organization, Texas House of Representatives), February 28, 2019, https://hro.house.texas.gov/pdf/focus/hwbill86.pdf; and for an account of 16 years of Senate service, see Sharon Navarro, *Latina Legislator: Leticia Van de Putte and the Road to Leadership* (College Station: Texas A&M University Press, 2008).

27. For more information on how committees work, see *House Committee Procedures: 84th Legislature*, Focus Report No. 84-3 (Austin: House Research Organization, Texas House of Representatives, March 4, 2015), http://www.hro.house.state.tx.us/pdf/focus/compro84.pdf; and Hugh L. Brady, ed., *Texas Senate Practice* (Austin, TX: Capitol Hill Books, 2013), 70–87.

28. Wendy Davis, *Forgetting to Be Afraid* (New York: Blue Rider Press, 2014), 261–291; and Caitlin Dewey, "Wendy Davis 'Tweetstorm' Was Planned in Advance," *Washington Post*, June 26, 2013. During the filibuster, Senator Davis wore her famous pink Mizuno running shoes. By contrast, Davis's Republican successor, former Tea Party leader and abortion opponent Konni Burton,

made her first Senate appearance wearing black cowboy boots marked "Stand for Life." See Dave Montgomery, "New Tarrant Senator Makes a Statement with Her Footwear," *Fort Worth Star-Telegram*, January 14, 2015.

29. As one authority explains, this difference in the two-thirds majorities required by Article IV, Section 14, represents "a mysterious error in the present constitution." See George D. Braden, *Citizens' Guide to the Proposed New Texas Constitution* (Austin: Sterling Swift, 1975), 15.

30. Terrence Stutz, "Senator Ripped for Killing Statewide Ban on Texting While Driving," *Dallas News*, May 28, 2013.

31. "Social Justice Requires Public Policy," https://everytexan.org

32. Dave Mann and Jake Bernstein, "UndemoCraddick," *Texas Observer*, February 18, 2005, 3.

33. "An Online Look at the Texas 83rd Legislative Session," *Influence Opinions*, June 2013, influenceopinions.com/white-paper-an-online-look-at-the-83rd-texas-legislative-session

34. For a veteran Texas journalist's account of four decades of reporting on the Texas legislature, see Dave McNeely, "A Press Corps on the Lege," *Texas Observer*, May 27, 2005, 8–11. See also the biography of Molly Ivins (1944–2007), a liberal journalist who covered the Texas legislature for many years: Bill Minutaglio and W. Michael Smith, *Molly Ivins: A Rebel Life* (New York: Public Affairs, 2009). Since 1973, *Texas Monthly* has published a biennial list of the best and worst Texas legislators. For the 87th Legislature, see Christopher Hooks, R.G. Ratcliffe and Andrea Zelinski, "The Best and Worst Legislators," *Texas Monthly*, July, 2021, 92–105.

Chapter 9

1. For a revisionist view of Davis and his administration, see Carl H. Moneyhon, *Edmund J. Davis of Texas: Civil War General, Republican Leader, Reconstruction Governor* (Fort Worth: Texas Christian University Press, 2010).

2. Brian McCall, *The Power of the Texas Governor: Connally to Bush* (Austin: University of Texas Press, 2009). For a broad view of governors across the country, see Alan Rosenthal, *The Best Job in Politics: Exploring How Governors Succeed as Policy Leaders*, rev. ed. (Washington, DC: CQ Press, 2012).

3. Rick Casey, "Shift in Power Lies Ahead for Government in Texas," *Houston Chronicle*, April 4, 2014, https://www.chron.com/opinion/outlook/article/Casey-Shift-in-power-lies-ahead-for-government-5374573.php

4. See James S. Olson and Sharon Phair, "Anatomy of a Race Riot: Beaumont, Texas, 1943," *Texana* 11 (1973): 64–72; James A. Burran, "Violence in an 'Arsenal of Democracy,'" *East Texas Historical Journal* 14 (Spring 1976): 39–51; and Valentine Belfiglio, *Honor, Pride, Duty: A History of the Texas State Guard* (Austin: Eakin Press, 1995), 64.

5. Christy Hoppe, "Amid Conspiracy Talk, Abbott Orders Texas Guard to Keep an Eye on Federal Military Training," *Dallas Morning News*, April 29, 2015, https://www.dallasnews.com/news/texas/2015/04/29/amid-conspiracy-talk-abbott-orders-texas-guard-to-keep-an-eye-on-federal-military-training/

6. Sig Christenson, "Texas Guard May See Its Copters Fly Away," *San Antonio Express-News*, January 19, 2014, https://www.expressnews.com/news/local/military/article/Texas-Guard-may-see-its-copters-fly-away-5155746.php

7. "Governor Abbott Directs DPS Resources To Dallas To Combat Spike In Violent Crime," *Office of the Texas Governor*, November 18, 2020, https://gov.texas.gov/news/post/governor-abbott-directs-dps-resources-to-dallas-to-combat-spike-in-violent-crime

8. Allie Morris, "Gov. Abbott makes good on threat to veto funding for Texas Legislature, staff as he signs $248.6 billion state budget," *Dallas Morning News*, June 18, 2021, https://www.dallasnews.com/news/politics/2021/06/18/texas-gov-abbott-follows-through-with-threat-to-veto-lawmakers-pay-as-he-signs-2486-billion-state-budget/

9. Steve Clark, "Perry Rejects Medicaid Expansion for Texas Residents," *Valley Morning Star*, July 10, 2012; and Edgar Walters, "With Hospital Funds in Question, Abbott Holds Firm On Medicaid Expansion," *Texas Tribune*, April 20, 2015, https://www.texastribune.org/2015/04/20/hospital-funds-question-abbott-holds-firm-against-

10. For all executive orders issued by Governor Abbott, see "Executive orders by Governor Greg Abbott," *Legislative Reference Library*, https://lrl.texas.gov/legeLeaders/governors/displayDocs.cfm?govdoctypeID=5&governorID=45

11. For all proclamations issued by Governor Abbott, see "Proclamations by Governor Greg Abbott," *Legislative Reference Library*, https://lrl.texas.gov/legeLeaders/governors/displayProcs.cfm?governorID=45

12. Office of the Governor, *Legislative Appropriations Request for Fiscal Years 2014 and 2015*, August 30, 2012, p. 1, available online at http://governor.state.tx.us/files/financial-services/LAR_AY_2014-15.pdf

13. Paul J. Weber, "Perry's Tech Fund Shows Gains Despite Bankruptcies," *NBCDFW,* February 4, 2014, https://www.nbcdfw.com/news/local/perrys-tech-fund-shows-gains-despite-bankruptcies/2010768/

14. Bill Hethcock, "'Tremendous Increase' in Corporate Relocations, Expansions to Texas Since Pandemic Hit," *Austin Business Journal*, September 25, 2020, https://www.bizjournals.com/austin/news/2020/09/25/corporate-relocation-texas.html. For the website of the Texas government's efforts to attract business to the state, see *GO BIG IN TEXAS*, https://businessintexas.com

15. Details of legislative-executive relations are found in Patrick Cox and Michael Phillips, *This House Will Come to Order: How the Texas Speaker Became a Power in State and National Politics* (Austin: University of Texas Press, 2010); Bill Hobby and Saralee Tiede, *How Things Really Work: Lessons from a Life in Politics* (Austin: Center for American History, University of Texas at Austin, 2010); and Dave McNeely and Jim Henderson, *Bob Bullock: God Bless Texas* (Austin: University of Texas Press, 2008).

16. See Dave Montgomery, "Perry Defends Ceremonial Bill Signings that Hutchison Blasts as 'Phony,'" *Fort Worth Star-Telegram*, August 21, 2009.

17. For all vetoes since 2001, see *Vetoes of Legislation*, House Research Organization, Texas House of Representatives, https://hro.house.texas.gov/vetoes.aspx. For all veto statements by Governor Abbott, see "Vetoed Bills – Governor Greg Abbott," *Legislative Reference Library of Texas,* https://lrl.texas.gov/legeLeaders/governors/vetoesByGovernor.cfm?governorID=45

18. Taylor Goldenstein, "'He's Decided He's the king': Gov. Greg Abbott's COVID Response Leaves Lawmakers on Sidelines," *Houston Chronicle*, September 8, 2020, https://www.houstonchronicle.com/news/article/Greg-Abbott-has-unilaterally-directed-COVID-15548794.php. See also Stacy Fernandez, "Texas Democrats Urge Abbott to Call Special Session as Details Emerge Showing Javier Ambler's Death at the Hands of Sheriff's Deputies," *Texas Tribune*, June 15, 2020, https://www.texastribune.org/2020/06/15/texas-greg-abbott-javier-ambler-police-brutality/

19. Sommer Ingram, "Perry's Texas Supreme Court Picks Criticized as Too Business-Friendly," *Dallas Morning News,* October 31, 2011, https://www.dallasnews.com/news/politics/2011/11/01/perrys-texas-supreme-court-picks-criticized-as-too-business-friendly/

20. Beth Brown, "Supreme Court Is Elected, but Bears Perry's Stamp," *New York Times,* August 12, 2011, https://www.nytimes.com/2011/08/12/us/12ttperry.html

21. For annual reports on the activities of the Texas Board of Pardons and Paroles, see "Publications," *Texas Board of Pardons and Paroles*, https://www.tdcj.texas.gov/bpp/publications/publications.html

22. "Governor Abbott Establishes Customized Clemency Application for Survivors of Human Trafficking And Domestic Abuse," *Office of the Texas Governor*, February 20, 2020, https://gov.texas.gov/news/post/governor-abbott-establishes-customized-clemency-application-for-survivors-of-human-trafficking-and-domestic-abuse

23. Brandi Grissom, "Perry Pardons Tim Cole," *Texas Tribune, March* 1, 2010, https://www.texastribune.org/2010/03/01/perry-pardons-tim-cole/

24. Justin Miller, "On Rodney Reed Case, Greg Abbott Gets a Political Reprieve," *Texas Observer,* November 19, 2020, https://www.texasobserver.org/on-rodney-reed-case-greg-abbott-gets-a-political-reprieve/

25. "Proclamation Commuting Death Sentence of Thomas Bartlett Whitaker," *Office of the Texas Governor*, February 22, 2018, https://gov.texas.gov/news/post/proclamation-commuting-death-sentence-of-thomas-bartlett-whitaker

26. For example, see Gov. Greg Abbott, "Franchise Tax Relief Is Essential to Texas Economy," *Austin American-Statesman*, April 15, 2015, https://www.statesman.com/news/20160924/abbott-franchise-tax-relief-is-essential-to-texas-economy?template=ampart

27. Jim Parker, "Gov. Abbott Visits El Paso on Its Deadliest Day of Virus Pandemic, Also Pays Tribute to Walmart Victims," *KVIA.com*, August 13, 2020, https://kvia.com/news/texas/2020/08/12/texas-gov-abbott-to-visit-el-paso-to-examine-virus-pandemic-impact/

28. Morgan Smith, "Gov. Abbott: I'm Keeping a List of Lawmakers Who Oppose Me during the Special Session," *Texas Tribune*, July 17, 2017, https://www.texastribune.org/2017/07/17/abbott-property-taxes-are-top-issue-special-session

29. Tom Benning, "Abuse-of-Power Case Against Rick Perry Officially Dismissed." *Dallas Morning News,* April 6, 2016, https://www.dallasnews.com/news/politics/2016/04/06/abuse-of-power-case-against-rick-perry-officially-dismissed/

30. See Abbott's social media accounts at https://gov.texas.gov/governor-abbott. Note that LinkedIn does not reveal a person's total number of connections, listing anything over 500 connections as "500+."

31. Ken Herman, "First Lady of Texas Takes a New Job," *Austin American-Statesman*, November 7, 2003. Concerning her salary, see "Anita Perry's Salary Comes Indirectly from Governor's Backers," *Austin American-Statesman*, September 14, 2011. For Anita Perry's responses to questions about her life in politics, see her interview by Evan Smith, "Anita Perry," *Texas Monthly*, September 2005, 178–180, 182, 184.

32. For more on Cecilia Abbott's endeavors as First Lady, see "Texas First Lady Cecilia Abbott," *Office of the Texas Governor*, https://gov.texas.gov/first-lady/

33. For the text of Abbott's plan, see http://gov.texas.gov/files/press-office/Restoring_The_Rule_Of_Law_01082016.pdf

34. See Governor Greg Abbott, *Broken but Unbowed: The Fight to Fix a Broken America* (New York: Threshold Editions of Simon and Schuster, 2016).

35. For an interactive list of government salaries, see "Government Salaries Explorer," *Texas Tribune*, https://salaries.texastribune.org

36. Jay Root, "In Texas, a Collapse of Ethics Reform," *USA Today*, June 1, 2015, https://www.usatoday.com/story/news/local/texas-news/2015/06/01/in-texas-a-collapse-of-ethics-reform/28307367/

37. Richard Dunham, "The Texas Supreme Court and Legislature Help Perry Cloak Travel Security Expenses," *Houston Chronicle*, July 10, 2011, https://blog.chron.com/txpotomac/2011/07/commentary-the-texas-supreme-court-and-legislature-help-rick-perry-cloak-travel-security-expenses/

38. R. G. Ratcliff, "Perry's a Long Way from the Cotton Farm," *Houston Chronicle*, July 26, 2009; Jay Root, "Spending on Perry's Austin Mansion Hits $800,000," *Texas Tribune*, November 23, 2011, https://www.texastribune.org/2011/11/23/governors-mansion-spending-hits-800000/

39. Wayne Slater, "Rick Perry Won't Rule Out Another Presidential Bid," *Dallas Morning News*, February 7, 2012; and Peggy Fikac, "Our Travelin' Governor Perry Will Spend Even More Time on the Road," *Houston Chronicle*, September 12, 2011.

40. Jim Nicar, "A Summer of Discontent," *Texas Alcalde*, September/October 1997, 83. For detailed accounts of Jim Ferguson's downfall, which opened the way for Miriam "Ma" Ferguson to be elected governor for two terms, see Bruce Rutherford, *The Impeachment of Jim Ferguson* (Austin: Eakin Press, 1983); and Cortez A. M. Ewing, "The Impeachment of James E. Ferguson," *Southwestern Social Science Quarterly* 48 (June 1933): 184–210.

41. For former Governor Dolph Briscoe's account of his election campaigns and six years (1973–1979) as governor, see his *Dolph Briscoe: My Life in Ranching and Politics*, as told to Don Carleton (Austin: Center for American History, University of Texas at Austin, 2008), 151–261. A biography that tells Governor Ann Richards's story is Jan Reid, *Let the People In: The Life and Times of Ann Richards* (Austin: University of Texas Press, 2012). For an insider's view of George W. Bush's years as governor, see Karl Rove, "A New Kind of Governor," in Rove's *Courage and Consequences: My Life as a Conservative in the Fight* (New York: Threshold Editions, 2010), chap. 6.

42. See Carolyn Barta, *Bill Clements: Texian to His Toenails* (Austin: Eakin Press, 1996); Bill Minutaglio, *First Son: George W. Bush and the Bush Family Dynasty* (New York: Times Books, 1999); and Clarke Rountree, *George W. Bush: A Biography* (Santa Barbara, CA: Greenwood, 2011).

43. For grades on Perry's leadership in eight public policy areas, see Nate Blakeslee, Pamela Colloff, Erica Grieder, Mimi Swartz, and Brian D. Sweany, "The Rick Perry Report Card," *Texas Monthly*, July 2014, 80–95. This same issue of *Texas Monthly* includes Paul Burka's assessment of Perry's administration (pp. 24, 26, and 28) and Brian D. Sweany's lengthy interview, "Face to Face with Rick Perry," (pp. 74–78, 150–155, 157–158), https://www.texasmonthly.com/issue/july-2014/. For *The Texas Tribune*'s analysis of Governor Perry's time in office, see "The Perry Legacy," https://apps.texastribune.org/perry-legacy

44. For campaign finance information about Governor Abbott and many other politicians, see *Project Vote Smart*, https://votesmart.org/candidate/campaign-finance/50168/gregory-abbott#.XHBn3S2ZPVp

45. Justin Miller, "Abbott Puts Cabal of His Billionaire Donors, Industry Lobbyists in Charge of Restarting Texas' Economy," *Texas Observer*, April 17, 2020, https://www.texasobserver.org/texas-economy-greg-abbott-coronavirus/

46. Patrick Svitek, "Valdez Has $222,000 for General Election, a Fraction of Abbott's Millions," *Texas Tribune*, July 17, 2018, https://www.texastribune.org/2018/07/17/lupe-valdez-greg-abbott-millions-november-election

47. Paul J. Weber, "Texas governor stockpiles cash but not for the usual reason," *Associated Press*, February 24, 2019, https://apnews.com/article/5a62516b5d544615b343d73198d0e459

48. Lyle Larson, "The Shape of Texas Government Needs an Extreme Makeover," *Star-Telegram*, May 13, 2016, https://www.star-telegram.com/opinion/opn-columns-blogs/other-voices/article77536762.html

49. For all Attorney General Opinions, see "Opinions," *Attorney General of Texas*, https://www.texasattorneygeneral.gov/opinions

50. WFAA Staff, "Greg Abbott: 'I Go Into the Office, I Sue the Federal Government,'" *WFAA.com*, October 30, 2013, https://www.wfaa.com/article/news/politics/greg-abbott-i-go-into-the-office-i-sue-the-federal-government/306072905

51. Chuck Lindell, "Ken Paxton Pivots from Suing Obama to Defending Trump Policies," *Austin American-Statesman*, September 25, 2018, https://www.statesman.com/NEWS/20180127/Ken-Paxton-pivots-from-suing-Obama-to-defending-Trump-policies

52. For the text of the amicus brief, see https://www.texasattorneygeneral.gov/sites/default/files/images/admin/2019/Press/Brief.pdf

53. See Emma Platoff, "Texas Attorney General Ken Paxton Wants Judge Recused from His Criminal Case, Promising Further Delays in Years-Old Prosecution," *Texas Tribune*, August 7, 2020, https://www.texastribune.org/2020/08/07/ken-paxton-criminal-case/ Kate McGee, "Ken Paxton asks appeals court to toss whistleblower case brought by former top aides," Texas Tribune, June 2, 2021, https://www.texastribune.org/2021/06/02/ken-paxton-whistleblower-appeal/

54. "Comptroller's Calm Is What State Needs Now," *Corpus Christi Caller-Times*, January 28, 2016, https://www.caller.com/story/opinion/editorials/2016/01/28/editorial-comptrollers-calm-is-what-state-needs-now/91195240/

55. Glenn Hegar, "New Budget Protects Texas Interests," *Austin American-Statesman*, September 23, 2016, https://www.statesman.com/news/20160923/glenn-hegar-new-budget-protects-texas-interests

56. Jeremy Blackman and Susan Carroll, "Lawmakers Agree to Fix Permanent School Fund, but George P. Bush Keeps Control," *Houston Chronicle*, May 29, 2019, https://www.houstonchronicle.com/news/houston-texas/houston/article/Lawmakers-agree-to-fix-Permanent-School-Fund-but-13902400.php

57. Asher Price, "Effort to Remove Warbler Protections Sees New Life," *Austin American-Statesman*, January 16, 2020, https://www.statesman.com/news/20200116/effort-to-remove-warbler-protections-sees-new-life. See also Asher Price and Eric Dexheimer, "How Texas Fights Endangered Species Protections, Critter by Critter," *Austin American-Statesman*, September 25, 2018, https://www.statesman.com/news/20180409/how-texas-fights-endangered-species-protections-critter-by-critter

58. For these and other stories about Commissioner Miller, see the directory home page "Agriculture Commissioner Sid Miller," *Texas Tribune*, https://www.texastribune.org/directory/sid-miller/

59. Alexa Ura, "Former Secretary of State David Whitley Back at Gov. Greg Abbott's Office," *Texas Tribune*, May 31, 2019, https://www.texastribune.org/2019/05/31/former-secretary-state-david-whitley-back-greg-abbotts-office/

60. For all activities of the Secretary of State, see *Texas Secretary of State*, https://www.sos.state.tx.us/index.html For a discussion of the resignation of Ruth Hughs, see Taylor Goldenstein and Jeremy Blackman, "Did a 'smooth and secure' 2020 election cost the Texas secretary of state her job?" *Houston Chronicle*, May 24, 2021, https://www.houstonchronicle.com/politics/texas/article/Texas-Secretary-of-State-Ruth-Hughs-resigns-under-16195586.php

61. For more on the commission, see *Texas Sunset Advisory Commission*, https://www.sunset.texas.gov/

62. For continuously updated information on public and private sector employment in Texas, see "Texas," *Southwest Information Office, Bureau of Labor Statistics*, https://www.bls.gov/regions/southwest/texas.htm

63. Harvey Kronberg, quoted in Jonathan Walters, "Life after Civil Service Reform," *Human Capital Series, IBM Endowment for the Business of Government*, October 2002, 20, https://www.businessofgovernment.org/sites/default/files/LIfeAfterCivilServiceReform.pdf

64. "An Annual Report on Classified Employee Turnover for Fiscal Year 2020," *The State of Texas State Auditor*, December 2020, https://sao.texas.gov/reports/main/21-703.pdf

65. J. David McSwane, "Losing Ground," *Dallas Morning News*, March 31, 2016, http://interactives.dallasnews.com/2016/pay-gap. The disparities noted in this study have continued each year through the most recent year of data, 2019. For these statistics, see "Equal Employment Opportunity Commission, State and Local Government Information (EEO-4), 2019, National Employment Summary," *U.S. Equal Employment Opportunity Commission*, https://www.eeoc.gov/equal-employment-opportunity-commission-state-and-local-government-information-eeo-4-2019-52

66. For a careful analysis of Texas education, including the SBOE, see Cal Jillson, *Lone Star Tarnished: A Critical Look at Texas Politics and Public Policy* (New York: Routledge, 2012), 103–127. For a discussion of recent controversies on the Board, see Kate Slater, "Who Chooses the History Textbooks?" *Today*, September 10, 2020, https://www.today.com/tmrw/who-chooses-history-textbooks-t190833

67. For more on the activities of the board and its members, see "SBOE-State Board of Education," *Texas Education Agency*, https://tea.texas.gov/node/106036. For a map of SBOE districts, see "Texas: State Board of Education Districts," *Texas Education Agency*, https://tea.texas.gov/sites/default/files/PlanE120%20large.pdf

68. For more on the TEA's accountability measures, see "Accountability," *Texas Education Agency*, https://tea.texas.gov/texas-schools/accountability

69. See "2020 Accountability Rating System," *Texas Education Agency*, https://tea.texas.gov/texas-schools/accountability/academic-accountability/performance-reporting/2020-accountability-rating-system

70. For more information about the board and the commissioner, see "Board / Commissioner," *Texas Higher Education Coordinating Board*, https://www.highered.texas.gov/about-us/board-commissioner/

71. More information for people served by HHS can be found at "Coronavirus (COVID-19) Information for People Receiving Services," *Texas Health and Human Services*, https://hhs.texas.gov/services/health/coronavirus-covid-19/coronavirus-covid-19-information-people-receiving-services

72. For more information on the TWC, see *Texas Workforce Commission*, https://www.twc.texas.gov/

73. "Press Release: Rep. Cuellar Works Hard to Deliver $27,685,179 in Federal Funds to the Texas Workforce Commission," *United States Congressman Henry Cuellar*, October 5, 2020, https://cuellar.house.gov/news/documentsingle.aspx?DocumentID=405812. See also Nick Natario, "Texas Looking to Collect $214 Million in Overpaid Unemployment Benefits," *ABC13: Eyewitness News*, October 2, 2020, https://abc13.com/careers/texas-is-taking-back-$214m-in-overpaid-unemployment-benefits/6720587/

74. Quoted in "Valley Senators, AFL-CIO Differ on Alvarez Appointment to TWC," *Rio Grande Guardian*, February 22, 2016, https://riograndeguardian.com/valley-senators-afl-cio-differ-on-alvarez-appointment-to-twc/

75. Office of the Texas Governor, "Governor Abbott Signs ERCOT Reforms, Power Grid Weatherization Legislation Into Law," June 8, 2021, https://gov.texas.gov/news/post/governor-abbott-signs-ercot-reforms-power-grid-weatherization-legislation-into-law

Chapter 10

1. Robert A. Carp, Ronald Stidham, Kenneth L. Manning, and Lisa M. Holmes, *Judicial Process in America,* 11th ed. (Thousand Oaks, CA: CQ Press, 2020), 9–10.

2. G. D. Walters and P. C. Bolger, "Procedural Justice Perceptions, Legitimacy Beliefs, and Compliance with the Law: A Meta-analysis. *Journal of Experimental Criminology* 15 (2019): 341–372. https://doi.org/10.1007/s11292-018-9338-2

3. Tom R. Tyler (2001). "A Psychological Perspective on the Legitimacy of Institutions and Authorities," in *The Psychology of Legitimacy: Emerging Perspectives on Ideology, Justice, and Intergroup Relations,* ed. John T. Jost and Brenda Major (New York: Cambridge University Press, 2001), 416.

4. Leo E. Strine, Jr., "Regular (Judicial) Order as Equity: The Enduring Value of the Distinct Judicial Role," *Temple Law Review* 87: 1 (2014): 91–100.

5. "Understanding Implicit Bias," *Kirwan Institute for the Study of Race and Ethnicity, The Ohio State University*, accessed September 27, 2020. http://kirwaninstitute.osu.edu/research/understanding-implicit-bias/. Harvard University's Project Implicit allows those who desire to do so to take an Implicit Association Test to measure their own implicit bias. The test can be accessed here: https://implicit.harvard.edu/implicit/takeatest.html

6. Mark Curriden, "Texas State Bar President under Fire for Facebook Post on Black Lives Matter," *Houston Chronicle*, July 22, 2020, https://www.houstonchronicle.com/business/article/Texas-State-Bar-president-under-fire-for-Facebook-15426130.php

7. An easy-to-understand book about Texas law is Richard Alderman's *Know Your Rights: Answers to Texans' Everyday Legal Questions*, 9th ed. (Dallas: Lone Star Books, 2018).

8. Annual statistics and other information on the Texas judicial system are available from the Texas Judicial Council and the Office of Court Administration, http://www.txcourts.gov/about-texas-courts.aspx

9. National Center for State Courts, "Legal Credentials, Qualifications to Serve as a Trial Court Judge, Trial Courts," *State Court Organization,* accessed on October 12, 2020. http://data.ncsc.org/QvAJAXZfc/opendoc.htm?document=Public%20App/SCO.qvw&host=QVS@qlikviewisa&anonymous=true

10. Many counties include instructions on how to prosecute a claim in justice courts. For example, Travis County (Austin) includes a page on its county website entitled "Guide & File for Pro Se Litigants" that outlines the procedure and includes forms for filing a claim in a Travis County justice court, available at https://www.traviscountytx.gov/justices-of-peace/guide-file-for-pro-se-litigants

11. See former Chief Justice Joe R. Greenhill, "The Constitutional Amendment Giving Criminal Jurisdiction to the Texas Courts of Civil Appeals and Recognizing the Inherent Power of the Texas Supreme Court," *Texas Tech Law Review* 33: 2 (2002): 377–404; Ben L. Mesches, "Bifurcated Appellate Review: The Texas Story of Two High Courts," *American Bar Association*, November 1, 2014, https://www.americanbar.org/groups/judicial/publications/judges_journal/2014/fall/bifurcated_appellate_review_the_texas_story_of_two_high_courts

12. SB 40, 86th Texas Legislature, introduced in Texas Senate, February 1, 2019, https://capitol.texas.gov/tlodocs/86R/billtext/pdf/SB00040F.pdf#navpanes=0

13. For an excellent chronology of actions taken by the Supreme Court and other agencies to manage the COVID-19 crisis from March to August 2020, see David Slayton, "Jury Trials During the COVID-19 Pandemic: Observations and Recommendations," Austin: Office of Court Administration, August 28, 2020, https://txcourts.gov/media/1449660/jury-report-to-scotx-final.pdf

14. Robert D. Morgan et al., "Specialty Courts: Who's In and Are They Working?" *Psychological Services* 13 (2016): 246–253; Frank A. Sloan et al., "Do Specialty Courts Achieve Better Outcomes for Children in Foster Care than General Courts?" *Evaluation Review* 37 (October 2013): 3–34.

15. David Beck, "A Civil Justice System with No Trials: Are We Sure We Want to Go There?" *Texas Bar Journal* 76 (December 2013): 1073–1076; David W. Elrod and Worthy Walker, "Fact or Fiction: Are There Less Jury Trials and Lawyers? If So, What Do We Do About It?" *Litigation Commentary & Review* 53 (June/July 2010), https://litigationcommentary.org/2010/2010-june-july/190-good-reads-david-elrod

16. Jeb Handelsman Shugerman, *The People's Courts: Pursuing Judicial Independence in America* (Cambridge, MA: Harvard University Press, 2012).

17. For a discussion of the way one attorney has supported opponents of judges who made unfavorable rulings against his clients, see Lisa Falkenberg, "System Appears to Let Lawyer Buy a Judge," *Houston Chronicle*, February 19, 2014.

18. Texas State Conference of NAACP Branches for Testimony of Gary L. Bledsoe to the Texas Commission on Judicial Selection, "Texas NAACP Addresses Important Issues to Facilitate the Discussion Regarding Proposed Changes for Selecting Members of Texas' Judiciary in the Aftermath of the George Floyd Tragedy," August 7, 2020, https://www.txcourts.gov/media/1449569/20200806_tx-naacp-on-judicial-selection.pdf

19. Roy A. Schotland, "New Challenges to States' Judicial Selection," *Georgetown Law Journal* 95 (2007): 1077–1105.

20. Brian T. Fitzpatrick, "The Politics of Merit Selection," *Missouri Law Review* 74 (2009): 675–709.

21. Wallace Jefferson, "The State of the Judiciary," *Texas Bar Journal* 74 (April 2011): 282–284.

22. "Public Warning, Michael McSpadden, CJC No. 18-0682," *State Commission on Judicial Conduct* (November 12, 2019), http://www.scjc.texas.gov/media/46781/mcspadden18-0682pubwarn111219.pdf

23. "Refraining from Inappropriate Judicial Conduct," Canon 5, *Texas Code of Judicial Conduct,* Canon 5, https://www.txcourts.gov/rules-forms/rules-standards/. Scroll to the Texas Code of Judicial Conduct on this site for the most current rules. The Texas Supreme Court promulgates the rules governing appropriate judicial conduct.

24. John G. Browning and Don Willett, "Rules of Engagement: Exploring Judicial Use of Social Media," *Texas Bar Journal* 79 (February 2016): 100–102 at 102.

25. Steve Miller, "Complaints against Texas Judges Are Piling Up – and So Are Complaints against the Agency Tasked with Handling Them," *Texas Monitor,* October 4, 2019, https://texasmonitor.org/complaints-against-texas-judges-are-piling-up-and-so-are-complaints-against-the-agency-tasked-with-handling-them/

26. Angela Morris, "'I Wasn't Good at My Job': Texas Bar Replaces Steve Fischer on Judicial Conduct Commission," *Texas Lawyer,* September 25, 2020, https://www.law.com/texaslawyer/2020/09/25/i-wasnt-good-at-my-job-texas-bar-replaces-steve-fischer-on-judicial-conduct-commission/

27. A discussion of the proceeding against Keller is available in Dave Montgomery, "Judge Who Refused to Keep Office Open in Death Row Case Shouldn't Be Removed, Ruling Says," *Fort Worth Star-Telegram*, January 21, 2010. The Special Court of Review's findings in this case can be accessed at http://caselaw.findlaw.com/tx-special-court-of-review-sct/1546619.html. For a discussion of the case against Chief Justice Nathan Hecht, see Paul Burka, "He's Doing a Hecht of a Job," *Texas Monthly,* July 31, 2007, http://www.texasmonthly.com/burka-blog/hes-doing-a-hecht-of-a-job. For a discussion of Justice Hecht's related case with the Texas Ethics Commission for soliciting funds to pay his lawyer's fees, see Chuck Lindell, "Nathan Hecht Pays $29,000 to End $1,000 Ethics Fine," *Austin American-Statesman,* October 28, 2015, http://www.statesman.com/news/news/nathan-hecht-pays-1000-to-end-29000-ethics-fine/npBNW/. All cases against Hecht were resolved in 2015.

28. Department of Research and Analysis, "2019 Population Trends of Racial/Ethnic Minorities in the State Bar of Texas," *State Bar of Texas,* https://www.texasbar.com/AM/Template.cfm?Section=Demographic_and_Economic_Trends&Template=/CM/ContentDisplaycfm&ContentID=48797; Department of Research and Analysis, "2019 Population Trends of Women in the State Bar of Texas," *State Bar of Texas,* https://www.texasbar.com/AM/Template.cfm?Section=Demographic_and_Economic_Trends&Template=/CM/ContentDisplay.cfm&ContentID=48799

29. Zach Wolfe, "Top 15 Proposed Changes to Texas Lawyer Advertising Rules," *Five Minute Law,* August 3, 2020, https://fiveminutelaw.com/author/zachwolfe99/

30. Lewis Powell, Address to the ABA Legal Services Program, American Bar Association Annual Meeting, August 10, 1976.

31. Betty Balli Torres, "The Justice System Fails Marginalized Texans When They Need It Most," Texas Access to Justice Foundation, June 9, 2020, https://www.teajf.org/news/releases/NoJusticeNoPeace.aspx

32. Eric Quitugua, "A New Way to Serve," *Texas Bar Journal* 82 (February 2019): 100–101.

33. In March 2020, Bexar County courts suspended in-person jury trials. The moratorium was originally set to expire on December 31, 2020, but was extended until April 1, 2021, by Local Administrative Judge, Ron Rangel. Slayton, "Jury Trials;" Paul Venema, "In-person Jury Trials in Bexar County Delayed until at Least April 1," KSAT, January 21, 2021, https://www.ksat.com/news/local/2021/01/21/in-person-jury-trials-in-bexar-county-delayed-until-at-least-april-1/

34. A Collin County (Plano) grand jury acted independently in investigating Attorney General Ken Paxton for stock fraud. After appointment of a special prosecutor, he was indicted. R. G. Ratcliffe, "Grand Jury Goes Rogue on Attorney General Ken Paxton," *Texas Monthly,* April 9, 2015, http://www.texasmonthly.com/burka-blog/grand-jury-goes-rogue-on-attorney-general-ken-paxton

35. Tommy Witherspoon, "Grand Jury Reindicts 59 after Challenges to Virtual Grand Jury Process," *Waco Tribune-Herald,* May 26, 2020, https://wacotrib.com/news/local/crime-and-courts/grand-jury-reindicts-59-after-challenges-to-virtual-grand-jury-process/article_c7fe7f50-53d3-5287-8504-f6d040e33382.html

36. For a discussion of the history of tort reform in Texas, see Mimi Swartz, "Hurt? Injured? Need a Lawyer? Too Bad!" *Texas Monthly*, November 2005, 164–169, 218–234, 254–258.

37. Joey Berlin, "Coming of Age: Celebrating 15 Years of Texas Tort Reform," *Texas Medicine,* September 2018, pp. 14–21, https://www.texmed.org/Template.aspx?id=48427

38. Ibid.

39. David Arkush, Peter Gosselar, Christine Hines, and Taylor Lincoln, "Liability Limits in Texas Fail to Curb Medical Costs," *Public Citizen,* December 2009, http://www.citizen.org/documents/Texas_Liability_Limits.pdf

40. Lana Shadwick, "Texas Court Filings Are Down 17 Percent: Tort Reform Is Blamed," *Breitbart*, March 8, 2015, http://www.breitbart.com/texas/2015/03/08/texas-court-filings-are-down-17-percent-tort-reform-is-blamed

41. Shawn Shinneman, "The Making of a $242 Million Verdict," *D Magazine,* January 2019, https://www.dmagazine.com/publications/d-magazine/2019/january/the-making-of-a-242-million-verdict/

42. Tex. R. Civ. P. 106 and 108(a). For an excellent discussion of the use of social media as an alternative method for service of process, see Emily Davis, "Social Media: A Good Alternative, for Alternative Service of Process," *Case W. Res. J. Int'l L.* 213 (2020), https://scholarlycommons.law.case.edu/jil/vol52/iss1/26

43. "Vexatious Litigants," *Office of Court Administration,* https://www.txcourts.gov/judicial-data/vexatious-litigants/

44. Beck, "A Civil Justice System"; Elrod and Walker, "Fact or Fiction."

45. Texas Association of Counties, "Indigent Defense," August 2020, https://www.county.org/Legislative/County-Legislative-Issues/Indigent-Defense

46. Tony Fabelo, Carl Reynolds, and Jessica Tyler, *Improving Indigent Defense: Evaluation of the Harris County Public Defender* (Austin: Council of Governments Justice Center, September 30, 2013).

47. Zach Despart and Keri Blakinger, "Harris County Judges Criticized over Pace of Court-Appointed Lawyer Reform," *Houston Chronicle,* October 7, 2019.

Chapter 11

1. Glenn Hegar, *Biennial Revenue Estimate 2020–2021 Biennium: 86th Texas Legislature,* Texas Comptroller of Public Accounts, January 2019, p. ii.

2. Ibid, p. 9.

3. "Texas Budget Challenges Are Not Over," Texas Taxpayers and Research Association, August 3, 2017, https://ttara.org/wp-content/uploads/2018/09/August2017TTARABudgetResearchReport_Final.pdf

4. Milton Friedman, *Dollars and Deficits: Inflation, Monetary Policy, and Balance of Payments* (Saddle Brook, NJ: Prentice-Hall, 1968), 7. For a different perspective on fiscal policy, see Kenneth P. Miller,

Texas vs. California: A History of Their Struggle for the Future of America (Oxford: Oxford University Press, 2020).

5. *Fiscal Note, 84th Legislative Regular Session, HB 32*, Legislative Budget Board, May 25, 2015, https://capitol.texas.gov/tlodocs/84R/fiscalnotes/pdf/HB00032F.pdf#navpanes=0

6. For a complete list of taxes and descriptions of each, see "Texas Taxes and Fees," *Taxes,* Texas Comptroller of Public Accounts, accessed December 21, 2020, https://www.comptroller.texas.gov/taxes/a-to-z.php

7. Glenn Hegar, *Tax Exemptions and Tax Incidence: A Report to the Governor and the 86th Legislature*, Texas Comptroller of Public Accounts, December 2020, p. 14, https://comptroller.texas.gov/transparency/reports/tax-exemptions-and-incidence/

8. "Fiscal 50: State Trends and Analysis," The Pew Charitable Trusts, November 5, 2020, https://www.pewtrusts.org/en/research-and-analysis/data-visualizations/2014/fiscal-50#ind6

9. *San Juan Cellular Telephone Company v. Public Service Corporation of Puerto Rico* (First Cir.), 967 F 2nd 683 (1992).

10. Art. III, Sec. 49a, Texas Constitution (1942, amended 1999).

11. Rodney Ellis and Sylvester Turner, "Short-Sighted Cuts Costly to Poor," *Houston Chronicle*, August 29, 2011.

12. For an excellent resource that includes descriptions of the state's major tax sources and amounts collected in 2019, see Glenn Hegar, *A Field Guide to the Taxes of Texas*, Texas Comptroller of Public Accounts, January 2020, https://comptroller.texas.gov/transparency/revenue/. Scroll to the document on this site.

13. Jannelle Cammenga, "State and Local Tax Rates, 2020," Tax Foundation, July 8, 2020, https://taxfoundation.org/state-and-local-sales-tax-rates-2020/

14. Hegar, *Tax Exemptions and Tax Incidence.*

15. Liz Farmer, "Here's Something Texas Government Did Right—And It Has To Do With E-Commerce Sales Taxes," *Forbes*, February 19, 2021, https://www.forbes.com/sites/lizfarmer/2021/02/19/heres-something-texas-government-did-right-and-it-has-to-do-with-e-commerce-sales-taxes/?sh=479f34a61754

16. "Amazon Announces First Fulfillment Center in Waco, TX," *Amazon Press Release*, October 23, 2020, https://press.aboutamazon.com/news-releases/news-release-details/amazon-announces-first-fulfillment-center-waco-tx

17. Chris Tomlinson, "Texas Needs to Drop Its Franchise Tax and Come Up with Something Better," *Houston Chronicle,* April 5, 2016, http://www.houstonchronicle.com/business/columnists/tomlinson/article/Franchise-tax-needs-to-go-better-business-tax-7230109.php For an excellent discussion of the history of the franchise tax, see Josh Haney and Chris Wright, "A History of the Texas Franchise Tax: The Complex Evolution of Our Main Business Tax," *Fiscal Notes,* May 2015, https://www.comptroller.texas.gov/economy/fiscal-notes/2015/may/franchisetax.php

18. Paul Flahive and Michael Taylor, "Oil Is in Trouble. So Is Texas," *Houston Public Media*, November 20, 2020, https://www.houstonpublicmedia.org/articles/news/energy-environment/2020/11/20/386632/oil-is-in-trouble-so-is-texas/

19. For articles on local protests to fracking and other concerns, see "Fracturing," *StateImpact: Texas—Reporting on Power, Policy, and the Planet,* http://stateimpact.npr.org/texas/tag/fracking

20. "Bill Analysis: Repealing the Inheritance Tax," House Research Organization, May 21, 2015, http://www.hro.house.state.tx.us/pdf/ba84r/sb0752.pdf#navpanes=0

21. *Fiscal Size-up: 2020–21 Biennium*, Legislative Budget Board, May 2020, p. 41, https://www.lbb.state.tx.us/Documents/Publications/Fiscal_SizeUp/Fiscal_SizeUp_2020-21.pdf

22. Jared Walczak and Jannelle Cammenga, "2021 State Business Tax Climate Index," Tax Foundation, https://taxfoundation.org/2021-state-business-tax-climate-index/. For a comparison among states of the total tax burden on businesses, see Jared Walczak, Katherine Loughead, Ulrik Boelson, and Jannelle Cammenga, "Location Matters 2021: The State Tax Costs of Doing Business," Tax Foundation, https://taxfoundation.org/state-tax-costs-of-doing-business-2021/#Interactive.

23. Tex. Business and Commerce Code Ann. Sec. 326.001-326.002 (2013).

24. "Legalized Sports Betting Unlikely in 3 Largest US States," *KXAN*, March 2, 2019, https://www.kxan.com/news/texas/legalized-sports-betting-unlikely-in-3-largest-us-states/

25. Brandi Grissom, "Lottery Pursued a Sports Play," *Dallas Morning News,* January 16, 2016.

26. I. C. Murrell, "Texas House to Consider Fantasy Sports Legislation," *Port Arthur News*, April 26, 2019, https://www.panews.com/2019/04/26/texas-house-to-consider-fantasy-sports-legislation/

27. Dave Montgomery, "On Second Thought Texas House Opts Not to Kill Lottery Commission," *Fort Worth Star-Telegram*, April 24, 2013.

28. Gromer Jeffers, "Gambling Bills Coming Up Losers in Legislature," *Dallas Morning News,* April 20, 2016.

29. Patrick Svitek, "Las Vegas Sands Went All in on Legalizing Casinos in Texas. Here's Why the Multimillion-dollar Effort Did Not Make It Far This Session," *Texas Tribune,* June 16, 2021, https://www.texastribune.org/2021/06/16/las-vegas-sands-texas-casino-gambling/; Patrick Svitek and Mitchell Ferman, "GOP Megadonor Sheldon Adelson Readies 2021 Lobbying Blitz to Bring Casinos to Texas," *Texas Tribune,* December 9, 2020, https://www.texastribune.org/2020/12/09/sheldon-adelson-texas-casinos/

30. Ken Paxton, "Opinion No. KP0057: The Legality of Fantasy Sports Leagues under Texas Law," Office of the Attorney General, January 19, 2016, https://www.texasattorneygeneral.gov/opinions/ken-paxton/kp-0057

31. Clay Carpenter, "Halls of Game," *Corpus Christi Caller-Times,* December 27, 2020, p. 1A, 6A; Mike Jimenez, "Drive-in Bingo Debuts While Halls Celebrate Short-Lived Reopening," *KVEO-TV,* May 4, 2020, https://www.valleycentral.com/news/drive-in-bingo-debuts-while-halls-celebrate-short-lived-reopening/

32. "Energy," General Land Office of Texas, http://www.glo.texas.gov/energy/index.html

33. *Annual Report 2020,* Texas Bond Review Board, December 2020, http://www.brb.state.tx.us/pub/bfo/AR/AR2020.pdf

34. Jim Malewitz, "Plan to Overhaul Texas Rainy Day Fund and Boost Returns Losing Steam," *Texas Tribune,* May 19, 2017, https://www.texastribune.org/2017/05/19/rainy-day-fund-overhaul-loses-steam-senate; Glenn Hegar, "Long-Term Obligations and the Texas Legacy Fund," *Fiscal Notes,* September/October 2018, https://comptroller.texas.gov/economy/fiscal-notes/2018/sep-oct/index.php#article

35. For an excellent description of the Texas budgeting process, see *Budget 101: A Guide to the Budget Process in Texas,* Senate Research Center, January 2021, https://senate.texas.gov/_assets/srcpub/87th_Budget_101.pdf

36. Governor Greg Abbott, *2022-2023 Governor's Budget,* February 2021, https://gov.texas.gov/uploads/files/press/Governors-Budget-FY-2022-2023.pdf

37. Governor's Office Budget Division and Legislative Budget Board, "Policy Letter for Legislative Appropriations Request," Office of the Governor, August 18, 2020, https://www.lbb.state.tx.us/Documents/Instructions/LAR/LAR_Policy_Letter.pdf

38. Texas Commission on the Arts, "Legislative Appropriations Request for Fiscal Years 2022 and 2023," Legislative Budget Board, https://www.arts.texas.gov/wp-content/uploads/2020/09/2022-2023_LAR_TCA_2020-09-11.pdf

39. "Senator Nelson Announces Zero-Based Budgeting for All Texas Agencies," Greater Arlington Chamber of Commerce, May 15, 2020, https://www.arlingtontx.com/blog/2020/05/page/3/

40. Mark Lisherorn, "Why Are Political Leaders Avoiding Naming a New Top Auditor?" *Texas Monitor,* February 7, 2019, https://texasmonitor.org/why-are-political-leaders-avoiding-naming-a-new-top-auditor/

41. U.S. Census Bureau, *Annual Survey of School System Finances Tables,* May 11, 2020, https://www.census.gov/content/census/en/programs-surveys/school-finances/data/tables.html/

42. Reynaldo Valencia, Sonia García, Henry Flores, and José Roberto Juárez, *Mexican Americans and the Law* (Tucson: University of Arizona Press, 2004), 29–37.

43. *Fiscal Note, 86th Legislative Regular Session (Conference Committee),* Legislative Budget Board, May 24, 2019, 7, https://capitol.texas.gov/tlodocs/86R/fiscalnotes/pdf/HB00003F.pdf#navpanes=0; *Fiscal Note, 87th Legislative Regular Session (Senate Committee Report),* Legislative Budget Board, May 13, 2021, 3.

44. "The Coronavirus Recession Is a School Funding Nightmare," Texas Association of School Boards, accessed December 26, 2020, https://www.tasb.org/members/enhance-district/coronavirus-recession-is-a-school-funding-nightmare.aspx

45. "Texas Higher Education Strategic Plan: 2015–2030, 60x30TX," Texas Higher Education Coordinating Board, July 2015, http://www.thecb.state.tx.us/reports/PDF/6862.PDF; "*60X30TX* Progress Report," Texas Higher Education Coordinating Board, July 2019, http://www.60x30tx.com/media/1518/2019-60x30tx-progress-report.pdf

46. "Public Schools Explorer," *Texas Tribune,* accessed December 26, 2020, https://schools.texastribune.org/about/

47. Alejandra Matos, "Texas Top-Ranked High Schools Don't Prepare Most Kids for College Data Shows," *Houston Chronicle,* September 28, 2018, https://www.houstonchronicle.com/news/local/article/Texas-top-ranked-high-schools-don-t-prepare-13266783.php

48. Leslie Helmcamp, *Sizing Up the 2014–2015 Texas Budget: Student Financial Aid* (Austin: Center for Public Policy Priorities, August 30, 2013), http://forabettertexas.org/images/EO_2013_08_PP_BudgetSeries_FinAid.pdf

49. Rick Perry, "State of the State Address, 2011," *House Journal of the Regular Session of the Eighty-Second Legislature,* February 8, 2011, 287, http://www.lrl.state.tx.us/scanned/govdocs/Rick%20Perry/2011/SOS_Perry_2011.pdf

50. Thomas L. Harnisch, *Performance-Based Funding: A Re-emerging Strategy in Public Higher Education Financing,* American Association of State Colleges and Universities, June 2011, https://www.aascu.org/uploadedFiles/AASCU/Content/Root/PolicyAndAdvocacy/PolicyPublications/Performance_Funding_AASCU_June2011.pdf

51. Ronald Trowbridge, "Community Colleges Get Short Shrift in Funding," *Houston Chronicle,* July 12, 2013.

52. The University of Texas System Office of Budget and Planning, "Available University Fund Report," December 2020, https://www.utsystem.edu/sites/default/files/documents/report-state/2020/available-university-fund-report-fy-2020/720-ut-sys-admin-2020-auf-report.pdf; Areeba Amer, "Permanent University Fund's Assets under UTIMCO Management Lose 5% in Market Value Since January Due to COVID-19," *Daily Texan,* June 22, 2020, https://thedailytexan. com/2020/06/22/permanent-university-fund%E2%80%99s-assets-under-utimco-management-lose-5-in-market-value-since/

53. John Sharp, *Bordering the Future: Higher Education, Setting the Framework* (Austin: Texas Comptroller of Public Accounts/Research Division, July 1998); and Richard R. Valencia, *Chicano Students and the Courts: The Mexican American Legal Struggle for Educational Equality* (New York: New York University Press, 2008), 255–267.

54. Julie Chang, "Dan Patrick: Lawmakers Should Regulate Tuition Again," *Austin American-Statesman,* April 26, 2016.

55. *The COVID-19 Pandemic and Resulting Economic Crash Have Caused the Greatest Health Insurance Losses in American History,* National Center for Coverage Innovation at Families USA, July 17, 2020, https://familiesusa.org/wp-content/uploads/2020/07/COV-254_Coverage-Loss_Report_7-17-20.pdf

56. "Child Poverty Tables," *The State of America's Children 2020,* Children's Defense Fund, https://www.childrensdefense.org/policy/resources/soac-2020-child-poverty-tables/

57. Joan Alker and Alexandra Corcoran, "Children's Uninsured Rate Rises by Largest Annual Jump in More Than a Decade," Georgetown University Health Policy Institute Center for Children and Families, October 9, 2020, https://ccf.georgetown.edu/wp-content/uploads/2020/10/ACS-Uninsured-Kids-2020_EMB-10-06-edit-1.pdf

58. Robin Rudowitz, Bradley Corallo, and Rachel Garfield, "New Incentive for States to Adopt the ACA Medicaid Expansion: Implications for State Spending," Kaiser Family Foundation, March 17, 2021, https://www.kff.org/medicaid/issue-brief/new-incentive-for-states-to-adopt-the-aca-medicaid-expansion-implications-for-state-spending/#:~:text=Under%20the%20ACA%2C%20states%20currently,to%2090%25%20over%20time; D. J. Wilson, "The Implications for Texas of CMS's Rescission of Its Medicaid Waiver Extension," *State of Reform,* April 19, 2021, https://stateofreform.com/news/texas/2021/04/the-implications-for-texas-of-cmss-rescission-of-its-medicaid-waiver-extension/

59. Kevin McPherson, Jessica Donald, and Bruce Wright, "Transportation Infrastructure: Keeping Texas Moving," *Fiscal Notes,* May 2018, https://comptroller.texas.gov/economy/fiscal-notes/2018/may/transportation.php#article

60. Texas Department of Transportation, *Texas Transportation Plan 2050,* June 25, 2020, https://ftp.txdot.gov/pub/txdot/tpp/2050/ttp-2050.pdf

61. Patrick Driscoll, "Gas Taxes Can't Fuel All Road Projects," *San Antonio Express-News,* December 4, 2005.

62. Texas Water Development Board, *Water for Texas: 2012 State Water Plan* (Austin: Texas Water Development Board, January 2012), http://www.twdb.texas.gov/waterplanning/swp/2012/index.asp, as amended by *Water for Texas: 2017 State Water Plan* (Austin: Texas Water Development Board, May 2016), http://www.twdb.texas.gov/waterplanning/swp/2017/doc/2017_SWP_Adopted.pdf. and *Water for Texas: 2022 State Water Plan (Draft),* accessed June 19, 2021, http://www.twdb.texas.gov/waterplanning/swp/2022/index.asp

63. Susan Combs, *Texas Water Report: Going Deeper for the Solution* (Austin: Office of the Comptroller of Public Accounts, January 2014).

64. Texas Water Development Board, *Water for Texas:2022.*

65. Ari Phillips, "What Happens When the First Texas Town to Run Out of Water Gets Rainfall," *ClimateProgress,* June 4, 2015.

66. "Population Projections," *Texas Demographic Center,* accessed December 28, 2020, https://demographics.texas.gov/data/TPEPP/Projections/

67. Spencer Grubbs, Shannon Halbrook, Jessica Donald, and Bruce Wright, "Texas Water: Planning for More," *Fiscal Notes,* April 2019, https://comptroller.texas.gov/economy/fiscal-notes/2019/apr/tx-water-planning.php

68. Lauren Mulverhill, "Texas' Digital Divide: The State of Broadband in Texas' Rural Communities," *Fiscal Notes,* October 2019, https://comptroller.texas.gov/economy/fiscal-notes/2019/oct/divide.php;

Connected Nation Texas, "Broadband in Texas: A Briefing Prepared for the Governor's Broadband Development Council," *Office of the Governor*, April 2020, https://gov.texas.gov/uploads/files/business/Texas_Broadband_Briefing_Book_-_April_2020.pdf.

69. "A Guide to the 2011 Texas Blackouts," *StateImpact*, accessed on May 30, 2021, https://stateimpact.npr.org/texas/tag/2011-blackouts/page/2/

Chapter 12

1. "S.B. No. 1 General Appropriations Act: Eighty-Seventh Legislature," May 2021, https://capitol.texas.gov/tlodocs/87R/billtext/pdf/SB00001F.pdf#navpanes=0

2. The classic Robert L. Lineberry, *American Public Policy* (New York: Harper & Row, 1977), 2; and Thomas R. Dye, *Understanding Public Policy*, 15th ed. (Boston: Pearson, 2017), 1.

3. Ross Ramsey, "UT/TT Poll: A Hard Line on Immigration, But Not on Deporting 'Dreamers,'" *Texas Tribune*, October 23, 2017, https://www.texastribune.org/2017/10/23/uttt-poll-hard-line-immigration-not-deporting-dreamers

4. For summaries of the research, see Rosalee A. Clawson and Zoe M. Oxley, *Public Opinion: Democratic Ideals, Democratic Practice*, 3rd ed. (Washington, DC: CQ Press, 2017), 352–356; and Carroll J. Glynn et al., *Public Opinion*, 3rd ed. (Boulder, CO: Westview Press, 2016), 295–319.

5. Martin Gilens and Benjamin I. Page, "Testing Theories of American Politics: Elites, Interest Groups, and Average Citizens," *Perspectives on Politics* 12 (2014): 575.

6. Darryl Fears, "Texas Official's Report Ignites a New Border Conflict," *Washington Post,* December 15, 2006, http://www.washingtonpost.com/wp-dyn/content/article/2006/12/14/AR2006121401552.html?noredirect=on%20 https://www.washingtonpost.com/wp-dyn/content/article/2006/12/14/AR2006121401552.html?noredirect=on%20 https://lawprofessors.typepad.com/immigration/files/TX.comptroller.report.pdf

7. Jose Ivan Rodriguez-Sanchez, "Undocumented Immigrants in Texas: A Cost-Benefit Assessment," (paper published by Rice University's Baker Institute for Public Policy, May 2020), https://www.bakerinstitute.org/media/files/files/47a234a5/usmx-pub-undocumentedresidents-050620.pdf

8. Maggie Flynn, "Bill to Boost Medicaid Rates for Texas Nursing Homes Dies Before a Vote," *Skilled Nursing News,* June 2, 2019, https://skillednursingnews.com/2019/06/bill-to-boost-medicaid-rates-for-texas-nursing-homes-dies-before-a-vote/

9. Andrew Schneider, "Report: Texas' Nursing Home Care Quality Is Poor, But Improving," *Houston Public Media,* December 9, 2019, https://www.houstonpublicmedia.org/articles/news/health-science/2019/12/09/353272/texas-nursing-home-care-quality-poor-but-improving/

10. Ben Elgin and Peter Waldman, "Nursing Homes Face Catastrophic Mix of Virus and Lax Oversight," *Claims Journal*, March 10, 2020, https://www.claimsjournal.com/news/national/2020/03/10/295920.htm

11. "COVID-19 Nursing Home Data," Data.CMS.gov, November 11, 2020, https://data.cms.gov/stories/s/COVID-19-Nursing-Home-Data/bkwz-xpvg/

12. "Coronavirus (COVID-19)," accessed October 19, 2020, https://hhs.texas.gov/services/health/coronavirus-covid-19

13. "Nursing Home Report Cards: Texas," Families for Better Care, 2019, https://familiesforbettercare.com/index.php/report-cards/details/tx

14. Jenny Deam, "Texas Ranks Last in U.S. in Nursing Home Care," *Houston Chronicle*, May 14, 2015, http://www.houstonchronicle.com/business/medical/article/Texas-ranks-last-in-U-S-in-nursing-home-care-6264584.php; Eric Nicholson, "Texas Leads the League in Bad Nursing Homes, Partly because It Won't Regulate the Offenders," *Dallas Observer*, December 18, 2012, http://www.dallasobserver.com/news/texas-leads-the-league-in-bad-nursing-homes-partly-because-it-wont-regulate-the-offenders-7139830; "Nursing Home Report Cards: Texas," *Families for Better Care*, 2014, https://nursinghomereportcards.com/state/tx/; Manuel Bojorquez, "Eleven States Get Failing Grades for Nursing Home Care," *CBS Evening News*, August 9, 2013, http://www.cbsnews.com/news/eleven-states-get-failing-grades-for-nursing-home-care; and "Long-Term Services & Supports State Scorecard," AARP, The Commonwealth Fund, and The SCAN Foundation, 2018, http://www.longtermscorecard.org/databystate/state?state=TX

15. The seminal work on demographic change in Texas in the 21st century and the consequences of not meeting the needs of Texas minorities is Steve H. Murdock et al., *The New Texas Challenge: Population Change and the Future of Texas* (College Station: Texas A&M University Press, 2003); updated in Steve H. Murdock et al., *Changing Texas: Implications of Addressing or Ignoring the Texas Challenge* (College Station: Texas A&M University Press, 2014).

16. "Best U.S. High Schools," *U.S. News and World Report*, 2021, https://www.usnews.com/education/best-high-schools/national-rankings?int=top_nav_National_Rankings

17. Bethany Blankley, "Texas Homeschool Coalition: 400 Percent Increase in Parents Withdrawing Students from Public Schools," *Corridor News*, September 15, 2020, https://smcorridornews.com/texas-homeschool-coalition-400-percent-increase-in-parents-withdrawing-students-from-public-schools/

18. "Summary of Charter Awards and Closures," Texas Education Agency Division of Charter School Administration, October 16, 2020, https://tea.texas.gov/sites/default/files/Summary_of_Awards_and_Closures.pdf

19. Christine F. Nishimura, "Tuition and Fees," Texas Charter Schools Association, August 9, 2017, https://txcharterschools.org/tuition-and-fees/

20. "What is a Charter School?" Texas Charter Schools Association, https://txcharterschools.org/. Although this is an advocacy group, earlier studies show similar results. Debra S. Haas examines 2005–2007 data in "An Analysis of Gaps in Funding for Charter Schools and Traditional Districts," Institute for Public School Initiative, The University of Texas System, http://utsystem.edu/ipsi. An analysis paid for by the Texas Charter School Association had similar conclusions for 2005–2009. See R. C. Wood & Associates, "Comparative Analyses of Revenues Generated from the Texas Foundation School Program for Independent School Districts and Charter School Districts," *ERIC* (February 2011), http://eric.ed.gov/?id=EJ990974

21. Kiah Collier, "Texas Supreme Court Upholds School Funding System," *Texas Tribune*, May 13, 2016, https://www.texastribune.org/2016/05/13/texas-supreme-court-issues-school-finance-ruling

22. "Charter Schools No Cure-All for Black Students, Says Study," *UT News*, April 11, 2012, https://news.utexas.edu/2012/04/11/charter-schools-no-cure-all-for-black-students-says-study/; "Failure Is an Option," *Houston Chronicle*, January 31, 2010; and Jennifer Radcliffe, "Study Supports KIPP Success," *Houston Chronicle*, June 22, 2010.

23. "Charter School Performance in Texas," Center for Research on Education Outcomes, July 22, 2015, http://Credo.stanford.edu

24. "News & Information Related to COVID-19," Texas Association of School Administrators, October 15, 2020, https://tasanet.org/resources-information-related-to-covid-19/

25. Melissa B. Taboada, "Texas School Coronavirus Cases Rising, New Data Show," Austin American-Statesman, September 23, 2020, https://www.statesman.com/news/20200923/texas-school-coronavirus-cases-rising-new-data-show

26. Morgan Smith, "Texas Schools Chief: Testing Has Gone Too Far," *Texas Tribune*, January 31, 2012, https://www.texastribune.org/2012/01/31/texas-school-chief-testing-has-gone-too-far

27. Holly K. Hacker, "Love or Hate Them, New A-F Letter Grades for Texas Schools Are Here to Stay, Lt. Gov. Dan Patrick Says," *Dallas Morning News*, January 2017, https://www.dallasnews.com/news/education/2017/01/11/love-hate-new-f-letter-grades-texas-schools-stay-lt-govdan-patrick-says

28. "News & Information Related to COVID-19," *Texas Association of School Administrators*, October 15, 2020, https://tasanet.org/resources-information-related-to-covid-19/

29. "2021 Best National University Rankings," *U. S. News and World Report*, https://www.usnews.com/best-colleges/rankings/national-universities?_sort=schoolName&_sortDirection=desc

30. Paul Burka, "General Admission," *Texas Monthly*, April 2012, http://www.texasmonthly.com/story/general-admission; see also *Sweatt v. Painter*, 339 U.S. 629 (1950).

31. "2018 Texas Public Higher Education Almanac," Texas Higher Education Coordinating Board (Spring 2018), http://www.thecb.state.tx.us/reports/PDF/10900.pdf

32. The Perryman Group, "A Tale of Two States—And One Million Jobs," Texas Higher Education Coordinating Board (March 2007), http://www.thecb.state.tx.us/reports/PDF/1345.PDF?CFID¼7562420&CFTOKEN¼51730738

33. *University of California Regents v. Bakke*, 438 U.S. 265 (1978).

34. *Hopwood v. Texas*, 78 F.3d 932 (1996).

35. *Fisher v. University of Texas at Austin*, 133 S. Ct. 2411 (2013).

36. *Fisher v. University of Texas* (2016), 579 U.S. ___ (2016).

37. Raga Justin, "UT-Austin Faces a Third Lawsuit Claiming that White Students were Unfairly Denied Admission under Affirmative Action," *Texas Tribune*, July 22, 2020, https://www.texastribune.org/2020/07/22/ut-austin-affirmative-action-lawsuit-white/

38. Jill Barshay, "Texas 10% Policy Didn't Expand Number of High Schools Feeding Students to Top Universities," *Hechinger Report*, July 8, 2019, https://hechingerreport.org/texas-top-10-policy-didnt-expand-number-of-high-schools-feeding-students-to-top-universities/

39. "A Red Flag," *Fort Worth Star-Telegram*, June 15, 2007. A similar argument is made by two health policy specialists from the University of Virginia, Arthur Garson Jr. and Carolyn Long Engelhard, "Texas Has Top Medical Centers but Provides Poor Health Care," *Houston Chronicle*, September 17,

2011, http://www.chron.com/opinion/outlook/article/Texas-has-top-medicalcentersbutprovides-poor-2174885.php

40. David C. Radley, Sara R. Collins, and Susan L. Hayes, "2019 Scorecard on State Health System Performance," The Commonwealth Fund (June 2019), https://www.commonwealthfund.org/sites/default/files/2019-06/Radley_State_Scorecard_2019.pdf

41. Robert T. Garrett, "Texas Faulted on Food Stamps," *Dallas Morning News*, January 13, 2010; and Editorial Board, "Privatization Failure Is Taxpayers' Burden," *Austin American-Statesman*, March 26, 2008.

42. Emily DePrang and Beth Cortez-Neavel, "Fostering Neglect," *Texas Observer*, June 2014, 19–25.

43. Emma Platoff and Edgar Walters, "Federal Appeals Court Finds Texas Foster Kids Were Endangered—But Strikes Down Some Attempts At Reform," *Texas Tribune*, October 18, 2018, https://www.texastribune.org/2018/10/18/foster-care-5th-circuit-order-reform

44. Eva DeLuna Castro, "Poverty 101," *Center for Public Policy Priorities*, November 2011, http://www.cppp.org/files/8/2011_11_Poverty101.pdf

45. Ali Safawi and Ife Floyd, "TANF Benefits Still Too Low to Help Families, Especially Black Families, Avoid Increased Hardship," Center on Budget and Policy Priorities, October 8, 2020,

46. For more information on these and other benefits, log on to *Your Texas Benefits* at http://www.yourtexasbenefits.com

47. Peter Clark, "Report: 659,000 More Texans Uninsured Ranking TX Last in US for Health Coverage," *Cover Texas Now!,* July 15, 2020, https://covertexasnow.org/posts/2020/7/14/report-659000-more-texans-uninsured-ranking-tx-last-in-us-for-health-coverage

48. Dr. Howard Brody, "Expand Medicaid, Save Lives," *Houston Chronicle*, October 12, 2012, http://www.chron.com/opinion/outlook/article/Expand-Medicaid-save-lives-3950778.php. For other consequences, see Rachel Garfield, Anthony Damico, and Kendal Orgera, "The Coverage Gap: Uninsured Poor Adults in States That Do Not Expand Medicaid," Kaiser Family Foundation, June, 12, 2018, https://www.kff.org/medicaid/issue-brief/the-coverage-gap-uninsured-poor-adults-in-states-that-do-not-expand-medicaid

49. Margot Sanger-Katz and Abby Goodnough, "Even as the Economy Grew, More Children Lost Health Insurance," *New York Times*, October 9, 2020, https://www.nytimes.com/2020/10/09/upshot/children-losing-health-insurance.html

50. Manny Fernandez, Mitch Smith, and James Dobbins, "5 South Texas Communities Have the Country's Highest New Infection Rates," *New York Times*, September 2, 2020, https://www.nytimes.com/2020/08/13/us/coronavirus-south-texas.html

51. "Ranking The States," Mental Health America, 2020, https://www.mhanational.org/issues/ranking-states#four

52. "Mental Health Spending by State Across the US," American Addiction Centers, 2020, https://www.rehabs.com/explore/mental-health-spending-by-state-across-the-us/

53. Edgar Walters, "State Spending More on Mental Health Care, but Waitlist for Beds Grows," *Texas Tribune*, May 1, 2016, https://www.texastribune.org/2016/05/01/despite-state-spending-dearth-pysch-hospital-beds

54. *Community Health Needs Assessment 2016* conducted by the Menninger Clinic, a psychiatric health system in Houston, https://www.menningerclinic.com/Assets/menninger-chna-final-report-6-30-16.pdf; Elizabeth Trovall, "Harris County Steps towards Mental Health Treatment Instead of Incarceration," *Houston Public Media*, October 10, 2018, https://www.houstonpublicmedia.org/articles/news/in-depth/2018/10/10/307457/harris-county-steps-towards-mental-health-treatment-instead-of-incarceration

55. Anna Novak, Mitchell Ferman, and Mandi Cai, "Texas' Unemployment Rate Has Fallen By Nearly Half Since the Record High in 2020," June 21, 2021, https://apps.texastribune.org/features/2020/texas-unemployment/

56. "Small Business Policy Index 2018," Small Business and Entrepreneurship Council, February 2018, https://sbecouncil.org/wp-content/uploads/2018/02/SBPI2018-SBECouncil.pdf "The 50-State Small Business Regulation Index," Pacific Research Institute, July 2015, www.pacificresearch.org

57. "Who Pays? A Distributional Analysis of the Tax Systems in All 50 States," 5th ed., Institute on Taxation and Economic Policy, January 2015, https://itep.org/whopays/; and "Measure of America: Human Development Index," Social Science Research Council, accessed July 5, 2016, www.measureofamerica.org/maps

58. Russell Gold, *The Boom: How Fracking Ignited the American Energy Revolution and Changed the World* (New York: Simon and Shuster, 2014); reviewed by Michael Ennis, "The Rough Guide to Frackistan," *Texas Monthly*, May 2014, 56–64.

59. Arthur Murray, "The Saveonenergy.com Electricity Bill Report: Who paid the most, least?," Save On Energy, January 21, 2021, https://www.saveonenergy.com/learning-center/post/electricity-bills-by-state/

60. "Short-Term Energy Outlook," U.S. Energy Information Administration, October 6, 2020, https://www.eia.gov/outlooks/steo/report/electricity.php

61. Jim Malewitz, "Deregulated Electricity a Mixed Bag for Consumers," *Texas Tribune*, August 12, 2015, https://www.texastribune.org/2015/08/12/report-deregulated-electric-utilities-narrowing-pr

62. Mark Fitzpatrick, "Average Cost of Car Insurance," *Value Penguin*, November 2, 2020, https://www.valuepenguin.com/average-cost-of-insurance

63. Terrence Stutz, "Texas Home Insurers See Another Strong Year But Still Seek Limits on Lawsuits," *Dallas Morning News*, April 20, 2015, https://www.dallasnews.com/news/texas/2015/04/21/texas-home-insurers-see-another-strong-year-but-still-seek-limits-on-lawsuits/

64. Stephanie K. Jones, "Texas 'Hailstorm' Litigation Bill Headed to Governor's Desk," *Insurance Journal*, May 17, 2017, https://www.insurancejournal.com/news/southcentral/2017/05/17/451407.htm

65. Ibid.

66. Kevin McPherson, Jessica Donald, and Bruce Wright, "Transportation Infrastructure: Keeping Texas Moving," Texas Comptroller of Public Accounts, May 2018, https://comptroller.texas.gov/economy/fiscal-notes/2018/may/transportation.php#:~:text=TxDOT's%20Texas%20Transportation%20Plan%202040,%2415%20billion%20annually%20through%202040

67. "2018 Texas Transit Statistics," *Texas Department of Transportation*, December 2018, https://ftp.dot.state.tx.us/pub/txdot-info/ptn/transit_stats/2018.pdf

68. Carlos Anchondo, "State Lawmakers Aim to Lock in Funding for Texas Parks, Historic Sites," *Texas Tribune*, January 30, 2019, https://www.texastribune.org/2019/01/30/state-push-to-fully-fund-Texas-state-parks-and-historic-sites

69. Forrest Wilder, "Agency of Destruction," *Texas Observer*, May 26, 2010, http://www.texasobserver.org/agency-of-destruction; and see Eliot Shapleigh, "Cronies at the Capitol: Connecting the Dots for TCEQ," in *Owner's Box* (El Paso: Shapleigh, 2010), 30–33.

70. Seamus McGraw, *A Thirsty Land: The Making of an American Water Crisis* (Austin: University of Texas Press, 2018).

71. "Billion-Dollar Weather and Climate Disaster: Events," National Centers for Environmental Information, accessed November 15, 2020, https://www.ncdc.noaa.gov/billions/events/TX/1980-2020

72. "Disposal Volume and Activity Table," Texas Low Level Radioactive Waste Disposal Compact Commission, 2017, http://www.tllrwdcc.org/reports-more/. Maine initially joined and then left the interstate compact before the disposal site was opened.

73. Christopher Helman, "Texas Billionaire Builds Giant Nuclear Waste Dump," *Forbes*, April 1, 2011, http://www.forbes.com/sites/christopherhelman/2011/04/01/texas-billionaire-builds-giant-nuclear-waste-dump; Julie Bykowicz, "Republican Donor Simmons Seeks Rule to Fill Texas Dump," *Bloomberg News*, April 5, 2012, http://www.bloomberg.com/news/articles/2012-04-05/republican-donor-simmons-seeks-rule-to-fill-texas-dump; and Kate Galbraith and Jay Root, "Texas Billionaire Nears Radioactive Waste Dump Victory," *Texas Tribune*, May 17, 2011, https://www.texastribune.org/2011/05/17/texas-billionaire-nears-radioactive-waste-dump-vic

74. "Editorial: Out of Austin, Mixed Messages on Illegal Immigration," *Dallas Morning News*, June 6, 2015, http://www.dallasnews.com/opinion/editorials/2015/06/06/editorial-out-of-austin-mixed-messages-on-illegal-immigration

75. Julián Aguilar, "Abbott Signs Sweeping Border Security Bill," *Texas Tribune*, June 9, 2015, https://www.texastribune.org/2015/06/09/abbott-signs-sweeping-border-security-bill

76. Ibid.

77. Benjy Sarlin, "How America's Harshest Immigration Law Failed," *MSNBC*, December 16, 2013, https://www.nbcnews.com/id/wbna53847137

78. "Editorial: Out of Austin."

79. Ibid.

80. Adam Liptak and Michael D. Shear, "Obama Immigration Plan Seems to Divide Supreme Court," *New York Times*, April 18, 2016, http://www.nytimes.com/2016/04/19/us/politics/supreme-court-immigration.html?_r=0

81. Nick Jimenez, "No Easy Answers in Resolving Immigration Problems," *Corpus Christi Caller-Times*, April 23, 2016, http://www.caller.com/columnists/nick-jimenez/no-easy-answers-in-resolving-immigration-problems-27aa034b-face-51df-e053-0100007f44e8-376786911.html

Chapter 13

1. Josiah Bates, "Amid Growing Support Campaign, Texas Death Row Inmate Rodney Reed's Planned Execution Has Been Stayed. Here's What You Need to Know," *Time*, November 15, 2019, https://time.com/5722795/rodney-reed-innocent-execution-protests/

2. Jordan Smith, "Texas Court Halts Rodney Reed Execution over Questions of Withheld Evidence, False Testimony," *Intercept*, November 17, 2019, https://theintercept.com/2019/11/17/rodney-reed-stay-of-execution/

3. William Mansell, "Rodney Reed's Execution Stayed by Texas Appeals Court," ABC News, November 15, 2019, https://abcnews.go.com/US/texas-parole-board-recommends-120-day-reprieve-rodney/story?id=67051452

4. Brian Duignan, "Habeas Corpus," Encyclopedia Britannica, accessed on November 23, 2020, https://www.britannica.com/topic/habeas-corpus

5. "Most States Have Ended SNAP Ban for Convicted Drug Felons," National Conference of State Legislatures, July 30, 2019, https://www.ncsl.org/blog/2019/07/30/most-states-have-ended-snap-ban-for-convicted-drug-felons.aspx

6. Kira Lerner, "This D.A. Election Could Bring a Big Change in How Austin, Texas Treats Drug Addiction," Appeal, March 2, 2020, https://theappeal.org/travis-county-district-attorney-election-drug-possession-addiction/

7. Jazmine Ulloa, "Drug Court Failing Black Offenders," *Austin American-Statesman,* September 25, 2018, https://www.statesman.com/NEWS/20160904/Drug-court-failing-black-offenders

8. "Ending the War on Drugs in Travis County, Texas," Texas Criminal Justice Coalition, accessed on November 24, 2020, https://www.texascjc.org/system/files/publications/Report%20-%20Ending%20the%20War%20on%20Drugs%20in%20Travis%20County%20Texas.pdf

9. Caitlin Dunklee, Travis Leete, and Jorge Antonio Renaud, "Effective Approaches to Drug Crimes in Texas: Strategies to Reduce Crime, Save Money, and Treat Addiction," *Texas Criminal Justice Coalition,* January 2013, https://www.texascjc.org/system/files/publications/TCJC%20Addiction%20Primer%20%28Jan%202013%29.pdf

10. Michael Balsamo, "Hate Crimes in U.S. Reach Highest Level in More Than a Decade," *U.S. News and World Report,* November 16, 2020, https://www.usnews.com/news/politics/articles/2020-11-16/hate-crimes-in-us-reach-highest-level-in-more-than-a-decade

11. Ibid.

12. Rebecca Salinas, "Map: Where the Most Hate Crimes Were Reported in Texas," KSAT 12 News, accessed November 24, 2020, https://www.ksat.com/news/local/2019/12/20/map-where-the-most-hate-crimes-were-reported-in-texas/

13. Andrew Weber, "Despite Oversized Risks, Transgender Texans Aren't Protected by the State's Hate Crime Law, KUT 90.5, January 10, 2019, https://www.kut.org/texas/2019-01-10/despite-outsized-risks-transgender-texans-arent-protected-by-the-states-hate-crime-law

14. Ryan McCrimmon, "Hate Crimes, Sodomy Law Before House Panel," *Texas Tribune,* May 6, 2015, https://www.texastribune.org/2015/05/06/house-committee-takes-hate-crimes-anti-sodomy-law/; Maggie Astor, "Violence Against Transgender People Is on the Rise, Advocates Say," *New York Times,* November 9, 2017, https://www.nytimes.com/2017/11/09/us/transgender-women-killed.html

15. Andrew Weber, "Despite Oversized Risks, Transgender Texans Aren't Protected by the State's Hate Crime Law, KUT 90.5, January 10, 2019, https://www.kut.org/texas/2019-01-10/despite-outsized-risks-transgender-texans-arent-protected-by-the-states-hate-crime-law

16. "Quick Facts: The Death Penalty System in Texas," *Texas Moratorium Network,* http://www.texasmoratorium.org/quick-facts

17. For insight into possible racial bias in the use of the death penalty and one lawyer's experiences in defending death row inmates, see Bryan Stevenson, *Just Mercy: A Story of Justice and Redemption* (New York: Spiegel and Grau, 2015); See also Bruce Jackson and Diane Christian, *In This Timeless Time: Living and Dying on Death Row in America* (Chapel Hill: University of North Carolina Press, 2012), which includes images of, and interviews with, Texas death row inmates. For a full discussion of the possible execution of an innocent man, see James Liebman, Shawn Crowley, Andrew Markquart, Lauren Rosenberg, Lauren Gallo White, and Daniel Zharkovsky, "Los Tocayos Carlos," *Columbia Human Rights Law Review* 43, (2012): 711–1152.

18. "Race and the Death Penalty in Texas," *New York Times,* April 2, 2016, http://www.nytimes.com/2016/04/03/opinion/sunday/race-and-the-death-penalty-in-texas.html; Lawrence Hurley, "U.S. Top Court Backs Texas Death Row Inmate in Race Case," *Reuters,* February 22, 2017, https://www.reuters.com/article/usa-court-deathpenalty-idUSL1N1G70VT

19. "The Death Penalty in Harris County," *Texas Coalition to Abolish the Death Penalty,* July 1, 2020, https://tcadp.org/wp-content/uploads/2020/07/Harris-County-fact-sheet-7-1-20.pdf

20. Jolie McCullough and Ben Hasson, "Faces of Death Row," *Texas Tribune,* May 12, 2016, https://apps.texastribune.org/death-row

21. Ken Herman, "Drugs, Death, and the OU Game," *Austin American-Statesman,* April 1, 2014.

22. For a discussion of the Danish manufacturer's response to the use of Nembutal as part of the execution process, see Ed Pilkington, "Florida Execution: Drug Firm Protests to Governor over Lethal Injection," *Guardian,* September 27, 2011, https://www.theguardian.com/world/2011/sep/27/death-penalty-florida-pentobarbital-lethal-injection. For details about Texas's purchase of the drug, see Mike Ward, "Records: Texas Bought Execution Drugs before Supply Dwindled," *Austin-American Statesman,* June 20, 2012.

23. Tom Dart, "Virgina to Execute Convicted Murderer after Texas Supplies Lethal Injection Drug," *Guardian,* September 25, 2015.

24. For a list of those states in which a moratorium is in force, see "Death Penalty in Flux," *Death Penalty Information Center,* http://www.deathpenaltyinfo.org/death-penalty-flux

25. To see a comparison between states with the death penalty and states without death penalty, see "Deterrence: States without the Death Penalty Have Had Consistently Lower Murder Rates," *Death Penalty Information Center,* https://deathpenaltyinfo.org/deterrence-states-without-death-penalty-have-had-consistently-lower-murder-rates

26. Traci L. Lacock and Michael L. Radelet, "Do Executions Lower Homicide Rates: The Views of Leading Criminologists," *Journal of Criminal Law and Criminology,* 99, (2009): 489–508.

27. Meghan Keneally, "4 of the 5 Counties with the Most Death Penalty Executions Are in Texas: Data," *ABC News,* March 23, 2019, https://abcnews.go.com/US/nationally-counties-responsible-executions/story?id=61679582

28. "Murder Rate of Death Penalty States Compared to Non-Death Penalty States," *Death Penalty Information Center,* 2018, https://deathpenaltyinfo.org/facts-and-research/murder-rates/murder-rate-of-death-penalty-states-compared-to-non-death-penalty-states

29. Texas Department of Criminal Justice, "Death Row Facts," *Death Row Information, Texas Department of Criminal Justice,* http://www.tdcj.state.tx.us/death_row/dr_facts.html

30. Richard C. Dieter, "On the Front Line: Law Enforcement Views on the Death Penalty," *Death Penalty Information Center,* February 1995, http://www.deathpenaltyinfo.org/front-line-law-enforcement-views-death-penalty#fn15

31. *Panetti v. Quarterman,* 551 U.S. 930 (2007).

32. Brandi Grissom, "Trouble in Mind: How Should Criminals Who Are Mentally Ill Be Punished?" *Texas Monthly,* March 2013, http://www.texasmonthly.com/story/trouble-mind

33. Jolie McCullough, "Execution Stayed for Dallas Accountant Who Killed Daughter," *Texas Tribune,* March 30, 2016; https://www.texastribune.org/2016/03/30/dallas-accountant-faces-execution-daughters-deaths; Tassneem Nashrulla and Chris Geidner, "Appeal Court Halts Texas Execution Amid Claims of Mental Illness," *Buzzfeednews.com,* March 30, 2016, https://www.buzzfeed.com/tasneemnashrulla/appeals-court-halts-texas-execution-amid-claims-of-mental-il?utm_term=.yilWZgzorm#.fixr07EWwk

34. Ronald Hopkins, "In 2019, Let's Resolve to Help More Americans Stay Out of Prison for Good [Opinion]," *Houston Chronicle,* January 17, 2019, https://www.houstonchronicle.com/opinion/outlook/article/In-2019-let-s-resolve-to-help-more-Americans-13538518.php#:~:text=Here%20in%20Texas%20the%20recidivism,to%20become%20a%20repeat%20offender

35. For a discussion of the history of the Texas prison system, see Robert Perkinson, *Texas Tough: The Rise of America's Prison Empire* (New York: Metropolitan, 2010); but some reviewers have faulted this book for not reflecting improvements in the Texas prison system in recent years; See Marc Levin, "More Criminal Justice Reform for Texas in 2018," *Houston Chronicle,* January 16, 2018, https://www.houstonchronicle.com/opinion/outlook/article/Levin-More-criminal-justice-reform-for-Texas-in-12499603.php

36. Nicole D. Porter, "The State of Sentencing 2015: Developments of Policy and Practice," *Sentencing Project,* February 10, 2016, http://www.sentencingproject.org/publications/the-state-of-sentencing-2015-developments-in-policy-and-practice

37. Jolie McCullough, "Texas to Shutter 3 More Prisons as Units Face Critical Staffing Shortages," *Texas Tribune,* December 2, 2020, https://www.kbtx.com/2020/12/02/texas-to-shutter-3-more-prisons-as-units-face-critical-staffing-shortages/

38. *Adult and Juvenile Correctional Population Projections: Fiscal Years 2019–2024* (Austin: Texas Legislative Budget Board, January 2019), https://www.lbb.state.tx.us/Documents/Publications/Policy_Report/4910_Correctional_Population_Projections_Jan_2019.pdf

39. "Texas Population 2013," *World Population Statistics,* http://www.worldpopulationstatistics.com/texas-population-2013

40. Mark Holden and Brooke Rollins, "Commentary: Texas Saved $3B Closing Prisons. Why Rehabilitation Works," *Austin American-Statesman,* September 25, 2018, https://www.statesman.com/news/20180209/commentary-texas-saved-3b-closing-prisons-why-rehabilitation-works

41. Gaby Galvin, "Underfunded, Overcrowded State Prisons Struggle with Reform," *U.S. News & World Report,* July 26, 2017, https://www.usnews.com/news/best-states/articles/2017-07-26/understaffed-and-overcrowded-state-prisons-crippled-by-budget-constraints-bad-leadership

42. Human Rights Clinic, University of Texas School of Law, *Reckless Indifference: Deadly Heat in Texas Prisons,* March 2015, https://law.utexas.edu/wp-content/uploads/sites/11/2015/04/2015-HRC-USA-Reckless-Indifference-Report.pdf; Lance Lowry, "Heat in Texas Prisons Is a Boiling Liability," *Austin American-Statesman,* January 2, 2014.

43. Ibid.

44. Dan Rosenzweig-Ziff, "Incarcerated Texans Are Dying from COVID-19 at a Rate 35% Higher than Rest of the U.S. Prison Population, UT Study Finds," *Texas Tribune*, November 10, 2020, https://www.texastribune.org/2020/11/10/texas-prison-deaths-coronavirus/

45. Jolie McCullough, "Texas to Shutter 3 More Prisons as Units Face Critical Staffing Shortages," *Texas Tribune*, December 2, 2020.

46. Ibid.

47. Michael Barajas, "The Prison Inside Prison," *Texas Observer*, January 21, 2020, https://www.texasobserver.org/solitary-confinement-texas/

48. Ibid.

49. Marc Levin, "Public Safety Requires Thinking Outside the Cell," *Newsweek,* July 29, 2020, https://www.newsweek.com/public-safety-requires-thinking-outside-cell-opinion-1521482

50. Marc Levin and Ann Yanez Correa, "Correcting the Texas Justice System," *Fort Worth Star-Telegram*, September 1, 2015.

51. Beth Avery and Han Lu, "Ban the Box: U.S. Cities, Counties, and States Adopt Fair Hiring Policies," *National Employment Law Project*, September 30, 2020, https://www.nelp.org/publication/ban-the-box-fair-chance-hiring-state-and-local-guide/; "Austin Becomes First Fair Chance Hiring City in the South," *City of Austin's Mayor Adler*, March 25, 2016, http://www.mayoradler.com/austin-becomes-first-fair-chance-hiring-city-in-the-south/

52. Gabrielle Banks, "Harris County Bail System Unconstitutional, Federal Judge Rules," *Chron*, February 14, 2018, https://www.chron.com/news/houston-texas/houston/article/Harris-County-bail-system-unconstitutional-11108210.php

53. Brian Rogers, "In Harris County, Punishment for Marijuana Depends on Where You're Caught," *Houston Chronicle*, January 24, 2018, https://www.houstonchronicle.com/news/houston-texas/article/Bay-area-law-enforcement-others-ignore-Harris-12511261.php

54. Brandi Grissom, "With Crime, Incarceration Rates Falling, Texas Closes Record Number of Prisons," *Dallas Morning News*, July 2017, https://www.dallasnews.com/news/texas-legislature/2017/07/05/crime-incarceration-rates-falling-texas-closes-record-number-lock-ups

55. John MacCormack, "Private Prison Boom Goes Bust," *San Antonio-Express News*, August 23, 2015.

56. Jolie McCullough, "Following Sexual Abuse Scandals, Texas Juvenile Justice Department Submits Plan to Revamp Agency," *Texas Tribune*, June 1, 2018, https://www.texastribune.org/2018/06/01/Texas-Juvenile-Justice-Department-greg-abbott

57. Dan Rosenzweig-Ziff, "'They Are Hurting Them'": Advocacy Groups Ask Feds to Investigate Sexual Assaults, Gang Violence in Texas Youth Lockups," *Texas Tribune*, October 21, 2020, https://www.texastribune.org/2020/10/21/texas-juvenile-justice-department-abuse/

58. "Juvenile Justice," *Texas Public Policy Foundation*, September 22, 2020, https://www.texaspolicy.com/legejuvenilejustice/

59. "Study Shows Community-Based Supervision, Not State-Run Incarceration, Leads to More Success for Texas Youth in Juvenile Justice System," *Justice Center Council of State Governments*, January 29, 2015, https://csgjusticecenter.org/youth/press-releases/study-shows-community-based-supervision-not-state-run-incarceration-leads-to-more-success-for-texas-youth-in-juvenile-justice-system

60. Ryan McCrimmon, "Study Touts Community Programs for Juvenile Offenders," *Texas Tribune,* January 29, 2015, https://www.texastribune.org/2015/01/29/study-keep-youth-offenders-in-their-community

61. Nicole Scialabba, "Should Juveniles Be Charged as Adults in the Criminal Justice System?" *American Bar Association*, October 3, 2016, https://www.americanbar.org/groups/litigation/committees/childrens-rights/articles/2016/should-juveniles-be-charged-as-adults

62. Office of Juvenile Justice and Delinquency Programs, "Statistical Briefing Book: Juvenile Justice System Structures and Process," *U.S. Department of Justice*, October 1, 2015, http://www.ojjdp.gov/ojstatbb/structure_process/qa04101.asp

63. Nils Franco, "Raise the Age Bills Flourish in 2016," *Campaign for Youth Justice: Research and Policy*, March 15, 2016, http://cfyj.org/news/blog/item/raise-the-age-bills-flourish-in-2016. See also, Patrick Michels, "Bringing 17-Year-Olds into Juvenile Justice System," *Texas Observer*, April 2, 2015, https://www.texasobserver.org/juvenile-justice-house-support-for-bringing-17-year-olds

64. Matt Clarke, "Texas Prison Population Drops as Guard Shortage Persists," *Prison Legal News*, January 10, 2015, https://www.prisonlegalnews.org/news/2015/jan/10/texas-prison-population-drops-guard-shortage-persists

65. Jolie McCullough, "'You're Not as Safe as You Should Be.' How Understaffing Is Affecting One Texas Prison," *Texas Tribune*, May 9, 2018, https://www.texastribune.org/2018/05/09/understaffing-texas-prisons-telford-maximum-security-prison-timothy-da

66. Jolie McCullough, "Three Texas Inmates Have Died at the Hands of Prison Officers as Use of Force Continues to Rise," *Texas Tribune*, February 7, 2020, https://www.texastribune.org/2020/02/07/texas-prison-deaths-come-staffers-use-force-against-inmates-increases/

67. Keri Blakinger, "Texas Prison Suicide Attempt Figures Drop on a Technicality," *Houston Chronicle*, December 19, 2019, https://www.houstonchronicle.com/news/houston-texas/houston/article/Texas-prison-suicide-attempt-figures-drop-on-a-14926073.php

68. "S.B. No. 1 General Appropriations Act: Eighty-Seventh Legislature," May 2021, https://capitol.texas.gov/tlodocs/87R/billtext/pdf/SB00001F.pdf#navpanes=0

69. Edgar Walters, "In Cellphone Contraband Cases, Few Face Charges," *Texas Tribune,* May 4, 2014, https://www.texastribune.org/2014/05/04/cellphone-contraband-cases-few-face-charges

70. Madlin Mekelburg, "New Prison Rule Means Texas Jailbirds Can't Tweet," *Texas Tribune,* April 14, 2016, https://www.texastribune.org/2016/04/14/criminal-justice-department-banning-inmates-social

71. Michael Morton, *Getting Life: An Innocent Man's 25-Year Journey from Prison to Peace* (New York: Simon and Schuster, 2014).

72. "Exoneration Map," *National Registry of Exonerations*, http://www.law.umich.edu/special/exoneration/Pages/Exonerations-in-the-United-States-Map.aspx

73. Daniele Selby, "These 8 States Had the Most Exonerations in 2019," *Innocence Project*, April 2, 2020, https://innocenceproject.org/these-8-states-had-the-most-exonerations-in-2019/#:~:text=In%20its%20annual%20report%2C%20the,the%20help%20of%20DNA%20evidence

74. "How Eyewitness Misidentification Can Send Innocent People to Prison," Innocence Project, April 15, 2020, https://innocenceproject.org/how-eyewitness-misidentification-can-send-innocent-people-to-prison/

75. Colin G. Tredoux, Christian A. Meisner, Roy S. Malpass, and Laura A. Zimmerman, "Eyewitness Identification," *Encyclopedia of Applied Psychology*, vol. 1, ed. C. D. Spielberg (New York: Elsevier Academic Press, 2004), 875–887.

76. Daniele Selby, "These 8 States Had the Most Exonerations in 2019," *Innocence Project*, April 2, 2020, https://innocenceproject.org/these-8-states-had-the-most-exonerations-in-2019/#:~:text=In%20its%20annual%20report%2C%20the,the%20help%20of%20DNA%20evidence

77. For a discussion of the criminal justice system's disparate impact on African Americans, see Michelle Alexander, *The New Jim Crow: Mass Incarceration in the Age of Colorblindness* (New York: New Press, 2010).

78. Brakkton Booker, "DOJ Unveils New Initiative to Help Police Departments, Offers Aid to Minneapolis," *National Public Radio*, October 20, 2020, https://www.npr.org/sections/live-updates-protests-for-racial-justice/2020/10/20/925778291/doj-unveils-new-initiative-to-help-police-departments-offers-aid-to-minneapolis

79. Eric Dexheimer, Taylor Goldenstein, and St. John Barned-Smith, "Texas Was Supposed to Collect Racial Profiling Data. It Left out Most of the 'Racial' Part," *Houston Chronicle*, June 25, 2020, https://www.houstonchronicle.com/news/houston-texas/texas/article/texas-race-profiling-data-cops-police-traffic-stop-15365887.php

80. Becky Fogel, "Texas Led the Nation in On-Duty Officer Deaths in 2019," *KUT 90.5*, December 31, 2019, https://www.kut.org/texas/2019-12-31/texas-led-the-nation-in-on-duty-officer-deaths-in-2019

81. Caitlin Clark, "Texas A&M Study: White Police Officers Use Force More often Than Non-White Colleagues," *Texas A&M Today*, June 24, 2020, https://today.tamu.edu/2020/06/24/texas-am-study-white-police-officers-use-force-more-often-than-non-white-colleagues/

82. Daniele Selby, "Only One Prosecutor Has Ever Been Jailed for Misconduct Leading to a Wrongful Conviction," *Innocence Project*, November 11, 2020, https://innocenceproject.org/ken-anderson-michael-morton-prosecutorial-misconduct-jail/

83. Matt Ferner, "Prosecutors Are Almost Never Disciplined for Misconduct," *Huffington Post*, February 11, 2016, http://www.huffingtonpost.com/entry/prosecutor-misconduct-justice_us_56bce00fe4b0c3c55050748a

84. Jon Herskovitz, "Former Texas Prosecutor Disbarred for Sending Innocent Man to Death Row," *Reuters*, February 8, 2016, 69, http://www.reuters.com/article/texas-prosecutor-idUSL2N15N253; Texas Appleseed and Texas Defender Service, *Towards More Transparent Justice: The Michael Morton Act's First Year* (Austin: Texas Appleseed and Texas Defender Service, 2015), https://www.texasdefender.org/wp-content/uploads/2019/12/Towards_More_Transparent_Justice.pdf

85. Tex. Code of Crim. Proc. Ann. Sec. 39.14 (2013).

Index